Medical Terminology
The Language of Health Care

Second Edition

Medical Terminology

The Language of Health Care

Second Edition

Marjorie Canfield Willis, CMA-AC

Program Director
Medical Assisting/Medical Transcription Programs
Orange Coast College
Costa Mesa, California

LIPPINCOTT WILLIAMS & WILKINS
A **Wolters Kluwer** Company

Philadelphia • Baltimore • New York • London
Buenos Aires • Hong Kong • Sydney • Tokyo

Editor: John Goucher
Managing Editor: Rebecca Kerins
Marketing Manager: Hilary Henderson
Production Editor: Bill Cady
Designer: Risa Clow
Compositor: Maryland Composition
Printer: R. R. Donnelley

Lippincott, Williams & Wilkins
351 West Camden Street
Baltimore, MD 21201

530 Walnut Street
Philadelphia, PA 19106

Printed in China

First Edition, 1996

Library of Congress Cataloging-in-Publication Data

Willis, Marjorie Canfield.
   Medical terminology : the language of health care / Marjorie Canfield Willis.—2nd ed.
    p. ; cm.
   Includes bibliographical references and index.
   ISBN 13: 978-1-4511-7676-6 (alk. paper)
   ISBN 10: 1-4511-7676-7 (alk. paper)
  1. Medicine—Terminology. I. Title.
   [DNLM: 1. Medicine—Terminology—English. W 15 W735m 2006]
R123.W476 2006
610'.1'4—dc22

                                     2005001177

To purchase additional copies of this book, call our customer service department at **(800) 638-3030** or fax orders to **(301) 824-7390**. International customers should call **(301) 714-2324**.

Visit Lippincott Williams & Wilkins on the Internet: http://www.LWW.com. Lippincott Williams & Wilkins customer service representatives are available from 8:30 am to 6:00 pm, EST.

18 19 20
4 5 6 7 8 9 10 11 12

RRS1803

Dedicated to the students and faculty of the
School of Allied Health Professions
Orange Coast College
Costa Mesa, California

Preface

The second edition of *Medical Terminology: The Language of Health Care* continues in its design to provide a framework for building a medical vocabulary, using an applied approach. Emphasis is on understanding basic medical terms and learning how they are used in documenting and reporting patient care procedures. Practical applications are provided by exercises and medical record analyses in each chapter. The goal is to develop a basic "working" knowledge of the language of health care to serve as a basis for individual expansion.

Text Overview

Chapter 1 identifies the need for the personal commitment that is required to develop a basic knowledge of medical language. Included are methods of time management, techniques for making use of the senses to reinforce memory, and preparation and use of flash cards.

Chapter 2 starts with the origin of medical language, then introduces basic term components (prefixes, suffixes, and a selected number of combining forms) illustrating how these structures are combined to form medical terms. Rules of pronunciation, spelling, and formation of singular and plural forms are included. Medical word components covered in this chapter are used repeatedly throughout the book.

Chapter 3 examines the evolution of the physician in medicine and identifies fields of medical practice, including scopes of practice and the expansion of allied health professions.

Chapter 4 establishes the basis for the application of learning medical terms covered throughout the text by introducing common forms, formats, abbreviations, symbols, and methods of documenting patient care. This enables the student to understand basic communication between professionals, including physician's orders and prescriptions. The content of this chapter is reinforced in medical record analyses in succeeding chapters.

Periodic review of Chapters 2 and 4 is essential for successful use of this book. Term components first encountered in these chapters are revisited in subsequent chapters to reinforce memory of common term components.

Chapters 5 through 17 cover terms related to the body systems. In each chapter, basic anatomical terms are outlined, additional combining forms related to the system are identified, and common terms and abbreviations related to symptoms, diagnoses, tests, procedures, surgeries, and therapies are identified. Practice exercises at the end of each chapter are designed to reinforce the memory of basic term components by repetitive word structure analysis. Answers to practice exercises are included in Appendix D.

Another feature of Chapters 5 through 17 is the medical record analysis. Each analysis requires reading a particular medical record and answering questions specific to each. Knowledge of Chapter 4 is a prerequisite for understanding questions presented in the medical record analyses.

New to This Edition

- Full color throughout
- Updated photographs of pathologies and images illustrating the latest in health care technology
- Additions and clarifications of pertinent terms
- Elimination of the possessive form of 's in all eponyms to match standardization initiated in medical dictionaries, e.g., Alzheimer disease, Kaposi sarcoma, and Cushing syndrome
- Current information regarding medical abbreviations and symbols deemed error prone
- Practice exercises now include a guided system of term analysis, addition of mini medical records, and anatomical labeling exercises

BONUS CD-ROM

The CD-ROM that accompanies this text provides a wealth of fun and interactive activities for learning reinforcement:

- A pronunciation glossary with audio pronunciations
- Spelling bees to help recognize and correctly spell terms
- Labeling exercises to reinforce and test knowledge of medical terms and anatomy
- Games in which terms or components are matched with definitions
- Scored and unscored section and chapter quizzes for knowledge assessment
- Interactive medical record exercises

ADDITIONAL BONUS: QUICK STUDY REFERENCE CARD

The laminated **Quick Study Reference** packaged with this textbook provides a portable study resource that includes key rules for learning medical terms and a summary list of term components with definitions. This invaluable tool facilitates "on the go" learning of critical information.

Other Special Features

Ancient Artifacts provide historical information about the origins of selected medical terms. More than 50 ancient artifacts are sprinkled in the margins throughout the text.

Appendix A summarizes medical term components (prefixes, suffixes, and combining forms) in two lists: (a) term component to English definition and (b) English definition to term component.

Appendix B provides a glossary of abbreviations and symbols.

Appendix C lists commonly prescribed drugs, including therapeutic classifications.

Appendix D includes answers to the practice exercises.

Answers to medical record analyses are provided in the CD-ROM packaged with the book.

Acknowledgments

I am so proud of the success of this text and hope the second edition will continue to play an important role in teaching medical terminology.

I want to thank the dedicated staff of Lippincott Williams & Wilkins who have combined their many talents to prepare this revision. In addition to those who are appropriately recognized on the copyright page, I especially want to thank my editor, John Goucher. His help was instrumental in the revision and the development of the many ancillaries. We will all benefit from the additional resources that enhance the original text.

I continue to enjoy the support of my colleagues at Orange Coast College and many others from professional and technical areas. Particularly, I'd like to acknowledge: Kevin Ballinger, Walt Banoczi, Dan Farrell, Fredra Kodama, Ann McClanahan, Eleanor Huang, Linda Harloe, Chrysty Hodson, Richard Reed, MD, Brian Coyne, MD, and Michael J. Deimling, RPh, PhD.

I'd also like to recognize the thoughtful assessment and suggestions submitted by the following reviewers:

Thomas J. Falen, MA, RHIA, LHRM
Undergraduate Program Director
Health Information Management
Health Services Administration
University of Central Florida
Orlando, Florida

Joan Fobbs, PhD
University of Maryland Eastern Shore
Princess Anne, Maryland

Alicia A. Hill, CMA, BS
Ivy Tech State College Northeast
Fort Wayne, Indiana

Craig Kallendorf, PhD
Professor of Classics and English
Texas A&M University
College Station, Texas

Merrilee McDuffie, MPH
Front Range Community College–
    Westminster
Westminster, Colorado

Theresa Offenberger, CMA-C, PhD
Professor, Medical Assisting
Cuyahoga Community College
Cleveland, Ohio

Tomma Parco, BA Education
Department Chair, Business
    Technologies
Pueblo Community College
Pueblo, Colorado

David Pearce
Baker College of Cadillac
Cadillac, Michigan

Charlene Thiessen, CMT
GateWay Community College
Phoenix, Arizona

Suzanne Trump, MDiv, OTR/L
University of the Sciences in
    Philadelphia
Philadelphia, Pennsylvania

Pam Ventgen, CMA, CCS-P, CPC
Professor, Medical Assisting
University of Alaska Anchorage
Anchorage, Alaska

Flynn W. Warren, MS
University of Georgia
College of Pharmacy
Athens, Georgia

I have enjoyed an incredible relationship with my students, and it is their feedback that has been incorporated in several of the clarifications and additions to this revision. Since the textbook was published, I have found myself responding to an even larger audience of students—all with the same need to learn and grow in the knowledge of the language of health care. I thank all these students and appreciate the fact that my book has played a part in their learning success.

Last to recognize is my family, who have been steadfast in their caring. I thank them with hugs and kisses: XXOO.

M.C.W.

USER'S GUIDE

Medical Terminology: The Language of Health Care, Second Edition is not just a textbook, it is a complete learning resource that will help you to understand important information and master medical terminology. To achieve this, the author and publisher have included features and tools throughout the text to help you work through the material presented. Please take a few moments to look through this User's Guide, which will introduce you to the features that will enhance your learning experience.

Chapter **6**

Musculoskeletal System

Objectives at the beginning of each chapter outline the skills you must know by the end of the chapter.

OBJECTIVES

After completion of this chapter you will be able to

- Define common combining forms used in relation to the musculoskeletal system
- Describe the basic functions of the musculoskeletal system
- Define the basic anatomical terms referring to the musculoskeletal system
- Describe the anatomical position
- List the planes of the body
- Define positional and directional terms
- Define the terms related to body movements
- Define common symptomatic and diagnostic terms related to the musculoskeletal system
- List common diagnostic tests and procedures related to the musculoskeletal system
- Identify common operative terms referring to the musculoskeletal system
- Identify common therapeutic terms including drug classifications related to the muscu-

System Overviews give a review of the anatomy and physiology in order to better understand the medical terminology in the chapter.

Musculoskeletal System Overview

The musculoskeletal system provides support and gives shape to the body. The skeleton gives structure to the body by providing a framework of bones and cartilage. Also, the bones store calcium and other minerals and produce certain blood cells within the bone marrow (Figs. 6.1 to 6.4).

The muscles cover the bones where they hinge (articulate) and supply the forces that make movement possible. They also provide a protective covering for internal organs and produce body heat (Figs. 6.5 and 6.6).

Ancient Artifacts boxes in the margins provide historical background for commonly used terms.

 ELBOW. Many terms referring to the elbow are based on the L-shape formed at the joint. This is the basis of the "el" of elbow. It is also the root of the Latin term ulna. An "ell" was an old measure of length, particularly of cloth, being the amount from the elbow (or shoulder) to the fingers, which was a convenient way of rapidly measuring lengths. Boga was a bending or a bow.

Anatomical Terms Related to Bones (Figs. 6.1 to 6.4)	
Term	Meaning
appendicular skeleton ap'en-dik'yū-lär	bones of shoulder, pelvis, and upper and lower extremities
axial skeleton ak'sē-āl	bones of skull, vertebral column, chest, and hyoid bone (U-shaped bone lying at the base of the tongue); refer to Figure 6.4 for abbreviated identification and numbering of cervical, thoracic, and lumbar vertebrae
bone	specialized connective tissue composed of osteocytes (bone cells) forming the skeleton
TYPES OF BONE TISSUE	
compact bone	tightly solid, strong bone tissue resistant to bending
spongy (cancellous) bone spŭn'jē kan'sē-lŭs	mesh-like bone tissue containing marrow and fine branching canals through which blood vessels run

Word Tables outline anatomical terms clearly and concisely with term, pronunciation, and meaning.

They never used the word in the modern meaning of the bony framework of the body. The first recorded use of the modern term in English occurred in 1578.

ELBOW. Many terms referring to the elbow are based on the L-shape formed at the joint. This is the basis of the "el" of elbow. It is also the root of the Latin term ulna. An "ell" was an old measure of length, particularly of cloth, being the amount from the

Musculoskeletal System Overview

The musculoskeletal system provides support and gives shape to the body. The skeleton gives structure to the body by providing a framework of bones and cartilage. Also, the bones store calcium and other minerals and produce certain blood cells within the bone marrow (Figs. 6.1 to 6.4).

The muscles cover the bones where they hinge (articulate) and supply the forces that make movement possible. They also provide a protective covering for internal organs and produce body heat (Figs. 6.5 and 6.6).

Anatomical Terms Related to Bones (Figs. 6.1 to 6.4)	
Term	Meaning
appendicular skeleton ap'en-dik'yū-lär	bones of shoulder, pelvis, and upper and extremities
axial skeleton ak'sē-āl	bones of skull, vertebral column, chest, a bone (U-shaped bone lying at the base of tongue); refer to Figure 6.4 for abbreviated identification and numbering of cervical, and lumbar vertebrae
bone	specialized connective tissue composed osteocytes (bone cells) forming the skele
TYPES OF BONE TISSUE	

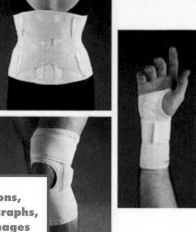

Examples of orthoses: back, knee, and wrist.

Numerous Illustrations,
photographs, radiographs,
micrographs, and images
help to illustrate medical terminology
and promote greater understanding.

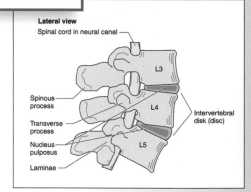

Lateral view
Spinal cord in neural canal

Spinous process

Transverse process

Nucleus pulposus

Laminae

L3

L4

L5

Intervertebral disk (disc)

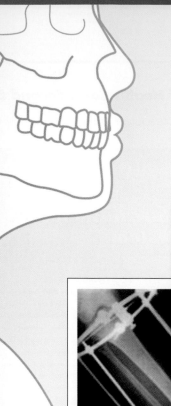

C1
C2
C3
C4
C5
C6
C7
T1
T2
T3
T4
T5
T6

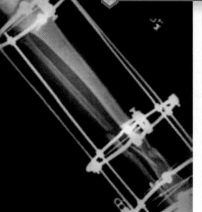

Figure 6.27 This radiograph, taken after closed reduction, percutaneous fixation of an open comminuted distal tibia/fibula fracture, shows placement of an external fixator to maintain pin placement during the healing process. The injury was the result of a gunshot to the right lower extremity.

Summaries of Acronyms/Abbreviations
appear at the end of each chapter.

Summary of Chapter 6 Acronyms/Abbreviations

A	anterior	MRI	magnetic resonance imaging
AKA	above-knee amputation	NSAID	nonsteroidal anti-inflammatory
AP	anterior-posterior	OA	osteoarthritis
BKA	below-knee amputation	ORIF	open reduction, internal fixation
CAT	computed axial tomography	P	posterior
CT	computed tomography	PT	physical therapy
DEXA	dual-energy x-ray absorptiometry	RA	rheumatoid arthritis
DJD	degenerative joint disease	ROM	range of motion
EMG	electromyogram	Tx	traction
Fx	fracture	x-ray	radiography

Numerous Practice Exercises
reinforce learning and retention.

PRACTICE EXERCISES

For the following terms, on the lines below the term, write out the indicated word parts: prefixes (P), combining forms (CF), roots (R), and suffixes (S). Then define the word.

EXAMPLE

hypertrophy

___ / ___ / ___
P   R   S

hyper/troph/y
P   R   S

DEFINITION: above or excessive/nourishment or development/condition or process of

1. thoracic

_____ / _____

Chapter 6 • Musculoskeletal System   **183**

Write in the missing anatomical terms on the blank lines in the following illustrations.

119–143.

119. {120. Face

- Hyoid
- 122. Manubrium
- 123.
- 124. Ribs
- 125.
- 126. Vertebral column
- Iliac crest
- 127.
- 128.
- 129.
- 130.
- 131.
- 132.
- 133.
- Pubic bone
- 134.
- 135.
- 136.
- 137.
- 141.
- 142.
- 143.

Posterior view

Chapter 6 • Musculoskeletal System   **191**

CENTRAL MEDICAL CENTER
211 Medical Center Drive • Central City, US 90000-1234 • PHONE: (012) 125-6784 • FAX: (012) 125-9999

X-RAY REPORT

LUMBOSACRAL SPINE:
Multiple views reveal no evidence of fracture. There is slight lumbar spondylosis with slight lipping and minimal bridging. The disc spaces appear maintained except for slight narrowing at L4-L5 and L5-S1. There is also a Grade 1 spondylolisthesis of L5 on S1 and evidence of spondylolysis at L5 on the left. There is also slight dextroscoliosis in the lumbar region and slight increased lordosis in the lumbosacral region. The bony architecture is unremarkable except for eburnation between the articulating facets at L5-S1. The SI joints appear unremarkable. Incidentally noted are slight osteoarthritic changes involving both hips.

CONCLUSION:
1. Slight lumbar spondylosis with hypertrophic lipping and slight narrowing of the L4-L5 and L5-S1 disc spaces, rule out discogenic disease. If clinically indicated, CT of the lumbosacral spine may prove helpful in further evaluation.

2. Grade 1 spondylolisthesis of L5 on S1 with evidence of spondylolysis at L5 on the left.

3. Slight dextroscoliosis in the lumbar region and slight increased lordosis in the lumbosacral region.

M. Volz, M.D.

MV:tj

D: 10/19/20xx
T: 10/20/20xx

X-RAY REPORT	PT. NAME: DORN, JAY F.
	ID NO: RL-483091
	ATT. PHYS: T. LIGHT, M.D.

Medical Record 6.3

MEDICAL RECORD 6.3

Jay Dorn, a retired construction worker, has had intermittent back pain for the last 2 months. When he began also having shooting pains in his legs, he went to his doctor at Central Medical Center. After a physical examination, Mr. Dorn underwent a series of back x-rays.

Directions

Read Medical Record 6.3 for Jay Dorn (page 191) and answer the following questions. This record is the radiographic report dictated by Dr. Mary Volz, the radiographer, after studying Mr. Dorn's x-rays and later transcribed for the record.

QUESTIONS ABOUT MEDICAL RECORD 6.3

Write your answers in the spaces provided.

1. Below are medical terms used in this record you have not yet encountered in this text. Underline each where it appears in the record and define below:

eburnation _____

_____

_____ one x-ray was taken?

_____

Does the report state how many x-rays were taken?

_____ no _____ yes If yes, how many?

_____

3. In your own words, not using medical terminology, describe the three diagnoses Dr. Volz makes.

Medical Records and Exercises in every chapter will help
you to apply medical terminology and build critical thinking skills.

USER'S GUIDE
Medical Terminology:
The Language of Health Care
Second Edition

Laminated Quick Review Guide is a great reference tool with Term Basics, and a comprehensive list of commonly used term components and their meanings.

Term Basics

Most medical terms have three basic components: **root**, **suffix**, and **prefix**.

The **root** is the **foundation** or **subject** of the term. All medical terms have one or more roots.

The **suffix** is the term **ending** that modifies and gives essential meaning to the root. All terms have a suffix.

The **prefix** is a term **beginning** used only when needed to further modify the root or roots. Not all medical terms have a prefix.

A **combining vowel** (usually *o* or *i*) connects a root to another root or to a suffix (term ending). A combining vowel is not used if the suffix begins with a vowel, but is retained when the suffix begins with a consonant.

A **combining form** is a **root plus** a combining **vowel**. Remembering combining forms makes it easy to form and spell medical terms.

Most medical terms can be defined by determining the meaning of the **suffix** first, then the **prefix** (if present), then the **root** or **roots**. Consult a good medical dictionary for the meaning of terms that are exceptions to this general rule.

Rules for Forming and Spelling Medical Terms

❶ A combining vowel is used to join root to root as well as root to any suffix beginning with a consonant, e.g., electr/o/cardi/o/gram.

❷ A combining vowel is *not* used before a suffix that begins with a vowel, e.g., vas/ectomy.

❸ If the root ends in a vowel and the suffix begins with the same vowel, drop the final vowel from the root and do not use a combining vowel, e.g., cardi/itis.

... a combining vowel ... een two roots even ... ot begins with a ... /esophageal.

... a prefix ends ... begins with ... s dropped ... enter/al.

---

acous/o	hearing
acr/o	extremity or topmost
-acusis	hearing condition
ad-	to, toward, or near
aden/o	gland
adip/o	fat
adren/o	adrenal gland
aer/o	air or gas
-al	pertaining to
albumin/o	protein
-algia	pain
allo-	other
alveol/o	alveolus (air sac)
ambi-	both
an-	without
ana-	up, apart
an/o	anus
andr/o	male
angi/o	vessel
ankyl/o	rooked or stiff
ante-	before
anti-	against or opposed to
aort/o	aorta
appendic/o	appendix
aque/o	water
-ar	pertaining to
-arche	beginning
arteri/o	artery
arthr/o	joint, articulation
articul/o	joint
-ary	pertaining to
-ase	enzyme
-asthenia	weakness
ather/o	fatty paste
-ation	process
atri/o	atrium
audi/o	hearing
aur/i	ear
auto-	self
bacteri/o	bacteria
balan/o	glans penis
bi-	two or both
bil/i	bile
-blast	germ or bud
blast/o	germ or bud
blephar/o	eyelid
brachi/o	arm
brady-	slow
bronch/o	bronchus (airway)
bronchi/o	bronchus (airway)
bronchiol/o	bronchiole (little airway)
bucc/o	cheek
capn/o	carbon dioxide
carb/o	carbon dioxide
carcin/o	cancer

-centesis	puncture for aspiration
cephal/o	head
cerebell/o	cerebellum (little brain)
cerebr/o	cerebrum (largest part of brain)
cerumin/o	wax
cervic/o	neck or cervix
cheil/o	lip
chol/e	bile
chondr/o	cartilage (gristle)
chrom/o	color
chromat/o	color
chyl/o	juice
circum-	around
cis/o	cut
col/o	colon
colon/o	colon
colp/o	vagina (sheath)
con-	together or with
conjunctiv/o	conjunctiva (to join together)
contra-	against or opposed to
corne/o	cornea
coron/o	circle or crown
cost/o	rib
crani/o	skull
crin/o	to secrete
cutane/o	skin
cyan/o	blue
cyst/o	bladder or sac
cyt/o	cell
dacry/o	tear
dactyl/o	digit (finger or toe)
de-	from, down, or not
dent/i	teeth
derm/o	skin
dermat/o	skin
-desis	binding
dextr/o	right, or on the right side
dia-	across or through
diaphor/o	profuse sweat
dips/o	thirst
dis-	separate from or apart
doch/o	du...
duoden/o	duod...
-dynia	painful, difficult, ...
dys-	painful, difficult, ...
-e	
e-	
-eal	
ec-	
-ectasis	expa...
ecto-	
-ectomy	
-emesis	

-emia	blood condition
en-	within
encephal/o	entire brain
endo-	within
enter/o	small intestine
epi-	upon
epididym/o	epididymis
episi/o	vulva (covering)
erythr/o	red
esophag/o	esophagus
esthesi/o	sensation
eu-	good or normal
ex-	out or away
exo-	outside
extra-	outside
fasci/o	fascia (a band)
femor/o	femur
fibr/o	fiber
gangli/o	ganglion (knot)
gastr/o	stomach
-gen	origin or production
gen/o	origin or production
ger/o	old age
-genesis	origin or production
gingiv/o	gums
gli/o	glue
glomerul/o	glomerulus (little ball)
gloss/o	tongue
glott/o	opening
gluc/o	sugar
glyc/o	sugar
glycos/o	sugar
gnos/o	knowing
-gram	record
-graph	instrument for recording
-graphy	process of recording
gynec/o	woman
hem/o	blood
hemat/o	blood
hemi-	half
hepat/o, hepatic/o	liver
herni/o	
hetera-	
hidr/o	
hist...	

Medical Terminology
The Language of Health Care
Marjorie Canfield Willis

Version 1.0   Second Edition

LIPPINCOTT WILLIAMS & WILKINS

Technical Support:
1-800-638-3030
or at techsupp@lww.com
Copyright©2006
Lippincott Williams & Wilkins,
A Wolters Kluwer Co.
All rights reserved.

A Bonus CD-ROM packaged with the book includes assessment exercises and Stedman's audio pronunciations.

Contents

Chapter 1

Building a Medical Vocabulary: Getting Started

OBJECTIVES

After completion of this chapter you will be able to

- Make a personal commitment to learn medical terminology
- Describe methods of study time management
- Explain the value of positive thinking in the learning process
- Choose a relaxing environment in which to study
- Explain how a healthy diet and regular exercise are beneficial to learning
- Use all senses to reinforce memory
- Prepare and use flash cards
- List suggested study tips
- Identify the learning tools that best fit your individual style

Personal Aspects of Successful Learning

To begin learning medical terminology, organize your study time and examine methods for efficient memorization. Consider the following personal aspects of successful learning.

COMMITMENT

Personal commitment is key to developing a solid knowledge of medical language. A strong pledge and lots of practice are necessary to memorize the basic building blocks of medical terms. Make that promise now!

TIME MANAGEMENT

Effective time management is essential. Other activities will always compete with the time available for study. Once committed to your goal, you must outline a reasonable plan for completion. Follow the study path this text and your instructor provide, and incorporate the necessary study time into your personal schedule.

Set aside *prime time* for study. Prime time is time during the day or evening when you feel most alert and at your finest, and it is when learning is best accomplished. Identify your personal prime time, and try your best to allot a concentrated block of it for memory work.

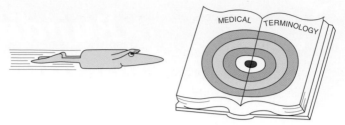

Figure 1.1   Focus on goals and plan for success.

The most common time-management problem is procrastination—putting tasks off until later. If you suffer from this affliction, you will need to act to curb this ineffective habit pattern and keep yourself on target. When you catch yourself procrastinating, focus immediately on the positive aspects of your commitment and the learning goals you have set. Try easing your way in by dividing studies into small segments you can reasonably complete. Take time to notice what you have accomplished, and reward yourself periodically for a job well done! Focus on your goals and the many rewards of accomplishment (Fig. 1.1).

ATTITUDE

Positive thinking is vital for effective learning. Feeling confident stems from positive thoughts. Negative thoughts always lead to defeat. Replace all negative thoughts with "can do" affirmatives that make confident thoughts a habit. A positive approach will help you to stay balanced when you encounter the inevitable hurdles and problems of life. Concentrate on what is "good"!

RELAXATION

Mental relaxation is indispensable for successful learning. The tension resulting from fear of failure or any other cause makes learning difficult or impossible. Give yourself a comfortable, relaxing atmosphere for studying. Consider listening to music you enjoy and find relaxing.

FITNESS

Regular, moderate exercise has been proven to reduce stress. Include it in your overall plan for successful learning. A healthy diet also provides the "fuel power" necessary for mental stamina.

Learning Tools

Part of setting the stage for learning is laying out effective tools and identifying the method of approach that meets one's individual needs. Sort out the following suggestions, and customize the ones that work best for you.

USING YOUR GOOD SENSES

When learning, the brain reinforces and retains facts as a result of interaction with the senses. The senses form mental images that are the basis for thought. We see (visual sense), we hear (auditory sense), we feel (kinesthetic sense), and, to a lesser degree, we taste (gustatory sense) and smell (olfactory sense).

An effective memory depends on intricate processes that recall mental images of sights, sounds, feelings, tastes, and smells. For this reason, try to include as many senses as possible in the process of reinforcing learning. Remember the three basics:

SEE IT	For visual reinforcement
SAY IT	For auditory reinforcement
WRITE IT	For kinesthetic reinforcement

FLASH CARDS FOR PREFIXES, SUFFIXES, AND COMBINING FORMS

Make a 3 × 5″ card for each prefix, suffix, and combining form listed in Chapter 2. Write each component on the front and its meaning on the back. Include a sample word or a drawing depicting the component to reinforce your visual sense (Fig. 1.2).

Use cards with different colors for each category, e.g., prefixes on blue cards, suffixes on green cards, and combining forms on pink cards. You can use pens of different colors for special emphasis, such as the prefix (blue card) in blue ink and the meaning on the reverse in red ink. Choose colors that are most pleasing to your visual and kinesthetic senses.

Also, within a category you can make distinctions; e.g., use green cards for all suffixes, but use different colors when writing meanings to indicate the types of suffixes [symptomatic suffixes (blue ink), diagnostic suffixes (green ink), operative/surgical suffixes (red ink), and general suffixes (black ink)]. These are just suggestions. Be as creative as you wish, and use colors that you find most pleasing or eye-catching.

Organizing Flash Cards

Punch a hole in the top of each flash card, and loop each card through a key chain or ring holder to make a "rotary file." This method keeps groups of cards together and prevents them from becoming lost or scattered. Within this file, you can group associated cards for components related to color, size, position, direction, etc.

Frugal Flash Cards

Preparing flash cards for each prefix, suffix, and combining form in Chapter 2 is well worth your effort and will pay off in memory reinforcement. Continue to make flash cards for each combining form added in Chapters 5 to 17.

Figure 1.2 Preparing flash cards.

Figure 1.3 Using the frugal flash card.

Also include abbreviations, symbols, and terms found throughout the text; however, if your stack of flash cards has become cumbersome, you may want to try the frugal flash card, so named because it consolidates paper and is inexpensive.

Fold a piece of $8\frac{1}{2} \times 11''$ lined paper in half lengthwise. Write the word component, symbol, or term on the first line of the first column and its definition on the same line in the second column. Skip a line and write the next word component, symbol, or term with its definition on the same line in the second column. Continue listing terms with corresponding definitions until you reach the bottom. Then fold the paper at the lengthwise crease so that the word component, symbol, or term is listed on one side and the definition appears on the same line on the other side. This lets you flip from one side to the other, "flashing" and reinforcing the meanings of the terms. Use the other side of the paper in the same way (Fig. 1.3).

Snatching Moments

Carry your flash cards with you at all times. During most days, there are times when you can snatch a moment to use your flash cards. You will feel less stress when waiting in a line or for an appointment if you know that you can use that time for study (Fig. 1.4).

Remember to use your good senses:

SEE IT	Employ your visual sense by making and repeatedly reviewing flash cards.
SAY IT	Pronounce each component out loud three times as you flash each card to reinforce your auditory sense.
WRITE IT	Make each flash card by hand using pleasant colored paper and ink to satisfy your kinesthetic sense.

DON'T HESITATE TO ANNOTATE!

Annotating simply refers to making notes as you read. Learning and reading research indicates that students retain information best after reflecting on what they've read and physically making notes with a pen or pencil that organize the material, clarify questions, and link new information to old. It is not enough to highlight or underline. As you read each chapter, and during lecture on related material, make notes in the

Figure 1.4 Snatching moments.

margins and look carefully at every new term or definition you encounter. Draw lines to separate the component parts of key terms, and write out their meanings.

MNEMONICS CAN HELP

Mnemonics, referring to any device for aiding memory, is named for the goddess of memory in Greek mythology. Mnemonic techniques link things to be remembered with clues for their recall using the stimulus of images, sounds, smell, touch, etc. Consider the following applications:

Draw pictures of word components for reinforcement. Often the most absurd associations can help you to remember. It does not matter if they make sense to no one but you (Fig. 1.5).

Make up rhymes or stories that help to differentiate between meanings. For example, "peri-," the prefix meaning *around*, is often confused with "para-," the prefix meaning *alongside of*. Use the two components in a sentence to compare their meanings; e.g., I sat "para" (**alongside of**) Sarah on the merry "peri" go-**around**.

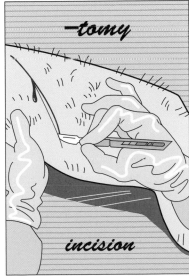

Figure 1.5 Draw pictures of word components for reinforcement.

Make up songs and rhythms to help remember facts. Take a song you are familiar with like "Row, row, row, your boat" and insert words with definitions that are in tune with the song.

Other Study Tips

Give yourself a memory drill by listing word components, symbols, or terms on one side of a paper and then filling in the definitions from memory. Write corrections in red ink. List the incorrectly defined components on a separate paper, and repeat the drill. Repeat this process until you have identified a list of those most continually found incorrect. Spend additional time on those troublesome terms.

Tape record lectures, and listen to pronunciations included in the CD-ROM that accompanies the text.

Find a study "buddy" or group from class. Compare notes, study techniques, quiz each other, and enjoy healthy competition.

Take advantage of the many fun and interactive learning activities this text provides in the CD-ROM, including:

- A pronunciation glossary with audio pronunciations
- Spelling bees to help you recognize and correctly spell terms
- Labeling exercises to reinforce and test your knowledge of medical terms and anatomy
- Games in which you match terms or components with definitions
- Scored and unscored chapter quizzes for knowledge assessment
- Interactive medical record exercises

Let your imagination be your guide. Be creative and make learning fun!

PRACTICE EXERCISES

1. Name the personal aspect that is key to developing a solid knowledge of medical language. _____

   _____

2. Identify your personal prime time. _____

3. Identify at least three methods for confronting procrastination. _____

   _____

   _____

   _____

   _____

4. How can a positive attitude help you with learning? _____

   _____

   _____

5. Give an example of a positive affirmation. _____

   _____

6. List at least three ways you can provide a relaxed environment in which to study.

   _____

   _____

   _____

   _____

7. How can a healthy diet and regular exercise help you learn? _____

   _____

   _____

8. List the three basic sensory rules for memorizing facts. _____

   _____

   _____

9. Describe the usefulness of preparing flash cards. _____

   _____

   _____

   _____

10. Explain what it means to annotate text material. _____

_____

_____

11. Identify at least three other study tips described in Chapter 1. _____

_____

_____

_____

Chapter 2

Basic Term Components

OBJECTIVES

After completion of this chapter you will be able to

- Describe the origin of medical language
- Analyze the component parts of a medical term
- List basic prefixes, suffixes, and combining forms
- Use basic prefixes, suffixes, and combining forms to build medical terms
- Explain common rules for proper medical term formation, pronunciation, and spelling

Most medical terms stem from Greek or Latin origins. These date to the founding of modern medicine by the Greeks and the influence of Latin when it was the universal language in the Western world. Other languages, such as German and French, have also influenced medical terms, and many new terms are derived from English, which is considered the universal language. Most terms related to diagnosis and surgery have Greek origin, and most anatomical terms can be traced to Latin.

Once you learn the basic medical term structure and memorize the most common term components (prefixes, suffixes, and combining forms), you can get the meaning of most medical terms by defining their parts. Those mysterious words, which are almost frightening at first, will soon no longer be a concern. You will analyze each term with your newly acquired knowledge and the help of a good medical dictionary.

This chapter lists common prefixes, suffixes, and a selected number of common combining forms. More combining forms and other pertinent prefixes and suffixes will be added in following chapters as you learn terms related to the body systems. The basic rules for proper medical term formation, pronunciation, and spelling are also presented here.

The key to success in building a medical vocabulary is the groundwork you do now by making flash cards and memorizing the basic term components in this chapter. The work will pay big dividends if you do.

ETYMOLOGY. The Greek root *etymon* refers to that which is true or genuine. Etymology is the study of the origin and development of words from the source language, original meaning, and history of usage.

Analysis of Term Components

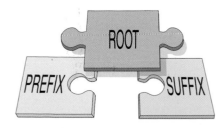

Most medical terms have three components: root, suffix, and prefix.

ROOT AND SUFFIX

Each term is formed by combining at least one root, the foundation or subject of the word, and a suffix, the ending that modifies and gives essential meaning to the root. For example, in lipemia,

$$\underset{\substack{\text{ROOT} \\ | \\ \text{fat}}}{\text{lip}} \Big/ \underset{\substack{\text{SUFFIX} \\ | \\ \text{blood condition}}}{\text{emia}}$$

Lip (fat), the root, is the subject. It is modified by the suffix (emia) to indicate a condition of fat in the blood. Note that each component is dependent on the other to express meaning.

Note: lipemia is synonymous with lipidemia (formed from lip, oid, and emia)

PREFIX

The prefix is a word structure placed at the beginning of a term when needed to further modify the root or roots. For example, in hyperlipemia

$$\underset{\substack{\text{PREFIX} \\ | \\ \text{excessive}}}{\text{hyper}} \Big/ \underset{\substack{\text{ROOT} \\ | \\ \text{fat}}}{\text{lip}} \Big/ \underset{\substack{\text{SUFFIX} \\ | \\ \text{blood condition}}}{\text{emia}}$$

The addition of the prefix, hyper, modifies the root to denote excessive fat in the blood.

ADDITIONAL ROOTS

Often a medical term is formed of two or more roots. For example, in hyperlipoproteinemia

$$\underset{\substack{\text{PREFIX} \\ | \\ \text{excessive}}}{\text{hyper}} \Big/ \underset{\substack{\text{ROOT} \\ | \\ \text{fat}}}{\text{lip}} \Big/ \underset{\substack{\text{VOWEL}}}{\text{o}} \Big/ \underset{\substack{\text{ROOT} \\ | \\ \text{protein}}}{\text{protein}} \Big/ \underset{\substack{\text{SUFFIX} \\ | \\ \text{blood condition}}}{\text{emia}}$$

In this term, the additional root, protein (joined to lip by the vowel "o"), further defines the word to indicate an excessive amount of fat and protein in the blood.

COMBINING VOWELS AND COMBINING FORMS

When a medical term has more than one root, each is joined by a vowel, usually an o. As shown in the term hyper/lip/o/protein/emia, the o links the two roots and fosters easier pronunciation. This vowel is known as a *combining vowel;* o is the most common combining vowel (i is the second most common) and is used so frequently to join root to root or root to suffix that it is routinely attached to the root and presented as a *combining form:*

lip   ROOT

lip/o   COMBINING FORM (ROOT WITH COMBINING VOWEL ATTACHED)

This text lists combining forms for easier term formation and analysis.

QUICK REVIEW

Complete the following sentences:

1. Most medical terms have three basic parts: the _____,

   _____, and _____.

2. The root is the _____ of the term.

3. The _____ is the word ending that modifies and gives essential meaning to the root.

4. The _____ is a word structure at the beginning of a term that further modifies the root.

5. Often a medical term is formed of _____ or more roots.

6. When a medical term has more than one root, it is joined together by a

   _____ (usually an ____).

7. A combining form is a _____ with a

   _____ attached.

QUICK REVIEW ANSWERS

1. root, suffix, prefix   4. prefix   7. root, vowel
2. foundation or subject   5. two
3. suffix   6. combining vowel, o

Required Activity

Using the guidelines found in Chapter 1 (see "Flash Cards for Prefixes, Suffixes, and Combining Forms", page 3), prepare flash cards for the basic term components listed in this chapter: prefixes (pages 20–22), combining forms (pages 23–25), and suffixes (pages 25–28). Memorize them in preparation for analysis of medical term formations, spelling considerations, and rules of pronunciation.

Rules for Forming and Spelling Medical Terms

Memorizing and spelling basic medical word components are the first steps for learning how to form medical terms. The next step is to construct the words using the following rules:

1. A combining vowel is used to join root to root as well as root to any suffix beginning with a consonant:

   e l e c t r   +   c a r d i   +   - g r a m
     ROOT   ROOT   SUFFIX
     electric   heart   record

   e l e c t r / o / c a r d i / o / g r a m

   e l e c t r o c a r d i o g r a m   (ELECTRICAL RECORD OF THE HEART)

2. A combining vowel is *not* used before a suffix that begins with a vowel:

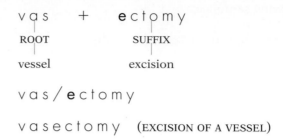

v a s   +   e c t o m y

ROOT   SUFFIX

vessel   excision

v a s / e c t o m y

v a s e c t o m y   (EXCISION OF A VESSEL)

3. If the root ends in a vowel and the suffix begins with the same vowel, drop the final vowel from the root and do not use a combining vowel:

c a r d i   +   i t i s

ROOT   SUFFIX

heart   inflammation

c a r d / i t i s

c a r d i t i s   (INFLAMMATION OF THE HEART)

4. Most often, a combining vowel is inserted between two roots even when the second root begins with a vowel:

c a r d i   +   e s o p h a g   +   e a l

ROOT   ROOT   SUFFIX

heart   esophagus   pertaining to

c a r d i / o / e s o p h a g e a l

c a r d i o e s o p h a g e a l   (PERTAINING TO THE HEART AND ESOPHAGUS)

5. Occasionally, when a prefix ends in a vowel and the root begins with a vowel, the final vowel is dropped from the prefix:

p a r a   +   e n t e r   +   a l

PREFIX   ROOT   SUFFIX

alongside of   intestine   pertaining to

p a r / e n t e r / a l

p a r e n t e r a l   (PERTAINING TO ALONGSIDE OF THE INTESTINE)

Breaking down and defining the components in a term often clues you to its meaning. Frequently, however, you must consult a medical dictionary to obtain a precise definition. Take a moment to look up *parenteral,* so you understand the complete meaning.

Note: There are many exceptions to these rules. Follow the basic guidelines, but be prepared to accept exceptions as you encounter them. Rely on your medical dictionary for additional guidance.

Defining Medical Terms Through Word Structure Analysis

You can usually define a term by interpreting the suffix first, then the prefix (if present), then the succeeding root or roots. For example, in pericarditis,

peri / card / itis

PREFIX	ROOT	SUFFIX
2	3	1
around	heart	inflammation

pericarditis   (INFLAMMATION AROUND THE HEART)

You sense the basic meaning of this term by understanding its components; however, the dictionary clarifies that the term refers to inflammation of the pericardium, the sac that encloses the heart.

Note: Beginning students often have difficulty differentiating between prefixes and roots (or combining forms) because the root appears first in a medical term when a prefix is not used. It is important to memorize the most common prefixes so that you can tell the difference. Also, keep in mind that a prefix is only used as needed to further modify the root or roots.

QUICK REVIEW

1. A combining vowel is used to join root to root as well as root to any suffix beginning with a consonant.
2. A combining vowel is not used before a suffix that begins with a vowel.
3. If the root ends in a vowel and the suffix begins with the same vowel, drop the final vowel from the root and do not use a combining vowel.
4. Most often, a combining vowel is inserted between two roots even when the second root begins with a vowel.
5. Occasionally, when a prefix ends in a vowel and the root begins with a vowel, the final vowel is dropped from the prefix.

Identify which of the rules listed above were applied when forming the following terms:

1. angi + -ectasis = angi/ectasis _____

2. hemat + -logy = hemato/logy _____

3. oste + -ectomy = ost/ectomy _____

4. electr + encephal + -gram = electro/encephalo/gram _____

5. para- + umbilic + -al = par/umbilic/al _____

6. vas + -ectomy = vas/ectomy _____

7. arteri + -itis = arter/itis _____

8. gastr + enter + -cele = gastro/entero/cele _____

9. gastr + -tomy = gastro/tomy _____

10. hypo + ox + -ia = hyp/ox/ia _____

Formation of Medical Terms

Most medical terms build from the root. Prefixes and suffixes are attached to the root to modify its meaning. Often two or more roots are linked before being modified. The following are examples of the various patterns of medical term formation using the root cardi (heart) as a base. Note the rules used for forming each term.

Root/Suffix

cardi / ac

HEART   PERTAINING TO
(pertaining to the heart)

Prefix/Root/Suffix

epi / card / ium

UPON   HEART   TISSUE
(tissue upon the heart, i.e., external lining of the heart)

Prefix/Prefix/Root/Suffix

sub / endo / cardi / al

BENEATH   WITHIN   HEART   PERTAINING TO
(pertaining to beneath and within the heart)

Root/Combining Vowel/Suffix

cardi / o / logy

HEART   STUDY OF
(study of the heart)

Root/Combining Vowel/Root/Suffix

cardi / o / pulmon / ary

HEART   LUNG   PERTAINING TO
(pertaining to the heart and lungs)

Root/Combining Vowel/Suffix (symptomatic)

cardi / o / dynia

HEART   PAIN
(pain in the heart)

Root/Combining Vowel/Suffix (diagnostic)

cardi / o / rrhexis

HEART   RUPTURE
(a rupture of the heart)

Root/Combining Vowel/Suffix (operative)

$$cardi / o / rrhaphy$$

HEART   SUTURE
(a suture of the heart)

A FEW EXCEPTIONS

As noted above, most medical terms are formed by the combination of a root or roots modified by suffixes and prefixes. Occasionally, terms are formed by a root alone or a combination of roots.

EXAMPLES

$$duct$$

ROOT

to lead

$$ovi / duct$$

ROOT   ROOT

egg   to lead

Oviduct refers to the uterine tube.

Sometimes, you will find a term formed from the combination of a prefix and a suffix.

EXAMPLE

meta   /   stasis

PREFIX   SUFFIX

beyond, after,   stop or stand
or change

Metastasis refers to the spread of a disease,
such as cancer, from one location to another.

QUICK REVIEW

Analyze the following terms by separating each component, and then define the individual elements:

1. gastric _____

2. epigastric _____

3. gastrocardiac _____

4. epigastralgia _____

5. gastroscopy _____

6. epigastrocele _____

7. gastrotomy _____

8. epigastrorrhaphy _____

QUICK REVIEW ANSWERS

1. gastr/ic   pertaining to the stomach
2. epi/gastr/ic   pertaining to upon the stomach
3. gastr/o/cardi/ac or gastro/cardi/ac   pertaining to the stomach and heart
4. epi/gastr/algia   pain upon the stomach
5. gastr/o/scopy or gastro/scopy   examination of the stomach
6. epi/gastr/o/cele or epi/gastro/cele   pouching or hernia upon the stomach
7. gastr/o/tomy or gastro/tomy   incision in the stomach
8. epi/gastr/o/rrhaphy or epi/gastro/rrhaphy   suture upon the stomach

Spelling Medical Terms

Correct spelling of medical terms is crucial for communication among health care professionals. Careless spelling causes misunderstandings that can have serious consequences. The following are some of the pitfalls to avoid.

1. Some words sound exactly the same but are spelled differently and have different meanings. Context is the clue to spelling. For example,

   i l e u m   (PART OF THE INTESTINE)   i l i u m   (PART OF THE HIP BONE)

   s i t o l o g y   (STUDY OF FOOD)   c y t o l o g y   (STUDY OF CELLS)

2. Other words sound similar but are spelled differently and have different meanings. For example,

   a b d u c t i o n   (TO DRAW AWAY FROM)   a d d u c t i o n   (TO DRAW TOWARD)

   h e p a t o m a   (LIVER TUMOR)   h e m a t o m a   (BLOOD TUMOR)

   a p h a g i a   (INABILITY TO SWALLOW)   a p h a s i a   (INABILITY TO SPEAK)

3. When letters are silent in a term, they risk being omitted when spelling the word. For example,

   pt has a "t" sound if found at the beginning of a term [e.g., pterygium, but both the "p" and "t" are pronounced when found within a term [e.g., nephroptosis (nef-rop-tō'sis)]

   ph has an "f" sound (e.g., diaphragm)

   ps has an "s" sound (e.g., psychology)

4. Some words have more than one accepted spelling. For example,

   o r t h o p e d i c   ORTHOPAEDIC (BRITISH)

   l e u k o c y t e   LEUCOCYTE (BRITISH)

5. Some combining forms have the same meaning but different origins that compete for usage. For example, there are three combining forms referring to the uterus:

hyster/o (GREEK)

metr/o (GREEK)

uter/o (LATIN)

ACCEPTABLE TERM FORMATIONS

As you learn medical terms, you can have fun experimenting with creating words, such as glyco (sweet) + cardio (heart) = sweetheart! However, in the real medical world, the word is formed when the term is coined. Often there seems to be no reason why a particular word form became acceptable. That is why you should check your medical dictionary when in doubt about the spelling, formation, or precise meaning.

Rules of Pronunciation

When you first learn to pronounce medical terms, the task can seem insurmountable. The first time you open your mouth to say a term is a tense moment for those who want to get it right! The best preparation is to study the basic rules of pronunciation, repeat the words after hearing them pronounced on the CD-ROM accompanying this text and/or after your instructor has said them, and try to keep the company of others who use medical language. There is nothing like the validation you get from the fact that no one laughed or snarled at you when you said something "medical" for the very first time! Your confidence will build with every word you use.

Following are some helpful shortcuts:

Shortcuts to Pronunciation

Consonant	Example
c (before a, o, u) = k	cavity colon cure
c (before e, i) = s	cephalic cirrhosis
ch = k	cholesterol
g (before a, o, u) = g	gallstone gonad gurney
g (before e, i) = j	generic giant
ph = f	phase
pn = n	pneumonia
ps = s	psychology
pt = t	ptosis pterygium

Consonant	Example
rh = r	rhythm
rrh = r	hemorrhoid
x = z (as first letter)	xerosis

THE PHONETIC SYSTEM

Phonetic spelling for pronunciation of most medical terms in this text is in parentheses below the term (beginning with Chapter 3). The phonetic system used is basic and has only a few standard rules. The macron and breve are the two diacritical marks used. The macron (¯) is placed over vowels that have a long sound:

ā	day
ē	be
ī	kite
ō	no
ū	unit

The breve (˘) is placed over vowels that have a short sound:

ă	alone
ĕ	ever
ĭ	pit
ŏ	ton
ŭ	sun

The primary accent (´) is placed after the syllable that is stressed when saying the word. Monosyllables do not have a stress mark. Other syllables are separated by hyphens.

QUICK REVIEW

1. The *pt* in *pterygium* has a/an ____ sound.

2. The *ch* in the word *chronic* has a/an ____ sound.

3. The *c* in the word *cirrhosis* has a/an ____ sound.

4. The *x* in *xerosis* has a/an ___ sound.

5. The *g* in *genital* has a/an ___ sound.

6. The *pn* in *pneumatic* has a/an ___ sound.

QUICK REVIEW ANSWERS

1. t	4. z
2. k	5. j
3. s	6. n

Singular and Plural Forms

Most often, plurals are formed by adding -s or -es to the end of a singular form. The following are common exceptions.

Singular		Plural	
ENDING	EXAMPLE	ENDING	EXAMPLE
-a	vertebra	-ae	vertebrae
-is	diagnosis	-es	diagnoses
-ma	condyloma	-mata	condylomata
-on	phenomenon	-a	phenomena
-um	bacterium	-a	bacteria
-us[a]	fungus	-i	fungi
-ax	thorax	-aces	thoraces
-ex	apex	-ices	apices
-ix	appendix	-ices	appendices
-y	myopathy	-ies	myopathies

[a]Viruses and sinuses are not exceptions.

QUICK REVIEW

Convert the following singular forms to plural:

1. bulla_____

2. speculum _____

3. fungus _____

4. stoma_____

5. anomaly _____

6. prognosis _____

QUICK REVIEW ANSWERS

1. bullae
2. specula
3. fungi
4. stomata
5. anomalies
6. prognoses

Common Prefixes

A list of commonly used prefixes organized within categories follows. A hyphen is placed after each prefix to indicate its link at the beginning of a medical term. Each includes a term example. Appendix A and the Quick Study Reference include a summary list of prefixes in alphabetical order.

Prefix	Meaning	Example
NEGATION		
a-, an-	without	aphonia (*without* voice or sound)
		anaerobic (pertaining to *without* air)
anti-, contra-	against or opposed to	anticoagulant (*against* clotting)
		contraception (*opposed* to becoming pregnant)
de-	from, down, or not	decapitate [separation of the head (caput) *from* the body]
POSITION/DIRECTION		
ab-	away from	abnormal (pertaining to *away from* normal)
ad-	to, toward, or near	adhesion (*to* stick to)
circum-, peri-	around	circumvascular (pertaining to *around* a vessel)
		periosteum (pertaining to *around* bone)
dia-, trans-	across or through	dialysis [dissolution *across* or *through* (a membrane)]
		transmission (to send *across* or *through*)
e-, ec-, ex-	out or away	edentia (condition of teeth *out*) [dent/o=teeth]
		eccentric (pertaining to *away* from center)
		excise (to cut *out*) [cis/o=to cut]
ecto-, exo-, extra-	outside	ectopic (pertaining to a place *outside*)
		exocrine (denoting secretion *outside*)
		extravascular (pertaining to *outside* a vessel)
en-, endo-, intra-	within	encapsulate (*within* little box)
		endoscope (instrument for examination *within*)
		intradermal (pertaining to *within* skin)

Prefix	Meaning	Example
epi-	upon	epidermal (pertaining to *upon* the skin)
inter-	between	intercostal (pertaining to *between* the ribs) [cost/o=rib]
meso-	middle	mesomorphic (pertaining to *middle* form)
meta-	beyond, after, or change	metastasis [*beyond* stopping or standing (spread of disease from one part of the body to another)]
		metamorphosis (condition of *change* in form)
para-	alongside of or abnormal	paramedic (pertaining to *alongside of* medicine)
		paranoia (condition of *abnormal* thinking)
retro-	backward or behind	retrograde (going *backward*)
sub-, infra-	below or under	infraumbilical (pertaining to *below* the navel) [umbilic/o=navel]
		sublingual (pertaining to *under* the tongue) [lingu/o=tongue]
QUANTITY OR MEASUREMENT		
bi-	two or both	bilateral (pertaining to *two or both* sides)
hemi-, semi-	half	hemicephalic (pertaining to *half* of the head)
		semilunar (pertaining to *half* moon) [luna=moon]
hyper-	above or excessive	hyperlipemia (*excessive* fat in blood)
hypo-	below or deficient	hypothermia (condition of *below* normal temperature) [therm/o=heat]
macro-	large or long	macrocyte (*large* cell)
micro-	small	microlith (*small* stone)
mono-, uni-	one	monochromatic (pertaining to *one* color) [chromat/o=color]
		unilateral (pertaining to *one* side)
oligo-	few or deficient	oliguria (condition of *deficient* urine)
pan-	all	panacea (a cure-*all*)

Prefix	Meaning	Example
poly-, multi-	many	polyphobia (condition of *many* fears)
		multicellular (pertaining to *many* cells)
quadri-	four	quadriplegia (paralysis of all *four* limbs)
super-, supra-	above or excessive	suprarenal (pertaining to *above* the kidney)
		supernumerary [*excessive* numbers (too many to count)]
tri-	three	triangle (*three* angles)
ultra-	beyond or excessive	ultrasonic (pertaining to *beyond* sound)
TIME		
ante-, pre-, pro-	before	antepartum (*before* labor)
		premature (*before* ripe)
		prognosis [*before* knowing (prediction of course and outcome of a disease)]
brady-	slow	bradycardia (condition of *slow* heart)
tachy-	fast	tachycardia (condition of *fast* heart)
post-	after or behind	postoperative [*after* operation (surgery)]
re-	again or back	reactivate (to make active *again*)
GENERAL		
con-, syn-, sym-	together or with	syndactylism (webbing *together* of toes or fingers) [dactyl/o= finger or toe]
		symbiosis (presence of life *together*) [bio=life]
		congenital (pertaining to being born *with*)
dys-	painful, difficult, or faulty	dysphonia [condition of *difficult* voice or sound (hoarseness)]
eu-	good or normal	eugenic (pertaining to *good* production)
neo-	new	neoplasia [a *new* (abnormal) formation]

Common Combining Forms

Following are selected combining forms (roots with combining vowels attached) to give you a start toward building medical terms. Additional combining forms are introduced at the beginning of Chapters 5 to 17 on body systems. Each is presented with a slash between the root and the combining vowel along with a term example. Appendix A and the Quick Study Reference include a summary list of combining forms in alphabetical order.

Combining Forms

Combining Form	Meaning	Example
abdomin/o	abdomen	abdominal (pertaining to *abdomen*)
lapar/o		laparotomy (incision into the *abdomen*)
acr/o	extremity or topmost	acrodynia (pain in an *extremity*)
		acrophobia [exaggerated fear of *topmost* places (heights)]
aden/o	gland	adenoma (*gland* tumor)
aer/o	air or gas	aerobic (pertaining to *air*)
angi/o	vessel	angioplasty (surgical repair of a blood *vessel*)
vas/o		vasectomy (excision of a *vessel*)
vascul/o		vascular (pertaining to a *vessel*)
carcin/o	cancer	carcinogenic (pertaining to production of *cancer*)
cardi/o	heart	cardiologist (one who specializes in treatment of the *heart*)
cephal/o	head	cephalic (pertaining to the *head*)
cyan/o	blue	cyanotic (pertaining to *blue*)
cyt/o	cell	cytology (study of *cells*)
derm/o	skin	dermal (pertaining to the *skin*)
dermat/o		dermatology (study of the *skin*)
cutane/o		cutaneous (pertaining to the *skin*)
dextr/o	right or on the right side	dextrocardia (condition of the heart *on the right side*)
erythr/o	red	erythrocyte (*red* cell)
fibr/o	fiber	fibroma (*fiber* tumor)
gastr/o	stomach	gastric (pertaining to the *stomach*)
gen/o	origin or production	osteogenic (pertaining to *origin or production* in bone)

 CANCER. Cancer is Latin for crab. The word is derived from the Greek word karkinos that was used by Hippocrates and other early writers and also means crab. Some authorities say the word was used because it describes the appearance of the disease; i.e., just as the crab's foot extend in all directions from its body, so can the disease extend in the human. Other authorities relate the term to the obstinacy of a crab in pursuing prey.

Combining Form	Meaning	Example
gluc/o	sugar	glucogenesis (origin or production of *sugar*)
glucos/o		glucose (*sugar*)
glyc/o		glycolysis (breakdown or dissolution of *sugar*)
hem/o	blood	hemogram (record of *blood*)
hemat/o		hematology (study of *blood*)
hepat/o	liver	hepatoma (tumor of the *liver*)
hydr/o	water	hydrophobia (exaggerated fear of *water*)
leuk/o	white	leukocyte (*white* cell)
lip/o	fat	lipoid (resembling *fat*)
lith/o	stone	lithiasis (formation or presence of a *stone*)
melan/o	black	melanoma (*black* tumor)
morph/o	form	morphology (study of *form*)
nas/o	nose	nasal (pertaining to the *nose*)
rhin/o		rhinitis (inflammation of the *nose*)
necr/o	death	necrocytosis (condition or increase of cell *death*)
or/o	mouth	oral (pertaining to the *mouth*)
orth/o	straight, normal, or correct	orthostatic (pertaining to standing *straight*)
oste/o	bone	osteal (pertaining to *bone*)
path/o	disease	pathology (study of *disease*)
ped/o	child or foot	pediatrics (treatment of *child*)
		pedal (pertaining to the *foot*)
phob/o	exaggerated fear or sensitivity	hydrophobia (*exaggerated fear* of water)
		photophobia (*sensitivity* to light)
phon/o	voice or sound	phonic (pertaining to *voice* or sound)
plas/o	formation	dysplasia (condition of faulty *formation*)
pod/o	foot	podiatry (treatment of the *foot*)
psych/o	mind	psychology (study of the *mind*)
py/o	pus	pyopoiesis (formation of *pus*)
ren/o	kidney	renal (pertaining to the *kidney*)
nephr/o		nephrosis (condition of the *kidney*)

Combining Form	Meaning	Example
scler/o	hard	sclerosis (a condition of *hardness*)
sinistr/o	left or on the left side	sinistropedal (pertaining to the *left* foot)
son/o	sound	sonometer (an instrument to measure *sound*)
sten/o	narrow	stenosis (a condition of *narrow*)
therm/o	heat	thermometer (instrument for measuring *heat*)
tox/o	poison	toxemia (*poison* in blood)
toxic/o		toxicology (study of *poison*)
troph/o	nourishment or development	trophocyte (a cell that provides *nourishment*)
		hypertrophy (condition of excessive *development*)
ur/o	urine	urology (study of *urine*)
urin/o		urinary (pertaining to *urine*)

 TOXIN. The Greek root toxicon means arrow poison and is derived from the word for the archer's bow. The Greeks often used darts and arrows coated with a poisonous substance.

Common Suffixes

Suffixes are endings that modify the root. They give the root essential meaning by forming a noun, verb, or adjective.

There are two types of suffixes: simple and compound. Simple suffixes form basic terms. For example, ic (pertaining to), a simple suffix, combined with the root gastr (stomach) forms the term gastric (pertaining to the stomach). Compound suffixes are formed by a combination of basic term components. For example, the root tom (to cut) combined with the simple suffix y (denoting a process of) forms the compound suffix tomy (incision); the compound suffix ectomy (excision or removal) is formed by a combination of the prefix ec (out) with the root tom (to cut) and the simple suffix y (a process of). Compound suffixes are added to the roots to provide a specific meaning. For example, hyster (a root meaning uterus) combined with ectomy forms hysterectomy (excision of the uterus). Noting the differences between simple and compound suffixes will help you analyze medical terms.

Suffixes in this text are divided into four categories:

- Symptomatic suffixes, which describe the evidence of illness

- Diagnostic suffixes, which provide the name of a medical condition

- Operative (surgical) suffixes, which describe a surgical treatment

- General suffixes, which have general application

Commonly used suffixes follow in alphabetical order except for groups with the same meaning. A hyphen is placed before each to indicate their link at the end of a term.

Appendix A and the Quick Study Reference include a summary list of suffixes in alphabetical order.

Suffix	Meaning	Example
SYMPTOMATIC SUFFIXES (WORD ENDINGS THAT DESCRIBE EVIDENCE OF ILLNESS)		
-algia	pain	cephalalgia [*pain* in the head (headache)]
-dynia		cephalodynia [*pain* in the head (headache)]
-genesis	origin or production	pathogenesis (*origin or production* of disease)
-lysis	breaking down or dissolution	hemolysis (*breakdown* of blood)
-megaly	enlargement	hepatomegaly (*enlargement* of the liver)
-oid	resembling	lipoid (*resembling* fat)
-penia	abnormal reduction	leukopenia [*abnormal reduction* of white (blood cells)]
-rrhea	discharge	rhinorrhea (runny *discharge* from nose)
-spasm	involuntary contraction	vasospasm (*involuntary contraction* of a blood vessel)
DIAGNOSTIC SUFFIXES (WORD ENDINGS THAT DESCRIBE A CONDITION OR DISEASE)		
-cele	pouching or hernia	gastrocele (*pouching* of the stomach)
-ectasis	expansion or dilation	angiectasis (*expansion or dilation* of a blood vessel)
-emia	blood condition	hyperlipemia (*blood condition* of excessive fat)
-iasis	formation or presence of	lithiasis (*formation or presence of* a stone or stones)
-itis	inflammation	hepatitis (*inflammation* of the liver)
-malacia	softening	osteomalacia (*softening* of bone)
-oma	tumor	carcinoma (cancer *tumor*)
-osis	condition or increase	sclerosis (*condition* of hard)
		leukocytosis (*increase* of white cells)
-phil	attraction for	basophil (cell with an *attraction for* basic dyes)
-philia		pneumophilia (condition that has an *attraction for* the lungs)

Suffix	Meaning	Example
-ptosis	falling or downward displacement	gastroptosis (*downward displacement* of the stomach)
-rrhage **-rrhagia**	to burst forth (usually blood)	hemorrhage (*to burst forth* blood)
-rrhexis	rupture	hepatorrhexis (*rupture* of the liver)

OPERATIVE SUFFIXES [WORD ENDINGS THAT DESCRIBE A SURGICAL (OPERATIVE) TREATMENT]

Suffix	Meaning	Example
-centesis	puncture for aspiration	abdominocentesis (*puncture for aspiration* of the abdomen)
-desis	binding	arthrodesis (*binding* together of a joint) [arthr/o=joint]
-ectomy	excision or removal	nephrectomy (*excision or removal* of a kidney)
-pexy	suspension or fixation	gastropexy [*fixation* of the stomach (to the abdominal wall)]
-plasty	surgical repair or reconstruction	rhinoplasty (*surgical repair* of the nose)
-rrhaphy	suture	osteorrhaphy (*suture* of bone)
-tomy	incision	laparotomy (*incision* into the abdomen)
-stomy	creation of an opening	gastrostomy (*creation of an opening* in the stomach)
-tripsy	crushing	lithotripsy (*crushing* of stone)

GENERAL SUFFIXES (SUFFIXES THAT HAVE GENERAL APPLICATIONS)

Noun Endings (suffixes that form a noun when combined with a root)

Suffix	Meaning	Example
-e	noun marker	erythrocyte (a red blood cell)
-ia	condition of	phobia (*condition of* an exaggerated fear or sensitivity)
-ism		alcoholism (*condition of* alcohol abuse)
-ium	structure or tissue	epigastrium [*structure* upon the stomach (region in the abdomen)]
		pericardium [*tissue* around the heart (sac enclosing the heart)]
-ation	condition or process of	starvation (*condition or process of* starving)
-y		adenopathy (*condition or process of* gland disease)

Suffix	Meaning	Example
Adjective Endings (suffixes that mean "pertaining to" and form an adjective when combined with a root)		
-ac		cardiac (*pertaining to* the heart)
-al		pedal (*pertaining to* the foot)
-ar		glandular (*pertaining to* a gland)
-ary		pulmonary (*pertaining to* the lung)
-eal		esophageal (*pertaining to* the esophagus)
-ic		toxic (*pertaining to* poison)
-ous		fibrous (*pertaining to* fiber)
-tic		cyanotic (*pertaining to* blue)
Diminutive Endings (suffixes meaning "small")		
-icle		ventricle (*small* belly or pouch)
-ole		bronchiole (*small* airway)
-ula		macula (*small* spot)
-ule		pustule (*small* pimple)
Other General Suffixes		
-gram	record	sonogram (*record* of sound)
-graph	instrument for recording	sonograph (*instrument for recording* sound)
-graphy	process of recording	sonography (*process of recording* sound)
-iatrics	treatment	pediatrics (*treatment* of children)
-iatry		psychiatry (*treatment* of the mind)
-logy	study of	cytology (*study of* cells)
-logist	one who specializes in the study or treatment of	psychologist (*one who specializes in the study or treatment of* the mind)
-ist	one who specializes in	pharmacist (*one who specializes in* drugs)
-meter	instrument for measuring	spirometer (*instrument for measuring* breathing) [spir/o= breathing]
-metry	process of measuring	spirometry (*process of measuring* breathing)
-poiesis	formation	hemopoiesis (*formation* of blood)
-scope	instrument for examination	endoscope (*instrument for examination* within)
-scopy	examination	endoscopy (*examination* within)
-stasis	stop or stand	hemostasis (*stop* blood)
		orthostasis (*stand* straight)

Don't Be Rolled Over by the

rr's

We have the Greeks to thank for the suffixes with **double rr's**. Take a careful look at each so that you will spell them correctly in a term!

Suffix	Meaning	Example
-rrhea	discharge	pyorrhea—a discharge of pus
-rrhage or -rrhagia	to burst forth (usually blood)	hemorrhage—a bursting forth of blood
		menorrhagia—a bursting forth of blood during menstruation
-rrhexis	rupture	angiorrhexis—rupture of a vessel
-rrhaphy	suture	nephrorrhaphy—suture of the kidney

Also note that each component also has an h and **-rrhaphy** has two!

PRACTICE EXERCISES

For the following words, draw a line or lines to separate prefixes, roots, combining forms, and suffixes. Then define the word according to the meaning of: **P=prefix; R=root; CF=combining form; S=suffix.**

EXAMPLE

hyperlipemia

_____ / _____ / _____
P   R   S

hyper/lip/emia
P R S

DEFINITION: above or excessive/fat/blood condition

1. pancytopenia

_____ / _____ / _____
P   CF   S

DEFINITION: _____

2. leukemia

_____ / _____
R   S

DEFINITION: _____

3. toxoid

_____ / _____
R   S

DEFINITION: _____

4. mesomorphic

_____ / _____ / _____
P   R   S

DEFINITION: _____

5. acrodynia

_____ / _____
CF   S

DEFINITION: _____

6. metastasis

_____ / _____
P   S

DEFINITION: _____

7. ultrasonography

_____ / _____ / _____
      P   CF   S

DEFINITION: _____

8. tachycardia

_____ / _____ / _____
      P   R   S

DEFINITION: _____

9. pyopoiesis

_____ / _____
      CF   S

DEFINITION: _____

10. adenitis

_____ / _____
      R   S

DEFINITION: _____

11. macrocephalous

_____ / _____ / _____
      P   R   S

DEFINITION: _____

12. paracentesis

_____ / _____
      P   S

DEFINITION: _____

13. microlithiasis

_____ / _____ / _____
      P   R   S

DEFINITION: _____

14. orthopedic

_____ / _____ / _____
      CF   R   S

DEFINITION: _____

15. angiomegaly

_____ / _____
      CF   S

DEFINITION: _____

16. psychiatry

_____ / _____
      R   S

DEFINITION: _____

17. carcinogenesis

_____ / _____
         CF   S

DEFINITION: _____

18. nephrologist

_____ / _____
         CF   S

DEFINITION: _____

19. rhinostenosis

_____ / _____ / _____
         CF   R   S

DEFINITION: _____

20. hypohydration

_____ / _____ / _____
          P   R   S

DEFINITION: _____

21. aerogastralgia

_____ / _____ / _____
         CF   R   S

DEFINITION: _____

22. fibroma

_____ / _____
          R   S

DEFINITION: _____

23. necrophilia

_____ / _____
         CF   S

DEFINITION: _____

24. sclerosis

_____ / _____
          R   S

DEFINITION: _____

25. hemolysis

_____ / _____
         CF   S

DEFINITION: _____

26. acrophobia

_____ / _____ / _____
         CF   R   S

DEFINITION: _____

27. cytometer

_____ / _____
       CF   S

DEFINITION: _____

28. cyanotic

_____ / _____
       CF   S

DEFINITION: _____

29. extravascular

_____ / _____ / _____
       P   R   S

DEFINITION: _____

30. hypertrophy

_____ / _____ / _____
       P   R   S

DEFINITION: _____

Write in the appropriate prefix to complete the following terms:

31. _____ nasal = *above* the nose
    a. para   b. peri   c. supra   d. infra   e. sub

32. _____ activate = make active *again*
    a. de   b. retro   c. pro   d. re   e. hyper

33. _____ operative = *before* surgery
    a. intra   b. post   c. pre   d. peri   e. circum

34. _____ hydrated = *not* watered
    a. anti   b. de   c. ec   d. dys   e. contra

35. _____ dermal = *across or through* the skin
    a. ecto   b. endo   c. intra   d. epi   e. trans

36. _____ acute = *excessively* severe
    a. sub   b. hypo   c. super   d. oligo   e. pan

37. _____ umbilical = *below or under* the navel
    a. hyper   b. infra   c. peri   d. para   e. pre

38. _____ cardia = *outside* the heart
    a. exo   b. endo   c. retro   d. para   e. peri

39. _____ phonia = *difficult* voice
    a. ab   b. dys   c. a   d. eu   e. para

40. _____ duction = to turn *away from*
    a. ad   b. ab   c. ecto   d. pro   e. ante

41. _____ phylaxis = to guard *before*
    a. retro   b. pro   c. post   d. peri   e. anti

42. _____ vascular = *around* a blood vessel
     a. intra   b. inter   c. para   d. circum   e. endo

43. _____ plegia = *half* paralysis
     a. quadri   b. peri   c. hemi   d. bi   e. mono

Match the following:

44. _____ away from   a. retro-

45. _____ between   b. peri-

46. _____ alongside of   c. anti-

47. _____ around   d. ecto-

48. _____ behind   e. dia-

49. _____ within   f. ab-

50. _____ against or opposed to   g. inter-

51. _____ without   h. para-

52. _____ outside   i. an-

53. _____ across or through   j. intra-

Give the meaning of the following prefixes:

54. poly- _____   60. bi-   _____

55. hypo- _____   61. quadri- _____

56. oligo- _____   62. semi-   _____

57. mono- _____   63. infra- _____

58. pan- _____   64. hyper- _____

59. ultra- _____

Match the following:

65. _____ before   a. brady-

66. _____ after   b. re-

67. _____ fast   c. ante-

68. _____ slow   d. post-

69. _____ again   e. tachy-

Circle the correct meaning for the following term components:

70. a-
    a. double   b. both   c. two   d. without   e. against

71. pod/o
    a. child   b. foot   c. voice   d. sound   e. pus

72. or/o
    a. lip   b. nourishment   c. gland   d. mouth   e. normal

73. neo-
    a. birth   b. death   c. origin   d. new   e. disease

74. -plasty
    a. surgical repair b. cancer   c. tumor   d. excision   e. incision

75. -ation
    a. measure   b. disease   c. tissue   d. pain   e. process

76. -tripsy
    a. nourishment   b. poison   c. crushing   d. incision   e. stone

77. -ectasis
    a. blood condition b. formation of c. expansion   d. rupture   e. discharge

78. dextr/o
    a. hard   b. straight   c. right   d. left   e. long

Match the following:

79. _____ black   a. tri-

80. _____ three   b. leuk/o

81. _____ red   c. cyan/o

82. _____ four   d. dextr/o

83. _____ white   e. uni-

84. _____ one   f. melan/o

85. _____ blue   g. quadri-

86. _____ two   h. sinistr/o

87. _____ few   i. oligo-

88. _____ right   j. erythr/o

89. _____ left   k. bi-

Circle the appropriate suffix for each of the following meanings:

90. record
    a. -meter   b. -metry   c. -gram   d. -graph   e. graphy

91. condition or increase
    a. -itis   b. -iasis   c. -osis   d. -ium   e. -ous

92. excision
    a. -tomy   b. -stomy   c. -ectomy   d. -centesis   e. cele

93. pertaining to
    a. -ia   b. -ar   c. -ism   d. -ium   e. -icle

94. rupture
    a. -rrhagia   b. -rrhea   c. -rrhagia   d. -rrhexis   e. -megaly

95. small
    a. -ous   b. -eal   c. -ula   d. -ia   e. -ary

96. condition of
    a. -ism   b. -ium   c. -ule   d. -ic   e. al

Match the following terms related to the kidney with the definitions listed below:

nephrolysis	nephrostomy	nephroptosis	nephrotomy
nephritis	nephropexy	nephroma	nephrocele
nephrogenous	nephrolithiasis	nephrorrhaphy	nephrectomy

97. inflammation of the kidney_____

98. dissolution or breakdown of the kidney_____

99. incision in the kidney _____

100. developing from the kidney _____

101. surgical fixation of the kidney _____

102. creation of an opening in the kidney _____

103. excision of the kidney_____

104. presence of kidney stones _____

105. kidney tumor _____

106. hernia of the kidney _____

107. suture of the kidney _____

108. downward displacement of the kidney _____

Circle the operative term in each of the following lists:

109. a. nephroptosis   b. hemolysis   c. angiectasis   d. colostomy
     e. necrosis

110. a. vasorrhaphy   b. hematoma   c. gastrocele   d. endoscope
     e. cardiorrhexis

111. a. morphologic   b. adenolysis   c. abdominocentesis   d. osteomalacia
     e. polyrrhea

Fill in the blanks for the following regarding singular/plural forms:

112. An ovum is an egg produced by an ovary. There are two _____ in the

female that produce eggs or _____.

113. The spread of cancer to a distant organ is called metastasis. The spread of

cancer to more than one organ is _____.

114. A verruca is a wart. The term for several warts is _____.

115. Condylomata are genital warts. One genital wart is a _____.

116. Indices is a plural form of _____.

117. A thrombus is a clot. Several clots are termed _____.

Circle the correct spelling:

118. a. nephoraphy   b. nephorrapy   c. nephrorrhaphy   d. nephorrhapy

119. a. abdominoscopy   b. abdemenoscopi   c. abdomenscopy   d. abdominoschope

120. a. perrycardium   b. pericardium   c. periocardium   d. parcardium

Chapter 3

Fields of Medical Practice

OBJECTIVES

After completion of this chapter you will be able to

- Define combining forms used in naming medical specialties
- Trace the evolution of medicine
- Identify the purpose of the American Board of Medical Specialties
- Define diplomate and fellow
- Describe the scope of medical practice for the medical specialties recognized by the American Board of Medical Specialties
- Identify other medical practitioners with the title of doctor and list their scope of practice
- List titles of other health professionals

Combining Forms

Combining Form	Meaning	Example
cardi/o	heart	cardiology kar-dē-ol'ō-jē
chir/o	hand	chiropractic kī-rō-prak'tik
crin/o	to secrete	endocrinology en'dō-kri-nol'ō-jē
dent/i	teeth	dentist den'tist
dermat/o	skin	dermatology der-mă-tol'ō-jē
enter/o	small intestine	gastroenterology gas'trō-en-ter-ol'ō-jē
esthesi/o	sensation	anesthesiology an'es-thē-zē-ol'ō-jē
gastr/o	stomach	gastroenterology gas'trō-en-ter-ol'ō-jē

Combining Form	Meaning	Example
gen/o	origin or production	gene jēn
ger/o	old age	geriatric jer-ē-at'rik
gynec/o	woman	gynecology gī-ně-kol'ō-jē
hemat/o	blood	hematology hē'mǎ-tol'ō-jē
immun/o	safe	immunology im'yū-nol'ō-jē
laryng/o	voicebox	otolaryngology ō'tō-lar-ing-gol'ō-jē
nephr/o	kidney	nephrology ne-frol'ō-jē
neur/o	nerve	neurologist noo-rol'ō-jist
obstetr/o	midwife	obstetric ob-stet'rik
onc/o	tumor	oncology ong-kol'ō-jē
ophthalm/o	eye	ophthalmology of-thal-mol'ō-jē
opt/o	eye	optometry op-tom'ě-trē
orth/o	straight, normal, or correct	orthopedics ōr-thō-pē'diks
ot/o	ear	otolaryngologist ō'tō-lar-ing-gol'ō-jist
path/o	disease	pathologist pa-thol'ō-jist
ped/o	child or foot	pediatrics pē-dē-at'riks orthopedics ōr-thō-pē'diks
physi/o	physical	physiatrist fiz-ī'ǎ-trist
plas/o	formation	plastic surgery plas'tik ser'jer-ē
pod/o	foot	podiatry pō-dī'ǎ-trē
psych/o	mind	psychiatry sī-kī'ǎ-trē

Combining Form	Meaning	Example
radi/o	x-ray	radiology rā-dē-ol′ō-jē
vascul/o	vessel	vascular vas′kyu-lăr

The Evolution of Medicine

Today's practice of medicine evolved from the customs of ancient times. Care for the *patient* (one who suffers) was often given by priests who gave homage to mythological gods and performed rituals designed to appease those gods to rid the body of disease.

Hippocrates, the ancient Greek physician who lived about 400 B.C., is known as the "Father of Medicine." He was the first to attempt to separate medicine from myth, and his writings include the first rational documentation of disease. He also wrote the Hippocratic Oath, which was the standard of medical ethics for physicians in his day and is the basis of modern ethical codes (Fig. 3.1).

Curiosity about the body and the causes of disease led to the study of anatomy and physiology and the art of healing practiced by medieval physicians. Scientific progress led to the development of surgery, pharmacy, pathology, and other aspects of medicine. Hospitals were built to care for the sick and dying, and universities were established to study disease (Fig. 3.2).

Medieval methods have evolved into the modern sophisticated health care system that provides comprehensive care. Physicians have branched out into many specialties of medicine and have been joined by a team of other health care professionals with highly developed training and skills.

The Physician

Today, health care is delivered by a complicated system involving many types of professionals. The most prominent professional responsible for meeting the medical needs of the patient is the physician, also called a medical doctor (Fig. 3.3).

HIPPOCRATES. Born on the island of Cos about 400 B.C. and known as the founder of medicine, this Greek physician created the art and science of medicine and removed it from the realm of superstition and magic. Our medical terminology really begins with Hippocrates because he was the first to write terms.

Qui dias memorem laudes, repetámque fideles
Ingenij dotes, Hippocratisque decus.
Democriti auditor Phœbea, ô, Coé propago,
Certius an quis te tradidit artis opes?

Figure 3.1 Hippocrates.

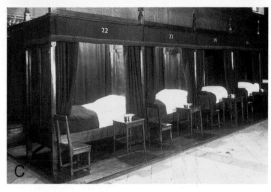

Figure 3.2 Three photographs of Hostel-Dieu, Beaune, France, a medieval hospital founded in 1443; it is now a museum. **A.** Entrance. **B.** Grand salle ("great room"—combination hospital ward and church). **C.** Bedsides.

 HOSPITAL. Hospital is derived from the Latin word meaning guest house. The words hospital, hospice, host, hostel, and hotel have the same origin but now have different meanings. It is unknown where special institutions for sick people originated. The Romans had military hospitals by 100 A.D. Christian hospitals seem to have originated from the tradition of a guest house for travelers. In 6th century France, an institution for the sick was called hostel Dieu (God's hotel). Most hospitals were run by religious orders whose members devoted themselves to the care of the sick. In the 19th century, hospitals became centers for treating disease for all classes of society, and they operated for both profit and nonprofit.

The Doctor of Medicine (M.D.) degree is earned by successfully completing medical school. To practice medicine, however, the graduate with an M.D. must be licensed. The license to practice medicine is granted after the applicant passes a specified medical licensing examination and meets any other requirements established by the medical board in the state where the applicant wants to practice.

The Doctor of Osteopathic Medicine (D.O.) is a medical practitioner similar to an M.D. but with a traditional emphasis on the role of the musculoskeletal system in

Figure 3.3 Luke Fildes' *The Doctor*.

maintaining function and balance in the body. Osteopathic physicians are trained at osteopathic colleges and are often affiliated with osteopathic hospitals. The licensing requirements for the osteopath are also similar to the M.D. and are established by medical boards in each state.

American Board of Medical Specialties

The licensed physician in the past was often both physician and surgeon. Today, with the rapid expansion of technology and the greater knowledge required to be proficient in treating patients, physicians have entered various nonsurgical and surgical specialty areas.

With increasing medical specialties, standards and monitoring of specialty practices were required. The American Board of Medical Specialties (ABMS) was founded in 1933 for this purpose. The 24 individual specialty boards recognized by ABMS have established criteria for specific training after medical school (3 to 7 years depending on the specialty). After the specialty training (called a residency or fellowship), the physician gains eligibility to take the specified board examination. A physician who has completed specialty requirements and passed the board examination is designated "board certified" and referred to as a "diplomate" (e.g., Joan Jones, M.D., Diplomate, American Board of Family Practice). A board's standards extend beyond the usual requirement for licensure.

Other organizations, such as the American College of Physicians (ACP) and the American College of Surgeons (ACS), recognize members who have met set published criteria for standards of distinction. These include Fellow of the American College of Physicians (F.A.C.P.) and Fellow of the American College of Surgeons (F.A.C.S.) (Fig. 3.4).

ABMS-approved specialty boards of the United States follow:

American Board of Allergy and Immunology

American Board of Anesthesiology

PHYSICIAN. Physician is derived from a Greek word for natural or according to the laws of nature. In ancient Greece, natural science, which included biology and medicine, was concerned with speculation about the origin and existence of things. Physic, in the sense of drug, especially a laxative made from herbs and natural sources, has the same origin. The teaching of medicine came under the general heading of physicus, and practitioners were called physicians.

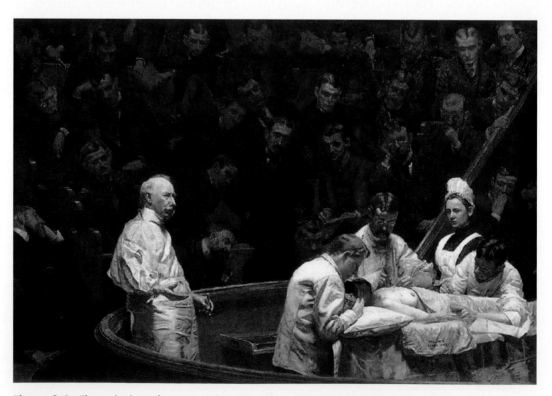

Figure 3.4   The early days of surgery and anesthesiology. Thomas Eakins' *The Agnew Clinic.*

American Board of Colon and Rectal Surgery

American Board of Dermatology

American Board of Emergency Medicine

American Board of Family Practice

American Board of Internal Medicine

American Board of Medical Genetics

American Board of Neurological Surgery

American Board of Nuclear Medicine

American Board of Obstetrics and Gynecology

American Board of Ophthalmology

American Board of Orthopaedic Surgery

American Board of Otolaryngology

American Board of Pathology

American Board of Pediatrics

American Board of Physical Medicine and Rehabilitation

American Board of Plastic Surgery

American Board of Preventive Medicine

American Board of Psychiatry and Neurology

American Board of Radiology

American Board of Surgery

American Board of Thoracic Surgery

American Board of Urology

Each specialty or subspecialty has its own scope of practice as follows. All earn the M.D. or D.O. degree. Ph.D. degrees are accepted by a few specialties/subspecialties, e.g., medical genetics, public health.

Special note: The American Osteopathic Association (AOA) also provides certification of osteopaths who have expertise in the following approved specialty and subspecialty areas: anesthesiology, dermatology, emergency medicine, family practice, internal medicine, neurology and psychiatry, neuromusculoskeletal medicine, nuclear medicine, obstetrics and gynecology, ophthalmology and otolaryngology, orthopedic surgery, pathology, pediatrics, preventive medicine, proctology, radiology, rehabilitation medicine, and surgery.

 CADUCEUS. The word for the staff of Mercury, an emblem in Greek mythology represented by two serpents twined around a staff, is the most common symbol of the medical profession. From earliest history, serpents have been symbols of wisdom and health and objects of worship. They appear as regular shrine equipment and were involved in ancient healing rituals. The significance of the caduceus for the medical profession is said to lie in the fact that the serpent symbolizes healing—some say because of its long life, others because the annual shedding of its skin suggests a renewal of youth and health, others because of its keen eyesight. The earliest representation of serpent and staff was the rod of Aesculapius, the god of medicine, which shows a single serpent twining around a rod or stick. Some argue that it is the true symbol of the medical profession (Fig. 3.5).

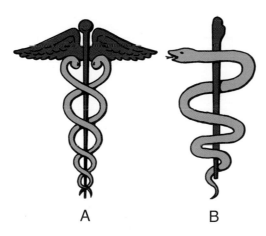

A   B

Figure 3.5 The caduceus. **A.** Staff of Mercury. **B.** Rod of Aesculapius.

ANESTHESIA. Anesthesia is a condition in which there is an absence of sensation [an (without)/esthesio (sensation)/ia (condition)]. The inhalation of various vapors to produce a sort of intoxication or stupefaction is an ancient practice. By the 14th century, methods of inducing sleep for surgical operations included the inhalation of hemlock, mandrake, and lettuce. Other attempts to produce anesthesia included the use of snow and ice. Interest in chemistry at the end of the 18th century resulted in the investigation of various chemicals that could be used for inhalation anesthesia. Early anesthetics included nitrous oxide, ether, and chloroform.

Physicians' Specialty Fields of Medical Practice

Specialty and Specialist	Scope of Practice
allergy and immunology al'er-jē and im'yū-nol'ō-jē **allergist/immunologist**	diagnosis, treatment, and prevention of allergic diseases, including asthma, and diagnosis, management, and therapy of immunologic diseases, e.g., autoimmune disorders
anesthesiology an'es-thē-zē-ol'ō-jē **anesthesiologist**	comprehensive medical management and anesthetic care before, during, and after surgery and long-term pain management and critical care related to cardiac and respiratory emergencies
colon and rectal surgery **colon and rectal surgeon**	diagnosis, medical care, and surgical treatment of conditions related to the small intestine, colon, and rectum
dermatology der-mă-tol'ō-jē **dermatologist**	medical and surgical treatment of disorders of the skin and its appendages, e.g., hair, nails, including cosmetic care
emergency medicine **emergency physician**	prehospital emergency medical care of acutely ill or injured patients; most commonly rendered in an emergency department of a hospital or a free-standing urgent care facility
family practice **family physician**	comprehensive general medical care of individuals of all ages and their families, with emphasis on disease prevention and health promotion
internal medicine **internist**	nonsurgical care centered around prevention, diagnosis, and treatment of diseases of adults
COMMON SUBSPECIALTIES OF INTERNAL MEDICINE	
cardiology kar-de-ol'ō-jē **(cardiovascular disease)** **cardiologist**	diagnosis and management of conditions related to the heart and blood vessels
endocrinology en'dō-kri-nol'ō-jē **endocrinologist**	diagnosis and management of diseases of the endocrine glands, e.g., diabetes, obesity, thyroid dysfunction

Specialty and Specialist	Scope of Practice
gastroenterology gas'trō-en-ter-ol'ō-jē gastroenterologist	diagnosis and management of conditions related to the digestive system
geriatric medicine geriatrician jer-ē-ă-trish'ŭn	diagnosis and medical management of conditions affecting the elderly; also a subspecialty of family practice
hematology hē-mă-tol'ō-jē hematologist	diagnosis and treatment of blood disorders
nephrology ne-frol'ō-jē nephrologist	nonsurgical treatment of kidney disorders
oncology ong-kol'ō-jē oncologist	treatment of tumors and cancer
rheumatology rū-mă-tol'ō-jē rheumatologist	treatment of arthritis and related disorders
medical genetics jĕ-net'iks geneticist jĕ-net'i-sist	diagnosis, treatment, and prevention of genetic (inherited) disorders; includes research, laboratory testing, and counseling
neurology nū-rol'ō-jē neurologist	nonsurgical treatment of diseases of the nervous system
neurological surgery neurosurgeon	surgical and nonsurgical treatment of diseases of the nervous system and supportive structures, including blood vessels
nuclear medicine nuclear medicine physician	use of radioactive substances to diagnose and treat disease; a dual specialty in other fields such as radiology, internal medicine, neurology, and cardiology is common
obstetrics and gynecology (OB/GYN)	
obstetrics ob-stet'riks obstetrician ob-stĕ-trish'ŭn	care and treatment of mother and fetus throughout pregnancy, childbirth, and immediate postpartum period

SURGEON. The Greek word chirurgeon (chiro, the hand; urgeon, to work) refers to one who works with the hands. The earliest conception of surgery was that diseases of an external nature were suitable for treatment by manual operations, as opposed to internal conditions that were treated with drugs, etc. The name surgeon has been in English since the 14th century. There was no distinction between barbers and surgeons until 1745 when the barbers and surgeons of London were separated and given individual charters.

Specialty and Specialist	Scope of Practice
gynecology gī-nĕ-kol'ō-jē gynecologist	medical and surgical treatment of disorders of the female reproductive and urinary system
ophthalmology of-thal-mol'ō-jē ophthalmologist	medical and surgical treatment of the eye, including vision care and services
orthopedic surgery ōr-thō-pē'dik orthopedic surgeon orthopedist (orthopaedist)	medical, surgical, and rehabilitative treatment of disorders of the musculoskeletal system, including the bones, joints, muscles, ligaments, tendons, and nerves
otolaryngology ō'tō-lar-ing-gol'ō-jē otolaryngologist ō'tō-lar-ing-gol'ō-jist ENT (ear, nose, throat) physician	medical and surgical treatment of diseases and disorders of the ear, nose, throat, and adjoining structures of the head and neck
pathology pa-thol'ō-jē pathologist	study of disease emphasizing examination of tissue for diagnosis, e.g., biopsy, autopsy
pediatrics pē-dē-at'riks pediatrician	comprehensive medical care of infants, children, and adolescents, with emphasis on disease prevention and healthful physical and mental development
physical medicine and rehabilitation physiatry fi-zī'ă-trē physiatrist fiz-ī'ă-trist	treatment of patients suffering from neuromusculoskeletal disorders caused by illness or injury, e.g., stroke, spinal cord injury
plastic surgery plastic surgeon	surgery for restoration, repair, or reconstruction of body structures, e.g., body contouring, skin grafting
preventive medicine	medical care that focuses on prevention of disease and health maintenance; specialty areas include: aerospace medicine, occupational medicine, public health, and general preventive medicine
psychiatry sī-kī'ă-trē psychiatrist	diagnosis, treatment, and prevention of mental, emotional, and behavioral disorders

Specialty and Specialist	Scope of Practice
radiology rā-dē-ol'ō-jē	use of ionizing and nonionizing imaging modalities, including x-ray, radionuclides, magnetic resonance, and ultrasound, to diagnose disease, or in therapies that involve imaging guidance; primary fields include diagnostic radiology, radiation oncology, and radiation physics
radiologist	
surgery	treatment of diseases and trauma requiring an operation;—subspecialty areas include vascular, pediatric, hand, and critical care surgery
general surgeon	
thoracic surgery thō-ras'ik	treatment of diseases, deformities, and trauma requiring an operation within the chest, including the heart and lungs
thoracic surgeon	
urology yū-rol'ō-jē	surgical and nonsurgical treatment of the male urinary and reproductive system and the female urinary system
urologist	

Other Fields of Medical Practice

Many other medical specialists are called doctors, even though they do not have an M.D. or D.O. degree. They have graduated from a college of podiatry, chiropractic, optometry, or dentistry and are licensed to practice. Because they commonly provide health care services in hospitals and/or medical clinics, you need a basic knowledge of their scope of practice.

Degree	Field of Practice	Scope of Practice
doctor of chiropractic medicine (D.C.)	chiropractic medicine kī-rō-prak'tik	treatment centered on manipulation of the spine to maintain function and balance in the body
	chiropractor kī-rō-prak'tor	(chir/o = hand; prattein = to do)
doctor of dental surgery (D.D.S.)	oral surgery	treatment of dental disorders requiring surgery
	oral surgeon	(or/o = mouth; dent/i = teeth)
doctor of podiatric medicine (D.P.M.) pō-dī'ă-trik	podiatry pō-dī'ă-trē podiatrist	diagnosis and treatment (including surgery) of disorders of the foot
doctor of optometry (O.D.)	optometry op-tom'ě-trē	diagnosis and nonsurgical treatment of the eye, including vision care and services
	optometrist op-tom'ě-trist	

Degree	Field of Practice	Scope of Practice
doctor of psychology (Psy.D. or Ph.D.)	psychology	counsel of patients with mental or emotional disorders
sī-kol′ō-jist	sī-kol′ō-jē	
	clinical psychologist sī-kol′ō-jist	

Other Health Care Professions

As a result of the major advances in health care technology, various licensed and non-licensed allied health professionals with specialized training and skill have emerged to meet the increasing needs of the population. They are integral to today's health care team. The following is a list of professions for which formal training is available.

acupuncturist
anesthesiologist assistant
art therapist
athletic trainer
audiologist
cardiovascular technologist
clinical exercise specialist
clinical laboratory scientist
cytogenetic technologist
cytotechnologist
dental assistant
dental hygienist
dental laboratory technologist
diagnostic medical sonographer
diagnostic molecular scientist
dialysis technician
dietetic technician
dietitian/nutritionist
electrocardiography technician
electroencephalographic technologist
electroneurodiagnostic technologist
emergency medical technician
fitness therapist
genetic counselor
geriatric home aide
gerontologist
health and fitness specialist
health information administrator
health information technician
histotechnician/histologic technician
home health aide
kinesiotherapy
marriage and family counselor/therapist

massage therapist
medical assistant
medical coding specialist
medical illustrator
medical laboratory technician
medical technologist
medical transcriptionist
medical unit coordinator (unit clerk/ secretary or ward clerk/secretary)
mental health counselor
mobility specialist
music therapist
nephrology technician
nuclear medicine technologist
nurse, licensed vocational or practical
nurse, registered
nurse anesthetist
nurse assistant
nurse midwife
nurse practitioner
nutrition care technologist
occupational therapist
occupational therapy assistant
operating room technician
ophthalmic dispensing optician
ophthalmic laboratory technician/ technologist
optician
orthoptist
orthotist/prosthetist
paramedic
pathologist assistant
perfusionist

NURSE. Derived from the Latin word nutrix, a nurse, from nutrire, to suckle or nourish, originally described one who suckled or cared for an infant, and by extension, now describes one who cares for any sick or helpless person.

pharmacist
pharmacologist
pharmacy technician/assistant
phlebotomy technician/phlebotomist
physical therapist
physical therapist assistant
physician assistant
polysomnographic technologist
psychiatric technician
radiation therapy technologist/
    radiation therapist
radiologic technologist/radiographer

recreational therapist
rehabilitation counselor
rehabilitation technologist
respiratory therapist
specialist in blood bank technology
speech-language pathologist
speech therapist
surgeon assistant
surgical technologist
therapeutic recreation specialist
veterinarian
veterinary assistant

Summary of Chapter 3 Acronyms/Abbreviations

ABMS	American Board of Medical Specialties
ACP	American College of Physicians
ACS	American College of Surgeons
AOA	American Osteopathic Association
D.C.	Doctor of Chiropractic Medicine
D.D.S.	Doctor of Dental Surgery
D.P.M.	Doctor of Podiatric Medicine
D.O.	Doctor of Osteopathic Medicine
ENT	ear, nose, throat
M.D.	Doctor of Medicine
OB/GYN	obstetrics and gynecology
O.D.	Doctor of Optometry
Ph.D.	Doctor of Psychology

PRACTICE EXERCISES

For the following words, draw a line or lines to separate prefixes, roots, combining forms, and suffixes. Then define the word according to the meaning of: **P=prefix; R=root; CF=combining form; S=suffix.**

EXAMPLE

psychiatry

_____ / _____
R   S

psych/iatry
R   S

DEFINITION: mind/treatment

1. oncology

_____ / _____
    CF   S

DEFINITION: _____

2. immunologist

_____ / _____
    CF   S

DEFINITION: _____

3. otolaryngology

_____ / _____ / _____
    CF   CF   S

DEFINITION: _____

4. optometry

_____ / _____
    CF   S

DEFINITION: _____

5. gynecology

_____ / _____
    CF   S

DEFINITION: _____

6. pathology

_____ / _____
    CF   S

DEFINITION: _____

7. orthopedic

_____ / _____ / _____
    CF   R   S

DEFINITION: _____

8. urologist

_____ / _____
　　　　CF　　　　　　　　　　S

DEFINITION: _____

9. neurology

_____ / _____
　　　　CF　　　　　　　　　　S

DEFINITION: _____

10. psychologist

_____ / _____
　　　　CF　　　　　　　　　　S

DEFINITION: _____

11. osteopathy

_____ / _____ / _____
　　　　CF　　　　　　　　　　R　　　　　　　　　　S

DEFINITION: _____

12. ophthalmologist

_____ / _____
　　　　CF　　　　　　　　　　S

DEFINITION: _____

13. obstetric

_____ / _____
　　　　R　　　　　　　　　　S

DEFINITION: _____

14. anesthesiology

_____ / _____ / _____
　　　　P　　　　　　　　　　CF　　　　　　　　　　S

DEFINITION: _____

15. cardiology

_____ / _____
　　　　CF　　　　　　　　　　S

DEFINITION: _____

16. dermatology

_____ / _____
　　　　CF　　　　　　　　　　S

DEFINITION: _____

17. pediatrics

_____ / _____
　　　　R　　　　　　　　　　S

DEFINITION: _____

18. endocrinologist

_____ / _____ / _____
         P   CF   S

DEFINITION: _____

19. nephrologist

_____ / _____
        CF   S

DEFINITION: _____

20. gastroenterology

_____ / _____ / _____
        CF   CF   S

DEFINITION: _____

21. hematologist

_____ / _____
        CF   S

DEFINITION: _____

Match the following specialists or specialties with the definition:

22. _____ emergency physician	a. doctor for adults
23. _____ chiropractor	b. treats foot disorders
24. _____ neurosurgeon	c. provides emotional counsel
25. _____ physiatrist	d. performs dental surgery
26. _____ radiologist	e. operates on heart and lungs
27. _____ plastic surgeon	f. interprets x-rays
28. _____ rheumatologist	g. uses radioactive isotopes
29. _____ thoracic surgeon	h. nonsurgical care of brain and spinal cord
30. _____ podiatrist	i. treats disease of the mind
31. _____ oral surgeon	j. cares for acutely ill
32. _____ psychiatrist	k. general practice
33. _____ neurology	l. performs brain surgery
34. _____ nuclear medicine	m. specialty for treatment of the elderly
35. _____ internist	n. performs reconstructive surgical repairs
36. _____ family practice	o. treats arthritis

37. _____ psychologist   p. rehabilitation specialist

38. _____ geriatrics   q. manipulates the spine

Write the full medical term for the following abbreviations:

39. OB/GYN _____

40. D.D.S. _____

41. ENT _____

42. ABMS _____

43. O.D. _____

44. F.A.C.S. _____

45. ACP _____

46. D.C. _____

47. D.P.M. _____

48. D.O. _____

49–53. From the following list, identify the five specialists who perform surgery:

gynecologist	cardiologist	gastroenterologist
neurologist	otolaryngologist	orthopaedist
allergist	rheumatologist	nephrologist
ophthalmologist	geneticist	endocrinologist
internist	pediatrician	urologist

Match the type of school with the degree it grants:

54. _____ dental   a. Ph.D.

55. _____ graduate   b. O.D.

56. _____ podiatric   c. D.D.S.

57. _____ medical   d. D.O.

58. _____ chiropractic   e. D.P.M.

59. _____ optometric   f. D.C.

60. _____ osteopathic   g. M.D.

Chapter 4

The Medical Record

OBJECTIVES

After completion of this chapter you will be able to

- Define basic terms and abbreviations used in documenting a history and physical
- Explain the concept of problem oriented medical record keeping and common format for documenting SOAP progress notes
- Identify common hospital records and patient care abbreviations
- Recognize types of diagnostic imaging modalities
- Define common terms related to disease
- Define common pharmacological terms
- Recognize abbreviations and symbols deemed error prone
- Define the symbols used in documenting a prescription or physician's order
- Record military date and time
- Follow legal guidelines when making corrections to a medical record entry
- Explain the terms used in documenting a medical history and physical record

Common Records Used in Documenting Care of a Patient

To put your knowledge of medical terminology to practical use, you need to see how this language is used in everyday communication about patients. Learning the common abbreviations, symbols, forms, and formats used in recording patient care will help you comprehend medical record documentation.

HISTORY AND PHYSICAL

CHART. The word originates from the Latin *charta,* a kind of paper made from papyrus. Charta came to mean any leaf or thin sheet of fine paper on which graphic illustrations were made. In medicine, the chart most often refers to patient record documentations.

The record that serves as a cornerstone for patient care is the *history and physical.* It documents the patient's medical history and findings from the physical examination. It is usually the first document generated when a patient presents for care, most often recorded at the time of a new patient visit (Fig. 4.1), or as part of a consultation (Fig. 4.2).

Subjective information is obtained from the patient and documented in the patient *history,* starting with the *chief complaint* (the reason for seeking care) along with the *history of present illness* (indicating duration and severity of the complaint) and any other symptoms that the patient is experiencing. Information about the patient's past *medical history, family history, social history,* and *occupational history* is then noted. The history is complete after documenting the patient's answers to questions related to the *review of systems,* which is intended to uncover any other significant evidence of disease.

Once subjective data have been recorded, the provider begins a physical examination to obtain *objective information,* facts that can be seen or detected by testing. Signs, or objective evidence of disease, are documented, and selected diagnostic tests are performed or ordered when further evaluation is necessary.

The *impression, diagnosis,* or *assessment* is made after evaluation of all subjective and objective data, including the results of the physical examination and diagnostic test findings. R/O (rule out) is the abbreviation used to indicate a differential diagnosis when two or more possible diagnoses are in question. Further tests are then necessary to rule out or eliminate these possibilities and verify the final diagnosis.

Final notations include the provider's *plan,* also called a *recommendation* or *disposition,* which outlines strategies designed to remedy the patient's condition.

Further documentation in the form of *progress notes* is made as care continues.

Most often, physicians are required to submit a current history and physical before admitting a patient to the hospital. When the patient is to have surgery, this report is often called a "preoperative" history and physical (see Figure 4.6).

Following are common terms and abbreviations used in documenting a history and physical examination.

Abbreviation	Meaning/Explanation
H & P	**History and Physical**
	documentation of patient history and physical examination findings
Hx	**History**
	record of subjective information regarding the patient's personal medical history, including past injuries, illnesses, operations, defects, and habits
subjective information	*information obtained from the patient including his or her personal perceptions*
CC	**Chief Complaint**
c/o	**complains of**
	patient's description of what brought him or her to the doctor or hospital; it is usually brief and is often documented in the patient's own words indicated within quotes
	For example:
	CC: left lower back pain; patient states, "I feel like I swallowed a stick and it got stuck in my back"
HPI (PI)	**History of Present Illness (Present Illness)**
	amplification of the chief complaint recording details of the duration and severity of the condition (how long the patient has had the complaint and how bad it is)
	For example:
	HPI: the patient has had left lower back pain for the past 2 weeks since slipping on a rug and landing on her left side; the pain worsens after sitting upright for any extended period but gradually subsides after lying in a supine position

Abbreviation	Meaning/Explanation
Sx	**symptom**
	subjective evidence (from the patient) that indicates an abnormality
PMH (PH)	**Past Medical History (Past History)**
	a record of information about the patient's past illnesses starting with childhood, including surgical operations, injuries, physical defects, medications, and allergies
UCHD	**usual childhood diseases**
	an abbreviation used to note that the patient had the "usual" or commonly contracted illnesses during childhood (e.g., measles, chickenpox, mumps)
NKA	**no known allergies**
NKDA	**no known drug allergies**
FH	**Family History**
	state of health of immediate family members
	A & W alive and well
	L & W living and well
	For example:
	FH: father, age 92, L & W; mother, age 91, died, stroke
SH	**Social History**
	a record of the patient's recreational interests, hobbies, and use of tobacco and drugs, including alcohol
	For example:
	SH: plays tennis twice/wk; tobacco—none; alcohol—drinks 1–2 beers per day
OH	**Occupational History**
	a record of work habits that may involve work-related risks
	For example:
	OH: the patient has been employed as a heavy equipment operator for the past 6 years
ROS (SR)	**Review Of Systems (Systems Review)**
	a documentation of the patient's response to questions organized by a head-to-toe review of the function of all body systems (note: this review allows evaluation of other symptoms that may not have been mentioned)

Abbreviation	Meaning/Explanation
objective information	*facts and observations noted*
PE (Px)	**Physical Examination** documentation of a physical examination of a patient, including notations of positive and negative objective findings
HEENT	**head, eyes, ears, nose, throat**
NAD	**no acute distress, no appreciable disease**
PERRLA	**pupils equal, round, and reactive to light and accommodation**
WNL	**within normal limits**
Dx	**Diagnosis**
IMP	**Impression**
A	**Assessment** identification of a disease or condition after evaluation of the patient's history, symptoms, signs, and results of laboratory tests and diagnostic procedures
R/O	**Rule Out** used to indicate a *differential diagnosis* when one or more diagnoses are suspect; each possible diagnosis is outlined and either verified or eliminated after further testing is performed For example: Diagnosis: R/O pancreatitis R/O gastroenteritis this indicates that either of these two diagnoses is suspected and further testing is required to verify or eliminate one or both possibilities
P	**Plan (also referred to as recommendation or disposition)** outline of the treatment plan designed to remedy the patient's condition, which includes instructions to the patient, orders for medications, diagnostic tests, or therapies

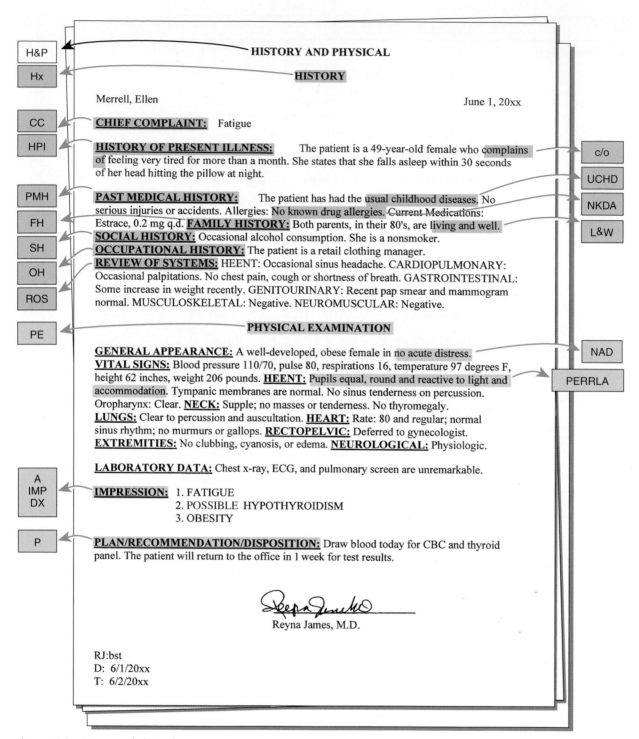

HISTORY AND PHYSICAL

HISTORY

Merrell, Ellen   June 1, 20xx

CHIEF COMPLAINT: Fatigue

HISTORY OF PRESENT ILLNESS: The patient is a 49-year-old female who complains of feeling very tired for more than a month. She states that she falls asleep within 30 seconds of her head hitting the pillow at night.

PAST MEDICAL HISTORY: The patient has had the usual childhood diseases. No serious injuries or accidents. Allergies: No known drug allergies. Current Medications: Estrace, 0.2 mg q.d. **FAMILY HISTORY:** Both parents, in their 80's, are living and well.
SOCIAL HISTORY: Occasional alcohol consumption. She is a nonsmoker.
OCCUPATIONAL HISTORY: The patient is a retail clothing manager.
REVIEW OF SYSTEMS: HEENT: Occasional sinus headache. CARDIOPULMONARY: Occasional palpitations. No chest pain, cough or shortness of breath. GASTROINTESTINAL: Some increase in weight recently. GENITOURINARY: Recent pap smear and mammogram normal. MUSCULOSKELETAL: Negative. NEUROMUSCULAR: Negative.

PHYSICAL EXAMINATION

GENERAL APPEARANCE: A well-developed, obese female in no acute distress.
VITAL SIGNS: Blood pressure 110/70, pulse 80, respirations 16, temperature 97 degrees F, height 62 inches, weight 206 pounds. **HEENT:** Pupils equal, round and reactive to light and accommodation. Tympanic membranes are normal. No sinus tenderness on percussion. Oropharynx: Clear. **NECK:** Supple; no masses or tenderness. No thyromegaly.
LUNGS: Clear to percussion and auscultation. **HEART:** Rate: 80 and regular; normal sinus rhythm; no murmurs or gallops. **RECTOPELVIC:** Deferred to gynecologist.
EXTREMITIES: No clubbing, cyanosis, or edema. **NEUROLOGICAL:** Physiologic.

LABORATORY DATA: Chest x-ray, ECG, and pulmonary screen are unremarkable.

IMPRESSION: 1. FATIGUE
                            2. POSSIBLE HYPOTHYROIDISM
                            3. OBESITY

PLAN/RECOMMENDATION/DISPOSITION: Draw blood today for CBC and thyroid panel. The patient will return to the office in 1 week for test results.

Reyna James, M.D.

RJ:bst
D: 6/1/20xx
T: 6/2/20xx

H&P
Hx
CC
HPI
PMH
FH
SH
OH
ROS
PE
A
IMP
DX
P

c/o
UCHD
NKDA
L&W
NAD
PERRLA

Figure 4.1   History and physical.

CENTRAL MEDICAL GROUP, INC.
Department of Otorhinolaryngology
201 Medical Center Drive • Central City, US 90000-1234 • PHONE: (012) 125-8888 • FAX: (012) 125-3434

Patient: Perron, Carleen   DATE: February 17, 20xx

Referring Physician: C. Camarillo, M.D.

CONSULTATION

REASON FOR CONSULTATION: This 28-year-old white female presents with a one week history of upper respiratory infection (URI), sinusitis, and some periorbital headaches in recent weeks. She also has expectorated yellow-green mucus occasionally and has had a history of tonsillitis.

MEDICATIONS: None. **ALLERGIES:** No known allergies (NKA). **SURGERIES:** None. **HOSPITALIZATIONS:** None.

PAST MEDICAL HISTORY/REVIEW OF SYSTEMS: Cardiopulmonary: There is no history of angina, dyspnea, hemoptysis, emphysema, asthma, chronic obstructive pulmonary disease (COPD), hypertension, or heart murmurs. Cardiovascular: There is no history of high blood pressure. Renal: There is no history of dysuria, polyuria, nocturia, hematuria, or cystoliths. Gastrointestinal: There is no history of gallbladder disease, hepatitis, pancreatitis, or colitis. Musculoskeletal: There is no history of arthritis. Endocrine: There is no history of diabetes. Hematologic: There is no history of anemia, blood transfusion, or easy bruising. Gynecological: The patient states her menses are regular, and the start of her last menstrual cycle occurred 15 days ago.

FAMILY HISTORY: The patient states her maternal grandmother has diabetes.

SOCIAL HISTORY: The patient is single and has no children. She denies smoking tobacco. She denies drinking alcoholic beverages. She denies taking drugs.

CHILDHOOD DISEASES: The patient has had the usual childhood diseases.

OTOLARYNGOLOGIC EXAMINATION: Otoscopy: Tympanic membranes (TMs) are dull and slightly congested. Sinuses: There is maxillary fullness. Rhinoscopic examination reveals mild nasoseptal deviation (NSD). Pharynx: There is moderate inflammation; no exudates. Oropharynx: No masses. Nasopharynx: No masses. Larynx: Clear. Neck: Supple. Cervical Adenopathy: There is mild adenopathy.

IMPRESSION:
1. MAXILLARY SINUSITIS.
2. PHARYNGITIS.
3. CHRONIC TONSILLITIS.

DISPOSITION:
1. Warm salt water gargle (WSWG).
2. Ery-Tab 333, #24, 1 t.i.d. p.c.
3. Robitussin.
4. Return to office (RTO) in one week.

P. Rodden MD
PATRICK RODDEN, M.D.

JR:ti
D: 2/17/20xx
T: 2/18/20xx   9:50 a.m.

Figure 4.2 History and physical documented as part of a consultation for a patient with an upper respiratory infection.

PROBLEM-ORIENTED MEDICAL RECORD

The problem-oriented medical record (POMR) is a method of record keeping introduced in the 1960s. It is a highly organized approach that encourages a precise method of documenting the logical thought processes of health care professionals. Data are organized so that information can be accessed readily at a glance, with a focus on the patient's health problem. The use of POMR and its adaptations has grown in many areas of medicine. The approach is often used in medical schools, hospitals, clinics, and private practices (Fig. 4.3).

The central concept is a medical record in which all information is linked to specific problems. The record has four sections:

- *Database* patient's history, physical examinations, and diagnostic test results; from the database, the problem is identified and a plan is developed to address it
- *Problem list* directory of the patient's problems; each problem is listed and often assigned a number; problems include
  1. a specific diagnosis
  2. a sign or symptom
  3. an abnormal diagnostic test result
  4. any other problem that may influence health or well-being

Once identified, each problem is evaluated, and a plan for treating it is written. When a problem is resolved, a notation is made to show its resolution, but the problem remains on the summary list. The original problem list is maintained in the record so that personnel can easily orient themselves to the patient's prior medical history.

- *Initial plan* the strategy employed to resolve each problem is listed. There are three subdivisions:
  1. *Diagnostic plan* orders are given for specific diagnostic testing to confirm suspicions
  2. *Therapeutic plan* goals for therapy are specified
  3. *Patient education* instructions communicated to the patient are notated

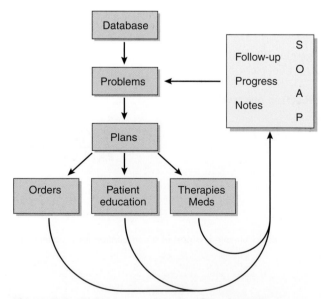

Figure 4.3 Problem-oriented medical record (POMR) diagram.

- *Progress notes* documentations of the progress concerning each problem are organized using the SOAP format (Figs. 4.4 and 4.5).

S—subjective	that which the patient describes
O—objective	observable information, e.g., test results, blood pressure readings
A—assessment	patient's progress and evaluation of the plan's effectiveness (note: any new problem identified is added to the problem list, and a separate plan for its treatment is recorded)
P—plan	decision to proceed or alter the plan strategy

The SOAP method of documenting a patient's progress appears to be the most popular adaptation to the entire system, and it is commonly utilized with or without assigning a number to the problem.

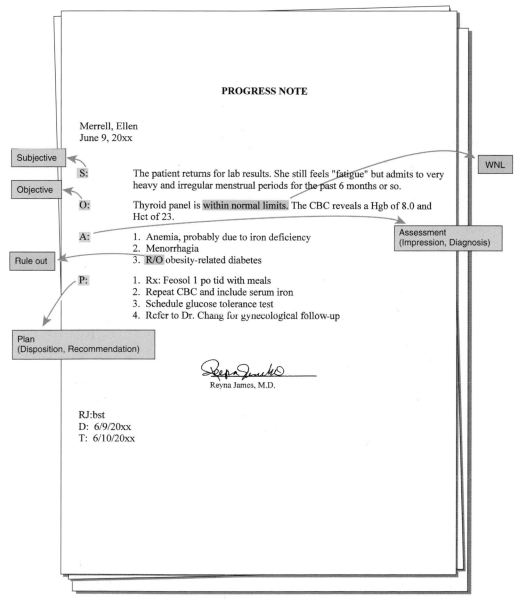

Figure 4.4 Progress note using SOAP format, representing follow-up visit after history and physical recorded in Figure 4.1.

CENTRAL MEDICAL GROUP, INC.

Department of Otorhinolaryngology

201 Medical Center Drive • Central City, US 90000-1234 • PHONE: (012) 125-8888 • FAX: (012) 125-3434

PROGRESS NOTES

Patient: PERRON, CARLEEN

03/30/20xx

S: The patient presents with a sore throat × 2 weeks.

O: Sinus exam: Maxillary and frontal congestion. Hypopharynx/adenoids: No inflammation.

A: Recurrent pharyngitis/sinusitis × 2 weeks.

P: 1) Ceftin 250 mg, #21, 1 t.i.d. p.o. p.c.

     2) Entex LA, #30, 1 b.i.d. p.o.

     3) Warm salt water gargle.

P Rodden MD
PATRICK RODDEN, M.D.

05/25/20xx

S: Recurrent sore throat every month.

O: Recurrent tonsillitis, cryptic tonsillitis. Sinus exam: Maxillary and frontal congestion.
Neck: Supple; no masses. Hypopharynx/Adenoids: No inflammation. Paranasal Sinus X-ray: Bilateral frontal and maxillary sinusitis.

A: Recurrent tonsillitis, 8-10 times per year. Chronic maxillary and frontal sinusitis.

P: 1) Tonsillectomy discussed with the patient. The risks of general and local anesthesia, as well as the surgical procedure, were discussed with the patient. The consent form was signed.

     2) An admitting order was given to the patient for CBC, UA, and basic metabolic panel to be done one day prior to being admitted.

     3) Ceftin 250 mg, #21, 1 t.i.d. p.o. p.c.

     4) Entex LA, #30, 1 b.i.d. p.o.

     5) Flonase nasal inhaler, 2 sprays each nostril b.i.d.

     6) Warm salt water gargle.

P Rodden MD
PATRICK RODDEN, M.D.

Figure 4.5 SOAP progress notes following consultation of a patient with an upper respiratory infection (Fig. 4.2).

HOSPITAL RECORDS

The *history and physical* is usually the first document entered into the patient's hospital record on admission. *Physician's orders* list the directives for care prescribed by the doctor attending the patient. The *nurse's notes* and *physician's progress* notes chronicle the care throughout the patient's stay, and *ancillary reports* note the various procedures and therapies, including *diagnostic tests* and *pathology reports*. In a difficult case, a specialist may be called in by the attending physician, and a *consultation report* is filed. If a surgical remedy is indicated, a narrative *operative report* is required of the primary surgeon. The anesthesiologist, who is in charge of life support during surgery, must file the *anesthesiologist's report*. The final document, which is recorded at the time of discharge from the hospital, is the *discharge summary*.

The following are descriptions of common forms used in documenting the care of a hospital patient.

history and physical	documentation of the patient's recent medical history and results of a physical examination required before hospital admission (e.g., before admission for surgery) (Fig. 4.6)
consent form	document signed by the patient or legal guardian giving permission for medical or surgical care
informed consent	consent of a patient after being informed of the risks and benefits of a procedure and alternatives—often required by law when a reasonable risk is involved (e.g., surgery)
physician's orders	a record of all orders directed by the attending physician (Fig. 4.7)
diagnostic tests/laboratory reports	records of results of various tests and procedures used in evaluating and treating a patient (e.g., laboratory tests, x-rays) (Fig. 4.8)
nurse's notes	documentation of patient care by the nursing staff (note: flow sheets and graphs are often used to display recordings of vital signs and other monitored procedures) (Fig. 4.9)
physician's progress notes	physician's daily account of patient's response to treatment, including results of tests, assessment, and future treatment plans (Fig. 4.10)
ancillary reports	miscellaneous records of procedures or therapies provided during a patient's care (e.g., physical therapy, respiratory therapy)
consultation report	report filed by a specialist asked by the attending physician to evaluate a difficult case; note: a patient may also see another physician in consultation as an outpatient (in a medical office or clinic)

operative report (op report)	surgeon's detailed account of the operation including the method of incision, technique, instruments used, types of sutures, method of closure, and the patient's responses during the procedure and at the time of transfer to recovery (Fig. 4.11)
pathology report	report of the findings of a pathologist after the study of tissue (e.g., a biopsy) (Fig. 4.12)
anesthesiologist's report	anesthesiologist's or anesthetist's report of the details of anesthesia during surgery, including the drugs used, dose and time given, and records indicating monitoring of the patient's vital status throughout the procedure
discharge summary, clinical resume, clinical summary, discharge abstract	four terms that describe an outline summary of the patient's hospital care, including date of admission, diagnosis, course of treatment, final diagnosis, and date of discharge (Fig. 4.13)

The sample medical records in Figures 4.6 to 4.13 chronicle the hospital care of Carleen Perron, a 28-year-old woman who was seen in consultation by Dr. Patrick Rodden, an ENT specialist, who recommended a surgical remedy for the repeated infections she has had over the past 6 months.

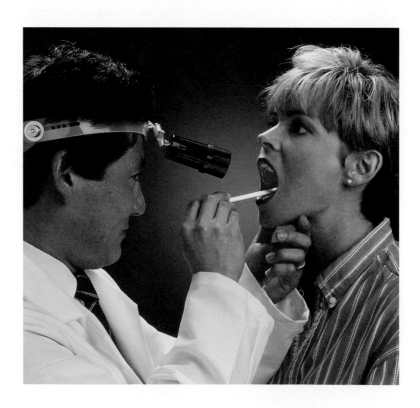

CENTRAL MEDICAL CENTER

211 Medical Center Drive • Central City, US 90000-1234 • PHONE: (012) 125-6784 • FAX: (012) 125-9999

PREOPERATIVE HISTORY AND PHYSICAL

HISTORY

DATE OF ADMISSION: June 3, 20xx

HISTORY OF PRESENT ILLNESS:
The patient is a 28-year-old white female with a chief complaint of frequent, recurrent, suppurative tonsillitis. She has had some eight infections over the last 6 months and is admitted at this time for elective tonsillectomy. The surgery has been discussed with the patient and family, including risks and complications. The patient's internist is C. Camarillo, M.D.

MEDICATIONS: None.

ALLERGIES: None known.

PAST SURGICAL HISTORY: None.

PAST MEDICAL HISTORY: UCHD (usual childhood diseases).

REVIEW OF SYSTEMS: CARDIOVASCULAR: No high blood pressure, heart murmurs, or shortness of breath. PULMONARY: No chronic lung disease; no asthma. GASTRO-INTESTINAL: No hepatitis. RENAL HISTORY: Negative for infections. ENDOCRINE: No diabetes or thyroid disease. MUSCULOSKELETAL: Negative for arthritis. HEMATOLOGIC: No history of anemia or bleeding tendencies.

FAMILY HISTORY: Grandmother has history of diabetes.

GYNECOLOGICAL HISTORY: Regular menses.

SOCIAL HISTORY: The patient is a nonsmoker. Alcohol use was denied, and drug use was denied.

(continued)

P. Rodden MD
PATRICK RODDEN, M.D.

JR:bst

D: 6/1/20xx
T: 6/2/20xx

HISTORY AND PHYSICAL Page 1	PT. NAME: PERRON, CARLEEN ID NO: 672894017 ROOM NO: ATT. PHYS: PATRICK RODDEN, M.D.

Figure 4.6 Preoperative history and physical. A documentation of a patient's presurgical history and physical, dictated and transcribed for the hospital record before admission.

CENTRAL MEDICAL CENTER

211 Medical Center Drive • Central City, US 90000-1234 • PHONE: (012) 125-6784 • FAX: (012) 125-9999

PREOPERATIVE HISTORY AND PHYSICAL

PHYSICAL EXAMINATION

VITAL SIGNS: Afebrile, alert, oriented, normotensive. Blood Pressure: 124/80. Pulse: 84. Respirations: 18.

HEENT: PERRLA (pupils equal, round, and reactive to light and accommodation). Tympanic membranes are clear. Light reflex is present. No sinus tenderness on percussion. Oropharynx: Clear. Hypertrophic tonsils. No exudates. Nasopharynx: No masses. Larynx: Clear.

NECK: Supple; no masses or tenderness. No cervical adenopathy.

LUNGS: Clear to percussion and auscultation.

HEART: Rate: 84 and regular; normal sinus rhythm; no murmurs or gallops.

RECTOPELVIC: Deferred.

EXTREMITIES: No peripheral edema. No ecchymoses.

NEUROLOGICAL: Physiologically intact.

IMPRESSION: Chronic, recurrent tonsillitis. The patient is admitted for an elective tonsillectomy.

P. Rodden MD
PATRICK RODDEN, M.D.

JR:bst
D: 6/1/20xx
T: 6/2/20xx

HISTORY AND PHYSICAL PAGE 2	PT. NAME: PERRON, CARLEEN ID NO: 672894017 ROOM NO: ATT. PHYS: PATRICK RODDEN, M.D.

Figure 4.6 *Continued.*

CENTRAL MEDICAL CENTER

211 Medical Center Drive • Central City, US 90000-1234 • PHONE: (012) 125-6784 • FAX: (012) 125-9999

PHYSICIAN'S ORDERS FOR:	PAGE
PREOPERATIVE ADMITTING ORDERS	1 OF 1

A THERAPEUTICALLY EQUIVALENT PRODUCT, WHICH HAS BEEN APPROVED BY THE PHARMACY AND THERAPEUTICS COMMITTEE OF THE MEDICAL STAFF, MAY BE DISPENSED AND ADMINISTERED UNLESS OTHERWISE SPECIFIED. PHYSICIAN: CROSS OUT ANY ORDERS WHICH DO NOT APPLY.

DOCTOR: PLEASE STATE PERTINENT CLINICAL INFORMATION WHEN ORDERING RADIOLOGY PROCEDURES.

DATE	TIME	[XX] Same Day Surgery [ ] Regular Inpatient Admission
06/02/20xx		(Admit to Observation if overnight stay req'd)

ADMIT DATE: _____JUNE 3, 20xx_____

ADMIT TO: [ ] Surgical Admit Unit _____ or [ ] _____
                                                (date)   (specific unit)   (date)

PATIENT'S NAME: PERRON, CARLEEN _____   ALLERGIES: ___NKA___

DIET: NPO   SURGEON: PATRICK RODDEN, M.D. _____

SURGERY CONSENT TO READ: TONSILLECTOMY _____

DATE AND TIME OF SURGERY: JUNE 3, 20xx at 9 a.m. _____

DATE TESTS TO BE DONE: JUNE 2, 20xx _____

TESTS: (Check box for desired tests)

```
    [ ] HGB      [XX] CBC      [XX] Basic metabolic panel    [ ] PT
    [ ] HCT      [XX] UA       [   ] Comp metabolic panel     [ ] PTT
    [ ] Other _____
    [ ] Group, Type, and Screen
    [ ] Prepare:      _____ units Autologous Red Blood Cells (packed cells)
    [ ] Crossmatch:   _____ units Directed Red Blood Cells (packed cells)
                      _____ units Red Blood Cells (packed cells)
    [ ] ECG
    [ ] CHEST FILM  Reason for x-ray; R/O active cardiopulmonary disease
    [ ] OTHER X-RAY _____
              Reason for x-ray: _____
```

OTHER:

MEDICATIONS: Pre-Meds by Anesthesia

_P Rodden MD_____
Physician's Signature

PERRON, CARLEEN   6/3/20xx
DOB 07/20/20xx   F284
672894017
Rodden, Patrick MD

PHYSICIAN'S ORDERS

Figure 4.7 Preoperative surgical admitting orders. A form completed by the admitting physician that is forwarded to the hospital before the date of surgery.

CENTRAL MEDICAL CENTER

211 Medical Center Drive • Central City, US 90000-1234 • PHONE: (012) 125-6784 • FAX: (012) 125-9999

DOCTOR: PLEASE STATE PERTINENT CLINICAL INFORMATION WHEN ORDERING RADIOLOGY PROCEDURES

WRITE WITH BALLPOINT INK PEN; PRESS HARD

DATE	TIME	
6/3/XX	0800	T. O. Dr Rodden / G. Glen RN
		Consent for tonsillectomy
		P. Rodden MD
		noted
		P Carson RN
		6/3/XX
		0800 Q Goodwer 6-3-XX 0830

Right margin: 6/3/20xx F 284 SURG 312 PERRON, CARLEEN DOB 07/20/xx 67289417 Rodden, Patrick MD

WRITE WITH BALLPOINT INK PEN; PRESS HARD

DATE	TIME	
6/3/XX	10⁰⁰	Anesthesia post-op care
		1) mask O2 8 L/min
		2) VS per PAR routine
		3) Demerol 20-40 mg IV q 5-15 min prn
		4) Droperidol 0.6-1.2 mg IV
		q 15-30 min prn
		5) maybe DC'd when awake & VS
		stable x 1 h
		noted Robert Jung, MD
		6-3-XX
		P Carson RN
		10¹⁰

Right margin: 6/3/20xx F 284 SURG 312 PERRON, CARLEEN DOB 07/20/xx 67289417 Rodden, Patrick MD

PHYSICIAN'S ORDERS

Figure 4.7 *Continued.* Physician's orders. Orders written by the anesthesiologist and surgeon and noted by the nursing staff during the patient's surgical care.

CENTRAL MEDICAL CENTER

211 Medical Center Drive • Central City, US 90000-1234 • PHONE: (012) 125-6784 • FAX: (012) 125-9999

DOCTOR: PLEASE STATE PERTINENT CLINICAL INFORMATION WHEN ORDERING RADIOLOGY PROCEDURES

WRITE WITH BALLPOINT INK PEN; PRESS HARD

DATE	TIME	
6-3-xx	10⁰⁰	POST-OP
		1) IVS q⁻¹h x4 then q 2h x4, then q 4h
		2) bed rest c̄ BRP when alert
		3) Continue IV's 80cc/hr 5°/₀ D/.2 NS until taking fluids well
		4) tylenol elixir c̄ cod ℥iii (sp q 4h po prn pain)
		5) Demerol 50mg ⎫ IM q 4h Vistaril 50mg ⎬ prn severepai
		6) Ice & liquids at bedside & encourage P.Rodden.MD
		noted W.Cliff. R.N. 6-3-xx 1130

Side column: 6/3/20xx F 284 SURG 312 PERRON, CARLEEN DOB 07/20/xx 67289017 Rodden, Patrick MD

WRITE WITH BALLPOINT INK PEN; PRESS HARD

DATE	TIME	
6-3-xx	12³⁰	1) full liquids requiring soft diet
		2) admit
		3) Dalmane 15 mg po qhs prn sleep MRX1 prn P.Rodden
		noted W. Cliff R.N. 12:30

Side column: 6/3/20xx F 284 SURG 312 PERRON, CARLEEN DOB 07/20/xx 67289017 Rodden, Patrick MD

PHYSICIAN'S ORDERS

Figure 4.7 *Continued.*

CENTRAL MEDICAL CENTER

211 Medical Center Drive • Central City, US 90000-1234 • PHONE: (012) 125-6784 • FAX: (012) 125-9999

DOCTOR: PLEASE STATE PERTINENT CLINICAL INFORMATION WHEN ORDERING RADIOLOGY PROCEDURES

WRITE WITH BALLPOINT INK PEN; PRESS HARD

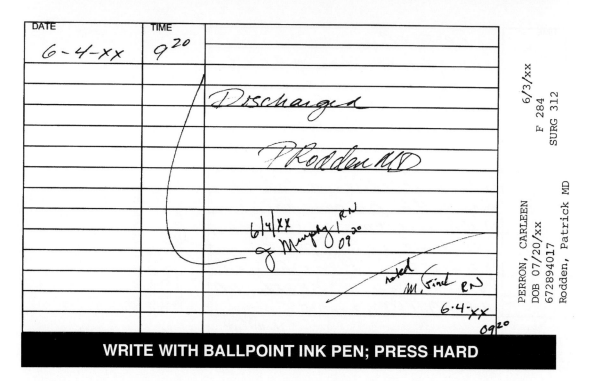

WRITE WITH BALLPOINT INK PEN; PRESS HARD

PHYSICIAN'S ORDERS

Figure 4.7 *Continued.*

CENTRAL MEDICAL CENTER

211 Medical Center Drive • Central City, US 90000-1234 • PHONE: (012) 125-6784 • FAX: (012) 125-9999

LABORATORY REPORT

June 2, 20xx 3 p.m.

Collect: 6/2/xx at 1500 (BLOOD)   28Y F - PERRON, CARLEEN
Service: 6/2/xx at 1450   PATRICK RODDEN, M.D.

CHEMISTRY

141	SODIUM	(135 - 145)	MMOL/L
3.7	POTASSIUM	(3.5 - 5.0)	MMOL/L
109	CHLORIDE	(100 - 110)	MMOL/L
29	CARBON DIOXIDE	(24 - 32)	MMOL/L
88	GLUCOSE	(65 - 110)	MG/DL
0.8	CREATININE	(0.4 - 1.5)	MG/DL
14	BUN	(7 - 22)	MG/DL

HEMATOLOGY

<<CBC>>

11.8*	WBC	(4.8 - 10.8)	1000/CUMM
4.1*	RBC	(4.20 - 5.40)	MIL/CUMM
12.9	HGB	(12.0 - 16.0)	G/DL
37.7	HCT	(37.0 - 47.0)	%
91.5	MCV	(80 - 100)	CU MICRON
31.0	MCH	(27 - 31)	MCMCG
34.1	MCHC	(32 - 37)	G/DL
12.8	RDW	(11.5 - 14.5)	RBC INDEX
253	PLT	(150 - 400)	1000/CUMM
20.1	LYM%	(14 - 51)	%
7.5	MONO%	(1 - 11)	%
70.2	NEUTRO%	(35 - 74)	%
1.5	EOS%	(0 - 6)	%
0.7	BASO%	(0 - 2)	%
2.3	LYM#	(1.5 - 4.0)	1000/CUMM
0.8	MONO#	(0.2 - 0.9)	1000/CUMM
7.9*	NEUTRO#	(1.0 - 7.0)	1000/CUMM
0.2	EOS#	(0 - 0.7)	1000/CUMM
0.1	BASO#	(0 - 0.2)	1000/CUMM

(continued)

LABORATORY REPORT   PATIENT: PERRON, CARLEEN   672894017

Figure 4.8 Diagnostic tests/laboratory reports. Reporting forms with results of blood and urine studies ordered before surgery.

CENTRAL MEDICAL CENTER

211 Medical Center Drive • Central City, US 90000-1234 • PHONE: (012) 125-6784 • FAX: (012) 125-9999

LABORATORY REPORT

June 2, 20xx 3 p.m.

URINALYSIS

Collect: 6/2/xx at 1500 (URINE)   28Y F - PERRON, CARLEEN
Service: 6/2/xx at 1450   PATRICK RODDEN, M.D.

<<BASIC URINALYSIS>>
SPECIFIC GRAVITY

1.024			
HAZY	APPEARANCE		
YELLOW	COLOR		
5.0	PH		
NEGATIVE	PROTEIN		
NEGATIVE	GLUCOSE		GM/DL
NEGATIVE	KETONE		
NORMAL	UROBILINOGEN	(0.1 - 1.0)	MG/DL
NEGATIVE	BLOOD		
NEGATIVE	LEUKOCYTES	(NEGATIVE)	
NEGATIVE	NITRITE	(NEGATIVE)	

<<MICROSCOPIC URINALYSIS>>

NONE	RBC	/HPF
0-3	WBC	/HPF
10-15	EPITHELIAL CELLS	/HPF
NONE	MUCUS	/HPF
3+	BACTERIA	/HPF
NONE	CASTS	/HPF
NONE	CRYSTALS	/HPF

LABORATORY REPORT   PATIENT: PERRON, CARLEEN   672894017

Figure 4.8 *Continued.*

DATE	TIME	REMARKS
6/3/XX	0615	admitted & oriented to room 312. In no acute distress. VS stable. Afebrile NPO maintained. Condition stable K. Brown RN
6/3/XX	0800	To OR via gurney - awake & oriented accompanied by her mother - condition stable K. Brown RN
6/3/XX	1110	Returned from PAR drowsy but arouses easily. Skin warm & dry. Color pink - VS stable - Throat dry unable to take sips of water very well - no nausea - c/o severe sore throat medicated x̄ with IM pain medication with desired effect - mother very supportive & remains @ bedside - Using a bedpan but unable to urinate - IV infusing well K. Brown RN

CENTRAL MEDICAL CENTER
PATIENT'S PROGRESS NOTES
GENERAL CARE & TREATMENT

PT. NAME: PERRON, CARLEEN
ID NO: 672894017
ROOM NO: 312
ATT. PHYS: PATRICK RODDEN, M.D.

Figure 4.9 Nurse's notes. A recording by the nursing staff of the patient's progress made during general care and treatment.

CENTRAL MEDICAL CENTER

211 Medical Center Drive • Central City, US 90000-1234 • PHONE: (012) 125-6784 • FAX: (012) 125-9999

VITAL SIGNS RECORD

DATE: 6-3-xx

NURSE'S INITIALS	TIME	PRESSURE	PULSE	RESP	TEMP	TIME	PRESSURE	PULSE	RESP	TEMP	NURSE'S INITIALS
PAR	11¹⁰	126/76	66	20							
KB	12¹⁰	123/78	59	18	97⁵						
KB	13¹⁰	115/74	65	16							
K.B	14¹⁰	123/66	64	16							
KB	15¹⁰	123/78	63	16	98						
KB	17¹⁰	109/56	91	16							
KB	19¹⁰	112/62	84	18	99³						

PT. NAME: PERRON, CARLEEN
ID NO: 672894017
ROOM NO: 312
ATT. PHYS: PATRICK RODDEN, M.D.

Figure 4.9 *Continued.* Vital signs record. A chart recording of the patient's vital signs documented by the nursing staff.

DATE	TIME	REMARKS
6/3/xx	10⁰⁵	op note
		Chronic, recurrent tonsillitis
		Procedure: tonsillectomy
		Surgeon: P. Rodden MD
		Anesthesiologist: Robert Jung MD
		Procedure tolerated well
		P Rodden MD
6/3/xx	12²⁰	post op check
		VS stable
		C/o pain & poor p o fluid intake
		Will keep pt overnight for observation
		Plan to DC in am
		P Rodden MD
6/4/xx	08⁰⁰	Doing much better – no bleeding
		taking liquids freely
		DC'd on fluids
		Given RX for tylenol.
		RTO in 48h
		P. Rodden MD

**CENTRAL MEDICAL CENTER
PHYSICIAN'S PROGRESS NOTES**

PT. NAME: PERRON, CARLEEN
ID NO: 672894017
ROOM NO: 312
ATT. PHYS: PATRICK RODDEN, M.D.

Figure 4.10 Physician's progress notes. Physician's notations of the patient's progress throughout care.

CENTRAL MEDICAL CENTER

211 Medical Center Drive • Central City, US 90000-1234 • PHONE: (012) 125-6784 • FAX: (012) 125-9999

OPERATIVE REPORT

DATE OF OPERATION: June 3, 20xx.

PREOPERATIVE DIAGNOSIS: Chronic tonsillitis.

POSTOPERATIVE DIAGNOSIS: Frequent, recurrent tonsillitis.

SURGEON: Patrick Rodden, M.D.

ASSISTANT SURGEON: None

ANESTHESIOLOGIST: Robert Jung, M.D.

ANESTHESIA: General.

SURGERY PERFORMED: Tonsillectomy.

DESCRIPTION OF OPERATION: After general anesthesia induction, with intubation, the McGivor mouth gag and tongue retractor were utilized for exposure of the oropharynx. Local anesthetic consisting of 6 cc of 0.5% Xylocaine with 1:100,000 epinephrine was utilized. Tonsillectomy was carried out using dissection and air technique. The right tonsillectomy electrocoagulation Bovie suction was utilized for hemostasis. Examination of the nasopharynx was normal.

The patient tolerated the procedure well and went to the recovery room in good condition.

P. Rodden MD
PATRICK RODDEN, M.D.

JR:as
D: 6/3/20xx
T: 6/4/20xx

OPERATIVE REPORT	PT. NAME:	PERRON, CARLEEN
	ID NO:	672894017
	ROOM NO:	312
	ATT. PHYS:	PATRICK RODDEN, M.D.

Figure 4.11 Operative report. Surgeon's account of a surgical procedure.

CENTRAL MEDICAL CENTER

211 Medical Center Drive • Central City, US 90000-1234 • PHONE: (012) 125-6784 • FAX: (012) 125-9999

PATHOLOGY REPORT

PATIENT: PERRON, CARLEEN
             28 Y (FEMALE)

DATE RECEIVED: June 3, 20xx.   DATE REPORTED: June 4, 20xx

GROSS:

Received are two tonsils each 2.5 cm in greatest diameter.

MICROSCOPIC:

The sections show deep tonsillar crypts associated with follicular lymphoid hyperplasia. No bacterial granules are seen.

DIAGNOSIS:

CHRONIC LYMPHOID HYPERPLASIA OF RIGHT AND LEFT TONSILS.

Mary Needham MD
MARY NEEDHAM, M.D.

MN:gds

D: 6/4/20xx
T: 6/5/20xx

Figure 4.12 Pathology report.

	MEDICAL RECORDS USE
THAT CONDITION WHICH AFTER STUDY IS DETERMINED TO BE THE REASON FOR ADMISSION TO THE HOSPITAL PRINCIPAL DIAGNOSIS - *Chronic tonsillitis*	
	474.00
FINAL DIAGNOSIS - NO ABBREVIATIONS	*474.00*
Same	
SECONDARY DIAGNOSIS:	
—	
COMPLICATIONS AND/OR COMORBIDITY:	
—	
PRINCIPAL OPERATION/PROCEDURES(S)/TREATMENT RENDERED:	
Tonsillectomy	
SECONDARY OPERATIONS/PROCEDURES:	

CONDITION ON DISCHARGE   *Stable*

☐ DISCHARGE INSTRUCTIONS   ☐ PRE-PRINTED INSTRUCTIONS GIVEN

MEDICATIONS   *Tylenol*

PHYSICAL ACTIVITY   *Bed rest*

DIET   *full liquid*

FOLLOW-UP   *office in 48 h*

DATE OF SUMMARY IF DICTATED:

DATE ADMITTED: *6/3/XX*		DATE DISCHARGED: *6/4/XX*		ATTENDING PHYSICIAN *P. Rodden*		M.D.

FOR MED. RECORDS USE ONLY	ASSEMBLY	ANALYSIS	CODED	KEYED	FINAL CHECK		
	SL	*ML/39*	*WL*	*Ly*	*CS*		*06/03/20XX*
CONSULTANTS:				AA	/		
				DP	*R48*		
				SC	*1212*		

CENTRAL MEDICAL CENTER

DIAGNOSIS RECORD/
DISCHARGE SUMMARY

Figure 4.13   Discharge summary (abstract). Final report documented at the time of discharge that includes the diagnostic record and diagnosis-related group (DRG)—the number assigned to the individual hospitalization based on the patient's diagnoses, complications, age, etc.—and that translates to a fixed dollar amount payable from a third-party payer, e.g., Medicare.

Medical Record Abbreviations

Following are common medical record abbreviations used in patient care documentations. They represent the "acceptable" terms used extensively throughout this text. It is important to note that individual medical facilities provide their own list of acceptable terms and abbreviations that may differ from site to site. Memorize the terms and abbreviations from this list, and plan on adapting them to the variations you encounter in the workplace.

ERROR-PRONE ABBREVIATIONS AND SYMBOLS

Medical errors caused by illegible entries and misinterpretations of medical abbreviations and symbols have led health care agencies, such as the Joint Commission on Accreditation of Healthcare Organizations (JCAHO), to require that medical facilities publish lists of authorized abbreviations for use by all personnel, including a list of those that are unacceptable.

In this text, the abbreviations and symbols that have been identified as error prone are **bolded red**. Depending on the medical facility, their use may or may not be deemed acceptable; therefore, it is very important to study them, too, so that you can properly interpret their meaning if they have been used in a medical record.

Abbreviation	Meaning
MEDICAL CARE FACILITIES	
CCU	coronary (cardiac) care unit
ECU	emergency care unit
ER	emergency room
ICU	intensive care unit
IP	inpatient (a registered bed patient)
OP	outpatient
OR	operating room
PACU	postanesthetic care unit
PAR	postanesthetic recovery
post-op/postop	postoperative (after surgery)
pre-op/preop	preoperative (before surgery)
RTC	return to clinic
RTO	return to office
PATIENT CARE	
BRP	bathroom privileges
CP	chest pain
DC, D/C	discharge, discontinue
ETOH	ethyl alcohol

Abbreviation	Meaning
Ⓛ	left
Ⓡ	right
pt	patient
RRR	regular rate and rhythm
SOB	shortness of breath
Tr	treatment
Tx	treatment or traction
VS	vital signs
T	temperature
P	pulse
R	respiration
BP	blood pressure
Ht	height
Wt	weight
WDWN	well-developed and well-nourished
y.o.	year old
#	number or pound: if before the numeral, it means number (e.g., #2 = number two); if after the numeral, it means pound (e.g., 150# = 150 pounds)
♀	female
♂	male
°	degree or hour
↑	increased
↓	decreased
ө	none or negative
♀	standing
♀	sitting
o—	lying

Common Diagnostic Tests and Procedures

Diagnostic tests and procedures are an integral part of patient care. Analyses of urine, stool, and blood specimens are recorded among the earliest efforts to understand conditions of disease. The advance of technology has led to the development of a myriad of highly sophisticated laboratory testing, examples of which will be featured in this text as they pertain to a specific body system. The two most common laboratory tests performed as part of a general health inquiry or to rule out a particular condition are the complete blood count, or CBC (see Fig. 4.8, Hematology, and Fig. 8.6 in Chapter 8) and urinalysis, or UA (see Fig. 4.8 Continued and Fig. 15.9 in Chapter 15).

It is valuable for health care professionals to recognize common diagnostic tests and procedures and the types of technology used to produce them.

Diagnostic Imaging Modalities

Methods of diagnostic imaging have rapidly expanded in the years since the discovery of x-rays by Wilhelm Roentgen in 1895. Radiation from x-rays, which pass through the body to produce images of the skeleton and other body structures, was found to be ionizing, a process that changes the electrical charge of atoms with a possible effect on body cells. Overexposure to ionizing radiation can have harmful side effects, e.g., cancer; however, technological advances have produced images requiring significantly lower doses of radiation to minimize risk.

Further advancement has led to the discovery and use of other imaging modalities (techniques) under the umbrella of the medical specialty known as radiology. Common ionizing modalities include radiography (x-ray), computed tomography, and nuclear medicine. Common nonionizing modalities that present no apparent risk include magnetic resonance imaging and sonography.

IONIZING IMAGING

Radiography (X-ray)

Radiography is a modality using x-rays (ionizing radiation) to provide images of the body's anatomy to diagnose a condition or impairment. An image is produced when a small amount of radiation is passed through the body to expose a sensitive film. The image is called a radiograph. (Note: -graph is the preferred suffix used in radiology to refer to an x-ray record. It is taken by a radiologic technologist [also known as a radiographer] and interpreted or read by a radiologist, a physician specializing in the study of radiology.) (See Figure 4.14.)

Computed Tomography or Computed Axial Tomography

Computed tomography (CT), also known as computed axial tomography (CAT), is a radiologic procedure that uses a machine (called a scanner) to examine a body site by taking a series of cross-sectional (tomographic) x-ray films in a full circle rotation. A computer then calculates and converts the rates of absorption and density of the x-rays into a three-dimensional picture on a screen (Fig. 4.15).

Nuclear Medicine Imaging or Radionuclide Organ Imaging

This diagnostic imaging technique uses an injected or ingested radioactive isotope, also called a radionuclide (a chemical that has been tagged with radioactive compounds that emit gamma rays). A gamma camera detects and produces an image of the

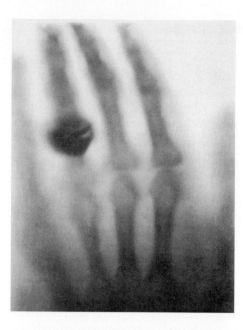

Figure 4.14 The first published x-ray image of the hand and signet ring of Professor Roentgen's wife. It was produced December 22, 1895.

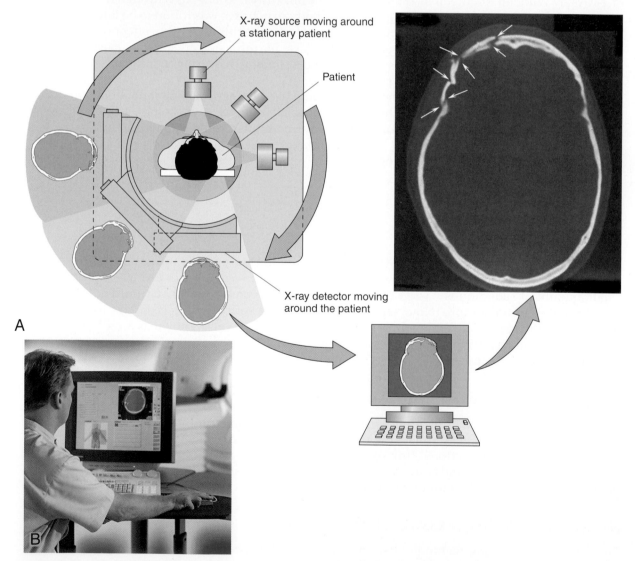

X-ray source moving around a stationary patient

Patient

X-ray detector moving around the patient

A

B

Figure 4.15 **A.** Principles of computed tomography (CT). *Inset*, CT showing multiple open fractures (*arrows*) of skull. **B.** CT imaging process.

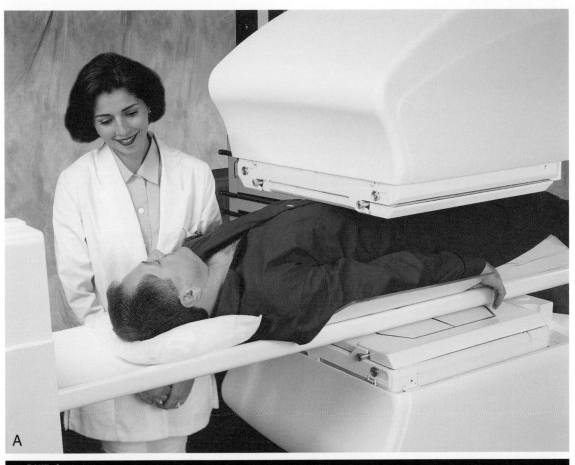

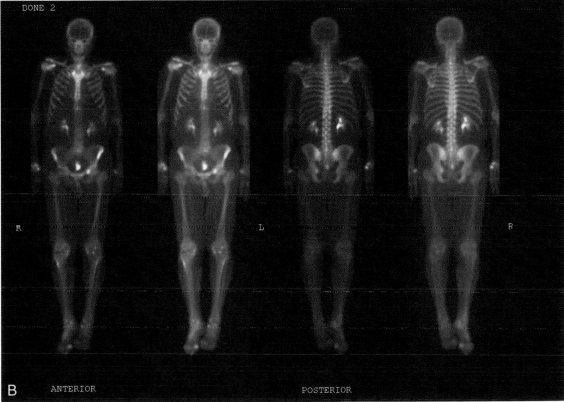

Figure 4.16 Nuclear medicine image. **A.** Gamma camera used to produce image. **B.** Radionuclide whole-body bone scan.

distribution of the gamma rays in the body. This is useful in determining the size, shape, location, and function of body organs such as the brain, lungs, bones, and heart (Fig. 4.16).

NONIONIZING IMAGING

Magnetic Resonance Imaging

Magnetic resonance imaging (MRI) is a nonionizing imaging technique using magnetic fields and radiofrequency waves to visualize anatomical structures within the body. A large magnet surrounds the patient as a scanner subjects the body to a radio signal that temporarily alters the alignment of the hydrogen atoms in the patient's tissue. As the radiowave signal is turned off, the atoms realign and the energy produced is absorbed by detectors and interpreted using computers to provide detailed anatomical images of the body part. MRI is particularly useful in examining soft tissues, joints, and the brain and spinal cord (Fig. 4.17).

Magnetic resonance angiography (MRA) applies MR technology in the study of blood flow (see Diagnostic Tests and Procedures in Chapters 7 and 10).

Sonography

Sonography (diagnostic ultrasound)[U/S or US] is the use of high-frequency sound waves (ultrasound) to visualize body tissues. Ultrasound waves sent through a scanning device, called a transducer, are reflected off structures within the body and analyzed by a computer to produce moving images on a monitor. Sonography is used to examine many parts of the body, including the abdomen, male and female reproductive organs, thyroid and parathyroid glands, and the cardiovascular system (Fig. 4.18).

USE OF CONTRAST

Some imaging procedures require the internal administration of a contrast medium to enhance the visualization of anatomical structures. There are many different kinds of contrast media, including barium, iodinated compounds, gasses (air, carbon dioxide), and other chemicals known to increase visual clarity. Depending on the medium, it may be injected, swallowed, or introduced through an enema or catheter. Compare Figures 15.5 and 15.8 (x-rays of the urinary tract) in Chapter 15, which show images taken with and without contrast.

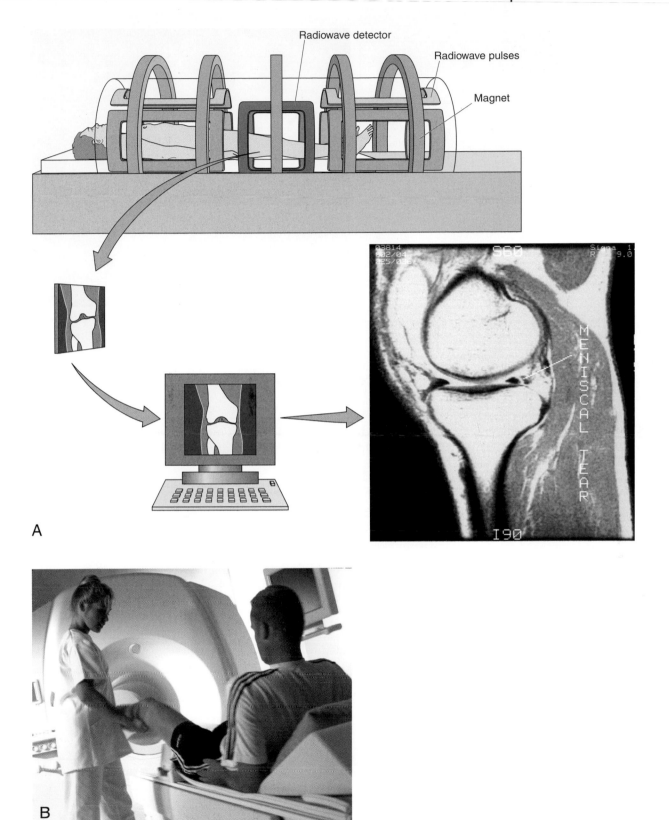

Figure 4.17 **A.** Principles of magnetic resonance imaging (MRI). Patient is positioned within a magnetic field as radiowave signals are conducted through the selected body part. Energy is absorbed by tissues and then released. A computer processes the released energy and formulates the image. *Inset,* MRI of the knee (lateral view) identifying a torn meniscus. **B.** MRI unit.

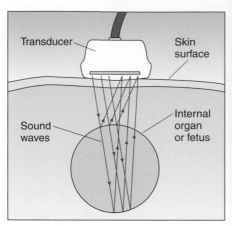

Energy in the form of sound waves is reflected off internal organs or, during pregnancy, the fetus and transformed into an image on a TV-type monitor.

A

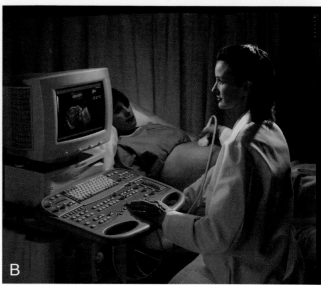

B

Figure 4.18 **A.** Principles of sonography. **B.** Obstetric sonography.

Common Medical Record Terms Related to Disease

NORMAL. The word stems from the Latin word normalis, referring to that which is made according to a carpenter's square, from norma, a carpenter's square; thus, normal refers to a rule or pattern. Abnormal is out of line, not conforming to the rule of pattern.

BENIGN VERSUS MALIGNANT. These antonyms, stemming from the Latin words benignus, meaning kind origin, and malignus, meaning bad origin, were first used to refer to conditions that were kind or mild as opposed to those that were bad or severe. Galen is credited for using the terms in reference to tumors. A tumor is considered malignant if cancerous and benign if not.

The following terms related to disease are common in medical records. Learn them as a foundation on which you will build as your vocabulary expands.

Term	Meaning
acute ă-kyūt′	sharp; having intense, often severe symptoms and a short course
chronic kronī′k	a condition developing slowly and persisting over time
benign bi-nīn′	mild or noncancerous
malignant mă-lig′nănt	harmful or cancerous
degeneration dē-jen-er-ā′shŭn	gradual deterioration of normal cells and body functions
degenerative disease	any disease in which there is deterioration of structure or function of tissue
diagnosis dī-ag-nō′sis	determination of the presence of a disease based on an evaluation of symptoms, signs, and test findings (results) (dia = through; gnosis = knowing)
etiology ē-tē-ol′ō-jē	cause of a disease (etio = cause)
exacerbation eg-zas-er-bā′shŭn	increase in severity of a disease with aggravation of symptoms (ex = out; acerbo = harsh)
remission rē-mish′ŭn	a period in which symptoms and signs stop or abate

Term	Meaning
febrile fe′brĭl	relating to a fever (elevated temperature)
gross	large; visible to the naked eye
idiopathic id′ē-ō-path′ik	a condition occurring without a clearly identified cause (idio = one's own)
localized lō′kăl-īzd	limited to a definite area or part
systemic sis-tem′ik	relating to the whole body rather than only a part
malaise mă-lāz′	a feeling of unwellness, often the first indication of illness
marked	significant
equivocal ē-kwīv′ō-kl	vague, questionable
morbidity mor-bid′i-tē	sick; a state of disease
morbidity rate	the number of cases of a disease in a given year; the ratio of sick to well individuals in a given population
mortality mor-tal′i-tē	the state of being subject to death
mortality rate	death rate; ratio of total number of deaths to total number in a given population
prognosis prog-nō′sis	foreknowledge; prediction of the likely outcome of a disease based on the general health status of the patient along with knowledge of the usual course of the disease
progressive prō-gres′iv	the advance of a condition as signs and symptoms increase in severity
prophylaxis pro-fi-lak′sis	a process or measure that prevents disease (pro = before; phylassein = to guard)
recurrent rē-kŭr′ent	to occur again; describes a return of symptoms and signs after a period of quiescence (rest or inactivity)
sequela sē-kwel′ă	a disorder or condition after, and usually resulting from, a previous disease or injury
sign	a mark; objective evidence of disease that can be seen or verified by an examiner
symptom simp′tŏm	occurrence; subjective evidence of disease that is perceived by the patient and often noted in his or her own words
syndrome sin′drōm	a running together; combination of symptoms and signs that give a distinct clinical picture indicating a particular condition or disease, e.g., menopausal syndrome

FEBRILE. Febrile is derived from the Latin febris, meaning "I am warm." In the ancient world, fever was considered a favorable symptom, and the origin of the word is associated with February (the month for cleansing or purifying). Before the clinical thermometer was developed, the method of estimating fever was to lay the hand on the skin.

Term	Meaning
noncontributory	not involved in bringing on the condition or result
unremarkable	not significant or worthy of noting

Pharmaceutical Abbreviations and Symbols

Pharmaceutical abbreviations and symbols are frequently used in documenting patient care. They are found throughout the medical record. Efficient medical record keeping and effective communication among health care workers depend on knowledge of commonly used pharmaceutical abbreviations and symbols.

UNITS OF MEASURE

The following are common metric and apothecary units of measurement. Consult your medical dictionary for a complete listing of units of measurement and conversion formulas.

Metric System

Metric is the most commonly used system of measurement in health care. It is a decimal system based on the following units.

meter (m)	length	39.37 inches
liter (L)	volume	1.0567 U.S. quarts
gram (g or gm)	weight	15.432 grains

Apothecary System

The apothecary system is an outdated method of liquid and weight measure used by the earliest chemists and pharmacists. The liquid measure was based on one drop. The weight measure was based on one grain of wheat. Although the small apothecary measures are rarely used, the larger ones, e.g., fluid ounces, are still common.

 DRUG. The Middle English drogge or drugge is derived from the Old French drogue, all meaning drug. Earlier origin is uncertain, possibly either a Teutonic root meaning dry or the Persian droa meaning odor because many drugs had a strong odor. Although the ancients listed the use of various medicines, the term drug did not appear until the end of the medieval period. The word druggist did not appear until the 16th century.

Common Abbreviations and Symbols

Abbreviation	Meaning
METRIC	
cc	cubic centimeter (1 cc = 1 mL)
cm	centimeter (2.5 cm = 1 inch)
g or gm	gram
kg	kilogram [1,000 grams (2.2 pounds)]
L	liter
mg	milligram [one-thousandth (0.001) of a gram]
ml, mL	milliliter [one-thousandth (0.001) of a liter]
mm	millimeter [one-thousandth (0.001) of a meter]
cu mm	cubic millimeter

Abbreviation	Meaning
APOTHECARY	
fl oz	fluid ounce
gr	grain
gt	drop (L. gutta = drop)
gtt	drops
dr	dram (1/8 ounce)
oz	ounce
lb or #	pound (16 ounces)
qt	quart (32 ounces)

MEDICATION ADMINISTRATION

Prescribed medications can be administered to patients in various ways, depending on the indication for the drug and the status of the patient. The following is an overview of forms of drugs and routes of administration, including abbreviations and symbols.

Drug Form	Route of Administration	
SOLID AND SEMISOLID FORMS		
tablet (tab) **capsule** (cap)	oral [per os (p.o.)] sublingual (SL) buccal	by mouth under the tongue in the cheek
suppository (suppos)	vaginal [per vagina (PV)] rectal [per rectum (PR)]	inserted in vagina inserted in rectum
LIQUID FORMS		
fluid	inhalation	inhaled through nose or mouth [e.g., aerosol (spray) or neblizer (device used to produce a fine spray or mist, often in a metered dose)]
parenteral	by injection (Fig. 4.19) *intradermal* (ID) *intramuscular* (IM) *intravenous* (IV) *subcutaneous* (Sub-Q, **SC, SQ**)	within the skin within the muscle within the vein under the skin
cream, lotion, ointment	topical	applied to the surface of the skin
other delivery systems	transdermal	absorption of a drug through unbroken skin
	implant	a drug reservoir imbedded in the body to provide continual infusion of a medication (see Chapter 11, Fig. 11.9)

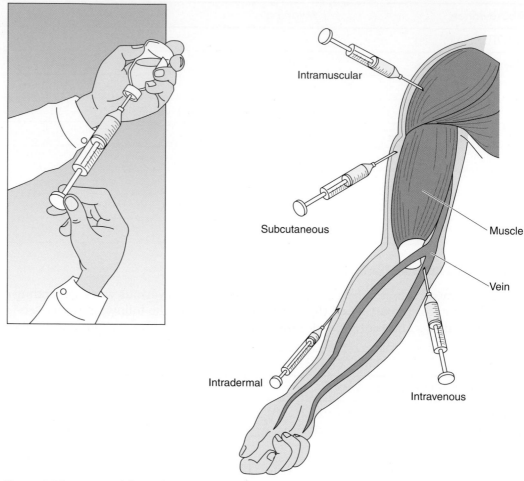

Figure 4.19 Parenteral drug administration.

Rx. The symbol found at the beginning of a prescription stands for recipe. The cross on the tail of the Rx incorporates the astrological sign of Jupiter, which has no connection with the word recipe. The sign of Jupiter was placed at the top of a formula to appease the chief Roman god so that the compound might act favorably. The period during the ascendancy of the planet Jupiter was considered a favorable time for the collection of herbs and the preparation of medicines.

The Prescription

A prescription is a written direction by a physician for dispensing or administering a medication to a patient. It is an order to supply a named patient with a particular drug of a specific strength and quantity along with specific instructions for administration. The prescription is a legal document that must be written in a specific format (Fig. 4.20).

DRUG NAMES

The *chemical name* is assigned to a drug in the laboratory at the time it is invented. It is the formula for the drug, which is written exactly according to its chemical structure. The *generic name* is the official, nonproprietary name given a drug. The *trade* or *brand* is the manufacturer's name for a drug. For example:

chemical name	*1-[[3-(6,7-dihydro-1-methyl-7-oxo-3-propyl-1H-pyrazolo[4,3-d]pyrimidin-5-yl)-4-ethoxyphenyl]sulfonyl]-4-methylpiperazine citrate*
generic name	*sildenafil*
trade or brand	*Viagra (Pfizer Pharmaceutical Company)*

```
                CENTRAL MEDICAL GROUP, INC.
                      Patrick Rodden, M.D.
                    DEA #:  AR 0000000
                     201 Medical Center Drive
                    Central City, US  90000-1234


Name of Patient  Carleen Perron        Date  6/4/xx

Address _____


Rx      Tylenol c codeine No. 3      #24

        Sig: tab i q4h p r n pain




_____ M.D.    Patrick Rodden M.D.
   SUBSTITUTION PERMITTED           DISPENSE AS WRITTEN


May refill ___3___ times
```

Figure 4.20 Sample prescription.

PRESCRIPTION ABBREVIATIONS

Many Latin abbreviations and symbols are commonly used in prescription writing as well as in physicians' orders. Being familiar with these symbols makes it possible to read a prescription or physician's order.

Historically, prescriptions were written in Latin. The words were abbreviated for convenience. For example, quater in die, Latin for four times a day, is abbreviated q.i.d. The periods were included to indicate the abbreviation of three words; if not carefully documented, however, they can be interpreted with drastic implications. For example, the period in q.d (meaning once a day) can be misinterpreted as q.i.d (four times a day) when handwritten. For the purpose of proper recognition, the periods were included in the abbreviations in this text, but the trend is to discourage their use, especially in writing, because they can be misinterpreted. In practice, you will find variations including or excluding the periods and the use of uppercase instead of lowercase letters, e.g., QID versus qid.

Roman numerals were used exclusively in the early days and are still used today; however, most pharmacy organizations now promote the use of Arabic numerals only.

Error-Prone Abbreviations and Symbols

Listed is a sampling of abbreviations and symbols deemed most error prone, including the risk for misinterpretation and preferred use.

Error-Prone Abbreviation	Meaning	Risk	Preferred Use
q.d	every day	mistaken for q.i.d. when the period after the "q" is sloppily written to look like an "i"	spell out "daily"
q.o.d.	every other day	mistaken for q.d when the "o" is mistaken for a period	spell out "every other day"
DC, D/C	discharge, discontinue	when used to mean "discharge," mistaken for "discontinue" when followed by medications prescribed at the time of discharge	spell out "discontinue" or "discharge"
AS, AD, AU	left ear, right ear, both ears	mistaken for each other	spell out
OS, OD, OU	left eye, right eye, both eyes	mistaken for each other	spell out
SC or SQ	subcutaneous	mistaken for SL (sublingual) or "5 every"	spell out "subcutaneously" or use Sub-Q
>, <	greater than, less than	mistaken for each other	spell out

Common Abbreviations and Symbols

Abbreviation	Meaning	Latin[a]
TIME AND FREQUENCY		
ā	before	ante
a.c.	before meals	ante cibum
a.m.	before noon	ante meridiem
b.i.d.	twice a day	bis in die
d	day	
h	hour	hora
h.s.	at hour of sleep (bedtime)	hora somni
noc.	night	noctis
p̄	after	post
p.c.	after meals	post cibum
p.m.	after noon	post meridiem
p.r.n.	as needed	pro re nata
q	every	quaque
q d	every day	quaque die
q h	every hour	quaque hora
q 2 h	every 2 hours	
q.i.d.	four times a day	quater in die
q.o.d.	every other day	quaque altera die
STAT	immediately	statim
t.i.d.	three times a day	ter in die
wk	week	
yr	year	
MISCELLANEOUS		
AD	right ear	auris dextra
AS	left ear	auris sinistra
AU	both ears	aures unitas
ad lib.	as desired	ad libitum
amt	amount	
aq	water	aqua
Ⓑ	bilateral	
C	Celsius, centigrade	
c̄	with	cum

DEXTER AND SINISTER. Dexter is Latin for right, and sinister is Latin for left. The origin of these terms, however, is earlier than ancient Rome. Sun worshippers facing the morning sun had the south on their right hand. The Sanskrit word for south is dekkan, allied to dhu, shining; thus, the right hand was the south or warm shining hand. The left hand was the north or cold hand. Therefore, dexterity or right-handedness was skill, whereas sinister was ill-omened. Among the Romans, sinisteritas (left-handedness) meant awkwardness.

Abbreviation	Meaning	Latin[a]
F	Fahrenheit	
(m)	murmur	
NPO	nothing by mouth	non per os
OD	right eye	oculus dexter
OS	left eye	oculus sinister
OU	both eyes	oculi unitas
per	by or through	
p.o.	by mouth	per os
PR	through rectum	per rectum
PV	through vagina	per vagina
q.n.s.	quantity not sufficient	
q.s.	quantity sufficient	
Rx	recipe; prescription	
Sig:	label; instruction to the patient	signa
$\bar{s}$	without	sine
$\overline{ss}$	one-half	semis
w.a.	while awake	
×	times or for [e.g., × 6 (six times), × 2 d (for 2 days)]	
>	greater than	
<	less than	
ī	one (modified lowercase Roman numeral i)	
īī	two (modified lowercase Roman numeral ii)	
īīī	three (modified lowercase Roman numeral iii)	
īv̄	four (modified lowercase Roman numeral iv)	
I, II, III, IV, V, VI, VII, VIII, IX, X	uppercase Roman numerals 1–10 (Note: Arabic numerals are preferred)	

[a]*Original Latin given when it is deemed helpful.*

Recording Date and Time

The date and time are usually required in entries in a medical record. Always include the month, day of the month, and the year (e.g., 12/25/xx); sometimes eight digits are required (e.g., 01/08/20xx). Often military time is used (Fig. 4.21).

Standard	Military	Standard	Military
1:00 a.m.	0100 zero one hundred	1:00 p.m.	1300 thirteen hundred
2:00 a.m.	0200 zero two hundred	2:00 p.m.	1400 fourteen hundred
2:15 a.m.	0215 zero two fifteen	3:00 p.m.	1500 fifteen hundred
3:00 a.m.	0300 zero three hundred	4:00 p.m.	1600 sixteen hundred
4:00 a.m.	0400 zero four hundred	5:00 p.m.	1700 seventeen hundred
4:30 a.m.	0430 zero four thirty	6:00 p.m.	1800 eighteen hundred
5:00 a.m.	0500 zero five hundred	7:00 p.m.	1900 nineteen hundred
6:00 a.m.	0600 zero six hundred	8:00 p.m.	2000 twenty hundred
7:00 a.m.	0700 zero seven hundred	9:00 p.m.	2100 twenty-one hundred
8:00 a.m.	0800 zero eight hundred	10:00 p.m.	2200 twenty-two hundred
9:00 a.m.	0900 zero nine hundred	11:00 p.m.	2300 twenty-three hundred
10:00 a.m.	1000 ten hundred		
11:00 a.m.	1100 eleven hundred	12:00 a.m. (midnight)	2400 twenty-four hundred hours
12:00 p.m. (noon)	1200 twelve hundred hours		

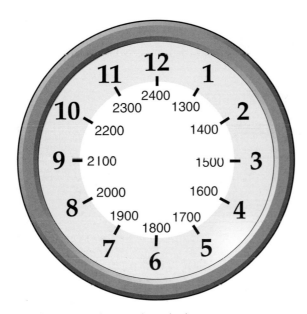

Figure 4.21 Military and standard time.

Regulations and Legal Considerations

Medical record documentations are made by physicians caring for the patient as well as other authorized health care professionals involved with care.

State, federal, and private accrediting agencies, e.g., the Joint Commission on Accreditation of Healthcare Organizations (JCAHO), provide specific guidelines that regulate how medical records are kept, including proper format for all forms, use of appropriate terminology and accepted abbreviations, protocol for personnel having access to records, and responsibilities for documentation.

Corrections

Sometimes mistakes are made when making an entry in a medical record. Careful clarification of the error is essential. If a mistake is made in a handwritten entry, it should be identified by drawing a single line through it, and the correction written in the margin above or immediately after. Include the date, the abbreviation "corr.," and the initials of the person making the correction. The use of correction fluid, e.g., Wite-Out, is forbidden!

The medical record often becomes evidence in medical malpractice cases. Obliterations and signs of possible tampering can be construed as trying to withhold information or covering up negligent wrongdoing. Complete and accurate record keeping is your best defense against any possible legal action (Fig. 4.22).

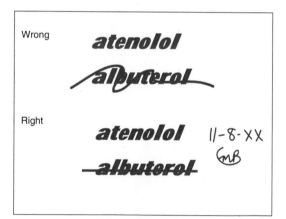

Figure 4.22   Proper correction of a medical record.

PRACTICE EXERCISES

Write the full medical term for the following abbreviations and symbols, and put an asterisk (*) next to those that are error prone:

1. CC _____

2. OH _____

3. PR _____

4. BRP _____

5. PACU _____

6. PH _____

7. D/C _____

8. Sig: _____

9. ER _____

10. ICU _____

11. R/O _____

12. NPO _____

13. L&W _____

14. BP _____

15. AU _____

16. Sx _____

17. VS _____

18. ROS _____

19. pt _____

20. OD _____

21. Sub-Q _____

22. H&P _____

23. Tx _____

24. Dx _____

25. HPI _____

26. ♀ _____

27. ↓ _____

Match the following terms with their meanings:

28. _____ febrile   a. period in which symptoms stop

29. _____ syndrome   b. probable outcome of a disease

30. _____ chronic   c. name of a disease based on history, exam, and testing

31. _____ remission   d. elevated temperature

32. _____ etiology   e. set of symptoms characteristic of a particular disease or condition

33. _____ malignant   f. increase in severity with aggravation of symptoms

34. _____ prognosis   g. developing slowly over time

35. _____ diagnosis   h. limited to a definite area or part

36. _____ exacerbation   i. cancerous

37. _____ localized   j. the study of the cause of a disease

Match the following definitions with their abbreviation or symbol:

38. _____ route of oral medications   a. pre-op

39. _____ place for surgery   b. prn

40. _____ as desired   c. parenteral

41. _____ progress note   d. po

42. _____ after surgery   e. STAT

43. _____ pound   f. ad lib

44. _____ as needed   g. post op

45. _____ by injection   h. OR

46. _____ before surgery   i. SOAP

47. _____ immediately   j. #

Write the meaning for the following pharmaceutical phrases:

48. VS q h × 4 h, then q 2 h _____

49. ℞ po qid pc hs _____

50. aspirin (ASA) gr $\overline{ii}$ $\overline{ss}$ _____

51. 650 mg po q 4 h prn temp >101° _____

52. † suppos PR q noc prn _____

53. gt † OU tid × 7 d _____

54. cap ̈ STAT, then † q 6 h _____

Write the standard pharmaceutical abbreviations for the following:

55. one tablet by mouth three times a day for 7 days

_____

56. one suppository in the vagina at bedtime

_____

57. five milliliters by mouth four times a day

_____

58. one or two by mouth every 3 to 4 hours as needed

_____

59. two drops in left ear every 3 hours

_____

60. one capsule by mouth two times a day, morning and evening

_____

61. two by mouth immediately, then one by mouth every 6 hours

_____

62. thirty milligrams by mouth at bedtime as needed

_____

Give the military time for the following:

63. 1:00 a.m.

64. 2:30 p.m.

65. midnight

66. 1:00 p.m.

67. 7:00 p.m.

68. 4:50 a.m.

Match the following chart entries with the corresponding health record abbreviations:

69. _____ works as a security officer

a. UCHD

70. _____ advised to lower salt intake

b. HPI

71. _____ father, age 88, L&W; mother, age 78, died, stroke

c. PE

72. _____ quit smoking 2 years ago, drinks alcohol socially

d. CC

73. _____ diagnosis: tonsillitis

e. OH

74. _____ c/o lower back pain

f. SH

75. _____ pain in lower back for 2 weeks, worse at night

g. FH

76. _____ no reaction to any previously administered drug

h. P

77. _____ had all commonly contracted childhood diseases

i. A

78. _____ lungs: clear; heart: regular rate and rhythm

j. NKA

Give the meaning for the following abbreviations deemed error prone, and list the preferred term for each:

Abbreviation	Meaning	Preferred Term
79. q.d	_____	_____
80. q.o.d.	_____	_____
81. OS	_____	_____
82. AD	_____	_____
83. AU	_____	_____
84. >	_____	_____
85. D/C	_____	_____

From the following list of diagnostic imaging modalities, circle those that *use* ionizing radiation:

86. computed tomography

87. magnetic resonance imaging

88. radiology

89. radionuclide organ imaging

90. sonography

Match the following imaging modalities with the type of radiation used:

91. _____ computed tomography   a. standard x-rays

92. _____ magnetic resonance imaging   b. gamma rays

93. _____ radiology   c. ultrasound waves

94. _____ radionuclide organ imaging   d. radio waves

95. _____ sonography   e. 3-D x-rays

MEDICAL RECORD ANALYSES

MEDICAL RECORD 4.1

Progress Note

CC: 37 y.o. ♂ c̄ diabetes c / o swelling of the (R) foot and calf × 3d

S: There is no Hx of trauma, pain, SOB, or cardiac Sx, smoker × 12 yr, s̄s̄ pkg q d, denies ETOH consumption

Meds: parenteral insulin qd, NKDA

O: Pt is afebrile, BP 140/84, P 72, R 16, lungs are clear; abdomen is benign s̄ organomegaly; muscle tone and strength are WNL; there is swelling of the (R) calf but s̄ erythema or tenderness

A: Edema of (R) calf of unknown etiology

P: Schedule STAT vascular sonogram of lower extremities; pt is to keep the leg elevated × ⅱ d, then RTC for follow-up and test results on Thursday (or sooner if ↑ edema, SOB, or CP)

1. What is the sex of the patient?

   a. male

   b. female

2. Where was the patient seen?

   a. emergency room

   b. outpatient office of clinic

   c. inpatient hospital

   d. not stated

3. What was the condition of the patient's abdomen?

   a. shows signs of cancer

   b. internal organs are enlarged

   c. internal organs are not enlarged

   d. muscle tone and strength are weak

4. How much does the patient smoke per day?

   a. one package

   b. two packages

   c. half a package

   d. none; patient quit smoking 12 years ago

5. How is the patient's insulin administered?

   a. orally

   b. transdermally

   c. infusion through implant

   d. by injection

6. What is the cause of the patient's complaint?

   a. unknown

   b. fever

   c. shortness of breath

   d. trauma

7. When should the sonogram be performed?

   a. immediately

   b. within two days

   c. at the time of follow-up

   d. only if symptoms persist

8. How long should the patient's leg be kept elevated?

   a. one week

   b. two weeks

   c. one day

   d. two days

MEDICAL RECORD 4.2

Postop Meds for Laparotomy

1. Vicodin, † tab p.o. q 3 h prn mild pain, or †† tab p.o. q 3 h prn moderate pain

2. Demerol, 100 mg IM q 3 h prn severe pain

3. Tylenol (acetaminophen) 650 mg p.o. q 4 h prn oral temp ↑ 100.4°F

4. Dalmane (flurazepam) 30 mg p.o. h.s. prn sleep

5. Mylicon (simethicone) 80 mg, † tab chewed and swallowed q.i.d.

6. Ducolax (bisacodyl) suppos, † PR in a.m.

1. How is the Demerol to be administered?
   a. by mouth
   b. within the vein
   c. under the skin
   d. within the muscle

2. What is the Sig: on the Mylicon?
   a. one every other day
   b. one twice a day
   c. one three times a day
   d. one four times a day

3. What is the Sig: on the Ducolax?
   a. one suppository in the rectum in the morning
   b. one suppository taken orally before noon
   c. two suppositories before breakfast
   d. one suppository as needed in the morning

4. When should the Dalmane be administered?
   a. each night
   b. at bedtime
   c. as needed
   d. every hour

5. What are the instructions for administering the Vicodin in the case of moderate pain?
   a. one tablet every three hours
   b. three tablets every hour
   c. two tablets every three hours
   d. three tablets every three hours

6. How should the Tylenol be administered?
   a. one dose every four hours as needed
   b. one dose every four hours only if patient has a temperature of 100.4°F or higher
   c. one dose every four hours as long as the patient's temperature does not go over 100.4°
   d. one dose every hour up to four per day

7. Laparotomy refers to
   a. a puncture of the abdomen
   b. excision of the stomach
   c. a puncture of the stomach
   d. an incision in the abdomen

MEDICAL RECORD 4.3

Michael Marsi has had chronic health problems in the past 2 years and has been seeing Dr. Spaulding, his personal physician, regularly in recent months. Dr. Spaulding uses problem-oriented medical records and writes a new SOAP progress note at each patient visit. Mr. Marsi has come to see Dr. Spaulding today because he feels worse than usual.

DIRECTIONS

Read Medical Record 4.3 (page 105) for Michael Marsi, and answer the following questions. This record is the progress note for today's visit, part of Dr. Spaulding's POMR for Mr. Marsi. Dr. Spaulding handwrote it herself during the patient's visit.

QUESTIONS ABOUT MEDICAL RECORD 4.3

Write your answers in the spaces provided.

1. How old is Mr. Marsi? _____

2. Where was the treatment rendered? _____

3. List the three elements of the patient's complaint

   a. _____

   b. _____

   c. _____

4. In your own words, not using medical terminology, briefly summarize Mr. Marsi's history:

   _____

   _____

   _____

5. Which of the following is *not* mentioned at all in this history?
   a. The prescription medication Mr. Marsi takes
   b. Mr. Marsi's smoking habit
   c. Mr. Marsi's activity level at work
   d. Mr. Marsi's consumption of alcohol

6. Dr. Spaulding and Mr. Marsi talked at length about Mr. Marsi's symptoms and how they've changed recently, and then Dr. Spaulding examined him. List three objective findings she noted in this examination.

   a. _____

   b. _____

   c. _____

PROGRESS NOTES

Patient Name: *MARSI, Michael*

DATE	FINDINGS
2-3-xx	CC: 51 y.o. ♂ c/o dizziness x 3 wk and headaches 5-6 x ↑ wk. Today he woke c̄ numbness in Ⓛ leg and hand
	S Hx of ↑ BP x 4 yrs Smoker x 20 yrs - 1 pkg/d MEDS: Dyazide ī q d. c̄ CP c̄ SOB occipital headaches in am mod fat diet 3 beers q noc. NKDA
	O BP 150/100 Ⓡ arm s̄ Ht 68" WT 198# T 98.7° P 76 R 15 Heart - RRR s̄ Ⓜ Lungs clear HEENT - WNL.
	A Hypertension (HTN) R/o Congestive heart failure (CHF)
	P Chest x-ray and electrocardiogram today ↓ ETO" to ī beer q noc. DC smoking Rx: Procardia XL 30 mg ī p.o. daily ↑ exercise to 3 x/wk for 20-30 min stop if CP, SOB or dizzy ↓ fat and cholesterol in diet rec̄ BP ī wk RTO sooner if CP, SOB or dizzy
	JR Spaulding MD

Medical Record 4.3

7. Dr. Spaulding's assessment is that Mr. Marsi has _____.

    But she also wants to make sure he does *not* have _____

    _____.

8. Dr. Spaulding's treatment plan involves four areas. List the specific plan(s) for each of these.

    Diagnostic tests ordered: _____

    _____

    Instruct patient to change (and how) these personal habits: _____

    _____

    _____

    _____

    _____

    Drug prescribed (and how much and when): _____

    _____

    Future diagnostic check and/or action to take: _____

    _____

9. When is Dr. Spaulding expecting to see Mr. Marsi again? _____

    _____

Chapter 5

Integumentary System

OBJECTIVES

After completion of this chapter you will be able to

- Define common combining forms used in relation to the integumentary system
- Describe the basic functions of the integumentary system
- Define basic anatomical terms related to the integumentary system
- Identify common symptomatic terms related to the integumentary system
- Identify common diagnostic terms related to the integumentary system
- List common diagnostic tests and procedures related to the integumentary system
- Identify common operative terms referring to the integumentary system
- Identify common therapeutic terms including drug classifications related to the integumentary system
- Explain common terms and abbreviations used in documenting medical records involving the integumentary system

Combining Forms

Combining Form	Meaning	Example
adip/o	fat	adiposis ad-i-pō′sis
lip/o		lipoma li-pō′ma
steat/o		steatoma stē-ā-tō′mă
derm/o	skin	hypodermic hī′pō-der′mik
dermat/o		dermatology der-mă-tol′ō-jē
cutane/o		subcutaneous sŭb-kyū-tā′nē-ŭs
erythr/o	red	erythrodermatitis ĕ-rith-rō-der′mă-tī′tis
hidr/o	sweat	anhidrosis an-hī-drō′sis

Combining Form	Meaning	Example
hist/o	tissue	histology his-tol'ō-jē
histi/o		histiogenic his'tē-ō-jen'ik
ichthy/o	fish	ichthyoid ik'thē-oyd
kerat/o	hard	keratosis ker-ă-tō'sis
scler/o		scleroderma sklĕr-ō-der'mă
leuk/o	white	leukonychia lū-kō-nik'ē-ă
melan/o	black	melanocyte mel'ă-nō-sīt
myc/o	fungus	mycosis mī-kō'sis
onych/o	nail	onychodystrophy on'i-kō-dis'trō-fē
plas/o	formation	dysplastic dis-plas'tik
purpur/o	purple	purpuric pŭr'pū'rik
seb/o	sebum (oil)	seborrhea seb-ō-rē'ă
squam/o	scale	squamous skwā'mūs
trich/o	hair	trichorrhexis trik-ō-rek'sis
xanth/o	yellow	xanthoma zan-thō'mă
xer/o	dry	xerosis zē-rō'sis

Integumentary System Overview

The integumentary system is composed of the skin (also called the *integument*) and its appendages, including hair, nails, sweat glands, and sebaceous glands. It protects the body from injury or intrusion of microorganisms, helps regulate body temperature, and houses the receptors for the sense of touch, including pain and sensation (Fig. 5.1).

The skin is the largest organ in the body. Skin layers are divided into an outer layer called the epidermis, an inner layer called the dermis, and a subcutaneous tissue layer beneath the dermis.

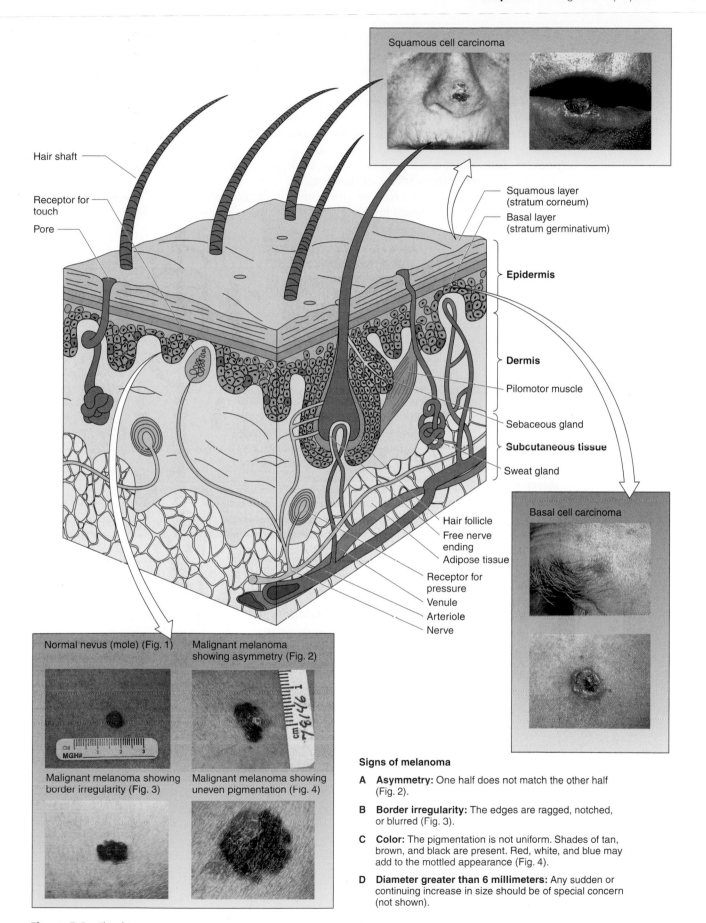

Squamous cell carcinoma

Hair shaft

Receptor for touch

Pore

Squamous layer (stratum corneum)

Basal layer (stratum germinativum)

Epidermis

Dermis

Pilomotor muscle

Sebaceous gland

Subcutaneous tissue

Sweat gland

Hair follicle

Free nerve ending

Adipose tissue

Receptor for pressure

Venule

Arteriole

Nerve

Basal cell carcinoma

Normal nevus (mole) (Fig. 1)

Malignant melanoma showing asymmetry (Fig. 2)

Malignant melanoma showing border irregularity (Fig. 3)

Malignant melanoma showing uneven pigmentation (Fig. 4)

Signs of melanoma

A   Asymmetry: One half does not match the other half (Fig. 2).

B   Border irregularity: The edges are ragged, notched, or blurred (Fig. 3).

C   Color: The pigmentation is not uniform. Shades of tan, brown, and black are present. Red, white, and blue may add to the mottled appearance (Fig. 4).

D   Diameter greater than 6 millimeters: Any sudden or continuing increase in size should be of special concern (not shown).

Figure 5.1   The skin.

Epidermis

The epidermis consists of several layers of stratified squamous (scale-like) epithelium. The two significant layers are the innermost layer, known as the *basal layer* (stratum germinativum), and the outermost layer, called the *squamous layer* (stratum corneum). The cells of the basal layer are constantly being produced, moving the older cells up toward the surface. As these cells are being pushed up, they flatten, become filled with a hard protein substance called *keratin,* and soon die. As a result, many layers of tightly packed dead cells accumulate in the outermost squamous layer, where they are sloughed off from the surface of the skin.

Melanocytes, which produce the pigment called *melanin* that gives color to the skin, are found in the basal layer.

Dermis

The dermis, also called the *corium,* is the connective tissue layer; it contains blood and lymphatic vessels, nerves and nerve endings, glands, and hair follicles within a network of elastic and collagen fibers. Collagen is a fibrous protein material that is tough and resistant. These fibers give the skin its qualities of toughness and elasticity.

Subcutaneous Tissue

The subcutaneous layer is below the dermis and is composed of loose connective tissue and adipose (fatty) tissue.

Anatomical Terms

Term	Meaning
epithelium ep-i-thē′lē-ŭm	cells covering external and internal surfaces of the body
epidermis ep-i-derm′is	thin, cellular outer layer of the skin
squamous cell layer skwā′mŭs	flat, scale-like epithelial cells comprising the outermost layers of the epidermis
basal layer bā′săl	deepest region of the epidermis
melanocyte mel′ă-nō-sīt	a cell found in the basal layer that gives color to the skin
melanin mel′ă-nin	dark brown to black pigment contained in melanocytes
dermis	dense, fibrous connective tissue layer of the skin (also known as the corium)
sebaceous glands sē-bā′shŭs	oil glands in the skin
sebum sē′bŭm	oily substance secreted by the sebaceous glands
sudoriferous glands sū-dō-rif′er-ŭs	sweat glands (sudor = sweat; ferre = to bear)

Term	Meaning
subcutaneous tissue sŭb-kyū-tā′nē-ŭs	connective and adipose tissue layer just under the dermis
collagen kol′lă-jen	protein substance found in skin and connective tissue (koila = glue; gen = producing)
hair	outgrowth of the skin composed of keratin
nail	outgrowth of the skin attached to the distal end of each finger and toe, composed of keratin
keratin ker′ă-tin	hard protein material found in the epidermis, hair, and nails

Symptomatic Terms

Term	Meaning
lesion lē′zhŭn	an area of pathologically altered tissue (two types: primary and secondary) (Fig. 5.2)
primary lesions	lesions arising from previously normal skin

flat, nonpalpable changes in skin color

macule (macula) mak′yul	a flat, discolored spot on the skin up to 1 cm across (e.g., a freckle) (Fig. 5.3A)
patch	a flat, discolored area on the skin larger than 1 cm (e.g., vitiligo) (Fig. 5.3B)

elevated, palpable, solid masses

papule pap′yūl	a solid mass on the skin up to 0.5 cm in diameter [e.g., a nevus (mole)] (Fig. 5.3C)
plaque plāk	a solid mass greater than 1 cm in diameter, limited to the surface of the skin (Fig. 5.3D)
nodule nod′yūl	a solid mass greater than 1 cm, which extends deeper into the epidermis (Fig. 5.3E)
tumor tu′mŏr	a solid mass larger than 1–2 cm (Fig. 5.3F)
wheal hwel	an area of localized skin edema (swelling) (e.g., a hive) (Fig. 5.3G)

elevation formed by fluid within a cavity

vesicle ves′ĭ-kl	little bladder; an elevated, fluid-filled sac (blister) within or under the epidermis up to 0.5 cm in diameter (e.g., a fever blister) (Fig. 5.3H)
bulla bul′ă	a blister larger than 0.5 cm (e.g., a second-degree burn) (bulla = bubble) (Fig. 5.3I)
pustule pŭs′chūl	a pus-filled sac (e.g., a pimple) (Fig. 5.3J)

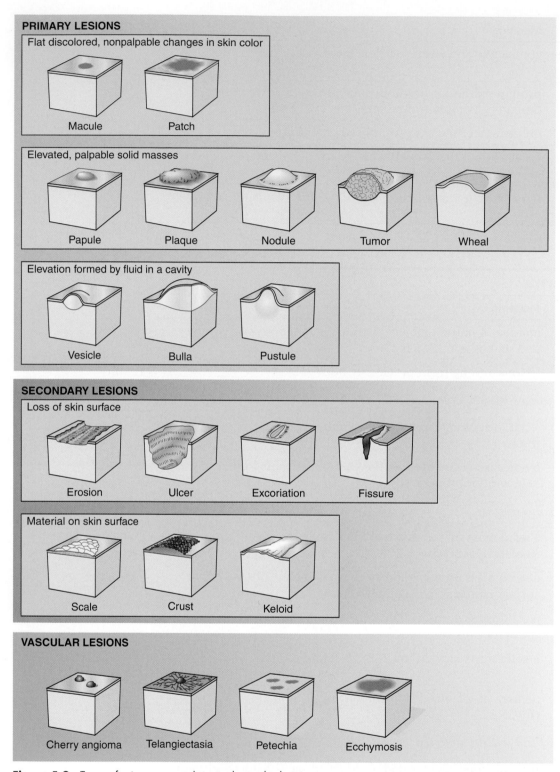

Figure 5.2 Types of primary, secondary, and vascular lesions.

Term	Meaning
secondary lesions	lesions that result in changes in primary lesions
loss of skin surface	
erosion ĕr-ō′zhŭn	to gnaw away; loss of superficial epidermis leaving an area of moisture but no bleeding (e.g., area of moisture after rupture of a vesicle) (Fig. 5.3K)

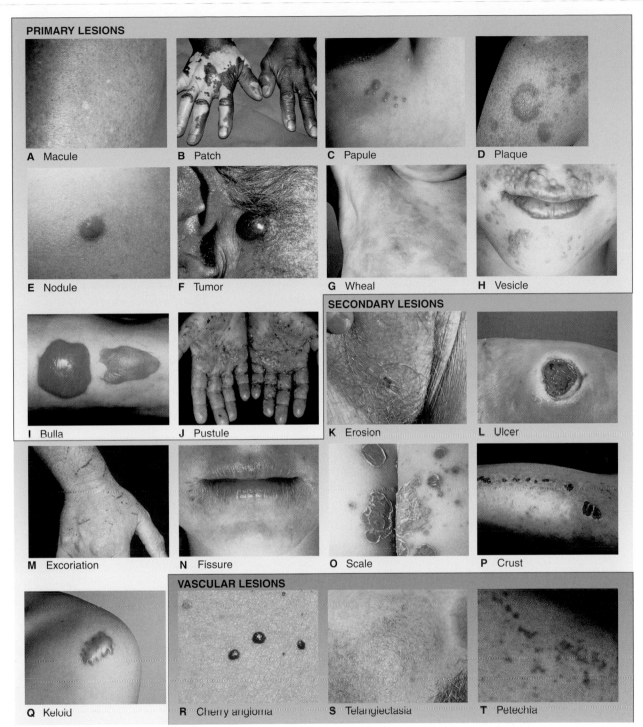

Figure 5.3 Skin lesions.

Term	Meaning
ulcer	an open sore on the skin or mucous membrane that can bleed and scar and is sometimes accompanied by infection (e.g., decubitus ulcer) (Fig. 5.3L)
excoriation eks-kō′rē-ā′shŭn	a scratch mark (e.g., from a cat scratch) (Fig. 5.3M)
fissure fish′ŭr	a linear crack in the skin (Fig. 5.3N)

Term	Meaning
material on skin surface	
scale	a thin flake of exfoliated epidermis (e.g., dandruff) (Fig. 5.3O)
crust	dried residue of serum (body liquid), pus, or blood on the skin (e.g., in impetigo) (Fig. 5.3P)
other secondary lesions	
cicatrix of the skin sik′ă-triks	a mark left by the healing of a sore or wound showing the replacement of destroyed tissue by fibrous tissue (cicatrix = scar)
keloid kē′loyd	an abnormal overgrowth of scar tissue that is thick and irregular (kele = tumor) (Fig. 5.3Q)
vascular lesions	lesions of a blood vessel
cherry angioma chār′ē an-jē-ō′mă	a small, round, bright-red blood vessel tumor on the skin, often on the trunk of the elderly ((Fig. 5.3R)
telangiectasia tel-an′jē-ek-tā′zē-ă **spider angioma** spī′der an-jē-ō′mă	a tiny, red blood vessel lesion formed by the dilation of a group of blood vessels radiating from a central arteriole, most commonly seen on the face, neck, or chest (telos = end) (Fig. 5.3S)
purpuric lesions pŭr′pū-rik	purpura; lesions as a result of hemorrhages into the skin
petechia pe-tē′kē-ă	spot; a reddish-brown, minute hemorrhagic spot on the skin that indicates a bleeding tendency—small purpura (Fig. 5.3T)
ecchymosis ek-i-mō′sis	bruise; a black and blue mark—large purpura (chymo = juice)
epidermal tumors	skin tumors arising from the epidermis
nevus nē′vŭs	a congenital malformation on the skin that can be epidermal or vascular—also called a mole (see Fig. 5.1)
dysplastic nevus dis-plas′tik nē′vŭs	a mole with precancerous changes
verruca vě-rū′kă	an epidermal tumor caused by a papilloma virus—also called a wart (Fig. 5.4)

GENERAL SYMPTOMATIC TERMS

alopecia al-ō-pē′shē-ă	baldness; natural or unnatural deficiency of hair
comedo **(pl. comedos,** **comedones)** kom′ē-dō	a plug of sebum (oil) within the opening of a hair follicle (Fig. 5.5)
closed comedo **(whitehead)**	below the skin surface with a white center
open comedo **(blackhead)**	open to the skin surface with a black center caused by the presence of melanin exposed to air

COMEDO, a plug of sebum within the opening of a hair follicle, also known as whitehead or blackhead, is derived from the Latin word meaning to eat up or consume. The material when expressed has a worm-like appearance, and ancient writers thought there was an actual worm eating into the flesh.

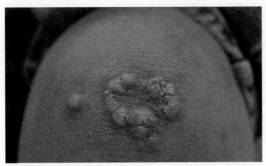

Figure 5.4 Verrucae on a knee. (From Dr. Barankin Dermatology Collection.)

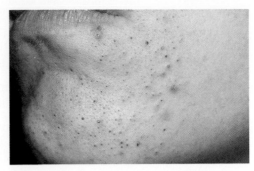

Figure 5.5 Open and closed comedones.

Term	Meaning
eruption ē-rŭp′shŭn	appearance of a skin lesion
erythema er-i-thē′mă	redness of skin
pruritus prū-rī′tŭs	severe itching
rash	a general term for skin eruption, most often associated with communicable disease
skin pigmentation	skin color due to the presence of melanin
depigmentation	loss of melanin pigment in the skin
hypopigmentation	areas of skin lacking color due to deficient amounts of melanin
hyperpigmentation	darkened areas of skin caused by excessive amounts of melanin
suppuration sŭp′yŭ-rā′shŭn	production of purulent matter (pus)
urticaria er′ti-kar′i-a	hives; an eruption of wheals on the skin accompanied by itch (urtica = stinging nettle) (see Fig. 5.3G)
xeroderma zēr′ō-der′mă	dry skin

Diagnostic Terms

Term	Meaning
acne ak′nē	an inflammation of the sebaceous glands and hair follicles of the skin evidenced by comedones, pustules, or nodules on the skin (acne = point) (Fig. 5.6)
albinism al′bi-nizm	a hereditary condition characterized by a partial or total lack of melanin pigment (particularly in the eyes, skin, and hair)

Term	Meaning
burn	any injury to body tissue caused by heat, chemicals, electricity, radiation, or gases
first-degree burn	a burn involving only the epidermis, characterized by erythema (redness) and hyperesthesia (excessive sensation)
second-degree burn	a burn involving the epidermis and the dermis, characterized by erythema, hyperesthesia, and vesications (blisters)
third-degree burn	a burn involving all layers of the skin, characterized by the destruction of the epidermis and dermis with damage or destruction of the subcutaneous tissue
cellulitis	an acute inflammation of subcutaneous tissue resulting from a bacterial invasion through a break in the skin (cellula = small storeroom)
dermatitis (eczema) der-mă-tī'tis	an inflammation of the skin characterized by redness, pruritus (itching), and various lesions
common types:	
atopic dermatitis (atopic eczema)	a chronic skin inflammation characterized by the appearance of inflamed, swollen papules and vesicles that crust and scale, with severe itching and burning; most outbreaks begin in infancy and are marked by exacerbations and remissions that usually clear up before adulthood; occurs in persons with atopy (a genetic hypersensitivity to environmental irritants or allergens)
contact dermatitis	an inflammation of the skin resulting from contact with a substance to which one is allergic (e.g., chemicals in dyes, preservatives, fragrances, rubber; allergic dermatitis); or one that is a known skin irritant (e.g., acid, solvent; irritant dermatitis) (Fig. 5.7)
seborrheic dermatitis	redness of the skin covered by a yellow, oily, itchy scale most commonly at the hairline, forehead, and around the nose, ears, or eyelashes and developing at any age; referred to as "cradle cap" in infants

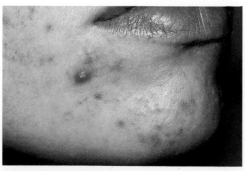

Figure 5.6 Acne lesions. Inflammatory papules, pustules, and closed comedones are present on the face of a patient diagnosed with acne vulgaris.

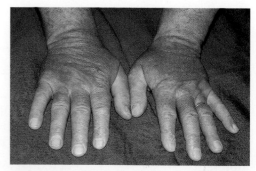

Figure 5.7 Contact dermatitis. This eczematous dermatitis on the dorsa of the hands was caused by exposure to lanolin.

Term	Meaning
dermatosis der-mă-tō′sis	any disorder of the skin
exanthematous viral disease eg-zan-them′ă-tŭs	eruption of the skin caused by a viral disease (exanthema = eruption)
rubella rū-bel′ă	reddish; German measles
rubeola rū-bē′ō-lă	reddish; 14-day measles
varicella var-ĭ-sel′ă	a tiny spot; chickenpox
eczema ek′ze-mă	to boil out; the term is often used interchangeably with dermatitis to denote a skin condition characterized by the appearance of inflamed, swollen papules and vesicles that crust and scale, often with sensations of itching and burning
furuncle fyū′rŭng-kl	a boil; a painful nodule formed in the skin by inflammation originating in a hair follicle—caused by staphylococcosis
carbuncle kar′bŭng-kl	a skin infection consisting of clusters of furuncles (carbo = small, glowing embers)
abscess ab′ses	a localized collection of pus in a cavity formed by the inflammation of surrounding tissues that heals when drained or excised (abscessus = a going away)
gangrene gang′grēn	an eating sore; death of tissue associated with a loss of blood supply resulting from trauma or an inflammatory or infectious process such as seen in complications of frostbite, severe burns, and conditions that affect circulation (e.g., diabetes)
herpes simplex virus type 1 (HSV-1) her′pēz	transient viral vesicles (e.g., cold sores, fever blisters) that infect the facial area, especially the mouth and nose (herpes = creeping skin disease)
herpes simplex virus type 2 (HSV-2)	sexually transmitted ulcer-like lesions of the genital and anorectal skin and mucosa; after initial infection, the virus lies dormant in the nerve cell root and may recur at times of stress (see Chapter 17, Fig. 17.9)
herpes zoster her′pēz zos′ter	a viral disease affecting the peripheral nerves characterized by painful blisters that spread over the skin following the affected nerves; usually unilateral—also known as shingles (zoster = girdle) (see Chapter 10, Fig. 10.10)
ichthyosis ik-thē-ō′sis	a skin condition caused by a gene defect that results in dry, thick, scaly skin; ichthyosis vulgaris is the most common of the many types (vulgaris is a Greek word meaning common)
impetigo im-pe-tī′gō	highly contagious, bacterial skin inflammation marked by pustules that rupture and become crusted—most often occurs around the mouth and nostrils

Term	Meaning
keratoses ker-ă-tō′sez	thickened areas of epidermis
actinic keratoses ak-tin′ik **solar keratoses**	localized thickening of the skin caused by excessive exposure to sunlight; a known precursor to cancer (actinic = ray; solar = sun) (Fig. 5.8)
seborrheic keratoses seb-ō-rē′ik	benign wart-like lesions (seen especially on elderly skin) (Fig. 5.9)
lupus lū′pŭs	a chronic autoimmune disease characterized by inflammation of various parts of the body (lupus = wolf)
cutaneous lupus kyū-tā′nē-ŭs	limited to the skin; evidenced by a characteristic rash especially on the face, neck, and scalp
systemic lupus erythematosus (SLE) sis-tem′ik lū′pŭs er-i-them′ă-tō-sis	a more severe form of lupus involving the skin, joints, and often the vital organs (e.g., lungs, kidneys)
malignant cutaneous neoplasm mă-lig′nănt kyū-tā′nē-ŭs nē′ō-plazm	skin cancer
squamous cell carcinoma (SCC) skwā′mŭs sel kar-si-nō′mă	a malignant tumor of squamous epithelium (see Fig. 5.1)
basal cell carcinoma (BCC) bā′săl sel kar-si-nō′mă	a malignant tumor of the basal layer of the epidermis [the most common type of skin cancer (see Fig. 5.1)]
malignant melanoma mă-lig′nănt mel′ă-nō′mă	a malignant tumor composed of melanocytes—most develop from a pigmented nevus over time (see Signs of Melanoma in Fig. 5.1)
Kaposi sarcoma kăp′ō-sē sar-kō′mă	a malignant tumor of the walls of blood vessels appearing as painless, dark bluish-purple plaques on the skin; often spreads to lymph nodes and internal organs (Fig. 5.10)
onychia ō-nik′ē-ă	inflammation of the fingernail or toenail

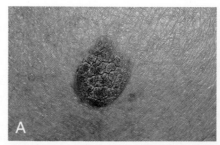

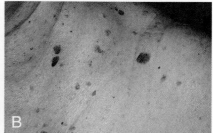

Figure 5.9   Seborrheic keratoses. **A.** Lesion with warty, stuck-on appearance. **B.** Multiple lesions showing various colors and sizes.

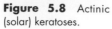

Figure 5.8 Actinic (solar) keratoses.

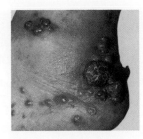

Figure 5.10 Skin lesions associated with Kaposi sarcoma.

Term	Meaning
paronychia par-ō-nik′ē-ă	inflammation of the nail fold (Fig. 5.11)
pediculosis pĕ-dik′yū-lō′sis	infestation with lice that causes itching and dermatitis (pediculo = louse) (Fig. 5.12)
pediculosis capitis pĕ-dik′yū-lō′sis kap′i-tis	head lice (capitis = head)
pediculosis pubis pĕ-dik′yū-lō′sis pyū′bis	lice that generally infect the pubic region, but hair of the axilla, eyebrows, lashes, beard, or other hairy body surfaces may also be involved—also called crabs (pubis = groin)
psoriasis sō-rī′ă-sis	an itching; a chronic, recurrent skin disease marked by silver-gray scales covering red patches on the skin that result from overproduction and thickening of skin cells—elbows, knees, genitals, arms, legs, scalp, and nails are common sites of involvement (Fig. 5.13)
scabies skā′bēz	a contagious disease caused by a parasite (mite) that invades the skin, causing an intense itch—most often found at articulations between the fingers or toes, elbow, etc. (scabo = to scratch)
seborrhea seb-ō-rē′ă	a skin condition marked by the hypersecretion of sebum from the sebaceous glands
tinea tin′ē-ă	a group of fungal skin diseases identified by the body part that is affected, including tinea corporis (body), commonly called ringworm, and tinea pedis (foot), also called athlete's foot
vitiligo vit-i-lī′gō	a condition caused by the destruction of melanin that results in the appearance of white patches on the skin, commonly the face, hands, legs, and genital areas (see Fig. 5.3B)

 TINEA. Tinea is Latin for a grub, a gnawing worm; it is used to describe the gnawed or moth-eaten appearance of the skin in this condition.

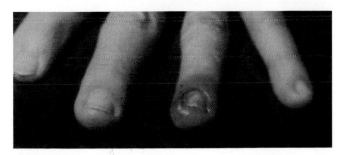

Figure 5.11 Chronic paronychia.

Pubic louse

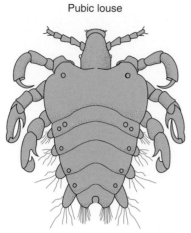

Head louse

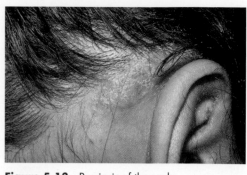

Figure 5.13 Psoriasis of the scalp.

Figure 5.12 Pediculosis.

SUTURE. Suture is derived from the Latin *sutura*, meaning a seam, a sewing together. In surgery, a suture is a thread or other material used for sewing. Also, to suture is to sew up or stitch together. Numbers indicate thickness of the thread (i.e., lower numbers denote thicker thread; higher numbers denote thinner thread).

Diagnostic Tests and Procedures

Term	Meaning
biopsy (Bx) bī′op-sē	removal of a small piece of tissue for microscopic pathological examination (Fig. 5.14)
excisional Bx	removal of an entire lesion
incisional Bx	removal of a selected portion of a lesion
shave Bx	a technique using a surgical blade to "shave" tissue from the epidermis and upper dermis
culture and sensitivity (C&S)	a technique of isolating and growing colonies of microorganisms to identify a pathogen and to determine which drugs might be effective in combating the infection it has caused
frozen section (FS)	a surgical method involving cutting a thin piece of tissue from a frozen specimen for immediate pathological examination

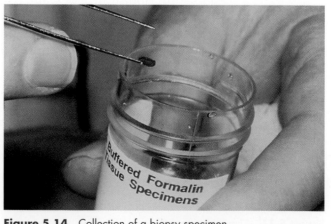

Figure 5.14 Collection of a biopsy specimen.

Term	Meaning
skin tests	methods for determining the reaction of the body to a given substance by applying it to, or injecting it into, the skin—commonly seen in treating allergy
scratch test	the substance is applied to the skin through a scratch
patch test	the substance is applied topically to the skin on a small piece of blotting paper or wet cloth

Operative Terms (Fig. 5.15)

Term	Meaning
chemosurgery kem′ō-ser-jer-ē chemical peel	a technique for restoring wrinkled, scarred, or blemished skin by application of an acid solution to "peel" away the top layers of the skin
cryosurgery krī-ō-ser′jer-ē	destruction of tissue by freezing—involves application of an extremely cold chemical (e.g., liquid nitrogen)
dermabrasion der-mă-brā′zhŭn	surgical removal of frozen epidermis using wire brushes and emery papers to remove scars, tattoos, and/or wrinkles; aerosol spray is used to freeze the skin
debridement dā-brēd-mon′	removal of dead tissue from a wound or burn site to promote healing and prevent infection
curettage kyū-rĕ-tahzh′	to clean; scraping of a wound using a spoon-like cutting instrument called a curette; this technique is used in debridement
electrosurgical procedures	use of electric currents to destroy tissue—the type and strength of the current and method of application varies
electrocautery ē-lek′trō-caw′ter-ē	use of an instrument heated by electric current (cautery) to coagulate bleeding areas by burning the tissue (e.g., to sear a blood vessel) (Fig. 5.16)
electrodesiccation ē-lek′trō-des-i-kā′shŭn	use of short, high-frequency, electric currents to destroy tissue by drying—the active electrode makes direct contact with the skin lesion (desicco = to dry up)
fulguration ful-gŭ-rā′shŭn	to lighten; use of long, high-frequency, electric sparks to destroy tissue; the active electrode does *not* touch the skin
incision and drainage (I&D)	incision and drainage of an infected skin lesion (e.g., an abscess)
laser surgery lā′zer	surgery using a laser in various dermatological procedures to remove lesions, scars, tattoos, etc.
laser	an acronym for light amplification by stimulated emission of radiation; an instrument that concentrates high frequencies of light into a small, extremely intense beam that is precise in depth and diameter; it is applied to body tissues to destroy lesions or for dissection (cutting of parts for study)

CAUTERY. A Greek word meaning branding iron refers to the surgical use of flame or heat to destroy tissue, control bleeding of wound sites, etc. The ancients used actual cautery with a metallic instrument heated in a flame and potential cautery with a caustic chemical.

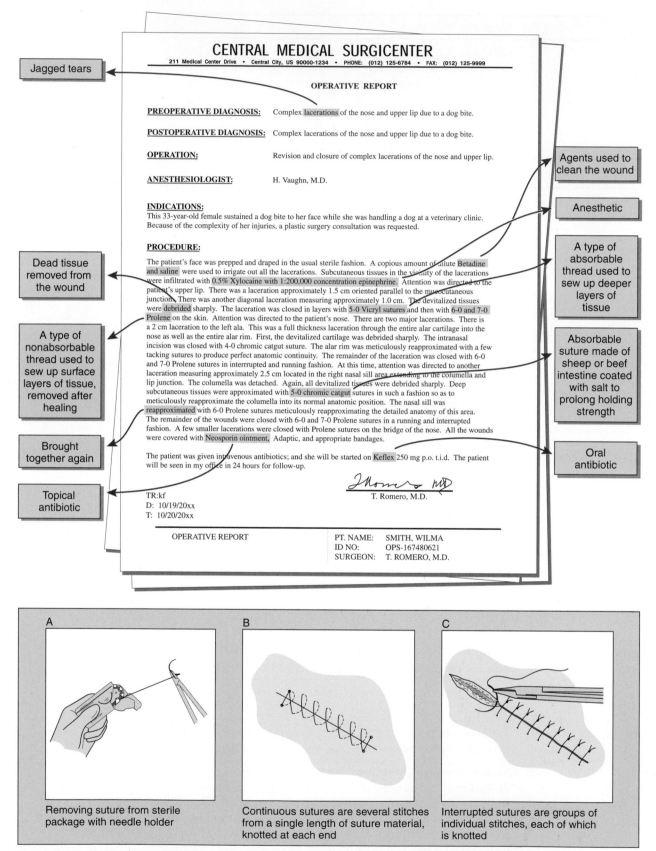

Jagged tears

Agents used to clean the wound

Anesthetic

A type of absorbable thread used to sew up deeper layers of tissue

Dead tissue removed from the wound

A type of nonabsorbable thread used to sew up surface layers of tissue, removed after healing

Absorbable suture made of sheep or beef intestine coated with salt to prolong holding strength

Brought together again

Oral antibiotic

Topical antibiotic

CENTRAL MEDICAL SURGICENTER

211 Medical Center Drive • Central City, US 90000-1234 • PHONE: (012) 125-6784 • FAX: (012) 125-9999

OPERATIVE REPORT

PREOPERATIVE DIAGNOSIS: Complex lacerations of the nose and upper lip due to a dog bite.

POSTOPERATIVE DIAGNOSIS: Complex lacerations of the nose and upper lip due to a dog bite.

OPERATION: Revision and closure of complex lacerations of the nose and upper lip.

ANESTHESIOLOGIST: H. Vaughn, M.D.

INDICATIONS:
This 33-year-old female sustained a dog bite to her face while she was handling a dog at a veterinary clinic. Because of the complexity of her injuries, a plastic surgery consultation was requested.

PROCEDURE:
The patient's face was prepped and draped in the usual sterile fashion. A copious amount of dilute Betadine and saline were used to irrigate out all the lacerations. Subcutaneous tissues in the vicinity of the lacerations were infiltrated with 0.5% Xylocaine with 1:200,000 concentration epinephrine. Attention was directed to the patient's upper lip. There was a laceration approximately 1.5 cm oriented parallel to the mucocutaneous junction. There was another diagonal laceration measuring approximately 1.0 cm. The devitalized tissues were debrided sharply. The laceration was closed in layers with 5-0 Vicryl sutures and then with 6-0 and 7-0 Prolene on the skin. Attention was directed to the patient's nose. There are two major lacerations. There is a 2 cm laceration to the left ala. This was a full thickness laceration through the entire alar cartilage into the nose as well as the entire alar rim. The devitalized cartilage was debrided sharply. The intranasal incision was closed with 4-0 chromic catgut suture. The alar rim was meticulously reapproximated with a few tacking sutures to produce perfect anatomic continuity. The remainder of the laceration was closed with 6-0 and 7-0 Prolene sutures in interrupted and running fashion. At this time, attention was directed to another laceration measuring approximately 2.5 cm located in the right nasal sill area extending to the columella and lip junction. The columella was detached. Again, all devitalized tissues were debrided sharply. Deep subcutaneous tissues were approximated with 5-0 chromic catgut sutures in such a fashion so as to meticulously reapproximate the columella into its normal anatomic position. The nasal sill was reapproximated with 6-0 Prolene sutures meticulously reapproximating the detailed anatomy of this area. The remainder of the wounds were closed with 6-0 and 7-0 Prolene sutures in a running and interrupted fashion. A few smaller lacerations were closed with Prolene sutures on the bridge of the nose. All the wounds were covered with Neosporin ointment, Adaptic, and appropriate bandages.

The patient was given intravenous antibiotics; and she will be started on Keflex 250 mg p.o. t.i.d. The patient will be seen in my office in 24 hours for follow-up.

T. Romero M.D.
T. Romero, M.D.

TR:kf
D: 10/19/20xx
T: 10/20/20xx

OPERATIVE REPORT

PT. NAME: SMITH, WILMA
ID NO: OPS-167480621
SURGEON: T. ROMERO, M.D.

A
Removing suture from sterile package with needle holder

B
Continuous sutures are several stitches from a single length of suture material, knotted at each end

C
Interrupted sutures are groups of individual stitches, each of which is knotted

Figure 5.15 Typical documentation of a surgical procedure. Suturing is also depicted.

Figure 5.16 Electrocautery. A cautery device is used to perform hemostasis during a surgical procedure.

Term	Meaning
Mohs surgery mōz	a technique used to excise tumors of the skin by removing fresh tissue layer by layer until a tumor-free plane is reached
skin grafting	transfer of skin from one body site to another to replace skin lost through burns or injury
autograft aw′to-graft	transfer to a new position in the body of the same person (auto = self)
homograft hŏ′mō-graft **allograft** al′ō-graft	donor transfer between individuals of the same species such as human to human (homo = same; allo=other)
xenograft zen′ō-graft **heterograft** het′er-ō-graft	a graft transfer from one animal species to one of another species (xeno = strange; hetero = different)

Therapeutic Terms

Term	Meaning
chemotherapy kēm′ō-ther-ă-pē	treatment of malignancies, infections, and other diseases with chemical agents that destroy selected cells or impair their ability to reproduce
radiation therapy rā′dē-ā′shŭn	treatment of neoplastic disease by using ionizing radiation to deter proliferation of malignant cells
sclerotherapy sklēr-ō-ther′ă-pē	use of sclerosing agents in treating diseases (e.g., injection of a saline solution into a dilated blood vessel tumor in the skin, resulting in hardening of the tissue within and eventual sloughing away of the lesion)
ultraviolet therapy ŭl-tră-vī′ō-let	use of ultraviolet light to promote healing of a skin lesion (e.g., an ulcer)
COMMON THERAPEUTIC DRUG CLASSIFICATIONS	
anesthetic an-es-thet′ik	a drug that temporarily blocks transmission of nerve conduction to produce a loss of sensations (e.g., pain)
antibiotic an′tē-bī-ot′ik	a drug that kills or inhibits the growth of microorganisms

Term	Meaning
antifungal an-tē-fŭng′ăl	a drug that kills or prevents the growth of fungi
antihistamine an-tē-his′tă-mēn	a drug that blocks the effects of histamine in the body
histamine his′tă-mēn	a regulating body substance released in excess during allergic reactions causing swelling and inflammation of tissues [e.g., in urticaria (hives), hay fever]
anti-inflammatory an′tē-in-flam′ă-tor-ē	a drug that reduces inflammation
antipruritic an′tē-prū-rit′ik	a drug that relieves itching
antiseptic isms an-tă-sep′tik	an agent that inhibits the growth of infectious microorgan-

Summary of Chapter 5 Acronyms/Abbreviations

BCC	basal cell carcinoma	**HSV-2**	herpes simplex virus type 2
Bx	biopsy	**I&D**	incision and drainage
C&S	culture and sensitivity	**SCC**	squamous cell carcinoma
FS	frozen section	**SLE**	systemic lupus erythematosus
HSV-1	herpes simplex virus type 1		

PRACTICE EXERCISES

For the following terms, on the lines below the term, write out the indicated word parts: prefixes (P), combining forms (CF), roots (R), and suffixes (S). Then define the word.

EXAMPLE

hypodermic

_____ / _____ / _____
　　P　　　　R　　　　S

hypo/derm/ic
　P　　R　　S

DEFINITION: below or deficient/skin/pertaining to

1. dermatologist

_____ / _____
　　　　CF　　　　　　　　　S

DEFINITION: _____

2. ichthyoid

_____ / _____
　　　　R　　　　　　　　　S

DEFINITION: _____

3. onycholysis

_____ / _____
　　　　CF　　　　　　　　　S

DEFINITION: _____

4. histotrophic

_____ / _____ / _____
　　　　CF　　　　　　　　R　　　　　　　　　S

DEFINITION: _____

5. dysplasia

_____ / _____ / _____
　　　　P　　　　　　　　　R　　　　　　　　　S

DEFINITION: _____

6. hyperkeratosis

_____ / _____ / _____
　　　　P　　　　　　　　　R　　　　　　　　　S

DEFINITION: _____

7. leukotrichia

_____ / _____ / _____
      CF   R   S
DEFINITION: _____

8. mycology

_____ / _____
      CF   S
DEFINITION: _____

9. epidermal

_____ / _____ / _____
      P   R   S
DEFINITION: _____

10. lipoma

_____ / _____
      R   S
DEFINITION: _____

11. subcutaneous

_____ / _____ / _____
      P   R   S
DEFINITION: _____

12. anhidrosis

_____ / _____ / _____
      P   R   S
DEFINITION: _____

13. histopathology

_____ / _____ / _____
      CF   CF   S
DEFINITION: _____

14. paronychia

_____ / _____ / _____
      P   R   S
DEFINITION: _____

15. adiposis

_____ / _____
      R   S
DEFINITION: _____

16. squamous

_____ / _____
      R   S
DEFINITION: _____

17. erythrodermatitis

_____ / _____ / _____
        CF   R   S

DEFINITION: _____

18. desquamation

_____ / _____ / _____
        P   R   S

DEFINITION: _____

19. histotoxic

_____ / _____ / _____
        CF   R   S

DEFINITION: _____

20. melanocyte

_____ / _____ / _____
        CF   R   S

DEFINITION: _____

21. xerosis

_____ / _____
        R   S

DEFINITION: _____

22. purpuric

_____ / _____
        R   S

DEFINITION: _____

23. seborrhea

_____ / _____
        CF   S

DEFINITION: _____

24. xanthoma

_____ / _____
        R   S

DEFINITION: _____

25. asteatosis

_____ / _____ / _____
        P   R   S

DEFINITION: _____

Complete the medical term by writing the missing part:

26. _____ oma = black tumor

27. _____ dermic = pertaining to below the skin

28. _____ angioma = bright-red, round blood vessel tumor

29. _____ coriation = scratch mark on the skin

30. _____ section = type of microscopic study of fresh tissue

31. _____ comedo = whitehead

32. anti_____ = a drug that relieves itching

33. _____ mycosis = condition of fungus of the fingernail or toenail

34. _____ biopsy = removal of an entire lesion for microscopic examination

35. _____ graft = transfer of skin to a new position in the body of the same person

36. _____ therapy = method of eliminating a dilated blood vessel tumor of the skin by injection of a hardening solution

37. _____ pigmentation = darkened areas of skin caused by excessive amounts of melanin

For each of the following, circle the combining form that corresponds to the meaning given:

38. **fat**	leuk/o	steat/o	seb/o
39. **black**	necr/o	trich/o	melan/o
40. **fungus**	seb/o	myc/o	onych/o
41. **nail**	onych/o	trich/o	squam/o
42. **red**	xanth/o	purpur/o	erythr/o
43. **hair**	trich/o	histi/o	fibr/o
44. **dry**	ichthy/o	xer/o	xanth/o
45. **oil**	py/o	hidr/o	seb/o

Write the correct medical term for each of the following definitions:

46. death of tissue associated with a loss of blood supply as a result of trauma or inflammatory or infectious process _____

47. severe itching _____

48. skin infection consisting of a cluster of furuncles _____

49. baldness _____

50. use of a spoon-like instrument to scrape tissue, such as that used in debridement of a wound _____

51. inflammation of the sebaceous glands and hair follicles of the skin evidenced by

    comedones, pustules, or nodules on the skin _____

52. chronic, recurrent skin disease marked by silver-gray scales covering red patches

    on the skin _____

53. acute inflammation of subcutaneous tissue as the result of bacterial invasion
    through a break in the skin (derived using the Latin word meaning *small
    storeroom*) _____

Match the lay terms with the appropriate medical terms:

54. _____ mole   a. pediculosis capitis

55. _____ black and blue mark   b. cicatrix

56. _____ blackhead   c. seborrheic dermatitis

57. _____ boil   d. urticaria

58. _____ crabs   e. verruca

59. _____ cradle cap   f. nevus

60. _____ head lice   g. furuncle

61. _____ hives   h. comedo

62. _____ scar   i. ecchymosis

63. _____ wart   j. pediculosis pubis

Using the suffix -derma, name the following conditions of the skin:

64. _____ white skin

65. _____ yellow skin

66. _____ dry skin

67. _____ red skin

68. _____ hard skin

Give the medical terms for the following exanthematous viral diseases:

69. German measles_____

70. chickenpox_____

71. 14-day measles _____

Match the following primary lesions with their descriptions:

72. _____ vesicle

    a. tiny, flat discolored spot on the skin, up to 1 cm diameter

73. _____ pustule

    b. large, flat discolored area on the skin, larger than 1 cm diameter

74. _____ papule

    c. solid mass on skin less than 0.5 cm diameter

75. _____ bulla

    d. solid mass greater than 1 cm that extends into the epidermis

76. _____ nodule

    e. solid mass greater than 1 cm limited to the skin's surface

77. _____ wheal

    f. small blister

78. _____ macule

    g. area of localized skin edema, such as a hive

79. _____ tumor

    h. large blister

80. _____ patch

    i. pus-filled sac

81. _____ plaque

    j. solid mass larger than 1–2 cm diameter

Write the abbreviation used to identify the following terms:

82. biopsy _____

83. incision and drainage _____

84. basal cell carcinoma _____

85. herpes virus that causes cold sores _____

86. culture and sensitivity _____

87. systemic lupus erythematosus _____

Match the following terms:

88. _____ scabies

    a. chemical peel

89. _____ cryosurgery

    b. purpuric lesion

90. _____ telangiectasia

    c. eczema

91. _____ tinea

    d. xenograft

92. _____ heterograft

    e. intense light

93. _____ actinic keratoses

    f. desiccation

94. _____ radiation therapy

    g. spider angioma

95. _____ petechia

    h. solar keratoses

96. _____ homograft

    i. allograft

97. _____ laser   j. cancer treatment

98. _____ chemosurgery   k. freezing treatment

99. _____ electrosurgery   l. mycosis

100. _____ dermatitis   m. mites

Write the plural forms of the following terms:

101. keratosis _____

102. bulla _____

103. nevus _____

104. macula _____

105. ecchymosis _____

Briefly describe the difference between the following terms:

106. electrodesiccation/fulguration _____

_____

_____

107. actinic keratoses/seborrheic keratoses _____

_____

_____

108. vitiligo/albinism _____

_____

_____

109. cicatrix/keloid _____

_____

_____

110. dermatosis/dermatitis _____

_____

_____

111. incisional biopsy/excisional biopsy _____

_____

_____

112. heterograft/allograft _____

_____

_____

113. closed comedo/open comedo _____

_____

_____

114. cutaneous lupus/systemic lupus erythematosus _____

_____

_____

115. dysplastic nevus/malignant melanoma _____

_____

_____

Write in the missing words on the blank lines in the following illustration of the skin.

116–120.

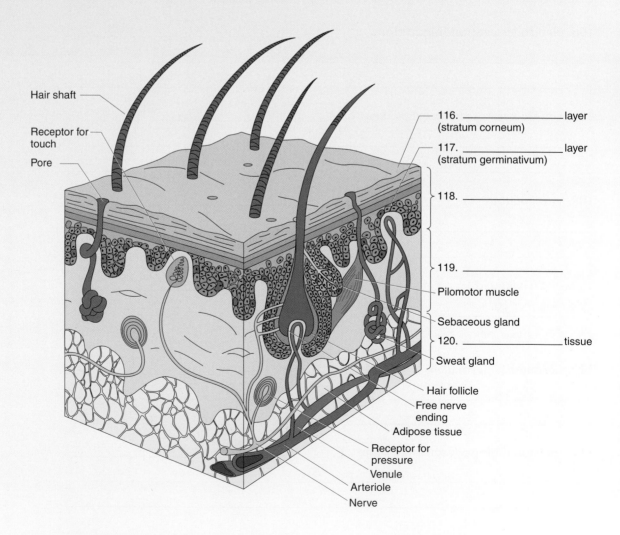

Hair shaft

Receptor for touch

Pore

116. _____ layer (stratum corneum)

117. _____ layer (stratum germinativum)

118. _____

119. _____

Pilomotor muscle

Sebaceous gland

120. _____ tissue

Sweat gland

Hair follicle

Free nerve ending

Adipose tissue

Receptor for pressure

Venule

Arteriole

Nerve

For each of the following, circle the correct spelling of the term:

121. cicatrix   scicatrix   cicatrex

122. pruritis   purritis   pruritus

123. petechia   patechia   petecchia

124. veruca   verucca   verruca

125. eckamosis   ecchymosis   eckemyosis

126. excission   excisison   excision

127. soriasis   psoreyeasis   psoriasis

128. impetigo   infantiego   impatiego

129. eggszema   eczema   ecczema

130. debridemant   debridement   debreedment

Give the noun that was used to form the following adjectives:

131. _____ keratotic

132. _____ bullous

133. _____ nodular

134. _____ seborrheic

135. _____ petechial

136. _____ ecchymotic

137. _____ urticarial

138. _____ eczematous

139. _____ macular

140. _____ suppurative

MEDICAL RECORD ANALYSES

MEDICAL RECORD 5.1

Progress Note

S: This is a 30 y.o. ♀ presenting with an erythematous and scaly eruption on the face and ears × 6 mo. Stress and emotional tensions aggravate the rash. Over-the-counter remedies provide no relief.

O: Patchy erythema with greasy, yellowish scaling appears over the nose and along the eyebrows. The external ears are similarly affected. Erythematous papules are scattered across the face, and there is ↑oiliness around the nose.

A: Seborrheic dermatitis

P: Rx: hydrocortisone cream, s̄s̄ oz tube
    Sig: apply to affected areas t.i.d.

1. What is the sex of the patient?

    a. male

    b. female

    c. not stated

2. What is the patient's CC?

    a. stress and emotional tension

    b. appearance of raised, yellow, pus-filled lesions on the skin

    c. appearance of red areas on the skin with flaking of the outer layers of the skin

    d. appearance of red areas on the skin with open sores

    e. appearance of a communicable rash on the face and ear

3. What is the diagnosis?

    a. inflammation of the sebaceous glands and hair follicles of the skin evidenced by comedones

    b. fungus of the skin

    c. inflammation of the skin with excessive secretion of sebum from the sebaceous glands

    d. highly contagious bacterial skin inflammation marked by pustules that rupture and become crusted

    e. transient, viral cold sores that infect the facial area

4. How much hydrocortisone cream was prescribed?

    a. one ounce

    b. two ounces

    c. one-half dram

    d. one dram

    e. one-half ounce

5. What is the Sig: on the prescription?

    a. apply to affected areas twice a day

    b. apply to affected areas three times a day

    c. apply to affected areas four times a day

    d. apply to affected areas every 2 hours

    e. apply to affected areas every 3 hours

MEDICAL RECORD 5.2

After ignoring various skin problems for months, Robert Fuller consulted his doctor in October when he became alarmed by what he saw happening on his right hand. His doctor referred him to Dr. Luong, a dermatologist, who then diagnosed and treated Mr. Fuller.

Directions

Read Medical Record 5.2 for Robert Fuller (page 136) and answer the following questions. This record is a SOAP progress note dictated by Dr. Luong immediately after the treatment of Mr. Fuller and transcribed the next day by his assistant.

QUESTIONS ABOUT MEDICAL RECORD 5.2

Write your answers in the spaces provided.

1. Below are medical terms used in this record that you have not yet encountered in this text. Underline each where it appears in the record and define below:

   vulgaris _____

   verruciform _____

2. In your own words, not using medical terminology, briefly describe Mr. Fuller's complaint.

   _____

   _____

   _____

3. In your own words, not using medical terminology, briefly describe Dr. Luong's three objective findings.

   a. _____

   b. _____

   c. _____

4. Define the three diagnoses for those three objective findings.

   a. _____

   b. _____

   c. _____

5. Briefly describe the treatments for those three diagnoses:

   a. _____

   b. _____

   c. _____

6. What did Dr. Luong tell Mr. Fuller might occur in the future? Check *all* that apply:

_____ scarring where the lesions were

_____ nausea and possible vomiting from the nitrogen

_____ red, freckle-like spots appearing on the right hand

_____ possible regrowth of lesions

_____ self-desiccating tissue destruction

CENTRAL MEDICAL GROUP, INC.

Department of Dermatology

201 Medical Center Drive • Central City, US 90000-1234 • PHONE: (012) 125-8888 • FAX: (012) 125-3434

CHART NOTE

PATIENT: FULLER, ROBERT K.

DATE: October 19, 20xx

SUBJECTIVE:	The patient presents with a growth on the right hand, multiple lesions, and other growths.
OBJECTIVE:	Ulcerated growth on the right hand, marked A; one verruciform tumor on the left hand; erythematous keratotic patches on the arms.
ASSESSMENT:	Basal cell carcinoma, verruca vulgaris, and actinic keratoses.
PLAN:	Following full counseling on healing with scarring, keloids, and possible recurrence, the growth from the right hand was excised. The site was anesthetized with Xylocaine 2% without epinephrine, 2 cc. Following excision, the bases of the growths were treated with fulguration and electrodesiccation. Desiccation was also performed on 0.3 cm of normal surrounding skin. The wart was treated with liquid nitrogen, two cycles. Freezing time: 8-10 seconds. Ten erythematous keratotic patches were also treated with liquid nitrogen, two cycles. Freezing time: 10-14 seconds.

D. Luong, M.D.

DL:ti

D: 10/19/20xx
T: 10/20/20xx

Medical Record 5.2

MEDICAL RECORD 5.3

About 5 months ago, Patricia Brown saw Dr. Luong, the dermatologist, and was treated for a skin problem. Since she was told then that there was a chance of recurrence, she has watched that area of her skin carefully. When what looked to her like a small dot appeared in the same area, she called Dr. Luong for another appointment.

Directions

Read Medical Record 5.3 for Patricia Brown (page 138) and answer the following questions. This record is the progress note dictated by Dr. Luong after treating her and transcribed the next day by his assistant.

QUESTIONS ABOUT MEDICAL RECORD 5.3

Write your answers in the spaces provided.

1. Below are medical terms used in this record you have not yet encountered in this text. Underline each where it appears in the record and define below:

   pigmented _____

   margin _____

   defect _____

2. In your own words, not using medical terminology, briefly describe what Dr. Luong found in the first visit 5 months ago and the treatment he then gave:

   _____

   _____

   _____

3. Dr. Malloy analyzed a tissue sample for Dr. Luong 5 months ago and diagnosed the lesion marked C. Translate her diagnosis into lay language:

   _____

   _____

   _____

4. Before initiating treatment of the recurrent lesion in this visit, Dr. Luong fully explained to Ms. Brown the likely and possible results. What three specific things (in nonmedical language) did she agree to accept as possible risks?

   a. _____

   b. _____

   c. _____

CENTRAL MEDICAL GROUP, INC.
Department of Dermatology

201 Medical Center Drive • Central City, US 90000-1234 • PHONE: (012) 125-8888 • FAX: (012) 125-3434

CHART NOTE

PATIENT: BROWN, PATRICIA D.

DATE: May 11, 20xx

SUBJECTIVE: Recurrence of growth on the patient's left leg. The patient was in my office on December 12, 20xx. At that time, three changing moles were excised: one on the left leg, marked C; one on the back; and one on the right of the chest. The one marked C was read by Dr. Malloy, the pathologist, as a pigmented compound nevus with mild atypical melanocytic hyperplasia, margins free and adequate.

OBJECTIVE: Very small pigmented lesion, approximately 2-3 mm in diameter, in the same area.

ASSESSMENT: Atypical and dysplastic nevus, possible recurrence.

PLAN: Fully counseled patient regarding healing with scarring and keloid; however, due to the nature of the nevus and the recurrence, we will need to remove a minimum of 4-5 mm of normal surrounding skin. With the patient's full acceptance of scarring, a keloid, and the possibility of recurrence, the tumor was re-excised with a large area surrounding the brown pigment, approximately 3-4 mm. The defect was then closed using 4-0 Vicryl x 3 and 4-0 Prolene x 4 interrupted. The specimen was marked C-1 and was sent to DermLab again to Dr. Malloy who read the patient's slide on December 12, 20xx. The patient is to return in two weeks for suture removal. An aftercare handout was given and discussed.

D. Luong, M.D.

DL:ti

D: 5/11/20xx
T: 5/12/20xx

Medical Record 5.3

5. Treatment of the recurrent lesion involved several steps. Put the following actions in correct order by numbering them 1 to 5:

_____ sample sent to lab

_____ suture removal

_____ excision of tumor and surrounding area

_____ patient's permission given

_____ suturing the wound

6. What, briefly, is Dr. Malloy's role *this* time? Is this the same as or different from her role in Ms. Brown's first treatment?

_____

_____

_____

MEDICAL RECORD 5.4

Mary Chen's physician, Dr. Ogawa, treated her for a skin lesion more than 2 months ago and more recently did a biopsy after that carcinoma apparently recurred. Dr. Ogawa then referred Mary to Dr. Volkman, a dermatologic surgeon.

Directions

Read Medical Record 5.4 (pages 141–142) for Mary Chen and answer the following questions. This record is the operative report dictated by Dr. Volkman after performing the surgery.

QUESTIONS ABOUT MEDICAL RECORD 5.4

Write your answers in the spaces provided.

1. Below are medical terms used in this record you have not yet encountered in this text. Underline each where it appears in the record and define below:

   supine _____

   gentian (crystal) violet _____

   hemostasis _____

   flap (full thickness) _____

2. In your own words, not using medical terminology, briefly describe Ms. Chen's preoperative diagnosis.

   _____

   Now describe the meaning of the addition to that diagnosis in the postoperative diagnosis.

   _____

3. In your own words, describe Dr. Ogawa's earlier treatment of Ms. Chen's lesion.

   _____

   _____

4. The surgery was performed with Ms. Chen in what position?

   a. lying flat, face down
   b. lying flat, face up
   c. lying on her side
   d. sitting

CENTRAL MEDICAL SURGICENTER

211 Medical Center Drive • Central City, US 90000-1234 • PHONE: (012) 125-6784 • FAX: (012) 125-9999

OPERATIVE REPORT

DATE OF OPERATION:	May 6, 20xx
LOCATION:	Mohs' surgery suite.
PREOPERATIVE DIAGNOSIS:	Recurrent basal cell carcinoma, left nasal tip.
POSTOPERATIVE DIAGNOSIS:	Recurrent basal cell carcinoma, left nasal tip, with extension and full-thickness loss.
OPERATION PERFORMED:	Mohs' histographic surgery, fresh tissue technique.
SURGEON:	E. Volkman, M.D.
ASSISTANT:	K. Ball, M.D.
ANESTHESIA:	Local.

INDICATIONS:
The patient is a 64-year-old white female with a history of a lesion over the left nasal tip, which was biopsied on March 27, 20xx, slide number K-476-xx. Findings revealed recurrent basal cell carcinoma. Examination revealed a 12 x 10 mm ill-defined area of the left tip with waxiness and indistinct margins. The patient was referred by Dr. Ogawa who performed the above biopsy and additionally had treated the patient in February 20xx for a basal cell carcinoma with a shave curettage and desiccation, slide number K-159-xx. In light of this, it was thought that Mohs' surgery would be appropriate. I discussed it with the patient. The patient fully understands the aims, risks, alternatives, and possible complications and elects to proceed. There are no medical or surgical contraindications to the procedure.

PROCEDURE:
The patient was placed in the supine position on the operating table in the Mohs' surgery suite. The area was prepared and draped in a standard manner. Gentian violet was used to outline the clinical margins of the tumor, and thereafter, local anesthesia with 1% Lidocaine with 1:100,000 epinephrine mixed with 0.5% Marcaine was administered; a total amount of 7.2 cc was used throughout the entire procedure. All of the grossly visible tumor was removed, and an underlying

(continued)

OPERATIVE REPORT
Page 1

PT. NAME:	CHEN, MARY S.
ID NO:	OP-078919
SURGEON:	EARL VOLKMAN, M.D.

Medical Record 5.4

CENTRAL MEDICAL SURGICENTER

211 Medical Center Drive • Central City, US 90000-1234 • PHONE: (012) 125-6784 • FAX: (012) 125-9999

OPERATIVE REPORT

layer was taken and was processed by the Mohs' technique. Hemostasis was obtained with electrocautery. The tumor was found to be present on the gross vertical and extended deep between cartilages and throughout the left alar tip. The first Mohs' layer consisted of seven sections with seven slides being evaluated. The second Mohs' layer consisted of seven sections with seven slides being evaluated. The third Mohs' layer consisted of three sections with three slides being evaluated. A total of the vertical and 17 slides were examined under the microscope via the Mohs' technique. A cancer-free plane was reached after the third layer. The final size of the defect was 25 x 23 mm. The wound was covered with an antibiotic ointment and a nonadherent dressing between stages.

Estimated blood loss for the total procedure was 4 cc.

Total operative time, including tissue processing in the Mohs' laboratory and microscopic Mohs' frozen section slide review per Dr. O'Connor, was four hours. The patient tolerated the procedure well and left the operating room in good condition. There was full-thickness loss of the left ala (wing-like flap of the nostril composed of cartilage). The patient was placed on Keflex 250 mg 1 p.o. q.i.d. and was referred to Dr. Jensen in plastic surgery who will see the patient later today for consideration of reconstructive repair which may indeed require a forehead flap. She is to take Tylenol with Codeine 1 q 4 h p.r.n. pain and will also be followed by Dr. Ogawa.

Earl Volkman, M.D.

EV:ti

D: 5/6/20xx
T: 5/7/20xx

OPERATIVE REPORT	PT. NAME:	CHEN, MARY S.
Page 2	ID NO:	OP-078919
	SURGEON:	EARL VOLKMAN, M.D.

Medical Record 5.4 *Continued.*

5. Put the following surgical actions in correct order to describe the surgery by numbering them 1 to 8:

_____ removing the gross tumor

_____ stopping the bleeding

_____ applying antibiotics

_____ outlining clinical margins of the tumor

_____ removing first underlying layer

_____ evaluating tissues microscopically

_____ administering local anesthetic

_____ removing second and third layers

6. Translate the surgeon's phrase "Hemostasis was obtained with electrocautery":

_____

_____

7. Describe a "frozen section": _____

_____

How many frozen sections were analyzed in this surgery? _____

8. For the other two physicians mentioned, give their specializations and their roles in treating Ms. Chen now and in the future:

Dr. O'Connor's specialization _____

role in treatment _____

Dr. Jensen's specialization _____

role in treatment _____

9. Translate the instructions for the two medications Ms. Chen will be taking postoperatively:

Drug Name	Route of Administration	Dose	Frequency of Dose
_____	_____	_____	_____
_____	_____	_____	_____

10. In your own words, not using medical terminology, briefly describe the additional treatment to be considered for Ms. Chen.

_____

_____

_____

Chapter **6**

Musculoskeletal System

OBJECTIVES

After completion of this chapter you will be able to

- Define common combining forms used in relation to the musculoskeletal system
- Describe the basic functions of the musculoskeletal system
- Define the basic anatomical terms referring to the musculoskeletal system
- Describe the anatomical position
- List the planes of the body
- Define positional and directional terms
- Define the terms related to body movements
- Define common symptomatic and diagnostic terms related to the musculoskeletal system
- List common diagnostic tests and procedures related to the musculoskeletal system
- Identify common operative terms referring to the musculoskeletal system
- Identify common therapeutic terms including drug classifications related to the musculoskeletal system
- Explain the terms and abbreviations used in documenting medical records involving the musculoskeletal system

Combining Forms

Combining Form	Meaning	Example
ankyl/o	crooked or stiff	ankylotic ang-ki-lot′ik
arthr/o	joint (articulation)	arthritis ar-thrī′tis
articul/o		articular ar-tik′yū-lăr
brachi/o	arm	brachium brā′kē-ŭm
cervic/o	neck	cervical ser′vĭ-kal
chondr/o	cartilage (gristle)	chondral kon′drăl

Combining Form	Meaning	Example
cost/o	rib	intercostal in-ter-kos′tăl
crani/o	skull	cranial krā′nē-ăl
dactyl/o	digit (finger or toe)	dactylomegaly dak′til-ō-meg′ă-lē
fasci/o	fascia (a band)	fasciodesis fas-ē-od′ĕ-sis
femor/o	femur	femoral fem′ŏ-răl
fibr/o	fiber	fibrous fi′brŭs
kyph/o	humpback	kyphosis kī-fō′sis
lei/o	smooth	leiomyoma lī′o-mī-ō′mă
lord/o	bent	lordosis lŏr-dō′sis
lumb/o	loin (lower back)	lumbar lŭm′bar
myel/o	bone marrow or spinal cord	myelitis mī-ĕ-lī′tis
my/o	muscle	myalgia mī-al′jē-ă
myos/o		myositis mī-ō-sī′tis
muscul/o		muscular mŭs′kyū-lăr
oste/o	bone	osteomyelitis os′tē-o-mī-ĕ-lī′tis
patell/o	knee cap	patellar pa-tel′ăr
pelv/i	hip bone or pelvic cavity	pelvimeter pel-vim′ĕ-ter
pelv/o		pelvic pel′vik
radi/o	radius	radial rā′dē-ăl
rhabd/o	rod shaped or striated (skeletal)	rhabdomyoma rab′dō-mī-ō′mă
sarc/o	flesh	sarcoma sar-kō′mă
scoli/o	twisted	scoliosis skō-lē-ō′sis

 DIGIT. The Latin term for finger or toe. Digit in the sense of a number was derived from the habit of counting on the fingers, which probably accounts for the decimal system. Digitalis, the heart drug, is an extract of the purple foxglove plant, also known as ladies fingers.

Combining Form	Meaning	Example
spondyl/o	vertebra	spondylitis spon-di-lī′tis
vertebr/o		vertebral ver′tĕ-brăl
stern/o	sternum (breastbone)	sternocostal ster′nō-kos′tăl
ten/o	tendon (to stretch)	tenodesis tĕ-nod′ē-sis
tend/o		tendolysis ten-dol′i-sis
tendin/o		tendinitis ten-di-nī′tis
thorac/o	chest	thoracic thō-ras′ik
ton/o	tone or tension	myotonia mī-ō-tō′nē-ă
uln/o	ulna	ulnar ŭl′năr

Musculoskeletal System Overview

The musculoskeletal system provides support and gives shape to the body. The skeleton gives structure to the body by providing a framework of bones and cartilage. Also, the bones store calcium and other minerals and produce certain blood cells within the bone marrow (Figs. 6.1 to 6.4).

The muscles cover the bones where they hinge (articulate) and supply the forces that make movement possible. They also provide a protective covering for internal organs and produce body heat (Figs. 6.5 and 6.6).

Anatomical Terms Related to Bones (Figs. 6.1 to 6.4)

Term	Meaning
appendicular skeleton ap′en-dik′yū-lăr	bones of shoulder, pelvis, and upper and lower extremities
axial skeleton ak′sē-ăl	bones of skull, vertebral column, chest, and hyoid bone (U-shaped bone lying at the base of the tongue); refer to Figure 6.4 for abbreviated identification and numbering of cervical, thoracic, and lumbar vertebrae
bone	specialized connective tissue composed of osteocytes (bone cells) forming the skeleton
TYPES OF BONE TISSUE	
compact bone	tightly solid, strong bone tissue resistant to bending
spongy (cancellous) bone spŭn′jē kan′sĕ-lŭs	mesh-like bone tissue containing marrow and fine branching canals through which blood vessels run

SKELETON. Skeleton is derived from a Greek word meaning "dried up." The Greeks used the term in reference to a mummy or dried-up body. They never used the word in the modern meaning of the bony framework of the body. The first recorded use of the modern term in English occurred in 1578.

ELBOW. Many terms referring to the elbow are based on the L-shape formed at the joint. This is the basis of the "el" of elbow. It is also the root of the Latin term ulna. An "ell" was an old measure of length, particularly of cloth, being the amount from the elbow (or shoulder) to the fingers, which was a convenient way of rapidly measuring lengths. Boga was a bending or a bow.

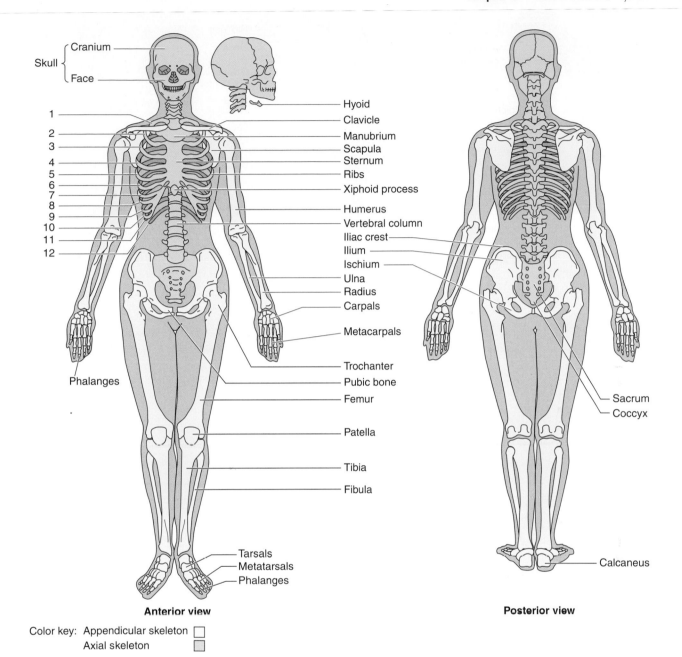

Figure 6.1 The skeleton.

Color key: Appendicular skeleton ☐
          Axial skeleton ☐

Term	Meaning
CLASSIFICATION OF BONES	
long bones	bones of arms and legs
short bones	bones of wrists and ankles
flat bones	bones of ribs, shoulder blades, pelvis, and skull
irregular bones	bones of vertebrae and face
sesamoid bones ses'ă-moyd	round bones found near joints (e.g., patella)

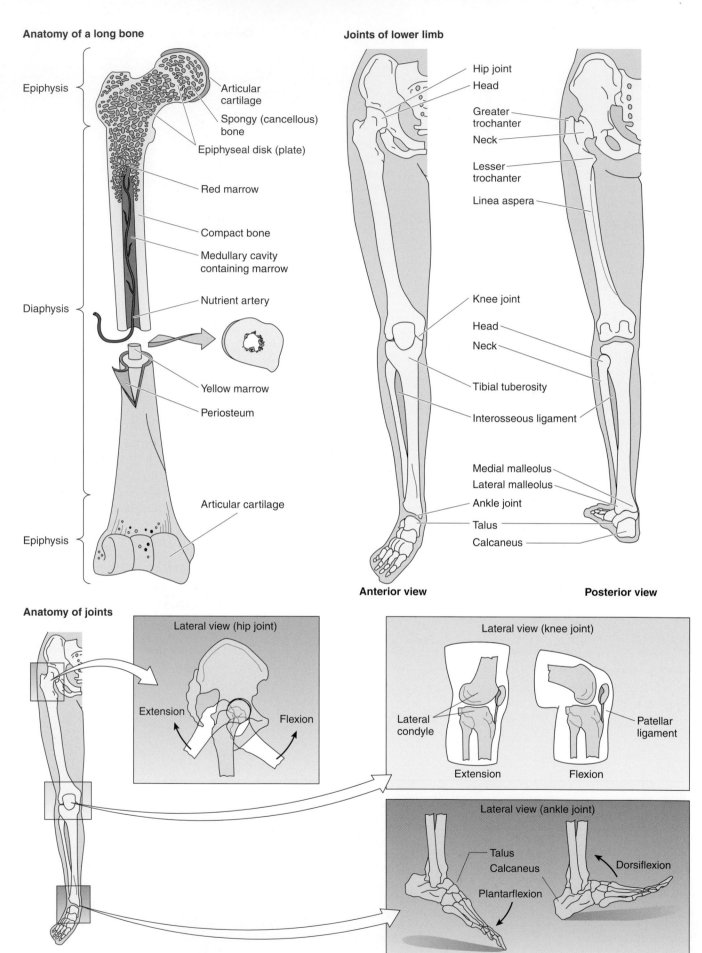

Anatomy of a long bone

Epiphysis

Articular cartilage

Spongy (cancellous) bone

Epiphyseal disk (plate)

Red marrow

Compact bone

Medullary cavity containing marrow

Diaphysis

Nutrient artery

Yellow marrow

Periosteum

Articular cartilage

Epiphysis

Joints of lower limb

Hip joint
Head
Greater trochanter
Neck
Lesser trochanter
Linea aspera

Knee joint
Head
Neck
Tibial tuberosity
Interosseous ligament

Medial malleolus
Lateral malleolus
Ankle joint
Talus
Calcaneus

Anterior view

Posterior view

Anatomy of joints

Lateral view (hip joint)

Extension   Flexion

Lateral view (knee joint)

Lateral condyle

Patellar ligament

Extension   Flexion

Lateral view (ankle joint)

Talus
Calcaneus
Dorsiflexion
Plantarflexion

Figure 6.2 Anatomy of bone and joints.

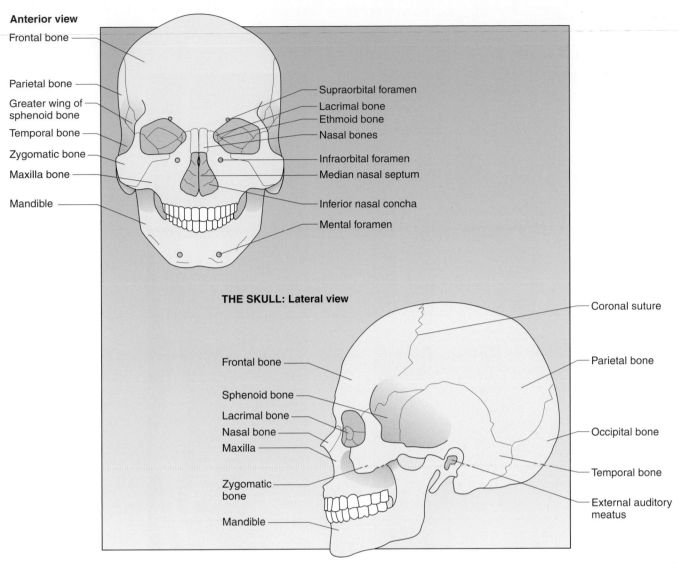

Anterior view

Frontal bone

Parietal bone

Greater wing of sphenoid bone

Temporal bone

Zygomatic bone

Maxilla bone

Mandible

Supraorbital foramen

Lacrimal bone

Ethmoid bone

Nasal bones

Infraorbital foramen

Median nasal septum

Inferior nasal concha

Mental foramen

THE SKULL: Lateral view

Frontal bone

Sphenoid bone

Lacrimal bone

Nasal bone

Maxilla

Zygomatic bone

Mandible

Coronal suture

Parietal bone

Occipital bone

Temporal bone

External auditory meatus

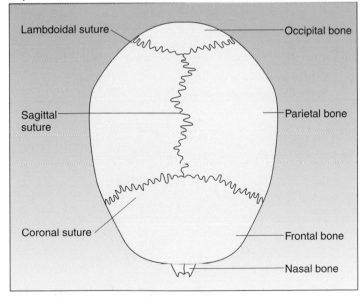

Superior view

Lambdoidal suture

Sagittal suture

Coronal suture

Occipital bone

Parietal bone

Frontal bone

Nasal bone

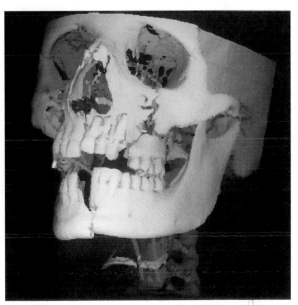

Three-dimensional CT reconstruction of a skull showing traumatic injury to facial bones suffered as the result of a motor vehicle accident.

Figure 6.3 The skull.

THE VERTEBRAE: Lateral view

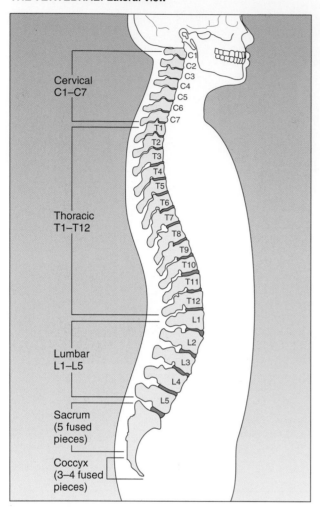

Cervical
C1–C7

Thoracic
T1–T12

Lumbar
L1–L5

Sacrum
(5 fused
pieces)

Coccyx
(3–4 fused
pieces)

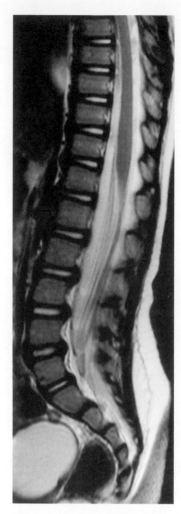

Magnetic resonance image of portions of the lower vertebrae (lower thoracic, lumbar, sacrum, and coccyx) demonstrating normal anatomy.

Superior view (L2)

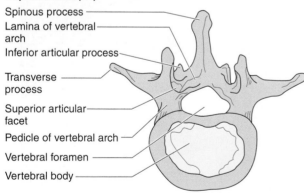

Spinous process
Lamina of vertebral arch
Inferior articular process
Transverse process
Superior articular facet
Pedicle of vertebral arch
Vertebral foramen
Vertebral body

Lateral view (L2)

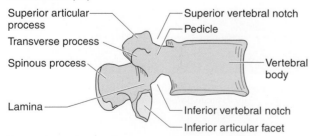

Superior articular process
Transverse process
Spinous process
Lamina
Superior vertebral notch
Pedicle
Vertebral body
Inferior vertebral notch
Inferior articular facet

Lateral view

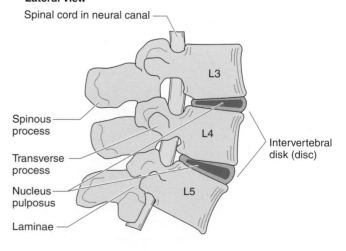

Spinal cord in neural canal
L3
L4
L5
Intervertebral disk (disc)
Spinous process
Transverse process
Nucleus pulposus
Laminae

Figure 6.4 The vertebrae.

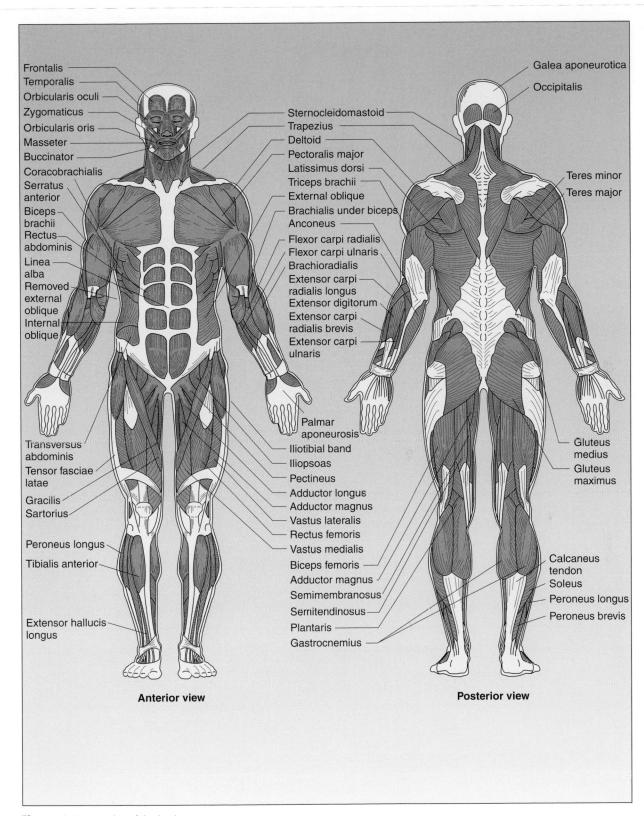

Frontalis
Temporalis
Orbicularis oculi
Zygomaticus
Orbicularis oris
Masseter
Buccinator
Coracobrachialis
Serratus anterior
Biceps brachii
Rectus abdominis
Linea alba
Removed external oblique
Internal oblique

Transversus abdominis
Tensor fasciae latae
Gracilis
Sartorius

Peroneus longus
Tibialis anterior

Extensor hallucis longus

Sternocleidomastoid
Trapezius
Deltoid
Pectoralis major
Latissimus dorsi
Triceps brachii
External oblique
Brachialis under biceps
Anconeus
Flexor carpi radialis
Flexor carpi ulnaris
Brachioradialis
Extensor carpi radialis longus
Extensor digitorum
Extensor carpi radialis brevis
Extensor carpi ulnaris

Palmar aponeurosis
Iliotibial band
Iliopsoas
Pectineus
Adductor longus
Adductor magnus
Vastus lateralis
Rectus femoris
Vastus medialis
Biceps femoris
Adductor magnus
Semimembranosus
Semitendinosus
Plantaris
Gastrocnemius

Galea aponeurotica
Occipitalis

Teres minor
Teres major

Gluteus medius
Gluteus maximus

Calcaneus tendon
Soleus
Peroneus longus
Peroneus brevis

Anterior view

Posterior view

Figure 6.5 Muscles of the body.

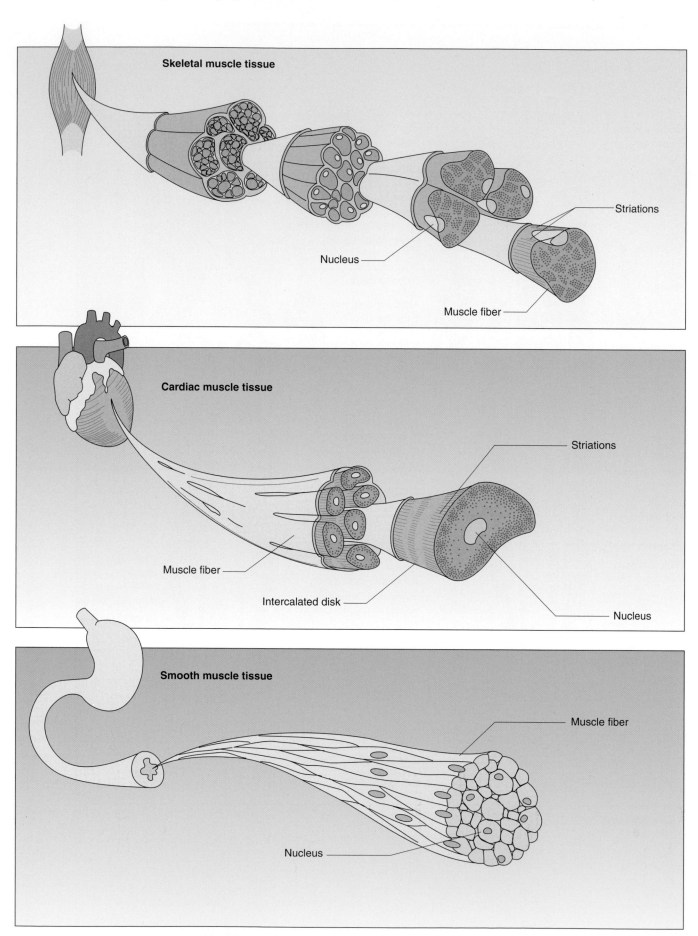

Figure 6.6 Architecture of the three types of muscle.

Term	Meaning
PARTS OF A LONG BONE (SEE FIG. 6.2)	
epiphysis e-pif'i-sis	wide ends of a long bone (physis = growth)
diaphysis dī-af'i-sis	shaft of a long bone
metaphysis mĕ-taf'i-sis	growth zone between epiphysis and diaphysis during development of a long bone
endosteum en-dos'tē-ŭm	membrane lining the medullary cavity of a bone
medullary cavity med'ŭ-lār-ē	cavity within the shaft of the long bones filled with bone marrow
bone marrow mar'ō	soft connective tissue within the medullary cavities of bones
red bone marrow	found in cavities of most bones in infants; functions in formation of red blood cells, some white blood cells, and platelets; in adults, red bone marrow is found most often in the flat bones
yellow bone marrow	gradually replaces red bone marrow in adult bones, functions as storage for fat tissue, and is inactive in formation of blood cells
periosteum per-ē-os'tē-ŭm	a fibrous, vascular membrane that covers the bone
articular cartilage ar-tik'yū-lăr kar'ti-lij	a gristle-like substance found on bones where they articulate

Anatomical Terms Related to Joints and Muscles (Figs. 6.2 to 6.7)

Term	Meaning
articulation ar'tik-yū-lā'shŭn	a joint; the point where two bones come together (Fig. 6.7)
bursa ber'să	a fibrous sac between certain tendons and bones that is lined with a synovial membrane that secretes synovial fluid
disk (disc)	a flat, plate-like structure composed of fibrocartilaginous tissue found between the vertebrae to reduce friction (see Fig. 6.4)
nucleus pulposus nu'klē-ŭs pŭl-pō'sŭs	the soft, fibrocartilaginous, central portion of intervertebral disk
ligament lig'ă-ment	a flexible band of fibrous tissue that connects bone to bone (Fig. 6.8)
synovial membrane si-nō'vē-ăl mem'brān	membrane lining the capsule of a joint
synovial fluid si-nō'vē-ăl flū'id	lubricating fluid secreted by the synovial membrane

 ANKLE. Ank, a very old Greek root meaning bend or angle, is the origin of the term for the ankle joint. It is also associated with ankyl/o, a combining form meaning crooked or bent.

 BURSA. A Latin word for a purse was given to the small synovial pouch associated with a joint. The meaning stems from the use of a purse by the bursar, the man who holds the purse in order to pay out of it. Most anatomical terms come from the names of familiar objects [e.g., patella (dish), acetabulum (bowl)].

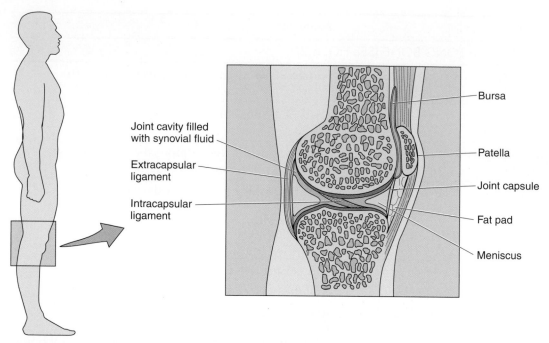

Figure 6.7 Lateral view of the knee joint.

Term	Meaning
muscle mŭs'ĕl	tissue composed of fibers that can contract, causing movement of an organ or part of the body (see Figs. 6.5 and 6.6)
striated (skeletal) muscle stri'ā-ted (skel'e-tăl)	voluntary striated muscle attached to the skeleton
smooth muscle	involuntary muscle found in internal organs
cardiac muscle	muscle of the heart
origin of a muscle	muscle end attached to the bone that does not move when the muscle contracts

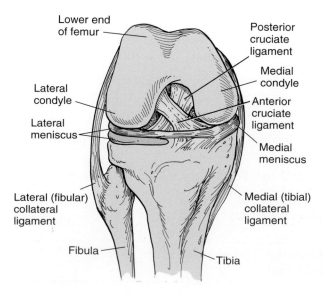

Figure 6.8 Posterior view of the knee and ligaments.

Term	Meaning
insertion of a muscle	muscle end attached to the bone that moves when the muscle contracts
tendon ten′dŏn	a band of fibrous tissue that connects muscle to bone
fascia fash′ē-ă	a band or sheet of fibrous connective tissue that covers, supports, and separates muscle

Anatomical Position and Terms of Reference

To communicate effectively about the body, health professionals use terms with specific meanings to refer to body positions, directions, and planes. These terms of reference are based on the body being in anatomical position, in which the person is assumed to be standing upright (erect), facing forward, feet pointed forward and slightly apart, arms at the sides with palms facing forward. The patient is visualized in this pose before applying any other term of reference.

With the body in an anatomical position, three different imaginary lines divide the body in half, forming body *planes*. In addition to the three body planes, *positional and directional terms* are used to indicate the location or direction of body parts in respect to each other (Fig. 6.9).

Term	Meaning
BODY PLANES	
coronal (frontal) plane kōr′ŏ-năl (frŭn′tăl)	vertical division of the body into front (anterior) and back (posterior) portions
sagittal plane saj′i-tăl	vertical division of the body into right and left portions
transverse plane trans-vers′	horizontal division of the body into upper and lower portions
TERMS OF POSITION AND DIRECTION	
anterior (A) (ventral) an-tēr′ē-ōr (ven′trăl)	front of the body
posterior (P) (dorsal) pos-tēr′ē-ōr (dor′săl)	back of the body
anterior-posterior (AP)	from front to back; commonly associated with the direction of an x-ray beam
posterior-anterior (PA)	from back to front; commonly associated with the direction of an x-ray beam
superior (cephalic) su-pēr′ē-ōr (se-fal′ik)	situated above another structure, toward the head
inferior (caudal) in-fē′rē-ōr (kaw′dăl)	situated below another structure, away from the head

FASCIA. Fascia is derived from a Latin word for a band or bandage derived from fascis, a bundle (the bandage that ties up a bundle, especially a band around a bundle of sticks). Fasces were bundles of sticks from which an ax projected; they were carried by Roman officials. In the 20th century, fasces were adopted in Italy as a political party badge, hence the term "fascist." In anatomy, the sheets of connective tissue that wrap the muscles or other parts are called fascia. Many are named for those who first described them, such as Camper, Scarpa, Colles.

Body planes

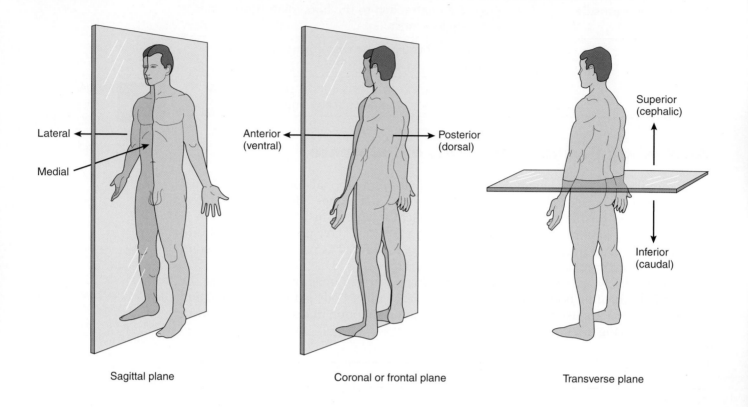

Sagittal plane

Coronal or frontal plane

Transverse plane

Body cavities

Thoracic cavity

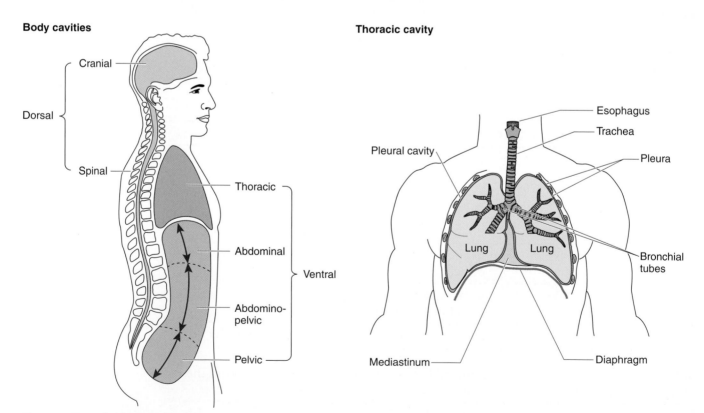

Figure 6.9   Body planes and cavities.

Term	Meaning
proximal prok′si-măl	toward the beginning or origin of a structure [e.g., the proximal aspect of the femur (thigh bone) is the area closest to where it attaches to the hip]
distal dis′tăl	away from the beginning or origin of a structure [e.g., the distal aspect of the femur (thigh bone) is the area at the end of the bone near the knee]
medial mē′dē-ăl	toward the middle (midline)
lateral lat′er-ăl	toward the side
axis ak′sis	line that runs through the center of the body or a body part

BODY POSITIONS

Term	Meaning
erect ĕ-rĕkt′	normal standing position
decubitus dē-kyū′bi-tŭs	lying down, especially in bed; i.e., lateral decubitus is lying on the side (decumbo = to lie down)
prone prōn	lying face down and flat
recumbent rē-kŭm′bent	lying down
supine sū-pīn′	horizontal recumbent; lying flat on the back— "on the spine" (Fig. 6.10)

BODY MOVEMENTS (FIG. 6.11)

Term	Meaning
flexion flek′shŭn	bending at the joint so that the angle between the bones is decreased
extension eks-ten′shŭn	straightening at the joint so that the angle between the bones is increased
abduction ab-dŭk′shŭn	movement away from the body
adduction ă-duk′shŭn	movement toward the body
rotation rō-lā′shŭn	circular movement around an axis
eversion ē-ver′zhŭn	turning outward, i.e., of a foot
inversion in-ver′zhŭn	turning inward, i.e., of a foot

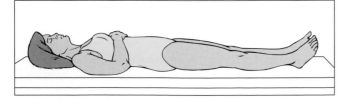

Figure 6.10 Supine (horizontal recumbent position). Patient lies on back with the legs extended.

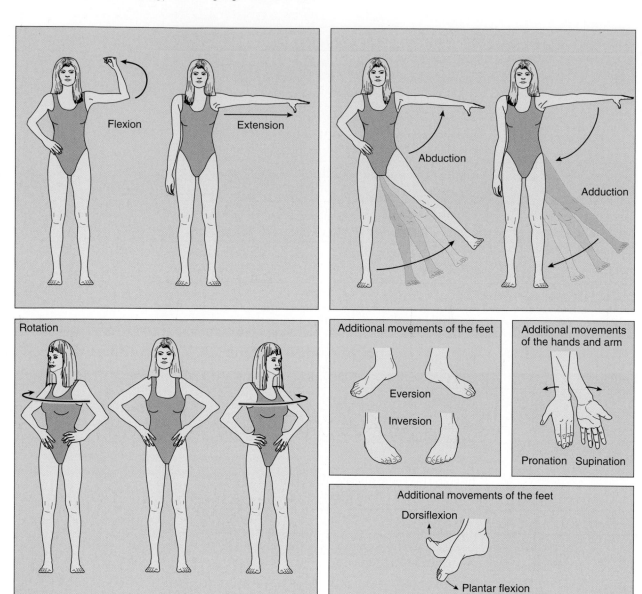

Figure 6.11 Body movements.

Term	Meaning
supination sū′pi-nā′shŭn	turning upward or forward of the palmar surface (palm of the hand) or plantar surface (sole of the foot)
pronation prō-nā′shŭn	turning downward or backward of the palmar surface (palm of the hand) or plantar surface (sole of the foot)
dorsiflexion dōr-si-flek′shŭn	bending of the foot or the toes upward
plantar flexion plan′tăr	bending of the sole of the foot by curling the toes toward the ground
range of motion (ROM)	total motion possible in a joint, described by the terms related to body movements, i.e., ability to flex, extend, abduct, or adduct; measured in degrees
goniometer gō-nē-om′ĕ-ter	instrument used to measure joint angles (gonio = angle) (Fig. 6.12)

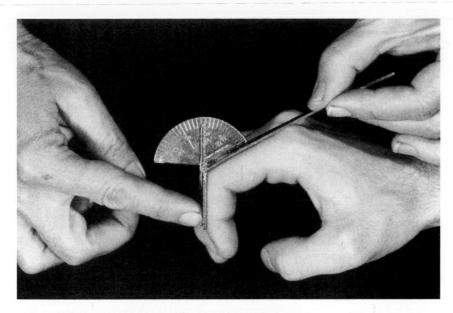

Figure 6.12 Dorsal placement of goniometer used when measuring digital motion.

Symptomatic and Diagnostic Terms

Term	Meaning
SYMPTOMATIC	
arthralgia ar-thral′jē-ă	joint pain
atrophy at′rō-fē	shrinking of tissue such as muscle
crepitation krep-i-tā′shŭn **crepitus** krep-i-tŭs	grating sound made by movement of some joints or broken bones
exostosis eks-os-tō′sis	a projection arising from a bone that develops from cartilage
flaccid flas′id	flabby, relaxed, or having defective or absent muscle tone
hypertrophy hī-per′trō-fē	increase in the size of tissue such as muscle
hypotonia hī′pō-tō′ne-ă	reduced muscle tone or tension
myalgia mī-al′jē-ă **myodynia** mī′ō-din′ē-ă	muscle pain
ostealgia os-tē-al′jē-ă **osteodynia** os-tē-o-din′ē-ă	bone pain
rigor or rigidity rig′er or ri-jid′i-tē	stiffness; stiff muscle

Term	Meaning
spasm spazm	drawing in; involuntary contraction of muscle
spastic spas'tik	uncontrolled contractions of skeletal muscles causing stiff and awkward movements (resembles spasm)
tetany tet'ă-nē	tension; prolonged, continuous muscle contraction
tremor trem'er	shaking; rhythmic muscular movement
DIAGNOSTIC	
ankylosis ang'ki-lō'sis	stiff joint condition
arthritis ar-thrī'tis	inflammation of the joints characterized by pain, swelling, redness, warmth, and limitation of motion—there are more than 100 different types of arthritis
osteoarthritis (OA) os'tē-ō-ar-thrī'tis	most common form of arthritis that especially affects weight-bearing joints (e.g., knee, hip); characterized by the erosion of articular cartilage (Fig. 6.13)
degenerative arthritis dē-jen'er-ă-tiv ar-thrī'tis	
degenerative joint disease (DJD) dē-jen'er-ă-tiv joynt di-zēz'	

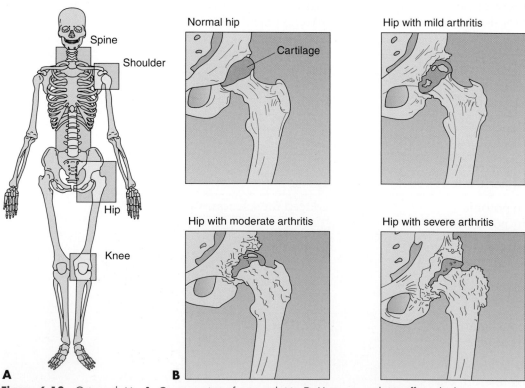

Figure 6.13 Osteoarthritis. **A.** Common sites of osteoarthritis. **B.** How osteoarthritis affects the hip.

Term	Meaning
rheumatoid arthritis (RA) rū′mă-toyd ar-thrī′tis	most crippling form of arthritis characterized by a chronic, systemic inflammation most often affecting joints and synovial membranes (especially in the hands and feet) causing ankylosis (stiff joints) and deformity (Fig. 6.14)
gouty arthritis gow′tē ar-thrī′tis	acute attacks of arthritis usually in a single joint (especially the great toe) caused by hyperuricemia (an excessive level of uric acid in the blood)

 GOUT. The term for gout stems from the Latin word meaning a drop. Known to the ancients, the condition was thought to be caused by a liquid secretion that was distilled drop by drop on the diseased part.

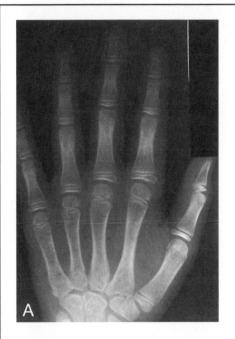

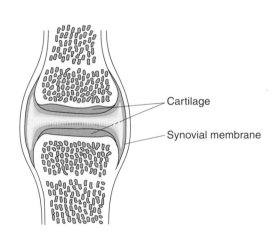

Cartilage

Synovial membrane

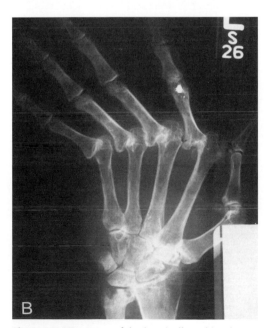

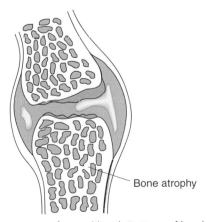

Bone atrophy

Figure 6.14 Joints of the hand affected by rheumatoid arthritis. **A.** X-ray of normal hand. **B.** X-ray of hand with rheumatoid arthritis.

Term	Meaning
bony necrosis ně-krō′sis **sequestrum** sē-kwes′trŭm	dead bone tissue from loss of blood supply such as can occur after a fracture (sequestrum = something laid aside)
bunion bŭn′yŭn	swelling of the joint at the base of the great toe caused by inflammation of the bursa
bursitis ber-sī′tis	inflammation of a bursa
carpal tunnel syndrome kar′păl	condition that results from compression of the median nerve within the carpal tunnel at the wrist, characterized by pain, numbness, and tingling in the wrist and fingers and weak grip; commonly seen as a result of cumulative trauma of surrounding tendons (Fig. 6.15)
chondromalacia kon′drō-mă-lā′shē-ă	softening of cartilage
epiphysitis e-pif-i-sī′tis	inflammation of epiphyseal regions of the long bone

Figure 6.15 Carpal tunnel containing the median nerve and the flexor tendons of the fingers and thumb.

Term	Meaning
fracture (Fx) frak′chūr	a broken or cracked bone (Fig. 6.16)
closed fracture	a broken bone with no open wound
open fracture	compound fracture; a broken bone with an open wound
simple fracture	a nondisplaced fracture involving one fracture line that does not require extensive treatment to repair (e.g., hairline Fx, stress Fx, or crack)
complex fracture	a displaced fracture that requires manipulation or surgery to repair
fracture line	line made by broken bone (e.g., oblique, spiral, or transverse)
comminuted fracture kom′i-nū-ted	broken in many little pieces
greenstick fracture	bending and incomplete break of a bone—most often seen in children
herniated disk or disc her′nē-ā-ted	protrusion of a degenerated or fragmented intervertebral disk so that the nucleus pulposus protrudes, causing compression on the nerve root (see Chapter 10, Fig. 10.9)
myeloma mī-ĕ-lō′mă	bone marrow tumor
myositis mī-ō-sī′tis	inflammation of muscle
myoma mī-ō′mă	muscle tumor
leiomyoma lī′ō-mī-ō′mă	smooth muscle tumor
leiomyosarcoma lī′ō-mī′ō-sar-kō′mă	malignant smooth muscle tumor
rhabdomyoma rab′dō-mī-o′mă	skeletal muscle tumor
rhabdomyosarcoma rab′dō-mī-ō-sar-kō′mă	malignant skeletal muscle tumor
muscular dystrophy mŭs′kyū-lăr dis′trō-fē	a category of genetically transmitted diseases characterized by progressive atrophy of skeletal muscles (Duchenne's type is most common)
osteoma os-tē-ō′mă	bone tumor
osteosarcoma os′tē-ō-sar-kō′mă	type of malignant bone tumor
osteomalacia os′tē-ō-mă-lā′shē-ă	disease marked by softening of the bone caused by calcium and vitamin D deficiency
rickets rik′ets	osteomalacia in children (causes bone deformity)

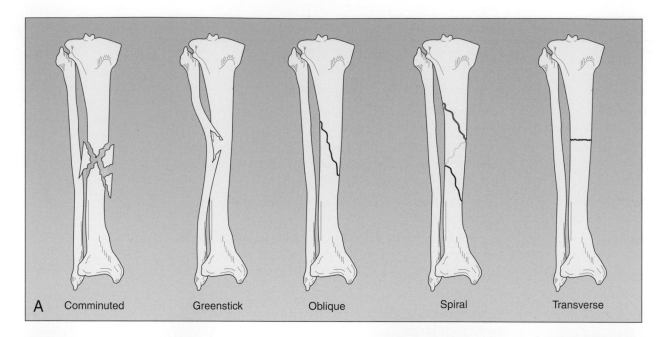

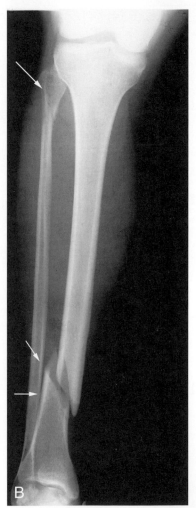

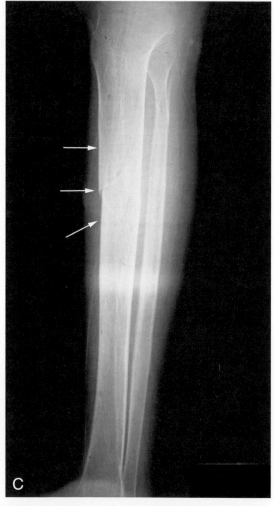

Figure 6.16 **A.** Types of common fracture. **B.** AP radiograph of lower leg demonstrating open fractures of the tibia and fibula (*arrows*). **C.** Lateral view radiograph demonstrating a closed spiral fracture of the tibia (*arrows*). (Note: -graph is the preferred suffix used in radiology to refer to an x-ray record.)

Term	Meaning
osteomyelitis os′tē-ō-mī-ĕ-lī′tis	infection of bone and bone marrow causing inflammation
osteoporosis os′tē-ō-pō-rō′sis	condition of decreased bone density and increased porosity, causing bones to become brittle and liable to fracture (porosis = passage) (Fig. 6.17)
spinal curvatures (Fig. 6.18) spī′năl	
kyphosis kī-fō′sis	abnormal posterior curvature of the thoracic spine (humpback condition)
lordosis lōr-dō′sis	abnormal anterior curvature of the lumbar spine (sway-back condition)
scoliosis skō-lē-ō′sis	abnormal lateral curvature of the spine (S-shaped curve) (Fig. 6.19)

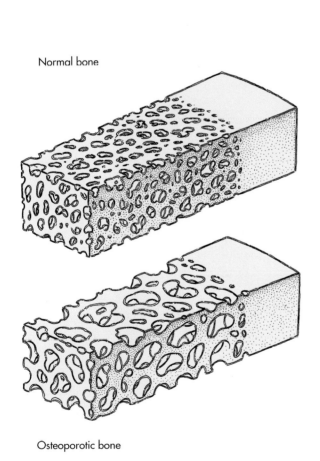

Normal bone

Osteoporotic bone

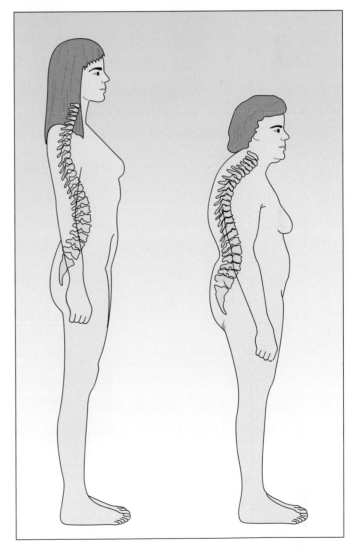

Normal spine in premenopausal woman

Spine compression and loss of height due to osteoporosis in postmenopausal woman

Figure 6.17 Osteoporosis.

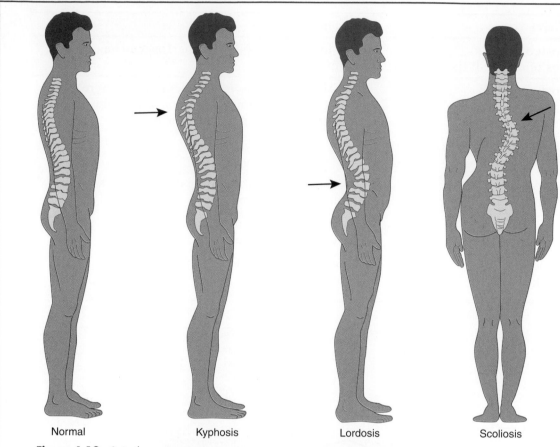

Normal   Kyphosis   Lordosis   Scoliosis

Figure 6.18 Spinal curvatures.

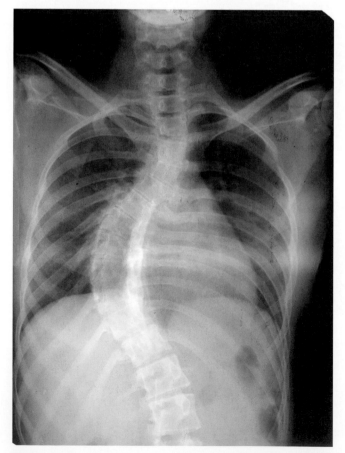

Figure 6.19 AP thoracic spine radiograph demonstrating scoliosis.

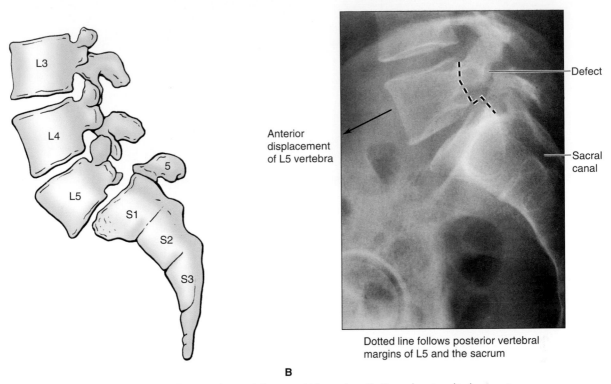

Figure 6.20   Spondylolisthesis. **A.** Drawing illustrates forward slipping of L5 vertebra. **B.** X-ray showing displacement.

Term	Meaning
spondylolisthesis spon′di-lō-lis-thē′sis	forward slipping of a lumbar vertebra (listhesis = slipping) (Fig 6.20)
spondylosis spon-di-lō′sis	stiff, immobile condition of vertebrae due to joint degeneration
sprain sprān	injury to a ligament caused by joint trauma but without joint dislocation or fracture
subluxation sŭb-lŭk-sā′shŭn	a partial dislocation (luxation = dislocation) (Fig. 6.21)
tendinitis ten-di-nī′tis	inflammation of a tendon
tendonitis ten-dō-nī′tis	

Diagnostic Tests and Procedures

Test or Procedure	Explanation
electromyogram (EMG) ē-lek-trō-mī′ō-gram	a neurodiagnostic graphic record of the electrical activity of muscle at rest and during contraction to diagnose neuromusculoskeletal disorders (e.g., muscular dystrophy); usually performed by a neurologist

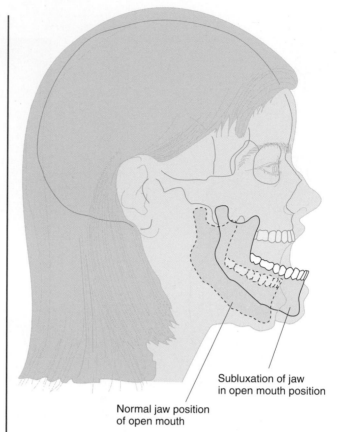

Subluxation of jaw
in open mouth position

Normal jaw position
of open mouth

Figure 6.21 Subluxation.

Test or Procedure	Explanation
magnetic resonance imaging (MRI)	a nonionizing imaging technique using magnetic fields and radiofrequency waves
măg-nĕt′ik rez′ō-nans im′ă-jing	to visualize anatomical structures—useful in orthopedics to detect joint, tendon, and vertebral disk disorders (see MRI of spine in Fig. 6.4 and MRI of knee in Chapter 4, Fig. 4.17A)
nuclear medicine nū′klē-er	ionizing imaging technique using radioactive isotopes
radionuclide organ imaging rā′dē-ō-nū′klīd	
bone scan	radionuclide image of bone tissue to detect tumor, malignancy, etc. (see whole-body bone scan in Chapter 4, Fig. 4.16B)
radiography (x-ray) rā′dē-og′ră-fē	x-ray imaging; an ionizing technique commonly used in orthopedics to visualize the extremities, ribs, back, shoulders, joints, etc. (see Fig. 6.19 and first radiograph in Chapter 4, Fig. 4.14)
arthrogram ar′thrō-gram	an x-ray of a joint taken after injection of a contrast medium
diskogram dis′kō-gram	an x-ray of an intervertebral disk after injection of a contrast medium

 X-RAYS. Wilhelm Roentgen discovered x-rays in 1895. He used the expression rays for the sake of brevity and named them x-rays to distinguish them from others of the same name. The first x-ray image was made of Roentgen's wife's hand.

Test or Procedure	Explanation
dual-energy x-ray absorptiometry (DEXA) ab-sōrp'tom'ĕ-trē	an x-ray scan that measures bone mineral density of the spine and extremities to diagnose osteoporosis, determine fracture risk, and monitor treatment; classifications of bone mass include normal, osteopenic, or osteoporotic as indicated by a T score (amount of bone mass of the patient compared to that of a normal young adult)
computed tomography (CT) tō-mog'ră-fē computed axial tomography (CAT)	a specialized x-ray procedure producing a series of cross-sectional images that are processed by a computer into a 2-dimensional or 3-dimensional image (see Fig. 6.3)
sonography sŏ-nog'ră-fē	ultrasound imaging; a nonionizing technique useful in orthopedics to visualize muscles, ligaments, displacements, and dislocations or to guide a therapeutic intervention such as that performed during arthroscopy

Operative Terms

Term	Meaning
amputation am-pyū-tā'shŭn	partial or complete removal of a limb; AKA, above-knee amputation; BKA, below-knee amputation
arthrocentesis ar'thrō-sen-tē'sis	puncture for aspiration of a joint
arthrodesis ăr-thrō-dē'sĭs	binding or fusing of joint surfaces
arthroplasty ar'thrō-plas-tē	repair or reconstruction of a joint
arthroscopy ar-thros'kă-pē	procedure using an arthroscope to examine, diagnose, and repair a joint from within (Fig. 6.22)
bone grafting	transplantation of a piece of bone from one site to another to repair a skeletal defect
bursectomy ber-sek'tō-mē	excision of a bursa
myoplasty mī'ō-plas-tē	repair of muscle
open reduction, internal fixation (ORIF) of a fracture	internal surgical repair of a fracture by bringing bones back into alignment and fixing them into place, often utilizing plates, screws, pins, etc. (Fig. 6.23)
osteoplasty os'tē-ō-plas-tē	repair of bone

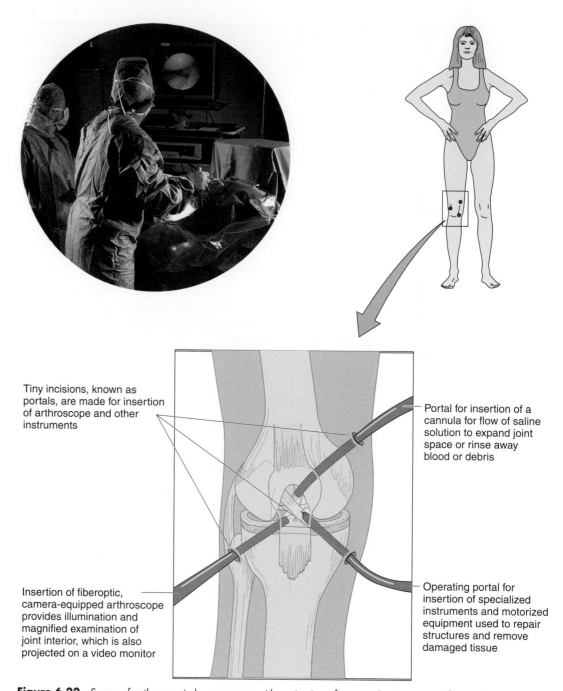

Tiny incisions, known as portals, are made for insertion of arthroscope and other instruments

Portal for insertion of a cannula for flow of saline solution to expand joint space or rinse away blood or debris

Insertion of fiberoptic, camera-equipped arthroscope provides illumination and magnified examination of joint interior, which is also projected on a video monitor

Operating portal for insertion of specialized instruments and motorized equipment used to repair structures and remove damaged tissue

Figure 6.22 Scene of arthroscopic knee surgery with projection of surgeon's view on a video monitor.

Term	Meaning
osteotomy os-tē-ot′ō-mē	an incision into bone
spondylosyndesis spon′di-lō-sin-dē′sis	spinal fusion (see Chapter 10, Fig. 10.24B)
tenotomy te-not′ō-mē	division by incision of a tendon to repair a deformity caused by shortening of a muscle

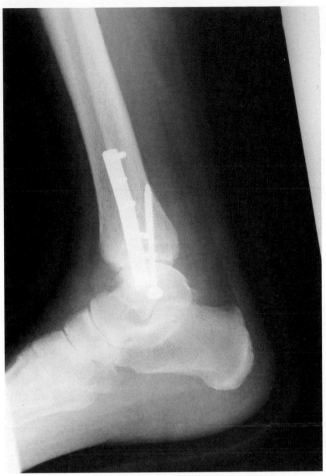

Figure 6.23 An x-ray image taken after open reduction, internal fixation (ORIF) of the right ankle (see Medical Record 6.2).

Therapeutic Terms

Term	Meaning
closed reduction, external fixation of a fracture	external manipulation of a fracture to regain alignment along with application of an external device to protect and hold the bone in place while healing
casting	use of a stiff, solid dressing around a limb or other body part to immobilize it during healing (Fig. 6.24)
splinting	use of a rigid device to immobilize or restrain a broken bone or injured body part; provides less support than a cast, but can be adjusted easier to accommodate for swelling from an injury (Fig. 6.25)
traction (Tx) trak′shŭn	application of a pulling force to a fractured bone or dislocated joint to maintain proper position during healing (Fig. 6.26)
closed reduction, percutaneous fixation of a fracture	external manipulation of a fracture to regain alignment, followed by insertion of one or more pins through the skin to maintain position—often includes use of an external device called a *fixator* to keep the fracture immobilized during healing (Fig. 6.27)

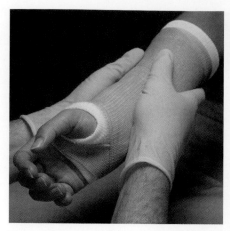

Figure 6.24 Applying a short arm cast.

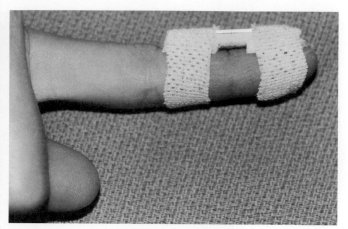

Figure 6.25 Finger splint.

BRACE. A Latin word from brachia, the arms, was originally used as a measure of length (the two extended arms), or a pair. The meaning was expanded to the idea of two arms that connect, support, or strengthen, i.e., to brace. Braces in the form of splints were used in ancient Egypt and by most surgeons throughout the centuries.

Term	Meaning
orthosis ōr-thō'sis	use of an orthopedic appliance to maintain a bone's position or provide limb support (e.g., back, knee, or wrist brace) (Fig. 6.28)
physical therapy (PT) fiz'i-kăl ther'ă-pē	treatment to rehabilitate patients disabled by illness or injury, involving many different modalities (methods), such as exercise, hydrotherapy, diathermy, and ultrasound
prosthesis pros'thē-sis	an artificial replacement for a diseased or missing body part such as a hip, joint, or limb (Fig. 6.29)

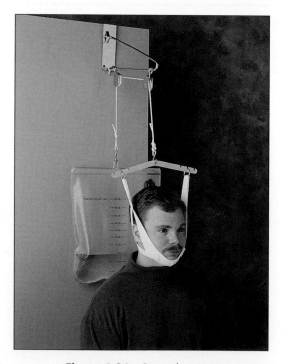

Figure 6.26 Cervical traction.

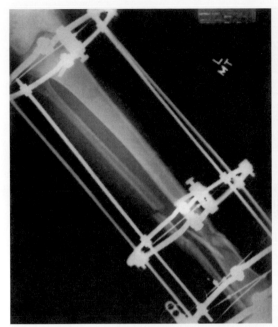

Figure 6.27 This radiograph, taken after closed reduction, percutaneous fixation of an open comminuted distal tibia/fibula fracture, shows placement of an external fixator to maintain pin placement during the healing process. The injury was the result of a gunshot to the right lower extremity.

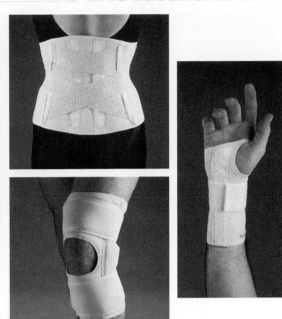

Figure 6.28 Examples of orthoses: back, knee, and wrist.

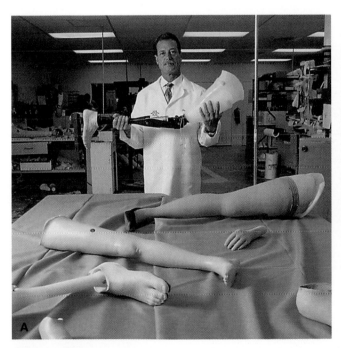

Figure 6.29 **A.** Prosthetist holding an above-the-knee prosthesis with an array of prostheses on the table in the foreground. **B.** A prosthetic leg makes it possible for an above-the-knee amputee to lead an active life.

COMMON THERAPEUTIC DRUG CLASSIFICATIONS

analgesic an-ăl-jē′zik	a drug that relieves pain
narcotic nar-kot′ik	a potent analgesic that has addictive properties
anti-inflammatory an′tē-in-flam′ă-tō-rē	a drug that reduces inflammation
antipyretic an′tē-pī-ret′ik	a drug that relieves fever
nonsteroidal anti-inflammatory drug (NSAID) non-stēr′oy-dăl	a group of drugs with analgesic, anti-inflammatory, and antipyretic properties (e.g., ibuprofen, aspirin) commonly used to treat arthritis

Summary of Chapter 6 Acronyms/Abbreviations

A	anterior	**MRI**	magnetic resonance imaging
AKA	above-knee amputation	**NSAID**	nonsteroidal anti-inflammatory drug
AP	anterior-posterior	**OA**	osteoarthritis
BKA	below-knee amputation	**ORIF**	open reduction, internal fixation
CAT	computed axial tomography	**P**	posterior
CT	computed tomography	**PT**	physical therapy
DEXA	dual-energy x-ray absorptiometry	**RA**	rheumatoid arthritis
DJD	degenerative joint disease	**ROM**	range of motion
EMG	electromyogram	**Tx**	traction
Fx	fracture	**x-ray**	radiography

PRACTICE EXERCISES

For the following terms, on the lines below the term, write out the indicated word parts: prefixes (P), combining forms (CF), roots (R), and suffixes (S). Then define the word.

EXAMPLE

hypertrophy

_____ / _____ / _____
  P   R   S

<u>hyper/troph/y</u>
  P   R   S

DEFINITION: above or excessive/nourishment or development/condition or process of

1. thoracic

_____ / _____
        R   S

DEFINITION: _____

2. myofascial

_____ / _____ / _____
        CF   R   S

DEFINITION: _____

3. arthropathy

_____ / _____ / _____
        CF   R   S

DEFINITION: _____

4. spondylolysis

_____ / _____
        CF   S

DEFINITION: _____

5. osteopenia

_____ / _____
        CF   S

DEFINITION: _____

6. achondroplasia

_____ / _____ / _____ / _____
        P   CF   R   S

DEFINITION: _____

7. ostealgia

_____ / _____
        R   S

DEFINITION: _____

8. polymyositis

_____ / _____ / _____
P   R   S

DEFINITION: _____

9. leiomyosarcoma

_____ / _____ / _____ / _____
CF   CF   R   S

DEFINITION: _____

10. myelocyte

_____ / _____ / _____
CF   R   S

DEFINITION: _____

11. costovertebral

_____ / _____ / _____
CF   R   S

DEFINITION: _____

12. musculotendinous

_____ / _____ / _____
CF   R   S

DEFINITION: _____

13. orthosis

_____ / _____
R   S

DEFINITION: _____

14. kyphoplasty

_____ / _____
CF   S

DEFINITION: _____

15. craniectomy

_____ / _____
R   S

DEFINITION: _____

16. arthrodesis

_____ / _____
CF   S

DEFINITION: _____

17. fibromyalgia

_____ / _____ / _____
CF   R   S

DEFINITION: _____

18. rhabdomyoma

_____ / _____ / _____
      CF   R   S

DEFINITION: _____

19. sternocostal

_____ / _____ / _____
      CF   R   S

DEFINITION: _____

20. intra-articular

_____ / _____ / _____
      P   R   S

DEFINITION: _____

21. syndactylism

_____ / _____ / _____
      P   R   S

DEFINITION: _____

22. lumbodynia

_____ / _____
      CF   S

DEFINITION: _____

23. cervicobrachial

_____ / _____ / _____
      CF   R   S

DEFINITION: _____

24. arthroscopy

_____ / _____
      CF   S

DEFINITION: _____

25. lordosis

_____ / _____
      R   S

DEFINITION: _____

Complete the medical term by writing the missing part:

26. inter _____ al = pertaining to between the *ribs*

27. _____ algia = *joint* pain

28. myo _____ = *incision* in a muscle

29. spondylosyn _____ = *binding* together of vertebrae

30. _____ myoma = *smooth* muscle tumor

31. osteo _____ = *softening* of bone

32. _____ listhesis = slipping of a *vertebra*

33. arthro _____ = *x-ray* of a joint

34. _____ tomy = incision into *bone*

35. epiphys _____ = *inflammation* of the ends of the long bones

36. _____ al = pertaining to the *neck*

37. bony _____ osis = *dead* bone tissue

38. _____ oma = tumor of *cartilage*

39. arthro _____ = *puncture for aspiration* of a joint

40. osteo _____ = *repair or reconstruction* of bone

For each of the following, circle the combining form that corresponds to the meaning given:

41. **cartilage**	crani/o	cost/o	chondr/o
42. **vertebra**	myel/o	spondyl/o	lumb/o
43. **bone marrow**	my/o	myel/o	muscul/o
44. **neck**	thorac/o	crani/o	cervic/o
45. **joint**	oste/o	arthr/o	ankyl/o
46. **chest**	thorac/o	cervic/o	spondyl/o
47. **muscle**	my/o	myel/o	lei/o
48. **rib**	stern/o	chondr/o	cost/o

Write the correct medical term for each of the following:

49. lateral curvature of the spine _____

50. bone tumor _____

51. grating sound made by movement of broken bones _____

52. synonym for bony necrosis _____

53. plane that divides the body into right and left portions _____

54. application of a pulling force to a fractured or dislocated joint to maintain proper position during healing _____

55. arthritis caused by hyperuricemia _____

56. a partial dislocation _____

57. toward the beginning of a structure _____

58. osteomalacia in children _____

59. physician specializing in x-ray technology _____

Match the following terms related to muscles with their meaning:

60. _____ atrophy

61. _____ tremor

62. _____ spasm

63. _____ rigidity

64. _____ spastic

65. _____ hypertrophy

66. _____ flaccid

67. _____ tetany

a. uncontrolled, stiff, and awkward muscle contractions

b. flabby muscle

c. involuntary muscle contraction

d. prolonged, continuous muscle contraction

e. stiff muscle

f. rhythmic muscle movement

g. increase in the size of a muscle

h. shrinking of muscle size

Briefly describe the difference between the following terms:

68. arthrogram/arthroscopy _____

_____

69. rhabdomyoma/rhabdomyosarcoma _____

_____

70. osteoarthritis/rheumatoid arthritis _____

_____

71. osteomalacia/osteoporosis _____

_____

72. orthosis/prosthesis_____

_____

73. closed reduction, external fixation of a Fx/open reduction, internal fixation of a Fx

_____

74. ankylosis/spondylosis _____

_____

75. leiomyoma/leiomyosarcoma _____

_____

76. lordosis/kyphosis _____

_____

77. spondylolisthesis/spondylosyndesis_____

_____

Match the following positions:

78. _____ erect

79. _____ supine

80. _____ decubitus

81. _____ prone

a. lying down, especially in bed

b. normal standing

c. face down and flat

d. horizontal recumbent ("on the spine")

Define the following abbreviations:

82. CT _____

83. PT_____

84. Tx_____

85. ROM _____

86. Fx_____

87. EMG _____

For each of the following, circle the correct spelling of the term:

88. spondelosis	spandalosis	spondylosis
89. scholiosis	scoliosis	scoleosis
90. arthrodynia	arthradynia	arthrodenia
91. osteoalgia	ostealgia	osstealgia
92. sagital	saggittal	sagittal

93. flaccid   flacid   flascid

94. sekquestrum   sequestrom   sequestrum

95. anklylosis   ankylosis   anklosis

96. chondral   chrondral   chondrel

97. dorsaflexion   dorsiflexion   dorsflexion

98. osteoparosis   osteoporosis   osteophorosis

99. rabdomyoma   rrhabdomyoma   rhabdomyoma

Write in the missing words on the blank lines in the following illustrations of body planes.

100–107.

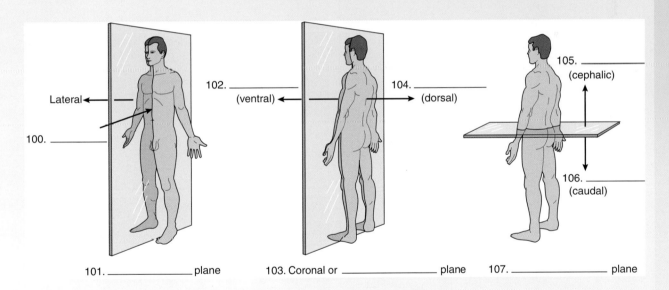

Lateral ←

100. _____

102. _____ ← (ventral)

104. _____ → (dorsal)

105. _____ (cephalic)

106. _____ (caudal)

101. _____ plane   103. Coronal or _____ plane   107. _____ plane

Write in the missing words on the blank lines in the following illustrations of body movements.

108–118.

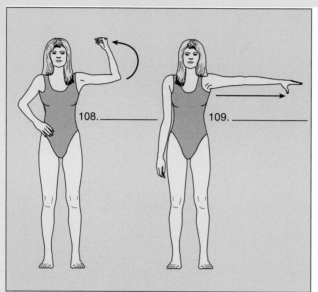

108. _____

109. _____

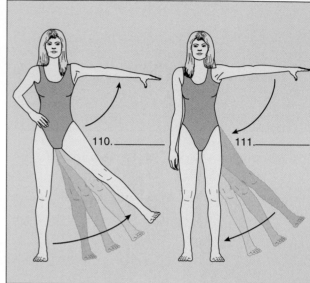

110. _____

111. _____

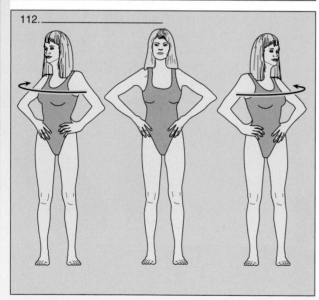

112. _____

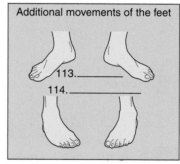

Additional movements of the feet

113. _____

114. _____

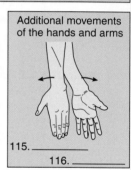

Additional movements of the hands and arms

115. _____

116. _____

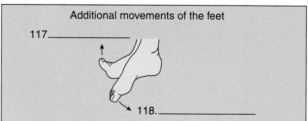

Additional movements of the feet

117. _____

118. _____

Write in the missing anatomical terms on the blank lines in the following illustrations.

119–143.

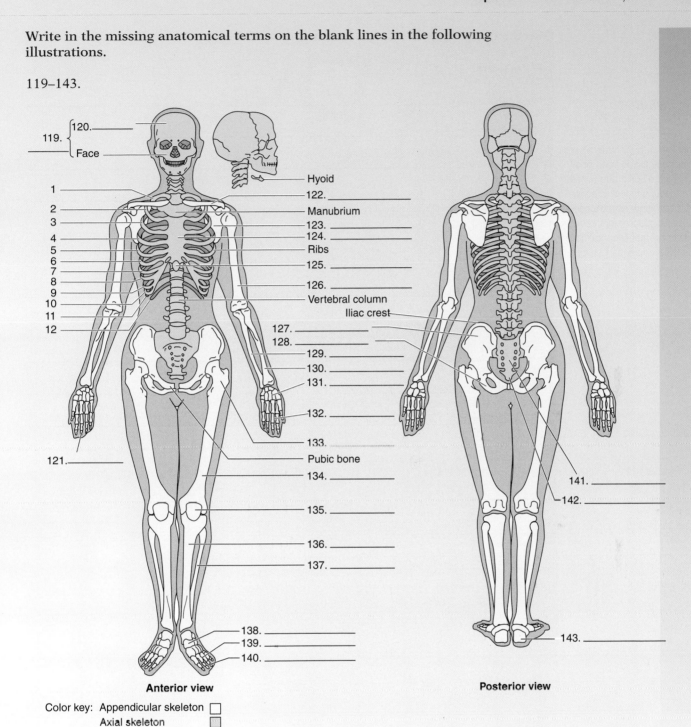

119. { 120._____
         Face

1 _____
2 _____
3 _____
4 _____
5 _____
6 _____
7 _____
8 _____
9 _____
10 _____
11 _____
12 _____

121._____

Hyoid
122. _____
Manubrium
123. _____
124. _____
Ribs
125. _____
126. _____
Vertebral column
Iliac crest
127. _____
128. _____
129. _____
130. _____
131. _____
132. _____
133. _____
Pubic bone
134. _____
135. _____
136. _____
137. _____
138. _____
139. _____
140. _____

141. _____
142. _____
143. _____

Anterior view

Posterior view

Color key: Appendicular skeleton ☐
            Axial skeleton   ▨

Give the noun that was used to form the following adjectives:

144. orthotic _____

145. hypertrophic _____

146. radial _____

147. kyphotic _____

148. bursal _____

149. dystrophic _____

150. necrotic _____

151. osteoporotic _____

152. lordotic _____

153. ulnar _____

154. scoliotic _____

155. prosthetic _____

MEDICAL RECORD ANALYSES

MEDICAL RECORD 6.1

History and Physical Examination

CC: "attacks" of right knee discomfort and instability

HPI: This 19 y/o ♂ presents with "attacks" of right knee pain and instability. Three years ago, while playing basketball, he turned sharply and felt his kneecap pop in and out. It was acutely swollen and painful and required manipulation to reduce it. He had a course of PT and did reasonably well for a few months until resuming athletic activities. Since then, he has had recurrent episodes of the knee slipping in and out, all related to twisting and turning while surfing or playing basketball. His primary complaint is the episodic discomfort and the inability to trust the knee. He is asymptomatic at this time.

PMH: NKDA. Hx of right ankle Fx in 20xx. Meds: none. Operations none.

SH: alcohol rarely used. FH: Father, age 49, Mother, age 43, both L&W.

ROS: noncontributory

PE: The patient is a cooperative male in NAD.

VS: T 97.2° F., P 64, R 14, BP 118/66

HEENT: WNL. Neck: supple, no tenderness, full ROM, no adenopathy.
Lungs, heart, abdomen: WNL. Back: no tenderness or deformity.
Extremities: unremarkable except for involved knee. Knee ROM is 0–45° equally.
There is no parapatellar tenderness.
Neurologic: Negative.
Radiographs show subluxation of the right knee.

IMP: RECURRENT RIGHT KNEE PATELLAR INSTABILITY

RECOMMENDATION: Patelloplasty is being discussed, and the risks and benefits of the procedure have been explained. The patient will return with his parents for further consultation before deciding whether to proceed with treatment.

1. Which describes the patient's symptoms at the time of the initial injury?

   a. severe pain over a short course

   b. pain that comes and goes

   c. pain that progressively gets worse

   d. pain that develops slowly over time

   e. no pain

2. What treatment was provided 3 years ago?

   a. puncture for aspiration of a joint

   b. transplantation of a piece of bone from one site to another

   c. examination of a joint from within

   d. physical rehabilitation including exercise

   e. binding or fusing joint surfaces

3. Which best describes the patient's symptoms at the time of this visit?
   a. severe pain
   b. moderate pain
   c. progressive pain
   d. mild pain
   e. no pain

4. Describe the orthopedic condition noted in the past history:
   a. forward slipping of a vertebra
   b. broken bone
   c. arthritis
   d. bone pain
   e. dislocation

5. What does full ROM indicate?
   a. swelling
   b. spasm
   c. inflammation
   d. bruising
   e. mobility

6. What did the radiographs indicate?
   a. no radiographs were mentioned
   b. patellar instability
   c. partial dislocation
   d. inflammation
   e. joint stiffness

7. What treatment did the physican recommend?
   a. surgical reconstruction of the knee cap
   b. physical therapy
   c. surgical repair of bone
   d. excision of the patella
   e. examination and repair of a joint from within using an endoscope

MEDICAL RECORD 6.2

As Alice Toohey was playing with her young granddaughter, she stepped on a toy dump truck and fell down her porch steps, wrenching her ankle violently. Because of the sharp pain and immediate swelling, Ms. Toohey was taken immediately to the hospital. After being seen by the emergency room physician, she was admitted and scheduled for surgery.

Directions

Read Medical Record 6.2 for Alice Toohey (page 189) and answer the following questions. This record is the operative report dictated by the surgeon, Dr. Ricardo Rodriguez, immediately after the operation and processed by a medical transcriptionist.

QUESTIONS ABOUT MEDICAL RECORD 6.2

Write your answers in the spaces provided.

1. Below are medical terms used in this record you have not yet encountered in this text. Underline each where it appears in the record and define below:

   malleolus _____

   oblique _____

   sterile_____

2. In your own words, not using medical terminology, briefly describe the preoperative diagnosis for Ms. Toohey.

   _____

   _____

   _____

3. Put the following operative steps in correct order by numbering them 1 to 10:

   _____ x-ray of the screws that were too long

   _____ incision on the outer side of the ankle

   _____ plate placed onto the fibula

   _____ sewing the incisions

   _____ x-ray of satisfactory screw position

   _____ towel clip positioned

   _____ removal of medial hematoma

   _____ removal of lateral hematoma

   _____ placement of a screw into the lower tibia

   _____ incision on the inner side of the right ankle

4. In this operation, the surgeon redid one step after using a diagnostic procedure to check whether that step was as effective as possible. In your own words, explain what Dr. Rodriguez changed and why.

_____

_____

_____

5. Describe the fracture line.

_____

6. When Dr. Rodriguez examined the ankle after making the first incision, he found a problem he could not and did not repair. In your own words, what had been destroyed in Ms. Toohey's injury?

_____

_____

7. Which of the following actions did *not* occur in this operation?
   a. washing the wound with antibiotic
   b. taping the fracture line
   c. drilling holes in the bone
   d. stapling the skin closed

8. Describe Ms. Toohey's condition when transferred to PAR after the operation.

_____

_____

_____

CENTRAL MEDICAL CENTER

211 Medical Center Drive • Central City, US 90000-1234 • PHONE: (012) 125-6784 • FAX: (012) 125-9999

OPERATIVE REPORT

PREOPERATIVE DIAGNOSIS: Trimalleolar fracture, right ankle/fracture dislocation.

POSTOPERATIVE DIAGNOSIS: Trimalleolar fracture, right ankle/fracture dislocation.

OPERATION PERFORMED: Open reduction and internal fixation of medial malleolus and lateral malleolus, right ankle.

ANESTHESIOLOGIST: K. Teglam, M.D.

ANESTHESIA: General.

DESCRIPTION OF OPERATION: After successful general anesthesia, the right lower extremity was prepped and draped in a sterile fashion. A pneumatic tourniquet was used in the case at 300 mm Hg (mercury) for 51 minutes. The medial side was opened first; the skin was incised, and this was carried down through the subcutaneous tissue down to the periosteum which was incised enough at the fracture site for visualization of a large transverse medial malleolar fracture. A hematoma was evacuated by curettage and irrigation. Unfortunately, there was some debris within the joint which was articular cartilage destruction and damage on the talus.

Attention was then directed laterally where an incision was made and carried through the skin and subcutaneous tissue. The fracture was brought into full view very easily. The fracture was long and oblique. This was curetted of hematoma and irrigated, and using a bone clamp, it was clamped in a reduced position. A 6-hole semitubular fibular-type plate was then bent to position and placed onto the fibula; and after predrilling, premeasuring, and pretapping, six cortical 3.5 mm diameter screws were used to hold the plate to the fractured fibula.

Attention was then directed medially. The fracture was reduced and held in place with a towel clip, and a 60 mm long malleolar screw was then inserted into the fragment into the distal tibia. X-rays revealed that three of the screws laterally were too long, and these were changed. The medial malleolus screw was also tightened down further. Repeat film revealed very satisfactory position of all the screws. The posterior malleolar fragment was felt to be adequately positioned. All the wounds were then irrigated with goodly amounts of antibiotic solution. Vicryl sutures, 0 and 2-0, were used to close the subcutaneous tissue on both sides; and staples were used for the skin. A bulky Jones dressing was applied with splints anteriorly and posteriorly.

The patient tolerated the procedure well and was transferred to the recovery room with stable vital signs.

R. Rodriguez, M.D.

RR:mb

D: 10/19/20xx
T: 10/20/20xx

OPERATIVE REPORT

PT. NAME: TOOHEY, ALICE M.
ID NO: IP-236701
ROOM NO: 729
ATT. PHYS: R. RODRIGUEZ, M.D.

Medical Record 6.2

MEDICAL RECORD 6.3

Jay Dorn, a retired construction worker, has had intermittent back pain for the last 2 months. When he began also having shooting pains in his legs, he went to his doctor at Central Medical Center. After a physical examination, Mr. Dorn underwent a series of back x-rays.

Directions

Read Medical Record 6.3 for Jay Dorn (page 191) and answer the following questions. This record is the radiographic report dictated by Dr. Mary Volz, the radiographer, after studying Mr. Dorn's x-rays and later transcribed for the record.

QUESTIONS ABOUT MEDICAL RECORD 6.3

Write your answers in the spaces provided.

1. Below are medical terms used in this record you have not yet encountered in this text. Underline each where it appears in the record and define below:

   eburnation _____

   lipping _____

   discogenic _____

2. What phrase in the report indicates that more than one x-ray was taken?

   _____

   Does the report state how many x-rays were taken?

   _____ no _____ yes   If yes, how many?

   _____

3. In your own words, not using medical terminology, describe the three diagnoses Dr. Volz makes.

   a._____

   b._____

   c._____

4. Not using any abbreviations, explain what test Dr. Volz says may be useful for Mr. Dorn to have next.

   _____

5. Which of the following is *not* mentioned in the report as a finding?
   a. lateral curvature of the spine
   b. forward slipping of a vertebra
   c. immobile condition of the spine
   d. inflammation of the bone marrow
   e. inflammation of both hips

CENTRAL MEDICAL CENTER

211 Medical Center Drive • Central City, US 90000-1234 • PHONE: (012) 125-6784 • FAX: (012) 125-9999

X-RAY REPORT

LUMBOSACRAL SPINE:
Multiple views reveal no evidence of fracture. There is slight lumbar spondylosis with slight lipping and minimal bridging. The disc spaces appear maintained except for slight narrowing at L4-L5 and L5-S1. There is also a Grade I spondylolisthesis of L5 on S1 and evidence of spondylolysis at L5 on the left. There is also slight dextroscoliosis in the lumbar region and slight increased lordosis in the lumbosacral region. The bony architecture is unremarkable except for eburnation between the articulating facets at L5-S1. The SI joints appear unremarkable. Incidentally noted are slight osteoarthritic changes involving both hips.

CONCLUSION:

1. Slight lumbar spondylosis with hypertrophic lipping and slight narrowing of the L4-L5 and L5-S1 disc spaces, rule out discogenic disease. If clinically indicated, CT of the lumbosacral spine may prove helpful in further evaluation.

2. Grade I spondylolisthesis of L5 on S1 with evidence of spondylolysis at L5 on the left.

3. Slight dextroscoliosis in the lumbar region and slight increased lordosis in the lumbosacral region.

M. Volz MD

M. Volz, M.D.

MV:ti

D: 10/19/20xx
T: 10/20/20xx

X-RAY REPORT	PT. NAME: DORN, JAY F.
	ID NO: RL-483091
	ATT. PHYS: T. LIGHT, M.D.

Medical Record 6.3

Chapter 7

Cardiovascular System

OBJECTIVES

After completion of this chapter you will be able to

- Define common combining forms used in relation to the cardiovascular system
- Identify basic anatomical terms referring to the heart and blood vessels
- Trace the flow of blood through the heart
- Define blood pressure and related terms
- Describe the pathway of electrical conduction in the heart and define related terms
- Define common symptomatic terms referring to the cardiovascular system
- Identify common diagnostic terms related to the cardiovascular system
- List the common diagnostic tests and procedures related to the cardiovascular system
- Identify common operative terms referring to the cardiovascular system
- Identify common therapeutic terms including drug classifications related to the cardiovascular system
- Explain terms and abbreviations used in documenting medical records involving the cardiovascular system

Combining Forms

Combining Form	Meaning	Example
angi/o	vessel	angiogram an′jē-ō-gram
vas/o		vasospasm vā′sō-spazm
vascul/o		vascular vas′ku-lar
aort/o	aorta	aortic ā-ōr′tik
arteri/o	artery	arteriosclerosis ar-tēr′ē′ō′skler-ō′sis
ather/o	fatty (lipid) paste	atheroma ath-er-ō′maă

Combining Form	Meaning	Example
atri/o	atrium	atrioventricular a'trē-ō-ven-trik'yū-lăr
cardi/o	heart	cardiology kar-dē-ol'ō-jē
coron/o	circle or crown	coronary kōr'o-nār-ē
my/o	muscle	myocardial mī-ō-kar'dē-ăl
pector/o	chest	pectoral pek'tŏ-ral
steth/o		stethoscope steth'ō-skōp
sphygm/o	pulse	sphygmomanometer sfig-mō-mă-nom'ĕ-ter
thrombo	clot	thrombocyte throm'bō-sīt
ven/o	vein	venous vē'nŭs
phleb/o		phlebitis flĕ-bī'tis
varic/o	swollen, twisted vein	varicosis vār-i-kō'sis
ventricul/o	ventricle (belly or pouch)	ventricular ven-trik'yū-lăr

Cardiovascular System Overview

The cardiovascular system consists of the heart and blood vessels that transport blood throughout the body.

The heart is the muscular organ that pumps blood throughout the body (Fig. 7.1). Its hollow interior has four chambers: the *right atrium* and *left atrium* (upper chambers) and the *right ventricle* and *left ventricle* (lower chambers). A partition, called the *septum,* divides the heart into right and left portions. The atria are separated by the *interatrial septum,* and the ventricles are separated by the *interventricular septum.* The valves of the heart open and close with the heartbeat to maintain the one-way flow of blood through the heart. They include the *tricuspid valve,* the *mitral (bicuspid) valve,* the *pulmonary semilunar valve,* and the *aortic valve.*

There are three layers of the heart: endocardium, myocardium, and epicardium. The *endocardium* is the membrane that lines the interior cavities of the heart; the *myocardium* is the thick, muscular layer; and the *epicardium* is the outer membrane. Surrounding and enclosing the heart is a loose, protective sac called the *pericardium.*

Blood transports essential elements within the body. It is circulated throughout the body via *arteries, arterioles, capillaries, venules,* and *veins.* (Blood is discussed separately in Chapter 8.) Blood flow through the heart is as follows.

Deoxygenated (depleted of oxygen) blood returning from circulation in the body enters the heart through the *superior vena cava* and *inferior vena cava* into the right atrium. During atrial contraction, the tricuspid valve opens to allow blood to flow into the right ventricle. Contraction of the ventricle pushes blood through the pulmonary

STRUCTURES OF THE HEART (arrows indicate path of blood flow)

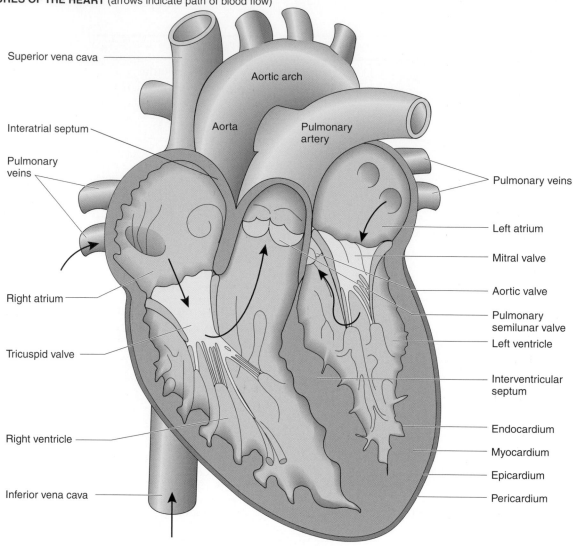

Superior vena cava

Aortic arch

Aorta

Pulmonary artery

Interatrial septum

Pulmonary veins

Pulmonary veins

Left atrium

Mitral valve

Aortic valve

Right atrium

Pulmonary semilunar valve

Left ventricle

Tricuspid valve

Interventricular septum

Endocardium

Myocardium

Right ventricle

Epicardium

Inferior vena cava

Pericardium

ECHOCARDIOGRAM
Normal, two-dimensional, apical four-chamber view

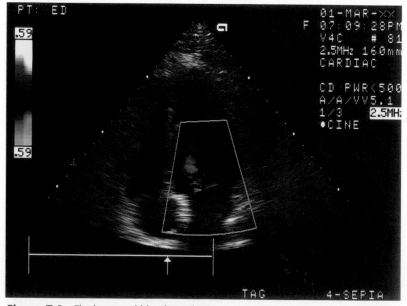

BLOOD CIRCULATION

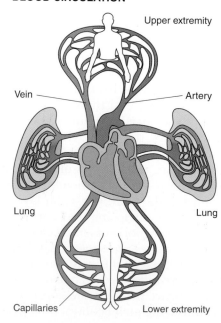

Upper extremity

Vein

Artery

Lung

Lung

Capillaries

Lower extremity

Figure 7.1 The heart and blood circulation.

semilunar valve into the pulmonary artery. The *pulmonary artery* carries the blood through two branches going to the lungs and on through the *pulmonary circulation* (a network of arteries, capillaries, air sacs, and veins in the lung), where it is oxygenated (supplied with oxygen) and gives off carbon dioxide waste. The oxygenated blood returns to the heart via the *pulmonary veins* into the left atrium. With atrial contraction, the mitral valve (also called bicuspid valve) opens to allow blood flow into the left ventricle. Contraction of the left ventricle pushes blood through the aortic valve into the aorta. Blood is then carried to all parts of the body through the *systemic circulation* (arteries, arterioles, capillaries, and veins) to provide transport for oxygen and nutrients. Note that the right side of the heart (right heart) handles deoxygenated blood and the left side of the heart (left heart) handles oxygenated blood.

The heart is the first organ to receive oxygenated blood via the coronary circulation. Branching from the aorta, the right and left coronary arteries divide to distribute blood throughout the entire heart (Fig. 7.2).

Anatomical Terms

Term	Meaning
SEPTA AND LAYERS OF THE HEART	
atrium ā′trē-ŭm	upper right and left chambers of the heart
endocardium en-dō-kar′dē-ŭm	membrane lining the cavities of the heart
epicardium ep-i-kar′dē-ŭm	membrane forming the outer layer of the heart
interatrial septum in-ter-ā′-trē-ăl sep′tŭm	partition between right and left atrium
interventricular septum in-ter-ven-trik′yū-lăr sep′tŭm	partition between right and left ventricle
myocardium mī-ō-kar′dē-ūm	heart muscle
pericardium per-i-kar′dē-ūm	protective sac enclosing the heart composed of two layers with fluid between
parietal pericardium pā-rī′ē-tāl	outer layer (parietal = pertaining to wall)
pericardial cavity pēr-ī-kar′dē-āl	fluid-filled cavity between the pericardial layers
visceral pericardium vıs′er-āl	layer closest to the heart (visceral = pertaining to organ)
ventricle ven′tri-kāl	lower right and left chambers of the heart
VALVES OF THE HEART AND VEINS	
heart valves	structures within the heart that open and close with the heartbeat to regulate the one-way flow of blood
aortic valve ā-ōr′tik	heart valve between the left ventricle and the aorta
mitral or bicuspid valve mī′trăl or bī-kŭs′pid	heart valve between the left atrium and left ventricle (cuspis = point)

MITRAL. Stems from mitre, the Latin word referring to a kind of cap or headband worn on the head and tied under the chin, and used to name the headdress of Christian bishops. In medicine, the term mitral is applied to the bicuspid valve of the heart because its two parallel cusps have a shape similar to a bishop's mitre.

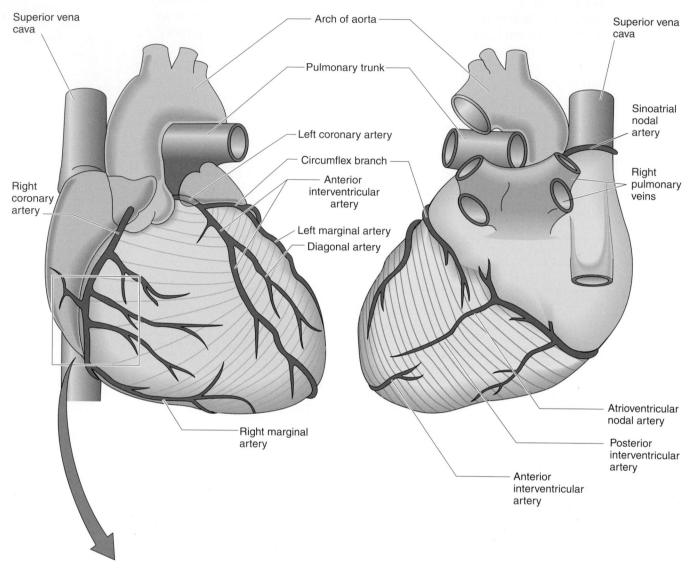

ANTERIOR VIEW OF CORONARY ARTERIES

POSTERIOR VIEW OF CORONARY ARTERIES

Superior vena cava

Arch of aorta

Pulmonary trunk

Superior vena cava

Left coronary artery

Circumflex branch

Anterior interventricular artery

Sinoatrial nodal artery

Right pulmonary veins

Right coronary artery

Left marginal artery

Diagonal artery

Right marginal artery

Atrioventricular nodal artery

Posterior interventricular artery

Anterior interventricular artery

PERCUTANEOUS TRANSLUMINAL CORONARY ANGIOPLASTY (PTCA)

Predilation angiogram revealing 99% stenosis of the right coronary artery (RCA).

PTCA procedure showing catheter placement and straddling of the balloon at the occluded site.

Post-PTCA angiogram showing successful dilation.

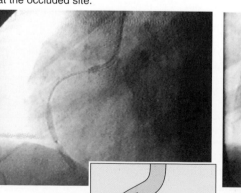

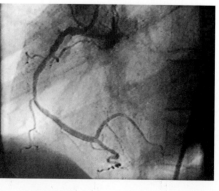

Catheter and wire placement with balloon inflation.

Figure 7.2. Coronary arteries and angiograms illustrating angioplasty.

Term	Meaning
pulmonary semilunar valve pŭl′mō-nār-ē sem-ē-lū′năr	heart valve opening from the right ventricle to the pulmonary artery (luna = moon)
tricuspid valve trī-kŭs′pid	valve between the right atrium and the right ventricle
valves of the veins	valves located at intervals within the lining of veins, especially in the legs, which constrict with muscle action to move the blood returning to the heart
BLOOD VESSELS (FIG. 7.3)	
arteries ăr′tĕr-ēz	vessels that carry blood *from* the heart to the arterioles (Fig. 7.4)
aorta ā-ōr′tă	large artery that is the main trunk of the arterial system branching from the left ventricle

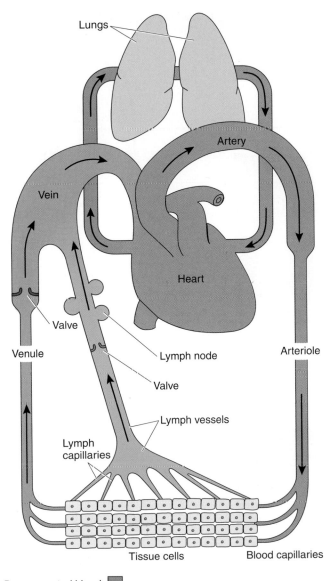

Figure 7.3 Blood and lymph circulation.

ARTERIAL BLOOD CIRCULATION

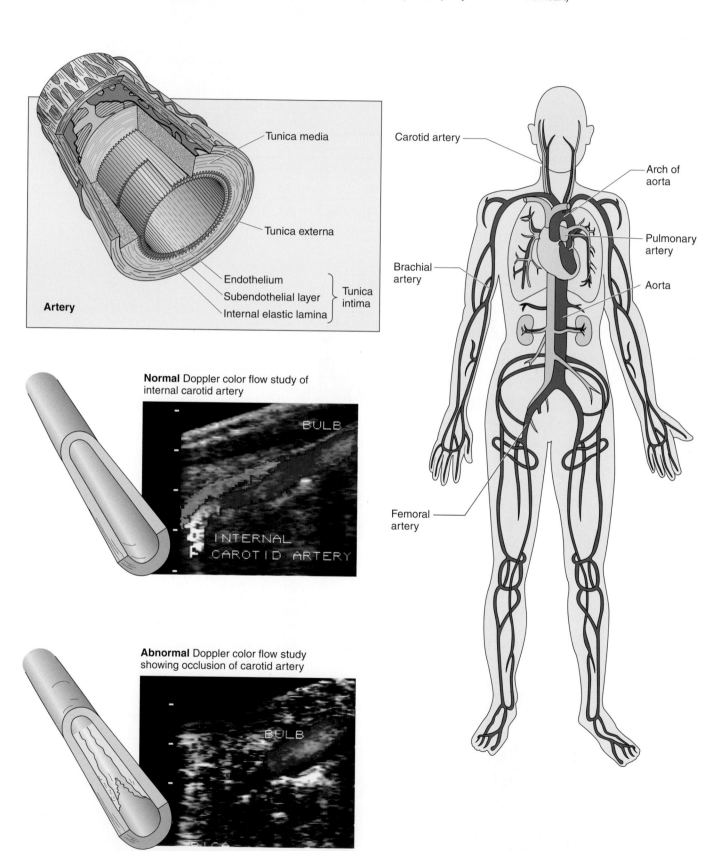

Arteries (carry blood from the heart)

Tunica media

Tunica externa

Endothelium
Subendothelial layer
Internal elastic lamina
} Tunica intima

Artery

Carotid artery

Arch of aorta

Pulmonary artery

Brachial artery

Aorta

Femoral artery

Normal Doppler color flow study of internal carotid artery

BULB

INTERNAL CAROTID ARTERY

Abnormal Doppler color flow study showing occlusion of carotid artery

BULB

Figure 7.4 Arteries.

Term	Meaning
arterioles ăr-tēr′ē-ōlz	small vessels that receive blood from the arteries
capillaries kap′i-lār-ēz	tiny vessels that join arterioles and venules
venules ven′yūlz	small vessels that gather blood from the capillaries into the veins
veins vānz	vessels that carry blood to the heart from the venules (Fig. 7.5)
CIRCULATION	
systemic circulation sis-tēm′ik	circulation of blood throughout the body through arteries, arterioles, capillaries, and veins to deliver oxygen and nutrients to body tissues
coronary circulation kōr′o-nār-ē	circulation of blood through the coronary blood vessels to deliver oxygen and nutrients to the heart muscle tissue
pulmonary circulation pūl′mō-nār-ē	circulation of blood from the pulmonary artery through the vessels in the lungs and back to the heart via the pulmonary vein, providing for the exchange of gases

CAPILLARY. A term formed from the Latin word capillus, a hair of the head (from caput, meaning head, and pilus, a hair), hence a very fine tube. Leonardo da Vinci was the first to make observations on capillary phenomena and spoke of capillary veins.

Blood Pressure

Blood pressure is the force exerted by circulating blood on the walls of the arteries, veins, and heart chambers. This pressure is determined by the volume of blood, the space within the arteries and arterioles, and the force of heart contractions (Fig. 7.6).

Blood pressure (BP) technique involves measuring pressure within the walls of an artery during the period of contraction of the heart, or *systole*, and during the period of relaxation of the heart, or *diastole*. When blood pressure is written, the systolic measurement is recorded first, followed by a slash, then the diastolic measurement (e.g., BP 120/80 means that the systolic reading is 120 and the diastolic reading is 80).

Blood Pressure Terms

Term	Meaning
diastole dī-as′tō-lē	to expand; period in the cardiac cycle when blood enters the relaxed ventricles from the atria
systole sis′tō-lē	to contract; period in the cardiac cycle when the heart is in contraction and blood is ejected through the aorta and pulmonary artery
normotension nōr-mō-ten′shŭn	normal blood pressure
hypotension hī′pō-ten′shŭn	low blood pressure
hypertension hī′per-ten′shŭn	high blood pressure

VENOUS CIRCULATION

Veins (carry blood to the heart)

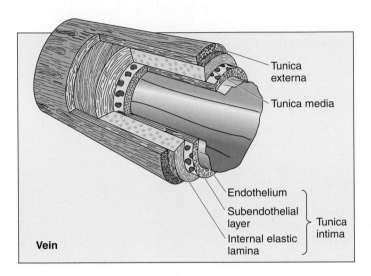

Tunica externa

Tunica media

Endothelium

Subendothelial layer

Internal elastic lamina

Tunica intima

Vein

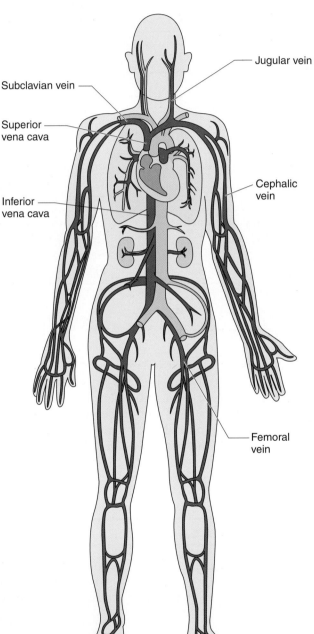

Jugular vein

Subclavian vein

Superior vena cava

Inferior vena cava

Cephalic vein

Femoral vein

FEMORAL THROMBUS

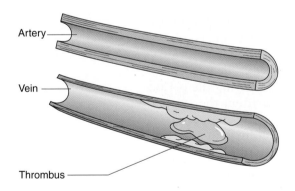

Artery

Vein

Thrombus

Color flow Doppler showing femoral vein thrombus

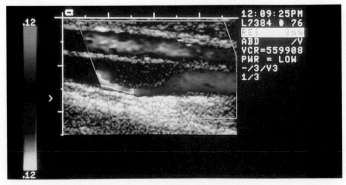

Figure 7.5 Veins.

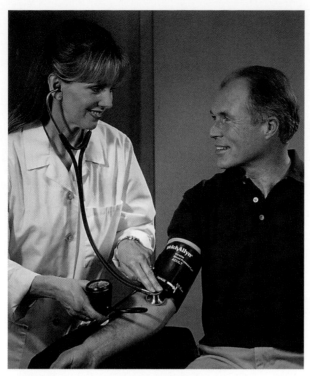

Figure 7.6 Blood pressure determination.

Cardiac Conduction

Movement of blood through the heart is made possible by cardiac conduction. The *cardiac cycle* is the repeated action of the heart during which an electrical impulse is conducted from the sinoatrial (SA) node (the pacemaker of the heart) to the atrioventricular (AV) node, to the bundle of His, to the left and right bundle branches, and to the Purkinje fibers, causing contraction of the heart and circulation of the blood (Fig. 7.7).

Initiated by the SA node, each myocardial cell responds to stimulation conducted by electrical impulses, changing from a resting state (polarized) to a state of contraction (depolarized) and then returning to a resting state by recharging (repolarizing); it is then ready again to begin the continuous cycle of contraction and relaxation of the myocardium that pumps blood through the heart.

Cardiac Conduction Terms

Term	Meaning
sinoatrial node (SA node) sī′nō-ā′trē-ăl nōd	the pacemaker; highly specialized neurological tissue, embedded in the wall of the right atrium, responsible for initiating electrical conduction of the heartbeat, causing the atria to contract and firing conduction of impulses to the AV node
atrioventricular node (AV node) ā′trē-ō-ven-trik′yū-lăr	neurological tissue in the center of the heart that receives and amplifies the conduction of impulses from the SA node to the bundle of His
bundle of His bŭn′dl	neurological fibers, extending from the AV node to the right and left bundle branches, that fire the impulse from the AV node to the Purkinje fibers

Term	Meaning
Purkinje fibers (network) pŭr-kin′jē fī′berz	fibers in the ventricles that transmit impulses to the right and left ventricles, causing them to contract
polarization pō′lăr-i-zā′shŭn	resting; resting state of a myocardial cell
depolarization dē-pō-lăr-i-zā′shŭn	change of a myocardial cell from a polarized (resting) state to a state of contraction (de = not; polarization = resting)
repolarization rē-pō-lăr-i-zā′shŭn	recharging of the myocardial cell from a contracted state back to a resting state (re = again; polarization = resting)
normal sinus rhythm (NSR)	regular rhythm of the heart cycle stimulated by the SA node (average rate of 60 to 100 beats/minute) (see Figs. 7.7 and 7.11)

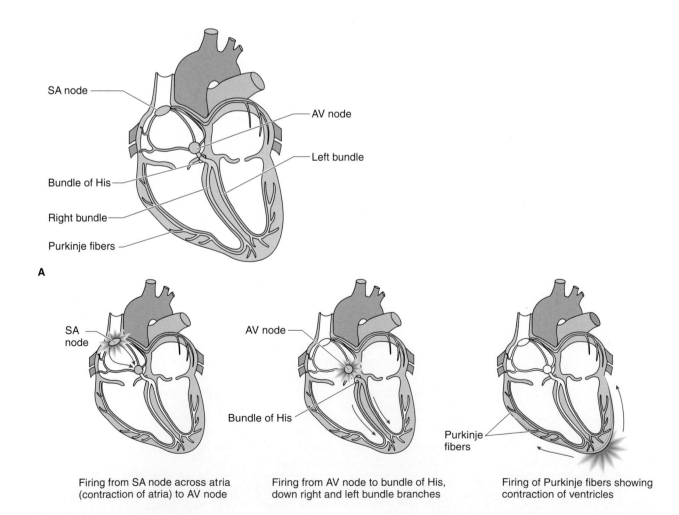

Figure 7.7 Cardiac conduction. **A.** Anatomy. **B.** Path of conduction.

Symptomatic and Diagnostic Terms

Term	Meaning
SYMPTOMATIC TERMS (FIG. 7.8)	
arteriosclerosis ar-tēr′ē′ō′skler-ō′sis	thickening, loss of elasticity, and calcification (hardening) of the arterial walls
atherosclerosis ath′er-ō-skler-ō′sis	buildup of fatty substances within the walls of arteries
atheromatous plaque ath-er-ō′mă-tŭs plak	a swollen area within the lining of an artery caused by the buildup of fat (lipids)
thrombus throm′bŭs	a stationary blood clot
embolus em′bō-lŭs	a clot (e.g., air, fat, foreign object) carried in the bloodstream that obstructs when it lodges (embolus = a stopper)
stenosis ste-nō-sis	condition of narrowing of a part
constriction kon-strik′shŭn	compression of a part
occlusion ŏ-klū′zhŭn	plugging; obstruction or a closing off
ischemia is-kē′mē-ă	to hold back blood; decreased blood flow to tissue caused by constriction or occlusion of a blood vessel

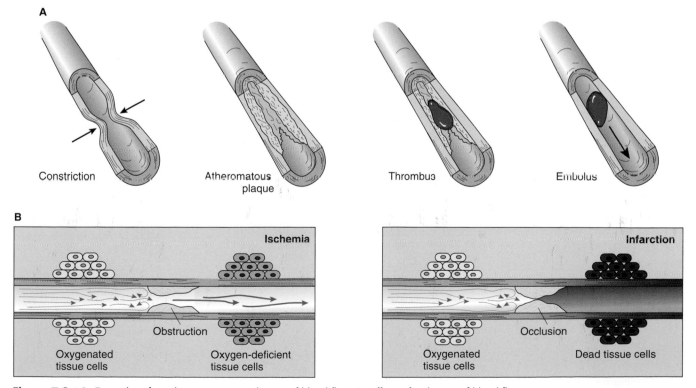

Figure 7.8   A. Examples of conditions causing reduction of blood flow. **B.** Effects of reduction of blood flow.

Term	Meaning
perfusion deficit per-fyū′zhŭn def′i-sit	a lack of flow through a blood vessel caused by narrowing, occlusion, etc.
infarct in′farkt	to stuff; a localized area of necrosis (condition of tissue death) caused by ischemia as a result of occlusion of a blood vessel
angina pectoris an′ji-nā pek′tō-ris	chest pain caused by a temporary loss of oxygenated blood to heart muscle often caused by narrowing of the coronary arteries (angina = to choke)
aneurysm an′yū-rizm	a widening; bulging of the wall of the heart, the aorta, or an artery caused by congenital defect or acquired weakness (Fig. 7.9)
saccular săk-ū-lăr	a sac-like bulge on one side
fusiform fū′zĭ-form	a spindle-shaped bulge
dissecting dī-sĕkt′ing	a split or tear of the vessel wall
claudication klaw-di-kā′shŭn	to limp; pain in a limb (especially the calf) while walking that subsides after rest; it is caused by inadequate blood supply
diaphoresis dī-ă-fō-rē′sis	profuse sweating
heart murmur hart mer′mer	an abnormal sound from the heart produced by defects in the chambers or valves
palpitation pal-pi-tā′shŭn	subjective experience of pounding, skipping, or racing heartbeats
vegetation vej-ĕ-tā′shŭn	to grow; an abnormal growth of tissue around a valve, generally a result of an infection such as bacterial endocarditis (Fig. 7.10)

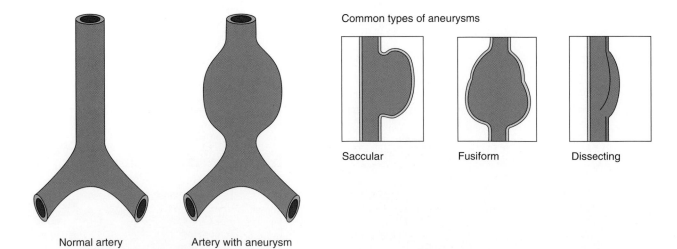

Common types of aneurysms

Normal artery   Artery with aneurysm   Saccular   Fusiform   Dissecting

Figure 7.9 Types of aneurysms.

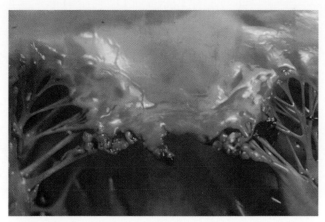

Figure 7.10 The mitral valve shows destructive vegetations, which have eroded through the free margins of the valve leaflets in a patient with bacterial endocarditis.

DIAGNOSTIC TERMS

arrhythmia ă-rith′mē-ă	any of several kinds of irregularity or loss of rhythm of the heartbeat (Fig. 7.11)
dysrhythmia dis-rith′mē-ă	
bradycardia brad-ē-kar′dē-ă	slow heart rate (<60 beats/minute)
fibrillation fib-ri-lā′shŭn	chaotic, irregular contractions of the heart, as in atrial or ventricular fibrillation
flutter flŭt′er	extremely rapid but regular contractions of the heart, as in atrial or ventricular flutter (typically from 250 to 350 beats/minute)
heart block hart blok	an interference with the normal electrical conduction of the heart defined by the location of the block (e.g., AV block)
premature ventricular contraction (PVC) prē-mă-tūr′ ven-trik′yū-lăr kon-trak′shun	a ventricular contraction preceding the normal impulse initiated by the SA node (pacemaker)
tachycardia tak′i′kar′dē-ă	fast heart rate (>100 beats/minute)
arteriosclerotic heart disease (ASHD) ar-tēr′ē-ō-skler-ot′ik	a degenerative condition of the arteries characterized by thickening of the inner lining, loss of elasticity, and susceptibility to rupture—seen most often in the aged or smokers
bacterial endocarditis bak-tēr′ē-ăl en′dō-kar-dī′tis	a bacterial inflammation that affects the endocardium or the heart valves (see Fig. 7.10)
cardiac tamponade kar′dē-ak tam-pŏ-nād′	compression of the heart produced by the accumulation of fluid in the pericardial sac as results from pericarditis or trauma, causing rupture of a blood vessel within the heart (tampon = a plug)

Normal sinus rhythm (NSR)

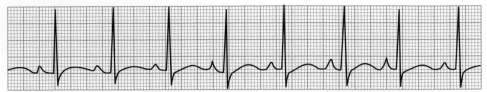

Bradycardia

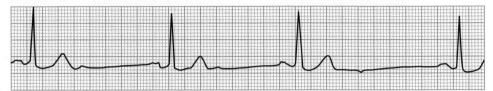

Fibrillation (ventricular)

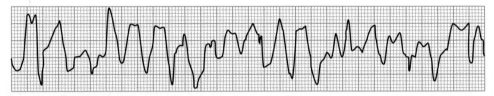

Flutter (atrial)

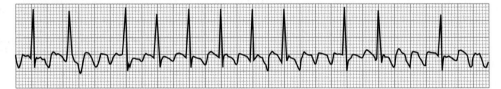

Heart block

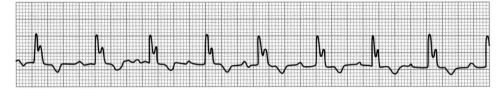

Premature ventricular contraction (PVC)

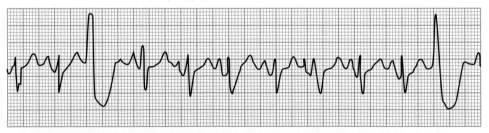

Tachycardia (sinus)

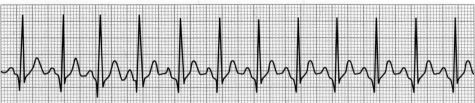

Figure 7.11 Electrocardiogram tracings showing common types of arrhythmia.

Term	Meaning
cardiomyopathy kar′dē-ō-mī-op′ă-thē	a general term for disease of the heart muscle [e.g., alcoholic cardiomyopathy (damage to the heart muscle caused by excessive consumption of alcohol)]
congenital anomaly of the heart kon-jen′i-tăl ă-nom′ă-lē	malformations of the heart present at birth (anomaly = irregularity)
atrial septal defect (ASD) ā′trē-ăl sep′tăl dē′fekt	an opening in the septum separating the atria
coarctation of the aorta kō-ark-tā′shŭn	narrowing of the descending portion of the aorta resulting in a limited flow of blood to the lower part of the body (Fig. 7.12)
patent ductus arteriosus (PDA) pā′tĕnt dŭk′tŭs ăr-tĕr-ē-ō′sŭs	an abnormal opening between the pulmonary artery and the aorta caused by the failure of the fetal ductus arteriosus to close after birth (patent = open) (Fig. 7.13)
tetralogy of Fallot tet-ral-ō-jē făl-ō	an anomaly that consists of four defects: pulmonary stenosis, ventricular septal defect, malposition of the aorta, and right ventricular hypertrophy—causes blood to bypass the pulmonary circulation so that deoxygenated blood goes into the systemic circulation, resulting in cyanosis (tetra = four)
ventricular septal defect (VSD) ven-trik′yū-lăr sep′tăl dē′fekt	an opening in the septum separating the ventricles
congestive heart failure (CHF) kon-jes′tiv **left ventricular failure**	failure of the left ventricle to pump an adequate amount of blood to meet the demands of the body, resulting in a "bottleneck" of congestion in the lungs that may extend to the veins, causing edema in lower portions of the body
cor pulmonale kōr pul-mō-nā′lē **right ventricular failure**	a condition of enlargement of the right ventricle as a result of chronic disease within the lungs that causes congestion within the pulmonary circulation and resistance of blood flow to the lungs (cor = heart)

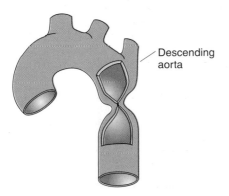

Descending aorta

Figure 7.12. Coarctation of the aorta.

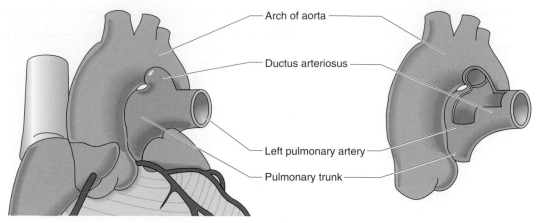

Arch of aorta

Ductus arteriosus

Left pulmonary artery

Pulmonary trunk

Figure 7.13. Patent ductus arteriosus.

Term	Meaning
coronary artery disease (CAD)	a condition affecting arteries of the heart that reduces the flow of blood and delivery of oxygen and nutrients to the myocardium—most often caused by atherosclerosis (Fig. 7.14)
hypertension (HTN) hī′per-ten′shŭn	persistently high blood pressure
essential (primary) hypertension ĕ-sen′shăl hī′per-ten′shŭn	high blood pressure attributed to no single cause, but risks include smoking, obesity, increased salt intake, hypercholesterolemia, and hereditary factors
secondary hypertension	high blood pressure caused by the effects of another disease (e.g., kidney disease)
mitral valve prolapse (MVP) mī′trăl	protrusion of one or both cusps of the mitral valve back into the left atrium during ventricular contraction, resulting in incomplete closure and backflow of blood

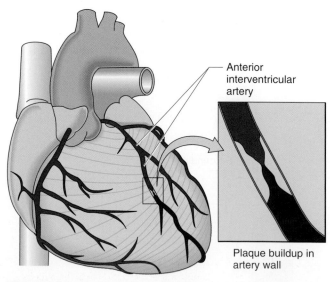

Anterior interventricular artery

Plaque buildup in artery wall

Figure 7.14 Coronary artery disease.

Term	Meaning
myocardial infarction (MI) mī-ō-kar′dē-ăl in-fark′shŭn	heart attack; death of myocardial tissue (infarction) owing to loss of blood flow (ischemia) as a result of an occlusion (plugging) of a coronary artery—usually caused by atherosclerosis; symptoms include pain in the chest or upper body (shoulders, neck, and jaw), shortness of breath, diaphoresis, and nausea (Fig. 7.15)
myocarditis mī′o-kar-dī′tis	inflammation of the myocardium most often caused by viral or bacterial infection
pericarditis per′i-kar-dī′tis	inflammation of the pericardium
phlebitis flĕ-bī′tis	inflammation of a vein
rheumatic heart disease rū-mat′ik	damage to heart muscle and heart valves by rheumatic fever (a streptococcal infection)
thrombophlebitis throm′bō-flĕ-bī′tis	inflammation of a vein associated with a clot formation
varicose veins văr′ĭ-kōs	abnormally swollen, twisted veins with defective valves, most often seen in the legs (Fig. 7.16)
deep vein thrombosis (DVT) throm-bō′sis	formation of a clot in a deep vein of the body, occurring most often in the femoral and iliac veins (see Fig 7.5)

Diagnostic Tests and Procedures

Test or Procedure	Explanation
auscultation aws-kŭl-tā′shŭn	a physical examination method of listening to sounds within the body with the aid of a stethoscope (e.g., auscultation of the chest for heart and lung sounds) (Fig. 7.17)

 AUSCULTATION. The Latin root means to listen or hear with attention. Listening to the sound of the breathing and of the beating of the heart is an ancient art that was current in Hippocrates' time. It was accomplished by placing the ear directly on the chest wall—direct or immediate auscultation. Indirect or mediate auscultation has been used in modern times since the invention of the stethoscope.

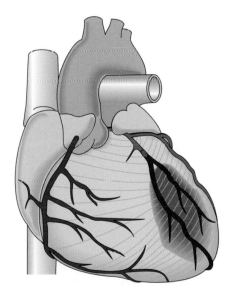

Figure 7.15 Anterolateral myocardial infarction (darkened area), caused by occlusion of the anterior descending branch of the left coronary artery.

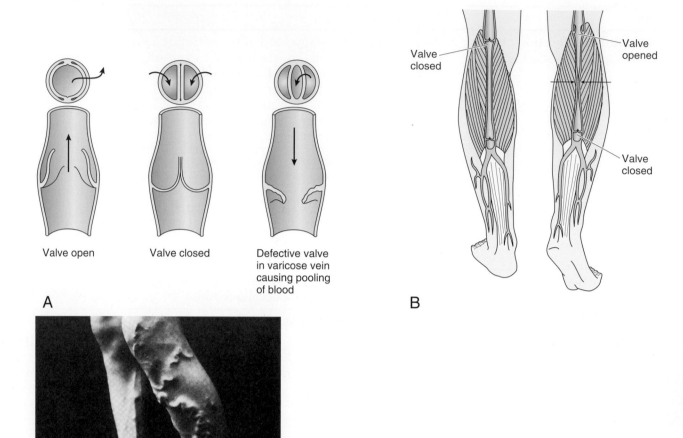

Valve open

Valve closed

Defective valve in varicose vein causing pooling of blood

A

Valve closed

Valve opened

Valve closed

B

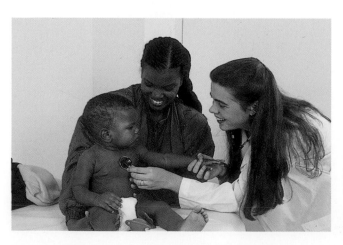

C

Figure 7.16 Varicose veins. **A.** Function of valves in the venous system. **B.** Contraction of skeletal muscle causes valves to open and close, preventing backflow of blood returning to the heart. **C.** Photo of patient with varicose veins.

Figure 7.17. Auscultating heart sounds.

Test or Procedure	Explanation
bruit brū-ē′	noise; an abnormal heart sound caused by turbulence within
gallop	an abnormal heart sound that mimics the gait of a horse; related to abnormal ventricular contraction
electrocardiogram **(ECG or EKG)** ē-lek-trō-kar′dē-ō-gram	an electrical picture of the heart represented by positive and negative deflections on a graph labeled with the letters P, Q, R, S, and T, corresponding to events of the cardiac cycle (Fig. 7.18)
stress electrocardiogram	an ECG of the heart recorded during the induction of controlled physical exercise using a treadmill or ergometer (bicycle); useful in detecting conditions such as ischemia and infarction (Fig. 7.19)
Holter ambulatory monitor hōlt′er am′byū-lă-tōr-ē mon′i-ter	a portable electrocardiograph worn by the patient that monitors electrical activity of the heart over 24 hours—useful in detecting periodic abnormalities
intracardiac electrophysiological study (EPS) in′tr ă-kar′dē-ak ē-lek′trō-fiz-ē-ō-loj′i-kăl stŭd′ē	invasive procedure involving placement of catheter-guided electrodes within the heart to evaluate and map the electrical conduction of cardiac arrhythmias; intracardiac catheter ablation may be performed at the same time to treat the arrhythmia

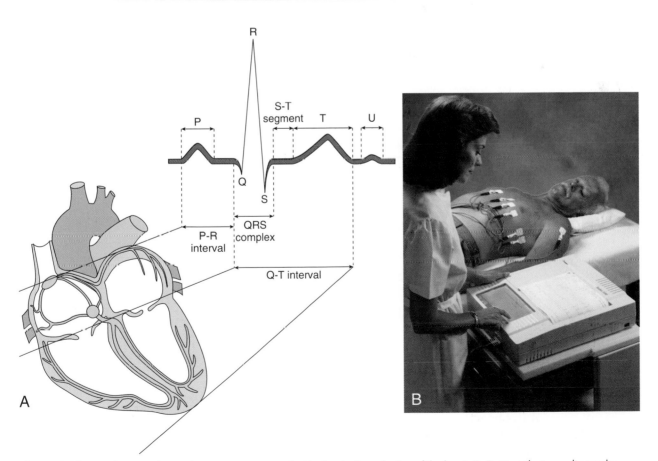

Figure 7.18 **A.** Electrocardiographic pattern associated with electrical conduction of the heart. **B.** Resting electrocardiography.

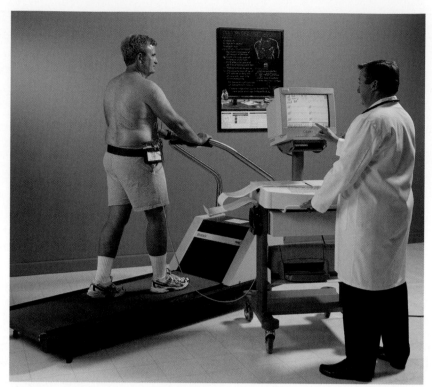

Figure 7.19 Stress electrocardiography.

Test or Procedure	Explanation
intracardiac catheter ablation in′tră-kar′dē-ak kath′ēter ab-lā′shŭn	use of radiofrequency waves sent through a catheter within the heart to treat arrhythmias by selectively destroying myocardial tissue at sites generating abnormal electrical pathways
magnetic resonance angiography (MRA) rez′ō-nans an-jē-og′ră-fē	magnetic resonance imaging of the heart and blood vessels for evaluation of pathology (see Chapter 10, Fig. 10.18)
nuclear medicine imaging of the heart nū′klē-ar med′i-sin im′ă-jing	radionuclide organ imaging of the heart after administration of radioactive isotopes to visualize structures and analyze functions
myocardial radionuclide perfusion scan mī-ō-kar′dē-ăl rā′dē-ō-nū′klīd per-fyū′zhŭn	a scan of the heart made after an intravenous injection of an isotope (e.g., thallium) that is absorbed by myocardial cells in proportion to blood flow throughout the heart
myocardial radionuclide perfusion stress scan	a nuclear scan of the heart taken after the induction of controlled physical exercise via treadmill or bicycle or administration of a pharmaceutical agent that produces the effect of exercise stress in patients unable to ambulate
positron emission tomography (PET) scan of the heart poz′i-tron ē̄-mish′shŭn tō-mog′ră-fē	use of nuclear isotopes and computed tomography techniques to produce perfusion (blood flow) images and study the cellular metabolism of the heart; can be taken at rest or with stress

Test or Procedure	Explanation
radiology	x-ray imaging
angiography an-jē-og′ră-fē	an x-ray of a blood vessel after injection of contrast medium
angiogram an′jē-ō-gram	a record obtained by angiography
coronary angiogram kōr′o-nār-ē an′jē-ō-gram	an x-ray of the blood vessels of the heart (see Fig. 7.2)
arteriogram ar-tēr′e-ō-gram	an x-ray of a particular artery (e.g., coronary arteriogram, renal arteriogram)
aortogram ā-ōr′tō-gram	an x-ray of the aorta
venogram vē′nō-gram	an x-ray of a vein
cardiac catheterization kar′dē-ak kath′ĕ-ter-ī-zā′shŭn	introduction of a flexible, narrow tube or *catheter* through a vein or artery into the heart to withdraw samples of blood, measure pressures within the heart chambers or vessels, and inject contrast media for fluoroscopic radiography and cine film (motion picture) imaging of the chambers of the heart and coronary arteries—very often includes interventional procedures such as angioplasty and atherectomy (see endovascular procedures listed under "Operative Terms") (Fig. 7.20)
left heart catheterization	an x-ray of the left ventricular cavity and coronary arteries
right heart catheterization	measurement of oxygen saturation and pressure readings of the right side of the heart
ventriculogram ven-trik′ū-lō-gram	an x-ray visualizing the ventricles
stroke volume (SV)	measurement of the amount of blood ejected from a ventricle in one contraction
cardiac output (CO)	measurement of the amount of blood ejected from either ventricle of the heart per minute
ejection fraction ē-jek′shŭn frak′shŭn	measurement of the volume percentage of left ventricular contents ejected with each contraction
sonography	sonographic imaging
echocardiography (ECHO) ek′ō-kar-dē-og′r ă-f ē	recording of sound waves through the heart to evaluate structure and motion (see Figs. 7.1 and 7.21)
stress echocardiogram **(stress ECHO)**	an echocardiogram of the heart recorded during the induction of controlled physical exercise via treadmill or bicycle or administration of a pharmaceutical agent that produces the effect of exercise stress in patients unable to ambulate—useful in detecting conditions such as ischemia and infarction

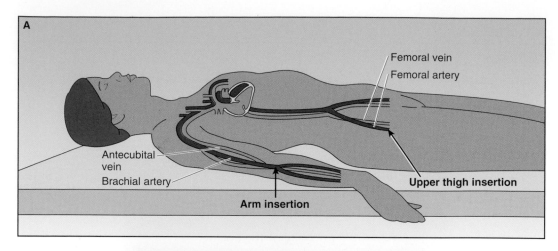

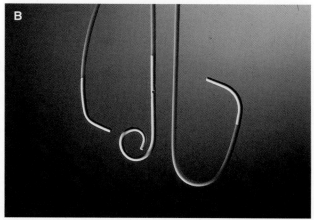

Figure 7.20 Cardiac catheterization. **A.** Possible insertion sites for cardiac catheterization. **B.** Cardiac catheterization catheters: *left,* 6 French JL4; *middle,* 6 French pigtail; *right,* 6 French JR4.**C.** Cardiac catheterization laboratory.

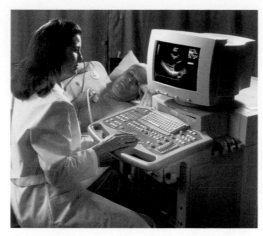

Figure 7.21 Echocardiography.

Test or Procedure	Explanation
transesophageal echocardiogram (TEE) trans-ē-sof′ă-jē′ăl	an echocardiographic image of the heart after placement of an ultrasonic transducer at the end of an endoscope inside the esophagus
Doppler sonography dōp′lĕr sō-nog′ră-fē	an ultrasound technique used to evaluate blood flow to determine the presence of a deep vein thrombosis (DVT) or carotid insufficiency, or flow through the heart, chambers, valves, etc. (see Figs. 7.4 and 7.5)
intravascular sonography in′tra-vas′kyū-lăr sŏ-nog′ră-fē	ultrasound images made after a sonographic transducer is placed at the tip of a catheter within a blood vessel—done to evaluate pathological conditions such as buildup of plaque

Operative Terms

Term	Meaning
coronary artery bypass graft (CABG)	grafting of a portion of a blood vessel retrieved from another part of the body (such as a length of saphenous vein from the leg or mammary artery from the chest wall) to bypass an occluded coronary artery, restoring circulation to myocardial tissue (Fig. 7.22); the traditional method includes temporary arrest of the heart with circulation (bypass) of the patient's blood through a heart-lung machine during the procedure—an alternative off-pump approach uses a stabilizer to perform the procedure on the beating heart
anastomosis ă-nas′tō-mō′sis	opening; joining of two blood vessels to allow flow from one to the other
endarterectomy end-ar-ter-ek′tō-mē	incision and coring of the lining of an artery to clear a blockage caused by a clot or atherosclerotic plaque buildup (e.g., carotid endarterectomy)

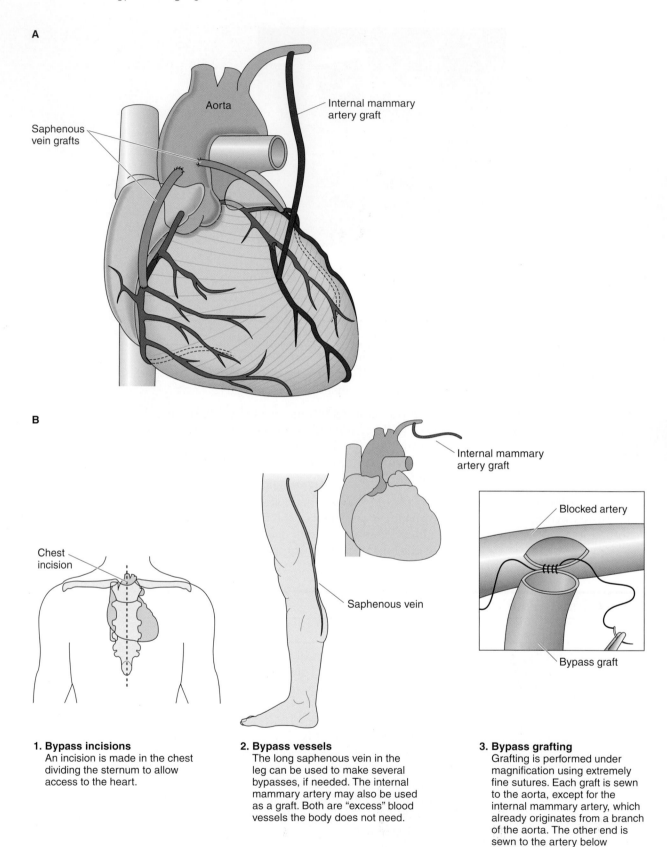

A

Aorta

Internal mammary
artery graft

Saphenous
vein grafts

B

Internal mammary
artery graft

Chest
incision

Blocked artery

Saphenous vein

Bypass graft

1. Bypass incisions
An incision is made in the chest dividing the sternum to allow access to the heart.

2. Bypass vessels
The long saphenous vein in the leg can be used to make several bypasses, if needed. The internal mammary artery may also be used as a graft. Both are "excess" blood vessels the body does not need.

3. Bypass grafting
Grafting is performed under magnification using extremely fine sutures. Each graft is sewn to the aorta, except for the internal mammary artery, which already originates from a branch of the aorta. The other end is sewn to the artery below the blockage.

Figure 7.22 Coronary artery bypass graft. **A.** Common sites for bypass grafts. **B.** Bypass process.

Term	Meaning
transmyocardial revascularization (TMR)	a laser technique used to open tiny channels in the heart muscle to restore blood flow, thereby relieving angina in patients with advanced coronary artery disease; an option for patients not treatable with angioplasty or coronary artery bypass
valve replacement	surgery to replace a diseased heart valve with an artificial one

types of artificial valves:

tissue—most commonly made from animal tissue such as porcine (pig) or bovine (cow)

mechanical—made from synthetic material (Fig. 7.23) |
valvuloplasty val′vyū-lō-plas-tē	repair of a heart valve
endovascular surgery	interventional procedures performed endoscopically at the time of cardiac catheterization (Fig. 7.24)
angioscopy (vascular endoscopy) an-jē-os′kō-pē	use of a flexible fiberoptic angioscope accompanied by an irrigation system, a camera, a video recorder, and a monitor that is guided through a specific blood vessel to visually assess a lesion and select the mode of therapy
atherectomy ăth-er-ek′tō-mē	excision of atheromatous plaque from within an artery utilizing a device housed in a flexible catheter that selectively cuts away or pulverizes tissue buildup (Fig. 7.24A)

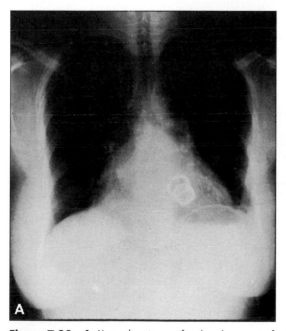 

Figure 7.23 **A.** X-ray showing artificial replacement of mitral valve (Starr-Edwards). **B.** Starr-Edwards Silastic ball mechanical valve.

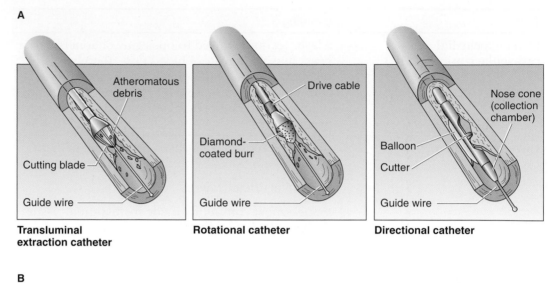

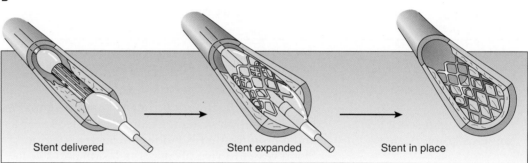

Figure 7.24 Examples of devices used in endovascular interventional procedures. **A.** Atherectomy devices. **B.** Intravascular stent.

Term	Meaning
percutaneous transluminal coronary angioplasty (PTCA) per-kyū-tā′nē-ŭs trăns-lū′mĭ-năl kōr′o-năr-ē an′jē-ō-plas-tē	a method of treating the narrowing of a coronary artery by inserting a specialized catheter with a balloon attachment, then inflating it to dilate and open the narrowed portion of the vessel and restore blood flow to the myocardium (see Fig. 7.2); most often includes placement of a stent
intravascular stent in′tra-vas′kyū-lăr	implantation of a device used to reinforce the wall of a vessel and ensure its patency (openness)—most often used to treat a stenosis or a dissection (a split or tear in the wall of a vessel) or to reinforce patency of a vessel after angioplasty (see Fig. 7.24B)

Therapeutic Terms

Term	Meaning
defibrillation dē-fib′ri-lā′shŭn	termination of ventricular fibrillation by delivery of an electrical stimulus to the heart, most commonly by applying electrodes of the defibrillator externally to the chest wall but can be performed internally at the time of open heart surgery or via an implanted device (Fig. 7.25)
defibrillator dē-fib′ri-lā′ter	a device that delivers the electrical stimulus in defibrillation

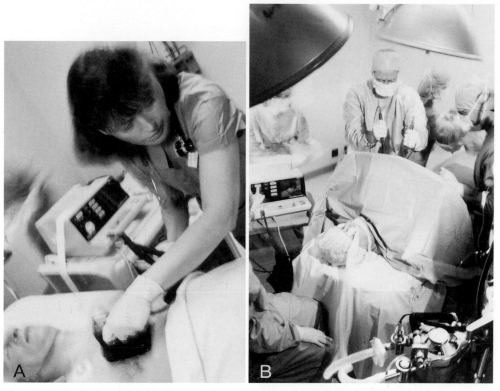

Figure 7.25 **A.** External defibrillation. **B.** Internal defibrillation performed in the operating room.

Term	Meaning
cardioversion kar′dē-ō-ver′zhŭn	termination of tachycardia either by pharmaceutical means or by delivery of electrical energy
implantable cardioverter defibrillator (ICD) kar′dē-ō-ver′ter dē fib′ri-lā′tcr	an implanted, battery-operated device with rate-sensing leads that monitors cardiac impulses and initiates an electrical stimulus as needed to stop ventricular fibrillation or tachycardia
pacemaker	a device used to treat slow heart rates (bradycardia) by electrically stimulating the heart to contract, most often implanted with lead wires and battery circuitry under the skin but can be temporarily placed externally with lead wires inserted into the heart via a vein (Fig. 7.26)
thrombolytic therapy throm-bō-lit′ik	dissolution of thrombi using drugs [e.g., streptokinase, tissue plasminogen activator (TPA)]

COMMON THERAPEUTIC DRUG CLASSIFICATIONS

angiotensin-converting enzyme (ACE) inhibitor ăn′jē-ō-tĕn′sin-kŏn-vĕr′ting ĕn′zīm	a drug that suppresses the conversion of angiotensin in the blood by the angiotensin-converting enzyme; used in the treatment of hypertension
antianginal an′tē-an′ji-năl	a drug that dilates coronary arteries, restoring oxygen to the tissues to relieve the pain of angina pectoris

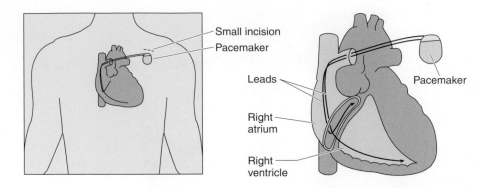

A small incision is made in the upper chest, below the clavicle, to access a large vein nearby.

A

The pacemaker leads are then guided through the vein and into the heart. After proper placement is determined, the leads are secured in position.

A small "pocket" to house the pacemaker is created just under the skin at the incision site. The leads are connected to the pacemaker that is secured in the "pocket." Finally, the incision is closed with a few sutures.

Figure 7.26 Pacemaker. **A.** Endocardial pacemaker. **B.** Teleradiology/critical care workstation. Chest x-rays on screen show pacemaker placement.

Term	Meaning
antiarrhythmic an′tē-ă-rith′mik	a drug that counteracts cardiac arrhythmia
anticoagulant an′tē-kō-ag′yū-lant	a drug that prevents clotting of the blood commonly used in treating thrombophlebitis and myocardial infarction
antihypertensive an′tē-hī-per-ten′siv	a drug that lowers blood pressure
beta-adrenergic blocking agents bā′tā ad-rĕ-ner′jik blok′ing **beta blockers** bā′tā blok′ers	agents that inhibit responses to sympathetic adrenergic nerve activity causing a slowing of electrical conduction and heart rate and a lowering of the pressure within the walls of the vessels; used to treat angina pectoris and hypertension

Term	Meaning
calcium channel blockers kal'sē-ŭm chan'ĕl blok'ers	agents that inhibit the entry of calcium ions in heart muscle cells causing a slowing of the heart rate, lessening the demand for oxygen and nutrients, and relaxing of the smooth muscle cells of the blood vessels to cause dilation; used to prevent or treat angina pectoris, some arrhythmias, and hypertension
cardiotonic kar'dē-ō-ton'ik	a drug that increases the force of myocardial contractions in the heart commonly used to treat congestive heart failure
diuretic dī-yū-ret'ik	a drug that increases the secretion of urine commonly prescribed in treating hypertension
hypolipidemic hī-pō-lip'i-dē'mik	a drug that reduces serum fat and cholesterol
statins	agents that lower cholesterol in the blood by inhibiting the effect of HMG-CoA reductase, a liver enzyme responsible for producing cholesterol
thrombolytic agents throm'bō-lit'ik	drugs used to dissolve thrombi (blood clots) (e.g., streptokinase, tissue plasminogen activator [TPA or tPA])
vasoconstrictor vā'sō-kon-strik'ter	a drug that causes narrowing of the blood vessels, decreasing blood flow
vasodilator vā'sō-dī-lā'ter	a drug that causes dilation of the blood vessels, increasing blood flow

Summary of Chapter 7 Acronyms/Abbreviations

ACE	angiotensin-converting enzyme	**MI**	myocardial infarction
ASD	atrial septal defect	**MRA**	magnetic resonance angiography
ASHD	arteriosclerotic heart disease	**MVP**	mitral valve prolapse
AV	atrioventricular	**NSR**	normal sinus rhythm
BP	blood pressure	**PDA**	patent ductus arteriosus
CABG	coronary artery bypass graft	**PET**	positron emission tomography
CAD	coronary artery disease	**PTCA**	percutaneous transluminal coronary angioplasty
CHF	congestive heart failure		
CO	cardiac output	**PVC**	premature ventricular contraction
DVT	deep vein thrombosis	**SA**	sinoatrial
ECG, EKG	electrocardiogram	**SV**	stroke volume
ECHO	echocardiography	**TEE**	transesophageal echocardiogram
EPS	electrophysiological study	**TMR**	transmyocardial revascularization
HTN	hypertension	**tPA, TPA**	tissue plasminogen activator
ICD	implantable cardioverter-defibrillator	**VSD**	ventricular septal defect

PRACTICE EXERCISES

For the following terms, on the lines below the term, write out the indicated word parts: prefixes (P), combining forms (CF), roots (R), and suffixes (S). Then define the term.

EXAMPLE

endocardial

_____ / _____ / _____
    P   R   S

<u>endo/cardi/al</u>
  P   R   S

DEFINITION: within/heart/pertaining to

1. angiography

_____ / _____
      CF   S

DEFINITION: _____

2. varicosis

_____ / _____
      R   S

DEFINITION: _____

3. pectoral

_____ / _____
      R   S

DEFINITION: _____

4. vasospasm

_____ / _____
      CF   S

DEFINITION: _____

5. venous

_____ / _____
      R   S

DEFINITION: _____

6. aortocoronary

_____ / _____ / _____
      CF   R   S

DEFINITION: _____

7. thrombophlebitis

_____ / _____ / _____
      CF   R   S

DEFINITION: _____

8. pericardiocentesis

_____ / _____ / _____
     P   R   S

DEFINITION: _____

9. vasculopathy

_____ / _____ / _____
     CF   R   S

DEFINITION: _____

10. atherogenesis

_____ / _____
     CF   S

DEFINITION: _____

11. stethoscope

_____ / _____
     CF   S

DEFINITION: _____

12. myocardium

_____ / _____ / _____
     CF   R   S

DEFINITION: _____

13. aortoplasty

_____ / _____
     CF   S

DEFINITION: _____

14. venostomy

_____ / _____
     CF   S

DEFINITION: _____

15. arteriostenosis

_____ / _____ / _____
     CF   R   S

DEFINITION: _____

16. phlebotomy

_____ / _____
     CF   S

DEFINITION: _____

17. cardioaortic

_____ / _____ / _____
     CF   R   S

DEFINITION: _____

18. ventriculogram

_____ / _____
       CF   S

DEFINITION: _____

19. phlebitis

_____ / _____
       R   S

DEFINITION: _____

20. angioplasty

_____ / _____
       CF   S

DEFINITION: _____

21. endovascular

_____ / _____ / _____
       P   R   S

DEFINITION: _____

22. cardiotoxic

_____ / _____ / _____
       CF   R   S

DEFINITION: _____

23. arteriogram

_____ / _____
       CF   S

DEFINITION: _____

24. atherectomy

_____ / _____
       R   S

DEFINITION: _____

25. atherothrombosis

_____ / _____ / _____
       CF   R   S

DEFINITION: _____

Fill in the blanks with the appropriate medical terms.

26. _____ anomalies = malformations of the heart present at birth

27. arterio _____ osis = thickening, loss of elasticity, and calcification (hardening) of arterial walls

28. _____ = irregularity or loss of rhythm of the heartbeat

29. cardiomyo _____ = general term for disease of the heart muscle

30. _____ = joining of two blood vessels to allow flow from one to the other

31. _____ = abnormal heart sound that mimics the gait of a horse

32. _____ cardiogram = a recording of sound waves directed through the heart to evaluate structure and motion

33. cor _____ = a condition of enlargement of the right ventricle as a result of chronic disease within the lungs

34. coronary _____ = an x-ray of the blood vessels of the heart made with the introduction of a catheter and release of a contrast medium

35. _____ ECG = electrocardiogram of the heart recorded during controlled physical exercise

36. intracardiac catheter _____ = treatment of arrhythmia by destroying myocardial tissue at sites generating abnormal electrical pathways

For each of the following, circle the combining form that corresponds to the meaning given:

37. **chest**	phleb/o	sphygm/o	pector/o
38. **vein**	aort/o	phleb/o	varic/o
39. **vessel**	angi/o	arteri/o	coron/o
40. **heart**	ven/o	coron/o	cardi/o
41. **fatty paste**	aor/o	ather/o	atri/o
42. **circle**	cardi/o	coron/o	sphygm/o
43. **pulse**	sphygm/o	steth/o	thromb/o
44. **clot**	atri/o	angi/o	thromb/o
45. **artery**	arteri/o	angi/o	aort/o
46. **belly or pouch**	varic/o	ventricul/o	ven/o

Match the following terms with their meanings:

47. _____ atherosclerosis

a. high blood pressure

48. _____ infarct

b. bulging of a vessel

49. _____ hypotension

c. stationary clot

50. _____ vegetation

d. cramp in leg muscle

51. _____ embolus

e. normal blood pressure

52. _____ occlusion

f. hard, nonelastic condition

53. _____ hypertension

g. traveling clot that obstructs when it lodges

54. _____ thrombus

h. buildup of fat

55. _____ constriction

i. growth of tissue

56. _____ normotension

j. a plugging

57. _____ angina

k. loss of blood flow

58. _____ claudication

l. compression

59. _____ ischemia

m. cramp in heart muscle

60. _____ arteriosclerosis

n. low blood pressure

61. _____ aneurysm

o. scar left by necrosis

Write the full medical term for the following abbreviations:

62. PVC _____

63. PDA _____

64. ASHD _____

65. ICD _____

66. CHF _____

67. CAD _____

68. HTN _____

69. MVP _____

70. MRA _____

71. VSD _____

Write in the missing words on the blank lines in the following illustration of the heart.

72–80.

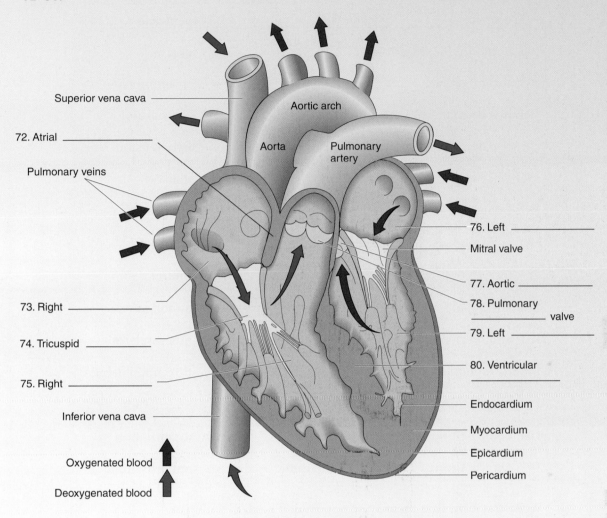

Superior vena cava

72. Atrial _____

Pulmonary veins

73. Right _____

74. Tricuspid _____

75. Right _____

Inferior vena cava

Oxygenated blood

Deoxygenated blood

Aortic arch

Aorta

Pulmonary artery

76. Left _____

Mitral valve

77. Aortic _____

78. Pulmonary _____ valve

79. Left _____

80. Ventricular _____

Endocardium

Myocardium

Epicardium

Pericardium

Match the following abbreviations with their meanings:

81. _____ ECG   a. balloon angioplasty

82. _____ tPA   b. magnetic resonance of blood vessels

83. _____ MRA   c. a clot in a vein

84. ___ PTCA   d. heart bypass surgery

85. _____ MI   e. electrical picture of heart

86. _____ DVT   f. echocardiogram directed through the esophagus

87. _____ ASD   g. left ventricular failure

88. _____ CABG   h. thrombolytic drug

89. _____ TEE   i. an abnormal opening in the atrial septum

90. _____ CHF   j. heart attack

For each of the following, circle the correct spelling of the term:

91. ventricel   ventrical   ventricle

92. aorta   aorto   aorrta

93. thrombos   thrombus   thrommbus

94. myocardial   mycardial   myocardiol

95. hypatension   hyptension   hypotension

96. diastolie   diastoly   diastole

97. ischemia   ishchemia   ishemia

98. oclusion   occlusion   ocllusion

99. infart   enfarct   infarct

100. anuerysm   aneurysm   annurysm

101. atherosclerotic   atherosclerrotic   atherasclerotic

102. thromboflebitus   thromboflebitis   thrombophlebitis

103. anngiogram   angiogram   angeogram

104. defibrillation   defibillation   defibrilation

105. antarhythmic   antiarrhythmic   antiarhythmic

Write the term that means the opposite of each given term:

106. vasoconstriction _____

107. coagulant _____

108. hypotension _____

109. bradycardia _____

110. diastole _____

MEDICAL RECORD ANALYSES

MEDICAL RECORD 7.1

Progress Note

S: This 54 y.o. ♂ was admitted to CCU with onset of acute anterior chest pain radiating to the left shoulder and SOB; pt underwent a CABG × 4 six months ago.

O: BP 190/110, P 100, R 72, T 38°C
On PE, pt was in moderate to severe distress. An ECG showed sinus tachycardia, and a CXR revealed left ventricular hypertrophy.

A: R/O MI

P: Order blood enzyme measurement STAT
echocardiogram
CT scan of chest

1. What is the patient's CC?

   a. severe angina

   b. angina developing slowly over time

   c. enlargement of the heart

   d. fast heart rate

   e. slow heart rate

2. Describe the procedure that the patient underwent 6 months ago:

   a. surgery to dilate and open narrowed portions of coronary arteries

   b. replacement of occluded arteries with transplanted portions of vein

   c. replacement of a diseased heart valve

   d. coring of the lining of an artery to remove a clot

   e. heart transplant

3. Where was the patient treated?

   a. outpatient medical office

   b. outpatient emergency room

   c. inpatient intensive care

   d. inpatient coronary care

   e. outpatient cardiology department

4. What type of physician is most appropriate to provide initial care and assessment of this patient?

   a. emergency room physician

   b. internist

   c. gerontologist

   d. cardiovascular surgeon

   e. cardiologist

5. What did the electrical picture of the heart reveal?

   a. extremely rapid but regular contractions of the heart

   b. slow heart rate

   c. chaotic, irregular contractions of the heart

   d. fast heart rate

   e. interference with normal electrical conduction of the heart known as a block

6. What was the assessment?

   a. patient may have had a heart attack

   b. patient may be suffering from right heart failure

   c. patient has congestive heart failure

   d. patient may have high blood pressure

   e. patient may have an enlarged heart

7. What were the objective findings of the chest radiograph?

   a. unknown

   b. increase in size of left ventricle

   c. vessel disease

   d. dead heart muscle

   e. fast heart rate

8. Identify the x-ray imaging procedure ordered in the plan:

   a. sonogram of heart

   b. chest radiography

   c. blood pressure

   d. computed tomography

   e. biochemistry panel

MEDICAL RECORD 7.2

Richard Stratten has had serious heart problems for more than 10 years. He has had two operations. During the past 6 months, he has developed increasing pain in the chest and is having more trouble breathing. His cardiologist, Dr. Charles Feingold, has now admitted him to Central Medical Center for further tests.

Directions

Read Medical Record 7.2 for Richard Stratten (pages 233–236) and answer the following questions. This record is the history and physical examination dictated by Dr. Feingold after his examination of Mr. Stratten.

QUESTIONS ABOUT MEDICAL RECORD 7.2

Write your answers in the spaces provided.

1. Below are medical terms used in this record you have not yet encountered in this text. Underline each where it appears in the record and define below:

   obtuse _____

   dyspnea (dyspneic) _____

   hiatal hernia _____

   basilar rales _____

   visceromegaly _____

   clubbing _____

2. In your own words, not using medical terminology, briefly describe why Mr. Stratten has been admitted to the hospital and what test he will be undergoing.

   _____

   _____

   _____

3. Name the diagnosis that underlies the nature of Mr. Stratten's heart conditions.

   _____

   _____

   _____

   Briefly describe this diagnosis using nonmedical language.

   _____

   _____

4. Identify the surgical procedure noted in the history that was *initially* performed to treat Mr. Stratten's heart disease.

   a. dilation of narrow occluded coronary arteries

   b. replacement of occluded arteries with transplanted portion of vein

   c. replacement of a diseased heart valve

   d. coring of the lining of an artery to remove a thrombus

   e. heart transplant

5. What were the patient's symptoms 8 years later on May 15, 20xx?

   _____

   Using nonmedical language, briefly describe the diagnosis made at that time.

   _____

   _____

   _____

6. Describe the test that showed changes consistent with the diagnosis.

   _____

   _____

7. Spell out TPA, and identify the reason why the drug was given to Mr. Stratten.

8. Which of the following were findings of the radiographic tests performed after the May 15 hospitalization? (Mark all that are appropriate.)

   a. hemorrhage of insertion site of obtuse marginal artery graft

   b. thromboembolism in the left anterior descending artery

   c. occluded circumflex artery

   d. torn sutures of the circumflex artery graft

   e. stenosis of the left anterior descending artery graft

   f. total occlusion of the left internal mammary vein graft

   g. dilated right coronary artery graft

9. List the arteries that were grafted in *both* bypass operations.

   _____

   _____

10. Using nonmedical language, list the three symptoms Mr. Stratten is now experiencing.

    a. _____

    b. _____

    c. _____

11. Mr. Stratten is taking eight different medications. Translate the medication instruction for these:

Drug Name	Dosage	Frequency of Dose
_____	_____	_____
_____	_____	_____
_____	_____	_____
_____	_____	_____
_____	_____	_____
_____	_____	_____
_____	_____	_____
_____	_____	_____

12. What family members have had a medical history of problems in the same body system?

_____

_____

13. In addition to Mr. Stratten's heart problems, Dr. Feingold's physical examination revealed abnormal findings in what other areas?

a. head

b. abdomen

c. extremities

d. all of the above

e. none of the above

14. What does "probable end-stage cardiomyopathy" mean? What treatment seems possible to Dr. Feingold, even though he had not yet performed the diagnostic tests for which he hospitalized Mr. Stratten?

_____

_____

_____

_____

CENTRAL MEDICAL CENTER
211 Medical Center Drive • Central City, US 90000-1234 • PHONE: (012) 125-6784 • FAX: (012) 125-9999

HISTORY

CHIEF COMPLAINT:
The patient is admitted for heart catheterization and coronary arteriography with a view of possible cardiac transplantation.

HISTORY OF PRESENT ILLNESS:
The patient is a 53-year-old Caucasian male who has had a known history of coronary artery disease. The patient had initial 4-vessel bypass surgery 10 years ago on July 18, 20xx, at which time the patient had a saphenous vein bypass graft to the left anterior descending, diagonal, obtuse marginal, and right coronary artery.

Eight years later, on May 15, 20xx, the patient was rehospitalized at Central Medical Center because of acute chest pain with electrocardiogram changes consistent with acute inferior wall infarction for which the patient was given TPA. Following that, the patient had dramatic improvement in terms of electrocardiogram changes and symptoms and subsequently underwent reevaluation, including heart catheterization and coronary arteriography. This revealed the following findings:

> Native right coronary artery, left anterior descending, and circumflex were all totally occluded. The bypass graft to the left anterior descending had an 80% stenosis proximally and was totally occluded distally. Circumflex was previously totally occluded. Bypass graft to the obtuse marginal had a 70% occlusion followed by 90% occlusion at the insertion site of the graft. The right coronary artery graft had 95-98% stenosis. This diagonal graft was previously demonstrated to be totally occluded.

Because of this, the patient underwent a second bypass surgery on May 25, 20xx, at which time the patient had a left internal mammary graft to the left anterior descending and right internal mammary graft to the diagonal. The patient also had a saphenous vein bypass graft to the obtuse marginal and right coronary artery.

Since that time, the patient has continued to have intermittent angina, particularly within the last six months or so. In addition, the patient has gotten progressively weaker and dyspneic.

(continued)

HISTORY AND PHYSICAL PAGE 1	PT. NAME: STRATTEN, R. ID NO: ROOM NO: ADM. DATE: October 15, 20xx ATT. PHYS: C. FEINGOLD, M.D.

Medical Record 7.2

CENTRAL MEDICAL CENTER
211 Medical Center Drive • Central City, US 90000-1234 • PHONE: (012) 125-6784 • FAX: (012) 125-9999

HISTORY

At the present time, the patient is taking Prinivil 5 mg daily in a.m., Procainamide 500 mg q 6 h, Lasix 80 mg b.i.d., Lipitor 10 mg daily, Lanoxin 0.25 mg daily, Aspirin 81 mg daily, Atenolol 10 mg daily, and Nitro-Dur 0.4 mg/hr patch, apply daily q a.m. and remove h.s.

Because of increasing symptoms, the patient is being evaluated for cardiac transplant. The patient is undergoing heart catheterization for evaluation.

PAST MEDICAL HISTORY:
PAST ILLNESSES: There is no prior history of hypertension or diabetes. See above regarding previous coronary bypass surgery and myocardial infarctions.

The patient has a known hiatal hernia, but it is asymptomatic at this time.

ALLERGIES: None known.

MEDICATIONS: See above.

PREVIOUS OPERATIONS: See above.

FAMILY HISTORY:
Father died of coronary artery disease at age 50. Paternal uncle also died of coronary artery disease. Maternal uncle and grandfather are both diabetic. The patient has no siblings. The remainder of family history is noncontributory.

SOCIAL HISTORY:
MARITAL HISTORY: Single.

HABITS: The patient is a nonsmoker and denies drinking ethanolic beverages.

INVENTORY BY SYSTEMS:
Noncontributory. There is no prior history of transient ischemic attack or claudication.

(continued)

HISTORY AND PHYSICAL PAGE 2	PT. NAME: STRATTEN, R. ID NO: ROOM NO: ADM. DATE: October 15, 20xx ATT. PHYS: C. FEINGOLD, M.D.

Medical Record 7.2 *Continued.*

CENTRAL MEDICAL CENTER
211 Medical Center Drive • Central City, US 90000-1234 • PHONE: (012) 125-6784 • FAX: (012) 125-9999

PHYSICAL EXAMINATION

GENERAL:
The patient is a well-developed, well-nourished Caucasian male who is not in acute distress.

VITAL SIGNS:
Blood Pressure: 120/80. Pulse: 70 and regular.

HEENT:
HEAD: Normocephalic, atraumatic.

NECK: Neck veins are essentially normal. There are no carotid bruits.

CHEST:
HEART: Revealed cardiomegaly. There is no murmur. There is an equivocal third heart sound.

LUNGS: There are a few basilar rales.

ABDOMEN:
No visceromegaly. The bowel sounds are normal. No masses or tenderness.

RECTAL:
Deferred.

EXTREMITIES:
No clubbing, cyanosis, or peripheral edema. The peripheral pulses are intact.

NEUROLOGIC:
Physiologic.

IMPRESSION:
CORONARY ARTERY DISEASE WITH PREVIOUS ANTERIOR AND INFERIOR WALL
INFARCTION STATUS POST PREVIOUS CORONARY BYPASS SURGERY x 2 WITH
PROGRESSIVE INCREASE IN SYMPTOMATOLOGY IN TERMS OF ANGINA AND
DYSPNEA WITH PROBABLE END-STAGE CARDIOMYOPATHY.

(continued)

HISTORY AND PHYSICAL PAGE 3	PT. NAME: STRATTEN, R. ID NO: ROOM NO: ADM. DATE: October 15, 20xx ATT. PHYS: C. FEINGOLD, M.D.

Medical Record 7.2 *Continued.*

CENTRAL MEDICAL CENTER
211 Medical Center Drive • Central City, US 90000-1234 • PHONE: (012) 125-6784 • FAX: (012) 125-9999

HISTORY AND PHYSICAL

The details of heart catheterization and coronary angiography have been discussed with the patient, including the risks and potential complications. The patient understands and wishes to proceed. This will be performed on October 16, 20xx.

C. Feingold, M.D.

CF:ti

D: 10/19/20xx
T: 10/20/20xx

HISTORY AND PHYSICAL Page 4	PT. NAME: STRATTEN, R. ID NO: ROOM NO: ADM. DATE: October 15, 20xx ATT. PHYS: C. FEINGOLD, M.D.

Medical Record 7.2 *Continued.*

MEDICAL RECORD 7.3

William Smith woke in the middle of the night with substernal chest heaviness that radiated to both arms. After getting no relief from taking aspirin and antacids, he went to the emergency room and was seen by Dr. Roland Galasso. The chest pain subsided only after administration of intravenous nitroglycerin. Dr. Galasso decided to admit Mr. Smith for further cardiac evaluation and treatment. A cardiac catheterization was performed the next day.

Directions

Read Medical Record 7.3 for William Smith (pages 239–240) and answer the following questions. This record is a report of the cardiac catheterization performed by Dr. Galasso and transcribed by a cardiology department transcriptionist.

QUESTIONS ABOUT MEDICAL RECORD 7.3

Write your answers in the spaces provided.

1. Below are medical terms used in this record you have not yet encountered in this text. Underline each where it appears in the record:

   ostium _____

   hemodynamic _____

   mitral regurgitation _____

   focal _____

2. In your own words, not using medical terminology, briefly describe the *indications* for performing the cardiac catheterization.

   _____

3. Put the following actions in correct order by numbering them 1 to 14:

   _____ pigtail catheter advanced to the left ventricle

   _____ hemostasis obtained by C-clamp pressure

   _____ right coronary arteriography performed

   _____ pigtail catheter exchanged for left coronary artery catheter

   _____ informed consent signed

   _____ arterial pressures recorded

   _____ right groin prepped and draped

   _____ left coronary arteriography performed

   _____ right femoral artery entered and Cordis sheath inserted

   _____ right coronary catheter and femoral artery sheath removed

_____ pigtail catheter inserted through sheath and guided to descending thoracic aorta

_____ left coronary catheter exchanged for right coronary catheter

_____ left ventriculography performed

_____ heparin administered

4. Briefly describe the conclusions of the procedure in nonmedical language:

a._____

b._____

5. From the recommendations, describe the test that will be performed right away.

_____

6. Identify the possible complications likely to occur in the future.

_____

_____

_____

Describe the procedure that is recommended should these complications occur.

_____

_____

_____

CENTRAL MEDICAL CENTER
211 Medical Center Drive • Central City, US 90000-1234 • PHONE: (012) 125-6784 • FAX: (012) 125-9999

CARDIAC CATHETERIZATION

DATE OF PROCEDURE: November 3, 20xx

PROCEDURE PERFORMED: Left heart catheterization with left ventriculography, left and right coronary arteriography.

INDICATIONS: Recent onset of angina pectoris.

CATHETERS USED: 6 French pigtail Cordis, 6 French JL4, 6 French JR4.

CONTRAST: Optiray-320.

MEDICATIONS GIVEN: None.

PROCEDURE IN DETAIL:
Informed consent was obtained. The patient was brought to the Cardiac Catheterization Laboratory where the right groin was prepped and draped in the usual sterile fashion. The skin was anesthetized with 1% Xylocaine. The right femoral artery was entered by Seldinger technique and a 7 French Cordis sheath was inserted through which a 7 French angled pigtail catheter was inserted and advanced under fluoroscopic guidance to the descending thoracic aorta. Heparin was administered. Arterial pressures were recorded. The pigtail catheter was then advanced across the aortic valve to the left ventricle. Pressures were recorded, and left ventriculography was performed by power injection of 40 cc of contrast at 12 cc per second with cine in the RAO projection. Post ventriculography pressures were recorded, and pullback across the aortic valve was performed. The pigtail catheter was exchanged for a left coronary catheter as listed above which was advanced to the ostium of the left coronary artery. Left coronary arteriography was performed by hand injections of 8-10 cc of contrast with cine in multiple views. The left coronary catheter was exchanged for the right coronary catheter, as listed above, and it was then advanced to the ostium of the right coronary artery. Right coronary arteriography was performed by hand injections of 8-10 cc of contrast with cine in multiple views. The right coronary catheter and femoral artery sheath were removed, and hemostasis was obtained by C-clamp pressure for 30-45 minutes. Complications: None. Fluoro time: 2.2 minutes. Contrast dose: 76 cc.

(continued)

CARDIAC CATHETERIZATION Page 1	PT. NAME: SMITH, W. ID NO: ROOM NO: ATT. PHYS: R. GALASSO, M.D.

Medical Record 7.3

CENTRAL MEDICAL CENTER
211 Medical Center Drive • Central City, US 90000-1234 • PHONE: (012) 125-6784 • FAX: (012) 125-9999

CARDIAC CATHETERIZATION

FINDINGS:

1. HEMODYNAMICS:
Left ventricle: 182/0; end-diastolic: 16 mm Hg. Aorta: 190/70; mean: 110 mm Hg.

2. LEFT VENTRICULOGRAPHY:
The left ventricle is normal in configuration, dimensions, and segmental wall motion with ejection fraction computed at 58% by area-length method. There is no evidence of mitral regurgitation.

3. CORONARY ARTERIOGRAPHY:
Left Main: Normal.

Left Anterior Descending: Seventy percent focal stenosis immediately after the first septal perforator branch. The remainder of the left anterior descending is within normal limits.

Ramus Intermedius: Normal.

Left Circumflex: Nondominant vessel with one marginal branch, all free of disease.

Right Coronary Artery: Large dominant vessel free of disease.

CONCLUSIONS:

1. MODERATE STENOSIS OF THE LEFT ANTERIOR DESCENDING CORONARY ARTERY.

2. NORMAL LEFT VENTRICULAR FUNCTION WITH EJECTION FRACTION 56%.

RECOMMENDATIONS:
The patient will be managed medically at this time. Radionuclide perfusion stress testing will be performed. If the patient has progressive anginal symptoms or has marked reversible ischemia in the distribution of the left anterior descending coronary artery, angioplasty of this vessel would be considered.

CARDIAC CATHETERIZATION Page 2	PT. NAME: SMITH, W. ID NO: ROOM NO: ATT. PHYS: R. GALASSO, M.D.

Medical Record 7.3 *Continued.*

Chapter 8

Blood and Lymph Systems

OBJECTIVES

After completion of this chapter, you will be able to

- Define common term components used in relation to the blood and lymph systems
- Describe the basic functions of the blood and lymph systems
- Define the basic anatomical terms referring to blood and lymph
- Define common symptomatic and diagnostic terms referring to the blood and lymph systems
- List common diagnostic tests and procedures related to the blood and lymph systems
- Identify common operative terms referring to the blood and lymph systems
- Identify common therapeutic terms including drug classifications related to the blood and lymph systems
- Explain terms and abbreviations used in documenting medical records involving the blood or lymph systems

Combining Forms

Combining Form	Meaning	Example
blast/o	germ or bud	erythroblastemia ĕ-rith´rō-blas-tē´mē-ă
-blast (also a suffix)		megaloblast meg´ă-lō-blast
chrom/o	color	chromic krō´mik
chromat/o		hemochromatosis hē´mō-krō-mă-tō´sis
chyl/o	juice	chylemia kī-lē´mē-ă
hem/o	blood	hemostat hē´mō-stat
hemat/o		hematopoiesis hē´mă-tō-poy-ē´sis

Combining Form	Meaning	Example
immun/o	safe	immunology im´yū-nol´ō-jē
lymph/o	clear fluid	lymphogenous lim-foj´ĕ-nŭs
morph/o	form	morphologic mōr-fō-loj´ik
myel/o	bone marrow (also spinal cord)	myelogenous mī-ĕ-loj´ĕ-nŭs
phag/o	eat or swallow	phagocytosis fag´ō-sī-tō´sis
plas/o	formation	aplastic ā-plas´tik
reticul/o	a net	reticulocyte re-tik´yū-lō-sīt
splen/o	spleen	splenomegaly splē-nō-meg´ă-lē
thromb/o	clot	thrombocyte throm´bō-sīt
thym/o	thymus gland	thymic thī´mik

Blood System Overview

The blood circulates through the blood vessels to transport oxygen, nutrients, and hormones to body cells and to carry away wastes. The liquid portion of the blood is called *plasma*. The cellular components suspended in the plasma are the *erythrocytes, leukocytes,* and *platelets*. The portion of the plasma that remains after the clotting process is called *serum* (Fig. 8.1).

Anatomical Terms

Term	Meaning
TERMS RELATED TO BLOOD FLUID	
plasma plaz´mah	liquid portion of the blood and lymph containing water, proteins, salts, nutrients, hormones, vitamins, and cellular components (leukocytes, erythrocytes, and platelets)
serum sēr´ŭm	liquid portion of the blood left after the clotting process
CELLULAR COMPONENTS OF THE BLOOD	
erythrocyte ĕ-rith´rō-sīt	red blood cell that transports oxygen and carbon dioxide within the bloodstream
hemoglobin hē´mō-glō´bin	protein-iron compound contained in the erythrocyte that has bonding capabilities for the transport of oxygen and carbon dioxide

SERUM. Serum is Latin for whey, the watery part of curdled milk, which looks similar to the watery part of clotted blood. The term was first recorded in English in 1672.

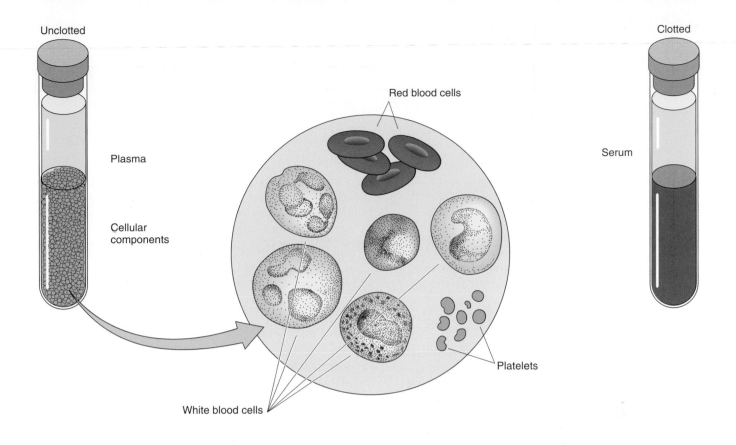

Unclotted

Plasma

Cellular components

Red blood cells

Platelets

White blood cells

Clotted

Serum

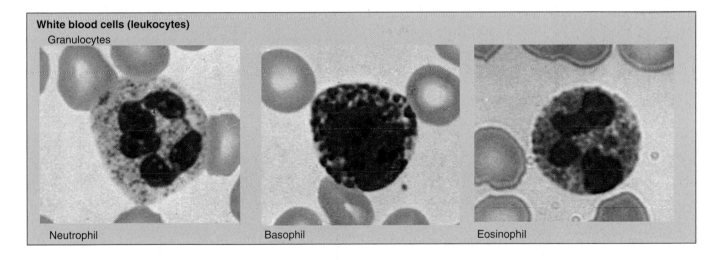

White blood cells (leukocytes)
Granulocytes

Neutrophil

Basophil

Eosinophil

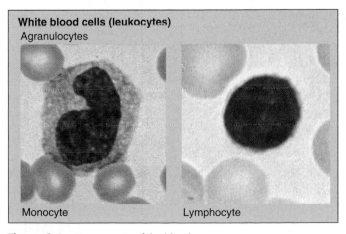

White blood cells (leukocytes)
Agranulocytes

Monocyte

Lymphocyte

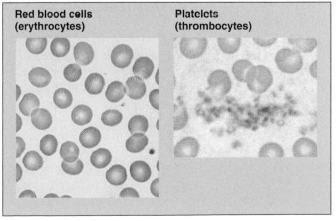

Red blood cells (erythrocytes)

Platelets (thrombocytes)

Figure 8.1 Components of the blood.

Term	Meaning
leukocyte lu´kō-sīt	white blood cell that protects the body from invasion of harmful substances
granulocytes gran´yū-lō-sīts	a group of leukocytes containing granules in their cytoplasm
neutrophil nū´trō-fil	a granular leukocyte, named for the neutral stain of its granules, that fights infection by swallowing bacteria (phagocytosis) (neutro = neither; phil = attraction for)
polymorphonuclear leukocyte (PMN) pol-ē-mōr´fō-nū´klē-ăr	another term for neutrophil, named for the many segments present in its nucleus (poly = many; morpho = form; nucleus = kernel)
band	an immature neutrophil
eosinophil ē-ō-sin´ō-fil	a granular leukocyte, named for the rose-color stain of its granules, that increases with allergy and some infections [eos = dawn-colored (rosy); phil = attraction for]
basophil bā´sō-fil	a granular leukocyte, named for the dark stain of its granules, that brings anticoagulant substances to inflamed tissues (baso = base; phil = attraction for)
agranulocytes ă-gran´yū-lō-sīts	a group of leukocytes without granules in their nuclei
lymphocyte lim´fō-sīt	an agranulocytic leukocyte that is active in the process of immunity—there are four categories of lymphocytes: T cells (thymus dependent) B cells (bone marrow derived) NK cells (natural killer) K-type cells
monocyte mon´ō-sīt	an agranulocytic leukocyte that performs phagocytosis to fight infection (mono = one)
platelets plāt´lets	thrombocytes; cell fragments in the blood essential for blood clotting (coagulation)

Lymphatic System Overview

The lymphatic system is made up of an intricate network of capillaries, vessels, valves, ducts, nodes, and organs. It protects the body by filtering microorganisms and foreign particles from the lymph and supporting the activities of the lymphocytes in the immune response. It also serves to maintain the body's internal fluid environment by acting as an intermediary between the blood in the capillaries and tissue cells. In addition, it is responsible for carrying fats away from the digestive organs (Fig. 8.2).

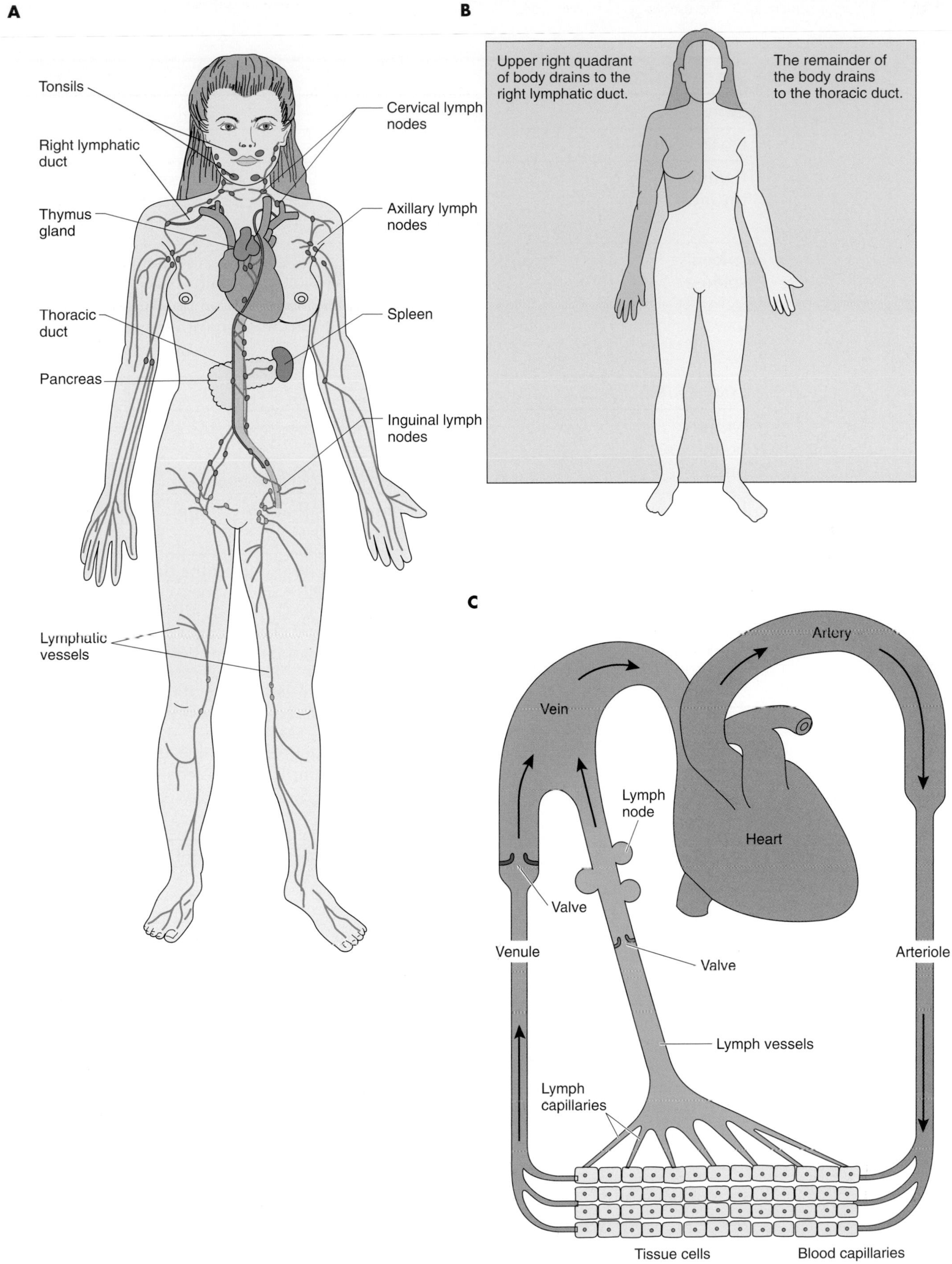

A

Tonsils

Right lymphatic duct

Thymus gland

Thoracic duct

Pancreas

Lymphatic vessels

Cervical lymph nodes

Axillary lymph nodes

Spleen

Inguinal lymph nodes

B

Upper right quadrant of body drains to the right lymphatic duct.

The remainder of the body drains to the thoracic duct.

C

Vein

Artery

Lymph node

Heart

Valve

Venule

Valve

Arteriole

Lymph vessels

Lymph capillaries

Tissue cells

Blood capillaries

Figure 8.2 Lymphatic system. **A.** Lymph structures. **B.** Lymph drainage. **C.** Blood and lymph circulation.

Anatomical Terms

Term	Meaning
LYMPH ORGANS	
thymus thī´mŭs	the primary gland of the lymphatic system, located within the mediastinum; helps maintain the body's immune response by producing T lymphocytes
spleen splēn	the organ between the stomach and diaphragm that filters out aging blood cells, removes cellular debris by performing phagocytosis, and provides the environment for the initiation of immune responses by lymphocytes
LYMPH STRUCTURES	
lymph body limf	fluid originating in the organs and tissues of the that is circulated through the lymph vessels
lymph capillaries limf kap´i-lār-ēz	microscopic vessels that draw lymph from the tissues to the lymph vessels
lymph vessels limf ves´ĕlz	vessels that receive lymph from the lymph capillaries and circulate it to the lymph nodes
lacteals lak´tē-ălz	specialized lymph vessels in the small intestine that absorb fat into the bloodstream (lacteus = milky)
chyle kīl	a white or pale yellow substance of the lymph that contains fatty substances absorbed by the lacteals
lymph nodes limf nōdz	many small oval structures that filter the lymph received from the lymph vessels—major locations include the cervical region, axillary region, and inguinal region
lymph ducts limf dŭktz	collecting channels that carry lymph from the lymph nodes to the veins
right lymphatic duct lim-fat´ik dŭkt	receives lymph from the upper-right part of the body
thoracic duct thō-ras´ik dŭkt	receives lymph from the left side of the head, neck, chest, abdomen, left arm, and lower extremities
IMMUNITY	
antigen an´ti-jen	a substance that, when introduced into the body, causes the formation of antibodies against it
antibody an´tē-bod-ē	a substance produced by the body that destroys or inactivates an antigen that has entered the body
immunoglobulins (Ig) im´yu-nō-glob´yu-lins	protein antibodies secreted by B lymphocytes that protect the body from invasion of foreign pathogens; the five major classes include IgA, IgD, IgE, IgG, and IgM

Term	Meaning
immunity i-myū´ni-tē	process of disease protection induced by exposure to an antigen
active immunity ak´tiv i-myū´ni-tē	an immunity that protects the body against a future infection, as the result of antibodies that develop *naturally* after contracting an infection or *artificially* after administration of a vaccine
passive immunity pas´iv i-myū´ni-tē	an immunity resulting from antibodies that are conveyed *naturally* through the placenta to a fetus or *artificially* by injection of a serum containing antibodies

Symptomatic and Diagnostic Terms

Term	Meaning
SYMPTOMATIC	
Related to Blood	
microcytosis mī´krō-sī-tō´sis	the presence of small red blood cells (Fig. 8.3)
macrocytosis mak´rō-sī-tō´sis	the presence of large red blood cells (see Fig. 8.4)
anisocytosis an-ī´sō-sī-tō´sis	the presence of red blood cells of unequal size (an = without; iso = equal) (see Fig. 8.4)
poikilocytosis poy´ki-lō-sī-tō´sis	the presence of large, irregularly shaped red blood cells (poikil/o = irregular) (Fig. 8.4)
reticulocytosis re-tik´yū-lō-sī-tō´sis	an increase of immature erythrocytes in the blood
erythropenia ĕ-rith-rō-pē´nē-ă	an abnormally reduced number of red blood cells
lymphocytopenia lim´fō-sī-tō-pē´nē-ă	an abnormally reduced number of lymphocytes
neutropenia nū´trō-pē´nē-ă	a decrease in the number of neutrophils
pancytopenia pan´sī-tō-pē´nē-ă	an abnormally reduced number of all cellular components in the blood
hemolysis hē-mol´i-sis	breakdown of the red blood cell membrane
Related to Lymph	
immunocompromised im´yū-nō-kom´pro-mīzd	impaired immunological defenses caused by an immunodeficiency disorder or therapy with immunosuppressive agents
immunosuppression im´yū-nō-sŭ-presh´ŭn	impaired ability to provide an immune response
lymphadenopathy lim-fad-ĕ-nop´ă-thē	the presence of enlarged (diseased) lymph nodes

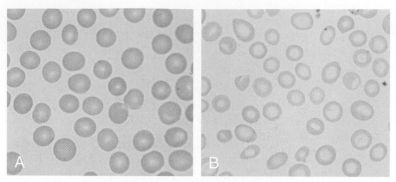

Figure 8.3 A blood smear showing normal erythrocytes (**A**) compared with a blood smear revealing microcytic-hypochromic erythrocytes in a patient with iron deficiency anemia (**B**).

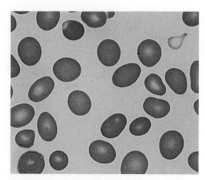

Figure 8.4 Photomicrograph of a blood smear from a patient with pernicious anemia reveals macrocytosis, anisocytosis, and poikilocytosis.

Term	Meaning
splenomegaly splē-nō-meg´ă-lē	enlargement of the spleen
DIAGNOSTIC	
acquired immunodeficiency syndrome (AIDS) ă-kwīrd´ i-myūn´o-dē-fish´en-sē sin´drōm	a syndrome caused by the human immunodeficiency virus (HIV) that renders immune cells ineffective, permitting opportunistic infections, malignancies, and neurological diseases to develop; it is transmitted sexually or through exposure to contaminated blood
anemia ă-nē´mē-ă	a condition in which there is a reduction in the number of red blood cells, the amount of hemoglobin, or the volume of packed red cells in the blood, resulting in a diminished ability of the red blood cells to transport oxygen to the tissues; common types follow:
aplastic anemia ā-plas´tik	a normocytic-normochromic type of anemia characterized by the failure of bone marrow to produce red blood cells
iron deficiency anemia i´ern dē-fish´en-sē	a microcytic-hypochromic type of anemia characterized by a lack of iron, affecting production of hemoglobin and characterized by small red blood cells containing low amounts of hemoglobin (see Fig. 8.3)
pernicious anemia per-nish´ŭs	a macrocytic-normochromic type of anemia characterized by an inadequate supply of vitamin B$_{12}$, causing red blood cells to become large, varied in shape, and reduced in number (see Fig. 8.4)
autoimmune disease aw-tō-i-myun´ di-zēz´	any disorder characterized by abnormal function of the immune system that causes the body to produce antibodies against itself, resulting in tissue destruction or loss of function; rheumatoid arthritis and lupus are examples of autoimmune diseases

Term	Meaning
erythroblastosis fetalis ĕ-rith′rō-blas-tō′sis fē′tă′lis	a disorder that results from the incompatibility of a fetus with an Rh-positive blood factor and a mother who is Rh negative, causing red blood cell destruction in the fetus; necessitates a blood transfusion to save the fetus
Rh factor	the presence, or lack, of antigens on the surface of red blood cells that may cause a reaction between the blood of the mother and fetus, resulting in fetal anemia
Rh positive	the presence of antigens
Rh negative	the absence of antigens
hemochromatosis hē′mō-krō-mă-tō′sis	a hereditary disorder that results in an excessive buildup of iron deposits in the body
hemophilia hē-mō-fil′ē-ă	a group of hereditary bleeding disorders in which there is a defect in clotting factors necessary for the coagulation of blood
leukemia lū-kē′mē-ă	a chronic or acute malignant (cancerous) disease of the blood-forming organs, marked by abnormal leukocytes in the blood and bone marrow; classified according to the types of white cells affected (e.g., myelocytic, lymphocytic)
myelodysplasia mī′ĕ-lō-dis-plā′zē-ă	a disorder within the bone marrow characterized by the proliferation of abnormal stem cells (cells that give rise to the different types of blood cells); usually develops into a specific type of leukemia
lymphoma lim-fō′mă	any neoplastic disorder of lymph tissue, usually malignant, as in Hodgkin disease
metastasis mĕ-tas′tă-sis	the process by which cancer cells are spread by blood or lymph circulation to distant organs
mononucleosis mon′ō-nū-klē-ō′sis	a condition caused by the Epstein-Barr virus characterized by an increase in mononuclear cells (monocytes and lymphocytes) in the blood, along with enlarged lymph nodes (lymphadenopathy), fatigue, and sore throat (pharyngitis)
polycythemia pol′ē-sī-thē′mē-ă	an increase in the number of erythrocytes and hemoglobin in the blood
septicemia sep-ti-sē′mē-ă	a systemic disease caused by the infection of microorganisms and their toxins in the circulating blood
thrombocytopenia throm′bō-sī-tō-pē′nē-ă	a bleeding disorder characterized by an abnormal decrease in the number of platelets in the blood, which impairs the clotting process

Diagnostic Tests and Procedures

Test or Procedure	Explanation
BLOOD STUDIES	
blood chemistry blŭd kem´is-trē	a test of the fluid portion of blood to measure the presence of a chemical constituent (e.g., glucose, cholesterol)
blood chemistry panels	specialized batteries of automated blood chemistry tests performed on a single sample of blood; used as a general screen for disease or to target specific organs or conditions (e.g., metabolic panel, lipid panel, arthritis panel)
basic metabolic panel met-ă-bol´ik	battery of tests used as a general screen for disease: calcium, carbon dioxide (CO_2), chloride, creatinine, glucose, potassium, sodium and blood urea nitrogen (BUN)
comprehensive metabolic panel	tests in addition to basic metabolic panel for expanded screening purposes: albumin, bilirubin, alkaline phosphatase, protein, ALT, and AST (Fig. 8.5)
blood culture blŭd kŭl´chŭr	a test to determine if infection is present in the bloodstream by isolating a specimen of blood in an environment that encourages the growth of microorganisms; the specimen is observed and the organisms that grow in the culture are identified
CD4 cell count	a measure of the number of CD4 cells (a subset of T lymphocytes) in the blood; used in monitoring the course of HIV and timing the treatment of AIDS; the normal adult range is 600–1,500 cells
complete blood count (CBC)	the most common laboratory blood test performed as a screen of general health or for diagnostic purposes; the following is a listing of the component tests included in a CBC (Fig. 8.6) (note: CBC results are usually reported with normal values so that the clinician can interpret the results based on the instrumentation used by the laboratory; normal ranges also may vary depending on factors such as the region and climate)
white blood count (WBC)	a count of the number of white blood cells per cubic millimeter obtained by manual or automated laboratory methods
red blood count (RBC)	a count of the number of red blood cells per cubic millimeter obtained by manual or automated laboratory methods
hemoglobin (HGB or Hgb) hē´mō-glō´bin	a test to determine the blood level of hemoglobin (expressed in grams)
hematocrit (HCT or Hct) hē´mă-tō-krit	a measurement of the percentage of packed red blood cells in a given volume of blood

CENTRAL MEDICAL CENTER
211 Medical Center Drive • Central City, US 90000-1234 • PHONE: (012) 125-6784 • FAX: (012) 125-9999

11/02/20xx
14:27

NAME : TEST, PATIENT LOC: TEST DOB: 02/03/xx AGE: 38Y
MR# : TEST-221 SEX: M
ACCT# : H111111111

M63561 COLL: 11/02/20xx 13:24 REC: 11/02/20xx 13:25

COMPREHENSIVE METABOLIC PANEL

Blood Urea Nitrogen (BUN)	*30	[5–25]	mg/dL
Sodium	139	[135–153]	mEq/L
Potassium	4.2	[3.5–5.3]	mEq/L
Chloride	105	[101–111]	mEq/L
Carbon Dioxide (CO$_2$)	27	[24–31]	mmol/L
Glucose, Random	*148	[70–110]	mg/dL
Creatinine	*1.5	[<1.5]	mg/dL
SGOT (AST)	18	[10–42]	U/L
SGPT (ALT)	*8	[10–60]	U/L
Alkaline Phosphatase	58	[42–121]	U/L
Total Protein	6.5	[6.0–8.0]	G/dL
Albumin	3.7	[3.5–5.0]	G/dL
Amylase	33	[<129]	U/L
Bilirubin, Total	0.7	[<1.5]	mg/dL
Calcium, Total	9.7	[8.6–10.6]	mg/dL

TEST, PATIENT TEST-221 END OF REPORT PAGE 1
11/02/20xx 14:27

INTERIM REPORT COMPLETED

Figure 8.5 Comprehensive metabolic panel report. Note: Normal ranges are in brackets [ ].

Test or Procedure	Explanation
blood indices in´di-sēz	calculations of RBC, HGB, and HCT results to determine the average size, hemoglobin concentration, and content of red blood cells for classification of anemia
mean corpuscular (cell) volume (MCV) kōr-pŭs´kyū-lăr	a calculation of the volume of individual cells in cubic microns using HCT and RBC results: MCV = HCT/RBC
mean corpuscular (cell) hemoglobin (MCH) kōr-pŭs´kyū-lăr hē´mō-glō´bin	a calculation of the content in weight of hemoglobin in the average red blood cell using HGB and RBC results: MCH = HGB/RBC
mean corpuscular (cell) hemoglobin concentration (MCHC) hē´mō-glō´bin kon-sen-trā´shŭn	a calculation of the average hemoglobin concentration in each red blood cell using HGB and HCT results: MCHC = HGB/HCT

CENTRAL MEDICAL CENTER
211 Medical Center Drive • Central City, US 90000-1234 • PHONE: (012) 125-6784 • FAX: (012) 125-9999

11/02/20xx
14:27

NAME	: TEST, PATIENT	LOC: TEST	DOB: 2/2/xx	AGE: 27Y
MR#	: TEST-221			SEX: M
ACCT#	: H111111111			

M63558 COLL: 11/2/20xx 13:23   REC: 11/2/20xx 13:24

HEMOGRAM
CBC

WBC	*11.5	[4.5–10.5]	K/UL
RBC	5.84	[4.6–6.2]	M/UL
HGB	17.2	[14.0–18.0]	G/DL
HCT	50.8	[42.0–52.0]	%
MCV	87	[82–92]	FL
MCH	29.5	[27–31]	PG
MCHC	33.9	[32–36]	G/DL
PLT	202	[150–450]	K/UL

Auto Lymph %	15	[20–40]	%
Auto Mono %	2	[1–11]	%
Auto Neutro %	82	[50–75]	%
Auto Eos %	1	[0–6]	%
Auto Baso %	0	[0–2]	%
Auto Lymph #	1.7	[1.5–4.0]	K/UL
Auto Mono #	0.2	[0.2–0.9]	K/UL
Auto Neutro #	9.4	[1.0–7.0]	K/UL
Auto Eos #	0.1	[0–0.7]	K/UL
Auto Baso #	0.0	[0–0.2]	K/UL

TEST, PATIENT	TEST-221	END OF REPORT	PAGE 1
11/02/20xx	14:27		INTERIM REPORT

INTERIM REPORT COMPLETE

Figure 8.6   Complete blood count (CBC) report.

Test or Procedure	Explanation
differential count	a determination of the number of each type of white blood cell (leukocyte) seen on a stained blood smear; each type is counted and reported as a percentage of the total examined

Type of Leukocyte	Normal Range
lymphocytes	25–33%
monocytes	3–7%
neutrophils	54–75%
eosinophils	1–3%
basophils	0–1%

red cell morphology mōr-fol´ō-jē	as part of identifying and counting the WBCs, the condition of the size and shape of the red blood cells in the background of the smeared slide is noted (e.g., anisocytosis, poikilocytosis)
platelet count (PLT) plāt´let	a calculation of the number of thrombocytes in the blood: normal range 150,000–450,000/cubic millimeters

Test or Procedure	Explanation
erythrocyte sedimentation rate (ESR) ĕ-rith´rō-sīt sed´i-men-tā´shŭn rāt	a timed test to measure the rate at which red blood cells settle or fall through a given volume of plasma
partial thromboplastin time (PTT)	a test to determine coagulation defects such as platelet disorders
thromboplastin throm-bō-plas´tin	a substance present in tissues, platelets, and leukocytes that is necessary for coagulation
prothrombin time (PT)	a test to measure the activity of prothrombin in the blood
prothrombin prō-throm´bin	a protein substance in the blood that is essential to the clotting process
venipuncture ven-i-pŭnk´chūr	an incision into or puncture of a vein to withdraw blood for testing
phlebotomy flĕ-bot´ō-mē	

BONE AND LYMPH STUDIES

bone marrow aspiration bōn mar´ō as-pi-rā´shŭn	a needle aspiration of bone marrow tissue for pathological examination (Fig. 8.7)
bone marrow biopsy bōn mar´ō bī´op-sē	a pathological examination of bone marrow tissue
lymphangiogram lim-fan´jē-ō-gram	an x-ray image of a lymph node or vessel taken after injection of a contrast medium

DIAGNOSTIC IMAGING

computed tomography (CT)	full-body x-ray CT images are used to detect tumors and cancers such as lymphoma
positron emission tomography (PET)	radionuclide scans, especially of the whole body, are useful in determining the recurrence of cancers or to measure response to therapy; commonly used in evaluating lymphoma

Operative Terms

Term	Meaning
bone marrow transplant bōn mar´ō tranz´plant	the transplantation of healthy bone marrow from a compatible donor to a diseased recipient to stimulate blood cell production
lymphadenectomy lim-fad-ĕ-nek´tō-mē	the removal of a lymph node
lymphadenotomy lim-fad-ĕ-not´ă-mē	an incision into a lymph node
lymph node dissection limf nōd di-sek´shŭn	the removal of possible cancer-carrying lymph nodes for pathological examination

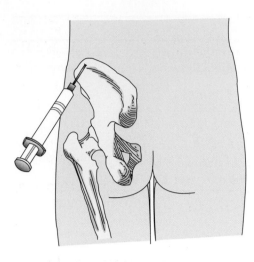

Figure 8.7 Bone marrow aspiration. Posterior view of the pelvic region showing common site.

Term	Meaning
splenectomy splē-nek´tō-mē	the removal of the spleen
thymectomy thī-mek´tō-mē	the removal of the thymus gland

Therapeutic Terms

Term	Meaning
blood transfusion	the introduction of blood products into the circulation of a recipient whose blood volume is reduced or deficient in some manner
autologous blood aw-tol´ŏ-gŭs blud	blood donated by, and stored for, a patient for future personal use (e.g., upcoming surgery)
homologous blood hŏ-mol´ō-gŭs blud	blood voluntarily donated by any person for transfusion to a compatible recipient
blood component therapy	the transfusion of specific blood components such as packed red blood cells, platelets, and plasma
crossmatching	a method of matching a donor's blood to the recipient by mixing a sample in a test tube to determine compatibility
chemotherapy kem´ō-thēr´ă-pē	the treatment of malignancies, infections, and other diseases with chemical agents that destroy selected cells or impair their ability to reproduce
immunotherapy im´ū-nō-thār´ă-pē	the use of biological agents to prevent or treat disease by stimulating the body's own defense mechanisms; as seen in the treatment of AIDS, cancer, and allergy
plasmapheresis plaz´mă-fĕ-rē´sis	the removal of plasma from the body with separation and extraction of specific elements (such as platelets) followed by reinfusion (apheresis = a withdrawal)

Term	Meaning
Common Therapeutic Drug Classifications	
anticoagulant an´tē-kō-ag´yū-lant	a drug that prevents clotting of the blood
hemostatic hē-mō-stat´ik	a drug that stops the flow of blood within the vessels
vasoconstrictor vā´sō-kon-strik´ter	a drug that causes a narrowing of blood vessels, decreasing blood flow
vasodilator vā´sō-dī´lā-ter	a drug that causes dilation of blood vessels, increasing blood flow

Summary of Chapter 8 Acronyms/Abbreviations

AIDS.............acquired immunodeficiency syndrome
ALT.............alanine aminotransferase (enzyme)
AST.............aspartate aminotransferase (enzyme)
BUN.............blood urea nitrogen
CBC.............complete blood count
CO₂.............carbon dioxide
CT.............computed tomography
ESR.............erythrocyte sedimentation rate
Fe.............iron (ferrous)
HCT or Hct.....hematocrit
HGB or Hgb.....hemoglobin

Ig.............immunoglobulin
MCH.............mean corpuscular (cell) hemoglobin
MCHC.............mean corpuscular (cell) hemoglobin concentration
MCV.............mean corpuscular (cell) volume
PET.............positron emission tomography
PLT.............platelet count
PMN.............polymorphonuclear leukocyte
PT.............prothrombin time
PTT.............partial thromboplastin time
RBC.............red blood cell or count
WBC.............white blood cell or count

PRACTICE EXERCISES

For the following terms, on the lines below the term, write out the indicated word parts: prefixes (P), combining forms (CF), roots (R), and suffixes (S). Then define the word.

EXAMPLE

dyshematopoiesis

———— / ———— / ————
   P   CF   S

<u>dys/hemato/poiesis</u>
   P   CF   S

DEFINITION: painful, difficult, or faulty/blood/formation

1. erythroblastosis

—————————— / —————————— / ——————————
     CF   R   S

DEFINITION: _____

2. myelodysplasia

—————————— / —————————— / —————————— / ——————————
    CF   P   R   S

DEFINITION: _____

3. hemocytometer

—————————— / —————————— / ——————————
    CF   CF   S

DEFINITION: _____

4. splenorrhagia

—————————— / ——————————
    CF   S

DEFINITION: _____

5. lymphadenitis

—————————— / —————————— / ——————————
    R   R   S

DEFINITION: _____

6. immunotoxic

—————————— / —————————— / ——————————
    CF   R   S

DEFINITION: _____

7. reticulocytosis

—————————— / —————————— / ——————————
    CF   R   S

DEFINITION: _____

8. thymopathy

_____ / _____ / _____
         CF   R   S

DEFINITION: _____

9. leukocytic

_____ / _____ / _____
         CF   R   S

DEFINITION: _____

10. lymphangiogram

_____ / _____ / _____
         R   CF   S

DEFINITION: _____

11. splenomegaly

_____ / _____
         CF   S

DEFINITION: _____

12. promyelocyte

_____ / _____ / _____ / _____
         P   CF   R   S

DEFINITION: _____

13. leukocytopenia

_____ / _____ / _____
         CF   CF   S

DEFINITION: _____

14. splenectomy

_____ / _____
         R   S

DEFINITION: _____

15. chylopoiesis

_____ / _____
         CF   S

DEFINITION: _____

16. lymphoma

_____ / _____
         R   S

DEFINITION: _____

17. cytomorphology

_____ / _____ / _____
         CF   CF   S

DEFINITION: _____

18. hemolysis

_____ / _____
            CF   S

DEFINITION: _____

19. anemia

_____ / _____
            P   S

DEFINITION: _____

20. metastasis

_____ / _____
            P   S

DEFINITION: _____

Complete the medical term by writing the missing part:

21. neutro_____ = abnormal reduction of neutrophils

22. _____ cyte = white blood cell

23. hemato_____ = formation of blood

24. spleno_____ = enlargement of the spleen

25. _____ penia = an abnormally reduced number of red blood cells

26. _____ ic = pertaining to the thymus gland

27. ____ granulocytes = white cells without granules in their nuclei

28. eosino_____ = a granular leukocyte named for its attraction to the rose-color stain of its granules

29. _____ cyte = red blood cell

30. _____ cytopenia = reduced number of all cellular components in the blood

For each of the following, circle the combining form that corresponds to the meaning given:

31. **eat or swallow**   phas/o   phag/o   plas/o

32. **clot**   thromb/o   thym/o   lymph/o

33. **juice**   lymph/o   hemat/o   chyl/o

34. **formation**   plas/o   troph/o   thromb/o

35. **color**   hem/o   chrom/o   cyan/o

36. **blood**   erythr/o   hem/o   lymph/o

37. **safe**   toxic/o   reticul/o   immun/o

38. **germ or bud**   blast/o   gen/o   crin/o

Fill in the blanks with the appropriate medical terms and abbreviations:

39. The procedure of counting the number of leukocytes in the blood is called a_____ _____ _____ and is abbreviated _____.

40. The blood study that determines the amount of pigment present in RBCs is called a _____ and is abbreviated _____.

41. The blood study that determines packed red blood cell volume is called a _____ and is abbreviated _____.

42. The classification of WBCs is performed in a _____ _____.

43. The calculations provided in blood indices, MCV_____ _____ _____, MCH_____ _____ _____, and MCHC_____ _____ _____ _____, are used to classify types of _____.

44. Venipuncture is also termed _____.

45. Hodgkin disease is a malignant type of _____.

Write the full medical term for the following abbreviations:

46. PT _____

47. ESR _____

48. PTT _____

49. CBC _____

Match the following terms with their meanings:

50. _____ microcytosis   a. large red blood cells

51. _____ poikilocytosis   b. thrombocyte

52. _____ neutrophil   c. WBC with rose-stained granules

53. _____ monocyte   d. RBC

54. _____ eosinophil   e. agranulocyte active in immunity

55. _____ lymphocyte   f. WBC with dark-stained granules

56. _____ basophil   g. WBC termed "one cell"

57. _____ platelet   h. RBCs of unequal size

58. _____ erythrocyte   i. WBC with granules

59. _____ granulocyte   j. large, irregular RBCs

60. _____ anisocytosis   k. polymorphonuclear WBC

61. _____ macrocytosis   l. small red blood cells

Write the correct medical term for each of the following:

62. impaired ability to provide an immune response _____

63. test tube method of matching a donor's blood to the recipient _____

64. syndrome caused by HIV _____

65. condition characterized by an increase in mononuclear cells caused by the Epstein-Barr virus _____

66. removal of plasma from the body, extraction of specific elements, then reinfusion

_____

Briefly describe the difference between the following terms:

67. plasma/serum _____

_____

68. anemia/leukemia _____

_____

69. autologous blood/homologous blood _____

_____

70. antibody/antigen _____

_____

71. vasoconstrictor/vasodilator _____

_____

72. anticoagulant/hemostatic _____

_____

73. polycythemia/hemochromatosis _____

_____

Write in the missing words on the lines in the following illustrations of the components of blood.

74–78.

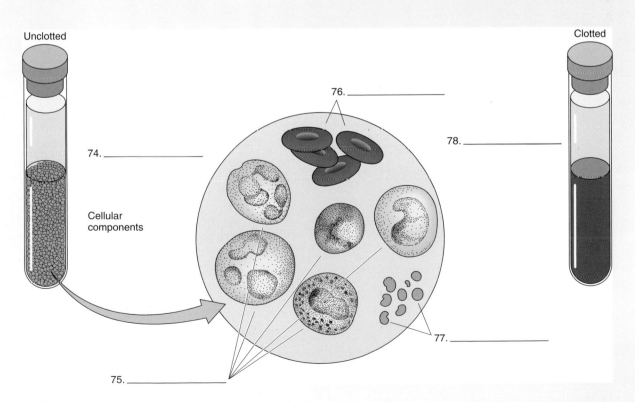

Unclotted

Clotted

76. _____

74. _____

78. _____

Cellular
components

77. _____

75. _____

Write in the missing words on the lines in the following illustrations of the lymphatic system.

79–84.

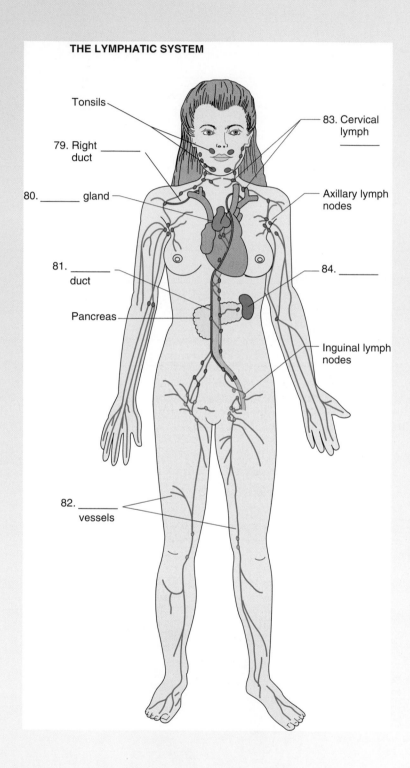

THE LYMPHATIC SYSTEM

Tonsils

79. Right _____ duct

80. _____ gland

81. _____ duct

Pancreas

82. _____ vessels

83. Cervical lymph _____

Axillary lymph nodes

84. _____

Inguinal lymph nodes

For each of the following, circle the correct spelling of the term:

85. hematopoesis   hematopoiesis   hematoepoisis

86. platelets   plattelets   plateletts

87. anissocytosis   aniscocytosis   anisocytosis

88. polkulocytosis   poikilocytosis   poiekilocytosis

89. hemalysis   hemoliesis   hemolysis

90. lymphadenpathy   lymphadenopathy   lymphoadenopathy

91. myelodysplasia   mylodysplaszia   myelodysphazia

92. thrombocytopnea   thrombocytopenia   throbocytpenia

93. hematocrit   hemacrit   hematocrete

94. splenecktomy   splenectomy   spleenectomy

95. plasmapheresis   plazmaphoresis   plasmophoresis

96. vasodialator   vasodilater   vasodilator

97. venipuncture   venapuncture   venepuncture

Give the noun that was used to form the following adjectives:

98. leukemic _____

99. immunosuppressive _____

100. thymic _____

101. hematopoietic _____

102. splenic _____

103. septicemic _____

104. hemophilic _____

105. myelodysplastic _____

MEDICAL RECORD ANALYSES

MEDICAL RECORD 8.1

Progress Note

CC: fatigue

S: This 43 y/o female c/o feeling rundown with lack of energy × 1 mo. Pt denies fever, chills, nausea, vomiting, diarrhea, constipation and reports no weight loss. She has had very heavy menstrual periods lasting 5 days since DC of birth control pills 1 year ago.
PMH: mononucleosis at age 14, NKDA. FH: father, age 68, died of MI
Mother, age 74, has myelodysplasia; sister, age 45, L&W
SH: married × 8 yr, no children; ETOH—wine with dinner, denies smoking.

O: VS: T 98.8°F, P 81, R 15, BP 136/62. WDWN female in NAD. HEENT-WNL
Neck: supple s̄ lymphadenopathy. Lungs: clear. Heart RRR s̄ murmur
Abdomen: soft and tender s̄ organomegaly. Extremities: no edema.

A: Etiology of fatigue and decreased energy unclear. Possible iron deficiency anemia in light of heavy menstrual periods.

P: Blood studies to include comprehensive metabolic panel, CBC c̄ differential. RTO in 1 wk for lab results.

1. Which of the following is not mentioned in the history?

   a. type of treatment the patient received for mononucleosis

   b. patient's consumption of alcohol

   c. how long the patient has been married

   d. health status of the patient's sister

2. Describe the condition of the patient's mother:

   a. she has leukemia

   b. she has a bleeding disorder characterized by an abnormally decreased number of platelets in the blood

   c. she has a hereditary disorder characterized by an excessive buildup of iron deposits in the body

   d. she has a disorder within the bone marrow characterized by a proliferation of abnormal stem cells, which usually develops into leukemia

3. Which of the following describes the findings of the physical examination?

   a. swollen lymph glands

   b. normal examination

   c. fast heart rate

   d. heart murmur

4. What is the possible cause of the patient's fatigue?

   a. viral condition characterized by an increase in mononuclear cells (monocytes and lymphocytes) in the blood

   b. macrocytic-normochromic type of anemia characterized by an inadequate supply of vitamin B_{12}, causing red blood cells to become large, varied in shape, and reduced in number

   c. microcytic-hypochromic type of anemia characterized by small red blood cells containing low amounts of hemoglobin because of lack of iron in the body

   d. normocytic-normochromic type of anemia characterized by the failure of bone marrow to produce red blood cells

5. Identify the subjective information most significantly linked to the assessment:

   a. enlarged lymph glands

   b. heavy menstrual periods

   c. fatigue

   d. the patient quit taking birth control pills

6. Of the following tests, which test is part of the plan?

   a. test to determine coagulation defects such as platelet disorders

   b. test to diagnose an infection in the bloodstream, by culturing a specimen of blood

   c. needle aspiration of bone marrow tissue for pathological examination

   d. expanded battery of automated blood chemistry tests used as a general screen for disease

MEDICAL RECORD 8.2

Henry Lin went to his personal physician after an extended period of feeling weak and tired, and starting to lose weight. His doctor admitted him to Central Medical Center hospital for additional tests after conducting a physical examination and blood tests. He is now being treated as an outpatient by his internist, Dr. Bradley, and an oncologist, Dr. Ellison, to whom he was referred for consultation and concurrent care.

Directions

Read Medical Record 8.2 for Mr. Lin (pages 267–268) and answer the following questions.

The progress note is the oncology/hematology progress note dictated by Dr. Ellison, the oncologist treating Mr. Lin, at the time of a follow-up visit 2 weeks after Mr. Lin's hospitalization. The second document is a hematology lab report, submitted before a second follow-up with Dr. Ellison 2 weeks later.

QUESTIONS ABOUT MEDICAL RECORD 8.2

Write your answers in the spaces provided.

1. Below are medical terms used in the progress note you have not yet encountered in this text. Underline each where it appears in the record and define below:

   edema _____

   scaphoid _____

   anorexia _____

2. In your own words, not using medical terminology, translate Mr. Lin's diagnosis:

   _____

3. Name the diagnostic test that confirmed this diagnosis:

   _____

4. Write the medical term for Mr. Lin's enlarged spleen:

   _____

5. Dr. Ellison's March 31 record includes the results of two CBC component tests from the earlier March 23 lab report, as well as results from the same tests for March 31. The April 15 lab report also contains the CBC component tests. In the spaces below, write the name of the tests and their results at these three times. Do not use abbreviations. Be sure to include units of measure.

	Result		
Test	March 23	March 31	April 15
_____	_____	_____	_____
_____	_____	_____	_____

6. What are the three elements Dr. Ellison includes in Mr. Lin's treatment plan?

a. _____

b. _____

c. _____

7. Study the April 15 laboratory report carefully and complete the following table of selected test results. Write the name of the component that is abbreviated and an N if the result for Mr. Lin is within the normal range or an A (abnormal) if the result is outside the normal range.

a. WBC _____

b. RBC _____

c. HGB _____

d. HCT _____

e. MCV _____

f. MCH _____

g. MCHC _____

h. PLT _____

i. lymph _____

j. mono _____

k. neutro _____

l. eos _____

m. baso _____

CENTRAL MEDICAL GROUP, INC.
Department of Oncology/Hematology
201 Medical Center Drive • Central City, US 90000-1234 • PHONE: (012) 125-8888 • FAX: (012) 125-3434

PROGRESS NOTE

PATIENT: LIN, HENRY N.

DATE: March 31, 20xx

Mr. Lin is a 69-year-old man seen for myelodysplasia while hospitalized on March 17, 20xx. He was transfused with 4.0 U of packed cells during that hospitalization. A bone marrow biopsy revealed histology consistent with chronic myelomonocytic leukemia (myelodysplasia).

A follow-up blood count was obtained through Dr. Bradley's office on March 23, 20xx, and revealed a hemoglobin of 11.0 G/DL and a hematocrit of 31.0%.

There have been no fevers, sweats, or anorexia; but he has noted some weight loss. There has been no bleeding. There has been no nausea, vomiting, or dark and bloody stools.

Exam: Weight: 172 lb. Blood Pressure: 120/50. Temperature: 98.6°F. Pulse: 88. Respirations: 18.

HEENT: Mild gum atrophy and inflammation. NECK: Supple. LYMPH NODES: There is no cervical or supraclavicular adenopathy. LUNGS: Clear. CARDIOVASCULAR: Normal. ABDOMEN: Scaphoid, soft, and nontender. The spleen is enlarged. EXTREMITIES: Without edema or petechiae.

TODAY'S LAB: Complete blood count reveals a total leukocyte count of 6600/cu mm, a hemoglobin of 8.0 G/DL, a hematocrit of 23.0%, and a platelet count of 149,000/cu mm.

CLINICAL DIAGNOSIS:
Chronic myelomonocytic leukemia (myelodysplastic syndrome). The patient is transfusion dependent.

The patient will be typed and crossmatched today and will be transfused with 2.0 U of packed red blood cells through the Oncology Day Facility tomorrow on April 1, 20xx.

I have asked the patient to follow up with Dr. Bradley next week and with me in two weeks.

A. Ellison, M.D.

AE:gds
cc: Blair Bradley, M.D.

D: 3/31/20xx
T: 4/3/20xx

Medical Record 8.2

CENTRAL MEDICAL CENTER
211 Medical Center Drive • Central City, US 90000-1234 • PHONE: (012) 125-6784 • FAX: (012) 125-9999

04/15/20xx
14:27

NAME	: Lin, Henry	LOC: TEST	DOB: 2/2/xx	AGE: 69Y
MR#	: TEST-226			SEX: M
ACCT#	: 168946701			

M63558 COLL: 04/15/20xx 13:23   REC: 04/15/20xx 13:25

HEMOGRAM

CBC

WBC	4.1	[4.5–10.5]	K/UL
RBC	2.93	[4.6–6.2]	M/UL
HGB	9.1	[14.0–18.0]	G/DL
HCT	25.3	[42.0–52.0]	%
MCV	86.2	[82–92]	FL
MCH	31.1	[27–31]	PG
MCHC	36.0	[32–36]	G/DL
PLT	90	[150–450]	K/UL

Auto Lymph %	8.3	[20–40]	%
Auto Mono %	32.6	[1–11]	%
Auto Neutro %	57.8	[50–75]	%
Auto Eos %	1.0	[0–6]	%
Auto Baso %	0.3	[0–2]	%
Auto Lymph #	0.3	[1.5–4.0]	K/UL
Auto Mono #	1.3	[0.2–0.9]	K/UL
Auto Neutro #	2.4	[1.0–7.0]	K/UL
Auto Eos #	0.0	[0–0.7]	K/UL
Auto Baso #	0.0	[0–0.2]	K/UL

TEST, PATIENT   TEST-221   END OF REPORT   PAGE 1
04/15/20xx 14:27   INTERIM REPORT

INTERIM REPORT COMPLETE

Medical Record 8.2   *Continued.*

Chapter 9

Respiratory System

OBJECTIVES

After completion of this chapter, you will be able to

- Define common term components used in relation to the respiratory system
- Describe the basic functions of the respiratory system
- Define the basic anatomical terms referring to the respiratory system
- Define common symptomatic and diagnostic terms referring to the respiratory system
- List the common diagnostic tests and procedures related to the respiratory system
- Identify common operative terms referring to the respiratory system
- Identify common therapeutic terms including drug classifications related to the respiratory system
- Explain the terms and abbreviations used in documenting medical records involving the respiratory system

Combining Forms

Combining Form	Meaning	Example
alveol/o	alveolus (air sac)	alveolar al-vē´ō-lăr
bronch/o	bronchus (airway)	bronchoscope brong´kō-skōp
bronchi/o		bronchiocele brong´kē-ō-sēl
bronchiol/o	bronchiole (little airway)	bronchiolitis brong-kē-ō-lī´tis
capn/o	carbon dioxide	hypercapnia hī-per-kap´nē-ă
carb/o		hypocarbia hī-pō-kar´bē-ă
laryng/o	larynx (voice box)	laryngospasm lă-ring´gō-spazm
lob/o	lobe (a portion)	lobectomy lō-bek´tō-mē
nas/o	nose	nasal nā´zăl
rhin/o		rhinorrhea rī-nō-rē´ă

Combining Form	Meaning	Example
or/o	mouth	oropharyngeal ōr-ō-fă-rin´jē-ăl
ox/o	oxygen	hypoxemia hī-pok-sē´mē-ă
palat/o	palate	palatoplasty pal´ă-tō-plas-tē
pharyng/o	pharynx (throat)	pharyngitis far-in-jī´tis
phren/o	diaphragm (also mind)	phrenospasm fren´ō-spazm
pleur/o	pleura	pleurisy plūr´i-sē
pneum/o	air or lung	pneumonia nū-mō´nē-ă
pneumon/o		pneumonectomy nū´mō-nek´tō-mē
pulmon/o	lung	pulmonologist pŭl´mō-nol´ŏ-jist
sinus/o	sinus (cavity)	sinusitis sī-nŭ-sī´tis
spir/o	breathing	spirometry spī-rom´ĕ-trē
thorac/o	chest	thoracotomy thōr-ă-kot´ō-mē
pector/o		pectoralgia pek-tō-ral´jē-ă
steth/o		stethoscope steth´ō-skōp
tonsill/o	tonsil (almond)	tonsillitis ton´si-lī´tis
trache/o	trachea (windpipe)	trachea trā´kē-ă
uvul/o	uvula	uvulitis yu-vyu-lī´tis
ADDITIONAL SUFFIX		
-pnea	breathing	dyspnea disp-nē´ă

Respiratory System Overview

The respiratory system is composed of the organs and structures that function to exchange gases within the body. The exchange of gases, called respiration, occurs when oxygen from the air is inhaled into the lungs and passes into the blood and carbon dioxide diffuses from the blood into the lungs and is exhaled into the air. Respiration is also known as *breathing* or *ventilation*. Intake of air is called *inspiration* or *inhalation,* and outflow of air is called *expiration* or *exhalation* (Fig. 9.1).

RESPIRATORY SYSTEM

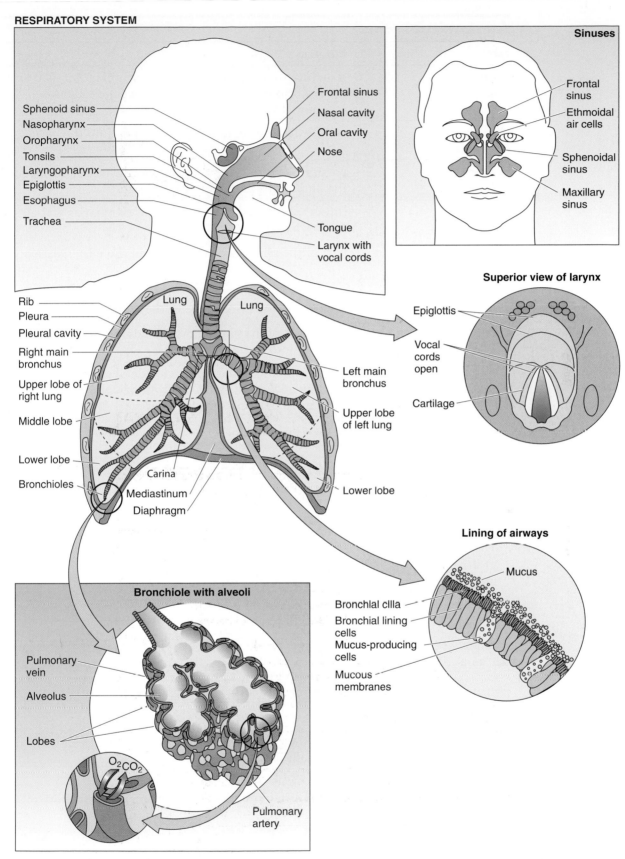

Sinuses

Superior view of larynx

Lining of airways

Bronchiole with alveoli

Figure 9.1. Respiratory tract.

Anatomical Terms

Term	Meaning
nose nōz	structure that warms, moistens, and filters air as it enters the respiratory tract and that houses the olfactory receptors for the sense of smell
sinuses sī´nŭs-ĕz	air-filled spaces in the skull that open into the nasal cavity
palate pal´ăt	partition between the oral and nasal cavities; divided into the hard and soft palate
pharynx far´ingks	throat; passageway for food to the esophagus and air to the larynx
nasopharynx nā´zō-far-ingks	part of the pharynx directly behind the nasal passages
oropharynx ŏr´ō-far-ingks	central portion of the pharynx between the roof of the mouth and the upper edge of the epiglottis
laryngopharynx lă-ring´gō-far-ingks	lower part of the pharynx just below the oropharynx opening into the larynx and the esophagus
tonsils ton´silz	oval lymphatic tissues on each side of the pharynx that filter air to protect the body from bacterial invasion—also called palatine tonsils
adenoid ad´ĕ-noyd	lymphatic tissue on the back of the pharynx behind the nose—also called pharyngeal tonsil
uvula yu´vyu-lă	small projection hanging from the back middle edge of the soft palate, named for its grape-like shape (see Chapter 14, Fig. 14.2)
larynx lar´ingks	voice box; passageway for air moving from pharynx to trachea; contains vocal cords
glottis glot´is	opening between the vocal cords in the larynx
epiglottis ep-i-glot´is	lid-like structure that covers the larynx during swallowing to prevent food from entering the airway
trachea tră´kē-ă	windpipe; passageway for air from the larynx to the area of the carina where it splits into the right and left bronchus
bronchial tree brong´kē-ăl	branched airways that lead from the trachea to the alveoli
right and left bronchus brong´kŭs	two primary airways branching from the area of the carina into the lungs
bronchioles brong´kē-ōlz	progressively smaller tubular branches of the airways
alveoli al-vē´ō-lī	thin-walled microscopic air sacs that exchange gases

Term	Meaning
lungs lŭngz	two spongy organs, located in the thoracic cavity enclosed by the diaphragm and rib cage, responsible for respiration
lobes lōbz	subdivisions of the lung, two on the left and three on the right
pleura plūr´ă	membranes enclosing the lung (visceral pleura) and lining the thoracic cavity (parietal pleura)
pleural cavity plūr´ăl kav´i-tē	potential space between the visceral and parietal layers of the pleura
diaphragm dī´ă-fram	muscular partition that separates the thoracic cavity from the abdominal cavity and aids in respiration by moving up and down
mediastinum me´dē-as-tī´nŭm	partition that separates the thorax into two compartments (that contain the right and left lungs) and encloses the heart, esophagus, trachea, and thymus gland
mucous membranes myū´kŭs mem´brānz	thin sheets of tissue that line the respiratory passages and secrete mucus, a viscid (sticky) fluid
cilia sil´ē-ă	hair-like processes from the surface of epithelial cells, such as those of the bronchi, that provide upward movement of mucus cell secretions
parenchyma pă-reng´ki-mă	functional tissues of any organ such as the tissues of the bronchioles, alveoli, ducts, and sacs that perform respiration

 LUNG. Lung is an Anglo-Saxon term derived from lungre, meaning *quickly* or *lightly*. The connection suggests that the lungs were named for their lightness and ability to float in water. The lungs were also called "lights."

Symptomatic and Diagnostic Terms

Term	Meaning
SYMPTOMATIC	
Breathing (Fig. 9.2)	
eupnea yūp-nē´ă	normal breathing
bradypnea brad-ip-nē´ă	slow breathing
tachypnea tak-ip-nē´ă	fast breathing
hypopnea hī-pop´nē-ă	shallow breathing
hyperpnea hi-perp-nē´ă	deep breathing
dyspnea disp-nē´ă	difficulty breathing
apnea ap´nē-ă	inability to breathe

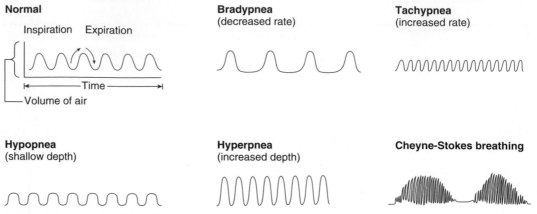

Figure 9.2 Examples of breathing patterns.

Term	Meaning
orthopnea ōr-thop-nē´ă	ability to breathe only in an upright position
Cheyne-Stokes respiration res-pi-rā´shŭn	pattern of breathing characterized by a gradual increase of depth and sometimes rate to a maximum level, followed by a decrease, resulting in apnea
Lung Sounds	
crackles krak´ĕlz **rales** rahlz	popping sounds heard on auscultation of the lung when air enters diseased airways and alveoli—occurs in disorders such as bronchiectasis or atelectasis
wheezes hwēz´ez **rhonchi** rong´kī	high-pitched, musical sounds heard on auscultation of the lung as air flows through a narrowed airway—occurs in disorders such as asthma or emphysema
stridor strī´dōr	a high-pitched crowing sound that is a sign of obstruction in the upper airway (trachea or larynx)
General Symptomatic Terms	
caseous necrosis kā´sē-ŭs nĕ-krō´sis	degeneration and death of tissue with a cheese-like appearance (characteristic of tuberculosis)
dysphonia dis-fō´nē-ă	hoarseness (phon/o = voice or sound)
epistaxis ep´i-stak´sis	nosebleed (epi = upon; stazo = to drip)
expectoration ek-spek-tō-rā´shŭn	coughing up and spitting out of material from the lungs
sputum spū´tŭm	material expelled from the lungs by coughing
hemoptysis hē-mop´ti-sis	coughing up and spitting out blood originating in the lungs (ptysis = to spit)

Term	Meaning
hypercapnia hī-per-kap′nē-ă **hypercarbia** hī-per-kar′bē-ă	excessive level of carbon dioxide in the blood (capno = smoke; carbo = coal)
hyperventilation hī′per-ven-ti-lā′shŭn	excessive movement of air in and out of the lungs causing hypocapnia
hypoventilation hī′pō-ven-ti-lā′shŭn	deficient movement of air in and out of the lungs causing hypercapnia
hypoxemia hī-pok-sē′mē-ă	deficient amount of oxygen in the blood
hypoxia hī-pok′sē-ă	deficient amount of oxygen in tissue cells
obstructive lung disorder lŭng dis-ōr′der	condition blocking the flow of air moving out of the lungs (Fig. 9.3C)
restrictive lung disorder	condition limiting the intake of air into the lungs (see Fig. 9.3B)
pulmonary edema pŭl′mō-nār-ē e-dē′mă	fluid filling of the spaces around the alveoli, even- tually flooding into the alveoli
pulmonary infiltrate pŭl′mō-nār-ē in-fil′trāt	density on an x-ray representing solid material within the air spaces of the lungs, usually indicating inflammatory changes (see Fig. 9.7)
rhinorrhea rī-nō-rē′ă	thin, watery discharge from the nose

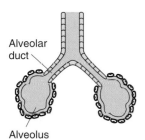

A   Normal
Bronchioles and alveolar ducts are open, allowing air to reach alveoli and alveolar capillaries; alveoli and ducts are elastic, pushing air out of the lungs during expiration.

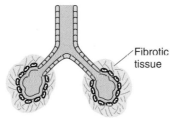

B   Pneumoconiosis
Chronic inhalation of dust particles results in the formation of fibrotic tissue surrounding the alveoli, limiting their ability to stretch and restricting the intake of air.

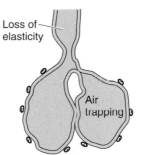

C   Emphysema
Alveoli lose their elasticity, making it difficult to push air out of the lungs and obstructing exhalation of air.

Figure 9.3 Comparison of normal alveoli **(A)** with alveoli in restrictive **(B)** and obstructive **(C)** lung disorders.

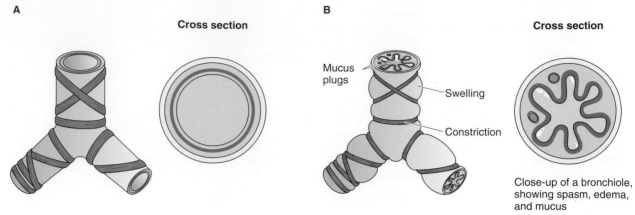

Figure 9.4 Constricted bronchial tubes in asthma. **A.** Normal. **B.** Asthma.

Term	Meaning
DIAGNOSTIC	
asthma az´mă	panting; obstructive pulmonary disease caused by a spasm of the bronchial tubes or by swelling of their mucous membrane, characterized by paroxysmal (sudden, periodic) attacks of wheezing, dyspnea, and cough (Fig. 9.4)
atelectasis at-ĕ-lek´tă-sis	collapse of lung tissue (alveoli) (atele = imperfect)
bronchiectasis brong-kē-ek´tă-sis	abnormal dilation of the bronchi with accumulation of mucus (Fig. 9.5)
bronchitis brong-kī´tis	inflammation of the bronchi
bronchogenic carcinoma brong-kō-jen´ik kar-si-nō´mă	lung cancer
bronchospasm brong´kō-spazm	constriction of bronchi caused by spasm of the peribronchial smooth muscle
emphysema em-fi-sē´mă	obstructive pulmonary disease characterized by overexpansion of the alveoli with air, with destructive changes in their walls resulting in loss of lung elasticity and gas exchange (emphysan = to inflate) (see Fig. 9.3C)
chronic obstructive pulmonary disease (COPD) kron´ik pŭl´mō-nār-ē di-zēz´	permanent, destructive pulmonary disorder that is a combination of chronic bronchitis and emphysema
cystic fibrosis sis´tik fī-brō´sis	inherited condition of exocrine gland malfunction causing secretion of abnormally thick, viscous (sticky) mucus that obstructs passageways within the body, commonly affecting the lungs and digestive tract; mucus that obstructs the airways leads to infection, inflammation, and lung tissue damage
laryngitis lar-in-jī´tis	inflammation of the larynx

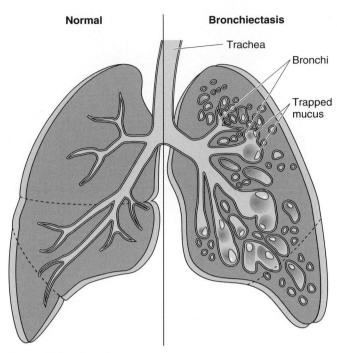

Figure 9.5. Bronchiectasis.

Term	Meaning
laryngotracheobronchitis (LTB) lăr-ing′gō-trā′kē-o-brong-kī′tis **croup** krūp	inflammation of the upper airways with swelling that creates a funnel-shaped elongation of tissue causing a distinct "seal bark" cough
laryngospasm lă-ring′gō-spazm	spasm of laryngeal muscles causing constriction
nasal polyposis nā′zăl pol′i-pō′sis	presence of numerous polyps in the nose (a polyp is a tumor on a stalk)
pharyngitis far-in-jī′tis	inflammation of the pharynx
pleural effusion plŭr′ăl e-fū′zhŭn	accumulation of fluid within the pleural cavity (Fig. 9.6)
empyema em-pī-ē′mă **pyothorax** pī-ō-thōr′aks	accumulation of pus in the pleural cavity
hemothorax hē-mō-thōr′aks	accumulation of blood in the pleural cavity
pleuritis plū-rī′tis **pleurisy** plūr′i-sē	inflammation of the pleura

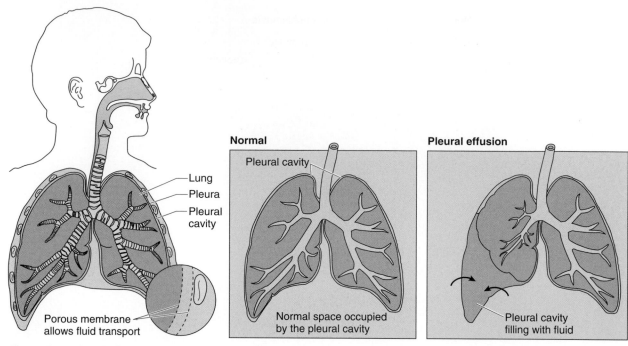

Lung
Pleura
Pleural cavity

Porous membrane allows fluid transport

Normal

Pleural cavity

Normal space occupied by the pleural cavity

Pleural effusion

Pleural cavity filling with fluid

Figure 9.6 Pleural effusion.

Term	Meaning
pneumoconiosis nū´mō-kō-nē-ō´sis	chronic restrictive pulmonary disease resulting from prolonged inhalation of fine dusts such as coal, asbestos (asbestosis), or silicone (silicosis) (conio = dust) (see Fig. 9.3B)
pneumonia nū-mō´nē-ă	inflammation in the lung caused by infection from bacteria, viruses, fungi, or parasites, or resulting from aspiration of chemicals (Fig. 9.7)
pneumocystis pneumonia nū-mō-sis´tis nū-mō´nē-ă	pneumonia caused by the *Pneumocystis carinii* organism—a common opportunistic infection seen in those with positive human immunodeficiency virus
pneumothorax nū-mō-thōr´aks	air in the pleural cavity caused by a puncture of the lung or chest wall (Fig. 9.8)
pneumohemothorax nū´mō-hē-mō-thōr´aks	air and blood in the pleural cavity
pneumonitis nū-mō-nī´tis	inflammation of the lung often caused by hypersensitivity to chemicals or dusts
pulmonary embolism (PE) pŭl´mō-nār-ē em´bō-lizm	occlusion in the pulmonary circulation, most often caused by a blood clot (see Figs. 9.11 and 9.15)
pulmonary tuberculosis (TB) pŭl´mō-nār-ē tū-ber-kyū-lō´sis	disease caused by the presence of *Mycobacterium tuberculosis* in the lungs characterized by the formation of tubercles, inflammation, and necrotizing caseous lesions (caseous necrosis) (Fig. 9.9)
sinusitis sī-nŭ-sī´tis	inflammation of the sinuses

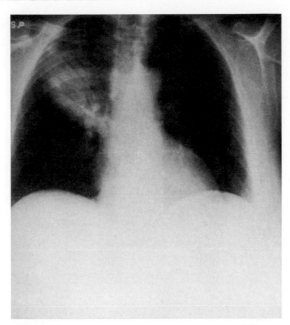

Figure 9.7 Chest x-ray showing pulmonary infiltrates in right upper lobe consistent with lobar pneumonia. Dense material (inflammatory exudate) absorbs radiation, whereas normal alveoli do not.

Term	Meaning
sleep apnea slēp ap´nē-ă	periods of breathing cessation (10 seconds or more) that occur during sleep, often causing snoring
tonsillitis ton´si-lī´tis	acute or chronic inflammation of the tonsils

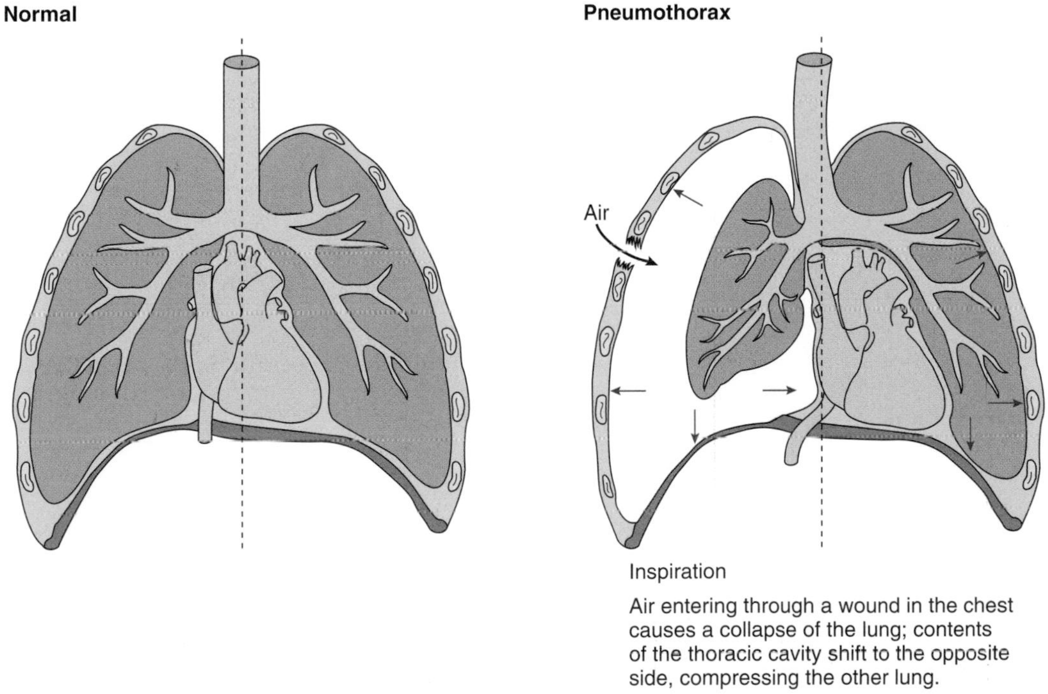

Normal   **Pneumothorax**

Air

Inspiration

Air entering through a wound in the chest causes a collapse of the lung; contents of the thoracic cavity shift to the opposite side, compressing the other lung.

Figure 9.8 Simple pneumothorax.

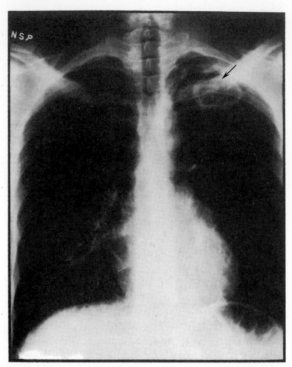

Figure 9.9 Chest x-ray showing presence of tuberculosis in the left upper lobe (*arrow*).

Term	Meaning
upper respiratory infection (URI) res´pi-ră-tōr-ē in-fek´shŭn	infectious disease of the upper respiratory tract involving the nasal passages, pharynx, and bronchi

Diagnostic Tests and Procedures

Test or Procedure	Explanation
arterial blood gases (ABGs) ar-tē´rē-ăl	analysis of arterial blood to determine the adequacy of lung function in the exchange of gases
pH	a measure of blood acidity or alkalinity
PaO_2	partial pressure of oxygen measuring the amount of oxygen in the blood
$PaCO_2$	partial pressure of carbon dioxide measuring the amount of carbon dioxide in the blood
endoscopy en-dos´kŏ-pē	examination of a body cavity with a flexible endoscope to examine within for diagnostic or treatment purposes
bronchoscopy brong-kos´kŏ-pē	use of a flexible endoscope, called a bronchoscope, to examine the airways (Fig. 9.10)
nasopharyngoscopy nā´zō-fa-ring-gos´kŏ-pē	use of a flexible endoscope to examine the nasal passages and the pharynx (throat) to diagnose structural abnormalities such as obstructions, growths, and cancers

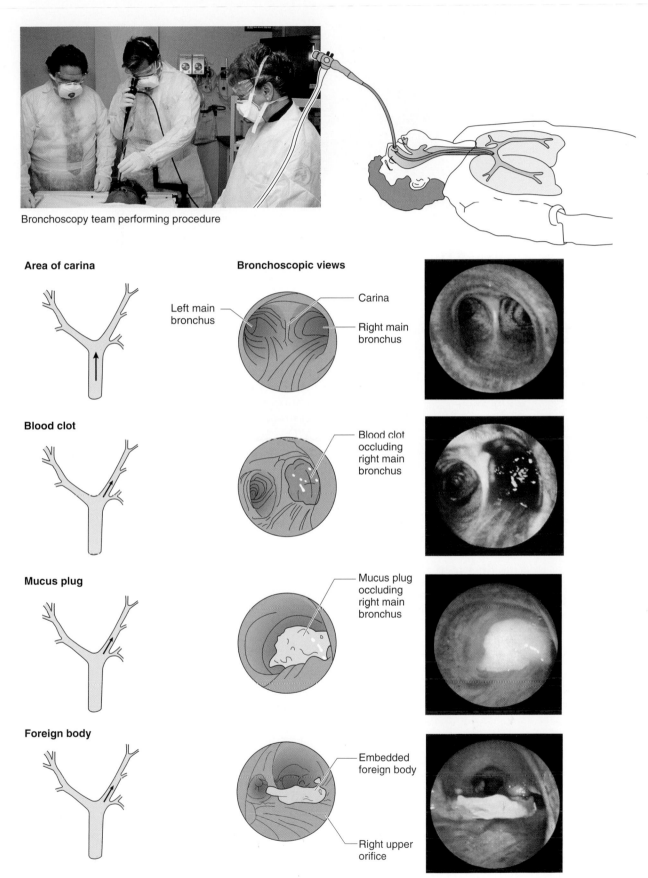

Bronchoscopy team performing procedure

Area of carina

Bronchoscopic views

Carina

Left main bronchus

Right main bronchus

Blood clot

Blood clot occluding right main bronchus

Mucus plug

Mucus plug occluding right main bronchus

Foreign body

Embedded foreign body

Right upper orifice

Figure 9.10   Bronchoscopy procedure.

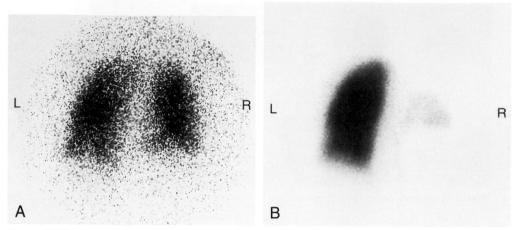

Figure 9.11 Posterior lung scan in a patient with an embolus in the right lung. Ventilation image **(A)** shows a normal pattern. Absence of blood flow to the right lung is apparent on perfusion scan **(B)**. *L*, left; *R*, right.

STETHOSCOPE. The Greek word stethos means chest and skopeo means to view. The stethoscope was invented by René Laënnec in 1816. He is said to have first thought of it when watching children playing; some of them listening at one end of a beam of wood could hear a pin scratching at the other end. He applied this principle to auscultation of the chest, which was then performed by placing the ear directly on the patient's chest. The first stethoscope was made of wood.

Test or Procedure	Explanation
lung biopsy (Bx) lŭng bī´op-sē	removal of a small piece of lung tissue for pathological examination
lung scan lŭng skan	two-part nuclear scan of the lungs to detect abnormalities of perfusion (blood flow) or ventilation (respiration), commonly called a $\dot{V}/\dot{Q}$ (ventilation/perfusion) scan (Fig. 9.11) ventilation scan—made as the patient breathes radioactive material into the airways perfusion scan—made after radioactive material is injected into the blood and circulates to the lungs
magnetic resonance image (MRI) mag-net´ic rez´ō-nans im´ij	nonionizing image of the lung to visualize lung lesions
polysomnography (PSG) pol´ē-som-nog´ră-fē	recording of various aspects of sleep (eye and muscle movements, respiration, brain wave patterns) for diagnosis of sleep disorders (somn/o = sleep) (see Chapter 10, Fig. 10.16)
physical examination methods	
auscultation aws-kŭl-tā´shŭn	to listen; physical examination method of listening to the sounds within the body with the aid of a stethoscope, such as auscultation of the chest for heart and lung sounds
percussion per-kŭsh´ŭn	physical examination method of tapping over the body to elicit vibrations and sounds to estimate the size, border, or fluid content of a cavity such as the chest
pulmonary function testing (PFT) pŭl´mō-nār-ē fŭngk´shŭn	direct and indirect measurements of lung volumes and capacities
spirometry spī-rom´ē-trē	portion of pulmonary function testing that is a direct measurement of lung volume and capacity (Fig. 9.12)

A

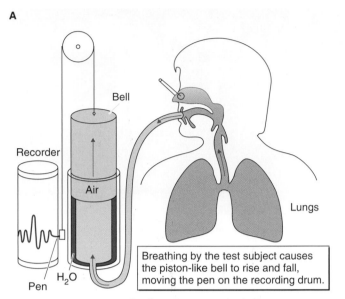

Breathing by the test subject causes the piston-like bell to rise and fall, moving the pen on the recording drum.

B

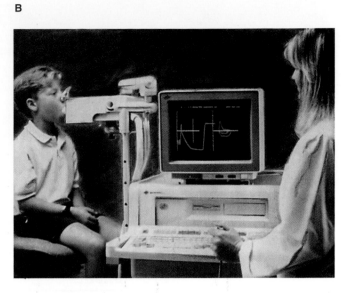

Figure 9.12 **A.** Principle of spirometry. **B.** Modern spirometry.

Test or Procedure	Explanation
tidal volume (TV or V_T) tī´dăl vol´yŭm	amount of air exhaled after a normal inspiration
vital capacity (VC) vīt´ăl kă-pas´i-tē	amount of air exhaled after a maximal inspiration
peak flow (PF) **peak expiratory flow rate** (PEFR) ek-spī´ră-tō-rē flō rāt	measure of the fastest flow of exhaled air after a maximal inspiration (Fig. 9.13)

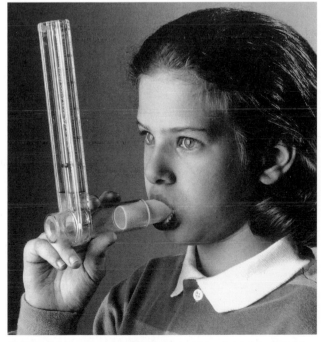

Figure 9.13. Routine peak flow monitoring by asthmatic adolescent female is performed to predict signs of an oncoming attack.

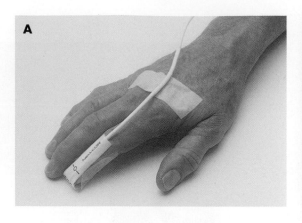

Figure 9.14 Pulse oximetry. **A.** Placement of a sensor on the patient's finger. **B.** Oxygen saturation reading on a portable monitor.

Test or Procedure	Explanation
pulse oximetry pŭls ok-sim´ĕ-trē	noninvasive method of estimating the percentage of oxygen saturation in the blood using an oximeter with a specialized probe attached to the skin at a site of arterial pulsation, commonly the finger; used to monitor hypoxemia (Fig. 9.14)
radiology rā-dē-ol´ō-jē	x-ray imaging
chest x-ray (CXR)	x-ray image of the chest to visualize the lungs
computed tomography (CT) tō-mog´ră-fē	computed x-ray imaging of the head is used to visualize the structures of the nose and sinuses; CT of the thorax is used to detect lesions in the lung
pulmonary angiography pŭl´mō-nār-ē an-jē-og´ră-fē	x-ray of the blood vessels of the lungs after injection of contrast material (Fig. 9.15)

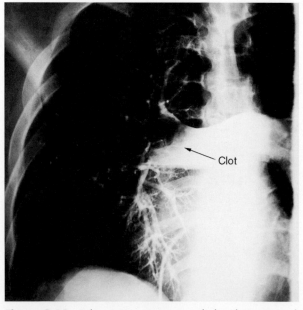

Figure 9.15 Pulmonary angiogram: embolus obstructing pulmonary circulation (*arrow*).

Operative Terms

Term	Meaning
adenoidectomy ad´ĕ-noy-dek´tō-mē	excision of the adenoids
lobectomy lō-bek´tō-mē	removal of a lobe of a lung
nasal polypectomy nā´zăl pol-i-pek´tō-mē	removal of a nasal polyp
pneumonectomy nū´mō-nek´tō-mē	removal of an entire lung
thoracentesis thōr´ă-sen-tē´sis	puncture for aspiration of the chest (Fig. 9.16)
thoracoplasty thōr´ă-kō-plas-tē	repair of the chest involving fixation of the ribs
thoracoscopy thōr-ă-kos´kŏ-pē	endoscopic examination of the pleural cavity using a thoracoscope
thoracostomy thōr-ă-kos´tō-mē	creation of an opening in the chest usually for insertion of a tube (see Fig. 9.16)
thoracotomy thōr-ă-kot´ō-mē	incision into the chest
tonsillectomy ton´si-lek´tō-mē	excision of the palatine tonsils
tonsillectomy and adenoidectomy (T & A) ad´ĕ-noy-dek´tō-mē	excision of the tonsils and adenoids
tracheostomy trā´kē-os´tō-mē	creation of an opening in the trachea, most often to insert a tube (Fig. 9.17)
tracheotomy trā´kē-ot´ō-mē	incision into the trachea (see Fig. 9.17)

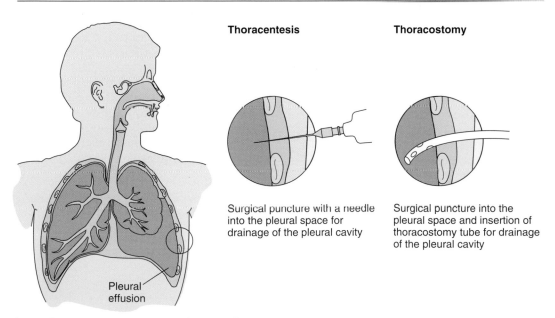

Thoracentesis

Surgical puncture with a needle into the pleural space for drainage of the pleural cavity

Thoracostomy

Surgical puncture into the pleural space and insertion of thoracostomy tube for drainage of the pleural cavity

Pleural effusion

Figure 9.16 Common treatments of pleural effusion.

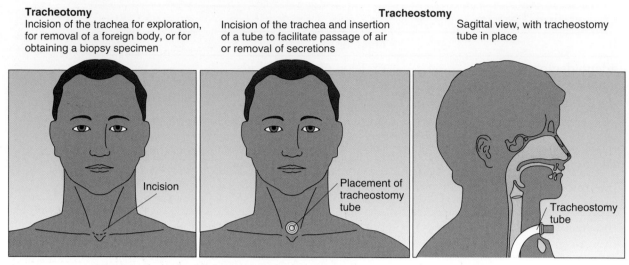

Tracheotomy
Incision of the trachea for exploration, for removal of a foreign body, or for obtaining a biopsy specimen

Tracheostomy
Incision of the trachea and insertion of a tube to facilitate passage of air or removal of secretions

Sagittal view, with tracheostomy tube in place

Incision

Placement of tracheostomy tube

Tracheostomy tube

Figure 9.17 Operative procedures related to the trachea.

Therapeutic Terms

Term	Meaning
cardiopulmonary resuscitation (CPR) kar´dē-ō-pŭl´mo-nār-ē rē-sŭs´i-tā´shŭn	method of artificial respiration and closed-chest massage used to restore breathing and cardiac output after cardiac arrest
continuous positive airway pressure (CPAP)	device that pumps a constant pressurized flow of air through the nasal passages, commonly used during sleep to prevent airway closure in sleep apnea (Fig. 9.18)
endotracheal intubation en´dō-trā´kē-ăl in-tū-bā´shŭn	passage of a tube into the trachea via the nose or mouth to open the airway for delivering gas mixtures to the lungs (e.g., oxygen, anesthetics, or air)
incentive spirometry in-sen´tiv spī-rom´ĕ-trē	common postoperative breathing therapy using a specially designed spirometer to encourage the patient to inhale and repeatedly sustain an inspiratory volume to exercise the lungs and prevent pulmonary complications (Fig. 9.19)
mechanical ventilation mĕ-kan´i-kăl ven-ti-lā´shŭn	mechanical method performed by a respiratory therapist to provide assisted breathing using a ventilator (Fig. 9.20)

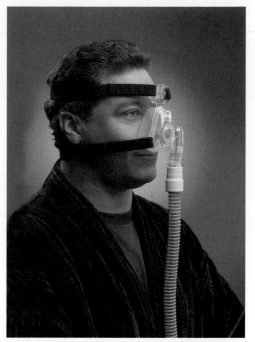

Figure 9.18 Patient wearing a CPAP mask.

Figure 9.19 Incentive spirometer.

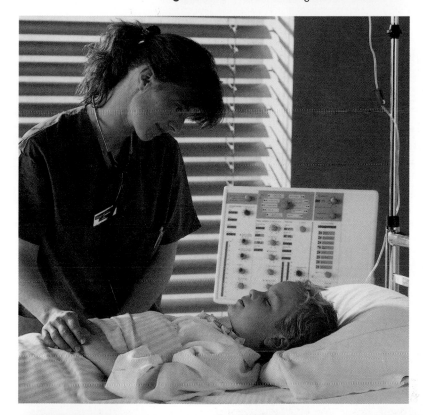

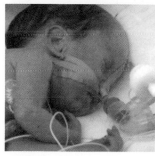

Neonate

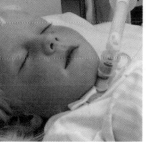

Pediatric

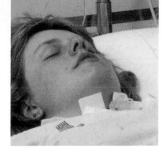

Adult

Figure 9.20 Mechanical ventilation.

Term	Meaning
COMMON THERAPEUTIC DRUG CLASSIFICATIONS	
antibiotic an´tē-bī-ot´ik	drug that kills or inhibits the growth of microorganisms
anticoagulant an´tē-kō-ag´yū-lant	drug that dissolves, or prevents the formation of, thrombi or emboli in the blood vessels (e.g., heparin)
antihistamine an-tē-his´tă-mēn	drug that neutralizes or inhibits the effects of histamine
histamine his´tă-mēn	compound in the body that is released by injured cells in allergic reactions, inflammation, etc., causing constriction of bronchial smooth muscle, dilation of blood vessels, etc.
bronchodilator brong-kō-dī-lā´ter	drug that dilates the muscular walls of the bronchi
expectorant ek-spek´tō-rănt	drug that breaks up mucus and promotes coughing

Summary of Chapter 9 Acronyms/Abbreviations

ABGs	arterial blood gases	**PaO₂**	partial pressure of oxygen
Bx	biopsy	**PE**	pulmonary embolism
COPD	chronic obstructive pulmonary disease	**PEFR**	peak expiratory flow rate
CPAP	continuous positive airway pressure	**PF**	peak flow
CPR	cardiopulmonary resuscitation	**PFT**	pulmonary function testing
CT	computed tomography	**pH**	potential of hydrogen
CXR	chest x-ray	**PSG**	polysomnography
HIV	human immunodeficiency virus	**T & A**	tonsillectomy and adenoidectomy
LTB	laryngotracheobronchitis	**TB**	tuberculosis
MRI	magnetic resonance image	**TV or V$_T$**	tidal volume
O₂	oxygen	**URI**	upper respiratory infection
PaCO₂	partial pressure of carbon dioxide	**VC**	vital capacity

PRACTICE EXERCISES

For the following terms, on the lines below the term, write out the indicated word parts: prefixes (P), combining forms (CF), roots (R), and suffixes (S). Then define the word.

EXAMPLE

intranasal

_____/ _____/ _____
　　　　P　　　　　　R　　　　　　S

intra/nas/al
　P　　R　　S

DEFINITION: within/nose/pertaining to

1. pulmonology

_____/ _____
　　　　CF　　　　　　　　　S

DEFINITION: _____

2. thoracocentesis

_____/ _____
　　　　CF　　　　　　　　　S

DEFINITION: _____

3. nasosinusitis

_____/ _____/ _____
　　　　CF　　　　　　　　R　　　　　　　　　S

DEFINITION: _____

4. hypoxemia

_____/ _____/ _____
　　　　P　　　　　　　　　R　　　　　　　　　S

DEFINITION: _____

5. pleuritis

_____/ _____
　　　　R　　　　　　　　　S

DEFINITION: _____

6. hypercarbia

_____/ _____/ _____
　　　　P　　　　　　　　　R　　　　　　　　　S

DEFINITION: _____

7. alveolar

_____ / _____
       R   S

DEFINITION: _____

8. tracheotomy

_____ / _____
      CF   S

DEFINITION: _____

9. oronasal

_____ / _____ / _____
      CF   R   S

DEFINITION: _____

10. rhinorrhea

_____ / _____
      CF   S

DEFINITION: _____

11. thoracostomy

_____ / _____
      CF   S

DEFINITION: _____

12. tonsillectomy

_____ / _____
       R   S

DEFINITION: _____

13. tracheobronchitis

_____ / _____ / _____
      CF   R   S

DEFINITION: _____

14. bronchospasm

_____ / _____
      CF   S

DEFINITION: _____

15. laryngostenosis

_____ / _____ / _____
      CF   R   S

DEFINITION: _____

16. spirogram

_____ / _____
      CF   S

DEFINITION: _____

17. lobectomy

   _____ / _____
          R   S

   DEFINITION: _____

18. peripleural

   _____ / _____ / _____
         P   R   S

   DEFINITION: _____

19. stethoscope

   _____ / _____
         CF   S

   DEFINITION: _____

20. pneumonic

   _____ / _____
          R   S

   DEFINITION: _____

21. nasopharyngoscopy

   _____ / _____ / _____
         CF   CF   S

   DEFINITION: _____

22. bronchiolectasis

   _____ / _____
          R   S

   DEFINITION: _____

23. phrenoptosis

   _____ / _____
         CF   S

   DEFINITION: _____

24. pectoral

   _____ / _____
          R   S

   DEFINITION: _____

25. uvulopalatopharyngoplasty

   _____ / _____ / _____ / _____
         CF   CF   CF   S

   DEFINITION: _____

Complete the medical term by writing the missing part:

26. _____coni_____ = lung condition caused by prolonged dust inhalation

27. bronchi_____ = dilation of bronchus

28. _____plasty = surgical repair of the chest

29. _____itis = inflammation of the lung

30. _____metry = process of measuring breathing

31. _____ventilation = deficient movement of air in and out of the lungs

32. _____pnea = normal breathing

33. _____pnea = slow breathing

34. _____pnea = difficulty breathing

35. _____pnea = inability to breathe except in an upright position

36. _____pnea = inability to breathe

37. _____pnea = fast breathing

For each of the following, circle the meaning that corresponds to the combining form given:

38. **nose**	ren/o	rhin/o	nos/o
39. **air or lung**	aden/o	pneum/o	thorac/o
40. **throat**	thorac/o	laryng/o	pharyng/o
41. **chest**	thorac/o	pneum/o	lapar/o
42. **voice box**	laryng/o	trache/o	pharyng/o
43. **breathing**	aer/o	spir/o	crin/o
44. **diaphragm**	phren/o	pleur/o	pneumon/o
45. **mouth**	ox/o	or/o	spir/o

Write the correct medical term for each of the following:

46. air in the pleural space

_____

47. pus in the pleural space

_____

48. blood in the pleural space

_____

49. listening to sounds within the body

_____

50. endoscope used to examine the airways

    _____

51. coughing up and spitting out material from the lungs

    _____

52. inflammation of the pleura

    _____

53. to elicit sounds or vibrations by tapping

    _____

54. puncture for aspiration of the chest

    _____

55. hoarseness

    _____

56. inflammation of the voice box

    _____

57. deficient amount of oxygen in tissue cells

    _____

58. disease characterized by overexpansion of the alveoli with air

    _____

59. nosebleed _____

60. cancer originating in the bronchus

    _____

61. inherited condition of exocrine gland malfunction that causes mucus to obstruct
    the airways _____

62. collapse of lung tissue

    _____

63. material expelled from the lungs by coughing

    _____

64. high-pitched crowing sound that is a sign of obstruction in the upper airway

    _____

65. blood clot in the lungs

    _____

66. surgical creation of an opening in the trachea

    _____

67. disease characterized by paroxysmal wheezing, dyspnea, and cough

    _____

68. excessive movement of air in and out of the lungs

    _____

69. common lung infection seen in those with positive HIV

    _____

70. disorder that is a combination of emphysema and chronic bronchitis

    _____

Write the full medical term for the following abbreviations:

71. PEFR _____

72. VC _____

73. TB _____

74. CPR _____

75. COPD _____

76. PaCO$_2$ _____

77. URI _____

78. V$_T$ _____

79. PFT _____

80. PSG _____

81. CPAP _____

Match the following:

82. _____ crackles   a. naso

83. _____ wheezes   b. hyperventilation

84. _____ pleurisy   c. LTB

85. _____ pneumoconiosis   d. thoraco

86. _____ empyema   e. CPAP

87. _____ hemothorax   f. asbestosis

88. _____ stetho   g. pleuritis

89. _____ sleep apnea   h. rhonchi

90. _____ hypocapnia   i. pyothorax

91. _____ rhino   j. hypoventilation

92. _____ hypercapnia   k. rales

93. _____ croup   l. thoracentesis

Write the standard abbreviations for the following:

94. chest x-ray _____

95. analysis of blood to determine the adequacy of lung function in exchange of gases _____

96. surgical removal of the tonsils and adenoids _____

Write in the missing words on the blank lines in the following illustration of the respiratory tract.

97–104.

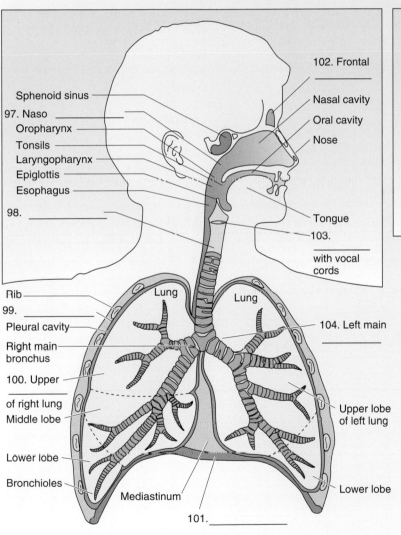

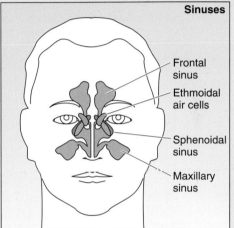

Sphenoid sinus

97. Naso _____

Oropharynx

Tonsils

Laryngopharynx

Epiglottis

Esophagus

98. _____

102. Frontal
_____

Nasal cavity

Oral cavity

Nose

Tongue

103. _____
with vocal cords

Sinuses

Frontal sinus

Ethmoidal air cells

Sphenoidal sinus

Maxillary sinus

Rib

99. _____

Pleural cavity

Right main bronchus

100. Upper _____ of right lung

Middle lobe

Lower lobe

Bronchioles

Mediastinum

101. _____

Lung   Lung

104. Left main _____

Upper lobe of left lung

Lower lobe

For each of the following, circle the correct spelling of the term:

105. auskucation	auscultation	ascultation
106. tackypnea	tachypenia	tachypnea
107. eupnea	eupenia	eupneia
108. plurisy	plurisey	pleurisy
109. hemathorax	hemothorax	hematothorex
110. stethoscope	stethescope	stethascope
111. epitaxes	epistaxes	epistaxis
112. ronchi	rhonchi	rhonkhi
113. hemoptysis	hemaptysis	hemoptsis
114. rhinorhea	rhinorrhea	rinorhea
115. imphasema	emphysema	emphasema
116. atelectasis	atalexisis	attelexis
117. bronkodielater	bronchodialator	bronchodilator

Give the noun that was used to form the following adjectives:

118. orthopneic _____

119. pleural _____

120. hypoxic _____

121. dyspneic _____

122. pharyngeal _____

123. apneic _____

124. tracheal _____

125. asthmatic _____

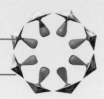

MEDICAL RECORD ANALYSES

MEDICAL RECORD 9.1

S: This is a 26 y.o. ♀ c/o a nonproductive cough, dyspnea, and fever × 2 d; pt does not smoke and has otherwise been in good health.

O: T 101°F, BP 100/64, R 25, 104
Tachypnea is accompanied by mild cyanosis, and inspiratory crackles are noted upon auscultation. WBC 31,000, Hct 37%, platelet count 109,000. CXR shows diffuse infiltrates at the bases of both lungs. An ABG taken while the patient was breathing room air showed a pH of 7.54, $PaCo_2$, of 20, PaO_2 of 74, sputum specimen contains 3+ WBC but no bacteria.

A: Pneumonia of unknown etiology

P: IV erythromycin STAT
admit to ICU
deliver O_2 by face mask and monitor for hypoxemia

1. What is the patient's chief complaint?
   a. afebrile with a dry cough and difficulty breathing
   b. febrile with a dry cough and difficulty breathing
   c. cannot breathe, fever, and coughing up material from the lungs
   d. hoarse throat, dry cough, and fever
   e. febrile, coughing up sputum, and breathing fast

2. What are the findings upon PE?
   a. slow breathing, blue skin, and rhonchi heard in the lungs as the patient exhales
   b. fast breathing, blue skin, and musical sounds heard in the lungs as the patient inhales
   c. slow breathing, blue skin, and rales heard in the lungs as the patient holds her breath
   d. fast heart, blue skin, and rales heard in the lungs as the patient inhales
   e. fast breathing, blue skin, and popping sounds heard in the lungs as the patient inhales

3. What did the chest x-ray show?
   a. tuberculosis
   b. asthma
   c. density representing solid material usually indicating inflammation
   d. fluid filling of spaces around the lungs
   e. lung cancer

4. What is the impression?
   a. dilation of the bronchi with an accumulation of mucus

   b. inflammation of the bronchi
   c. inflammation of the pleura
   d. inflammation of the lungs due to sensitivity to dust or chemicals
   e. inflammation of the lungs of unknown cause

5. What is an ABG?
   a. analysis of blood to determine the adequacy of lung function in the exchange of gases
   b. meausurement of lung volume and capacity
   c. measure of the flow of air during inspiration
   d. scan to detect breathing abnormalities
   e. image of the lungs used to visualize lung lesions

6. Describe the condition for which the patient was monitored while undergoing oxygen therapy:
   a. blockage of airflow out of the lungs
   b. excessive movement of air in and out of the lungs
   c. deficient amount of oxygen in the blood
   d. deficient amount of oxygen in the tissue cells
   e. excessive level of carbon dioxide in the blood

7. What is the Sig: on the erythromycin?
   a. not mentioned
   b. inject into a vein immediately
   c. take four immediately
   d. insert into the vagina immediately
   e. inject into a muscle immediately

MEDICAL RECORD 9.2

Angelica Torrance, a retired painter who for years has boasted to friends that she has the good health of a 30-year-old, suffered a broken ankle when she slipped off a footstool in her basement. The surgical repair of her fracture at Central Medical Center was routine, but soon after surgery Ms. Torrance developed other problems, and a pulmonologist was eventually called in for a consultation.

Directions

Read Medical Record 9.2 for Ms. Torrance (pages 300–302) and answer the following questions. This record is the history and physical examination report from Dr. Carl Brownley, the pulmonologist who consulted with Ms. Torrance's doctors after she developed breathing problems.

QUESTIONS ABOUT MEDICAL RECORD 9.2

Write your answers in the spaces provided.

1. Below are medical terms used in this record you have not yet encountered in this text. Underline each where it appears in the record and define below:

   morphine _____

   heparin _____

   obese _____

2. In your own words, not using medical terminology, describe what surgery Ms. Torrance had for her broken ankle:

   _____

   _____

   _____

3. Describe in your own words the four symptoms that Ms. Torrance developed postsurgically:

   a. _____
   b. _____
   c. _____
   d. _____

4. Before Ms. Torrance's acute "sense of suffocating," she was being treated with what three pharmacological treatments?

   a. _____
   b. _____
   c. _____

5. Immediately after her reported "sense of suffocating," she was given what two treatments?

   a. _____
   b. _____

6. Put the following events that occurred in the hospital in correct order by numbering them 1 to 8:

   _____ postoperative pulmonary symptoms

   _____ transport to intensive care

   _____ sense of suffocation

   _____ episode of tachycardia

   _____ nuclear lung scan showing high probability of embolus

   _____ evaluation for complications in the lungs

   _____ open reduction, internal fixation

   _____ intravenous drugs first administered

7. In your own words, not using medical terminology, describe the two diagnostic imaging studies performed the morning of 10/24:

   a. _____

   b. _____

8. Name and describe the test that was performed to monitor Ms. Torrance's heparin therapy:

   _____

   _____

   _____

9. Translate into lay language Dr. Brownley's first four assessments from the examination:

   a. _____

   b. _____

   c. _____

   d. _____

10. Dr. Brownley's recommendations include requests for certain tests to be run (or run again) and certain other actions to be taken while Ms. Torrance stays in the hospital. Without using abbreviations, list the tests to be performed and the actions to be taken:

    Tests:

    a. _____

    b. _____

    c. _____

    d. _____

    e. _____

    f. _____

    Actions:

    g. _____

    h. _____

CENTRAL MEDICAL CENTER

211 Medical Center Drive • Central City, US 90000-1234 • PHONE: (012) 125-6784 • FAX: (012) 125-9999

HISTORY

DATE OF CONSULTATION:
October 24, 20xx

HISTORY:
The patient is a 75-year-old woman who is admitted to this hospital on October 18, 20xx, after having fractured her right ankle. She underwent an ORIF of this lesion. Upon emerging from surgery, it was noted that she was quite wheezy and was having copious, purulent secretions. She was started on antibiotics; however, fever, cough, and breathlessness persisted. Finally, she was evaluated on October 20, 20xx, for possible pulmonary complications. A V/Q scan at that time showed a high probability for pulmonary emboli, and she was started on IV Heparin along with her antibiotics and bronchodilators. The patient did well with resolution of symptoms and fever and was progressing to the point of discharge.

Late yesterday evening, however, the patient developed the acute onset of "a sense of suffocating." This lasted for about 20-30 minutes and did resolve somewhat with the application of nasal oxygen and morphine sulfate 2 mg. The patient denies any cough, mucus, or actual chest pressure or pain. She denies any wheezing during this episode. Her heart rate went as high as 115-120; however, she was normotensive.

She was transported to ICU for further evaluation and management. An ECG obtained at that time revealed slight ST segment depression and T wave flattening at V4-6 with sinus tachycardia. Arterial blood gases done during the episode on 7 L O_2 showed a PaO_2 of 78, a pH of 7.44, and a $PaCO_2$ of 35. This morning, a chest x-ray revealed continuing resolution of the right upper and right lower lobe infiltrates. A V/Q scan showed evidence of resolving multiple perfusion defects on the right that appeared to actually match the defects noted on the chest x-ray. PTT, which had been continually in control during her Heparin therapy, was as high as 150 on 7 units of Heparin per hour.

PAST MEDICAL HISTORY:
The patient denies a past history of chronic respiratory disease but did have severe pneumonia about 30 years ago. The patient is a nonsmoker who has never smoked, and she has an essentially negative past medical history.

ALLERGIES:
The patient denies any personal allergies, but her family all suffer from chronic post nasal drip.

(continued)

PULMONARY CONSULTATION
Page 1

PT. NAME:	TORRANCE, ANGELICA W.
ID NO:	IP-228904
ROOM NO:	663
ATT. PHYS.	C. BROWNLEY, M.D.

Medical Record 9.2

CENTRAL MEDICAL CENTER

211 Medical Center Drive • Central City, US 90000-1234 • PHONE: (012) 125-6784 • FAX: (012) 125-9999

PHYSICAL EXAMINATION

GENERAL:
Well-nourished, somewhat overweight woman in no acute distress, having recently come back from x-ray with no undue dyspnea.

VITAL SIGNS:
BP: 110/70. Respirations: 16. Heart Rate: 80 and regular. Temperature: 99°.

CHEST:
LUNGS: Fair expansion bilaterally. Percussion node is normal. There are rare, distant end inspiratory rales at both bases.

HEART: No clinical cardiomegaly. There are no murmurs or gallops.

ABDOMEN:
Obese, soft, nontender.

EXTREMITIES:
1+ pretibial edema on the left with a cast on the right.

ASSESSMENT:
1. ACUTE ONSET OF SHORTNESS OF BREATH OF UNCLEAR ETIOLOGY.
2. HYPOXIA.
3. HYPOTHROMBINEMIA (PATIENT ON HEPARIN).
4. STATUS POST PULMONARY EMBOLISM WITH RESOLUTION AND NO EVIDENCE OF RECURRENCE.
5. STATUS POST OPEN REDUCTION INTERNAL FIXATION OF TRIMALLEOLAR FRACTURE ON THE RIGHT.
6. RULE OUT ACUTE MYOCARDIAL INFARCTION VERSUS ISCHEMIA.
7. POSSIBLE MUCUS PLUG.

(continued)

PULMONARY CONSULTATION Page 2	PT. NAME: TORRANCE, ANGELICA W. ID NO: IP-228904 ROOM NO: 663 ATT. PHYS. C. BROWNLEY, M.D.

Medical Record 9.2 *Continued.*

CENTRAL MEDICAL CENTER

211 Medical Center Drive • Central City, US 90000-1234 • PHONE: (012) 125-6784 • FAX: (012) 125-9999

PHYSICAL EXAMINATION

RECOMMENDATIONS:

Cardiac enzymes should be obtained, and the ECG should be repeated as well. Recheck ABGs. Recheck PTT and discontinue Heparin until PTT diminishes to the 60s. Check CBC and comprehensive metabolic panel. Continue to observe in the ICU.

It is somewhat unclear as to what is the etiology of the episode of dyspnea. A possibility might be a mucous plug which has mobilized into the central airway and momentarily caused increased respiratory distress.

Thank you for the opportunity to assist in the management of this patient.

C. Brownley

C. Brownley, M.D.
Pulmonologist

CB:im

D: 10/24/20xx
T: 10/25/20xx

PULMONARY CONSULTATION Page 3	PT. NAME:	TORRANCE, ANGELICA W.
	ID NO:	IP-228904
	ROOM NO:	663
	ATT. PHYS.	C. BROWNLEY, M.D.

Medical Record 9.2 *Continued.*

MEDICAL RECORD 9.3

Richard Puma, a heavy smoker until recently, had been treated for pneumonia in the last month. Even though his condition had deteriorated in the last few days, he refused to be hospitalized. Today, May 18, having much trouble breathing, he came to Central Medical Center and was seen by Dr. Theresa Cunningham.

Directions

Read Medical Record 9.3 for Richard Puma (pages 306–309) and answer the following questions. This record includes the history, physical examination, and discharge summary dictated by Dr. Cunningham and transcribed the next day.

QUESTIONS ABOUT MEDICAL RECORD 9.3

Write your answers in the spaces provided.

1. Below are medical terms used in these records you have not yet encountered in this text. Underline each where it appears in the record and define below:

   hepatosplenomegaly _____

   precordial _____

   fulminant _____

   respiratory acidosis _____

   cardiac arrest _____

2. In your own words, not using medical terminology, describe Mr. Puma's chief complaint to Dr. Cunningham:

   _____

   _____

   _____

3. Following are various elements from the history of Mr. Puma's present illness. Put them in correct chronological order by numbering them 1 to 7, starting with the event that occurred first:

   ___ productive cough with some show of blood

   ___ seen at the Bradford Emergiclinic

   ___ progressively worsening with marked SOB

   ___ diagnosis of pneumonia

   ___ refusal to be hospitalized

   ___ administration of Cipro began

   ___ administration of Cipro started a second time

4. In your own words, not using medical terminology, describe how Mr. Puma looked in general at the time of examination:

_____

_____

_____

5. Although examination of the abdomen produced no negative findings, Dr. Cunningham's auscultation of the lungs and heart was more significant. In your own words, what were her findings?

_____

_____

_____

6. Dr. Cunningham concluded her examination with a diagnosis and treatment plan. Although the cause of Mr. Puma's condition is unclear, the diagnosis statement itself is definite. Describe it in your own words:

_____

_____

_____

7. In the history and physical examination, Dr. Cunningham's treatment plan called for what immediate action?

_____

_____

_____

8. As noted in the discharge summary, Dr. Anderson was next to see Mr. Puma. In your own words, describe Dr. Anderson's specialty:

_____

9. What diagnostic test was first to be performed on admission to the CCU?

_____

10. During the CCU examination, what happened to Mr. Puma?

_____

How did Dr. Anderson respond?

_____

11. Put Dr. Cunningham's final three diagnoses in your own words (do not include history or treatment information):

    a. _____

    b. _____

    c. _____

CENTRAL MEDICAL CENTER

211 Medical Center Drive • Central City, US 90000-1234 • PHONE: (012) 125-6784

HISTORY

CHIEF COMPLAINT:
Marked respiratory distress.

HISTORY OF PRESENT ILLNESS:
The patient is a 62-year-old white male with a history of pneumonia diagnosed four weeks ago. He appeared to have a favorable response to a two-week course of Cipro; however, after being off the medication for two days, symptoms including hemoptysis and yellow sputum returned. He was restarted on half a dose of the antibiotic for five more days with some improvement. This was finished 1½ weeks ago. Over the past 10 days, he has become progressively worse with a marked increase in shortness of breath and orthopnea. Two days ago, he was seen at the Bradford Emergiclinic because of the progressive nature of his shortness of breath. At that time, hospitalization was recommended, but the patient refused.

PAST MEDICAL HISTORY:
The patient states there is no prior history of heart disease, although he says an electrocardiogram showed a possible old heart attack in the past; this was noted approximately 14 years ago. He has a history of possible hypertension in the past.

ALLERGIES: He has no known allergies.

HABITS: He smoked two packs of cigarettes per day for 35 years; he stopped one month ago. He drinks approximately one beer a month.

SURGERIES: He had several hernia surgeries in the past.

FAMILY HISTORY: The patient's father died at age 42 of heart problems.

REVIEW OF SYSTEMS:
Noncontributory to the present illness.

(continued)

HISTORY AND PHYSICAL
Page 1

PT. NAME: PUMA, RICHARD G.
ID NO: 077321
ADM. DATE: May 18, 20xx
ATT. PHYS. T. CUNNINGHAM, M.D.

Medical Record 9.3

CENTRAL MEDICAL CENTER

211 Medical Center Drive • Central City, US 90000-1234 • PHONE: (012) 125-6784

PHYSICAL EXAMINATION

GENERAL APPEARANCE:
Markedly tachypneic, thin, cyanotic white male in marked respiratory distress. VITAL SIGNS:
Blood pressure: 90/50.

HEENT:
Eyes: Pupils are equal and reactive to light and accommodation. Extraocular movements are
normal. Ears, nose, and throat are negative.

NECK: Supple. Jugular venous pulsations are normal. Carotids are 2+ and equal bilaterally
without bruit.

CHEST:
LUNGS: There is a very rapid rate with a few basilar rales and decreased breath sounds in the
bases.

HEART: It was difficult to auscultate because of the marked tachypnea and respiratory noises.
There were no obvious murmurs heard.

ABDOMEN: Soft and nontender. No hepatosplenomegaly or masses were noted.

GENITALIA/RECTAL:
Normal male. The rectal examination was not performed due to the acute nature of the patient's
illness.

EXTREMITIES:
There was no edema. Peripheral pulses are barely palpable. There was no marked cyanosis.

LABORATORY AND X-RAY DATA:
An electrocardiogram shows regular sinus rhythm with PVCs and fusion beats, nonspecific interior
ventricular conduction delay, right axis deviation, poor precordial R-wave progression, and
nonspecific ST-T wave changes.

(continued)

HISTORY AND PHYSICAL Page 2	PT. NAME: PUMA, RICHARD G. ID NO: 077321 ADM. DATE: May 18, 20xx ATT. PHYS. T. CUNNINGHAM, M.D.

Medical Record 9.3 *Continued.*

CENTRAL MEDICAL CENTER

211 Medical Center Drive · Central City, US 90000-1234 · PHONE: (012) 125-6784

PHYSICAL EXAMINATION

IMPRESSION:

1. MARKED, SEVERE RESPIRATORY DISTRESS WITH CYANOSIS DUE TO UNKNOWN ETIOLOGY. RULE OUT FULMINANT PNEUMONIA, RULE OUT CONGESTIVE HEART FAILURE, RULE OUT OTHER CAUSES.

2. CHRONIC OBSTRUCTIVE PULMONARY DISEASE.

3. POSSIBLE HISTORY OF HYPERTENSION, PRESENTLY HYPOTENSIVE.

PLAN:

The patient is admitted to the CCU immediately after being seen in the office. Upon admission, he will be seen by Dr. Anderson in pulmonary consult. Further evaluation and treatment will depend upon the results of the studies.

T. Cunningham, M.D.

T. Cunningham, M.D.

TC:ti

D: 5/18/xx
T: 5/19/xx

HISTORY AND PHYSICAL PAGE 3	PT. NAME: PUMA, RICHARD G. ID NO: 077321 ADM. DATE: May 18, 20xx ATT. PHYS. T. CUNNINGHAM, M.D.

Medical Record 9.3 _Continued._

CENTRAL MEDICAL CENTER

211 Medical Center Drive • Central City, US 90000-1234 • PHONE: (012) 125-6784

DISCHARGE SUMMARY

DATE OF ADMISSION: May 18, 20xx   **DATE OF DISCHARGE:** May 18, 20xx

DIAGNOSES:
1. ACUTE SEVERE RESPIRATORY DISTRESS, WITH RESPIRATORY FAILURE, TREATED, DIED.
2. CARDIAC ARREST, DUE TO UNKNOWN ETIOLOGY, PROBABLY SECONDARY TO MARKED PULMONARY DISEASE, TREATED WITH CARDIOPULMONARY RESUSCITATION, UNSUCCESSFUL.
3. CHRONIC OBSTRUCTIVE PULMONARY DISEASE WITH A LONG HISTORY OF TOBACCO ABUSE.

SUMMARY:
This patient was seen in the office on the morning of admission in marked respiratory distress. He was markedly tachypneic and cyanotic, and he had a history of pneumonia which was treated one month ago with progressive symptoms over the past week.

The patient was admitted immediately to the CCU where he was met by M. Anderson, M.D., a pulmonologist, who saw him in consultation. During the initial evaluation, while the patient was getting ready for a CXR in the CCU, he suddenly had a cardiac arrest.

Resuscitation was begun immediately. The patient was seen by me at that time; however, he did not respond to any measures. An arterial line was placed. He had marked respiratory acidosis, and after no response to resuscitation, he was pronounced dead.

T. Cunningham, M.D.

TC:ti

D: 5/18/xx
T: 5/19/xx

DISCHARGE SUMMARY	PT. NAME:	PUMA, RICHARD G.
	ID NO:	077321
	ROOM:	CCU
	ATT. PHYS.	T. CUNNINGHAM, M.D.

Medical Record 9.3 *Continued.*

Chapter 10

Nervous System

OBJECTIVES

After completion of this chapter you will be able to

- Define common term components used in relation to the nervous system and psychiatry
- Describe the basic functions of the nervous system
- Define the basic anatomical terms referring to the nervous system
- Define common symptomatic and diagnostic terms related to the nervous system
- Define common diagnostic terms related to the nervous system
- List common diagnostic tests and procedures related to the nervous system
- Define common operative terms related to the nervous system
- Define common therapeutic terms including drug classifications related to the nervous system
- Define common symptomatic terms related to psychiatry
- Define common diagnostic terms related to psychiatry
- Define common therapeutic terms related to psychiatry
- Explain common terms and abbreviations used in documenting medical records involving the nervous system or field of psychiatry

Combining Forms

Combining Form	Meaning	Example
arthr/o	articulation	dysarthria
cerebell/o	cerebellum (little brain)	cerebellar ser-e-bel′ar
cerebr/o	cerebrum (largest part of brain)	cerebrospinal ser′ĕ-brō-spī-năl
crani/o	skull	cranium krā′nē-ŭm
encephal/o	entire brain	encephalography en-sef-ă-log′ră-fĕ
esthesi/o	sensation	hyperesthesia hī′per-es-thē′zē-ă
gangli/o	ganglion (knot)	ganglioneuroma gang′glē-ō-nū-rō′mă

Combining Form	Meaning	Example
gli/o	glue	glial glī′ăl
gnos/o	knowing	gnosia nō′sēă
hypn/o	sleep	hypnosis hip-nō′sis
somn/i		somnipathy som-nip′ă-thē
somn/o		polysomnography pol′ē-som-nog′ră-fē
kinesi/o	movement	kinesiology ki-nē-sē-ol′ō-jē
lex/o	word or phrase	dyslexia dis-lek′sē-ă
mening/o	meninges (membrane)	meningocele mě-ning′gō-sēl
meningi/o		meningitis men-in-jī′tis
myel/o	spinal cord or bone marrow	myeloma mī-ě-lō′mă
narc/o	stupor, sleep	narcotic nar-kot′ik
neur/o	nerve	neuralgia nū-ral′jē-ă
phas/o	speech	dysphasia dis-fā′zē-ă
phob/o	exaggerated fear or sensitivity	phobia fō′bē-ă
phor/o	carry or bear	euphoria yu-fōr′ē-ă
phren/o	mind	schizophrenia skiz′-ō-frē′nē-ă
psych/o		psychotic sī-kot′ik
thym/o		dysthymia dis-thī′mē-ă
schiz/o	split	schizoid skiz′oyd
somat/o	body	psychosomatic sī′kō-sō-mat′ik
spin/o	spine (thorn)	spinal spī′năl
spondyl/o	vertebra	spondylosyndesis spon′di-lō-sin-dē′sis
vertebr/o		vertebral ver′te-brăl

Combining Form	Meaning	Example
stere/o	three dimensional or solid	stereotaxic ster′ē-ō-tak′sik
tax/o	order or coordination	ataxic ă-tak′sik
thalam/o	thalamus (a room)	thalamotomy thal-ă-mot′ō-mē
ton/o	tone or tension	tonic ton′ik
top/o	place	topesthesia top′es-thē′-zē-ă
ventricul/o	ventricle (belly or pouch)	ventriculostomy ven-trik-yū-los′tō-mē
ADDITIONAL PREFIX		
cata-	down	catatonic kat-ă-ton′ik
ADDITIONAL SUFFIXES		
-asthenia	weakness	neurasthenia nūr-as-thē′nē-ă
-lepsy	seizure	narcolepsy nar′kō-lep-sē
-mania	condition of abnormal impulse toward	necromania nek-rō-mā′nē-ă
-paresis	slight paralysis	hemiparesis hem′ē-pa-rē′sis
-plegia	paralysis	paraplegia par-ă-plē′jē-ă

Nervous System Overview

The nervous system is an intricate communication network of structures that activates and controls all functions of the body and receives all input from the environment.

There are two major classes of cells that make up the nervous system: the *neuron,* the basic structure, and the *neuroglia,* the supporting cells (Fig. 10.1).

Each neuron is made up of a *soma* (the body of the neuron), *dendrites* (the afferent branches of the soma), and an *axon* (the efferent branch of the soma), which are linked via terminals called *synapses.* At the synapse, chemicals known as *neurotransmitters* are released to effect changes that inhibit or excite cells. They function within the vast complex of impulse-carrying fibers called *nerves.* A ganglion is a collection of somas in the peripheral nervous system, and a nucleus is a collection of somas in the central nervous system.

Four types of neuroglia perform essential functions in the nervous system: *ependymal cells* make the cerebrospinal fluid that circulates in and around the brain and spinal cord. The star-shaped *astrocytes* have the responsibility of passing nutrients from blood to neurons. *Myelin,* the lipid that surrounds nerve fibers and helps to conduct neuronal impulses, is produced by the *oligodendroglia.* The small, branching *microglia* perform phagocytosis.

The nervous system has three divisions: (*a*) central nervous system, (*b*) peripheral nervous system, and (*c*) autonomic nervous system.

NEURON

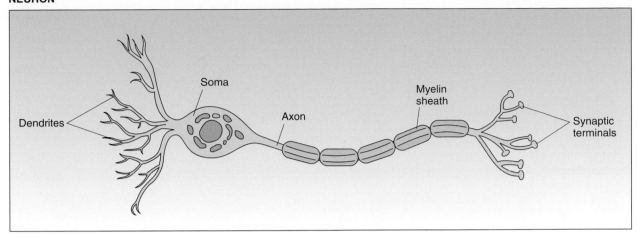

GLIAL CELLS

Ependymal cells
(line brain ventricles)

Oligodendrocytes
(wrap axons: myelination)

Astrocytes
(support capillaries)

Microglial cells
(engulf invading
microorganisms
and dead tissues)

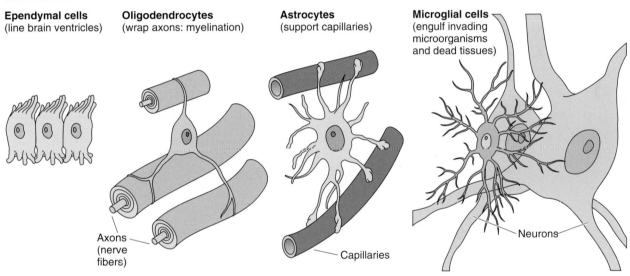

Figure 10.1 Basic components of the nervous system.

Anatomical Terms

Term	Meaning
central nervous system (CNS)	brain and spinal cord
brain	portion of the central nervous system contained within the cranium
cerebrum sĕr-ē′brum	largest portion of the brain; it is divided into right and left halves known as *cerebral hemispheres* that are connected by a bridge of nerve fibers called the *corpus callosum;* lobes of the cerebrum are named after the skull bones they underlie (Fig. 10.2)
frontal lobe frŭn′tăl lōb	anterior section of each cerebral hemisphere responsible for voluntary muscle movement and personality
parietal lobe pă-rī′ĕ-tăl lōb	portion posterior to the frontal lobe, responsible for sensations such as pain, temperature, and touch

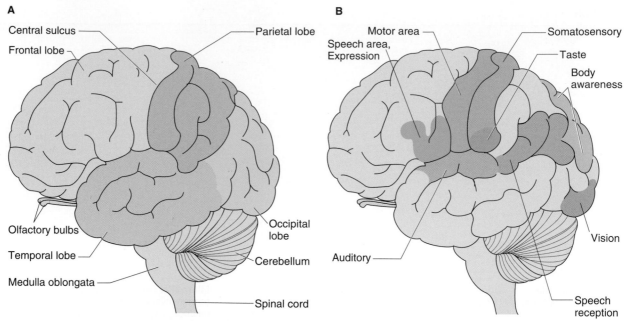

Figure 10.2 **A.** Lobes of the brain. **B.** Localized functions of the cerebrum.

Term	Meaning
temporal lobe tem′pŏ-răl lōb	portion that lies below the frontal lobe, responsible for hearing, taste, and smell
occipital lobe ok-sip′i-tăl lōb	portion posterior to the parietal and temporal lobes, responsible for vision
cerebral cortex ser′ĕ-brăl kōr′teks	outer layer of the cerebrum consisting of gray matter, responsible for higher mental functions (cortex = bark)
thalamus (diencephalon) thal′ă-mŭs dī-en-sef′ă-lon	two gray matter nuclei deep within the brain, responsible for relaying sensory information to the cortex
gyri jī′rī	ring or circle; convolutions (mounds) of the cerebral hemispheres
sulci sŭl′sī	ditch; shallow grooves that separate gyri
fissures fish′ŭrz	splitting crack; deep grooves in the brain
cerebellum ser-ĕ-bel′ŭm	portion of the brain located below the occipital lobes of the cerebrum, responsible for control and coordination of skeletal muscles (Fig. 10.3)
brainstem brān′stem	region of the brain that serves as a relay between the cerebrum, cerebellum, and spinal cord, responsible for breathing, heart rate, and body temperature; there are three levels: mesencephalon (midbrain), pons, and medulla oblongata
ventricles ven′tri-klz	series of interconnected cavities within the cerebral hemispheres and brainstem filled with cerebrospinal fluid (Fig. 10.4)

THE BRAIN

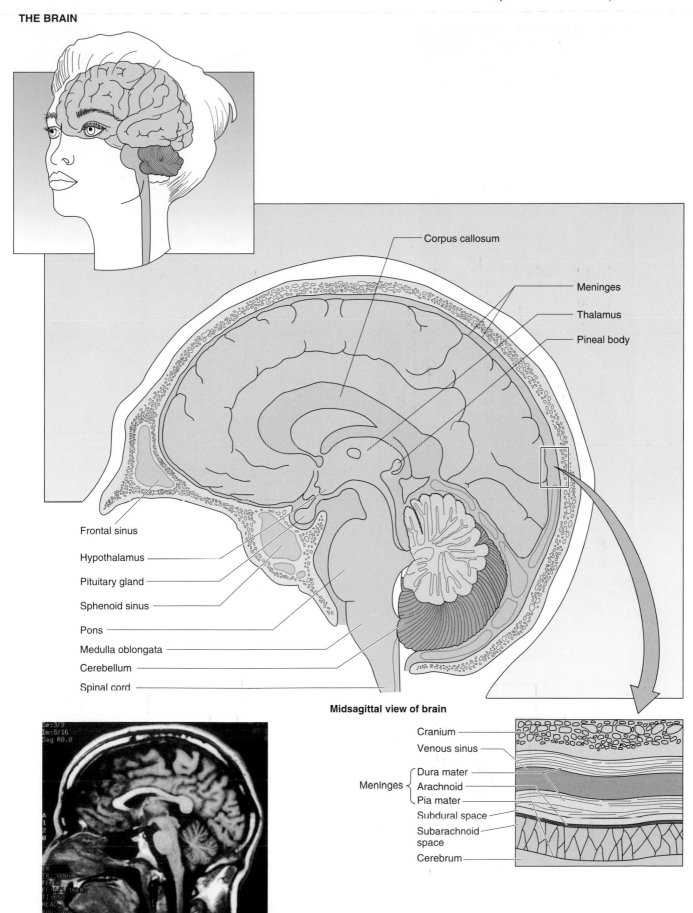

Corpus callosum

Meninges

Thalamus

Pineal body

Frontal sinus

Hypothalamus

Pituitary gland

Sphenoid sinus

Pons

Medulla oblongata

Cerebellum

Spinal cord

Midsagittal view of brain

Cranium

Venous sinus

Dura mater

Arachnoid

Pia mater

Meninges

Subdural space

Subarachnoid space

Cerebrum

Magnetic resonance imaging (MRI) of normal brain, midsagittal view

Figure 10.3 Midsagittal view of the brain.

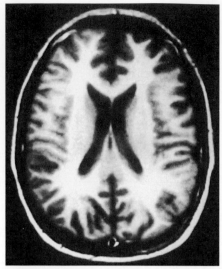

Magnetic resonance image, horizontal view A

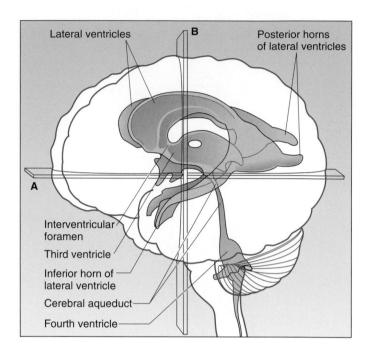

Lateral ventricles

B

Posterior horns
of lateral ventricles

Interventricular
foramen

Third ventricle

Inferior horn of
lateral ventricle

Cerebral aqueduct

Fourth ventricle

A

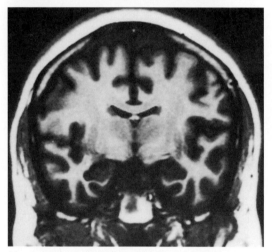

Magnetic resonance image, coronal view B

Figure 10.4 Ventricles of the brain.

Term	Meaning
cerebrospinal fluid (CSF) ser′ĕ-brō-spī-năl flū′id	plasma-like clear fluid circulating in and around the brain and spinal cord
spinal cord spī′năl kōrd	column of nervous tissue from the brainstem through the vertebrae, responsible for nerve conduction to and from the brain and the body
meninges mĕ-nin′jēz	three membranes that cover the brain and spinal cord, consisting of the dura mater, pia mater, and arachnoid
peripheral nervous system (PNS)	nerves that branch from the central nervous system, including nerves of the brain (cranial nerves) and spinal cord (spinal nerves) (Fig. 10.5)
cranial nerves krā′nē-ăl nervz	12 pairs of nerves arising from the brain

THE PERIPHERAL NERVOUS SYSTEM

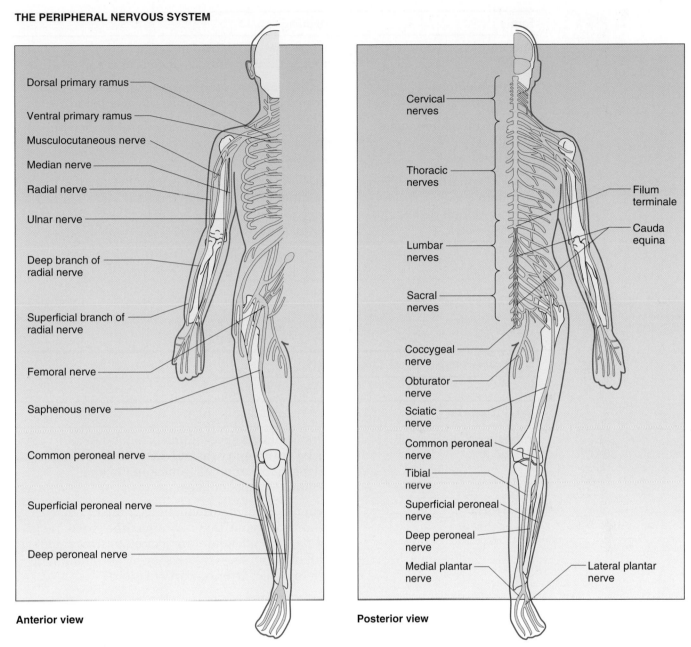

Dorsal primary ramus

Ventral primary ramus

Musculocutaneous nerve

Median nerve

Radial nerve

Ulnar nerve

Deep branch of
radial nerve

Superficial branch of
radial nerve

Femoral nerve

Saphenous nerve

Common peroneal nerve

Superficial peroneal nerve

Deep peroneal nerve

Anterior view

Cervical
nerves

Thoracic
nerves

Lumbar
nerves

Sacral
nerves

Coccygeal
nerve

Obturator
nerve

Sciatic
nerve

Common peroneal
nerve

Tibial
nerve

Superficial peroneal
nerve

Deep peroneal
nerve

Medial plantar
nerve

Filum
terminale

Cauda
equina

Lateral plantar
nerve

Posterior view

Figure 10.5 Peripheral nervous system.

Term	Meaning
spinal nerves	31 pairs of nerves arising from the spinal cord
sensory nerves sen′sŏ-rē nervz	nerves that conduct impulses from body parts and carry sensory information to the brain—also called afferent nerves (ad = toward; ferre = carry)
motor nerves	nerves that conduct motor impulses from the brain to muscles and glands; also called efferent nerves (e = out; ferre = carry)

Term	Meaning
autonomic nervous system (ANS)	nerves that carry involuntary impulses to smooth muscle, cardiac muscle, and various glands
hypothalamus hī′pō-thal′ă-mŭs	control center for the autonomic nervous system located below the thalamus (diencephalon)
sympathetic nervous system sim-pă-thet′ik	division of the ANS concerned primarily with preparing the body in stressful or emergency situations
parasympathetic nervous system par-ă-sim-pă-thet′ik	division of the ANS that is most active in ordinary conditions; it counterbalances the effects of the sympathetic system by restoring the body to a restful state after a stressful experience

Symptomatic and Diagnostic Terms

Term	Meaning
SYMPTOMATIC	
aphasia ă-fā′zē-ă	condition without speech; impairment due to localized brain injury that affects understanding, retrieving, and formulating meaningful and sequential elements of language
dysarthria dis-ar′thrē-ă	condition of difficult articulation; group of related speech impairments that may affect the speed, range, direction, strength, and timing of motor movement as a result of paralysis, weakness, or incoordination of speech muscles (arthr/o = articulation)
dysphasia dis-fā′zē-ă	difficulty speaking
coma kō′mă	general term referring to levels of decreased consciousness with varying responsiveness; a common method of assessment is the Glasgow coma scale (Fig. 10.6)
delirium dē-lir′ē-ŭm	state of mental confusion due to disturbances in cerebral function—there are many causes, including fever, shock, or drug overdose (deliro = to draw the furrow awry in plowing, i.e., to go off the rails)
dementia dē-men′shē-ă	impairment of intellectual function characterized by memory loss, disorientation, and confusion (dementio = to be mad)
motor deficit mō′ter def′i-sit	loss or impairment of muscle function
sensory deficit sen′sŏ-rē def′i-sit	loss or impairment of sensation

COMA. Coma is derived from a Greek word meaning a deep sleep, a state of unconsciousness from which one cannot be roused. In Greek mythology, Comus was the guardian of banquets who indulged in nightly orgies that resulted in a state of profound insensibility caused by a drunken stupor. The ingestion of a toxin such as alcohol is only one of many causes of coma. The words comic and comical share the same origin with coma.

Glasgow Coma Scale			A.M.	P.M.				A.M.					
Assessment	Reaction	Score	8	10	12	2	4	6	8	10	12	2	4	6	8
Eye Opening	Spontaneously	4	X							X	X	X	X	X
Response	To speech	3		X				X						
	To pain	2			X	X	X							
	No response	1												
Motor Response	Obeys verbal command	6	X							X	X	X	X	X
	Localizes pain	5		X	X									
	Flexion withdrawal	4				X		X						
	Flexion	3					X							
	Extension	2												
	No response	1												
Verbal Response	Oriented x3	5	X							X	X	X	X	X
	Conversation confused	4		X				X						
	Inappropriate speech	3		X										
	Incomprehensible sounds	2			X	X								
	No response	1												

Figure 10.6 Glasgow Coma Scale scoring for a child. A score of 3 to 8 denotes severe trauma; a score of 9 to 12 denotes moderate trauma; and a score of 13 to 15 denotes slight trauma. Notice the gradual improvement from coma in this example.

Term	Meaning
neuralgia nū-ral′jē-ă	pain along the course of a nerve
paralysis	temporary or permanent loss of motor control
flaccid paralysis flas′sid pă-ral′i-sis	defective (flabby) or absent muscle control caused by a nerve lesion
spastic paralysis spas′tik pă-ral′i-sis	stiff and awkward muscle control caused by a central nervous system disorder
hemiparesis hem-ē-pa-rē′sis	partial paralysis of the right or left half of the body
sciatica sī-at′i-kă	pain that follows the pathway of the sciatic nerve caused by compression or trauma of the nerve or its roots
seizure sē′zher	sudden, transient disturbances in brain function resulting from abnormal firing of nerve impulses (may or may not be associated with convulsion)
convulsion kon-vŭl′shŭn	to pull together; type of seizure that causes a series of sudden, involuntary contractions of muscles
syncope sin′kŏ-pē	fainting
tactile stimulation tak′til	evoking a response by touching

Term	Meaning
hyperesthesia hī′per-es-thē′zē-ă	increased sensitivity to stimulation such as touch or pain
paresthesia par-es-thē′zē-ă	abnormal sensation of numbness and tingling without objective cause

DIAGNOSTIC

Term	Meaning
agnosia ag-nō′sē-ă	any of many types of loss of neurological function associated with interpretation of sensory information
astereognosis ă-stēr′ē-og-nō′sis	inability to judge the form of an object by touch (e.g., a coin from a key)
atopognosis ă-top-og-nō′sis	inability to locate a sensation properly, such as to locate a point touched on the body
Alzheimer disease	disease of structural changes in the brain resulting in an irreversible deterioration that progresses from forgetfulness and disorientation to loss of all intellectual functions, total disability, and death (see Fig. 10.19)
amyotrophic lateral sclerosis (ALS) ā-mī-ō-trō′fik	a condition of progressive deterioration of motor nerve cells resulting in total loss of voluntary muscle control; symptoms advance from muscle weakness in the arms, legs, muscles of speech, swallowing, and breathing to total paralysis and death—also known as Lou Gehrig disease
cerebral palsy (CP) ser′ĕ-brăl pawl′zē	condition of motor dysfunction caused by damage to the cerebrum during development or injury at birth, characterized by partial paralysis and lack of muscle coordination (palsy = paralysis)
cerebrovascular disease	disorder resulting from a change within one or more blood vessels of the brain
cerebral arteriosclerosis ar-tēr′ē-ō-skler-ō′sis	hardening of the arteries of the brain
cerebral atherosclerosis ath′er-ō-skler-ō′sis	condition of lipid (fat) buildup within the blood vessels of the brain (ather/o = fatty [lipid] paste)
cerebral aneurysm an′yū-rizm	dilation of a blood vessel in the brain (aneurysm = dilation or widening)
cerebral thrombosis throm-bō′sis	presence of a stationary clot in a blood vessel of the brain
cerebral embolism em′bō-lizm	obstruction of a blood vessel in the brain by an embolus transported through the circulation
cerebrovascular accident (CVA) stroke	damage to the brain caused by cerebrovascular disease (e.g., occlusion of a blood vessel by an embolus or thrombus or intracranial hemorrhage after rupture of an aneurysm) (Fig. 10.7)
transient ischemic attack (TIA) tran′zē-ĕnt is-kē′mik	brief episode of loss of blood flow to the brain usually caused by a partial occlusion that results in temporary neurological deficit (impairment)—often precedes a CVA (Fig. 10.8)

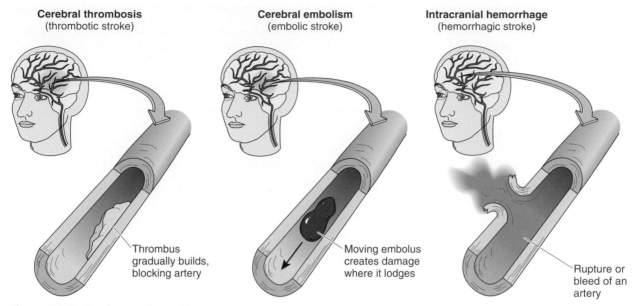

Cerebral thrombosis
(thrombotic stroke)

Cerebral embolism
(embolic stroke)

Intracranial hemorrhage
(hemorrhagic stroke)

Thrombus gradually builds, blocking artery

Moving embolus creates damage where it lodges

Rupture or bleed of an artery

Figure 10.7 Cerebrovascular accident.

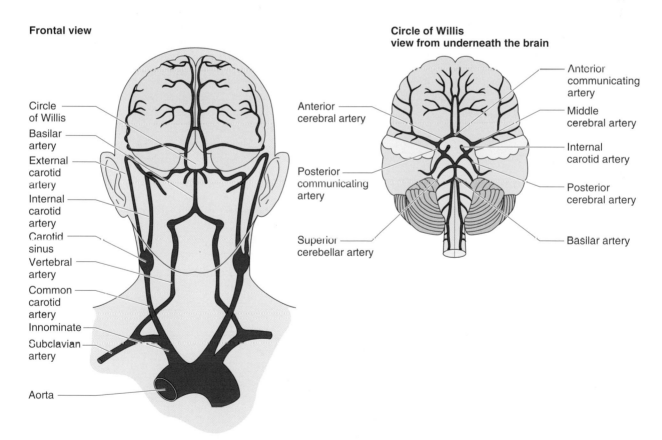

Frontal view

Circle of Willis view from underneath the brain

Circle of Willis
Basilar artery
External carotid artery
Internal carotid artery
Carotid sinus
Vertebral artery
Common carotid artery
Innominate
Subclavian artery
Aorta

Anterior cerebral artery

Posterior communicating artery

Superior cerebellar artery

Anterior communicating artery
Middle cerebral artery
Internal carotid artery
Posterior cerebral artery
Basilar artery

Figure 10.8 Sites of transient ischemic attack: carotid and vertebrobasilar circulation.

CAROTID.
Carotid stems from the Greek word meaning to stupefy or throttle. The ancients used the term to describe the arteries in the neck because they believed that when they were pressed hard, one became sleepy.

EPILEPSY.
Epilepsy comes from a Greek word for seizure. Aristotle used the word to mean a convulsive seizure, a condition that came to be called epilepsy. It was regarded in ancient times as an infliction from the gods, hence the Roman term, morbus sacer (sacred disease). Many other terms were applied to epilepsy, such as "disease of Hercules" because sufferers seemed to have superhuman strength.

Term	Meaning
carotid TIA ka-rot'id	ischemia of the anterior circulation of the brain
vertebrobasilar TIA ver'tĕ-brō-bas'i-lăr	ischemia of the posterior circulation of the brain
encephalitis en-sef-ă-lī'tis	inflammation of the brain
epilepsy ep'i-lep'sē	disorder affecting the central nervous system characterized by recurrent seizures
tonic-clonic ton'ik-klon'ik	stiffening-jerking; a major motor seizure involving all muscle groups—previously termed grand mal (big bad) seizure
absence ab'sens	seizure involving a brief loss of consciousness without motor involvement—previously termed petit mal (little bad) seizure
partial	seizure involving only limited areas of the brain with localized symptoms
glioma glī-ō'mă	tumor of glial cells graded by degree of malignancy
herniated disk her'nē-ā-ted	protrusion of a degenerated or fragmented intervertebral disk so that the nucleus pulposus protrudes, causing compression on the nerve root (Fig. 10.9)
herpes zoster her'pēz zos'ter	viral disease affecting the peripheral nerves, characterized by painful blisters that spread over the skin following the affected nerves, usually unilaterally—also known as shingles (Fig. 10.10)
Huntington disease (HD)	hereditary disease of the central nervous system
Huntington chorea kōr-ē'ă	characterized by bizarre involuntary body movements and progressive dementia (choros = dance)

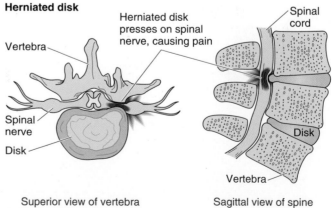

Superior view of vertebra   Sagittal view of spine

Figure 10.9 Herniated disk.

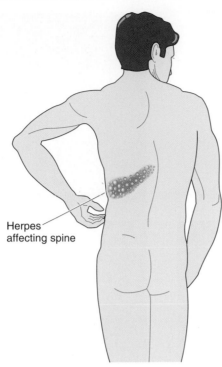

Herpes
affecting spine

Figure 10.10 Herpes zoster: typical eruption site.

Term	Meaning
hydrocephalus hī-drō-sef′ă-lŭs **hydrocephaly**	abnormal accumulation of cerebrospinal fluid in the ventricles of the brain as a result of developmental anomalies, infection, injury, or tumor (Fig. 10.11; also see Fig. 10.13)
meningioma mě-nin′jē-ō′mă	benign tumor of the coverings of the brain (meninges)
meningitis men-in-jī′tis	inflammation of the meninges
migraine headache mī′grān	paroxysmal attacks of mostly unilateral headache often accompanied by disordered vision, nausea, and/or vomiting, lasting hours or days and caused by dilation of arteries
multiple sclerosis (MS) sklě-rō′sis	disease of the central nervous system characterized by the demyelination (deterioration of the myelin sheath) of nerve fibers, with episodes of neurological dysfunction (exacerbation) followed by recovery (remission) (Fig. 10.12)
myasthenia gravis mī-as-thē′nē-ă gra′văs	autoimmune disorder that affects the neuromuscular junction, causing a progressive decrease in muscle strength with activity and a return of strength after a period of rest
myelitis mī-ě-lī′tis	inflammation of the spinal cord

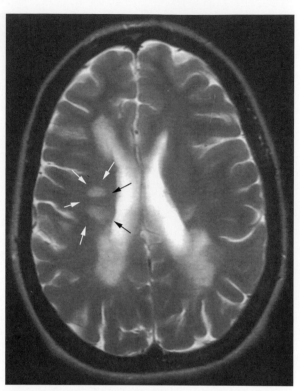

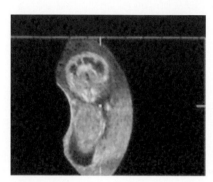

Figure 10.11 Sonogram of fetus with hydrocephalus.

Figure 10.12 Magnetic resonance image of the brain. *Arrows,* plaque formation in a patient with multiple sclerosis.

Term	Meaning
narcolepsy nar′kō-lep-sē	sleep disorder characterized by a sudden, uncontrollable need to sleep, attacks of paralysis (cataplexy), and dreams intruding while awake (hypnagogic hallucinations)
Parkinson disease	condition of slowly progressive degeneration of an area of the brainstem (substantia nigra) resulting in a decrease of dopamine (a chemical neurotransmitter that is necessary for proper movement); characterized by tremor, rigidity of muscles, and slow movements (bradykinesia), usually occurring later in life
plegia plē′jē-ă	paralysis
hemiplegia hem-ē-plē′jē-ă	paralysis on one side of the body
paraplegia par-ă-plē′jē-ă	paralysis from the waist down
quadriplegia kwah′dri-plē′jē-ă	paralysis of all four limbs
poliomyelitis po′lē-ō-mi′ě-lī′tis	inflammation of the gray matter of the spinal cord caused by a virus, often resulting in spinal and muscle deformity and paralysis (polio = gray)

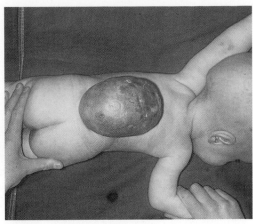

Figure 10.13 Spina bifida with myelomeningocele. The infant also has hydrocephaly.

Term	Meaning
polyneuritis pol′ē-nū-rī′tis	inflammation involving two or more nerves, often owing to a nutritional deficiency such as lack of thiamine
reflex sympathetic dystrophy (RSD) rē′fleks sim-pă-thet′ik dis′trŏ-fē	condition of abnormal function of the sympathetic nervous system in response to pain perception, usually as the result of an injury to an extremity; symptoms include persistent burning pain, tissue edema, joint tenderness, changes in skin color and temperature, and abnormal sweating at the pain site—decreased mobility caused by pain can lead to muscle atrophy and loss of motor function
sleep apnea ap′nē-ă	periods of breathing cessation that occur during sleep, often causing snoring
spina bifida spī′nă bi′fă-dă	congenital defect in the spinal column characterized by the absence of vertebral arches, often resulting in pouching of spinal membranes or tissue (Fig. 10.13)

Diagnostic Tests and Procedures

Test or Procedure	Explanation
electrodiagnostic procedures ē-lek′trō-dī-ag-nōs′tik	
electroencephalogram (EEG) ē-lek′trō-en-sef′ă-lō-gram	record of the minute electrical impulses of the brain used to identify neurological conditions that affect brain function and level of consciousness (Fig. 10.14)
evoked potentials ē-vokt′ pō-ten′shăls	record of minute electrical potentials (waves) that are extracted from ongoing EEG activity to diagnose auditory, visual, and sensory pathway disorders—also used to monitor the neurological function of patients during surgery (Fig. 10.15)

Electroencephalography (EEG)

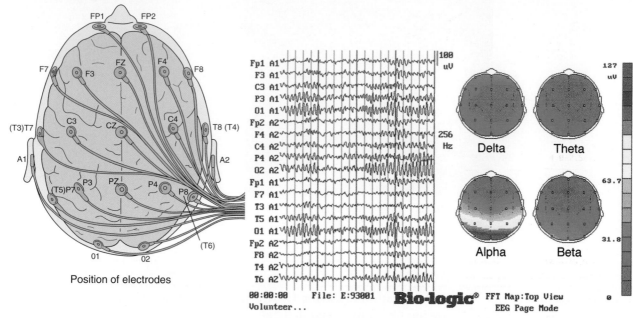

Position of electrodes

Normal EEG wave forms shown on left and computer compilation of frequency bands (delta, theta, alpha, and beta) mapped on right

Figure 10.14 Electroencephalography.

SOMNUS.
Somnus is a Latin word for sleep that was derived from ancient mythology. Somnus was the poetical god of sleep, the son of Nox (night), who lived with his brother Thanatos (death) in a palace at the western end of the world.

Test or Procedure	Explanation
nerve conduction velocity (NCV) nerv kon-dŭk′shŭn	electrical shock of peripheral nerves to record time of conduction; used to diagnose various peripheral nervous system diseases
polysomnography (PSG) pol′ē-som-nog′ră-fē	recording of various aspects of sleep (e.g., eye and muscle movements, respiration, EEG patterns) to diagnose sleep disorders (Fig. 10.16)

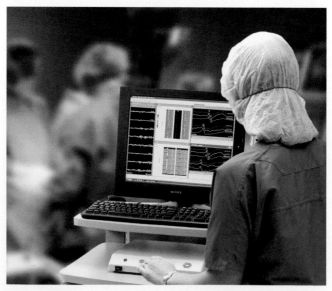

Figure 10.15 Use of evoked potentials to monitor neurological function during surgery.

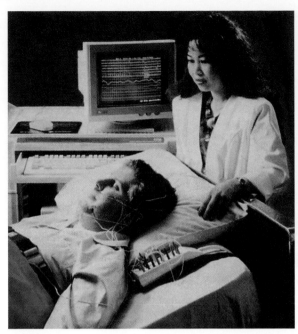

Figure 10.16   Polysomnography.

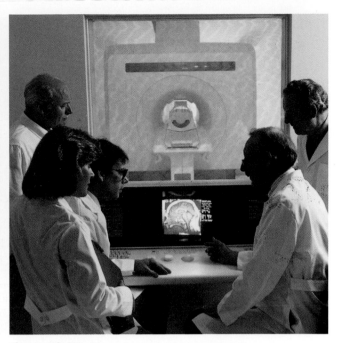

Figure 10.17   Magnetic resonance imaging unit.

Test or Procedure	Explanation
lumbar puncture (LP) lŭm′bar pŭnk′chūr	introduction of a specialized needle into the spine in the lumbar region for diagnostic or therapeutic purpose, such as to obtain cerebrospinal fluid for testing; also called spinal tap
magnetic resonance imaging (MRI) mag-net′ic rez′ō-nans im′ă-jing	nonionizing imaging technique using magnetic fields and radiofrequency waves to visualize anatomical structures (especially soft tissue), such as the tissues of the brain and spinal cord (Fig. 10.17; also see Figs. 10.3, 10.4, and 10.12)
magnetic resonance angiography (MRA) mag-net′ic rez′ō-nans an-jē-og′ră-fē	use of magnetic resonance in imaging of the blood vessels—useful in detecting pathological conditions such as atherosclerosis and thrombosis
intracranial MRA in′tră-krā′nē-ăl	magnetic resonance image of the head to visualize the vessels of the circle of Willis (common site of cerebral aneurysm, stenosis, or occlusion) (Fig. 10.18A)
extracranial MRA eks′tră-krā′nē-ăl	magnetic resonance image of the neck to visualize the carotid artery (Fig. 10.18B)
nuclear medicine imaging	radionuclide organ imaging
SPECT brain scan (single photon emission computed tomography)	scan combining nuclear medicine and computed tomography technology to produce images of the brain after administration of radioactive isotopes

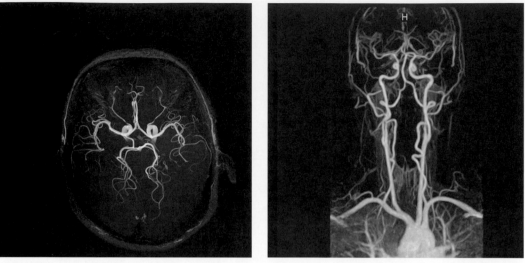

A **B**

Figure 10.18 **A.** Contrast-enhanced intracranial magnetic resonance angiography showing circulation of the circle of Willis. **B.** Contrast-enhanced extracranial magnetic resonance angiography showing carotid circulation.

Test or Procedure	Explanation
positron emission tomography (PET) poz′i-tron ē-mish′ŭn tō-mog′ră-fē	technique combining nuclear medicine and computed tomography technology to produce images of brain anatomy and corresponding physiology—used to study stroke, Alzheimer disease, epilepsy, metabolic brain disorders, chemistry of nerve transmissions in the brain, etc.; it provides greater accuracy than SPECT but is used less often because of cost and limited availability of the radioisotopes (Fig. 10.19)

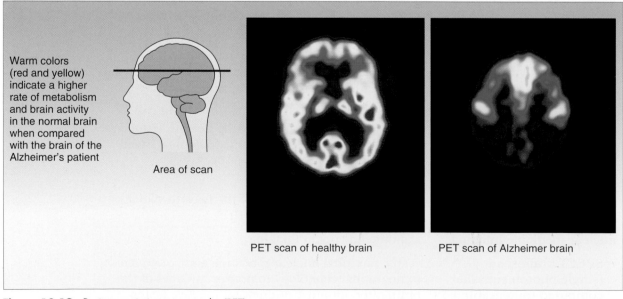

Warm colors (red and yellow) indicate a higher rate of metabolism and brain activity in the normal brain when compared with the brain of the Alzheimer's patient

Area of scan

PET scan of healthy brain

PET scan of Alzheimer brain

Figure 10.19 Positron emission tomography (PET) scans.

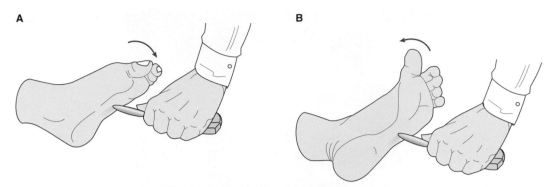

A   **B**

Figure 10.20   Reflex testing. **A.** Normal plantar reflex. **B.** Babinski sign.

Test or Procedure	Explanation
radiography rā′dē-og′ră-fē	x-ray imaging
cerebral angiogram ser′ĕ-brăl an′jē-ō-gram	x-ray of blood vessels in the brain after intracarotid injection of contrast medium
computed tomography (of the head)	computed tomographic x-ray images of the head used to visualize abnormalities within (e.g., brain tumors, malformations)
myelogram	x-ray of the spinal cord made after intraspinal injection of contrast medium
reflex testing	test performed to observe the body's response to a stimulus (Fig. 10.20A)

deep tendon reflexes (DTR)	involuntary muscle contraction after percussion at a tendon (e.g., patella, Achilles) indicating function; positive findings are noted when there is either no reflex response or an exaggerated response to stimulus; numbers are often used to record responses:
	    no response
	    1+ diminished response
	    2+ normal response
	    3+ more brisk than average response
	    4+ hyperactive response

Babinski sign or reflex	pathological response to stimulation of the plantar surface of the foot; a positive sign is indicated when the toes dorsiflex (curl upward) (Fig. 10.20B)
transcranial sonogram trans-krā′nē-ăl	image made by sending ultrasound beams through the skull to assess blood flow in intracranial vessels—used in diagnosis and management of stroke and head trauma (Fig. 10.21)

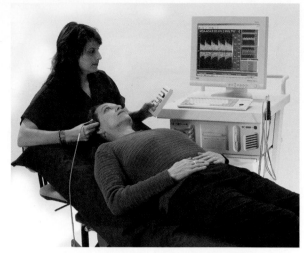

Figure 10.21 Transcranial sonography procedure.

Operative Terms

Term	Meaning
craniectomy krā′nē-ek′tō-mē	excision of part of the skull to approach the brain
craniotomy krā-nē-ot′ō-mē	incision into the skull to approach the brain
diskectomy (discectomy) dis-ek′tō-mē	removal of a herniated disk often done percutaneously (Fig. 10.22)
laminectomy lam′i-nek′tō-mē	excision of one or more laminae of the vertebrae to approach the spinal cord
vertebral lamina	flattened posterior portion of the vertebral arch (see Chapter 6, Figure 6.4)

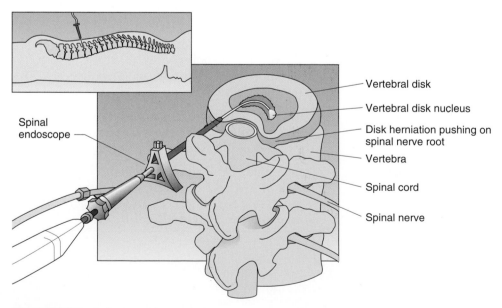

Spinal endoscope

Vertebral disk

Vertebral disk nucleus

Disk herniation pushing on spinal nerve root

Vertebra

Spinal cord

Spinal nerve

Figure 10.22 Diskectomy (discectomy).

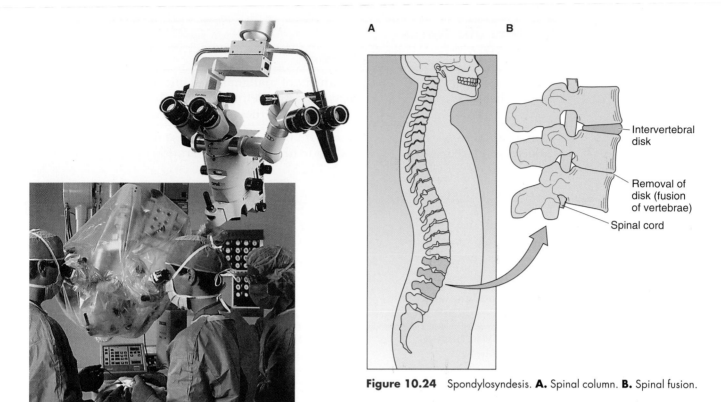

Figure 10.23 Microscope designed for neurological surgery.

Figure 10.24 Spondylosyndesis. **A.** Spinal column. **B.** Spinal fusion.

Term	Meaning
microsurgery mī-krō-ser′jer-ē	utilization of a microscope to dissect minute structures during surgery (Fig. 10.23)
neuroendovascular surgery nūr′ō-en-do-vas′kyu-lăr ser′jer-ē	diagnosis and treatment of disorders within cerebral blood vessels performed in a specialized angiographic laboratory by interventional neuroradiologists; common procedures include: • cerebral angioplasty and stent to restore blood flow through narrowed vessels such as the carotid artery, middle cerebral, and vertebrobasilar arteries • embolization (plugging) of intracranial aneurysms and other malformations
neuroplasty nūr′ō-plas-tē	surgical repair of a nerve
spondylosyndesis spon′di-lō-sin-dē′sis	spinal fusion (Fig. 10.24)

Therapeutic Terms

Term	Meaning
chemotherapy kem′ō-thār′ă-pē	treatment of malignancies, infections, and other diseases with chemical agents that destroy selected cells or impair their ability to reproduce
radiation therapy rā′dē-ā′shŭn thār′ă-pē	treatment of neoplastic disease using ionizing radiation to impede proliferation of malignant cells (Fig. 10.25)
stereotactic (stereotaxic) radiosurgery ster′ē-ō-tak′tik (ster′ē-ō-tak′sik) rā′dē-ō-ser′jer-ē	radiation treatment to inactivate malignant lesions involving the focus of multiple, precise external radiation beams on a target with the aid of a stereotactic frame and imaging such as CT, MRI, or angiography; used to treat inoperable brain tumors and other lesions
stereotactic (stereotaxic) frame	mechanical device used to localize a point in space targeting a precise site (Fig. 10.26)
thrombolytic therapy throm-bō-lit′ik	dissolution of thrombi using drugs [e.g., tissue plasminogen activator (tPA)] used to treat acute ischemic stroke

COMMON THERAPEUTIC DRUG CLASSIFICATIONS

analgesic an-ăl-jē′zik	agent that relieves pain
anticoagulant an′tē-kō-ag′yū-lant	drug that prevents clotting of the blood; commonly used to prevent heart attack and ischemic stroke

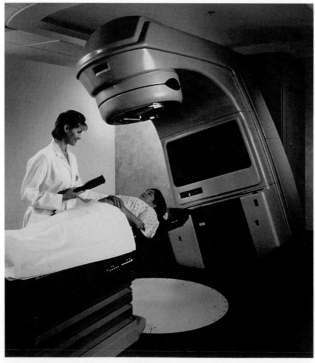

Figure 10.25 Radiation therapy: linear accelerator.

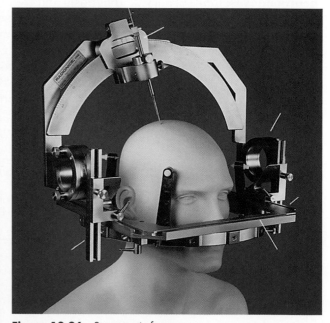

Figure 10.26 Stereotactic frame.

Term	Meaning
anticonvulsant an′tē-kon-vŭl′sant	agent that prevents or lessens convulsion
hypnotic hip-not′ik	agent that induces sleep
sedative sed′ă-tiv	agent that has a calming effect

Psychiatric Terms

Term	Meaning
SYMPTOMATIC TERMS	
affect af′fekt	emotional feeling or mood
flat affect	significantly dulled emotional tone or outward reaction
apathy ap′ă-thē	lack of interest or display of emotion
catatonia kat-ă-tō′nē-ă	state of unresponsiveness to one's outside environment, usually including muscle rigidity, staring, and inability to communicate
delusion dē-loo′zhŭn	persistent belief that has no basis in reality
grandiose delusion	person's false belief that he or she possesses great wealth, intelligence, or power
persecutory delusion	person's false belief that someone is plotting against him or her with intent to harm
dysphoria dis-fōr′ē-ă	restless, dissatisfied mood
euphoria yu-fōr′ē-ă	exaggerated, unfounded feeling of well-being
hallucination ha-loo′si-nā′shŭn	false perception of the senses for which there is no reality, most commonly hearing or seeing things (alucinor = to wander in mind)
ideation ī-dē-ā′shŭn	formation of thoughts or ideas [e.g., suicidal ideation (thoughts of suicide)]
mania mā′nē-ă	state of abnormal elation and increased activity
neurosis noo-rō′sis	psychological condition in which anxiety is prominent
psychosis sī-kō′sis	mental condition characterized by distortion of reality, resulting in the inability to communicate or function within one's environment
thought disorder	thought that lacks clear processing or logical direction

Psychiatric Diagnostic Terms

Term	Meaning
MOOD DISORDERS	
major depression **major depressive illness** **clinical depression** **major affective disorder** **unipolar disorder**	disorder causing periodic disturbances in mood that affect concentration, sleep, activity, appetite, and social behavior; characterized by feelings of worthlessness, fatigue, and loss of interest
dysthymia dis-thī′mē-ă	milder affective disorder characterized by a chronic depression persisting for at least 2 years
manic depression **bipolar disorder (BD)**	affective disorder characterized by mood swings of mania and depression (extreme up and down states)
seasonal affective disorder (SAD)	affective disorder marked by episodes of depression that most often occur during the fall and winter and remit in the spring
ANXIETY DISORDERS	
generalized anxiety disorder (GAD)	most common anxiety disorder, characterized by chronic, excessive, and uncontrollable worry about everyday problems that affects the ability to relax or concentrate but does not usually interfere with social interactions or employment; physical symptoms include muscle tension, trembling, twitching, fatigue, headaches, nausea, and insomnia—symptoms must exist for at least 6 months before a diagnosis can be made
panic disorder (PD)	disorder of sudden, recurrent attacks of intense feelings including physical symptoms that mimic a heart attack such as rapid heart rate, chest pain, shortness of breath, chills, sweating, and dizziness, with a general sense of loss of control or feeling that death is imminent; often progresses to agoraphobia

Term	Meaning
phobia fō′bē-ă	exaggerated fear of a specific object or circumstance that causes anxiety and panic; named for the object or circumstance, such as agoraphobia (marketplace), claustrophobia (confinement), or acrophobia (high places)
posttraumatic stress disorder (PTSD)	condition resulting from an extremely traumatic experience, injury, or illness that leaves the sufferer with persistent thoughts and memories of the ordeal; may occur after a war, violent personal assault, physical or sexual abuse, serious accident, natural disaster, etc.; symptoms include feelings of fear, detachment, exaggerated startle response, restlessness, nightmares, and avoidance of anything or anyone who triggers the painful recollections
obsessive-compulsive disorder (OCD)	anxiety disorder featuring unwanted, senseless obsessions accompanied by repeated compulsions, which can interfere with all aspects of a person's daily life (e.g., the thought that a door is not locked, with repetitive checking to make sure that it is locked; thoughts that one's body has been contaminated, with repetitive washing)
hypochondriasis hī′pō-kon-drī′ă-sis	preoccupation with thoughts of disease and concern that one is suffering from a serious condition that persists despite medical reassurance to the contrary
DISORDERS USUALLY DIAGNOSED IN CHILDHOOD	
autism aw′tizm	developmental disability commonly appearing during the first 3 years of life, resulting from a neurological disorder affecting brain function, evidenced by difficulties with verbal and nonverbal communication, and an inability to relate to anything beyond oneself (auto = self) in social interactions; individuals with autism often exhibit body movements such as rocking, repetitive hand movements, and commonly become preoccupied with observing parts of small objects or moving parts or performing meaningless rituals
dyslexia dis-lek′sē-ă	developmental disability characterized by a difficulty understanding written or spoken words, sentences, or paragraphs, affecting reading, spelling, and self-expression
attention-deficit/ hyperactivity disorder (ADHD)	dysfunction characterized by consistent hyperactivity, distractibility, and lack of control over impulses, which interferes with the ability to function normally at school, home, or work; specific criteria must be met before a diagnosis is made
mental retardation	condition of subaverage intelligence characterized by an IQ of 70 or below, resulting in the inability to adapt to normal social activities

Term	Meaning
EATING DISORDERS	
anorexia nervosa an-ō-rek′sē-ă ner′vōs-ă	severe disturbance in eating behavior caused by abnormal perceptions about one's body weight, evidenced by an overwhelming fear of becoming fat that results in a refusal to eat and body weight well below normal
bulimia nervosa boo-lim′ē-ă	eating disorder characterized by binge eating followed by efforts to limit digestion through induced vomiting, use of laxatives, or excessive exercise
SUBSTANCE ABUSE DISORDERS	
substance abuse disorders	mental disorders resulting from abuse of substances such as drugs, alcohol, or other toxins causing personal and social dysfunction; identified by the abused substance, such as alcohol abuse, amphetamine abuse, opioid (narcotic) abuse, or polysubstance abuse
PSYCHOTIC DISORDERS	
schizophrenia skiz′ō-frē′nē-ă	disease of brain chemistry causing a distorted cognitive and emotional perception of one's environment characterized by a broad range of "positive" and "negative" symptoms
	positive symptoms include distortions of normal function (behaviors that are absent in normal people, e.g., disorganized thought, delusions, hallucinations, catatonic behavior)
	negative symptoms (normal reactions missing in persons with schizophrenia) including flat affect, apathy, and withdrawal from reality
types: **disorganized**	featuring disorganized speech, behavior, and flat or inappropriate affect
catatonic	featuring catatonia
paranoid par′ă-noyd	featuring delusions, most often persecutory or grandiose types
schizoaffective disorder skiz′ō-ă-fek′tiv	concurrent with major depression or manic depression

Psychiatric Therapeutic Terms

Term	Meaning
electroconvulsive therapy (ECT) ē-lek′trō-kon-vŭl′siv	electrical shock applied to the brain to induce convulsions; used to treat severely depressed patients
light therapy	use of specialized illuminating light boxes and visors to treat seasonal affective disorder

Term	Meaning
psychotherapy sī′kō-thār′ă-pē	treatment of psychiatric disorders using verbal and nonverbal interaction with patients, individually or in a group, employing specific actions and techniques
behavioral therapy bē-hāv′ver-ăl thār′ă-pē	treatment to decrease or stop unwanted behavior
cognitive therapy kog′ni-tiv	treatment to change unwanted patterns of thinking
COMMON THERAPEUTIC DRUG CLASSIFICATIONS	
psychotropic drugs sī′kō-trōp′ik	medications used to treat mental illnesses (trop/o = a turning)
antianxiety agents an′tē-ang-zī′ě-tē	drugs used to reduce anxiety
anxiolytic agents ang′zē-ō-lit′ik	
antidepressant an′tē-dē-pres′ănt	agent that counteracts depression
neuroleptic agents noor-ō-lep′tik	drugs used to treat psychosis, especially schizophrenia

Summary of Chapter 10 Acronyms/Abbreviations

ADHD .....attention-deficit/hyperactivity disorder
ALS ....amyotrophic lateral sclerosis
ANS ....autonomic nervous system
BD ....bipolar disorder
CNS ....central nervous system
CP ....cerebral palsy
CSF ....cerebrospinal fluid
CVA ....cerebrovascular accident
DTR ....deep tendon reflexes
ECT ....electroconvulsive therapy
EEG ....electroencephalogram
GAD ....generalized anxiety disorder
HD ....Huntington disease
LP ....lumbar puncture
MRA ....magnetic resonance angiography

MRI ....magnetic resonance imaging
MS ....multiple sclerosis
NCV ....nerve conduction velocity
OCD ....obsessive-compulsive disorder
PD ....panic disorder
PET ....positron emission tomography
PNS ....peripheral nervous system
PSG ....polysomnography
PTSD ....posttraumatic stress disorder
RSD ....reflex sympathetic dystrophy
SAD ....seasonal affective disorder
SPECT ....single photon emission computed tomography
TIA ....transient ischemic attack

PRACTICE EXERCISES

For the following terms, on the lines below the term, write out the indicated word parts: prefixes (P), combining forms (CF), roots (R), and suffixes (S). Then define the word.

EXAMPLE

anencephaly

_____ / _____ / _____
   P   R   S

<u>an/encephal/y</u>
  P   R   S

DEFINITION: without/entire brain/condition or process of

1. ganglioma

_____ / _____
        R   S

DEFINITION: _____

2. atopognosia

_____ / _____ / _____ / _____
      P   CF   R   S

DEFINITION: _____

3. catatonic

_____ / _____ / _____
      P   R   S

DEFINITION: _____

4. dystaxia

_____ / _____ / _____
      P   R   S

DEFINITION: _____

5. bradykinesia

_____ / _____ / _____
      P   R   S

DEFINITION: _____

6. meningocele

_____ / _____
      CF   S

DEFINITION: _____

7. dysthymia

   _____ / _____ / _____
   　　　　P　　　　　　　　　　R　　　　　　　　　　S

   DEFINITION: _____

8. polysomnogram

   _____ / _____ / _____
   　　　　P　　　　　　　　　　CF　　　　　　　　　S

   DEFINITION: _____

9. spondylosyndesis

   _____ / _____ / _____
   　　　　CF　　　　　　　　　　P　　　　　　　　　S

   DEFINITION: _____

10. hemiplegia

    _____ / _____
    　　　　P　　　　　　　　　　S

    DEFINITION: _____

11. craniotomy

    _____ / _____
    　　　　CF　　　　　　　　　　S

    DEFINITION: _____

12. thalamic

    _____ / _____
    　　　　R　　　　　　　　　　S

    DEFINITION: _____

13. neuroglial

    _____ / _____ / _____
    　　　　CF　　　　　　　　　　R　　　　　　　　　S

    DEFINITION: _____

14. dyslexia

    _____ / _____ / _____
    　　　　P　　　　　　　　　　R　　　　　　　　　S

    DEFINITION: _____

15. somnipathy

    _____ / _____ / _____
    　　　　CF　　　　　　　　　　R　　　　　　　　　S

    DEFINITION: _____

16. hydrocephalic

    _____ / _____ / _____
    　　　　CF　　　　　　　　　　R　　　　　　　　　S

    DEFINITION: _____

17. dysarthria

_____ / _____ / _____
      P   R   S

DEFINITION: _____

18. acrophobia

_____ / _____ / _____
      CF   R   S

DEFINITION: _____

19. hypnotic

_____ / _____
      CF   S

DEFINITION: _____

20. euphoria

_____ / _____ / _____
      P   R   S

DEFINITION: _____

21. parasomnia

_____ / _____ / _____
      P   R   S

DEFINITION: _____

22. narcolepsy

_____ / _____
      CF   S

DEFINITION: _____

23. stereotaxy

_____ / _____ / _____
      CF   R   S

DEFINITION: _____

24. hemiparesis

_____ / _____
      P   S

DEFINITION: _____

25. neurasthenia

_____ / _____
      R   S

DEFINITION: _____

26. myelopathy

_____ / _____ / _____
      CF   R   S

DEFINITION: _____

27. intracranial

_____ / _____ / _____
    P   R   S

DEFINITION: _____

28. aphasia

_____ / _____ / _____
    P   R   S

DEFINITION: _____

29. schizophrenia

_____ / _____ / _____
    CF   R   S

DEFINITION: _____

30. cerebrospinal

_____ / _____ / _____
    CF   R   S

DEFINITION: _____

Complete the medical term by writing the missing part:

31. electro_____ gram = record of electrical brain impulses

32. _____ syndesis = spinal fusion

33. crani_____ = excision of part of the skull

34. cerebral _____ sclerosis = fat buildup in blood vessels of the brain

35. hyper_____ = increased sensations

36. dys_____ = condition of difficulty speaking

37. _____ algesia = loss of sense of pain

38. a_____ gnosis = inability to judge the form of an object by touch (e.g., to tell a coin from a key)

For each of the following, circle the combining form that corresponds to the meaning given:

39. **brain**	encephal/o	crani/o	neur/o
40. **movement**	esthesi/o	kinesi/o	somat/o
41. **speech**	lex/o	gnos/o	phor/o
42. **body**	somn/o	somat/o	phren/o
43. **spinal cord**	vertebr/o	spondyl/o	myel/o

44. **mind**	cerebr/o	thym/o	thalm/o
45. **sensation**	esthesi/o	neur/o	kinesi/o
46. **place**	top/o	tax/o	phor/o
47. **sleep**	somat/o	hypn/o	esthesi/o
48. **knowing**	phren/o	phas/o	gnos/o

Write the correct medical term for each of the following:

49. inflammation of the meninges _____

50. excision of a herniated disk_____

51. slowly progressive degeneration of nerves in the brain characterized by tremor, rigidity of muscles, and slow movements _____

52. pathological response to stimulation of the plantar surface of the foot indicated by dorsiflexion of the toes _____

53. numbness and tingling_____

54. state of unconsciousness _____

55. congenital defect of the spinal column resulting in pouching of spinal membranes

_____

Match the following neurological terms with their abbreviations:

56. _____ amyotrophic lateral sclerosis   a. PSG

57. _____ herpes zoster   b. tonic-clonic

58. _____ spinal tap   c. CVA

59. _____ faint   d. Alzheimer disease

60. _____ grand mal   e. Lou Gehrig disease

61. _____ petit mal   f. flaccid

62. _____ cerebral thrombus   g. absence

63. _____ flabby   h. clot

64. _____ stroke   i. LP

65. _____ dementia   j. shingles

66. _____ sleep study   k. syncope

Write the full medical term for the following abbreviations:

67. CT _____

68. MRI _____

69. PET _____

70. MS _____

71. CNS _____

72. CP _____

73. TIA _____

74. EEG _____

75. DTR _____

76. CSF _____

77. MRA _____

78. CVA _____

Write in the missing words on the blank lines in the following illustration of brain anatomy.

79–86.

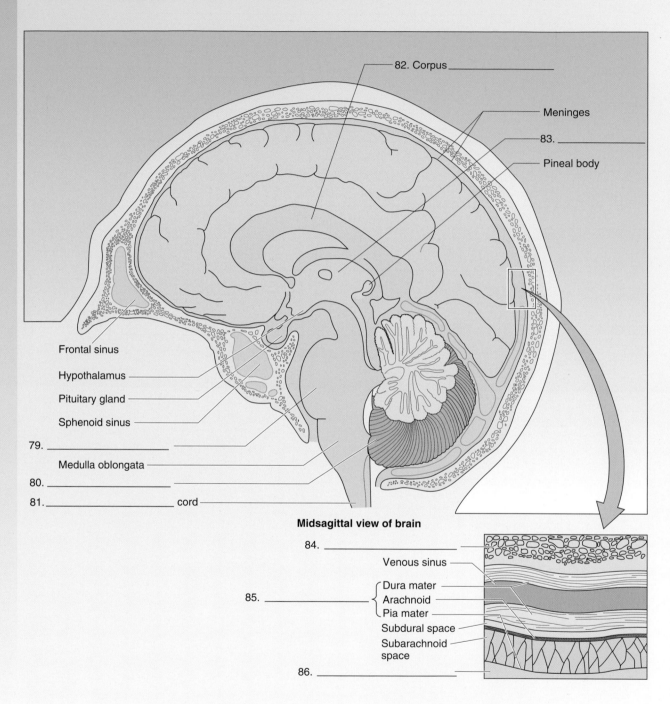

82. Corpus _____

Meninges

83. _____

Pineal body

Frontal sinus

Hypothalamus

Pituitary gland

Sphenoid sinus

79. _____

Medulla oblongata

80. _____

81. _____ cord

Midsagittal view of brain

84. _____

Venous sinus

Dura mater

Arachnoid

Pia mater

Subdural space

Subarachnoid space

85. _____

86. _____

Match the following psychiatric terms with their meanings:

87. _____ hallucination

a. exaggerated, unfounded feeling of well-being

88. _____ persecutory delusion

b. dull emotional tone or outward reaction

89. _____ catatonia

c. false belief that one is very wealthy, intelligent, or powerful

90. _____ apathy

d. false belief that one is being plotted against

91. _____ euphoria

e. state of abnormal elation and increased activity

92. _____ mania

f. lack of interest or display of emotion

93. _____ flat affect

g. thoughts that lack clear process or logical direction

94. _____ dysphoria

h. state of unresponsiveness including muscle rigidity, staring, and inability to communicate

95. _____ thought disorder

i. restless, dissatisfied mood

96. _____ grandiose delusion

j. hearing or seeing things

Write the full medical term for the following abbreviations:

97. GAD_____

98. ADHD_____

99. OCD _____

100. ECT_____

101. PD _____

102. BD _____

103. PTSD_____

Match the following psychiatric diagnoses:

104. _____ unipolar disorder

a. hypochondriasis

105. _____ anxiety disorder

b. anorexia nervosa

106. _____ bipolar disorder

c. clinical depression

107. _____ psychosis

d. dysthymia

108. _____ disorder identified in childhood

e. schizophrenia

109. _____ eating disorder

f. manic depression

110. _____ mild depression

g. autism

Match the following psychiatric conditions with therapeutic terms:

111. _____ anxiety   a. behavioral therapy

112. _____ schizophrenia   b. light therapy

113. _____ seasonal affective disorder   c. anxiolytic agent

114. _____ major affective disorder   d. electroconvulsive therapy

115. _____ bulimia   e. neuroleptic agent

For each of the following, circle the correct spelling of the term:

116. Alsheimer	Alzheimer	Alshiemer
117. skitzoprenia	skizophrenia	schizophrenia
118. polysomnography	polysonography	polysolemography
119. parenoia	paranoia	paranoyea
120. atopagnosis	atopegnosis	atopognosis
121. demensha	dementia	dimentia
122. epilapsey	epilepsey	epilepsy
123. catonia	catatonia	catetonia
124. delushion	dilusion	delusion
125. hellucination	hallucination	hallucinashun
126. poliomyalitis	poliomyelitis	poleiomyalitis

Give the noun that was used to form the following adjectives:

127. epileptic _____

128. euphoric _____

129. delusional _____

130. syncopal _____

131. autistic _____

132. psychotic _____

133. cerebral _____

134. dysphasic _____

135. paranoid _____

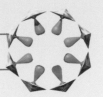

MEDICAL RECORD ANALYSES

MEDICAL RECORD 10.1

Progress Note

OP H&P

Neurological Services

CC: numbness and tingling in feet and hands

HPI: This 44 y.o. right-handed female c/o numbness in her feet for the past two weeks with "pockets" of numbness in the abdomen. Her legs feel heavy and numb. Her hands started tingling a week ago and she is feeling very nervous. She has had similar episodes over the past 3 years, lasting about a week at a time, often after stressful events, or during hot weather.

PMH: Operations: none. No serious illnesses/accidents
        FH: Father, age 71, L&W; Mother, age 66, is bipolar;
        Her only sibling, a sister, age 28, has cerebral palsy.
        SH: Denies smoking or use of street drugs, but drinks socially
        OH: certified public accountant. Marital Status: single
        ROS: noncontributory.
        VS: T 98.2° F., P 82, R 16, BP 110/68, Ht 5'2", Wt 138#

PE: HEENT: WNL. Neck: negative. Heart/Lungs: normal.
        Cranial nerves intact. Reflexes: DTR's are increased, greater on the left than the right without spasticity.
        Toes upgoing bilaterally.
        There is numbness to tactile pin stimulation over both extremities. She has no finger-to-nose ataxia. Her gait is steady.

A: R/O MS

P: Schedule MRI of the brain with and without gaolinium (contrast) RTO for report and further evaluation × 1 wk

1. Which medical term best describes the patient's symptoms:
   a. hyperesthesia
   b. paresthesia
   c. ataxia
   d. hemiparesis
   e. neuralgia

2. What is noted in the history about the patient's mother?
   a. she is alive and well
   b. she suffers from depression
   c. she has mood swings of mania and depression
   d. she suffers from generalized anxiety
   e. she is a hypochondriac

3. Describe the sister's condition:
   a. disorder affecting the central nervous system characterized by seizures
   b. hereditary disease of the central nervous system characterized by bizarre involuntary body movements and progressive dementia
   c. abnormal accumulation of cerebrospinal fluid in the ventricles of the brain as a result of developmental abnormality
   d. condition of motor dysfunction caused by damage to the cerebrum during development or injury at birth
   e. slowly progressive degeneration of nerves in the brain characterized by tremor, rigidity, and slow movements

4. Which medical term describes the positive finding of the "toes upgoing" bilaterally?

a. Babinski sign

b. neuralgia

c. hemiparesis

d. spastic paralysis

e. flaccid paralysis

5. What is the doctor's impression?

a. the patient has multiple sclerosis

b. the patient does not have multiple sclerosis

c. the patient may have multiple sclerosis

d. the patient may have hardening of the arteries in the brain

e. the patient does not have hardening of the arteries in the brain

6. Describe the test noted in the plan:

a. x-ray

b. nuclear image

c. ultrasound scan

d. tomographic radiograph

e. scan produced by magnetic fields and radiofrequency waves

MEDICAL RECORD 10.2

Mary Clarke came into the living room where her father, Bob Clarke, had been watching television and found him slumped back in his chair, apparently asleep. When she could not wake him, she realized he was unconscious and called 911. The ambulance rushed him to the Central Medical Center emergency room, where he was seen by Dr. Gregory Kincaid.

Directions

Read Medical Record 10.2 for Mr. Clarke (pages 351–353) and answer the following questions. This record is the history and physical examination report dictated by Dr. Kincaid after his examination and initial treatment of Mr. Clarke.

QUESTIONS ABOUT MEDICAL RECORD 10.2

Write your answers in the spaces provided.

1. Below are medical terms used in this record you have not encountered in this text so far. Underline each where it appears in the record and define below:

   abrasion _____

   foci of atrophy _____

   ambulate _____

   cataract _____

2. In your own words, not using medical terminology, briefly describe Mr. Clarke's condition from the time he was found at home:

   _____

   Describe his condition after he arrived at the ER:

   _____

3. Which of the following was *not* an emergency treatment provided for Mr. Clarke?
   a. administration of Valium
   b. assessment of respiratory rate
   c. CPR
   d. assistance with breathing

4. Define "postictal": _____

5. Mr. Clarke has a past medical history of several different illnesses. On the following list, check all health problems Mr. Clarke has experienced:

   _____ skin bruising

   _____ heart attacks

   _____ excessive thyroid secretion

_____ COPD

_____ skin scrapes

_____ headaches

_____ nausea and vomiting

_____ atrial fibrillation

_____ pulmonary embolus

6. From the list of medications Mr. Clarke is taking, one includes an abbreviation that has been deemed error prone. Identify the abbreviation, potential problem, and preferred wording.

Abbreviation   *Potential Problem*   *Preferred Wording*

_____   _____   _____

7. In your own words, describe the surgery Mr. Clarke had in the past:

_____

_____

_____

8. In lay language, what nervous system disorder did a family member experience?

_____

_____

_____

9. Dr. Kincaid's diagnosis identifies three possible conditions that may have led to Mr. Clarke's seizure. Put each in your own words:

a._____

b._____

c._____

10. What three actions will now occur in the ICU?

a._____

b._____

c._____

CENTRAL MEDICAL CENTER

211 Medical Center Drive • Central City, US 90000-1234 • PHONE: (012) 125-6784

HISTORY

DATE OF ADMISSION: August 1, 20xx

REASON FOR ADMISSION: Seizure episode.

HISTORY OF PRESENT ILLNESS: The patient is a 76-year-old male brought to the emergency room following a seizure episode at home where he was found to be in mild tonic condition and was given intravenous Valium at which time his respiratory rate dropped, and he required some ventilatory assistance. He remained unresponsive postictal until an hour after emergency room arrival. He has a past history of a similar seizure in 20xx which was treated with Dilantin for a year and was then discontinued. No focal abnormality was noted at that time with the exception of an abnormality on CT showing small foci of atrophy possibly secondary to vascular disease. He has been evaluated by Dr. Levy, a neurologist. Please refer to Dr. Levy's consultation report.

PAST MEDICAL HISTORY: The patient has a past medical history of severe chronic obstructive airways disease; he is on multiple medications. He takes Slo-Bid 300 mg b.i.d., Medrol 5 mg q.o.d., and p.r.n. inhalation of albuterol up to q.i.d. He has a long history of being steroid dependent and is daily symptomatic. He has a history of coronary artery disease with myocardial infarctions, questionable congestive heart failure, and chronic atrial fibrillation. He is being seen by Dr. Foley, a cardiologist. He is on Lanoxin 0.25 mg, Verelan 120 mg, Lasix 40 mg, and Micro-K 750 mg on a daily basis. He also has a history of hypothyroidism and takes Synthroid 0.1 mg. He has a history of steroid-dependent skin fragility with multiple ecchymoses; a recent fall resulted in a number of abrasions which were under treatment by Dr. Depmore, a family practitioner, with good healing.

PAST SURGICAL HISTORY: Septoplasty.

MEDICATIONS: As mentioned above.

ALLERGIES: The patient does not report any allergies to medications.

REVIEW OF SYSTEMS: The patient is not reported to have problems with headaches or dizzy spells. He does have exertional shortness of breath that he maintains control of with medications, and he is able to ambulate at least a mile a day. No abdominal or gastrointestinal symptoms are noted. There is no arthralgia.

(continued)

HISTORY AND PHYSICAL
Page 1

PT. NAME:	CLARKE, ROBERT B.
ID NO:	088676
ROOM NO:	ICU
ATT. PHYS.	G. KINCAID, M.D.

Medical Record 10.2

CENTRAL MEDICAL CENTER

211 Medical Center Drive • Central City, US 90000-1234 • PHONE: (012) 125-6784 • FAX: (012) 125-9999

HISTORY

FAMILY HISTORY: The patient's parents lived into their late 80s and died of old age. His brother died at age 70 of a cerebral vascular accident (CVA). There is no family history of diabetes, cardiac, pulmonary, renal, hepatic, or hematologic disorder; but his father did have cancer of the prostate.

PHYSICAL EXAMINATION

VITAL SIGNS: Blood Pressure: 173/78. Pulse: 90-100. Respirations: 12.

GENERAL APPEARANCE: The patient is able to respond to some degree to voice but poorly follows directions, this being due to the fact that he is still somewhat under the influence of Valium.

SKIN: Multiple ecchymoses of extremities. Only his back, abdomen, and head are free of signs of injury. The skin is dry. There are active abrasions from his seizure episode on the right ankle and both forearms.

HEENT: Tympanic membranes, nose, and throat appear to be normal. His teeth are in good condition. Both eyes are reactive to light. The right fundus is normal; however, the left fundus is not visualized secondary to cataract.

NECK: There is no cervical adenopathy or thyroid enlargement.

CHEST:
LUNGS: The patient's lungs are clear to percussion and auscultation. There are no rales, rhonchi, or wheezes.

HEART: Tones are regular without murmur.

ABDOMEN: The abdomen is flat, soft, and nontender without organ enlargement or masses. The bowel sounds are active.

RECTAL/GENITALIA: The rectal examination is normal. The patient has normal circumcised external genitalia.

(continued)

HISTORY AND PHYSICAL Page 2	PT. NAME: CLARKE, ROBERT B. ID NO: 088676 ROOM NO: ICU ATT. PHYS. G. KINCAID, M.D.

Medical Record 10.2 *Continued.*

CENTRAL MEDICAL CENTER
211 Medical Center Drive • Central City, US 90000-1234 • PHONE: (012) 125-6784

PHYSICAL EXAMINATION

EXTREMITIES: There are multiple ecchymoses. Deep tendon reflexes are absent. The patient is able to move all four extremities without any evidence of motor deficit. He is unable to report sensory activity. There was no Babinski sign.

IMPRESSION:
SEIZURE DISORDER, POSSIBLY SECONDARY TO CEREBRAL EMBOLI, HYPOXIA, OR UNKNOWN CAUSES, POSSIBLY DUE TO INTRACEREBRAL DISEASE.

PLAN: Recommend observation in Intensive Care Unit as workup proceeds and will ask for neurologic and pulmonary support from specialists R. Wilson, M.D., and E. Wong, M.D.

G. Kincaid, M.D.

GK:wq

D: 8/2/20xx
T: 8/5/20xx

Medical Record 10.2 *Continued.*

MEDICAL RECORD 10.3

Anne Cross had been fairly healthy until she had a stroke about 2 months ago. She was treated by Dr. Paul Jiang, her personal physician, at that time and was discharged from the hospital on medication. At the request of Ms. Cross, Dr. Jiang called for a consultation from a neurologist, Dr. Melvin Classen.

Directions

Read Medical Record 10.3 for Ms. Cross (pages 356–357) and answer the following questions. This record is a consultation report written by Dr. Classen as a letter back to Ms. Cross's physician, Dr. Jiang, after his consultation.

QUESTIONS ABOUT MEDICAL RECORD 10.3

Write your answers in the spaces provided.

1. Below are medical terms used in this record you have not yet encountered. Underline each where it appears in the record and define below:

   homonymous hemianopsia _____

   finger-nose test _____

   apraxia _____

   clonus _____

2. In your own words, not using medical terminology, briefly describe Ms. Cross's symptoms in April before she was admitted to the hospital:

   _____

   _____

   _____

3. Write the missing parts in this table summarizing the diagnostic tests performed in April:

Test	*Definition of Test*	*Findings*
CT	_____	_____
_____	sound waves through heart	_____
carotid ultrasound	_____	_____
_____	_____	slowed electrical pulses on right side

4. What family member had a problem perhaps similar to Ms. Cross's?

   _____

5. For each of the following medications given to Ms. Cross, translate the dosage instructions:

   Persantine _____

   aspirin _____

   Proventil _____

   Procardia _____

6. Dr. Classen recommends two diagnostic studies. Describe both in your own words:

   a. _____

   b. _____

   In one sentence, describe Dr. Classen's rationale for recommending the combination of these two tests:

   _____

   _____

7. Name the preventive surgical procedure Dr. Classen suggests that may be appropriate if changes are found in the carotid blood vessels:

   _____

   Describe that procedure in your own words:

   _____

   _____

CENTRAL MEDICAL GROUP, INC.

Department of Neurology

201 Medical Center Drive • Central City, US 90000-1234 • PHONE: (012) 125-8888 • FAX: (012) 125-3434

June 9, 20xx

Paul Jiang, M.D.
1409 West Ninth Street
Central City, US 90000-1233

Dear Dr. Jiang:

RE: Anne Cross

I had the pleasure of meeting Mrs. Cross today. As you know, she is a 65-year-old right-handed female who began to have difficulties on or about April 17, 20xx. She experienced dizziness that she described as occurring in the midday; there was also some associated slurring of speech. By the next morning, she seemed to have some disorientation with putting on her clothes, and she had some difficulties using the left side of her body. She had no headache or other problems. Prior to that time, she denied having any symptomatology. She was admitted to the hospital, as you are aware, and underwent a series of studies. A CT scan was reviewed and showed evidence of a right ischemic occipital infarct. In addition, she underwent an echocardiogram that was normal and an electroencephalogram that showed some right-sided slowing. A carotid ultrasound study suggested 60-70% stenosis of the bifurcation and/or internal carotids.

The patient was discharged on a combination of Persantine 50 mg t.i.d, enteric-coated aspirin 81 mg daily, Proventil 1 q 12 h p.r.n. for chronic obstructive pulmonary disease, and Procardia XL 1 daily for hypertension. The patient also has stopped smoking.

The patient reports that in the past, she has been essentially well except for some eye surgery. Additionally, after her discharge, she underwent visual field studies which confirmed the presence of an incomplete left-sided homonymous hemianopsia.

By way of family background, her brother died from complications of a stroke at age 78. Her mother died from liver cancer, and her father died from a myocardial infarction.

The patient has no specific allergy to drugs.

The patient's risk factors have been otherwise unremarkable.

On examination today, the patient is a slender female in no acute distress.

Blood pressure from the left arm in a sitting position is 130/95 and from the right arm in the sitting position is 145/95. Her pulse rate is 76 and regular.

No bruits are present over the carotid distributions. The temporal arteries are not enlarged or tender.

On examination of the eyes, the patient showed some mild arteriolar narrowing without hemorrhage or exudate. Gross visual confrontation suggests a neglect of left hemianopsia. The extraocular movements are full. The pupils are symmetrical. There is no ptosis. Facial movements are normal, and speech is normal.

Medical Record 10.3

CENTRAL MEDICAL GROUP, INC.
Department of Neurology
201 Medical Center Drive • Central City, US 90000-1234 • PHONE: (012) 125-8888 • FAX: (012) 125-3434

There is no drift to the outstretched hands. Finger-to-nose test is performed symmetrically.

The patient does not have any asymmetrical topagnosis. She has no evidence of apraxia.

The patient's reflexes are physiologic: they are 2+ at the biceps, triceps, and brachioradialis. The knee and ankle jerks are 2+. No clonus is elicited.

Gait and stance are normal.

OVERALL ASSESSMENT:

Without prior warning, this woman had a new onset of a cerebral infarct. By her description, it is likely that she had a posterior circulatory infarct in the area of the occipital lobe. There may have been an association zone in the parietal area as well. Since that time, she has had some residual hemianopsia as described.

PLAN:

At this time, it is suggested that the most prudent approach would be to do an MRA and an MRI. This should include the great vessels of the neck and the vertebrobasilar system. The MRI would allow us to see the nature of residuals of the stroke, the distribution of the stroke, and would allow us to determine if there are any asymptomatic lesions, including microvascular infarcts which would not be seen on the CAT scan. The MRA would allow us to determine the overall anatomy of the vasculature--including the neck, the bifurcations, and the posterior circulation--in a noninvasive way. Depending on the results of both of these studies, we would have to consider if she needs a full angiogram done with selective views. If, in fact, she has had an infarct of the posterior occipital lobe, then the current treatment with aspirin and Persantine would be adequate. If, by the nature of the MRA, it is determined that there are significant changes or irregularity of the contour of the intima of the vessels at the bifurcations, then there may be an indication for prophylaxis for an endarterectomy despite not having a stroke in that distribution of the vessels. This, of course, would all be determined by the results of this study. The advantage of the MRA-MRI combined would allow us to visualize adequately the vessels combined with the detailed evaluation of her brain.

I think this would be the patient's best and most prudent approach to the patient's health and would help to prevent recurrence of this problem.

Please do not hesitate to call me if there are any questions regarding this patient's evaluation.

Sincerely,

Melvin Classen, M.D.
Department of Neurology
(012) 125-6899

MC:mar
DOT:6/10/20xx

cc: Mrs. Anne Cross

Medical Record 10.3 *Continued.*

Chapter 11

Endocrine System

OBJECTIVES

After completion of this chapter you will be able to

- Define common term components used in relation to the endocrine system
- Describe the basic functions of the endocrine system
- Define the basic anatomical terms referring to the endocrine system
- Define common symptomatic and diagnostic terms referring to the endocrine system
- List the common diagnostic tests and procedures related to the endocrine system
- Identify common operative terms referring to the endocrine system
- Identify common therapeutic terms including drug classifications related to the endocrine system
- Explain the terms and abbreviations used in documenting medical records involving the endocrine system

Combining Forms

Combining Form	Meaning	Example
aden/o	gland	adenoma ad-ĕ-nō′mă
adren/o	adrenal gland	adrenotrophic ă-drē-nō-trō′fik
adrenal/o		adrenalopathy ă-drē-nă-lop′ă-thē
andr/o	male	androgenous an-droj′ĕ-nŭs
crin/o	to secrete	endocrine en′dō-krin
dips/o	thirst	polydipsia pol-ē-dip′sē-ă
gluc/o	sugar	glucogenic glū-kō-jen′ik
glucos/o		glucose gloo′kōs
glyc/o		hyperglycemia hi′per-glī-sē′mē-ă
glycos/o		glycosuria glī-kō-sū′rē-ă

Combining Form	Meaning	Example
hormon/o	hormone (an urging on)	**hormonal** hōr-mōn′ăl
ket/o	ketone bodies	**ketogenic** kē-tō-jen′ik
keton/o		**ketonuria** kē-tō-nū′rē-ă
pancreat/o	pancreas	**pancreatitis** pan′krē-ă-tī′tis
thym/o	thymus gland	**thymoma** thī-mō′mă
thyr/o	thyroid gland (shield)	**thyrotoxic** thī-rō-tok′sik
thyroid/o		**thyroiditis** thī-roy-dī′tis

THYMUS. Derived from the Greek word for an offer or sacrifice, the thyme plant was burnt on altars because of its sweet smell. The term was applied to the thymus gland because of its likeness to a bunch of thyme.

THYROID. Thyroid is from a Greek word referring to a large oblong shield carried by soldiers. It had a deep notch at the top for the chin. The thyroid gland and the thyroid cartilage in the neck were named for this shield because of their similar appearance.

Endocrine System Overview

The endocrine system is a network of ductless glands and other structures that affect the function of targeted organs by the secreting *hormones*. Figure 11.1 shows the locations of the endocrine glands. The hormones secreted by these glands and their functions are described under "Anatomical Terms" and in Figure 11.2.

Anatomical Terms

Gland or Hormone	Location or Function
adrenal glands ă-drē′năl **suprarenal glands** sū′pră-rē′năl	located next to each kidney, the adrenal cortex secretes steroid hormones and the adrenal medulla secretes epinephrine and norepinephrine
steroid hormones stēr′oyd **glucocorticoids** glū-kō-kōr′ti-koydz	regulate carbohydrate metabolism and salt and water balance; some effect on sexual characteristics
mineral corticosteroids min′er-ăl kōr′ti-kō-stēr′oydz	
androgens an′drō-jenz	
epinephrine ep′i-nef′rin	affect sympathetic nervous system in stress response
norepinephrine nōr′ep-i-nef′rin	
ovaries ō′vă-rēz	located one on each side of the uterus in the female pelvis, functioning to secrete estrogen and progesterone

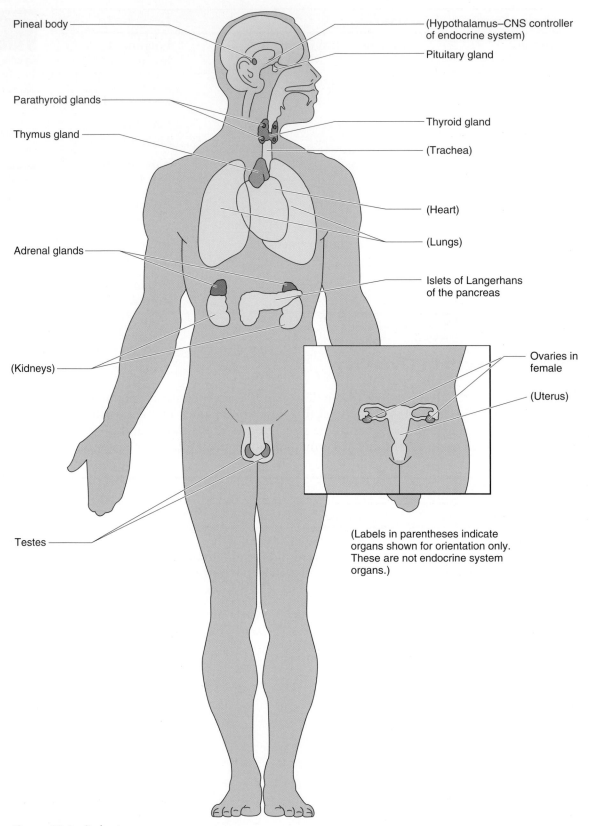

Pineal body

(Hypothalamus–CNS controller of endocrine system)

Pituitary gland

Parathyroid glands

Thyroid gland

Thymus gland

(Trachea)

(Heart)

(Lungs)

Adrenal glands

Islets of Langerhans of the pancreas

(Kidneys)

Ovaries in female

(Uterus)

Testes

(Labels in parentheses indicate organs shown for orientation only. These are not endocrine system organs.)

Figure 11.1 Endocrine system.

Endocrine gland	Secretions	Function
* Anterior pituitary (adenohypophysis)	Thyroid-stimulating hormone (TSH)	Stimulates secretion from thyroid gland
	Adrenocorticotropic hormone (ACTH)	Stimulates secretion from adrenal cortex
	Follicle-stimulating hormone (FSH)	Initiates growth of ovarian follicle; stimulates secretion of estrogen in females and sperm production in males
	Luteinizing hormone (LH)	Causes ovulation; stimulates secretion of progesterone by corpus luteum; causes secretion of testosterone in testes
	Melanocyte-stimulating hormone (MSH)	Affects skin pigmentation
	Growth hormone (GH)	Influences growth
	Prolactin (lactogenic hormone)	Stimulates breast development and milk production during pregnancy
* Posterior pituitary (neurohypophysis)	Antidiuretic hormone (ADH)	Influences the absorption of water by kidney tubules
	Oxytocin	Influences uterine contraction
Pineal body	Melatonin	Exact function unknown, affects onset of puberty
	Serotonin	Serves as a precursor to melatonin
Thyroid gland	Triiodothyronine (T_3), thyroxine (T_4)	Regulate metabolism
	Calcitonin	Regulates calcium and phosphorus metabolism
Parathyroid glands	Parathyroid hormone (PTH)	Regulates calcium and phosphorus metabolism
Pancreas (islets of Langerhans)	Insulin, glucagon	Regulates carbohydrate/sugar metabolism
Thymus gland	Thymosin	Regulates immune response
Adrenal glands (suprarenal glands)	Steroid hormones: glucocorticoids, mineral corticosteroids, androgens	Regulate carbohydrate metabolism and salt and water balance; some effect on sexual characteristics
	Epinephrine, norepinephrine	Affect sympathetic nervous system in stress response
Ovaries	Estrogen, progesterone	Responsible for the development of female secondary sex characteristics and for the regulation of reproduction
Testes	Testosterone	Affects masculinization and reproduction

* Release of hormones in pituitary is controlled by hypothalamus

Figure 11.2 Functions of the endocrine glands.

Gland or Hormone	Location or Function
estrogen es′trō-jen **progesterone** prō-jes′ter-ōn	responsible for the development of female secondary sex characteristics and the regulation of reproduction
pancreas **(islets of Langerhans)** pan′krē-as	located behind the stomach in front of the first and second lumbar vertebrae, functioning to secrete insulin and glucagon
insulin in′sŭ-lin **glucagon** glū′kă-gon	regulate carbohydrate/sugar metabolism
parathyroid glands par-ă-thī′royd	located on the posterior aspect of the thyroid gland in the neck, functioning to secrete parathyroid hormone (PTH)
parathyroid **hormone (PTH)**	regulates calcium and phosphorus metabolism
pineal gland pin′ē-ăl	located in the center of the brain, functioning to secrete melatonin and serotonin
melatonin mel-ă-tōn′in	exact function unknown; affects onset of puberty
serotonin	a neurotransmitter that serves as the precursor to melatonin
pituitary gland pi-tū′i-tār-ē **hypophysis** hī-pof′i-sis	located at the base of the brain, the anterior pituitary secretes thyroid-stimulating hormone, adrenocorticotropic hormone, follicle-stimulating hormone, luteinizing hormone, melanocyte-stimulating hormone, growth hormone, and prolactin; the posterior pituitary releases antidiuretic hormone and oxytocin
anterior pituitary **(adenohypophysis)** ad′ĕ-nō-hī-pof′i-sis	
thyroid-stimulating **hormone (TSH)**	stimulates secretion from thyroid gland
adrenocorticotropic **hormone (ACTH)** ă-drē′nō-kōr′ti-kō-trō′fik	stimulates secretion from adrenal cortex
follicle-stimulating **hormone (FSH)** fol′i-kl	initiates growth of ovarian follicle; stimulates secretion of estrogen in females and sperm production in males
luteinizing hormone (LH) lū′tē-ī-nīz-ing	causes ovulation; stimulates secretion of progesterone by corpus luteum; causes secretion of testosterone in testes

Gland or Hormone	Location or Function
melanocyte-stimulating hormone (MSH) mel'ă-nō-sīt	affects skin pigmentation
growth hormone (GH)	influences growth
prolactin (lactogenic hormone) prō-lak'tin	stimulates breast development and milk production during pregnancy
posterior pituitary (neurohypophysis) nūr'ō-hī-pof'i-sis	
antidiuretic hormone (ADH) an'tē-dī-yū-ret'ik	influences the absorption of water by kidney tubules
oxytocin ok-sē-tō'sin	influences uterine contraction
testes tes'tēz	located one on each side within the scrotum in the male, functioning to secrete testosterone
testosterone tes-tos'tĕ-rōn	affects masculinization and reproduction
thymus gland thī'mŭs	located in the mediastinal cavity anterior to and above the heart, functioning to secrete thymosin
thymosin thī'mō-sin	regulates immune response
thyroid gland	located in front of the neck, functioning to secrete triiodothyronine (T$_3$), thyroxine (T$_4$), and calcitonin
triiodothyronine (T$_3$) trī-ī'ō-dō-thī'rō-nēn	known as the thyroid hormones; regulate metabolism
thyroxine (T$_4$) thī-rok'sēn	
calcitonin kal-si-tō'nin	regulates calcium and phosphorus metabolism

Symptomatic and Diagnostic Terms

Term	Meaning
SYMPTOMATIC	
exophthalmos ek-sof-thal'mos exophthalmus	protrusion of one or both eyeballs, often because of thyroid dysfunction or a tumor behind the eyeball (see Fig. 11.6B)

Term	Meaning
glucosuria glū-kō-sū′rē-ă **glycosuria** glī-kō-sū′rē-ă	glucose (sugar) in the urine
hirsutism her′sū-tizm	shaggy; an excessive growth of hair especially in unusual places (e.g., a woman with a beard)
hypercalcemia hī′per-kal-sē′mē-ă	an abnormally high level of calcium in the blood
hypocalcemia hi′pō-kal-sē′mē-ă	an abnormally low level of calcium in the blood
hyperglycemia hī′per-glī-sē′mē-ă	high blood sugar
hypoglycemia hī′pō-glī-sē′mē-ă	low blood sugar
hyperkalemia hī′per-kă-lē′mē-ă	an abnormally high level of potassium in the blood (kalium = potassium)
hypokalemia hī′pō-ka-lē′mē-ă	deficient level of potassium in the blood
hypernatremia hī′per-nă-trē′mē-ă	excessive level of sodium ions in the blood (natro = sodium)
hyponatremia hī′pō-nă-trē′mē-ă	low level of sodium ions in the blood
hypersecretion hī′per-se-krē′shŭn	abnormally increased secretion
hyposecretion hī′pō-se-krē′shŭn	decreased secretion
ketosis kē-tō′sis **ketoacidosis** kē-tō-as-i-dō′sis **diabetic ketoacidosis (DKA)**	presence of an abnormal amount of ketone bodies (acetone, beta-hydroxybutyric acid, and acetoacetic acid) in the blood and urine indicating an abnormal utilization of carbohydrates as seen in uncontrolled diabetes and starvation (keto = alter)
metabolism mĕ-tab′ō-lizm	all chemical processes in the body that result in growth, generation of energy, elimination of waste, and other body functions
polydipsia pol-ē-dip′sē-ă	excessive thirst
polyuria pol-ē-yū′rē-ă	excessive urination

Term	Meaning
DIAGNOSTIC	
Adrenal Glands	
Cushing syndrome	collection of signs and symptoms caused by an excessive level of cortisol hormone from any cause, such as a result of excessive production by the adrenal gland (often caused by a tumor), or more commonly as a side effect of treatment with glucocorticoid (steroid) hormones such as prednisone for asthma, rheumatoid arthritis, lupus or other inflammatory diseases; symptoms include upper body obesity, facial puffiness (moon-shaped appearance), hyperglycemia, weakness, thin and easily bruised skin with stria (stretch marks), hypertension, and osteoporosis (Fig. 11.3)
adrenal virilism ă-drē′năl vir′i-lizm	excessive output of the adrenal secretion of androgen (male sex hormone) in adult women owing to tumor or hyperplasia; evidenced by amenorrhea (absence of menstruation), acne, hirsutism, and deepening of the voice (virilis = masculine)
Pancreas (pan′krē-as)	
diabetes mellitus (DM) di-ă-bē′tēz mel′i-tŭs	metabolic disorder caused by an abnormal utilization of insulin secreted by the pancreas; evidenced by hyperglycemia and glucosuria (diabetes = passing through; mellitus = sugar)
insulin in′sŭ-lin	hormone secreted by the beta cells of the islets of Langerhans of the pancreas responsible for regulating the metabolism of glucose (insulin = island)
type 1 diabetes mellitus	diabetes in which there is no beta cell production of insulin—the patient is dependent on insulin for survival

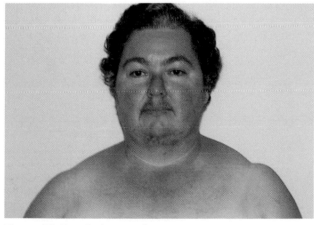

Figure 11.3   Cushing syndrome.

Term	Meaning
type 2 diabetes mellitus	diabetes in which the body produces insulin, but not enough, or there is insulin resistance (a defective use of the insulin that is produced)—the patient usually is not dependent on insulin for survival
hyperinsulinism hī′per-in′sū-lin-izm	condition resulting from an excessive amount of insulin in the blood that draws sugar out of the bloodstream, resulting in hypoglycemia, fainting, and convulsions; often caused by an overdose of insulin or by a tumor of the pancreas
pancreatitis pan′krē-ă-tī′tis	inflammation of the pancreas
Parathyroid Glands (par-ă-thī′royd)	
hyperparathyroidism hī′per-par-ă-thī′royd-izm	hypersecretion of the parathyroid glands, usually caused by a tumor
hypoparathyroidism hi′pō-par-ă-thī′royd-izm	hyposecretion of the parathyroid glands
Pituitary Gland (Hypophysis)	considered the master gland because it secretes hormones that regulate the function of other glands, such as the thyroid gland, adrenal glands, ovaries, and testicles
acromegaly ak-rō-meg′ă-lē	disease characterized by enlarged features, especially the face and hands, caused by hypersecretion of the pituitary hormone after puberty, when normal bone growth has stopped; most often caused by a pituitary tumor (Fig. 11.4)

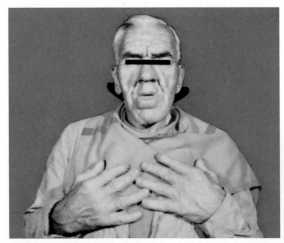

Figure 11.4 Enlarged hands and facial features in a patient with acromegaly.

Figure 11.5 Normal male (extreme right) and three types of dwarfism. (1) On the extreme left is a child who has failed to grow because of the congenital absence of the thyroid gland (cretinism). (2) The next two dwarfs have normal proportions but are half normal size (pituitary dwarfism). The next two dwarfs on the right show disproportionately short extremities but normal-size trunk and head (disproportionate dwarfism).

Term	Meaning
diabetes insipidus di-ă-bē′tēz in-sip′id-ŭs	condition of abnormal increase in urine output most commonly caused by inadequate secretion of pituitary antidiuretic hormone (vasopressin); symptoms include polyuria and polydipsia; urine appears colorless due to the inability of the kidneys to concentrate urine (insipid = without taste)
pituitary dwarfism dwōrf′izm	condition of congenital hyposecretion of growth hormone slowing growth and causing a short yet proportionate stature (not affecting intelligence)—often treated during childhood with growth hormone (Fig. 11.5) [note: there are many other forms of dwarfism, a condition of being markedly undersized; disproportionate types (short limb or short trunk) are most often caused by gene defects (see Fig. 11.5)]
pituitary gigantism jī′gan-tizm	condition of hypersecretion of growth hormone during childhood bone development that leads to an abnormal overgrowth of bone, especially of the long bones; most often caused by a pituitary tumor
Thyroid Gland	
goiter goy′ter	enlargement of the thyroid gland caused by thyroid dysfunction, tumor, lack of iodine in the diet, or inflammation (goiter = throat) (Fig. 11.6A)
hyperthyroidism hī-per-thī′royd-izm **Graves disease** grāvz di-zēz′ **thyrotoxicosis** thī′rō-tok-si-kō′sis	condition of hypersecretion of the thyroid gland characterized by exophthalmia, tachycardia, goiter, and tumor (see Fig. 11.6 and Fig. 11.7A)

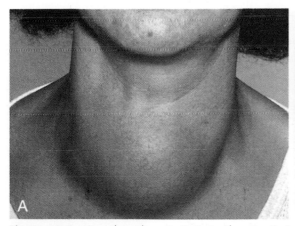
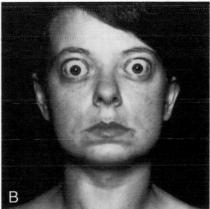

Figure 11.6 Hyperthyroidism. **A.** Patient with goiter. **B.** Patient with exophthalmos.

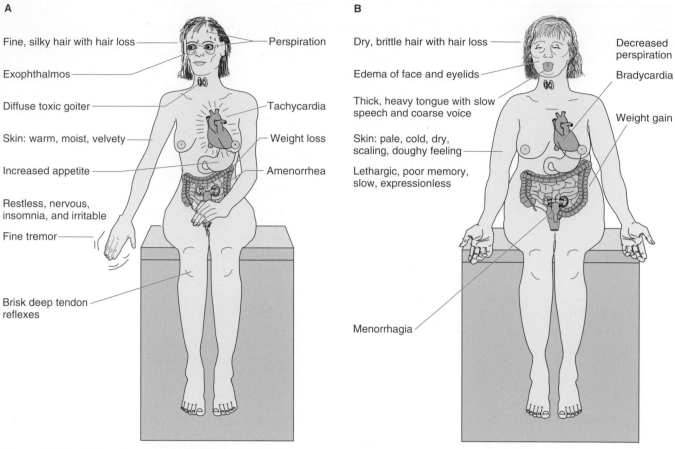

A

Fine, silky hair with hair loss

Exophthalmos

Diffuse toxic goiter

Skin: warm, moist, velvety

Increased appetite

Restless, nervous, insomnia, and irritable

Fine tremor

Brisk deep tendon reflexes

Perspiration

Tachycardia

Weight loss

Amenorrhea

B

Dry, brittle hair with hair loss

Edema of face and eyelids

Thick, heavy tongue with slow speech and coarse voice

Skin: pale, cold, dry, scaling, doughy feeling

Lethargic, poor memory, slow, expressionless

Menorrhagia

Decreased perspiration

Bradycardia

Weight gain

Figure 11.7 **A.** Hyperthyroidism. **B.** Hypothyroidism.

Term	Meaning
hypothyroidism hī′pō-thī′royd-izm	condition of hyposecretion of the thyroid gland causing low thyroid levels in the blood that result in sluggishness, slow pulse, and often obesity (Fig. 11.7B)
myxedema mik-se-dē′mă	advanced hypothyroidism in adults characterized by sluggishness, slow pulse, puffiness in the hands and face, and dry skin (myx = mucous)
cretinism krē′tin-izm	condition of congenital hypothyroidism in children that results in a lack of mental development and dwarfed physical stature; the thyroid gland is either congenitally absent or imperfectly developed (see Fig. 11.5)

Diagnostic Tests and Procedures

Test or Procedure	Explanation
LABORATORY TESTING	
blood sugar (BS) **blood glucose**	measurement of the level of sugar (glucose) in the blood
fasting blood sugar (FBS)	measurement of blood sugar level after a fast of 12 hours
postprandial blood sugar (PPBS)	measurement of blood sugar level after a meal, commonly after 2 hours
glucose tolerance test (GTT)	measurement of the body's ability to metabolize carbohydrates by administering a prescribed amount of glucose after a fasting period, then measuring blood and urine for glucose levels every hour thereafter—usually for 4 to 6 hours
glycohemoglobin glī-kō-hē-mō-glō'bin	molecule (fraction) in hemoglobin that rises in the blood as a result of an increased level of blood sugar; it is a common blood test used in diagnosing and treating diabetes, also known as glycosylated hemoglobin (HbA_{1c})
electrolytes ē-lek'tro-lītz	measurement of the level of specific ions (sodium, potassium, CO_2, and chloride) in the blood; electrolyte balance is essential for normal metabolism
thyroid function study	measurement of thyroid hormone levels in blood plasma to determine efficiency of glandular secretions, including T_3, T_4, and TSH
urine sugar and ketone studies kē'tōn	chemical tests to determine the presence of sugar or ketone bodies in the urine; used as a screen for diabetes (note: to void means to urinate)
IMAGING PROCEDURES	
computed tomography (CT)	CT of the head is used to obtain a transverse view of the pituitary gland
magnetic resonance imaging (MRI)	nonionizing images of magnetic resonance are useful in identifying abnormalities of pituitary, pancreas, adrenal, and thyroid glands
sonography	sonographic images are used to identify endocrine pathology, such as with thyroid ultrasound
thyroid uptake and image	nuclear image involving scan of the thyroid to visualize the radioactive accumulation of previously ingested isotopes to detect thyroid nodules or tumors (Fig. 11.8)

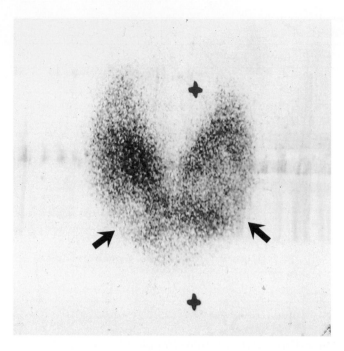

Figure 11.8 Thyroid uptake and image detecting presence of multiple nodules (*arrows*).

Operative Terms

Term	Meaning
adrenalectomy ă-drē-năl-ek′tō-mē	excision of adrenal gland
hypophysectomy hī′pof-i-sek′tō-mē	excision of pituitary gland
pancreatectomy pan′krē-ă-tek′tō-mē	excision of pancreas
parathyroidectomy pa′ră-thī-roy-dek′tō-mē	excision of parathyroid gland
thymectomy thī-mek′tō-mē	excision of thymus gland
thyroidectomy thī-roy-dek′tō-mē	excision of thyroid gland

Therapeutic Terms

Term	Meaning
continuous subcutaneous insulin infusion (CSII) **insulin pump therapy**	use of an insulin-delivery device worn on the body (usually the abdomen) that subcutaneously infuses doses of insulin programmed according to the individual needs of the diabetic patient (Fig. 11.9)
radioiodine therapy rā′dē-ō-ī′ō-din	use of radioactive iodine to treat disease, such as to eradicate thyroid tumor cells

Figure 11.9 Abdominal placement of insulin pump (continuous subcutaneous insulin infusion).

Term	Meaning
COMMON THERAPEUTIC DRUG CLASSIFICATIONS	
antihypoglycemic an'tē-hī'pō-glī-sē'mik	drug that raises blood glucose
antithyroid drug	agent that blocks the production of thyroid hormones; used to treat hyperthyroidism
hormone replacement hōr'mōn	drug that replaces a hormone deficiency (e.g., estrogen, testosterone, thyroid)
hypoglycemic **antihyperglycemic** hī'pō-glī-sē'mik an'tē-hī'per-glī-sē'mik	drug that lowers blood glucose (e.g., insulin)

Summary of Chapter 11 Acronyms/Abbreviations

ACTH .... adrenocorticotropic hormone
ADH ..... antidiuretic hormone
BS blood sugar
CO₂ ...... carbon dioxide
CSII ...... continuous subcutaneous insulin infusion
CT .... computed tomography
DKA ..... diabetic ketoacidosis
DM .... diabetes mellitus
FBS ...... fasting blood sugar
FSH ...... follicle-stimulating hormone

GH .... growth hormone
GTT ...... glucose tolerance test
LH .... luteinizing hormone
MRI ...... magnetic resonance imaging
MSH ..... melanocyte-stimulating hormone
PPBS .... postprandial blood sugar
PTH ...... parathyroid hormone
T₃ .... triiodothyronine
T₄ .... thyroxine
TSH ...... thyroid-stimulating hormone

PRACTICE EXERCISES

For the following terms, on the lines below the term, write out the indicated word parts: prefixes (P), combining forms (CF), roots (R), and suffixes (S). Then define the word.

EXAMPLE

parathyroid

_____ / _____ / _____
    P   R   S

para/thyr/oid
  P   R   S

DEFINITION: alongside of/thyroid gland/resembling

1. adenitis

_____ / _____
     R   S

DEFINITION: _____

2. euglycemia

_____ / _____ / _____
    P   R   S

DEFINITION: _____

3. thyrotoxicosis

_____ / _____ / _____
    CF   R   S

DEFINITION: _____

4. polydipsia

_____ / _____ / _____
    P   R   S

DEFINITION: _____

5. hormonal

_____ / _____
     R   S

DEFINITION: _____

6. ketosis

_____ / _____
     R   S

DEFINITION: _____

7. polyuria

_____ / _____ / _____
    P   R   S

DEFINITION: _____

8. endocrine

_____ / _____ / _____
        P   R   S

DEFINITION: _____

9. thyroptosis

_____ / _____
      CF   S

DEFINITION: _____

10. thymoma

_____ / _____
      R   S

DEFINITION: _____

11. acromegaly

_____ / _____
      CF   S

DEFINITION: _____

12. android

_____ / _____
      R   S

DEFINITION: _____

13. adrenotrophic

_____ / _____ / _____
      CF   R   S

DEFINITION: _____

14. pancreatogenic

_____ / _____ / _____
      CF   R   S

DEFINITION: _____

15. glycosuria

_____ / _____ / _____
      R   R   S

DEFINITION: _____

16. dipsogenic

_____ / _____ / _____
      CF   R   S

DEFINITION: _____

Complete the medical term by writing the missing part:

17. _____secretion = abnormally increased secretion

18. _____glycemia = low blood sugar

19. _____ syndrome = condition resulting from hypersecretion of the adrenal cortex causing obesity, hyperglycemia, and weakness

20. _____secretion = decreased secretion

21. _____glycemia = high blood sugar

22. _____graphy = ultrasound imaging

For each of the following, circle the meaning that corresponds to the combining form given:

23. **adren/o**	male	extremity	adrenal gland
24. **thyr/o**	nourishment	shield	chest
25. **crin/o**	blue	cell	secrete
26. **gluc/o**	stomach	sugar	pancreas
27. **dips/o**	thirst	ketones	secrete
28. **thym/o**	shield	hormone	thymus gland
29. **hormon/o**	development	urging on	ketones
30. **aden/o**	male	extremity	gland

Write the correct medical term for each of the following:

31. another name for Graves disease _____

32. protrusion of one or both eyeballs _____

33. disease characterized by enlarged features caused by hypersecretion of the

    pituitary hormone after puberty _____

34. enlargement of the thyroid gland _____

35. condition of congenital hyposecretion of growth hormone _____

36. nuclear image of the thyroid _____

Match the following:

37. _____ cretinism

38. _____ polydipsia

39. _____ hyperthyroidism

40. _____ pituitary gland

41. _____ thyromegaly

42. _____ myxedema

43. _____ hypokalemia

44. _____ type 2 diabetes

45. _____ pituitary hypersecretion

46. _____ adrenal virilism

47. _____ hypernatremia

48. _____ type 1 diabetes

49. _____ diabetes insipidus

a. gigantism

b. inadequate antidiuretic hormone

c. excessive sodium

d. depends on insulin

e. congenital hypothyroidism

f. hypophysis

g. not usually insulin dependent

h. excessive thirst

i. goiter

j. low potassium

k. advanced adult hypothyroidism

l. thyrotoxicosis

m. hirsutism

Write the full medical term for the following abbreviations:

50. BS _____

51. HRT _____

52. FBS _____

53. DM _____

54. PPBS _____

55. GTT _____

56. DKA _____

Write in the missing words on the blank lines in the following illustration of the endocrine glands.

57–62.

THE ENDOCRINE SYSTEM

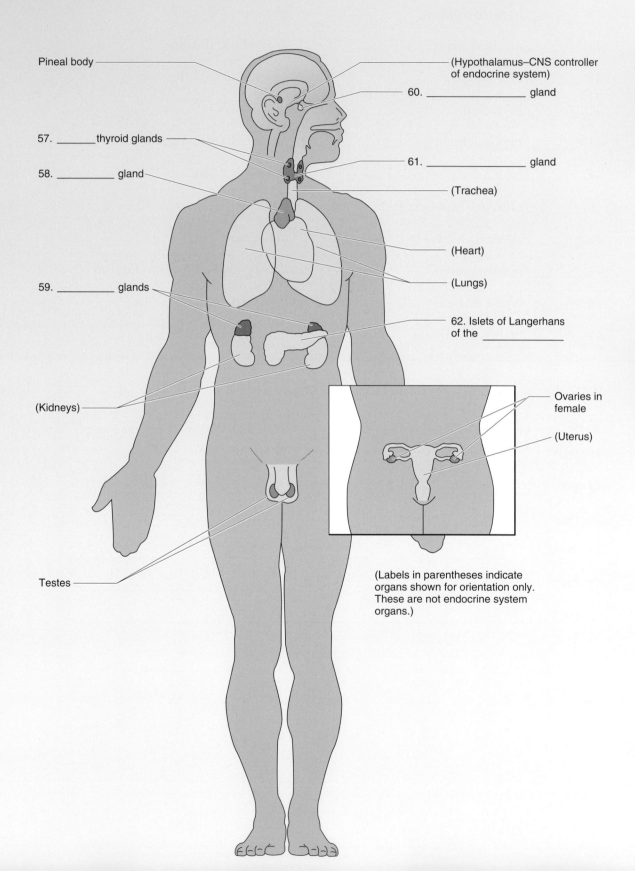

Pineal body

(Hypothalamus–CNS controller of endocrine system)

60. _____ gland

57. _____ thyroid glands

58. _____ gland

61. _____ gland

(Trachea)

(Heart)

(Lungs)

59. _____ glands

62. Islets of Langerhans of the _____

(Kidneys)

Ovaries in female

(Uterus)

Testes

(Labels in parentheses indicate organs shown for orientation only. These are not endocrine system organs.)

For each of the following, circle the correct spelling of the term:

63. hirsutism   hirsuitism   hirsitism

64. exopthalmos   exopthamamos   exophthalmos

65. myexedema   myxedema   myxadema

66. goiter   goyter   goitir

67. androgenius   androgenous   andreogenous

68. virillism   virilism   viralism

69. epinephrine   epinefrine   epineprine

70. hypoglicemic   hypoglicemic   hypoglycemic

Give the noun that was used to form the following adjectives:

71. _____ acromegalic

72. _____ exophthalmic

73. _____ metabolic

74. _____ diabetic

75. _____ hypoglycemic

MEDICAL RECORD ANALYSES

MEDICAL RECORD 11.1

S: This is a 27 y.o. ♀ c̄ a known Hx of diabetes seen in the ER with nausea and vomiting for the past three hours. She has skipped two doses of her insulin because BS levels monitored at home have been low. She is now experiencing a cephalalgia similar to what she has had in the past before coma.

O: T 35.5° C, P 90, R 20, BP 126/68
Lab blood studies: sodium 130, potassium 4.1, CO_2 9, chloride 102, glucose 296

A: Diabetic ketoacidosis

P: Admit to ICU: give 10 units insulin IV; measure BS 1° p̄ insulin given, then q 4 h; check urine for sugar and ketosis q void; repeat electrolytes in a.m.

1. What is the CC?

   a. nausea, vomiting, and headache

   b. nausea, vomiting, and dizziness

   c. nausea, vomiting, and high blood pressure

   d. nausea, vomiting, and ringing in the ears

   e. nausea, vomiting, and unconsciousness

2. What is the diagnosis?

   a. hyperglycemia

   b. hypoglycemia

   c. type 1 DM with presence of ketone bodies in the blood

   d. type 2 DM without the presence of ketone bodies in the blood

   e. combination of hyperglycemia and glucosuria

3. As an inpatient, where was treatment provided?

   a. neuropsychiatric facility

   b. coronary care facility

   c. emergency room

   d. recovery room

   e. critical care facility

4. Which of the following are electrolytes? 1. sodium 2. potassium 3. chloride 4. glucose

   a. only 1, 2, and 3 are correct

   b. only 1 and 3 are correct

   c. only 2 and 4 are correct

   d. only 4 is correct

   e. all are correct

5. Why were the blood electrolyte studies performed?

   a. to examine the electrical impulses of the brain

   b. to measure the level of ions in the blood in evaluation of metabolism

   c. to measure hormone levels and determine glandular efficiency

   d. to visualize the accumulation of radioactive isotopes to eliminate the presence of tumor

   e. to measure the level of glucose in the blood

6. How should the insulin be administered?

   a. within the skin

   b. absorption through unbroken skin

   c. within the muscle

   d. within the vein

   e. under the skin

7. How often should the blood glucose be measured?

   a. one hour after insulin administration, then every four hours

   b. once each morning

   c. each time the patient urinates

   d. one hour before insulin administration, then four times a day

   e. one hour before insulin administration, then every four hours thereafter

MEDICAL RECORD 11.2

Tara Nguyen had a long history of hyperthyroidism that was managed by pharmacological treatment for more than 5 years. She was often unhappy with how she felt, however, and decided on her own to stop taking the drug. Two months ago, the symptoms of hyperthyroidism recurred, and she sought medical attention.

Directions

Read Medical Record 11.2 for Ms. Nguyen (page 380) and answer the following questions. This record is the report by Dr. Rincon, who analyzed Ms. Nguyen's thyroid uptake and imaging study.

QUESTIONS ABOUT MEDICAL RECORD 11.2

Write your answers in the spaces provided.

1. Below are medical terms used in this record you have not yet encountered in this text. Underline each where it appears in the record and define below:

   propylthiouracil (PTU) _____

   uptake _____

   baseline (nonmedical term) _____

2. In your own words, not using medical terminology, briefly describe what seems to have been missing in Ms. Nguyen's past medical management:

   _____

   _____

3. In nonmedical terms, explain how the sodium iodide was administered:

   _____

4. In your own words, not using medical terminology, briefly describe Dr. Rincon's diagnosis:

   _____

   _____

   _____

5. What additional test did Dr. Rincon order on his own authority?
   a. thyroid function study
   b. fasting blood sugar
   c. thyroid MRI
   d. thyroid ultrasound

6. Which of the following tests is recommended to be performed in 6 months?
   a. thyroid function study
   b. fasting blood sugar
   c. thyroid MRI
   d. thyroid ultrasound

CENTRAL MEDICAL CENTER

211 Medical Center Drive • Central City, US 90000-1234 • PHONE: (012) 125-6784 • FAX: (012) 125-9999

THYROID UPTAKE AND IMAGING STUDY

Date of Exam: 5/29/20xx

CLINICAL HISTORY: The patient has more than a six year history of hyperthyroidism which was treated until approximately one year ago with propylthiouracil (PTU). The patient relates some instability in symptomatology during the treatment. She had no previous uptake and imaging study, and radioiodine therapy was never discussed with the patient. She spontaneously discontinued taking the PTU approximately one year ago and has had recurrent symptoms of hyperthyroidism in the last two months.

TECHNIQUE: The patient ingested a capsule containing 200 μCi^{123}I sodium iodide. Uptakes in the neck were measured at 6 and 24 hours. Images of the thyroid were obtained in multiple projections at 6 hours.

FINDINGS: Radioiodine uptake at 6 hours was 37% (normal: 0-15%), and at 24 hours, uptake was 57% (normal: 5-35%). Thyroid images reveal the gland to be diffusely modestly enlarged. Multiple areas of reduced function correlating with palpable nodules are present in both thyroid lobes with the largest nodule being present in the lower poles of both lobes but with the right lobe being somewhat more severely overall affected than the left lobe. No dominant functioning thyroid nodule is evident.

CONCLUSION:

TOXIC MULTINODULAR GOITER

NOTE: Because of the presence of the multiple nodules which are likely on a benign basis, I took the liberty of ordering a thyroid ultrasound as a baseline. This will be separately reported, and it is suggested that the thyroid ultrasound be repeated in six months to one year.

_____
C. Rincon, M.D.

CR:se

D: 5/29/20xx   T: 5/31/20xx

THYROID UPTAKE AND IMAGING STUDY	PT. NAME: NGUYEN, TARA T. ID NO: NM-384023 Sex: F Age: 58 Y DOB: 02/18/xx ATT. PHYS. T. Hutton

Medical Record 11.2

MEDICAL RECORD 11.3

Jane Dano, an 11-year-old girl, started experiencing a constant thirst accompanied by frequent urination. Gradually, she lost weight. At the suggestion of Dr. Freeman, her family doctor, she was admitted to Central Medical Center for tests. Shortly after admission, her care was referred to Dr. Gallegos.

Directions

Read Medical Record 11.3 regarding Jane Dano (pages 383–385) and answer the following questions. These records represent the physician's orders from Dr. Gallegos, who assumed the care of Jane at the time of her admission, and his clinical summary dictated at the time of her discharge.

QUESTIONS ABOUT MEDICAL RECORD 11.3

Write your answers in the spaces provided.

1. Below are medical terms used in this record you have not yet encountered in this text. Underline each where it appears in the records and define below:

   void _____

   urinalysis _____

   nocturia _____

   dietitian_____

   Kussmaul respiration _____

2. In your own words, not using medical terminology, briefly describe Jane's condition as identified by the admitting and final diagnosis:

   _____

   _____

   _____

3. Dr. Gallegos requested that the unit nurses take Jane's blood pressure every ___ hours.

4. Explain in lay language Dr. Gallegos' instructions to the nurses for Jane's fluid intake:

   _____

   _____

5. Every nurse helping care for Jane needs to know to check her urine for acetone and sugar at what times?

   _____

6. Part of Jane's care involves teaching her and others how to manage her diabetes when she returns home after discharge. The nurses and dietician provided this education to which of the following people (check all that apply):

_____ Jane's stepmother

_____ Jane's father

_____ Jane's teachers

_____ Jane's older brother

_____ a neighbor

_____ Dr. Gallegos

_____ the twins

7. Explain in lay language the two symptoms Jane had for 2 months before being admitted:

_____

What two additional symptoms occurred in the last 3 weeks?

_____

_____

8. At the time of discharge, Jane weighed:
   a. 40 lb
   b. 148 lb
   c. 89 lb
   d. 148 kg

9. Which of the following diagnostic tests will Jane and her family be performing at home?
   a. blood glucose monitoring
   b. vital signs
   c. body weight
   d. insulin injections

10. If you were Jane's parent, what guidance would you give about how active she can be at school? (Put in terms an 11-year-old can understand.)

_____

_____

_____

CENTRAL MEDICAL CENTER

211 Medical Center Drive • Central City, US 90000-1234 • PHONE: (012) 125-6784 • FAX: (012) 125-9999

DOCTOR: PLEASE STATE PERTINENT CLINICAL INFORMATION WHEN ORDERING RADIOLOGY PROCEDURES

WRITE WITH BALLPOINT INK PEN; PRESS HARD

DATE	TIME	AUTHORIZATION IS GIVEN TO DISPENSE ANOTHER BRAND OF DRUG IDENTICAL IN FORM AND CONTENT UNLESS CHECKED
11-11-XX	1400	1. STAT Comprehensive metabolic panel 2. glyco hemoglobin (HbA1c) 3. anti-islet cell antibodies R. Gallegos M.D Noted 11/11/xx B. Hill, RN 1425
11-11-XX	1430	1. admit to 6 north 2. Dx: Type 1 DM new onset 3. VS per routine BP q 4° during day 4. daily wt 5. encourage p.o. fluids 1200 cc q 8° 6. a.m. insulin to be Novolin Regular and NPH Please have Available on floor 7. U.A 8. accu check (blood sugar test) at 07-11-17-22-02 9. Give 7 units of Regular insulin now 10. Check urine for sugar, acetone and volume q void 11. accu check 1° p̄ above insulin given R. Gallegos M.D C. Wells 11-11-xx 1500 Noted 11/11/xx B. Hill, RN 1600
11-11-XX	1530	1800-Calorie diet based on USDA Dietary Guidelines c̄ 3 meals and 2 snacks – no A.M. snack R. Gallegos M.D C. Wells 11-11-xx 1830

PHYSICIAN'S ORDERS

PT. NAME: DANO, J.
ID NO: 4038315
SEX: F AGE: 11 DOB: 02/13/20xx
ATT. PHYS: R. GALLEGOS, M.D.

Medical Record 11.3

CENTRAL MEDICAL CENTER

211 Medical Center Drive • Central City, US 90000-1234 • PHONE: (012) 125-6784 • FAX: (012) 125-9999

DISCHARGE SUMMARY

ADMITTING DIAGNOSIS: New onset Type 1 diabetes mellitus.

FINAL DIAGNOSIS: New onset Type 1 diabetes mellitus.

HISTORY OF PRESENT ILLNESS: The patient is an 11-year-old white female who presented with a 3-week history of polyuria and polydipsia. She has also had nocturia for the past two months and associated weight loss. She was seen by E. Freeman, M.D., her private physician, on the day of admission. A urinalysis was positive for glucose. The patient was then referred to this examiner for further evaluation and management of new onset diabetes mellitus.

HOSPITAL COURSE: The patient was admitted to the third floor. She was initially treated with regular insulin and then progressed to a 2-shot regimen with regular insulin and NPH before breakfast and regular insulin and NPH before dinner. She also required some spot dosing at lunch time for hyperglycemia. Prior to discharge, her blood sugars had stabilized. She did not have any overnight hypoglycemia. She had spilled 10 gm of glucose in her urine but no ketones. Also, during the course of hospitalization, the parents, the patient, and a neighbor underwent extensive education with nursing and the dietitian. The patient lives with her father and stepmother. Her stepmother is due to deliver twins in January, and her father travels quite a bit in his work; therefore, a neighbor was also trained to help in taking care of her diabetes. Prior to discharge, the patient and her parents have been able to give insulin injections and also do home blood glucose monitoring.

LABORATORY DATA: Initial laboratory studies showed the following: Sodium: 134. Potassium: 4.0. Chloride: 102. CO_2: 28. Blood urea nitrogen (BUN): 9. Creatinine: 0.7. Serum glucose: 517. Thyroid function was normal with: T_4: 6.5; free thyroxine index (FTI): 7.8; T_3: 1.02; TSH: 2.0. Total cholesterol was 146. Liver function tests were normal. Glycohemoglobin was 19.5. Anti-islet cell antibodies were sent out and are pending at the time of discharge. [islet cell antibodies commonly occur in newly diagnosed insulin dependent diabetics].

(continued)

DISCHARGE SUMMARY	PT. NAME:	DANO, JANE V.
Page 1	ID NO:	IP-403831
	ROOM NO:	610
	ADM. DATE:	November 11, 20xx
	DIS. DATE:	November 18, 20xx
	ATT. PHYS:	R. GALLEGOS, M.D.

Medical Record 11.3 *Continued.*

CENTRAL MEDICAL CENTER

211 Medical Center Drive • Central City, US 90000-1234 • PHONE: (012) 125-6784 • FAX: (012) 125-9999

DISCHARGE SUMMARY

PHYSICAL EXAMINATION: Temperature: 36.9°C. Heart rate: 68. Respirations: 18. Discharge weight: 40.4 kg. Height: 148 cm. GENERAL: The patient is awake and alert and in no acute distress. Eyes reveal normal funduscopic examination. The neck is supple. The thyroid gland is nonpalpable. The chest is clear to percussion and auscultation. No Kussmaul's respirations were noted at discharge. CARDIOVASCULAR: Apical pulse is regular without murmur. ABDOMEN: The abdomen is soft and nontender. No enlargement or mass is noted. GENITOURINARY: Normal external female genitalia. EXTREMITIES: The patient did have significant improvement of the dryness on her hands and also around her mouth.

DISCHARGE PROGRAM: The patient is to be seen in the Diabetic Clinic in approximately two weeks. DIET: She is on a 2000-calorie diet based on USDA Dietary Guidelines with three meals and two snacks. Physical activity is ad lib. The patient may return to school at the end of the week. SPECIAL INSTRUCTIONS: The parents are to check blood sugar at 2 a.m. for the first two nights at home. They are also to call for insulin dose adjustments daily for the first week after discharge.

DISCHARGE MEDICATIONS: Novolin Human Insulin, 12 units of regular and 12 units of NPH, to be given 20 minutes before breakfast; 10 units of regular and 6 units of NPH to be given 20 minutes before dinner.

R. Gallegos M.D.

R. Gallegos, M.D.

RG:ti

D: 11/18/xx
T: 11/19/xx

DISCHARGE SUMMARY	PT. NAME: DANO, JANE V.
Page 2	ID NO: IP-403831
	ROOM NO: 610
	ADM. DATE: November 11, 20xx
	DIS. DATE: November 18, 20xx
	ATT. PHYS: R. GALLEGOS, M.D.

Medical Record 11.3   *Continued.*

Chapter **12**

Eye

OBJECTIVES

After completion of this chapter you will be able to

- Define the common term components used in relation to the eye
- Locate and name the major structures of the eye and list their functions
- Define common symptomatic and diagnostic terms referring to the eye
- List the common diagnostic tests and procedures related to the eye
- Identify common operative terms referring to the eye
- Identify common therapeutic terms including drug classifications related to the eye
- Explain the terms and abbreviations used in documenting medical records involving the eye

Combining Forms

Combining Form	Meaning	Example
aque/o	water	**aqueous** ak′wē-ŭs
blephar/o	eyelid	**blepharospasm** blef′ă-rō-spazm
conjunctiv/o	conjunctiva (to join together)	**conjunctival** kon-jŭnk-tī′văl
corne/o	cornea	**corneal** kōr′nē-ăl
kerat/o		**keratoplasty** ker′ă-tō-plas-tē
cycl/o	ciliary body (circle)	**cycloplegia** sī-klō-plē′jē-ă
ir/o irid/o	iris (colored circle)	**iritis** ī-rī′tis
		iridectomy ir′i-dek′tō-mē
lacrim/o	tear	**lacrimal** lak′ri-măl
dacry/o		**dacryocyst** dak′rē-ō-sist

Combining Form	Meaning	Example
ocul/o	eye	ocular ok′yū-lăr
ophthalm/o		ophthalmology of-thal-mol′ō-jē
opt/o		optometry op-tom′ĕ-trē
phac/o	lens (lentil)	phacolysis fă-kol′i-sis
phak/o		phakoma fa-kō′mă
phot/o	light	photophobia fō-tō-fō′bē-ă
presby/o	old age	presbyopia prez-bē-ō′pē-ă
retin/o	retina	retinopathy ret-i-nop′ă-thē
scler/o	sclera (hard)	scleritis sklĕ-rī′tis
vitre/o	glassy	vitreous vit′rē-ŭs
ADDITIONAL SUFFIX		
-opia	condition of vision	hyperopia hī-per-ō′pē-ă

Eye Overview

The eye is the organ of sight that through pairing provides three-dimensional vision (Fig. 12.1). Each eye is located in a bony orbit (cavity) of the skull and is covered by the protective fold of the eyelid.

The *sclera,* the white of the eye, and the *cornea,* the transparent anterior coating, are part of the outer fibrous *tunic* (layer) that *refracts* (bends) light that enters the eye.

The *choroid,* a vascular layer located just beneath the sclera, contains blood vessels that nourish the outer portion of the retina. The *iris* contains blood vessels, pigment cells, and muscle fibers. Muscles of the iris regulate the amount of light that enters through the central opening known as the *pupil.* Melanin, the pigment present in the epithelial cells that cover the iris, gives color to the eyes. The *ciliary body* is a ring of muscle located behind the peripheral iris that controls the power of the lens. The elastic, transparent *lens,* located behind the pupil, focuses light rays on the *retina* in the inner, posterior part of the eye. *Aqueous humor,* produced by the surface epithelium of the ciliary body, provides nutrition to the avascular lens and cornea. *Vitreous* is the jelly-like material that occupies the space between the lens and retina.

The *retina* is the nerve tissue layer that contains cells for visual reception. The visual receptor neurons of the retina are the rods and cones. *Rods* are responsible for vision in dim light, and *cones* are responsible for vision in bright light. The *macula lutea* is the central region of the retina. It has a yellowish color caused by its pigment. At the center of the macula, a tiny, pinpoint depression known as the fovea centralis is the site of sharpest, central vision. The *optic disk* is the area in the retina where nerve fibers form the *optic nerve* for transmission to the optic tracts in the brain.

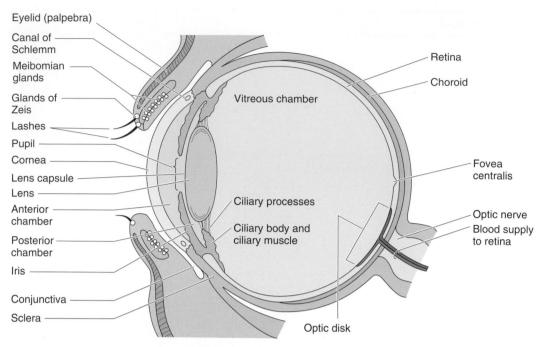

Figure 12.1 Anatomy of the eye (sagittal view).

The *conjunctiva* provides a lining for the eye and eyelid. The *lacrimal gland,* located in the orbit above each eye, secretes tears that lubricate and protect the eye. Tears constantly flow across the eye and downward to the *lacrimal ducts,* to the *lacrimal sac,* and then into the *nasolacrimal duct* that drains into the nose. The *meibomian glands* are sebaceous glands located within the rim of the eyelid that secrete sebum to keep the lids from sticking together, and the *glands of Zeis* are sebaceous glands surrounding the hair follicles of the eyelashes.

Anatomical Terms

Term	Meaning
anterior chamber	fluid-filled space between the cornea and iris
aqueous humor ak′wē-ŭs hyū′mer	watery liquid secreted at the ciliary body that fills the anterior and posterior chambers of the eye and provides nourishment for the cornea, iris, and lens (humor = fluid)
canal of Schlemm	duct in the anterior chamber that carries filtered aqueous humor to the veins and bloodstream
choroid kō′royd	vascular layer beneath the sclera that provides nourishment to the outer portion of the retina
ciliary body sil′ē-ar-ē	ring of muscle behind the peripheral iris that controls the power of the lens
ciliary muscle	smooth muscle portion of the ciliary body, which contracts to assist in near-vision capability
ciliary processes	epithelial tissue folds on the inner surface of the ciliary body that secrete aqueous humor
conjunctiva kon-jŭnk-tī′vă	joining together; mucous membrane that lines the eyelids and outer surface of the eyeball

Term	Meaning
cornea kōr′nē-ă	transparent, anterior part of the eyeball covering the iris, pupil, and anterior chamber that functions to refract (bend) light to focus a visual image
eyelid (palpebra) pal-pē′bră	movable protective fold that opens and closes, covering the eye
fovea centralis fō′vē-ă sen-trā′lis	pinpoint depression in the center of the macula lutea that is the site of sharpest vision (fovea = pit)
fundus (base) fŭn′dŭs	interior surface of the eyeball including the retina, optic disk, macula, and posterior pole (curvature at the back of the eye)
glands of Zeis	oil glands surrounding the eyelashes
meibomian glands mī-bō′mē-an	oil glands located along the rim of the eyelids
iris ī′ris	colored circle; colored part of the eye located behind the cornea that contracts and dilates to regulate light passing through the pupil
lacrimal gland lak′ri-măl	gland located in the upper outer region above the eyeball that secretes tears (Fig. 12.2)
lacrimal ducts	tubes that carry tears to the lacrimal sac
lacrimal sac	structure that collects tears before emptying into the nasolacrimal duct
lens	transparent structure behind the pupil that bends and focuses light rays on the retina
lens capsule	capsule that encloses the lens
macula lutea (macula) mak′yū-lă	central region of the retina responsible for central vision; yellow pigment provides its color (lutea = yellow) (see Fig. 12.13B)

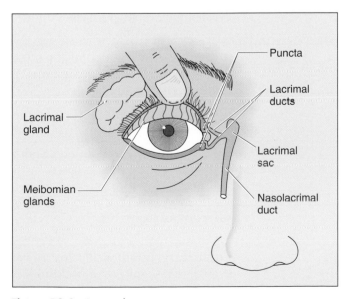

Figure 12.2 Lacrimal apparatus.

Term	Meaning
nasolacrimal duct nā-zō-lak′ri-măl	passageway for tears from the lacrimal sac into the nose
optic disk op′tik	exit site of retinal nerve fibers, as well as the entrance point for retinal arteries and the exit point for retinal veins (see Fig. 12.13B)
optic nerve	nerve responsible for carrying impulses for the sense of sight from the retina to the brain
posterior chamber	space between the back of the iris and the front of the vitreous filled with aqueous fluid
pupil pyū′pīl	black circular opening in the center of the iris through which light passes as it enters the eye
retina ret′i-nă	innermost layer that perceives and transmits light to the optic nerve (see Fig. 12.13B)
cones	cone-shaped cells within the retina that are color sensitive and respond to bright light
rods	rod-shaped cells within the retina that respond to dim light
sclera sklēr′ă	tough, fibrous, white outer coat extending from the cornea to the optic nerve
trabecular meshwork tră-bek′yū-lăr	mesh-like structure in the anterior chamber that filters the aqueous humor as it flows into the canal of Schlemm
vitreous vit′rē-ŭs	jelly-like mass filling the inner chamber between the lens and retina that gives bulk to the eye

PUPIL. The Latin word, pupilla, the pupil of the eye, is derived from pupa, meaning a doll or little girl. The name is said to have been given to the pupil of the eye because a tiny image of the beholder may be seen reflected in it.

Symptomatic and Diagnostic Terms

Term	Meaning
SYMPTOMATIC	
asthenopia as-thĕ-nō′pē-ă	eyestrain (asthenia = weak condition)
blepharospasm blef′ă-rō-spazm	involuntary contraction of the muscles surrounding the eye, causing uncontrolled blinking and lid squeezing
diplopia di-plō′pē-ă	double vision
exophthalmos ek-sof-thal′mos **exophthalmus**	abnormal protrusion of one or both eyeballs
lacrimation lak-ri-mā′shŭn	secretion of tears
nystagmus nis-tag′mŭs	involuntary, rapid oscillating movement of the eyeball (nystagmos = a nodding)
photophobia fō-tō-fō′bē-ă	extreme sensitivity to, and discomfort from, light

Term	Meaning
scotoma skō-tō′mă	blind spot in vision (skotos = darkness)
DIAGNOSTIC	
refractive errors rē-frak′tiv	defects in the bending of light as it enters the eye, causing an improper focus on the retina
astigmatism ă-stig′mă-tizm	distorted vision caused by an oblong or cylindrical curvature of the lens or cornea that prevents light rays from coming to a single focus on the retina (stigma = point)
hyperopia hī-per-ō′pē-ă	farsightedness; difficulty seeing close objects when light rays extend beyond the proper focus on the retina (Fig. 12.3A and B)
myopia mī-ō′pē-ă	nearsightedness; difficulty seeing distant objects when light rays fall short of the proper focus on the retina (Fig. 12.3A and C)
presbyopia prez-bē-ō′pē-ă	impaired vision owing to old-age loss of accommodation
accommodation ă-kom′ŏ-dā′shŭn	ability of the eye to adjust focus on near objects
amblyopia am-blē-ō′pē-ă	decreased vision in early life due to a functional defect that can occur as a result of strabismus, refractive errors (when one eye is more nearsighted, farsighted, or astigmatic than the other), or trauma; usually occurs in one eye, also known as lazy eye (ambly/o = dim)
aphakia ă-fā′kē-ă	absence of the lens, usually after cataract extraction
blepharitis blef′ă-rī′tis	inflammation of the eyelid
blepharochalasis blef′ă-rō-kal′ă-sis dermatochalasis der′mă-tō-kal′ă-sis	baggy eyelid; overabundance and loss of elasticity of skin on the upper eyelid, causing a fold of skin to hang down over the edge of the eyelid when the eyes are open (chalasis = a slackening)
blepharoptosis blef′ă-rop′tō-sis ptosis	drooping of the eyelid usually caused by paralysis

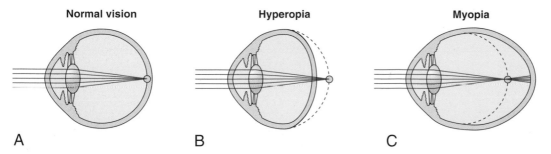

Figure 12.3 **A.** Proper focus of light rays on the retina. **B.** Light rays extend beyond proper focus in hyperopia. **C.** Light rays fall short of proper focus in myopia.

CATARACT. This Greek word meaning waterfall, or something that rushes down to form an obstruction, like a portcullis, was probably related to the obstruction of vision that is symptomatic of a cataract. It was an ancient belief that the interference with vision occurred between the lens and the iris (like a veil).

Term	Meaning
chalazion ka-lā′zē-on (shǎ-lā′zē-on)	chronic nodular inflammation of a meibomian gland, usually the result of a blocked duct; commonly presents as a swelling on the upper or lower eyelid (chalaza = hailstone) (Fig. 12.4)
cataract kat′ǎ-rakt	opaque clouding of the lens causing decreased vision (Figs. 12.5 and 12.6B)
conjunctivitis kon-jŭnk-ti-vī′tis	pinkeye; inflammation of the conjunctiva
dacryoadenitis dak′rē-ō-ad-ĕ-nī′tis	inflammation of the lacrimal gland
dacryocystitis dak′rē-ō′sis-tī′tis	inflammation of the tear sac (cyst/o = sac)
diabetic retinopathy dī-ǎ-bet′ik ret-i-nop′ǎ-thē	disease of the retina in diabetics characterized by capillary leakage, bleeding, and new vessel formation (neovascularization), leading to scarring and loss of vision (Figs. 12.6C and 12.13C)
ectropion ek-trō′pē-on	outward turning of the rim of the eyelid (trop/o = turning) (Fig. 12.7A)
entropion en-trō′pē-on	inward turning of the rim of the eyelid (Fig. 12.7B)
epiphora ē-pif′ō-rǎ	abnormal overflow of tears caused by blockage of the lacrimal duct (epi = upon; phor/o = to carry or bear)
glaucoma glaw-kō′mǎ	group of diseases of the eye characterized by increased intraocular pressure that results in damage to the optic nerve, producing defects in vision (Fig. 12.6D)
hordeolum hōr-dē′ō-lŭm	sty; an acute infection of a sebaceous gland of the eyelid (hordeum = barley) (Fig. 12.8)
iritis ī-rī′tis	inflammation of the iris
keratitis ker-ǎ-tī′tis	inflammation of the cornea

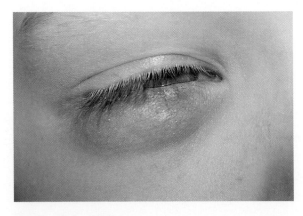

Figure 12.4 Chalazion.

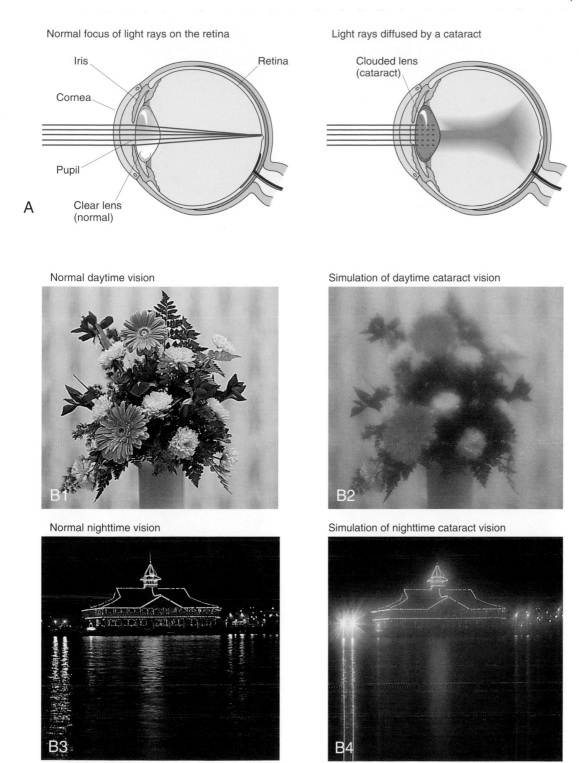

Figure 12.5 Cataract. **A.** Normal light focus compared with light focus interference caused by a cataract. **B.** Simulation of cataract vision.

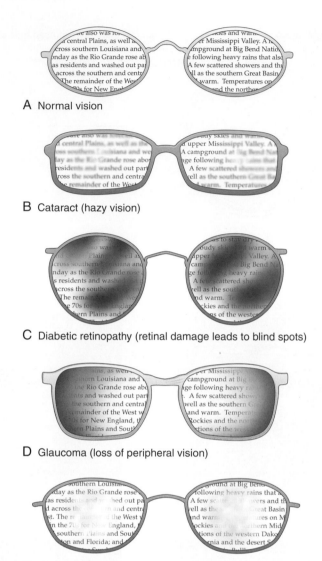

A Normal vision

B Cataract (hazy vision)

C Diabetic retinopathy (retinal damage leads to blind spots)

D Glaucoma (loss of peripheral vision)

E Macular degeneration (loss of central vision)

Figure 12.6 Simulations of vision loss.

Term	Meaning
macular degeneration mak′yū-lăr dē-jen-er-ā′shŭn	breakdown or thinning of the tissues in the macula, resulting in partial or complete loss of central vision (see Fig. 12.6E)
pseudophakia sū-dō-fak′ē-ă	eye in which the natural lens is replaced with an artificial lens implant (pseudo = false)
pterygium tĕ-rij′ēŭm	fibrous growth of conjunctival tissue that extends onto the cornea (Fig. 12.9)
retinal detachment ret-i-nal	separation of the retina from the underlying epithelium, disrupting vision and resulting in blindness if not repaired surgically (Fig. 12.13D)
retinitis ret-i-nī′tis	inflammation of the retina

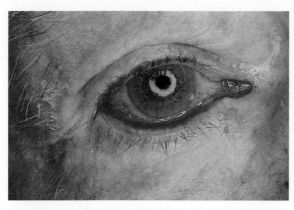
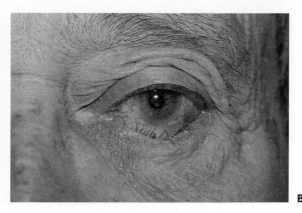

Figure 12.7 Eyelid abnormalities. **A.** Severe bilateral lower lid ectropion. **B.** Lower lid entropion causing the lashes to rub on the cornea.

Term	Meaning
strabismus stra-biz′mŭs	crossed eyes; a condition of eye misalignment caused by intraocular muscle imbalance (strabismus = a squinting; hetero = other) (Fig. 12.10)
heterotropia het′er-ō-trō′pē-ă	
esotropia es-ō-trō′pē-ă	right or left eye deviates inward toward the nose (eso = inward; tropo = turning)
exotropia ek-sō-trō′pē-ă	right or left eye deviates outward away from the nose (exo = out; tropo = turning)
scleritis sklĕ-rī′tis	inflammation of the sclera
trichiasis trī-kī′ă-sis	misdirected eyelashes that rub on the conjunctiva or cornea

STRABISMUS. Strabo, a geographer and prominent figure in Alexandria during the Roman period, suffered from a peculiar and noticeable squint. Any man with the same type of squint was called Strabo, which led to the word strabismus.

Figure 12.8 Upper lid hordeolum.

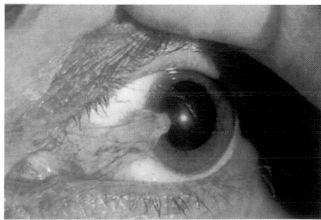

Figure 12.9 Pterygium caused by ultraviolet exposure and drying.

Esotropia

Exotropia

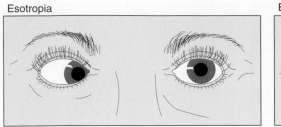
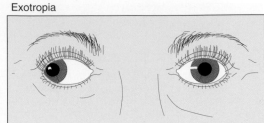

Figure 12.10 Strabismus.

Diagnostic Tests and Procedures

Test or Procedure	Explanation
distance visual acuity	measure of the ability to see the details and shape of identifiable objects from a specified distance (usually 20 feet), typically using a Snellen chart (Fig. 12.11)
fluorescein angiography flūr-es′ē-in an-jē-og′ră-fē	visualization and photography of retinal and choroidal vessels made as fluorescein dye, which is injected into a vein, circulates through the eye (Fig. 12.12)
ophthalmoscopy of-thal-mos′kō-pē	use of an ophthalmoscope to view the interior of the eye (Fig. 12.13)
refraction rē-frak′shŭn	measurement of refractive errors using a phoropter to determine best corrected vision and prescription for eye glasses or contact lenses
phoropter fŏ-rop′ter	instrument that holds corrective lenses in front of the eye to determine optical correction

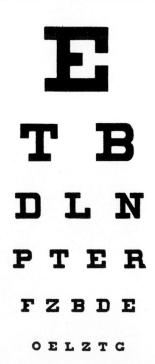

Figure 12.11 Snellen eye chart for testing distance visual acuity.

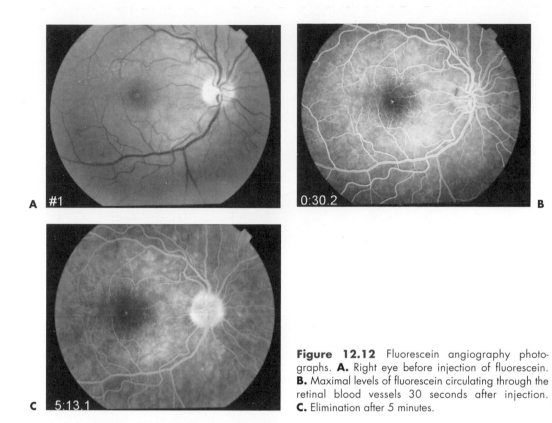

Figure 12.12 Fluorescein angiography photographs. **A.** Right eye before injection of fluorescein. **B.** Maximal levels of fluorescein circulating through the retinal blood vessels 30 seconds after injection. **C.** Elimination after 5 minutes.

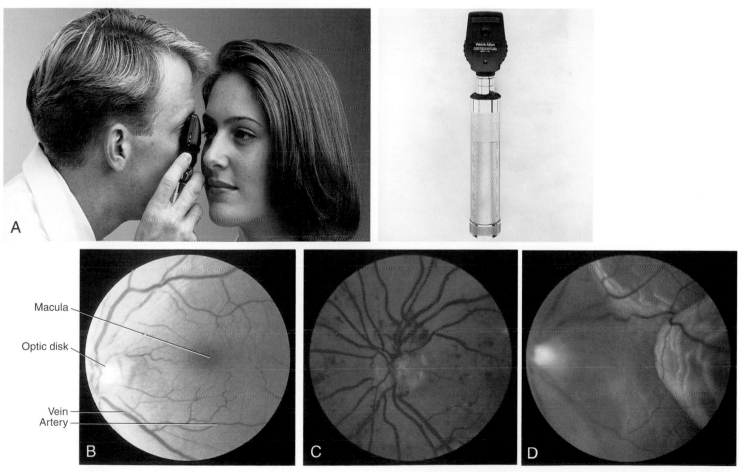

Macula
Optic disk
Vein
Artery

Figure 12.13 **A.** Doctor performing ophthalmoscopy using an ophthalmoscope. **B.** Normal retina. **C.** Aneurysms seen in diabetic retinopathy. **D.** Retinal detachment.

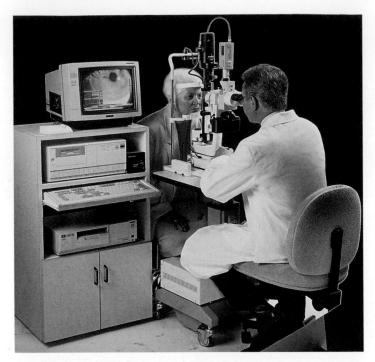

Figure 12.14 Slit-lamp biomicroscope.

Test or Procedure	Explanation
slit-lamp biomicroscopy bi′ō-mi-kros′kŏ-pē	use of a tabletop microscope to examine the eye, especially the cornea, lens, fluids, and membranes (Fig. 12.14)
sonography sŏ-nog′ră-fē	use of high-frequency sound waves to detect pathology within the eye such as foreign bodies or a detached retina
tonometry tō-nom′ĕ-trē	use of a tonometer to measure intraocular pressure, which is elevated in glaucoma (Fig. 12.15)

Operative Terms

Term	Meaning
blepharoplasty blef′ă-ro-plast-tē	surgical repair of an eyelid
cataract extraction kat′ă-rakt ek-strak′shŭn	excision of a cloudy lens from the eye
cryoretinopexy krī-ō-ret′i-nō-pek-se **cryopexy**	use of intense cold to seal a hole or tear in the retina; used to treat retinal detachment
dacryocystectomy dak′rē-ō-sis-tek′tō-mē	excision of a lacrimal sac

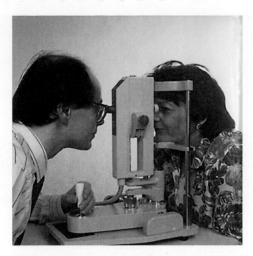

Figure 12.15.   Tonometer/tonometry.

Term	Meaning
enucleation ē-nū-klē-ā′shŭn	excision of an eyeball
iridectomy ir′i-dek′tō-mē	excision of a portion of iris tissue
iridotomy ir-i-dot′ō-mē	incision into the iris (usually with a laser) to allow for drainage of aqueous humor from the posterior to anterior chamber; used to treat a type of glaucoma
keratoplasty ker′ă-tō-plas-tē	corneal transplant; replacement of a diseased or scarred cornea with a healthy one from a matched donor
laser surgery	use of a laser to make incisions or destroy tissues (e.g., to create fluid passages, to obliterate tumors or aneurysms) (Fig. 12.16)
laser-assisted in situ keratomileusis (LASIK) in sī′tū ker′ă-tō-mil-oo′sis	technique using the excimer laser to reshape the surface of the cornea to correct refractive errors such as myopia, hyperopia, and astigmatism (smileusis = carving)

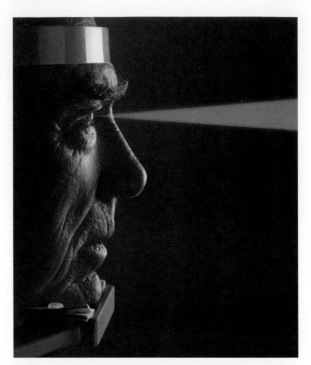

Figure 12.16. Simulation of laser application.

Term	Meaning
intraocular lens (IOL) implant in′tră-ok′yū-lăr	implantation of an artificial lens to replace a defective natural lens (e.g., after cataract extraction) (Fig. 12.17)
phacoemulsification fak′ō-ē-mŭl-si-fi-kā′shŭn	use of ultrasound to shatter and break up a cataract with aspiration and removal
scleral buckling sklĕr′ăl bŭk′ling	surgery to treat retinal detachment by placing a band of silicone around the sclera to cinch it toward the middle of the eye and relieve pull on the retina—often combined with other techniques to seal retinal tears such as cryoretinopexy
trabeculectomy tră-bek′yū-lek′tō-mē	removal of a portion of the trabecular meshwork to increase the flow of aqueous humor from the eye; used in treatment of acute glaucoma or glaucoma not treatable with medication

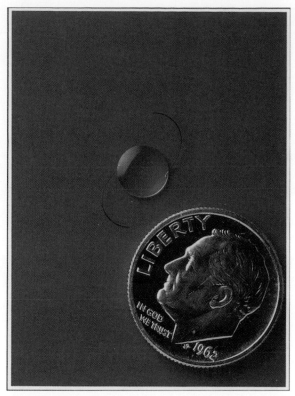

Figure 12.17. Size comparison of an intraocular lens to a dime.

Therapeutic Terms

Term	Meaning
contact lens	small plastic curved disk with optical correction that fits over the cornea; used to correct refractive errors
eye instillation	introduction of a medicated solution in the eye
eye irrigation	washing of the eye with water or other fluid (e.g., saline)

COMMON THERAPEUTIC DRUG CLASSIFICATIONS	
antibiotic ophthalmic solution an'tē-bī-ot'ik of-thal'mik	antimicrobial agent in solution, used to treat bacterial infections (e.g., conjunctivitis, corneal ulcers)
cycloplegic sī-klō-plē'jik	agent that paralyzes the ciliary muscle and powers of accommodation; commonly used in pediatric eye examinations
mydriatic (dilation of pupil) mi-drē-at'ik	agent that causes dilation of the pupil (e.g., for certain eye examinations)
miotic mī-ot'ik	agent that causes the pupil to contract (mio = less)

Summary of Chapter 12 Acronyms/Abbreviations

IOL............intraocular lens   **LASIK**.......laser-assisted in situ keratomileusis

PRACTICE EXERCISES

For the following terms, on the lines below the term, write out the indicated word parts: prefixes (P), combining forms (CF), roots (R), and suffixes (S). Then define the word.

EXAMPLE

epikeratophakia

_____ / _____ / _____ / _____
P   CF   R   S

<u>epi/kerato/phak/ia</u>
P   CF   R   S

DEFINITION: upon/cornea/lens/condition of

1. blepharoptosis

_____ / _____
CF   S

DEFINITION: _____

2. iridotomy

_____ / _____
CF   S

DEFINITION: _____

3. ophthalmology

_____ / _____
CF   S

DEFINITION: _____

4. vitrectomy

_____ / _____
R   S

DEFINITION: _____

5. dacryolithiasis

_____ / _____ / _____
CF   R   S

DEFINITION: _____

6. lacrimal

_____ / _____
R   S

DEFINITION: _____

7. photophobia

_____ / _____ / _____
        CF   R   S

DEFINITION: _____

8. keratoplasty

_____ / _____
        CF   S

DEFINITION: _____

9. aqueous

_____ / _____
        R   S

DEFINITION: _____

10. iritis

_____ / _____
        R   S

DEFINITION: _____

11. corneal

_____ / _____
        R   S

DEFINITION: _____

12. phacolysis

_____ / _____
        CF   S

DEFINITION: _____

13. retinopathy

_____ / _____ / _____
        CF   R   S

DEFINITION: _____

14. ocular

_____ / _____
        R   S

DEFINITION: _____

15. conjunctivitis

_____ / _____
        R   S

DEFINITION: _____

16. presbyopia

_____ / _____
        R   S

DEFINITION: _____

17. optometry

_____ / _____
       CF   S

DEFINITION: _____

18. aphakia

_____ / _____ / _____
       P   R   S

DEFINITION: _____

19. hyperopia

_____ / _____
       P   S

DEFINITION: _____

20. scleromalacia

_____ / _____
       CF   S

DEFINITION: _____

Complete the following medical term by writing the missing part:

21. _____phakia = absence of the lens of the eye

22. _____ophthalmos = protrusion of the eyeball

23. _____chalasis = baggy eyelids

24. _____ buckling = surgical placement of a band of silicone around the sclera to cinch it toward the middle of the eye

25. blepharo_____ = involuntary contraction of the muscles surrounding the eye

For each of the following, circle the combining form that corresponds to the meaning given:

26. **eye**   or/o   opt/o   ot/o

27. **old age**   presby/o   scler/o   phas/o

28. **glassy**   aque/o   vitre/o   hydr/o

29. **light**   phon/o   phot/o   opt/o

30. **hard or sclera**	corne/o	vitre/o	scler/o
31. **lens (lentil)**	phac/o	scler/o	conjunctiv/o
32. **colored circle**	chrom/o	irid/o	corne/o
33. **tear**	dacry/o	hydr/o	aque/o
34. **eyelid**	ocul/o	ophthalm/o	blephar/o
35. **water**	aque/o	hidr/o	vitre/o

Write the correct medical term for each of the following:

36. pinkeye _____

37. inflammation of the eyelid _____

38. eyestrain _____

39. an agent that causes dilation of the pupil _____

40. a sty; acute infection of a meibomian gland of the eyelid _____

41. clouding of the lens causing decreased vision _____

42. breakdown or thinning of the tissues in the macula, resulting in partial or complete loss of central vision _____

Match the surgical procedures with diagnoses:

43. _____ keratoplasty   a. myopia

44. _____ phacoemulsification   b. retinal detachment

45. _____ LASIK   c. cataract

46. _____ trabeculectomy   d. dermatochalasis

47. _____ blepharoplasty   e. scarred cornea

48. _____ cryoretinopexy   f. acute glaucoma

Briefly define the following medical terms:

49. entropion _____

50. tonometer _____

51. ectropion _____

52. nystagmus _____

Match the following:

53. _____ myopia

a. old-age loss of accommodation

54. _____ strabismus

b. lazy eye

55. _____ presbyopia

c. pink eye

56. _____ astigmatism

d. double vision

57. _____ hyperopia

e. distorted vision

58. _____ amblyopia

f. nearsightedness

59. _____ scotoma

g. sty

60. _____ diplopia

h. crossed eyes

61. _____ conjunctivitis

i. farsightedness

62. _____ hordeolum

j. blind spot in vision

Write in the missing words on the blank lines in the following illustration of the eye's anatomy.

63–70.

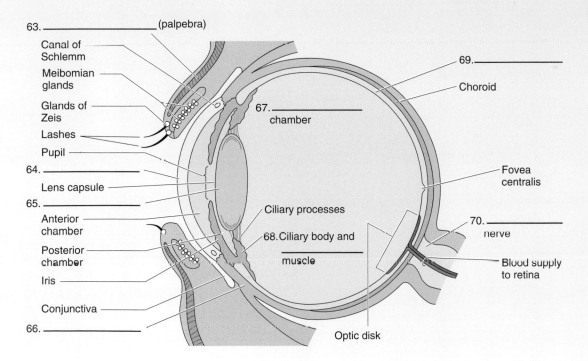

63. _____ (palpebra)

Canal of Schlemm

Meibomian glands

Glands of Zeis

Lashes

Pupil

64. _____

Lens capsule

65. _____

Anterior chamber

Posterior chamber

Iris

Conjunctiva

66. _____

67. _____ chamber

Ciliary processes

68. Ciliary body and _____ muscle

Optic disk

69. _____

Choroid

Fovea centralis

70. _____ nerve

Blood supply to retina

For each of the following, circle the correct spelling of the term:

71. asthenopia   assthinopia   asthinopia

72. terigium   pterygium   pteregium

73.	horadeolum	hordeolum	hordeaolum
74.	nistagmis	nystagmis	nystagmus
75.	chalazion	shalazion	calazion
76.	mydriatic	midriatic	myadriatic
77.	skotoma	scotoma	schotoma
78.	epiphora	epifora	epifhora
79.	dakryeocyst	dacryocyst	dacreyocyst
80.	opthalmoscope	ofthalmoscope	ophthalmoscope

Give the noun that was used to form the following adjectives:

81. conjunctival _____

82. myopic _____

83. scleral _____

84. macular _____

85. exophthalmic _____

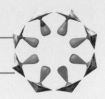

MEDICAL RECORD ANALYSES

MEDICAL RECORD 12.1

S: This 51 y/o ♀ c/o a growth in the corner of her right eye that is dry and irritated. She has had the feeling that there was "something in the eye" for about four months before actually noticing the growth three weeks ago. She wears contacts to correct farsightedness, but has recently switched to eyeglasses because of the discomfort. She is active physically and loves tennis and water sports, but does not frequently wear sunglasses.

O: Inspection of the right eye reveals an inflamed, raised, whitish, triangular wedge of fibrovascular tissue, whose base lies within the interpalpebral conjunctiva and whose apex encroaches the cornea. A photo documentation is made and included in the chart.

A: INFLAMED PTERYGIUM, RIGHT EYE

P: 1) The patient is advised that the pterygium is not dangerous, but further growth could interfere with vision and warrant surgical excision. She was counseled on the importance of wearing UV blocking sunglasses and advised to avoid smoky or dusty areas as much as possible.

2) RX: fluorometholone, 0.1% suspension, 1 gt q 4h OD during the day for inflammation; OTC artificial tears solution, prn dryness/irritation

3) RTO in 3 months for slit lamp evaluation, or sooner if symptoms persist.

1. Describe the refractive error noted in the subjective information:

   a. eyestrain

   b. inflammation of the cornea

   c. difficulty seeing distant objects

   d. difficulty seeing close objects

   e. blind spot in vision

2. Which action on the part of the patient likely contributed to the condition?

   a. wearing contact lenses

   b. removing contact lenses

   c. playing tennis

   d. not routinely wearing sunglasses

   e. strenuous physical activity

3. Which ophthalmological procedure is included in the plan?

   a. use of a laser to reshape the surface of the cornea

   b. use of an ophthalmoscope to view the interior of the eye

   c. use of a tabletop microscope to examine the eye, especially the cornea

   d. implantation of an artificial lens

   e. use of a tonometer to measure intraocular pressure

4. How should the fluorometholone be administered?

   a. one drop every 4 hours

   b. four drops in the eye every morning

   c. one drop every day for 4 days

   d. as needed during the day

   e. one drop every other day for 4 days

5. When should the patient instill the artificial tears?

   a. every day

   b. every night

   c. during the day

   d. only as needed

   e. when feeling the need to cry

6. What caused the pterygium?
   a. misdirected eyelashes that rub on the conjunctiva or cornea
   b. intraocular muscle imbalance
   c. separation of the retina from the underlying epithelium
   d. abnormal overflow of tears
   e. ultraviolet exposure and drying

7. What was the patient told about the pterygium?
   a. it is cancerous
   b. it is not cancerous
   c. it must be removed
   d. both a and c

MEDICAL RECORD 12.2

Not long ago, Cassandre Aquero had cataract surgery for her left eye, and she is now losing vision in her right eye because of another cataract. She is consulting an ophthalmologist, Dr. Oanh Tran, about surgery on the right eye.

Directions

Read Medical Record 12.2 for Ms. Aquero (pages 413–414) and answer the following questions. This record is the history and physical examination written by Dr. Tran in planning for Ms. Aquero's surgery.

QUESTIONS ABOUT MEDICAL RECORD 12.2

Write your answers in the spaces provided.

1. Below are medical terms used in this record you have not yet encountered in this text. Underline each where it appears in the record and define below:

   appendectomy _____

   irides _____

2. In your own words, briefly describe Ms. Aquero's current complaint and diagnosis noted under "History of Present Illness":

   _____

   _____

   _____

3. Describe in lay language the two medical conditions Ms. Aquero has in addition to her current problem and past surgeries:

   _____

   _____

   _____

4. Which of the following findings on physical examination is related to her general medical condition in addition to her eye problems?

   a. rales on auscultation
   b. disoriented consciousness
   c. BP 180/100
   d. weight 135 lb

5. The planned operation involves several risks that the patient has accepted in the hopes of regaining good eyesight. Which of the following was *not* mentioned by Dr. Tran as a risk?

   a. hypertensive crisis

   b. retinal detachment

   c. edema of the macula

   d. bleeding

6. The preoperative nursing staff will ensure that Ms. Aquero receives five medications before surgery. Translate the instructions for these:

   a. _____

   b. _____

   c. _____

   d. _____

   e. _____

7. In your own words, not using medical terminology, briefly describe what will occur in the surgery:

   _____

   _____

   _____

CENTRAL MEDICAL GROUP, INC.
Department of Ophthalmology
201 Medical Center Drive • Central City, US 90000-1234 • PHONE: (012) 125-8888

HISTORY

HISTORY OF PRESENT ILLNESS:
This 57-year-old female complains of progressive loss of vision in the right eye over the last two years which has been diagnosed as a cataract. The patient recently underwent cataract surgery in the left eye and is currently scheduled for surgery in the right eye due to her decreased vision.

PAST MEDICAL HISTORY:
The patient has had the normal childhood diseases and has essential hypertension and hypothyroidism.

SURGERIES:
Appendectomy 40 years ago. Tonsillectomy and adenoidectomy as a child. Cataract surgery in the left eye with a posterior chamber lens implant in 199x.

ALLERGIES:
None.

MEDICATIONS:
Propranolol 80 mg b.i.d. Hydrochlorothiazide 50 mg b.i.d. Clonidine, 0.1 mg, 2 tablets p.o. t.i.d. Synthroid 0.1 mg daily Slow-K 2 tablets p.o. daily

PHYSICAL EXAMINATION

VITAL SIGNS:
WEIGHT: 135 lb. BLOOD PRESSURE: 180/100.

HEENT:
HEAD, EARS, EYES, NOSE, THROAT: Normal.

EYES: Best corrected visual acuity in the right eye is counting fingers at two feet and 20/50 in the left eye. Pinhole vision in the left eye is 20/30. Slit lamp examination reveals normal lids, conjunctivae, and sclerae. Corneas are clear. Anterior chambers are clear and deep. Irides are within normal limits in the right eye. Evaluation of the lens reveals a 4+ posterior subcapsular plaquing with 3-4+ nuclear sclerosis, and in the left eye, there is a posterior chamber lens that is in place with posterior lens capsular plaquing. Intraocular pressure: OD: 18. OS: 17. Fundus examination in the right eye was severely hindered due to the dense cataract. However, evaluation of the posterior pole in the right eye was within normal limits.

(continued)

HISTORY AND PHYSICAL
Page 1

PT. NAME:	AQUERO, CASSANDRE D.
ID NO:	008654
ATT PHYS:	O. TRAN, M.D.

Medical Record 12.2

CENTRAL MEDICAL GROUP, INC.

Department of Ophthalmology

201 Medical Center Drive • Central City, US 90000-1234 • PHONE: (012) 125-8888

PHYSICAL EXAMINATION

CHEST:
Clear to percussion and auscultation. The breasts were normal, and the lungs were clear.

PELVIC/RECTAL:
Within normal limits.

EXTREMITIES:
Within normal limits.

NEUROLOGICAL:
Within normal limits.

IMPRESSION:
1)   Cataract, right eye.
2)   Pseudophakia, left eye.
3)   Essential hypertension.
4)   Hypothyroidism.

RISKS/BENEFITS:
The patient is aware of the alternatives, risks, benefits, and possible complications of the procedure that include hemorrhage, infection, loss of vision, reoperation, retinal detachment, macular edema; and the patient still desires to undergo the procedure.

PLAN:
Extracapsular cataract extraction with posterior chamber lens implant under local anesthesia using a +21 diopter posterior chamber lens with the ultraviolet filter. Preoperative medication will consist of the patient's morning dose of Propranolol, 80 mg; Hydrochlorothiazide, 50 mg; Clonidine, 0.2 mg; and Diamox, 250 mg with ¼ glass of water at approximately 10 a.m. on the day of surgery. The patient was also instructed to take Maxitrol, 1 gt OD, q 3 h starting 24 hours prior to the procedure, while awake.

O. Tran, M.D.

OT:mk
D: 10/19/20xx   T: 10/20/20xx

HISTORY AND PHYSICAL Page 2	PT. NAME: AQUERO, CASSANDRE D. ID NO: 008654 ATT PHYS: O. TRAN, M.D.

Medical Record 12.2   *Continued.*

Chapter 13

Ear

OBJECTIVES

After completion of this chapter you will be able to

- Define the common term components used in relation to the ear
- Locate and name the major structures of the ear and list their functions
- Define common symptomatic and diagnostic terms referring to the ear
- List the common diagnostic tests and procedures related to the ear
- Identify common operative terms referring to the ear
- Identify common therapeutic terms including drug classifications related to the ear
- Explain the terms and abbreviations used in documenting medical records involving the ear

Combining Forms

Combining Form	Meaning	Example
acous/o	hearing	acoustic ă-kŭs′tik
audi/o		audiometry aw-dē-om′ĕ-trē
aer/o	air or gas	aerotitis ār-ō-tī′tis
aur/i	ear	auricle aw′ri-kl
ot/o		otology ō-tol′ŏ-jē
cerumin/o	wax	ceruminosis se-rū-mi-nō′sis
salping/o	eustachian tube or uterine tube	salpingoscope sal-ping′gō-skōp
tympan/o	eardrum	tympanic tim-pan′ik
myring/o		myringotomy mir-ing-got′ō-mē

ADDITIONAL SUFFIX

-acusis	hearing condition	presbyacusis prez′bē-ă-kū′sis

TYMPANUM. Tympanum is the Latin word for tambourine or kettledrum, percussion instruments that are struck or beaten. Use of the term for eardrum was first introduced in 1255 and was adopted by the famous anatomist, Gabrielle Fallopius, because of the likeness of the eardrum to a tambourine.

OSSICLE. Ossicle means a little bone; it is a diminutive of the Latin ossiculum, meaning bone. Specifically, ossicle means one of the small bones in the middle ear. The first authentic records indicate that the malleus and the incus were the first two to be discovered in 1514. The stapes was discovered around 1546.

Overview of the Ear

The sense of hearing occurs through the mechanical action of the ear and its three divisions: outer ear, middle ear, and inner ear (Fig. 13.1).

Sounds are gathered by the projections of the *external ear* called the *pinna*, or auricle, and then dispersed through the external auditory meatus (canal) to the *tympanum*, or eardrum, of the middle ear. Glands located throughout the external canal secrete a protective, waxy substance called *cerumen*.

The tympanum transmits sound vibrations through the auditory ossicles— *malleus*, *incus*, and *stapes*—to the oval window. Vibrations are increased as they are distributed from the tympanum to the malleus, incus, and stapes. When the stapes, held by a ligament called the *oval window*, vibrates, it stimulates the motion of the auditory fluids in the inner ear.

Within the *middle ear*, the *eustachian tube* or *auditory tube* provides a passageway to the throat, allowing air to pass to and from the outside of the body. This process is important for maintaining equal air pressure.

Located within the temporal bone of the skull, the *inner ear* receives sound vibrations passed from the oval window to the *cochlea*, the outer structure of the inner ear, which is part of the intricate intercommunicating tubes and chambers known as the *labyrinth*. Vibrations are passed through *perilymph*, a fluid within an area of the cochlea called the *scala vestibuli*, to the cochlear duct, which is filled with a fluid called *endolymph*. Finally, the vibrations are passed through the *organ of Corti*, where hairs along its lining stimulate surrounding nerve fibers, generating impulses that then travel to the brain for processing of hearing.

THE EAR

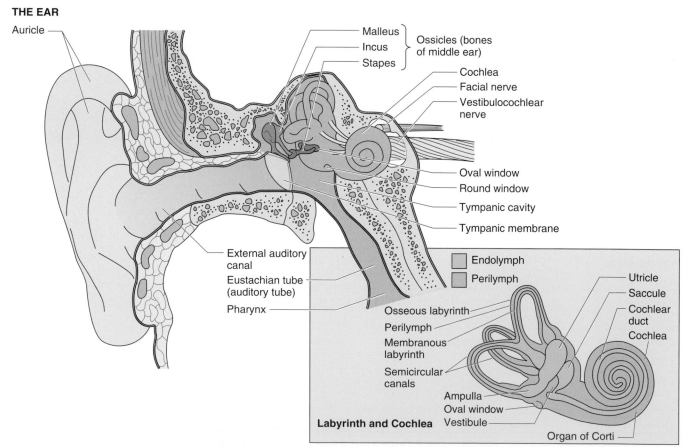

Figure 13.1. Anatomy of the ear.

In addition to hearing, the labyrinth is responsible for the equilibrium within the body. Within the labyrinth, the *semicircular canals* are connected to the cochlea by a cavity called the *vestibule*. Within the vestibule are structures known as the *utricle* and *saccule*. Hair cells and surrounding nerve fibers within the canals that connect with the utricle respond to and are moved by endolymph to stimulate nerve conduction when changes in movement occur.

Anatomical Terms

Term	Meaning
external ear	
pinna pin′ă	auricle (little ear); projected part of the external ear (pinna = feather)
external auditory meatus (canal)	external passage for sounds collected from the pinna to the tympanum (meat/o = opening)
cerumen sĕ-rū′men	waxy substance secreted by glands located throughout the external canal
middle ear	
tympanic membrane (TM) tim-pan′ik mem′brān	eardrum; drum-like structure that receives sound collected in the external auditory meatus (canal) and amplifies it through the middle ear (see Fig. 13.3B)
malleus mal′ē-ŭs	hammer; first of the three auditory ossicles of the middle ear
incus ing′kŭs	anvil; middle of the three auditory ossicles of the middle ear
stapes stā′pēz	stirrup; last of the three auditory ossicles of the middle ear
eustachian tube yū-stā′shŭn	tube connecting the middle ear to the pharynx (throat)
auditory tube	
mastoid process mas′toyd	projection of the temporal bone located behind the ear containing air cells that connect to the middle ear (masto = breast)
oval window	membrane that covers the opening between the middle ear and inner ear
inner ear	structures and liquids that relay sound waves to the auditory nerve fibers on a path to the brain for interpretation of sound
labyrinth lab′i-rinth	maze; inner ear consisting of bony and membranous labyrinths
cochlea kok′lē-ă	coiled tubular structure of the inner ear that contains the organ of Corti (cochlea = snail)
perilymph per′i-limf	fluid that fills the bony labyrinth of the ear
endolymph en′dō-limf	fluid within the cochlear duct of the inner ear (labyrinth)

Term	Meaning
organ of Corti	organ located in the cochlea that contains receptors (hair cells) that receive vibrations and generate nerve impulses for hearing
vestibule ves′ti-būl	middle part of the inner ear in front of the semicircular canals and behind the cochlea that contains the utricle and saccule
utricle ū′tri-kl	larger of two sacs within the membranous labyrinth of the vestibule in the inner ear (uter = leather bag)
saccule sak′yūl	smaller of two sacs within the membranous labyrinth of the vestibule in the inner ear (sacculus = small bag)
semicircular canals sem′ē-sir′kyū-lăr kă-nalz′	three canals within the inner ear that contain specialized receptor cells that generate nerve impulses with body movement

Symptomatic and Diagnostic Terms

Term	Meaning
SYMPTOMATIC	
otalgia ō-tal′jē-ă	earache
otodynia ō-tō-din′ē-ă	
otorrhagia ō-tō-rā′jē-ă	bleeding from the ear
otorrhea ō-tō-rē′ă	purulent drainage from the ear
tinnitus ti-nī′tŭs	a jingling; ringing or buzzing in the ear
vertigo ver′ti-gō	a turning round; dizziness
DIAGNOSTIC	
External Ear	
otitis externa ō-tī′tis eks-ter′nă	inflammation of the external auditory meatus (canal) (Fig. 13.2B)
cerumen impaction sĕ-rū′men im-pak′shŭn	excessive buildup of wax in the ear
Middle Ear	
myringitis mir-in-jī′tis	inflammation of the eardrum
tympanitis tim-pă-nī′tis	

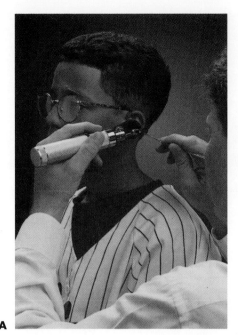
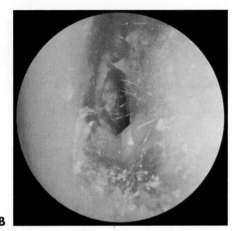

A   **B**

Figure 13.2.   **A.** Otoscopic examination of the external auditory meatus (canal). **B.** Otitis externa.

Term	Meaning
otitis media ō-tī′tis mē′dē-ă	inflammation of the middle ear (Fig. 13.3C)
aerotitis media ār-ō-tī′tis mē′dē-ă	inflammation of the middle ear from changes in atmospheric pressure; often occurs in frequent air travel
otosclerosis ō′tō-sklē-rō′sis	hardening of the bony tissue in the ear
mastoiditis mas-toy-dī′tis	inflammation of the mastoid process; most commonly seen as a result of the spread of inflammation and infection in otitis media
eustachian obstruction yū-stā′shŭn ob-strŭk′shŭn	blockage of the eustachian tube usually as a result of infection, as in otitis media
Inner Ear	
acoustic neuroma ă-kŭs′tik noo-ro′mă	benign tumor on the auditory nerve (8th cranial nerve) that causes vertigo, tinnitus, and hearing loss
aplasia ă-plā′zē-ă	condition of absence or malformation of inner ear structures during embryonic development, resulting in hearing loss
labyrinthitis lab′ĭ-rin-thī′tis	inflammation of the labyrinth
Ménière disease měn-yer′z	disorder of the inner ear due to an excessive buildup of endolymphatic fluid causing episodes of vertigo, tinnitus, nausea, vomiting, and hearing loss; one or both ears can be affected, and attacks vary in frequency and intensity

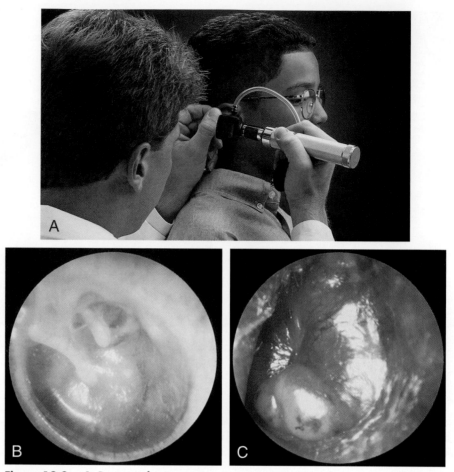

Figure 13.3. **A.** Doctor performing pneumatic otoscopy. **B.** Normal tympanic membrane. **C.** Otitis media.

Term	Meaning
General	
deafness def′nes	general term for partial or complete hearing loss
conductive hearing loss kon-dŭk′tiv	hearing impairment caused by interference with sound or vibratory energy in the external canal, middle ear, or ossicles
sensorineural hearing loss sen′sōr-i-nū′răl	hearing impairment caused by lesions or dysfunction of the cochlea or auditory nerve
mixed hearing loss	combination of sensorineural and conductive hearing loss
presbyacusis prez′bē-ă-kū′sis **presbycusis** prez-bē-kū′sis	hearing impairment in old age

Diagnostic Tests and Procedures

Test or Procedure	Explanation
audiometry aw-dē-om′ĕ-trē	process of measuring hearing (Fig. 13.4)
audiometer aw-dē-om′ĕ-ter	instrument to measure hearing
audiogram aw′dē-ō-gram	record of hearing measurement
audiologist aw-dē-ol′ō-jist	person who specializes in the study of hearing impairments
auditory acuity testing aw′di-tōr-ē ă-kyū′i-tē	physical assessment of hearing; useful in differentiating between conductive and sensorineural hearing loss (Fig. 13.5)
tuning fork	two-pronged, fork-like instrument that vibrates when struck: used to test for hearing, especially bone conduction

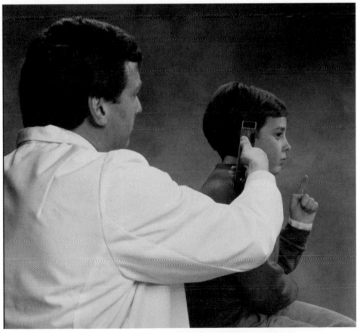

Figure 13.4. Audiometry: hearing screening.

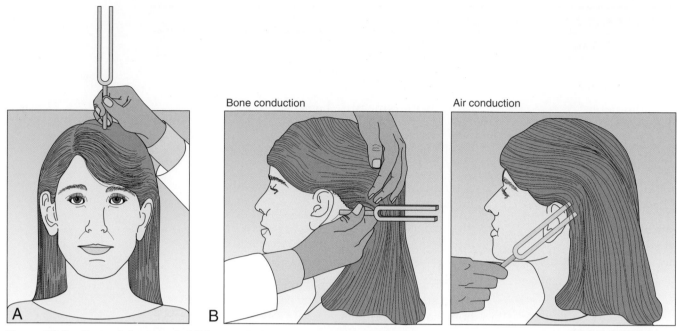

Bone conduction

Air conduction

Figure 13.5. Tuning fork testing. **A.** Weber test. **B.** Rinne test.

Test or Procedure	Explanation
brainstem auditory evoked potentials (BAEP)	electrodiagnostic testing using computerized equipment to measure involuntary responses to sound within the auditory nervous system—commonly used to assess hearing in newborns (Fig. 13.6)
otoscopy ō-tos′kŏ-pē	use of an otoscope to examine the external auditory meatus (canal) and tympanic membrane (Figs. 13.2A and Fig. 13.7)

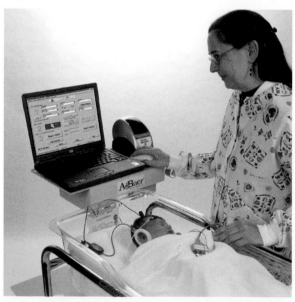

Figure 13.6. Brainstem auditory evoked potentials (BAEP) testing of a newborn.

Test or Procedure	Explanation
pneumatic otoscopy noo-mat′ik ō-tos′kŏ-pē	otoscopic observation of the tympanic membrane as air is released into the external auditory meatus (canal); immobility indicates the presence of middle ear effusion (fluid buildup) as occurs as a result of otitis media (see Fig. 13.3A)
tympanometry tim′pă-nom′ĕ-trē	measurement of the compliance and mobility (conductibility) of the tympanic membrane and ossicles of the middle ear by monitoring the response after exposure to external airflow pressures

Operative Terms

Term	Meaning
microsurgery mī-krō-ser′jer-ē	surgery with the use of a microscope; used in procedures involving delicate tissue such as the ear
myringotomy mir-ing-got′ŏ-mē **tympanostomy** tim′păn-os′tō-mē	incision into the eardrum, most often for insertion of a small metal or plastic tube [e.g., polyethylene (PE) tube], to keep the meatus (canal) open, avoiding fluid buildup (effusion) as that which occurs as a result of otitis media (Fig. 13.8)
otoplasty ō′tō-plas-tē	surgical repair of the external ear
stapedectomy stā-pĕ-dek′tō-mē	excision of the stapes to correct otosclerosis
tympanoplasty tim′pă-nō-plas-tē	vein graft of a scarred tympanic membrane to improve sound conduction

Figure 13.7. Otoscope.

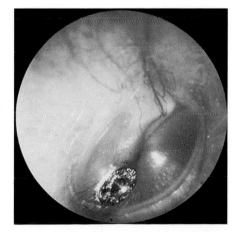

Figure 13.8. View through otoscope shows placement of tympanostomy tube.

Therapeutic Terms

Term	Meaning
auditory prosthesis pros'thē-sis	any internal or external device that improves or substitutes for natural hearing
hearing aid	external amplifying device designed to improve hearing by more effective collection of sound into the ear
cochlear implant kok'lē-ăr	electronic device implanted in the cochlea that provides sound perception to patients with severe or profound sensorineural (nerve) hearing loss in both ears (Fig. 13.9)
ear lavage lă-vahzh'	irrigation of the external ear canal, commonly done to remove excessive buildup of cerumen
ear instillation in-sti-lā'shŭn	introduction of a medicated solution into the external canal
COMMON THERAPEUTIC DRUG CLASSIFICATIONS	
antibiotic an'tē-bī-ot'ik	drug that inhibits the growth of or destroys microorganisms; used to treat diseases caused by bacteria (e.g., otitis media)
antihistamine an-tē-his'tă-mēn	drug that blocks the effects of histamine
histamine his'tă-mēn	regulating body substance released in excess during allergic reactions that cause swelling and inflammation of tissues; seen in hay fever, urticaria (hives), etc.
anti-inflammatory an'tē-in-flam'ă-tō-rē	drug that reduces inflammation
decongestant dē-kon-jes'tant	drug that reduces congestion and swelling of membranes, such as those of the nose and eustachian tube after infection

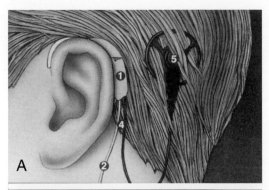

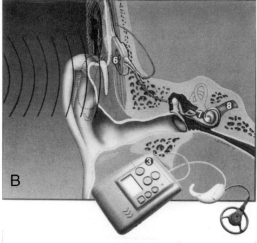

Figure 13.9.   A and **B.** Operation of a cochlear implant. (1) Directional microphone. (2) Sound is carried from the microphone by a cord to the speech processor worn on the belt or pocket. (3) The speech processor filters, analyzes, and digitizes the sound into coded signals and sends it (4) to the transmitting coil (5). The coil sends the coded signals as FM radio signals to the cochlear implant inserted under the skin. The cochlear implant (6) delivers the electrical energy to the array of electrodes surgically inserted into the cochlea (7). The electrodes stimulate the remaining auditory nerve fibers (8), and sound information is sent to the brain for interpretation.

Summary of Chapter 13 Acronyms/Abbreviations

BAEP ......brainstem auditory evoked potentials   **TM** ....tympanic membrane
PE ....polyethylene

PRACTICE EXERCISES

For the following terms, on the lines below the term, write out the indicated word parts: prefixes (P), combining forms (CF), roots (R), and suffixes (S). Then define the word.

EXAMPLE

macrotia

_____ / _____ / _____
   P   R   S

<u>macr/ot/ia</u>
P R S

DEFINITION: large or long/ear/condition of

1. acoustic

_____ / _____
       R   S

DEFINITION: _____

2. otorrhea

_____ / _____
      CF   S

DEFINITION: _____

3. myringoplasty

_____ / _____
      CF   S

DEFINITION: _____

4. aerotitis

_____ / _____ / _____
       R   R   S

DEFINITION: _____

5. ototoxic

_____ / _____ / _____
      CF   R   S

DEFINITION: _____

6. ceruminolysis

_____ / _____
      CF   S

DEFINITION: _____

7. salpingoscope

_____ / _____
      CF   S

DEFINITION: _____

8. hyperacusis

_____ / _____
         P   S

DEFINITION: _____

9. audiometry

_____ / _____
        CF   S

DEFINITION: _____

10. tympanocentesis

_____ / _____
        CF   S

DEFINITION: _____

11. otodynia

_____ / _____
        CF   S

DEFINITION: _____

12. auricle

_____ / _____
         R   S

DEFINITION: _____

13. myringotomy

_____ / _____
        CF   S

DEFINITION: _____

14. ceruminosis

_____ / _____
         R   S

DEFINITION: _____

15. audiology

_____ / _____
        CF   S

DEFINITION: _____

Complete the medical term by writing the missing part:

16. oto_____osis = condition of hardening of the bony tissue of the ear

17. _____scope = instrument used to view the ear canal and tympanum

18. _____ disease = disorder of the inner ear due to an excessive buildup of endolymphatic fluid

19. _____neuroma = tumor of the auditory nerve affecting hearing

For each of the following, circle the combining form that corresponds to the meaning given:

20. **eardrum**   salping/o   ot/o   myring/o

21. **hearing**   ot/o   audi/o   angi/o

22. **wax**   cerumin/o   crin/o   scler/o

23. **eustachian tube**   tympan/o   myring/o   salping/o

24. **ear**   rhin/o   ot/o   or/o

25. **air**   acr/o   aur/i   aer/o

Match the following:

26. _____ conductive hearing loss   a. presbyacusis

27. _____ one who studies hearing impairments   b. aplasia

28. _____ bleeding from the ear   c. otalgia

29. _____ partial or complete hearing loss   d. cochlear implant

30. _____ sensorineural hearing loss   e. otorrhea

31. _____ hearing impairment of old age   f. nerve conduction

32. _____ discharge from the ear   g. otorrhagia

33. _____ auditory prosthetic   h. deafness

34. _____ earache   i. audiologist

35. _____ absence of inner ear structures   j. bone conduction

Write the correct medical term for each of the following:

36. _____ = inflammation of labyrinth

37. _____ = dizziness

38. _____ = ringing in the ear

39. _____ = excision of stapes to correct otosclerosis

40. _____ = excessive buildup of earwax

41. _____ = the study of hearing

42. The introduction of a medicated solution into the external canal is called ear instillation. Irrigation of the external ear canal is called ear _____.

Write in the missing words on the blank lines in the following illustration of the ear.

43–50.

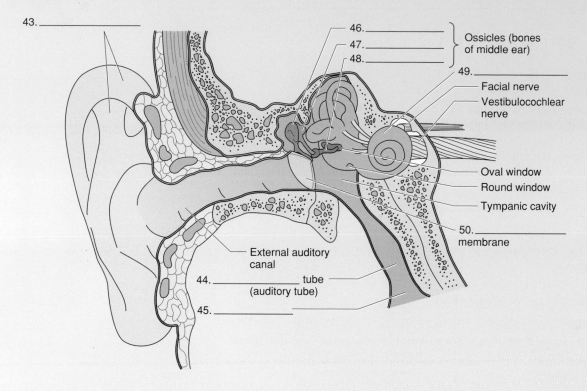

For each of the following, circle the correct spelling of the term:

51. aerotitus	aerotitis	airotitis
52. cerumen	ceramen	ceruman
53. myrimogotomy	mirongotomy	myringotomy
54. presbyecusis	presbyacusis	presbeacusis
55. vertigo	vertago	verttigo
56. antihestamine	antihistamine	antehistamine
57. tinnitis	tinitus	tinnitus
58. stapedectomy	stapesectomy	stapedecktomy
59. defness	deafnass	deafness
60. eustation	eustachian	euhstation

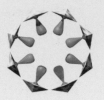

MEDICAL RECORD ANALYSES

MEDICAL RECORD 13.1

Progress Note

S: This 21 y.o white male c/o a clogged Ⓡ ear c̄ increasing tinnitus. He has had a slight pharyngitis and nasal congestion ×7 d.

O: On PE there was moist infectious debris in the Ⓡ ear that was suctioned clear. The Ⓡ tympanum was dull and thickened. The Ⓛ external ear was clear and the tympanic membrane intact.

A: Otitis media Ⓡ ear

P: *(1)* Keep ears dry; *(2)* Rx Pen VK 250 mg #24 ŧ q.i.d. p.c. and h.s.; *(3)* RTO in 10 d for followup (f/u)

1. Summarize the subjective information:
   a. patient complains of clogged, ringing ears; sore throat; and stuffy nose
   b. patient has a clogged right ear, sore throat, stuffy nose, and dizziness
   c. patient's right eardrum is thick and dull and clogged with infectious matter, causing dizziness
   d. patient complains of a sore throat, stuffy nose, and a clogged right ear that is buzzing
   e. patient has a sore throat, stuffy nose, and purulent drainage from the right ear

2. What was the assessment?
   a. clogged right ear, sore throat, and stuffy nose
   b. inflammation of the right middle ear
   c. inflammation of the right external ear canal
   d. blockage of the eustachian tube
   e. inflammation of the right eardrum

3. When should the patient take the prescribed medication?
   a. twice in 24 hours
   b. before meals
   c. at bedtime
   d. four times a day
   e. every 4 hours

4. Which is true of the plan?
   a. patient should return to the office immediately if a fever develops
   b. patient is given ear drops and advised not to get the ears wet for 10 days
   c. doctor wants to examine the patient again in 10 days
   d. patient is given an antibiotic and advised to increase fluid intake
   e. if not better in 10 days, the patient will be referred to an otolaryngologist

MEDICAL RECORD 13.2

Hank Ball, a preschooler, has had recurrent ear infections for 1 year that his doctor has not been able to treat successfully with antibiotics and other drugs. His preschool teacher also identified nasal speech patterns that his doctor later confirmed were related to his medical problems. After Hank saw several doctors who recommended surgery, his parents have admitted him to Central Medical Center.

Directions

Read Medical Record 13.2 for Hank Ball (pages 434–436) and answer the following questions. These records are the history and physical examination before surgery and the subsequent operative report, both dictated by Dr. Baird, the surgeon.

QUESTIONS ABOUT MEDICAL RECORD 13.2

Write your answers in the spaces provided.

1. Below are medical terms used in this record you have not yet encountered in this text. Underline each where it appears in the record and define below:

   hepatosplenomegaly _____

   turbinates _____

   extubation _____

2. In the left column, list the patient's medical problems noted in the HPI; in the right column, write the diagnosis that pertains to each.

Medical Problem	*Diagnosis*
a. _____	_____
_____	_____
b. _____	_____
_____	_____

3. In your own words, explain how Hank's social history is related to his medical history:

   _____

   _____

   _____

4. Under the "Review of Systems," were any additional medical symptoms or problems identified? If so, list below.

   _____

   _____

5. What does it mean that at the time of the examination Hank was afebrile?

_____

6. Carefully read the physical examination. Mark the body areas/systems in which Dr. Baird found any abnormalities:

_____ general

_____ HEENT

_____ chest

_____ back

_____ rectal/genitalia

_____ extremities

7. List the surgical procedures identified under "Plan," and briefly describe them in your own words, not using medical terminology:

a. _____

_____

_____

_____

b. _____

_____

_____

_____

c. _____

_____

_____

_____

8. In your own words, not using medical terminology, briefly describe oral intubation.

_____

_____

_____

9. Put the following operative actions in correct order by numbering them 1 to 11:

_____ removal of adenoids

_____ incision in right eardrum

_____ PE tube placement in right tympanum

_____ repositioning in Rose's position

_____ incision in left eardrum

_____ aspiration of right middle ear

_____ extubation

_____ removal of wax in right ear

_____ nasopharynx examination

_____ polyethylene tube placement in left tympanum

_____ intubation

10. In your own words, not using medical terminology, briefly describe the condition of Hank's adenoids before adenoidectomy:

_____

_____

_____

CENTRAL MEDICAL CENTER

211 Medical Center Drive • Central City, US 90000-1234 • PHONE: (012) 125-6784 • FAX: (012) 125-9999

HISTORY

DATE OF ADMISSION: August 28, 20xx

HISTORY OF PRESENT ILLNESS: The patient is a 4-year-old white male with recurrent ear infections and ear congestion nonresponsive to antibiotic and decongestant therapy over the past 12 months. The patient also has a history of nasal obstruction and nasal speech. The patient is being admitted for myringotomy, polyethylene tubes, and examination of the nasopharynx and adenoidectomy. The patient has also seen other doctors who have recommended surgery, including Dr. Feldman and Dr. Saunders.

PAST MEDICAL HISTORY: Medications: None. Allergies: None. Hospitalizations: None. Surgeries: None. Childhood Diseases: Normal.

FAMILY HISTORY: No cancer or diabetes, although the patient's grandparents have a history of adult-onset diabetes.

SOCIAL HISTORY: Normal development except for speech.

REVIEW OF SYSTEMS: CARDIOVASCULAR: No hypertension and no heart murmurs. PULMONARY: No croup or asthma. GASTROINTESTINAL: No hepatitis. RENAL: Negative. ENDOCRINE: No diabetes. MUSCULOSKELETAL: No joint disease. HEMATOLOGIC: No anemia or bleeding tendencies.

(continued)

R. Baird, M.D.

RB:nn

D: 8/28/20xx
T: 8/29/20xx

HISTORY AND PHYSICAL Page 1	PT. NAME:	BALL, HANK F.
	ID NO:	OP-372201
	ROOM:	OPS
	ADM. DATE:	August 28, 20xx
	ATT. PHYS:	R. BAIRD, M.D.

Medical Record 13.2

CENTRAL MEDICAL CENTER

211 Medical Center Drive • Central City, US 90000-1234 • PHONE: (012) 125-6784 • FAX: (012) 125-9999

PHYSICAL EXAMINATION

GENERAL: The patient is alert and afebrile.

HEENT: TMs are dull and slightly retracted; there is decreased mobility. There is dull light reflex bilaterally. No sinus tenderness on percussion of the maxillary or frontal sinuses; there are swollen turbinates on nasal examination. The oropharynx shows hypertrophic tonsils, and there are hypertrophic adenoids on examination of the nasopharynx.

CHEST: LUNGS: Clear to percussion and auscultation. HEART: Pulse: 88 and regular. There are no murmurs, gallops, or rubs. ABDOMEN: There are no masses or tenderness. No hepatosplenomegaly was noted. There was no costovertebral angle (CVA) tenderness.

BACK: Supple. There are no masses or tenderness. There is mild anterior cervical adenopathy.

RECTAL/GENITALIA: Deferred.

EXTREMITIES: There was no peripheral edema, and there were no ecchymoses.

IMPRESSION: CHRONIC OTITIS MEDIA WITH EFFUSION, NASAL SPEECH, AND NASAL OBSTRUCTION SECONDARY TO ADENOID HYPERTROPHY.

PLAN: The patient is to be admitted as an outpatient for adenoidectomy, myringotomy, and polyethylene (PE) tubes as noted above. The surgery and potential risks and complications have been discussed with the grandfather and mother as well as the possible need for further repeat myringotomy and PE tubes.

R. Baird, M.D.

RB:nn

D: 8/28/20xx
T: 8/29/20xx

HISTORY AND PHYSICAL	PT. NAME: BALL, HANK F.
Page 2	ID NO: OP-372201
	ROOM NO: OPS
	ADM. DATE: August 28, 20xx
	ATT. PHYS: R. BAIRD, M.D.

Medical Record 13.2 *Continued.*

CENTRAL MEDICAL CENTER

211 Medical Center Drive • Central City, US 90000-1234 • PHONE: (012) 125-6784 • FAX: (012) 125-9999

OPERATIVE REPORT

DATE OF OPERATION: August 28, 20xx

PREOPERATIVE DIAGNOSIS: Chronic otitis media with effusion bilaterally and nasal obstruction with chronic adenoiditis and adenoid hypertrophy.

POSTOPERATIVE DIAGNOSIS: Chronic otitis media with effusion bilaterally and adenoid hypertrophy and chronic adenoiditis.

OPERATION PERFORMED: Bilateral myringotomy and tubes with adenoidectomy.

SURGEON: R. Baird, M.D.

ANESTHESIOLOGIST: F. Kodama, M.D.

PROCEDURE AND FINDINGS: After general anesthesia induction and oral intubation, the patient's ears were prepped and draped in the usual manner for microscopic myringotomy surgery. A myringotomy in the right ear was carried out following debridement of cerumen. Incision of the circumferential inferior anterior quadrant was carried out. Mucoid material was aspirated from the middle ear. A Shepard polyethylene tube was placed in position without difficulty. Cotton dressing was applied to the ear. The left ear was examined. A similar dull, nonmobile TM was noted. An inferior anterior myringotomy was carried out again, and thick mucoid material was aspirated. A Shepard polyethylene tube was inserted again in the left ear. Cotton dressing was applied to the ear canal. The patient was repositioned in the Rose's position for examination of the nasopharynx which was carried out with a palate retractor, McIvor mouth gag, tongue retractor, and was stabilized with the Mayo stand. The marked adenoid hypertrophy was noted, and the adenoidectomy was carried out with curette technique. The patient tolerated the procedure well, and following extubation, he was sent back to the recovery room in satisfactory postoperative condition.

FINAL DIAGNOSIS: Chronic otitis media with effusion bilaterally, with chronic adenoiditis, adenoid hypertrophy, and nasal obstruction.

R. Baird, M.D.

RB:as
D: 8/28/20xx   T: 8/29/20xx

OPERATIVE REPORT Page 1	PT. NAME: BALL, HANK F. ID NO: OP-372201 ROOM NO: OPS ATT. PHYS: R. BAIRD, M.D.

Medical Record 13.2 *Continued.*

Chapter 14

Gastrointestinal System

OBJECTIVES

After completion of this chapter you will be able to

- Define common term components used in relation to the gastrointestinal system
- Describe the basic functions of the gastrointestinal system
- Define the basic anatomical terms referring to the gastrointestinal system and accessory organs
- Identify the anatomical and clinical divisions of the abdomen
- Define common symptomatic and diagnostic terms referring to the gastrointestinal system
- List the common diagnostic tests and procedures related to the gastrointestinal system
- Identify common operative terms referring to the gastrointestinal system
- Identify common therapeutic terms including drug classifications related to the gastrointestinal system
- Explain the terms and abbreviations used in documenting medical records involving the gastrointestinal system

Combining Forms

Combining Form	Meaning	Example
abdomin/o	abdomen	abdominocentesis ab-dom′i-nō-sen-tē′sis
celi/o		celiac sē′lē-ak
lapar/o		laparoscopy lap-ă-ros′kŏ-pē
an/o	anus	anal ā′năl
appendic/o	appendix	appendical ă-pen′di-kăl
bil/i	bile	biligenic bil-i-jen′ik
chol/e		cholelithiasis kō′lē-li-thī′ă-sis

Combining Form	Meaning	Example
bucc/o	cheek	buccal bŭk′ăl
cheil/o	lip	cheiloplasty kī′lō-plas-tē
col/o	colon	colitis kō-lī′tis
colon/o		colonoscopy kō-lon-os′kŏ-pē
cyst/o	bladder or sac	cholecystectomy kō′lē-sis-tek′tō-mē
dent/i	teeth	dental den′tăl
doch/o	duct	choledochotomy kō-led-ō-kot′ō-mē
duoden/o	duodenum	duodenal dū′ō-dē′năl
enter/o	small intestine	enterocele en′ter-ō-sēl
esophag/o	esophagus	esophageal ē-sof′ă-jē′ăl
gastr/o	stomach	gastritis gas-trī′tis
gingiv/o	gum	gingivitis jin-ji-vī′tis
gloss/o	tongue	glossitis glo-sī′tis
lingu/o		lingual ling′gwăl
hepat/o	liver	hepatomegaly hep′ă-tō-meg′ă-lē
hepatic/o		hepaticotomy he-pat-i-kot′ō-mē
herni/o	hernia	herniorrhaphy her′nē-ōr′ă-fē
ile/o	ileum	ileostomy il′ē-os′tō-mē
inguin/o	groin	inguinal ing′gwi-năl
jejun/o	jejunum (empty)	jejunitis je-jū-nī′tis
lith/o	stone	lithiasis li-thī′ă-sis

Combining Form	Meaning	Example
or/o	mouth	oral or′ăl
stomat/o		stomatosis stō-mă-tō′sis
pancreat/o	pancreas	pancreatitis pan′krē-ă-tī′tis
peritone/o	peritoneum	peritoneoscopy per′i-tō-nē-os′kŏ-pē
phag/o	eat or swallow	aphagia ă-fā′jē-ă
proct/o	anus and rectum	proctologic prok-tō-loj′ik
pylor/o	pylorus (gatekeeper)	pyloric pī-lōr′ik
rect/o	rectum	rectal rek′tăl
sial/o	saliva	sialolithiasis sī′ă-lō-li-thī′ă-sis
sigmoid/o	sigmoid colon (resembles s)	sigmoidoscopy sig′moy-dos′kŏ-pē
steat/o	fat	steatolysis stē-ă-tol′i-sis
ADDITIONAL SUFFIX		
-emesis	vomiting	hematemesis hē-mă-tem′ĕ-sis

Gastrointestinal System Overview

The gastrointestinal (GI) system processes and transports nutrients and various wastes. The organs form a tube or tract, known as the *alimentary canal,* extending from the mouth to the anus. The alimentary canal is composed of the mouth, pharynx, esophagus, stomach, and intestines (Fig. 14.1).

The gastrointestinal system has three functions: digestion, absorption, and excretion. *Digestion* is the process by which food is broken down by chewing and swallowing and is then mixed with digestive juices in the stomach to convert some of the food into absorbable molecules. *Absorption* is the passage of digested food molecules through the walls of the intestines into the bloodstream to be carried to the body cells. *Excretion* is the elimination of materials that are not absorbed (waste products) by transporting them outside the body.

The accessory organs that aid in the digestion and absorption of food are the teeth, salivary glands, liver, gallbladder, and pancreas.

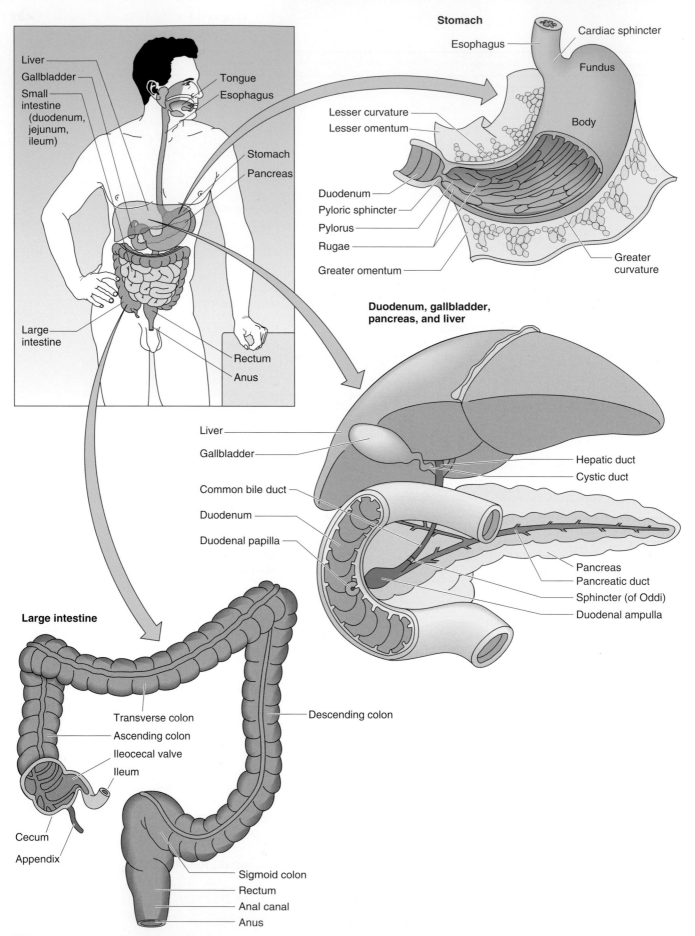

Stomach

Esophagus
Cardiac sphincter
Fundus
Body
Lesser curvature
Lesser omentum
Duodenum
Pyloric sphincter
Pylorus
Rugae
Greater omentum
Greater curvature

Liver
Gallbladder
Small intestine (duodenum, jejunum, ileum)
Tongue
Esophagus
Stomach
Pancreas
Large intestine
Rectum
Anus

Duodenum, gallbladder, pancreas, and liver

Liver
Gallbladder
Common bile duct
Duodenum
Duodenal papilla
Hepatic duct
Cystic duct
Pancreas
Pancreatic duct
Sphincter (of Oddi)
Duodenal ampulla

Large intestine

Transverse colon
Ascending colon
Ileocecal valve
Ileum
Cecum
Appendix
Descending colon
Sigmoid colon
Rectum
Anal canal
Anus

Figure 14.1 Gastrointestinal system.

Anterior view

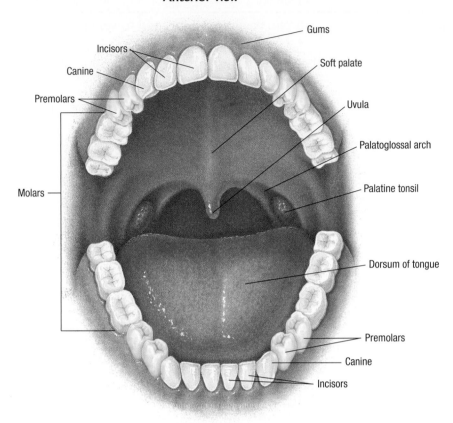

Figure 14.2 Oral cavity.

Anatomical Terms

Term	Meaning
oral cavity	cavity that receives food for digestion (Fig. 14.2)
mouth	
salivary glands sal'i-vār-ē	three pairs of exocrine glands in the mouth that secrete saliva: parotid, submandibular (submaxillary), and sublingual
cheeks	lateral walls of the mouth
lips	fleshy structures surrounding the mouth
palate pal'ăt	structure that forms the roof of the mouth; it is divided into the hard and soft palate
uvula yū'vyū-lă	small projection hanging from the back middle edge of the soft palate
tongue	muscular structure of the floor of the mouth covered by mucous membrane and held down by a band-like membrane known as the *frenulum*
gums	tissue covering the processes of the jaws
teeth	hard bony projections in the jaws that serve to masticate (chew) food

Term	Meaning
pharynx far′ingks	throat; passageway for food traveling to the esophagus and air traveling to the larynx
esophagus ē-sof′ă-gŭs	muscular tube that moves food from the pharynx to the stomach
stomach stŭm′ŭk	sac-like organ that chemically mixes and prepares food received from the esophagus
cardiac sphincter kar′dē-ak sfingk′ter	opening from the esophagus to the stomach (sphincter = band)
pyloric sphincter pī-lōr′ik sfingk′ter	opening of the stomach into the duodenum
small intestine in-tes′tin	tubular structure that digests food received from the stomach
duodenum dū-ō-dē′nŭm	first portion of the small intestine
jejunum jĕ-jū′nŭm	second portion of the small intestine
ileum il′ē-ŭm	third portion of the small intestine
large intestine	larger tubular structure that receives the liquid waste products of digestion, reabsorbs water and minerals, and forms and stores feces for defecation
cecum se′kŭm	first part of the large intestine
vermiform appendix ver′mi-fōrm ă-pen′diks	worm-like projection of lymphatic tissue hanging off the cecum with no digestive function—may serve to resist infection (vermi = worm)
colon kō′lon	portions of the large intestine extending from the cecum to the rectum; identified by direction or shape
ascending colon as-send′ing	portion that extends upward from the cecum
transverse colon trans-vers′	portion that extends across from the ascending colon
descending colon dē-send′ing	portion that extends down from the transverse colon
sigmoid colon sig′moyd	portion (resembling an s) that terminates at the rectum
rectum rek′tŭm	distal (end) portion of the large intestine
rectal ampulla rek′tăl am-pūl′lă	dilated portion of the rectum just above the anal canal
anus ā′nŭs	opening of the rectum to the outside of the body
feces fē′sēz	refuse; solid waste formed in the large intestine

DUODENUM. The Latin word for 12 is the origin of the name for the first part of the small intestine because the length of the structure was estimated to be 12 fingerbreadths.

JEJUNUM. The Latin word meaning empty or hungry was used for the portion of the small intestine that follows the duodenum because the ancients noted it was always empty after death.

Term	Meaning
defecation def-ĕ-kā′shŭn	evacuation of feces from the rectum
peritoneum per′i-tō-ne′ŭm	membrane surrounding the entire abdominal cavity consisting of the parietal layer (lining the abdominal wall) and visceral layer (covering each organ in the abdomen)
peritoneal cavity per-i-tō-nē′ăl	space between the parietal and visceral peritoneum
omentum ō-men′tŭm	a covering; an extension of the peritoneum attached to the stomach and connecting it with other abdominal organs
liver	organ in the upper right quadrant that produces bile, which is secreted into the duodenum during digestion
gallbladder gawl′blad-er	receptacle that stores and concentrates the bile produced in the liver
pancreas pan′krē-as	gland that secretes pancreatic juice into the duodenum, where it mixes with bile to digest food
biliary ducts bil′ē-ār-ē	ducts that convey bile, including hepatic, cystic, and common bile ducts

 PANCREAS. The Greek word for sweetbread is formed by the combination of -creas, meaning flesh, and pan-, meaning all. The organ was so named because of its meaty or fleshy character. Aristotle used the term.

Anatomical and Clinical Divisions of the Abdomen

Anatomical and clinical divisions of the abdomen provide specific or general reference for descriptive purposes. There are nine specific anatomical divisions and four general clinical divisions (Figs. 14.3–14.5). All references are based on the *patient's* right or left.

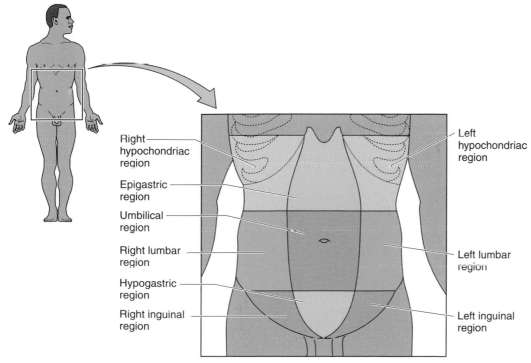

Figure 14.3 Anatomical divisions of the abdomen.

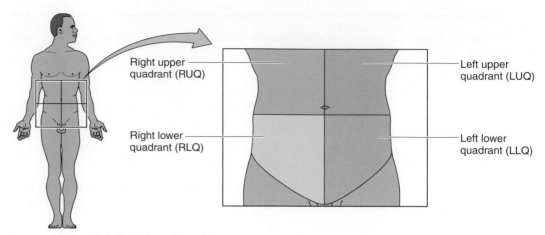

Figure 14.4 Clinical divisions of the abdomen.

HYPOCHONDRIAC. This Greek word meaning below the cartilage was used to refer to regions below the cartilages of the ribs. In these hypochondriac regions, various sensations of a distressing nature were sometimes experienced without apparent organic disease. People with such complaints were called hypochondriacs. Today, hypochondria refers to one who has an abnormal concern for one's health with the false belief that he or she is suffering from disease.

Anatomical Divisions

Region	Location
hypochondriac regions hī-pō-kon′drē-ak	upper lateral regions beneath the ribs
epigastric region ep-i-gas′trik	upper middle region below the sternum
lumbar regions lŭm′bar	middle lateral regions

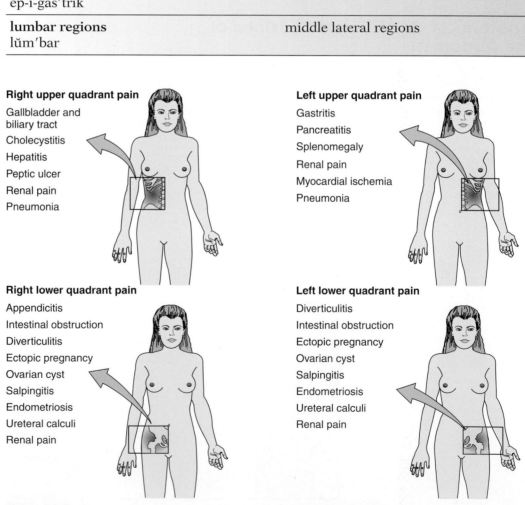

Right upper quadrant pain
Gallbladder and biliary tract
Cholecystitis
Hepatitis
Peptic ulcer
Renal pain
Pneumonia

Left upper quadrant pain
Gastritis
Pancreatitis
Splenomegaly
Renal pain
Myocardial ischemia
Pneumonia

Right lower quadrant pain
Appendicitis
Intestinal obstruction
Diverticulitis
Ectopic pregnancy
Ovarian cyst
Salpingitis
Endometriosis
Ureteral calculi
Renal pain

Left lower quadrant pain
Diverticulitis
Intestinal obstruction
Ectopic pregnancy
Ovarian cyst
Salpingitis
Endometriosis
Ureteral calculi
Renal pain

Figure 14.5 Common sites of abdominal pain characteristic of various conditions.

Region	Location
umbilical region ŭm-bil′i-kăl	region of the navel
inguinal regions ing′gwi-năl	lower lateral groin regions
hypogastric region hī-pō-gas′trik	region below the navel

Symptomatic and Diagnostic Terms

Term	Meaning
SYMPTOMATIC	
anorexia an-ō-rek′sē-ă	loss of appetite (orexia = appetite)
aphagia ă-fā′jē-ă	inability to swallow
ascites ă-sī′tēz	accumulation of fluid in the peritoneal cavity (ascos = bag) (Fig. 14.6)
buccal bŭk′ăl	in the cheek

ASCITES. A Greek word for pouch or sac referring to the appearance of the abdomen with the collection of fluid in the peritoneal cavity.

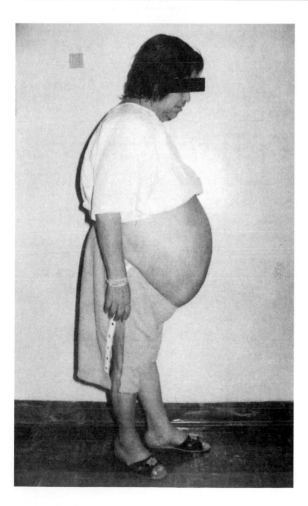

Figure 14.6 Side view of a patient showing massive ascites and distention of abdomen.

Term	Meaning
constipation kon-sti-pā′shŭn	infrequent or incomplete bowel movements characterized by hardened, dry stool that is difficult to pass (constipo = to press together)
diarrhea dī-ă-rē′ă	frequent loose or liquid stools
dyspepsia dis-pep′sē-ă	indigestion (peptein = to digest)
dysphagia dis-fā′jē-ă	difficulty in swallowing
eructation ē-rūk-tā′shŭn	belch
flatulence flat′yū-lens	gas in the stomach or intestines (flatus = a blowing)
halitosis hal-i-tō′sis	bad breath (halitus = breath)
hematochezia hē′mă-tō-kē′zē-ă	red blood in the stool (chezo = defecate)
hematemesis hē-mă-tem′ĕ-sis	vomiting blood
hepatomegaly hep′ă-tō-meg′ă-lē	enlargement of the liver
hyperbilirubinemia hī′per-bil′i-rū-bi-nē′mē-ă	excessive level of bilirubin (bile pigment) in the blood
icterus ik′ter-ŭs jaundice jawn′dis	yellow discoloration of the skin, sclera (white of the eye), and other tissues caused by excessive bilirubin in the blood (jaundice = yellow) (Fig. 14.7)
melena me-lē′nă	dark-colored, tarry stool caused by old blood
nausea naw′zē-ă	sick in the stomach
steatorrhea ste′ă-tō-rē′ă	feces containing fat

ICTERUS. Icterus is a Greek word for jaundice meaning yellow bird. The yellow color associated with the condition was thought similar to the color of this bird. It was said that if a person suffering from jaundice looks at the bird, the bird dies and the patient recovers.

NAUSEA. Nausea is derived from a Greek word for ship referring to "ship sickness." Hippocrates used the term for seasickness; later, it became generally applied to the sick and uneasy feeling that precedes vomiting.

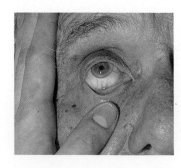

Figure 14.7 The yellow color of jaundice (icterus) is easily seen in the sclera of this patient and also in the skin as contrasted with the examiner's hand.

Term	Meaning
sublingual sŭb-ling′gwăl	under the tongue
hypoglossal hī-pō-glos′ăl	
DIAGNOSTIC	
stomatitis stō-mă-tī′tis	inflammation of the mouth
sialoadenitis si′ă-lō-ad-ĕ-nī′tis	inflammation of a salivary gland
parotitis (parotiditis) par-ō-tī′tis	inflammation of the parotid gland; also called mumps
cheilitis kī-lī′tis	inflammation of the lip
glossitis glo-sī′tis	inflammation of the tongue
ankyloglossia ang′ki-lō-glos′ē-ă	tongue-tie; a defect of the tongue characterized by a short, thick frenulum (ankyl/o = crooked or stiff)
gingivitis jin-ji-vī′tis	inflammation of the gums
esophageal varices ē-sof′ă-jē′ăl	swollen, twisted veins in the esophagus especially susceptible to ulceration and hemorrhage (see Fig. 14.15)
esophagitis ē-sof-ă-jī′tis	inflammation of the esophagus
gastritis gas-trī′tis	inflammation of the stomach (see Fig. 14.15)
gastroesophageal reflux disease (GERD) gas′trō-ē-sof′ă-jē′ăl rē′flŭks di-zēz′	backflow of stomach contents into the esophagus, often as a result of abnormal function of the lower esophageal sphincter; causes burning pain in the esophagus
pyloric stenosis pī-lōr′ik ste-nō′sis	narrowed condition of the pylorus
peptic ulcer disease (PUD) pep′tik ŭl′ser di-zēz′	a sore on the mucous membrane of the stomach, duodenum, or any other part of the gastrointestinal system exposed to gastric juices; commonly caused by infection with *Helicobacter pylori* bacteria (pept/o = to digest) (Fig. 14.8)
gastric ulcer gas′trik	ulcer located in the stomach
duodenal ulcer dū′ō-dē′năl	ulcer located in the duodenum

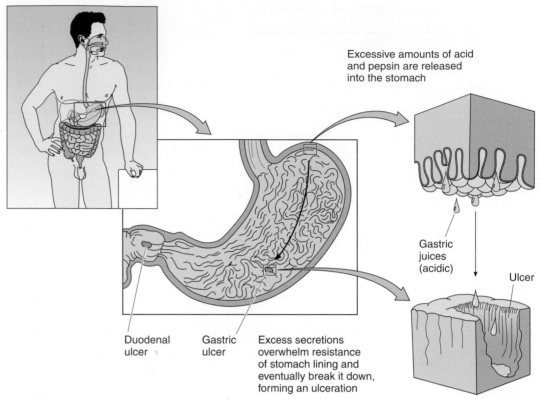

Figure 14.8   Peptic ulcer disease.

Term	Meaning
gastroenteritis gas′trō-en-ter-ī′tis	inflammation of the stomach and small intestine
enteritis en-ter-ī′tis	inflammation of the small intestine
ileitis il-ē-ī′tis	inflammation of the lower portion of the small intestine
colitis kō-lī′tis	inflammation of the colon (large intestine)
ulcerative colitis ŭl′ser-ă-tiv	chronic inflammation of the colon along with ulcerations
diverticulum dī-ver-tik′yū-lŭm	a by-way; an abnormal side pocket in the gastrointestinal tract usually related to a lack of dietary fiber
diverticulosis dī′ver-tik-yū-lō′sis	presence of diverticula in the gastrointestinal tract, especially in the bowel (Fig. 14.9; also see Fig. 14.15)
diverticulitis dī′ver-tik-yū-lī′tis	inflammation of diverticula
dysentery dis′en-tār-ē	inflammation of the intestine characterized by frequent, bloody stools, most often caused by bacteria or protozoa (e.g., amebic dysentery)

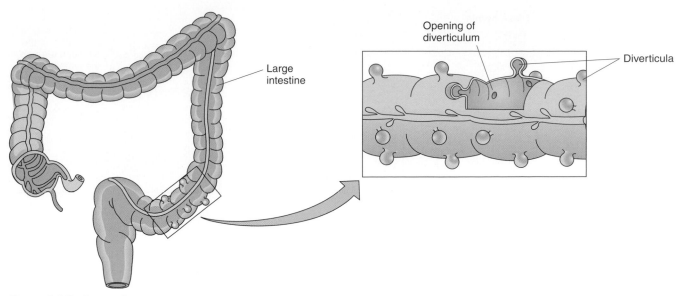

Figure 14.9 Diverticulosis.

Term	Meaning
appendicitis ă-pen-di-sī′tis	inflammation of the appendix
hernia her′nē-ă	protrusion of a part from its normal location
hiatal hernia hī-ā′tăl	protrusion of part of the stomach upward through the hiatal opening in the diaphragm (Fig. 14.10)
inguinal hernia ing′gwi-năl	protrusion of a loop of the intestine through layers of the abdominal wall in the inguinal region (see Fig. 14.10)
incarcerated hernia in-kar′ser-ā-ted	hernia that is swollen and fixed within a sac, causing an obstruction
strangulated hernia strang′gyū-lā-ted	hernia that is constricted, cut off from circulation, and likely to become gangrenous
umbilical hernia ŭm-bil′i-kăl	protrusion of the intestine through a weakness in the abdominal wall around the umbilicus (navel)
intussusception in′tŭs-sŭ-sep′shŭn	prolapse of one part of the intestine into the lumen of the adjoining part (intus = within; suscipiens = to take up) (Fig. 14.11)
volvulus vol′vū-lŭs	twisting of the bowel on itself, causing obstruction (volvo = to roll) (Fig. 14.12)
polyposis pol′i-pō′sis	multiple polyps in the intestine and rectum with a high malignancy potential (see Fig. 14.15)
polyp pol′ip	tumor on a stalk
proctitis prok-tī′tis	inflammation of the rectum and anus
anal fistula ā′năl fis′tyū-lă	abnormal tube-like passageway from the anus that may connect with the rectum (fistula = pipe) (Fig. 14.13)

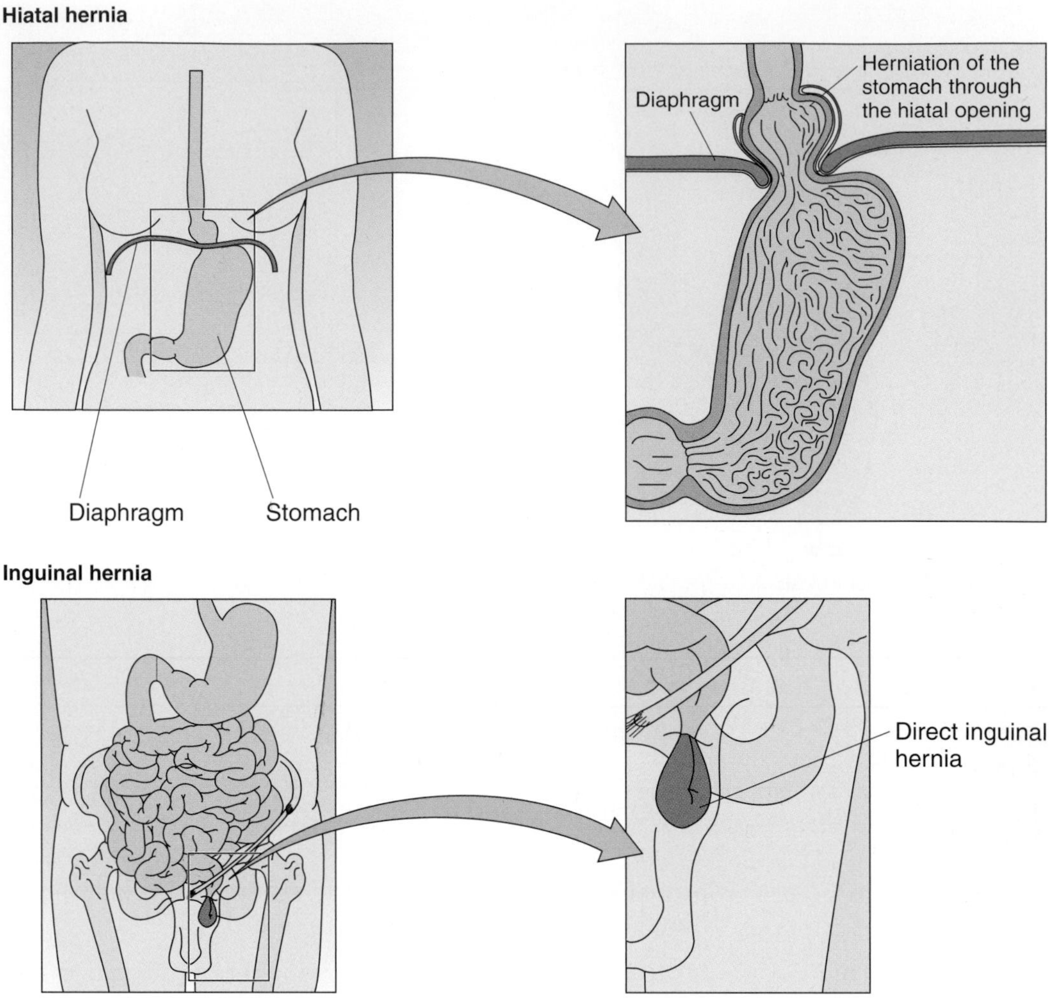

Hiatal hernia

Diaphragm

Stomach

Diaphragm

Herniation of the stomach through the hiatal opening

Inguinal hernia

Direct inguinal hernia

Figure 14.10   Common hernias.

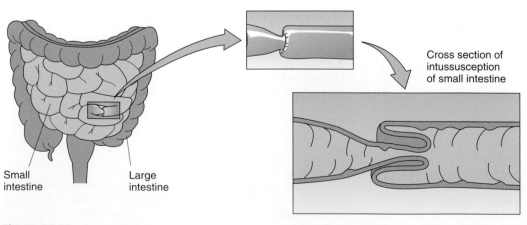

Small intestine

Large intestine

Cross section of intussusception of small intestine

Figure 14.11   Intussusception.

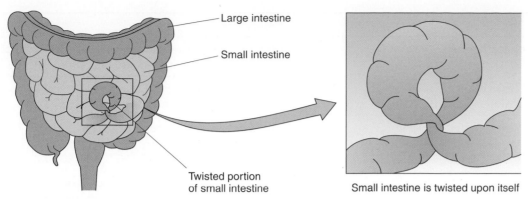

Figure 14.12 Volvulus.

Term	Meaning
hemorrhoid hem'ŏ-royd	swollen, twisted vein (varicosity) in the anal region (haimorrhois = a vein likely to bleed)
peritonitis per'i-tō-nī'tis	inflammation of the peritoneum
hepatitis hep-ă-tī'tis	inflammation of the liver
hepatitis A	infectious inflammation of the liver caused by the hepatitis A virus (HAV), usually transmitted orally through fecal contamination of food or water
hepatitis B	infectious inflammation of the liver caused by the hepatitis B virus (HBV) that is transmitted sexually or by exposure to contaminated blood or body fluids
hepatitis C	inflammation of the liver caused by the hepatitis C virus (HCV) transmitted by exposure to infected blood (rarely contracted sexually)
cirrhosis sir-rō'sis	chronic disease characterized by degeneration of liver tissue, most often caused by alcoholism or a nutritional deficiency (cirrho = yellow)
cholangitis kō-lan-jī'tis	inflammation of the bile ducts
cholecystitis kō'lē-sis-tī'tis	inflammation of the gallbladder

CIRRHOSIS. A Greek word referring to a yellow condition, cirrhosis was first applied to the fibrosis of the liver in alcoholics because the granular deposits in the organ looked yellow.

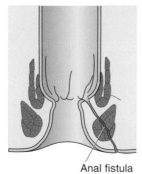

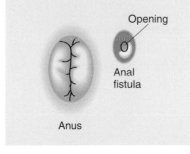

Figure 14.13 Anal fistula.

Term	Meaning
cholelithiasis kō′lē-li-thī′ă-sis	presence of stones in the gallbladder or bile ducts (Fig. 14.14; also see Fig. 14.21B)
choledocholithiasis kō-led′ō-kō-lith-ī′ă-sis	presence of stones in the common bile duct (see Figs. 14.14 and 14.15)
pancreatitis pan′krē-ă-tī′tis	inflammation of the pancreas

Diagnostic Tests and Procedures

Test or Procedure	Explanation
endoscopy en-dos′kŏ-pē	examination within a body cavity with a flexible endoscope for diagnosis or treatment; used in the gastrointestinal tract to detect abnormalities and perform procedures such as biopsies, excision of lesions, dilations of narrowed areas, and removal of swallowed objects (Fig. 14.15)
esophagoscopy ē-sof-ă-gos′kŏ-pē	examination of the esophagus with an esophagoscope
gastroscopy gas-tros′kŏ-pē	examination of the stomach with a gastroscope
upper gastrointestinal endoscopy gas′trō-in-tes′tin-ăl	examination of the lining of the esophagus, stomach, and duodenum with a flexible endoscope; also known as esophagogastroduodenoscopy (EGD) or panendoscopy (see Fig. 14.15)
endoscopic retrograde cholangiopancreatography (ERCP) en-dos′kŏp′ik ret′rō-grād kō-lan′jē-ō-pan-krē-ă-tog′ră-fē	endoscopic procedure including x-ray fluoroscopy to examine the ducts of the liver, gallbladder, and pancreas (biliary ducts)

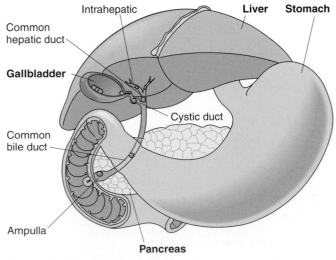

Intrahepatic

Common hepatic duct

Liver   **Stomach**

Gallbladder

Cystic duct

Common bile duct

Ampulla

Pancreas

Figure 14.14   Sites of gallstones.

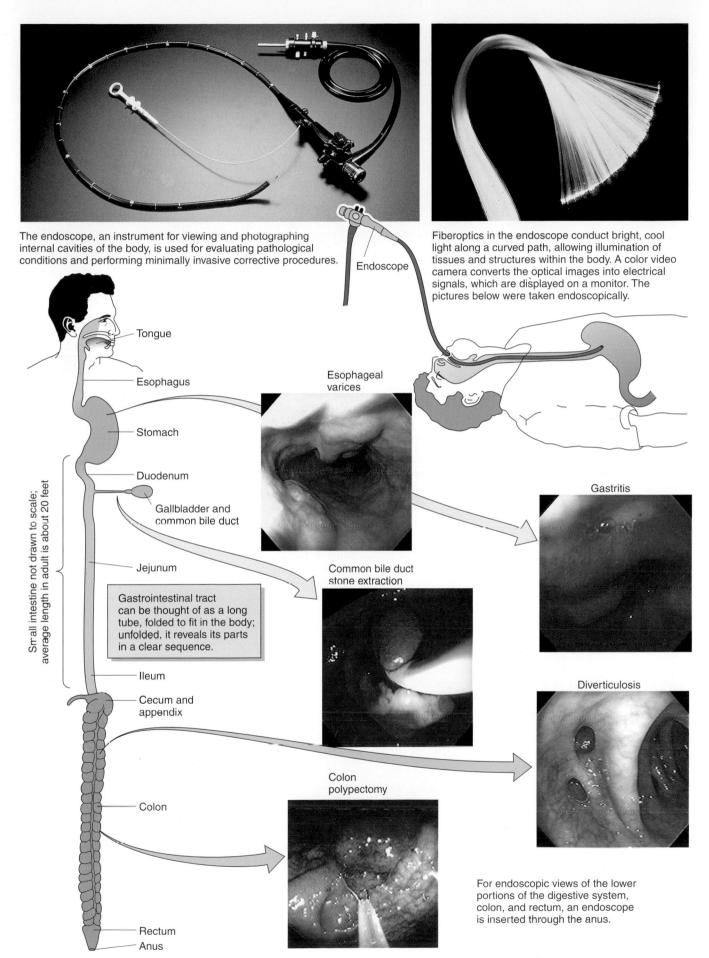

The endoscope, an instrument for viewing and photographing internal cavities of the body, is used for evaluating pathological conditions and performing minimally invasive corrective procedures.

Endoscope

Fiberoptics in the endoscope conduct bright, cool light along a curved path, allowing illumination of tissues and structures within the body. A color video camera converts the optical images into electrical signals, which are displayed on a monitor. The pictures below were taken endoscopically.

Tongue

Esophagus

Esophageal varices

Stomach

Duodenum

Gallbladder and common bile duct

Gastritis

Small intestine not drawn to scale; average length in adult is about 20 feet

Jejunum

Common bile duct stone extraction

Gastrointestinal tract can be thought of as a long tube, folded to fit in the body; unfolded, it reveals its parts in a clear sequence.

Ileum

Cecum and appendix

Diverticulosis

Colon polypectomy

Colon

For endoscopic views of the lower portions of the digestive system, colon, and rectum, an endoscope is inserted through the anus.

Rectum

Anus

Figure 14.15 Endoscopy of gastrointestinal system.

Test or Procedure	Explanation
laparoscopy lap-ă-ros′kŏ-pē	examination of the abdominal cavity with a laparoscope—often including interventional surgical procedures (Fig. 14.16)
peritoneoscopy per′i-tō-nē-os′kŏ-pē	examination of the peritoneal cavity with a peritoneoscope; often performed to examine the liver and obtain a biopsy specimen
capsule endoscopy kap′sool	examination of the small intestine made by a tiny video camera placed in a capsule and swallowed; images are transmitted to a waist-belt recorder and downloaded onto a computer for assessment of possible abnormalities; traditional endoscopy cannot completely access the small intestine because of its length and complexity
colonoscopy kō-lon-os′kŏ-pē	examination of the colon using a flexible colonoscope (see Fig. 14.15)
sigmoidoscopy sig′moy-dos′kŏ-pē	examination of the sigmoid colon with a rigid or flexible sigmoidoscope
proctoscopy prok-tos′kŏ-pē	examination of the rectum and anus with a proctoscope
DIAGNOSTIC IMAGING	
magnetic resonance image of the abdomen	nonionizing imaging technique for visualizing the abdominal cavity to identify disease or deformity in the gastrointestinal tract
nuclear medicine	radionuclide organ imaging
liver scan	scan of the liver made after injection of radioactive tracers into the bloodstream; used to detect tumors and functional abnormalities

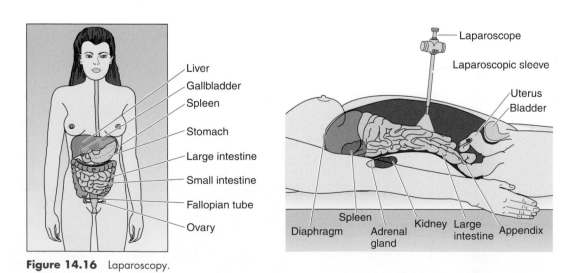

Figure 14.16 Laparoscopy.

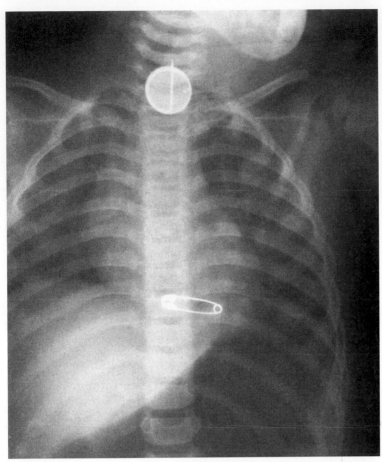

Figure 14.17 Plain radiograph (without contrast) showing two impacted foreign bodies in a child, aged 2 1/2 years. This child has ingested a safety pin and an ornamental pin. Endoscopic removal was required.

Test or Procedure	Explanation
radiography rā′dē-og′ră-fē	x-ray imaging (Fig. 14.17)
upper GI series	x-ray of the esophagus, stomach, and duodenum after the patient has swallowed a contrast medium (barium is most commonly used) (Fig. 14.18)
barium swallow ba′rē-ŭm	x-ray of the esophagus only; often used to locate swallowed objects
fluoroscopy flūr-os′kŏ-pe	x-ray using a fluorescent screen to visualize structures in motion (such as during a barium swallow)
small bowel series	x-ray exam of the small intestine—generally done in conjunction with an upper GI series
lower GI series barium enema en′ĕ-mă	x-ray of the colon after administration of an enema containing a contrast medium (Fig. 14.19)
cholangiogram kō-lan′jē-ō-gram	x-ray of the bile ducts; often performed during surgery
cholecystogram kō-lē-sis′tō-gram	x-ray of the gallbladder taken after oral ingestion of iodine

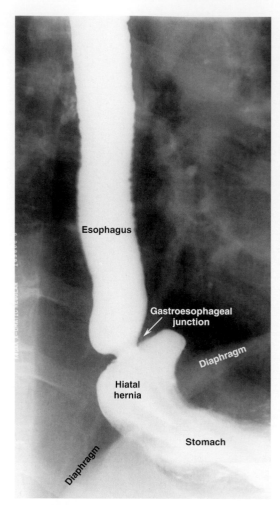

Figure 14.18 Upper gastrointestinal radiograph showing a hiatal hernia.

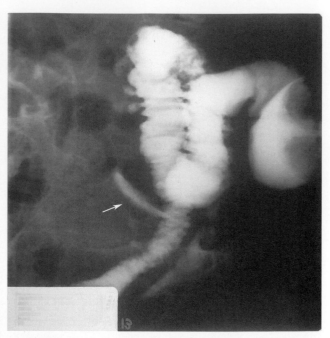

Figure 14.19 Barium enema radiograph of the colon showing a ruptured diverticulum. Its elongated appearance is similar to that of a deflated balloon.

Test or Procedure	Explanation
computed tomography (CT) of abdomen tō-mog′ră-fē	cross-sectional x-ray of the abdomen used to identify a condition or anomaly within the gastrointestinal tract (e.g., tumor, injury) (Fig. 14.20)
CT colonography	computed tomographic image of the colon performed as an alternative to traditional invasive colonoscopy; also known as virtual colonoscopy
sonography sŏ-nog′ră-fē	ultrasound imaging
abdominal sonogram son′ō-gram	ultrasound image of the abdomen to detect disease or deformity in organs and vascular structures (e.g., liver, pancreas, gallbladder, spleen, aorta) (Fig. 14.21)
endoscopic sonography en′dō-skŏp′ik	endoscopic procedure using a sonographic transducer within an endoscope to examine a body cavity and make sonographic images of structures and tissues

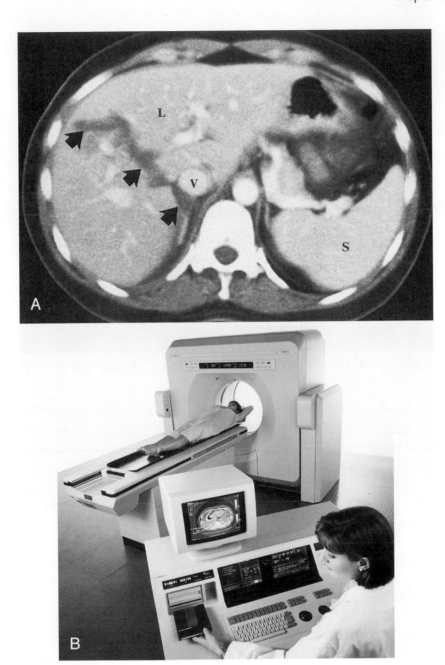

Figure 14.20 **A.** CT scan of a patient involved in a motor vehicle accident demonstrates a jagged laceration (*arrows*) extending from the posterior to inferior vena cava (*V*) through the right lobe of the liver (*L*). *S*, spleen. **B.** CT scanner.

Test or Procedure	Explanation
LABORATORY STUDIES	
biopsy (Bx) bī′op-sē	removal of tissue for microscopic pathological examination
endoscopic biopsy	removal of a specimen for biopsy during an endoscopic procedure (e.g., colonoscopy)
excisional biopsy ek-sizh′ŭn-ăl	removal of an entire lesion for examination

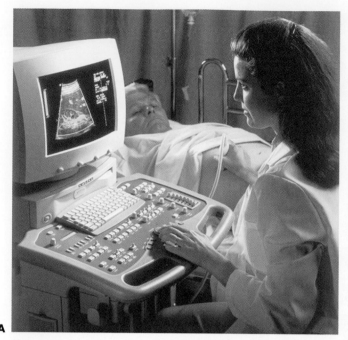

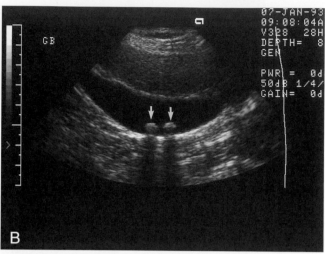

Figure 14.21 **A.** Abdominal sonography procedure. **B.** Abdominal sonogram of two stones present in the gallbladder (*arrows*).

Test or Procedure	Explanation
incisional biopsy in-sizh′ŭn-ăl	removal of a portion of a lesion for examination
needle biopsy	percutaneous removal of a core specimen of tissue using a special hollow needle (e.g., liver biopsy) (Fig. 14.22)
stool culture and sensitivity (C&S)	isolation of a stool specimen in a culture medium to identify disease-causing organisms; if present, the drugs to which they are sensitive are listed
stool occult blood study	chemical test of a stool specimen to detect the presence of blood; positive findings indicate bleeding in the gastrointestinal tract

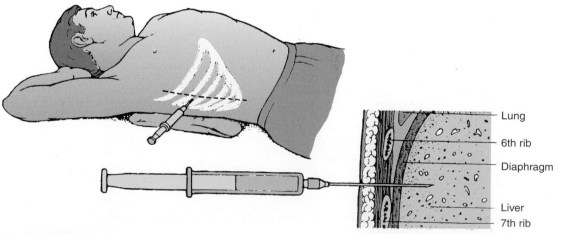

Figure 14.22 Liver biopsy procedure.

Operative Terms

Term	Meaning
bariatric surgery bar-ē-at′rik	treatment of morbid obesity by surgery to the stomach and/or intestines; procedures include restrictive techniques that limit the size of the stomach and malabsorptive techniques that limit the absorption of food (baros = weight; iatric = pertains to treatment)
cheiloplasty kī′lō-plas-tē	repair of the lip
glossectomy glo-sek′tō-mē	excision of all or part of the tongue
glossorrhaphy glo-sōr′ă-fē	suture of the tongue
esophagoplasty ē-sof′ă-gō-plas-tē	repair of the esophagus
gastrectomy gas-trek′tō-mē	partial or complete removal of the stomach
gastric resection gas′trik rē-sek′shŭn	partial removal and repair of the stomach
abdominocentesis ab-dom′i-nō-sen-tē′sis **paracentesis** par′ă-sen-tē′sis	puncture of the abdomen for aspiration of fluid (e.g., fluid accumulated in ascites)
laparotomy lap′ă-rot′ō-mē	incision into the abdomen
laparoscopic surgery lap′ă-rō-skōp′ik	abdominal surgery using a laparoscope
herniorrhaphy her′nō-ōr′ă-fē **hernioplasty** her′nē-ō-plas-tē	repair of a hernia
colostomy kō-los′tō-mē	creation of an opening in the colon through the abdominal wall to create an abdominal anus allowing stool to bypass a diseased portion of the colon; performed to treat ulcerative colitis, cancer, or obstructions (Fig. 14.23)
anastomosis ă-nas′tō-mō′sis	union of two hollow vessels; used in bowel surgery
ileostomy il′ē-os′tō-mē	surgical creation of an opening on the abdomen to which the end of the ileum is attached, providing a passageway for ileal discharges; performed after removal of the colon (e.g., to treat chronic inflammatory bowel diseases such as ulcerative colitis)

1. Ascending colostomy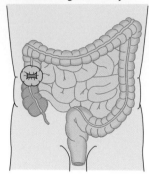

2. Transverse colostomy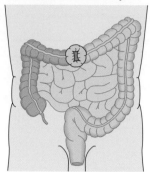

3. Descending colostomy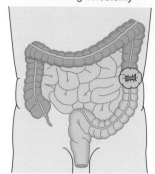

4. Sigmoid colostomy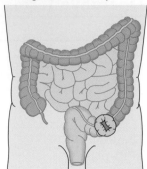

Figure 14.23 Common colostomy sites.

Term	Meaning
appendectomy ap-pen-dek'tō-mē	excision of a diseased appendix
incidental appendectomy	removal of the appendix during abdominal surgery for another procedure (e.g., a hysterectomy)
polypectomy pol-i-pek'tō-mē	excision of polyps
proctoplasty prok'tō-plas-tē	repair of the anus and rectum
anal fistulectomy fis-tyū-lek'tō-mē	excision of an anal fistula
hemorrhoidectomy hem'ō-roy-dek'tō-mē	excision of hemorrhoids
hepatic lobectomy he-pat'ik lō-bek'tō-mē	excision of a lobe of the liver
cholecystectomy kō'lē-sis-tek'tō-mē	excision of the gallbladder
laparoscopic cholecystectomy lap'ă-rō-skŏp'ik	excision of the gallbladder through a laparoscope
cholelithotomy kō'le-li-thot'ō-mē	incision for removal of gallstones
choledocholithotomy kō-led'ō-kō-li-thot'ō-mē	incision of the common bile duct for extraction of gallstones
cholelithotripsy kō-lē-lith'ō-trip-sē	crushing of gallstones
pancreatectomy pan'krē-ă-tek'tō-mē	excision of the pancreas

Therapeutic Terms

Term	Meaning
gastric lavage gas'trik lă-vahzh'	oral insertion of a tube into the stomach for examination and treatment [e.g., to remove blood clots from the stomach and monitor bleeding (lavage = to wash)]
nasogastric (NG) intubation nā-zō-gas'trik in-tū-bā'shŭn	insertion of a tube through the nose into the stomach for various purposes (e.g., to obtain a gastric fluid specimen for analysis)

COMMON THERAPEUTIC DRUG CLASSIFICATIONS

antacid ant-as'id	drug that neutralizes stomach acid
antiemetic an'tē-ĕ-met'ik	drug that prevents or stops vomiting
antispasmodic an'tē-spaz-mod'ik	drug that decreases motility in the gastrointestinal tract to arrest spasm or diarrhea
cathartic kă-thar'tik	drug that causes movement of the bowels; also called a laxative

Summary of Chapter 14 Acronyms/Abbreviations

Bx	biopsy	**HBV**	hepatitis B virus
C&S	culture and sensitivity	**HCV**	hepatitis C virus
CT	computed tomography	**LLQ**	left lower quadrant
EGD	esophagogastroduodenoscopy	**LUQ**	left upper quadrant
ERCP	endoscopic retrograde cholangiopancreatography	**MRI**	magnetic resonance imaging
		NG	nasogastric
GERD	gastroesophageal reflux disease	**PUD**	peptic ulcer disease
GI	gastrointestinal	**RLQ**	right lower quadrant
HAV	hepatitis A virus	**RUQ**	right upper quadrant

PRACTICE EXERCISES

For the following terms, on the lines below the term, write out the indicated word parts: prefixes (P), combining forms (CF), roots (R), and suffixes (S). Then define the word.

EXAMPLE

sublingual

_____/ _____/ _____
P   R   S

<u>sub/lingu/al</u>
P   R   S

DEFINITION: below or under/tongue/pertaining to

1. transabdominal

_____/ _____/ _____
     P   R   S

DEFINITION: _____

2. gastroenterostomy

_____/ _____/ _____
     CF   CF   S

DEFINITION: _____

3. sialolithotomy

_____/ _____/ _____
     CF   CF   S

DEFINITION: _____

4. glossorrhaphy

_____/ _____
     CF   S

DEFINITION: _____

5. hematemesis

_____/ _____
     R   S

DEFINITION: _____

6. cheilostomatoplasty

_____/ _____/ _____
     CF   CF   S

DEFINITION: _____

7. appendicitis

_____ / _____
          R   S
DEFINITION: _____

8. celiotomy

_____ / _____
          CF   S
DEFINITION: _____

9. cholangiogram

_____ / _____ / _____
      R   CF   S
DEFINITION: _____

10. colonoscopy

_____ / _____
          CF   S
DEFINITION: _____

11. anorectal

_____ / _____ / _____
      CF   R   S
DEFINITION: _____

12. enterocolitis

_____ / _____ / _____
      CF   R   S
DEFINITION: _____

13. orolingual

_____ / _____ / _____
      CF   R   S
DEFINITION: _____

14. proctosigmoidoscopy

_____ / _____ / _____
      CF   CF   S
DEFINITION: _____

15. laparoscope

_____ / _____
          CF   S
DEFINITION: _____

16. dysphagia

_____ / _____ / _____
      P   R   S
DEFINITION: _____

17. pancreatoduodenostomy

_____ / _____ / _____
CF   CF   S

DEFINITION: _____

18. hernioplasty

_____ / _____
CF   S

DEFINITION: _____

19. biliary

_____ / _____
R   S

DEFINITION: _____

20. gastroesophageal

_____ / _____ / _____
CF   R   S

DEFINITION: _____

21. choledochotomy

_____ / _____ / _____
CF   CF   S

DEFINITION: _____

22. steatorrhea

_____ / _____
CF   S

DEFINITION: _____

23. dentalgia

_____ / _____
R   S

DEFINITION: _____

24. pylorospasm

_____ / _____
CF   S

DEFINITION: _____

25. hepatotoxic

_____ / _____ / _____
CF   R   S

DEFINITION: _____

26. ileojejunitis

_____ / _____ / _____
CF   R   S

DEFINITION: _____

27. peritoneocentesis

_____ / _____
CF   S

DEFINITION: _____

28. buccogingival

_____ / _____ / _____
CF   R   S

DEFINITION: _____

29. cholecystectomy

_____ / _____ / _____
CF   R   S

DEFINITION: _____

30. perirectal

_____ / _____ / _____
P   R   S

DEFINITION: _____

Complete the medical term by writing the missing part or word:

31. hemi _____ ectomy = removal of half of the colon

32. _____ itis = inflammation of the appendix

33. _____ rrhaphy = suture of the lip

34. cholelitho _____ = incision for removal of gallstones

35. _____ plasty = surgical repair of the mouth

36. chol _____ gram = x-ray of bile ducts (vessels)

37. _____ bilirubin _____ = excessive level of bilirubin in the blood

38. gastric _____ = partial removal and repair of the stomach

39. diverticulo _____ = the presence of diverticula

For each of the following, circle the combining form that corresponds to the meaning given:

40. **abdomen**   gastr/o   lapar/o   stomat/o

41. **tongue**   gloss/o   proct/o   gingiv/o

42. **small intestine**   col/o   appendic/o   enter/o

43. **teeth**   dent/i   chol/e   lingu/o

44. **stomach**	lapar/o	stomat/o	gastr/o
45. **cheek**	bucc/o	or/o	proct/o
46. **bile**	col/o	celi/o	chol/e
47. **mouth**	gastr/o	stomat/o	lapar/o
48. **liver**	hepat/o	nephr/o	ren/o
49. **eat**	phas/o	phag/o	gloss/o
50. **stone**	scler/o	steat/o	lith/o
51. **rectum**	an/o	proct/o	col/o

Write the correct medical term for each of the following:

52. inflammation of the stomach _____

53. loss of appetite _____

54. inability to swallow _____

55. in the cheek _____

56. gas in the stomach or intestines _____

57. rupture or protrusion of a part from its normal location _____

58. black tarry stool _____

59. belch _____

60. instrument used to examine the rectum _____

61. inflammation of the large intestine _____

62. portion of upper GI series x-ray used to examine the esophagus only _____

63. accumulation of fluid in the peritoneal cavity _____

64. inflammation of the gallbladder _____

65. feces containing fat _____

66. presence of inflamed abnormal side pockets in gastrointestinal tract _____

67. peptic ulcer located in the stomach _____

68. enlargement of the liver _____

69. tongue-tie condition _____

Name the anatomical divisions of the abdomen:

70. lower lateral groin regions _____

71. upper lateral regions beneath the ribs _____

72. upper middle region below the sternum _____

73. region below the navel _____

74. middle lateral regions _____

75. region of the navel _____

Name the clinical divisions of the abdomen:

76. _____

77. _____

78. _____

79. _____

Match the following terms:

80. _____ cathartic

81. _____ herniorrhaphy

82. _____ appendicitis

83. _____ lower GI series

84. _____ icterus

85. _____ peptic ulcer disease

86. _____ abdominocentesis

87. _____ parotitis

88. _____ sublingual

89. _____ upper GI series

90. _____ ulcerative colitis

91. _____ cholelithiasis

92. _____ morbid obesity

a. cholelithotripsy

b. barium swallow

c. bariatric surgery

d. appendectomy

e. colostomy

f. hernioplasty

g. *H. pylori* bacterial infection

h. barium enema

i. mumps

j. paracentesis

k. jaundice

l. hypoglossal

m. laxative

An endoscope is an instrument used to examine within the body. Name the specific type of endoscope used to examine the following body parts:

93. abdomen _____

94. anus _____

95. stomach _____

96. colon _____

97. peritoneal cavity _____

98. esophagus _____

99. Which type of hernia is swollen and fixed within a sac, causing obstruction?
_____

100. Which type of biopsy involves the removal of an entire growth? _____

Write the full medical term for the following abbreviations:

101. NG tube _____

102. ERCP _____

103. GERD _____

104. LUQ _____

105. GI _____

106. MRI _____

107. EGD _____

Write in the term components related to each of the gastrointestinal organs on the blank lines provided in the following illustration.

108–115.

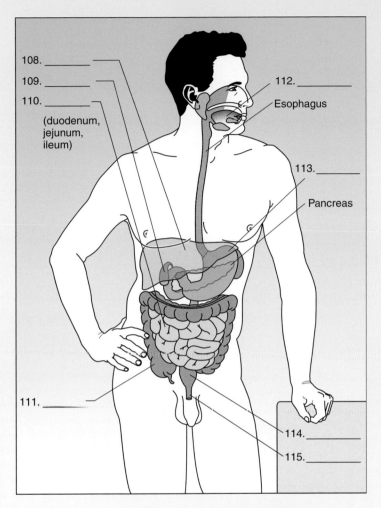

108. _____
109. _____
110. _____
(duodenum, jejunum, ileum)

112. _____
Esophagus

113. _____

Pancreas

111. _____

114. _____
115. _____

For each of the following, circle the correct spelling of the term:

116. anorexia	annorexia	anorrexia
117. asites	ascitis	ascites
118. hematochesia	hemochezia	hematochezia
119. icterus	ickterus	icteris
120. ankleoglossia	ankyloglosia	ankyloglossia
121. volvulis	volvulus	volvolus
122. cirhosis	cirrhosus	cirrhosis
123. glossectomy	glozectomy	glosectomy
124. hernniorhaphy	herniorraphy	herniorrhaphy
125. hemorroidectomy	hemroidectomy	hemorrhoidectomy

126. anteacid   anacid   antacid

127. antiemetic   antemetic   antaemetic

128. cathartik   cathartic   catarthic

129. melena   melenna   melana

Give the noun that was used to form the following adjectives:

130. fecal _____

131. icteric _____

132. ileal _____

133. endoscopic _____

134. hemorrhoidal _____

135. pancreatic _____

MEDICAL RECORD ANALYSES

MEDICAL RECORD 14.1

S: This is a 36 y.o. ♂ with a complaint of abdominal pain. He describes having lifted a 75# beam yesterday at work. He noticed a sharp pain in his navel but continued to work. The pain intensified as the day went on and persisted through last night and today. He claims his navel now bulges forward. He denies fever, chills, dysphagia, anorexia, or vomiting.
PMH: No hospitalizations or surgeries
Meds: none
Allergies: NKDA

O: T 97.5°F, P 87, R18, BP 128/86
WDWN male in moderate distress secondary to abdominal pain. Upon palpation, the abdomen is soft with spasm of the muscles in the periumbilical region, and there is an obvious bulge in the umbilicus. The omentum is also palapable. There is no hepatosplenomegaly.

A: Incarcerated umbilical hernia

P: Admit for STAT umbilical hernia repair

1. Summarize the subjective information:
   a. pain in stomach
   b. pain in abdomen
   c. pain in the groin area
   d. generalized abdominal pain with chills and fever
   e. stomach pain and has difficulty swallowing

2. What kind of an appetite does the patient have?
   a. normal
   b. increased
   c. decreased

3. What is the condition of the patient's liver?
   a. not stated
   b. enlarged
   c. not enlarged
   d. inflamed
   e. ruptured

4. What were the objective findings?
   a. involuntary contraction of the muscles around the navel
   b. pouching of the muscles under the navel
   c. contraction of abdominal muscles and enlargement of the spleen
   d. protrusion of the navel and enlargement of the liver
   e. pouching of the stomach and omentum

5. Which of the following best describes the diagnosis?
   a. portion of the bowel has protruded through the abdominal wall and has been cut off from circulation
   b. prolapse of one part of the intestine into the lumen of the adjoining part
   c. portion of the intestine has protruded through a weakness in the abdominal wall around the navel and is swollen and fixed in a sac
   d. portion of the bowel has twisted on itself causing obstruction
   e. inflammation of the stomach and small intestine

6. Which of the following medical terms describes the planned surgery?
   a. laparotomy
   b. gastroenterostomy
   c. hernioplasty
   d. ileostomy
   e. abdominocentesis

MEDICAL RECORD 14.2

Mr. Antonio Villata undergoes a comprehensive physical examination each year as part of a wellness program promoted by his employer. This year, after a routine sigmoidoscopic exam revealed a polyp in his intestine, he was referred to Dr. Blain, a gastroenterologist at Central Medical Center, for evaluation.

Directions

Read Medical Record 14.2 for Antonio Villata (page 475) and answer the following questions. This record is a procedure report dictated by Dr. Blain after his evaluation and treatment of Mr. Villata in the endoscopy suite at Central Medical Center.

QUESTIONS ABOUT MEDICAL RECORD 14.2

Write your answers in the spaces provided.

1. Below are medical terms used in the progress note you have not yet encountered in this text. Underline each where it appears in the record and define below:

   cannulated _____

   pediculated _____

   verge _____

   snare _____

2. Describe the screening procedure performed by Dr. Kolima prior to Mr. Villata's referral to Dr. Blain:

   _____

   _____

   _____

3. In your own words, not using medical terminology, briefly describe the procedure performed by Dr. Blain and the indications for which the patient was referred:

   _____

   _____

   _____

4. The procedure was performed with Mr. Villata in what position?
   a. lying flat, face down
   b. lying flat, face up
   c. lying on his side
   d. sitting

5. Put the following actions in order by numbering them 1 to 12:

_____ location of the cecum was confirmed by internal and external landmarks

_____ video colonoscope was inserted in the rectum and advanced carefully to the cecum

_____ hemorrhoids were noted

_____ terminal ileum was then cannulated

_____ scope was straightened, air was aspirated, and scope was withdrawn

_____ scattered diverticula were noted in the sigmoid colon

_____ lining of the colon was thoroughly inspected

_____ polyp was removed using a snare and submitted to pathology lab for biopsy

_____ pediculated 4 mm polyp was seen in the sigmoid colon

_____ scope was brought back to the rectum and retroflexed

_____ patient was placed in the left lateral decubitus position

_____ scope was brought back to the cecum and then gradually withdrawn

6. Translate the statement noting that "a pediculated 4-mm polyp was seen in the sigmoid colon":

_____

_____

_____

7. How many inches from the anal verge was the polyp? _____

8. Write the sentence that describes the polypectomy that was performed:

_____

_____

_____

9. Name and describe the condition for which a high-fiber diet was indicated in the Plan:

_____

_____

_____

10. Describe the third condition Dr. Blain listed in his assessment of Mr. Villata. Include the degree of severity and any treatment planned:

_____

_____

_____

11. In your own words, describe the recommendations outlined in the Plan that will be made depending on the results of the biopsy:

_____

_____

_____

CENTRAL MEDICAL CENTER

211 Medical Center Drive • Central City, US 90000-1234 • PHONE: (012) 125-6784 • FAX: (012) 125-9999

ENDOSCOPY LABORATORY REPORT

PATIENT: Villata, Antonio   DATE: 4/29/20xx

PROCEDURE PERFORMED: COLONOSCOPY WITH BIOPSY

INDICATIONS: This is a 54-year-old white male referred to me for evaluation of a polyp found during a screening sigmoidoscopy by Dr. Kolima. A complete colonoscopy is being done to remove the polyp and rule out other concurrent lesions.

CONSENT: The procedure and its risks including bleeding, infection, perforation, and sedative reaction have been explained to the patient, and informed consent was obtained.

INSTRUMENT USED: Olympus video colonoscope.

MEDICATIONS GIVEN: Demerol 50 mg and Versed 3 mg in divided doses. The patient had stable vital signs. A Fleets Phospho-Soda prep provided good visualization.

PROCEDURE: The patient was placed in the left lateral decubitus position. After adequate sedation, a rectal examination was performed. No masses were felt. The video colonoscope was inserted in the rectum and advanced carefully to the cecum. The location of the cecum was confirmed by internal and external landmarks, and photographic documentation was obtained. The terminal ileum was then cannulated. This was normal to about 2 cm. The scope was brought back to the cecum and then gradually withdrawn. The lining of the colon was thoroughly inspected. There were scattered diverticula noted in the sigmoid colon. A pediculated 4 mm polyp was seen in the sigmoid colon at 30 cm from the anal verge. This was removed using a snare and submitted to pathology lab for biopsy. The scope was brought back to the rectum and retroflexed. Minimal hemorrhoids were noted. The scope was straightened, air was aspirated, and the scope was withdrawn. The patient tolerated the procedure well.

IMPRESSION:
1. POLYP ON SIGMOID COLON AT 30 CM.
2. SIGMOID DIVERTICULAR DISEASE.
3. HEMORRHOIDS.

PLAN:
1. A high-fiber diet is indicated.
2. Await pathology results. If adenomatous, a full colonoscopy is indicated in 3 years. If hyperplastic or normal, a colonoscopy is indicated in 10 years.

Roger Blain, M.D.

RB:mw
D: 4/29/xx
T: 5/1/xx
cc: R. Kolima, M.D.

Medical Record 14.2

MEDICAL RECORD 14.3

At age 77, Kathleen Hillman has been in fairly good health. But 1 week ago, she developed what she called "stomach problems" that led to frequent vomiting. She refused to seek medical help at first, until her daughter coaxed her into calling her family practitioner, Dr. Shigeda. Once she learned how serious Ms. Hillman's problem had become, Dr. Shigeda urged her to go to the emergency room immediately.

Directions

Read Medical Record 14.3 for Kathleen Hillman (pages 479–481) and answer the following questions. This record is the consultation report dictated by Dr. Flagstone after he examined her in the emergency room at Central Medical Center.

QUESTIONS ABOUT MEDICAL RECORD 14.3

Write your answers in the spaces provided.

1. Below are medical terms used in this record you have not yet encountered in this text. Underline each where it appears in the record and define below:

   rebound tenderness _____

   abdominal guarding _____

   dehydration _____

   stasis dermatitis _____

   intractable _____

2. What was Ms. Hillman's complaint that led her to call Dr. Shigeda, who then sent her to the emergency room at Central Medical Center?

   _____

   _____

   _____

3. From the list of medications Ms. Hillman is taking, one includes an abbreviation that has been deemed error prone. Identify the abbreviation, potential problem, and preferred wording.

Abbreviation	*Potential Problem*	*Preferred Wording*
_____	_____	_____

4. According to Dr. Flagstone's initial impression, which factor in Ms. Hillman's present history might be a cause of her gastrointestinal symptoms?
   a. her drinking
   b. stress from living with her daughter
   c. her allergies
   d. her arthritis medications

5. Describe the two previous operations Ms. Hillman has had involving the musculoskeletal system:

_____

_____

_____

6. Using nonmedical language, explain what Ms. Hillman does not remember exactly about her gastrointestinal history two decades ago:

_____

_____

_____

7. Check all of the findings below that Dr. Flagstone noted in the physical examination of Ms. Hillman:

_____ dehydration

_____ pulse 98

_____ icterus in the whites of the eyes

_____ chronic stasis dermatitis

_____ varicose veins

_____ irregular heart rate

_____ vaginal infection

_____ possible atrial fibrillation

_____ parotitis

_____ yellowing of the skin

_____ multiple ecchymoses

_____ clear lungs

8. Does Ms. Hillman have blood in her stool? Write the phrase from the medical record that indicates this:

_____

_____

_____

9. In your own words, explain the initial diagnoses, including the possibilities to eliminate:

   a. _____

   b. _____

   c. _____

10. Dr. Flagstone's plan calls for administering medications, checking tests, and performing a procedure. Fill in the details below:

    Administered to Ms. Hillman

    a. _____

    b. _____

    c. _____

    Check Ms. Hillman's

    d. _____

    e. _____

    f. _____

    Perform

    g. _____

11. In your own words, describe stool culture and sensitivity:

    _____

    _____

    _____

CENTRAL MEDICAL CENTER

211 Medical Center Drive • Central City, US 90000-1234 • PHONE: (012) 125-6784 • FAX: (012) 125-9999

CONSULTATION

REASON FOR CONSULTATION:
This 77-year-old female presented herself to the emergency room with a one-week history of rather severe nausea and vomiting and also diarrhea and epigastric pain; she was sent by Dr. Shigeda, her family practitioner. The most troubling symptom for her is the vomiting and nausea because she vomits everything she drinks and eats. The epigastric pains are tolerable. The diarrhea also has somewhat improved. The patient's bowel movements usually are normal without history of black or bloody stools. Her appetite has been down markedly, and she has lost at least two to three pounds in the last several days. Her urination is normal. She does not drink or smoke. Her last admission was about a month ago after a fall.

MEDICATIONS: Prednisone, 10 mg, 1 q.i.d.; Naprosyn, 250 mg, 1 q noc; Voltaren 1 q d; penicillamine t.i.d.; and Mylanta and Tylenol p.r.n.

ALLERGIES: Demerol, which gives her severe confusion lasting for days.

PAST MEDICAL HISTORY/REVIEW OF SYSTEMS:
The patient has reading glasses. There is no history of cephalalgia, diplopia, or tinnitus. There is no history of thyroid disease. CARDIOPULMONARY: There is no history of angina, dyspnea, hemoptysis, emphysema, hypertension, or heart murmurs. GASTROINTESTINAL: The patient had peptic ulcer disease about 20 years ago, nonbleeding, and does not remember whether it was gastric or duodenal. It was healed by diet and antacids. There has been no recurrence since. There is no history of gallbladder disease, hepatitis, pancreatitis, or colitis. However, years ago, she was told she had diverticulosis. GENITOURINARY: She is Gravida III Para III (3 pregnancies and 3 live births). Her last menstrual period was some 25 years ago. There is no history of dysuria, hematuria, or nephrolithiasis. MUSCULOSKELETAL: The patient has had severe rheumatoid arthritis for about 20 years and has been in treatment with Dr. Clemons. The disease is relatively well controlled with the above-mentioned medications. She had a right hip replacement in 20xx and left knee arthroscopy. NEUROMUSCULAR: There is no history of loss of consciousness or seizure disorder. PSYCHIATRIC REVIEW: Negative.

FAMILY HISTORY:
All siblings and parents died of old age.

SOCIAL HISTORY:
The patient is a widow. She lives with her daughter.

(continued)

CONSULTATION Page 1 October 19, 20xx	PT. NAME: HILLMAN, KATHLEEN E. ID NO: IP-990960 ROOM NO: 508 ATT. PHYS: R. FLAGSTONE, M.D.

Medical Record 14.3

CENTRAL MEDICAL CENTER

211 Medical Center Drive • Central City, US 90000-1234 • PHONE: (012) 125-6784 • FAX: (012) 125-9999

CONSULTATION

PHYSICAL EXAMINATION:

GENERAL: The patient appeared to be in moderate to severe distress, appearing pale, chronically ill, with dehydration.

VITAL SIGNS: Blood pressure, lying: 100/70. Blood pressure, sitting: 90/65. Temperature: 98°C. Pulse: 80; went to 100 on sitting up. Respirations: 12.

HEENT: Head: Normocephalic. Eyes: Pupils equal, round, reactive to light and accommodation. No scleral icterus. Fundi benign. Ears, nose, throat, and mouth were unremarkable.

NECK: Supple. No lymphadenopathy. No thyromegaly.

CHEST: Chest, costovertebral angle, and back were nontender.

LUNGS: Clear to percussion and auscultation.

HEART: There was an irregular rate, possibly atrial fibrillation, with a II/VI systolic ejection-type murmur mostly along the left sternal border.

ABDOMEN: Soft. There was moderate epigastric tenderness. There was no hepatosplenomegaly, no guarding, no rebound tenderness, no masses, no ascites, and no abdominal bruits.

VAGINAL EXAMINATION: Refused.

RECTAL EXAMINATION: Good sphincter tone. Light brown, semiformed stool in the rectal ampulla, which was occult blood negative.

EXTREMITIES: No edema. No varicose veins. Good peripheral pulses. No clubbing. No palmar erythema. There were, however, brownish changes of chronic stasis dermatitis.

SKIN: The skin showed 10–15% dehydration without jaundice. There were multiple ecchymoses secondary to the patient's prednisone.

(continued)

CONSULTATION Page 2 October 19, 20xx	PT. NAME: HILLMAN, KATHLEEN E. ID NO: IP-990960 ROOM NO: 508 ATT. PHYS: R. FLAGSTONE, M.D.

Medical Record 14.3 *Continued.*

CENTRAL MEDICAL CENTER

211 Medical Center Drive • Central City, US 90000-1234 • PHONE: (012) 125-6784 • FAX: (012) 125-9999

CONSULTATION

INITIAL IMPRESSION:

1. SEVERE NAUSEA AND VOMITING, INTRACTABLE, WITH DEHYDRATION, PROBABLY SECONDARY TO MEDICATION-INDUCED GASTRITIS OR POSSIBLE RECURRENT PEPTIC ULCER DISEASE.

2. R/O POSSIBLE PANCREATITIS SECONDARY TO PREDNISONE OR PENICILLAMINE.

3. R/O POSSIBLE VIRAL GASTROENTERITIS, THOUGH LESS LIKELY.

SECONDARY DIAGNOSES:

1. HISTORY OF LONG-STANDING, ADVANCED RHEUMATOID ARTHRITIS WITH LEFT KNEE SURGERY AND RIGHT HIP REPLACEMENT.

2. HISTORY OF DIVERTICULOSIS AND PREVIOUS PEPTIC ULCER DISEASE.

PLAN:

The patient will be admitted at least for a 23-hour hold and is then to be reevaluated and will receive fluid volume replacement and potassium replacement; she will have her electrolytes checked, as well as her blood count, and will also be placed on Zantac intravenously. She will then have a gastroscopy in the morning. Her stools will also be checked, if they are still loose, for further occult blood, ova, and parasites, and a possible culture and sensitivity.

R. Flagstone, M.D.

RF:ti

D: 10/19/20xx
T: 10/20/20xx

CONSULTATION	PT. NAME:	HILLMAN, KATHLEEN E.
Page 3	ID NO:	IP-990960
October 19, 20xx	ROOM NO:	508
	ATT. PHYS:	R. FLAGSTONE, M.D.

Medical Record 14.3   *Continued.*

Chapter **15**

Urinary System

OBJECTIVES

After completion of this chapter you will be able to

- 🔹 Define common term components used in relation to the urinary system
- 🔹 Describe the basic functions of the urinary system
- 🔹 Define the basic anatomical terms referring to the urinary system
- 🔹 Define common symptomatic and diagnostic terms referring to the urinary system
- 🔹 List the common diagnostic tests and procedures related to the urinary system
- 🔹 Define common operative terms referring to the male reproductive system
- 🔹 Identify common therapeutic terms including drug classifications related to the urinary system
- 🔹 Explain terms and abbreviations used in documenting medical records involving the urinary system

Combining Forms

Combining Form	Meaning	Example
albumin/o	protein	**albuminoid** al-byū′min-oyd
bacteri/o	bacteria	**bacterium** bak-tēr′ē-ŭm
cyst/o	bladder or sac	**cystoscope** sis′tō-skōp
vesic/o		**vesicotomy** ves′i-kot′ō-mē
dips/o	thirst	**polydipsia** pol-ē-dip′sē-ă
glomerul/o	glomerulus (little ball)	**glomerular** glō-mār′yū-lăr
gluc/o	sugar	**glucogenic** gloo-kō-jen′ik
glucos/o		**glucose** glū′kōs
glyc/o		**glycolysis** glī-kol′i-sis

Combining Form	Meaning	Example
ket/o	ketone bodies	ketosis kē-tō'sis
keton/o		ketonuria kē-tō-nū'rē-ă
lith/o	stone	lithiasis li-thī'ă-sis
meat/o	meatus (opening)	meatal mē-ā'tăl
nephr/o	kidney	nephrosis ne-frō'sis
ren/o		renal rē'năl
pub/o	pubic bone (lower front portion of hip bone) (see Figs. 6.1 and 15.1)	suprapubic soo-pră-pyu'bik
pyel/o	renal pelvis (basin)	pyelonephrosis pī'ĕ-lō-ne-frō'sis
py/o	pus	pyonephritis pī'ĕ-lō-ne-frī'tis
ureter/o	ureter	ureterolithiasis yū-rē'ter-ō-li-thī'ă-sis
urethr/o	urethra	urethrodynia yū-rē-thrō-din'ē-ă
ur/o	urine	urologist yū-rol'ō-jist
urin/o		urinary yūr'i-nār-ē

Urinary System Overview

The urinary system includes the organs and structures involved in the secretion and elimination of urine: kidneys, ureters, urinary bladder, and urethra (Fig. 15.1). The principal organs of the urinary system, the *kidneys,* are located on each side of the lumbar region. They filter the blood and secrete water and nitrogenous wastes (e.g., urea, creatinine) in the form of *urine.*

The functional unit of the kidney is called the *nephron.* Each nephron consists of a *glomerulus,* the little ball-shaped cluster of capillaries at the top; *Bowman's capsule,* the top part that encloses the nephron; and a *renal tubule,* the stem portion of the nephron. Approximately one million nephrons make up the *cortex,* the outer part of each kidney. They gather waste substances by filtering the blood that enters the kidney through the *renal artery* at the *hilum,* the prominent indented portion. In the *medulla,* the inner portion of the kidney, the *calyces* collect urine from the tubules of the nephrons and drain their contents into the *renal pelvis,* the basin-like portion of the ureter within the kidney.

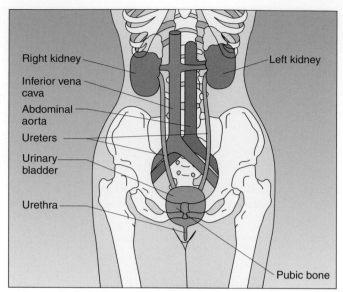

Figure 15.1 Urinary system.

The *ureters,* usually one for each kidney, are tubes that carry the urine from the kidney to the *urinary bladder,* where it is held until being expelled during *urination* (micturition). The *urethra* is the single canal that carries urine from the bladder to the outside of the body. The *urethral meatus* is the opening in the urethra to the outside of the body.

In addition to excreting waste products such as urea and creatinine, the kidneys play an essential life-sustaining role by regulating the levels of critical elements such as water, sodium, and potassium.

Anatomical Terms

Term	Meaning
kidneys kid′nēz	two structures located on each side of the lumbar region that filter blood and secrete impurities, forming urine (Fig. 15.2)
cortex kōr′teks	outer part of the kidney (cortex = bark)
hilum hī′lŭm	indented opening in the kidney where vessels enter and leave
medulla me-dūl′ă	inner part of the kidney
calyces (calices) kal′i-sēz	system of ducts carrying urine from the nephrons to the renal pelvis (kalyx = cup of a flower)
nephron nef′ron	microscopic functional units of the kidney, comprised of kidney cells and capillaries, each capable of forming urine (see Fig. 15.2)
glomerulus glō-mār′yū-lŭs	little ball-shaped cluster of capillaries located at the top of each nephron
Bowman's capsule bō-mĕnz kap′sūl	top part of the nephron that encloses the glomerulus

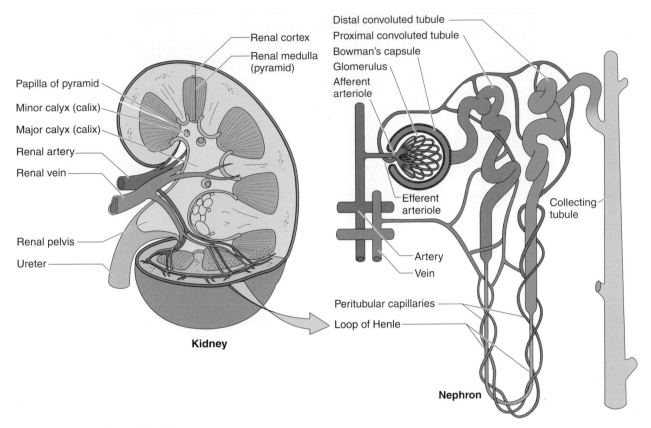

Figure 15.2 Kidney and nephron.

Term	Meaning
renal tubule rē′năl tū′byūl	stem portion of the nephron
ureter ū-rē′ter	tube that carries urine from the kidney to the bladder
renal pelvis rē′năl pel′vis	basin-like portion of the ureter within the kidney
ureteropelvic junction yū′rē′ter-ō-pel′vik	point of connection between the renal pelvis and ureter
urinary bladder yūr′i-nār-ē	sac that holds the urine
urethra yū-rē′thră	single canal that carries urine to the outside of the body
urethral meatus mē-ā′tŭs	opening in the urethra to the outside of the body
urine yūr′in	fluid produced by the kidneys containing water and waste products
urea yū-rē′ă	waste product formed in the liver, filtered out of the blood by the kidneys, and excreted in urine
creatinine krē-at′i-nēn	waste product of muscle metabolism filtered out of the blood by the kidneys and excreted in urine

Symptomatic and Diagnostic Terms

Term	Meaning
SYMPTOMATIC	
albuminuria al-byū-mi-nū′rē-ă **proteinuria** prō-tē-nū′rē-ă	presence of albumin in the urine; occurs in renal disease or in normal urine after heavy exercise
anuria an-yū′rē-ă	absence of urine formation
bacteriuria bak-tēr-ē-ū′rē-ă	presence of bacteria in the urine
dysuria dis-yū′rē-ă	painful urination
enuresis en-yū-rē′sis	to void urine; involuntary discharge of urine, most often refers to a lack of bladder control
nocturnal enuresis nok-ter′năl	bed wetting during sleep
hematuria hē-mă-tū′rē-ă	presence of blood in the urine (Fig. 15.3)
glucosuria gloo-kōs-yur′ē-ă	glucose (sugar) in the urine
incontinence in-kon′ti-nens	involuntary discharge of urine or feces
stress urinary incontinence (SUI)	involuntary discharge of urine at the time of cough, sneeze, and/or strained exercise
ketonuria kē-tō-nū′rē-ă	presence of ketone bodies in the urine
ketone bodies kē′tōn **ketone compounds**	acetone, beta-hydroxybutyric acid, and acetoacetic acid are products of metabolism that appear in the urine as a result of an abnormal utilization of carbohydrates; seen in uncontrolled diabetes and starvation

INCONTINENCE. The Latin word continent means to hold in, and the prefix in- means not. In Shakespeare's time, incontinently was used to mean immediately. Today, incontinence specifically refers to the inability to prevent the discharge of excretions, especially urine or feces.

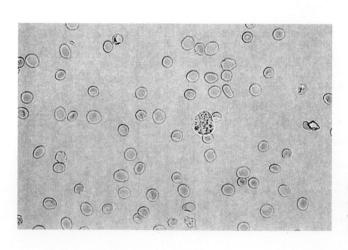

Figure 15.3 Hematuria. Microscopic urine showing a large number of red blood cells. One lone white blood cell is present in the center of the field.

Term	Meaning
nocturia nok-tū′rē-ă	urination at night
oliguria ol-i-gū′rē-ă	scanty production of urine
polyuria pol-ē-yū′rē-ă	condition of excessive urination
pyuria pī-yū′rē-ă	presence of white cells in the urine, usually indicating infection (Fig. 15.4)
urinary retention yūr′i-nār-ē rē-ten′shŭn	retention of urine owing to the inability to void (urinate) naturally because of spasm, obstruction, etc.
DIAGNOSTIC	
adult polycystic kidney disease (APKD)	inherited condition of multiple cysts that gradually form in the kidney, causing destruction of normal tissue that leads to renal failure—diagnosed in adults presenting with hypertension, kidney enlargement, and recurrent urinary tract infections
glomerulonephritis glō-mār′yū-lō-nef-rī′tis	form of nephritis involving the glomerulus
hydronephrosis hī′drō-ne-frō′sis	dilation and pooling of urine in the renal pelvis and calyces of one or both kidneys caused by an obstruction in the outflow of urine (Fig. 15.5)
nephritis ne-frī′tis	inflammation of the kidney
pyelonephritis pī′ĕ-lō-ne-frī′tis	inflammation of the renal pelvis

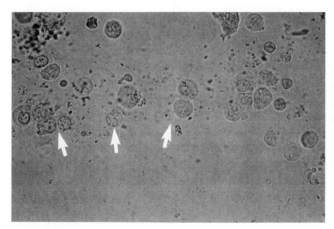

Figure 15.4 Pyuria. Microscopic urine showing the presence of white blood cells (*arrows*).

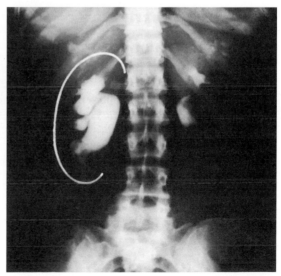

Figure 15.5 Collection of contrast media in the kidney displays an extraordinary amount of material, which indicates right-sided hydronephrosis caused by obstruction in the ureter.

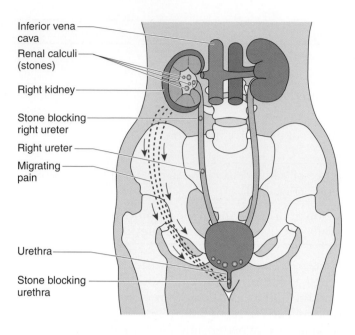

Inferior vena cava
Renal calculi (stones)
Right kidney
Stone blocking right ureter
Right ureter
Migrating pain
Urethra
Stone blocking urethra

Figure 15.6 Kidney stone formation.

Term	Meaning
nephrosis ne-frō´sis	degenerative disease of the renal tubules
nephrolithiasis nef´rō-li-thī´ă-sis	presence of renal stone or stones caused by mineral buildup in the kidneys—most commonly as a result of hyperuricuria (excessive amount of uric acid in the urine) or hypercalciuria (excessive amount of calcium in the urine) (Fig. 15.6)
cystitis sis´tī´tis	inflammation of the bladder
urethritis yū-rē-thrī´tis	inflammation of the urethra
urethrocystitis yū-rē´thrō-sis-tī´tis	inflammation of the urethra and bladder
urethral stenosis yū-rē´thrăl ste-nō´sis	narrowed condition of the urethra
urinary tract infection (UTI)	invasion of pathogenic organisms (commonly bacteria) in the structures of the urinary tract, especially the urethra and bladder; symptoms include dysuria, urinary frequency, and malaise
uremia yū-rē´mē-ă	excess of urea and other nitrogenous waste in the blood as a result of kidney failure
azotemia az-ō-tē´mē-ă	

Diagnostic Tests and Procedures

Test or Procedure	Explanation
cystometrogram sis-tō-met´rō-gram	record that measures urinary volume, bladder pressure, and capacity to evaluate urinary dysfunction such as incontinence

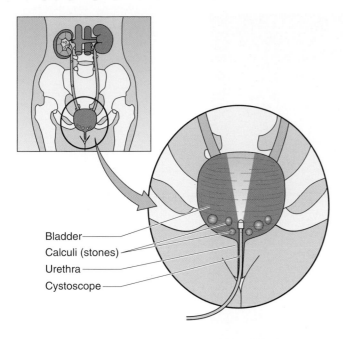

Bladder
Calculi (stones)
Urethra
Cystoscope

Figure 15.7. Cystoscopy.

Test or Procedure	Explanation
cystoscopy sis-tos′kŏ-pē	examination of the bladder using a rigid or flexible cystoscope (Fig. 15.7)
kidney biopsy (Bx) **renal biopsy**	removal of kidney tissue for pathological examination
radiography rā′dē-og′ră-fē	x-ray studies commonly used in urology
intravenous pyelogram (IVP) in′tră-vē′nŭs pī′el-ō-gram **intravenous urogram**	x-rays of the urinary tract taken after iodine is injected into the bloodstream and as the contrast passes through the kidney, revealing obstruction, evidence of trauma, etc. (see Fig. 15.5)
kidney, ureter, bladder (KUB)	abdominal x-ray of kidney, ureter, and bladder typically used as a scout film before doing an IVP (Fig. 15.8)
scout film	plain x-ray taken to detect any obvious pathology before further imaging (e.g., a KUB before an IVP)
renal angiogram (arteriogram) an′jē-ō-gram	x-ray of the renal artery made after injecting contrast material into a catheter in the artery
retrograde pyelogram (RP) ret′rō-grād	x-ray of the upper urinary tract taken after contrast medium is injected up to the kidney by way of a small catheter passed through a cystoscope—done to detect the presence of stones or obstruction
voiding (urinating) **cystourethrogram** **(VCU or VCUG)** sis-tō-yū-rēth′rō-gram	x-ray of the bladder and urethra taken during urination
abdominal sonogram son′ō-gram	ultrasound image of the urinary tract including the kidney, ureters, and bladder

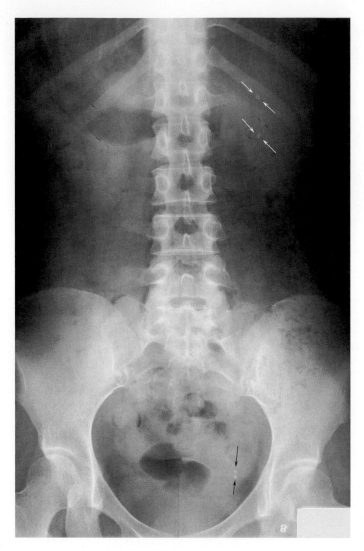

Figure 15.8 KUB showing kidney stones in ureters and bladder (*arrows*).

LABORATORY TESTING

Test or Procedure	Explanation
urinalysis (UA) yū-ri-nal′i-sis	physical, chemical, and microscopic examination of urine (Fig. 15.9)
specific gravity (SpGr)	measure of the kidney's ability to concentrate or dilute urine
pH	measure of the acidity or alkalinity of urine
glucose (sugar) glū′kōs	chemical test used to detect sugar in the urine, used most often to screen for diabetes
albumin (alb) al-byū′min **protein**	chemical test used to detect albumin in the urine
ketones	chemical test used to detect ketone bodies in the urine; if positive, fats are being utilized by the body instead of carbohydrates, which occurs in starvation or an unstable diabetic state

CENTRAL MEDICAL CENTER

211 Medical Center Drive • Central City, US 90000-1234 • PHONE: (012) 125-6784 • FAX: (012) 125-9999

11/02/20xx
13:49

NAME :   TEST, PATIENT   LOC: TEST   DOB: 2/2/XX   AGE: 38Y
MR#   :   TEST-221   SEX: M
ACCT #   :   H111111111

M63560 COLL: 11/2/20xx 13:24   REC: 11/2/20xx   13:25

URINE BASIC
   Color   STRAW
   Appearance   CLEAR
   Specific Gravity   1.010   [1.003 - 1.035]
   pH   5.5   [5.0 - 9.0]
   Protein   NEG   [0 - 10]   MG/DL
   Glucose   NEG   [NEG]
   Ketones   NEG   [NEG]
   Bilirubin   NEG   [NEG]
   Urine Occult Blood   NEG   [NEG]
   Nitrites   NEG

URINE MICROSCOPIC
   Epithelial Cells   3 to 4   /HPF
   WBCs   0 to 1   /HPF
   RBCs   0   /HPF
   Bacteria   0
   Mucous Threads   0

TEST, PATIENT   TEST-221   END OF REPORT   PAGE 1
11/02/20xx   13:49   INTERIM REPORT
INTERIM REPORT COMPLETED

Figure 15.9 Sample urinalysis report.

Test or Procedure	Explanation
occult blood, urine	chemical test used to detect hidden blood in the urine resulting from red blood cell hemolysis—indicates bleeding in the kidneys (occult = hidden)
bilirubin bil-i-rū′bin	chemical test used to detect bilirubin in the urine—seen in gallbladder and liver disease
urobilinogen yūr-ō-bī-lin′ō-jen	chemical test used to detect bile pigment in the urine—increased amounts seen in gallbladder and liver disease
nitrite nī′trīt	chemical test used to detect bacteria in the urine
microscopic findings mī-krō-skop′ik	microscopic identification of abnormal constituents in the urine (e.g., red blood cells, white blood cells, casts) as reported per high- or low-power field (hpf or lpf) (see Figs. 15.3 and 15.4)
urine culture and sensitivity (C&S)	isolation of a urine specimen in a culture medium that propagates the growth of microorganisms; organisms that grow in the culture are identified, and drugs to which they are sensitive are listed
blood urea nitrogen (BUN) yū-rē′ănī′trō-jen	blood test to determine the level of urea in the blood—a high BUN indicates the kidney's inability to excrete urea
creatinine, serum krē-at′i-nēn sēr′ŭm	test to determine the level of creatinine in the blood—useful in assessing kidney function
creatinine, urine	test to determine the level of creatinine in the urine
creatinine clearance testing	measurements of the level of creatinine in the blood and a 24-hour urine specimen to determine the rate that creatinine is "cleared" from the blood by the kidneys

Operative Terms

Term	Meaning
urologic endoscopic surgery yū-rō-loj′ik-ăl	use of specialized endoscopes (e.g., resectoscope) within the urinary tract to perform various surgical procedures, such as resection of a tumor, repair of an obstruction, stone retrieval, or placement of a stent (Fig. 15.10)
resectoscope rē-sek′tō-skōp	urologic endoscope sent through the urethra to resect (cut and remove) lesions of the bladder, urethra, or prostate
intracorporeal lithotripsy in′tră-kōr-pō′rē-ăl lith′ō-trip-sē	method of destroying stones within the urinary tract using electrical energy discharges transmitted to a probe within a flexible endoscope—most commonly used to pulverize bladder stones (Fig. 15.11)
nephrotomy ne-frot′ō-mē	incision into the kidney

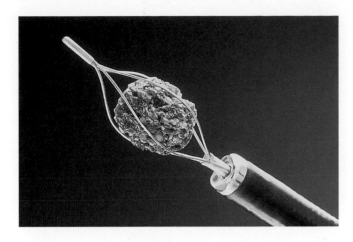

Figure 15.10   Stone basket used in kidney stone retrieval.

Term	Meaning
nephrorrhaphy nef-rōr′ă-fē	suture of an injured kidney
nephrolithotomy nef′rō-li-thot′ō-mē	incision into the kidney for the removal of stones
nephrectomy ne-frek′tō-mē	excision of a kidney
pyeloplasty pī′e-lō-plas-tē	surgical reconstruction of the renal pelvis
stent placement	use of a device to hold open vessels or tubes (e.g., an obstructed ureter) (Fig. 15.12)
kidney transplantation **renal transplantation**	transfer of a kidney from the body of one person (donor) to another (recipient) (Fig. 15.13)
urinary diversion	creation of a temporary or permanent diversion of the urinary tract to provide a new passage through which urine exits the body—used to treat defects or disease such as bladder cancer

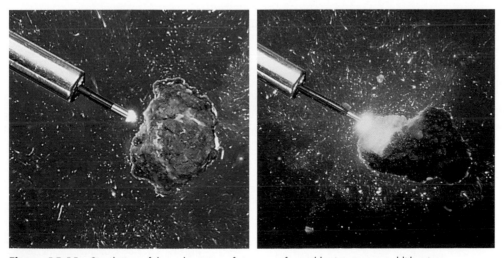

Figure 15.11   Simulation of the pulverizing of stones performed by intracorporeal lithotripsy.

Before

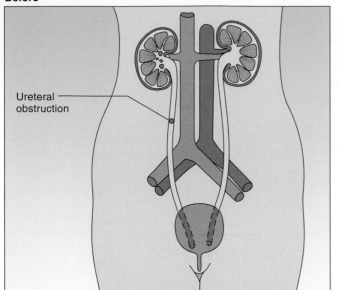

Ureteral obstruction

After

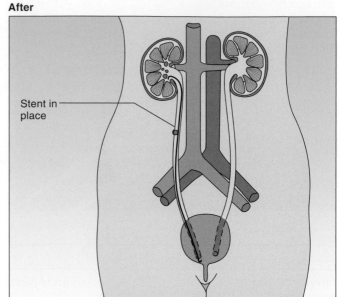

Stent in place

Figure 15.12 Placement of a double-J stent to relieve ureteral obstruction.

Term	Meaning
common types of urinary diversion:	
noncontinent ileal conduit non-kon′ti-nent il′ē-ăl kon′dū-it	removal of a portion of the ileum to use as a conduit to which the ureters are attached at one end; the other end is brought through an opening (stoma) created in the abdomen—urine drains continually into an external appliance (bag) (Fig 15.14)
continent urostomy kon′ti-nent yūr-os′tō-mē	internal reservoir (pouch) constructed from a segment of intestine that diverts urine through an opening (stoma) that is brought through the abdominal wall; a valve is created internally to prevent leakage, and the patient empties the pouch by catheterization
orthotopic bladder (neobladder)	bladder constructed from portions of intestine connected to the urethra, allowing "natural" voiding

__Continent__ refers to the ability to hold or retain urine. __Noncontinent__ indicates that urine cannot be held and drains continually.

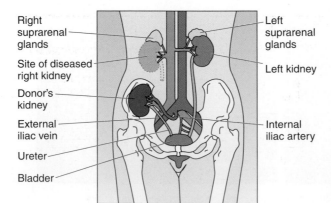

Right suprarenal glands

Site of diseased right kidney

Donor's kidney

External iliac vein

Ureter

Bladder

Left suprarenal glands

Left kidney

Internal iliac artery

Figure 15.13 Common site for donor kidney transplantation.

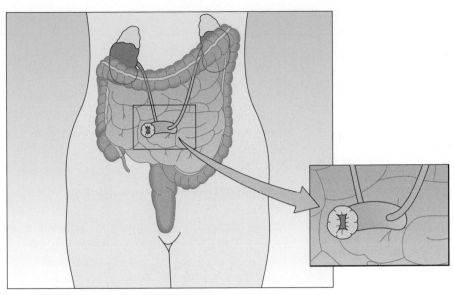

Figure 15.14   Urostomy: ileal conduit.

Therapeutic Terms

Term	Meaning
extracorporeal shock wave lithotripsy (ESWL) eks′tră-kōr-pō′rē-ăl lith′ō-trip-sē	procedure using ultrasound to penetrate the body from outside and bombard and disintegrate a stone within—most commonly used to treat urinary stones above the bladder (Fig. 15.15)
kidney dialysis dī-al′i-sis	methods of filtering impurities from the blood to replace the function of one or both kidneys due to renal failure
hemodialysis hē-mō-dī-al′i-sis	method to remove impurities by pumping the patient's blood through a dialyzer, the specialized filter of the artificial kidney machine (hemodialyzer)

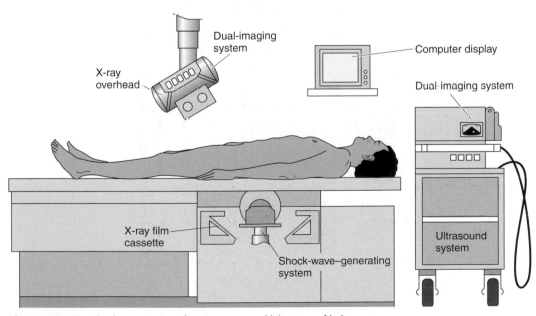

Figure 15.15   Shock wave system for extracorporeal lithotripsy of kidney stones.

Term	Meaning
peritoneal dialysis per-i-tō-nē'ăl	method of removing impurities using the peritoneum as the filter; catheter insertion in the peritoneal cavity is required to deliver cleansing fluid (dialysate) that is washed in and out in cycles
Kegel exercises	specific exercises that strengthen the muscles of the pelvic floor to maintain proper organ placement and retain urine
urinary catheterization	methods of placing a tube into the bladder to drain or collect urine
common types: **straight catheter**	inserted through the urethra into the bladder to relieve urinary retention or collect a sterile specimen of urine for testing—removed immediately after the procedure
Foley catheter	indwelling catheter inserted through the urethra into the bladder; includes a collection system that allows urine to be drained into a bag—can remain in place for an extended time
suprapubic catheter	indwelling catheter inserted directly into the bladder through an abdominal incision above the pubic bone; includes a collection system that allows urine to be drained into a bag—used in patients requiring long-term catheterization
COMMON THERAPEUTIC DRUG CLASSIFICATIONS	
analgesic an-ăl-jē'zik	drug that relieves pain
antibiotic an'tē-bī-ot'ik	drug that kills or inhibits the growth of microorganisms
antispasmodic an'tē-spaz-mod'ik	drug that relieves spasm
diuretic dī-yū-ret'ik	drug that increases the secretion of urine

Summary of Chapter 15 Acronyms/Abbreviations

alb	albumin	KUB	kidney, ureter, bladder
APKD	adult polycystic kidney disease	RP	retrograde pyelogram
BUN	blood urea nitrogen	SpGr	specific gravity
Bx	biopsy	SUI	stress urinary incontinence
C&S	urine culture and sensitivity	UA	urinalysis
ESWL	extracorporeal shock wave lithotripsy	UTI	urinary tract infection
IVP	intravenous pyelogram	VCU, VCUG	voiding cystourethrogram

PRACTICE EXERCISES

For the following terms, on the lines below the term, write out the indicated word parts: prefixes (P), combining forms (CF), roots (R), and suffixes (S). Then define the word.

example

pericystitis

_____ / _____ / _____
P   R   S

<u>peri/cyst/itis</u>
P R S
DEFINITION: around/bladder or sac/inflammation

1. vesicoureteric

_____ / _____ / _____
CF   R   S

DEFINITION: _____

2. bacteriosis

_____ / _____
R   S

DEFINITION: _____

3. transurethral

_____ / _____ / _____
P   R   S

DEFINITION: _____

4. urogram

_____ / _____
CF   S

DEFINITION: _____

5. urethrocystitis

_____ / _____ / _____
CF   R   S

DEFINITION: _____

6. nephroptosis

_____ / _____
CF   S

DEFINITION: _____

7. polydipsia

_____ / _____ / _____
P   R   S

DEFINITION: _____

8. glomerulosclerosis

_____ / _____ / _____
         CF   R   S

DEFINITION: _____

9. pyonephritis

_____ / _____ / _____
         CF   R   S

DEFINITION: _____

10. urology

_____ / _____
         CF   S

DEFINITION: _____

11. ureterovesicostomy

_____ / _____ / _____
         CF   CF   S

DEFINITION: _____

12. glycorrhea

_____ / _____
         CF   S

DEFINITION: _____

13. meatotomy

_____ / _____
         CF   S

DEFINITION: _____

14. pyelonephrosis

_____ / _____ / _____
         CF   R   S

DEFINITION: _____

15. cystoscopy

_____ / _____
         CF   S

DEFINITION: _____

16. suprarenal

_____ / _____ / _____
         P   R   S

DEFINITION: _____

17. nephrolithiasis

_____ / _____ / _____
         CF   R   S

DEFINITION: _____

18. ureterocele

_____ / _____
          CF   S

DEFINITION: _____

19. albuminous

_____ / _____
          R   S

DEFINITION: _____

20. pyelography

_____ / _____
          CF   S

DEFINITION: _____

Using nephr/o, the Greek combining form meaning kidney, identify the medical term for the following:

21. _____ inflammation of the kidney

22. _____ degenerative condition of the kidney

23. _____ incision in the kidney

24. _____ suture of a kidney

25. _____ removal of the kidney

26. _____ incision into the kidney for the removal of stones

Complete the following:

27. urethral _____osis = a narrowed condition of the urethra

28. extracorporeal shock wave _____ = procedure for disintegration of kidney stones

29. _____ catheter = indwelling catheter inserted in the bladder through an abdominal incision above the pubic bone

30. _____scope = specialized endoscope to remove lesions from the bladder, prostate gland, and urethra

31. _____ exercises = strengthen muscles of the pelvic floor to maintain proper organ placement and retain urine

32. _____blood = hidden blood

33. _____ = a record that measures urinary volume, bladder pressure, and capacity

34. peritoneal _____ = method of replacing the function of the kidneys to removing impurities from the blood using the peritoneum as a filter

35. _____ film = plain x-ray taken to detect obvious pathology before further imaging

Identify the medical term for the following:

36. _____ inflammation of the bladder

37. _____ involuntary discharge of urine or feces

38. _____ involuntary discharge of urine

39. _____ bed wetting during sleep

40. _____ dilation and pooling of urine in the kidney caused by obstruction of outflow of urine

41. _____ inherited condition of multiple cysts that gradually form in the kidney in adult life

Using the suffix -uria, name the following conditions of urine:

42. _____ urinating at night

43. _____ scanty urination

44. _____ painful urination

45. _____ presence of ketone bodies in the urine

46. _____ presence of blood in the urine

47. _____ presence of pus (white cells/infection) in the urine

Match the following:

48. _____ sugar   a. cyst/o

49. _____ proteinuria   b. bacteriuria

50. _____ uremia   c. renal Bx

51. _____ ren/o   d. albuminuria

52. _____ vesic/o   e. neobladder

53. _____ diuretic   f. Foley

54. _____ kidney biopsy   g. glyc/o

55. _____ nitrite   h. nephr/o

56. _____ catheter   i. azotemia

57. _____ urinary diversion   j. urobilinogen

58. _____ bile pigment   k. urination

Define the following abbreviations:

59. alb _____

60. IVP_____

61. ESWL _____

62. UTI_____

63. SUI_____

64. BUN_____

For each of the following, circle the combining form that corresponds to the meaning given:

65. **urine**	hydr/o	ur/o	ren/o
66. **thirst**	dips/o	crin/o	hidr/o
67. **pus**	pyel/o	py/o	albumin/o
68. **bladder**	cyt/o	vesic/o	nephr/o
69. **protein**	albumin/o	lip/o	bacteri/o
70. **kidney**	hepat/o	cyst/o	nephr/o
71. **opening**	or/o	meat/o	orth/o
72. **basin**	meat/o	vesic/o	pyel/o
73. **stone**	scler/o	lip/o	lith/o

Write in the missing words on the blank lines in the following illustration of the urinary anatomy.

74–78.

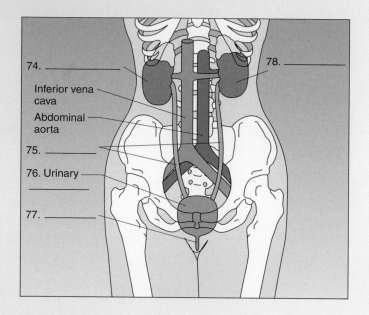

74. _____

Inferior vena cava

Abdominal aorta

75. _____

76. Urinary _____

77. _____

78. _____

For each of the following, circle the correct spelling of the term:

79. cystascope   cystoskope   cystoscope

80. pyleogram   pyelogram   pielogram

81. oliguria   oleguria   oligouria

82. hydronefrosis   hidronephrosis   hydronephrosis

83. azootemia   azothemia   azotemia

84. urinalysis   urinelysis   uranalysis

85. glowmerular   glomerular   glomarular

86. nefrectomy   nephrecktomy   nephrectomy

87. diuretic   dyuretic   diuretik

88. hemadialysis   hemodialysis   hemidialysis

89. cathetersation   catheterization   cathterization

Give the noun that was used to form the following adjectives:

90. urinary _____

91. glomerular _____

92. meatal _____

93. uremic _____

94. urethral _____

95. nephrotic _____

Write the abbreviation for the following terms:

96. urinalysis _____

97. urine culture and sensitivity _____

98. retrograde pyelogram _____

99. x-ray of kidneys, ureters, and bladder _____

100. voiding cystourethrogram _____

MEDICAL RECORD ANALYSES

MEDICAL RECORD 15.1

S: This 70 y.o. female has had polyuria, nocturia, and dysuria × 2-3 days. She had a
similar infection 6 months ago and was treated with Macrobid, 50 mg, qid × 3d.
She has occasional stress incontinence with hard sneezing.

O: The patient is afebrile. UA shows a trace of leukocytes and blood

A: R/O recurrent UTI

P: C&S
Cipro 500 mg tab po bid pending culture
pt instructed to ↑ fluid intake and call for culture results in 48 h

1. What is the patient's CC?

  a. the presence of red and white blood cells in
  her urine

  b. a urinary tract infection

  c. pain when she urinates with the need to go
  often, even at night

  d. urinary tract infection

2. What were the objective findings?

  a. culture showed leukocytes and blood in the
  urine

  b. urinalysis indicated red and white blood cells
  present in urine

  c. bladder infection

  d. return of bladder infection

3. What was the doctor's impression?

  a. there were leukocytes and blood in the
  patient's urine

  b. the patient has pain when she urinates with
  the need to go often, even at night

  c. the pain has a bladder infection

  d. the patient may have another bladder
  infection

4. Which medical terms describe the UA findings?

  a. pyuria and hematuria

  b. dysuria and enuresis

  c. bacteriuria and hematuria

  d. bacteriuria and nocturia

5. To what does C&S refer?

  a. a condition of urinary stress

  b. the isolation of microorganisms in the urine

  c. inflammation of the bladder

  d. physical, chemical, and microscopic study of
  urine

6. How should the Cipro be administered?

  a. two, by mouth every day

  b. one, by mouth two times a day

  c. one, by mouth three times a day

  d. one, by mouth four times a day

7. Was the patient's temperature elevated?

  a. yes

  b. no

  c. nothing is stated about the patient's
  temperature

MEDICAL RECORD 15.2

Charles Mercier had urination problems and abdominal pain when he saw his doctor, who referred him to Central Medical Center for a possible kidney infection. Dr. Zlatkin performed surgery, and Mr. Mercier was soon doing fine and was discharged. As planned, he later returned for surgical removal of a device that had been temporarily placed during the first surgery.

Directions

Read Medical Record 15.2 for Mr. Mercier (pages 507–508) and answer the following questions. The first record is the discharge summary from the first surgery, dictated by Dr. Zlatkin. The second record is the operative report for Mr. Mercier's return surgery 6 weeks later, also dictated by Dr. Zlatkin.

QUESTIONS ABOUT MEDICAL RECORD 15.2

Write your answers in the spaces provided.

1. Below are medical terms used in this record you have not yet encountered in this text. Underline each where it appears in the record and define below:

   stent (double J) _____

   drain (Jackson-Pratt)_____

   lithotomy position _____

   ureteral catheter_____

   patency _____

2. In your own words, not using medical terminology, briefly describe the history of Mr. Mercier's medical problems identified in the "Discharge Summary":

   _____

   _____

   _____

3. Put the following events reported in the "Discharge Summary" in chronological order by numbering them from 1 to 5:

   _____ removal of drain

   _____ reconstruction of renal pelvis

   _____ difficulty with micturition

   _____ urine test for microorganisms

   _____ insertion of stent

4. While at home after the operation, Mr. Mercier is instructed to do two things and *not* to do three things. List them below:

Mr. Mercier should _____

_____

Mr. Mercier should not_____

_____

5. When Mr. Mercier returned 6 weeks later for follow-up surgery, describe in your own words the preoperative diagnosis:

_____

_____

_____

6. During the second surgery, an endoscopic procedure and two different x-ray procedures were used to visualize internal structures. List and define each procedure and describe the findings:

Procedure	*Definition*	*Finding*
_____	_____	_____
_____	_____	_____
_____	_____	_____
_____	_____	_____
_____	_____	_____
_____	_____	_____
_____	_____	_____
_____	_____	_____
_____	_____	_____
_____	_____	_____

7. The first surgery included insertion of a specialized device that was then removed in the second surgery. What was this device, and what function did it perform during the time between the two surgeries?

_____

_____

_____

8. In the second surgery, did Mr. Mercier experience any complications? Write the sentence that supports your answer:

_____

_____

CENTRAL MEDICAL CENTER

211 Medical Center Drive • Central City, US 90000-1234

DISCHARGE SUMMARY

DATE OF ADMISSION: 10/25/20xx   DATE OF DISCHARGE: 10/29/20xx

ADMITTING DIAGNOSIS:
Left ureteropelvic junction obstruction.

DISCHARGE DIAGNOSIS:
Left ureteropelvic junction obstruction.

PROCEDURE PERFORMED:
Left dismembered pyeloplasty and placement of stent.

BRIEF SUMMARY:
The patient is a 19-year-old male who was admitted to the hospital a month ago with left pyelonephritis. He was found to have a left ureteropelvic junction obstruction. The patient was brought to the hospital at this time for repair of the moderately to severely obstructed left kidney. A preoperative urine culture was sterile. The patient underwent the procedure without complication. A double-J stent was placed. The Jackson-Pratt drain was removed on the second postoperative day because of minimal drainage. The patient initially had urinary retention, but this resolved by the third postoperative day. He was doing fine at the time of discharge. His condition on discharge is good.

INSTRUCTIONS TO THE PATIENT:
1) Regular diet. 2) No heavy lifting, straining, or driving an automobile for six weeks from the day of surgery. He should also keep the incision relatively dry this week. 3) Follow-up in my office in three weeks. 4) It is anticipated the stent will remain indwelling for six weeks and then will be removed cystoscopically at that time. 5) Discharge medication is Tylenol #3, 1-2 q 4 h p.r.n. pain.

L. Zlatkin, M.D.

LZ:mr

D: 10/29/20xx
T: 10/30/20xx

DISCHARGE SUMMARY	PT. NAME:	MERCIER, CHARLES F.
	ID NO:	IP-392689
	ROOM NO:	444
	ATT. PHYS:	L. ZLATKIN, M.D.

Medical Record 15.2

CENTRAL MEDICAL CENTER

211 Medical Center Drive • Central City, US 90000-1234

OPERATIVE REPORT

DATE: December 7, 20xx

PREOPERATIVE DIAGNOSIS: Congenital left ureteropelvic junction obstruction status post pyeloplasty. Indwelling left ureteral stent.

POSTOPERATIVE DIAGNOSIS: Congenital left ureteropelvic junction obstruction status post pyeloplasty. Indwelling left ureteral stent, removed.

OPERATION: Cystoscopy, removal of left ureteral stent, and left retrograde pyelogram.

PROCEDURE: The patient was identified, was placed on the operating table, and was administered a general anesthetic. He was placed in the lithotomy position, and a KUB was obtained. The genitalia were prepped and draped in a sterile fashion. After reviewing the KUB, it was noted at this time that the position of the stent was normal. Cystoscopy was performed with a #22 French cystoscope. The stent was identified coming from the left ureteral orifice, and the end was grasped with forceps and removed through the cystoscope. A #8 French cone-tipped ureteral catheter was then placed in the left ureteral orifice and passed to 10 cm. Then, 20 cm^3 of contrast was injected into a left collecting system. A film was exposed, and this showed patency without extravasation at the left ureteropelvic junction. There was some filling of calyces and partial filling of the dilated renal pelvis. A drainage film was subsequently obtained showing complete emptying of the pelvis and partial emptying of the mid and distal ureters. Dilated calyces were noted in the kidney. The patient was allowed to awaken and was returned to the recovery room in satisfactory condition. There were no intraoperative complications. He had no bleeding. The patient did receive 1 gm Ancef one-half hour prior to the onset of the procedure.

L. Zlatkin, M.D.

LZ:mr
D: 12/07/20xx
T: 12/08/20xx

OPERATIVE REPORT	PT. NAME:	MERCIER, CHARLES F.
	ID NO:	OP-912689
	ROOM NO:	ASC
	ATT. PHYS:	L. ZLATKIN, M.D.

Medical Record 15.2 *Continued.*

Chapter 16

Male Reproductive System

OBJECTIVES

After completion of this chapter you will be able to

- Define common term components used in relation to the male reproductive system

- Describe the basic functions of the male reproductive system

- Define the basic anatomical terms referring to the male reproductive system

- Define common symptomatic and diagnostic terms referring to the male reproductive system

- List the common diagnostic tests and procedures related to the male reproductive system

- Define common operative terms referring to the male reproductive system

- Identify common therapeutic terms including drug classifications related to the male reproductive system

- Explain terms and abbreviations used in documenting medical records involving the male reproductive system

Combining Forms

Combining Form	Meaning	Example
balan/o	glans penis	balanoplasty bal′an-ō-plas-tē
epididym/o	epididymis	epididymitis ep-i-did-i-mī′tis
orch/o	testis or testicle	orchitis ōr-kī′tis
orchi/o		orchiopexy ōr′kē-ō-pek′sē
orchid/o		orchidectomy ōr-ki-dek′tō-mē
test/o		testicle tes′tĭ-kl
perine/o	perineum	perineal per′i-nē′ăl

ORCHIO. Orchio is a Greek root for testicle, so named for the resemblance of the gland to the root of the orchid plant. At one time, orchid root was used to treat diseases of the testicle.

Combining Form	Meaning	Example
prostat/o	prostate	prostatodynia pros′tă-tō-din′ē-ă
sperm/o	sperm (seed)	oligospermia ol-i-gō-sper′mē-ă
spermat/o		spermatic sper-mat′ik
vas/o	vessel	vasorrhaphy vas-ōr′ă-fē

Male Reproductive System Overview

The male reproductive system includes the *scrotum, testes, epididymides, vas deferens, seminal vesicles, prostate gland, bulbourethral glands, urethra,* and *penis* (Fig. 16.1). These parts produce and maintain *sperm,* the male reproductive cells, and introduce them into the female reproductive tract for the purpose of fertilizing the female ovum. The male reproductive organs also secrete certain hormones necessary for the maintenance of secondary sexual characteristics in the male.

TESTICLE. Testicle is from the Latin testis, a word that also meant a witness or one who testifies. The presence of the testicles was evidence of virility, and it is said that under Roman law, no man could witness in court unless his testicles were present. An oath was taken with a hand on the testicles. The testicles are also associated with the swearing of oaths in the Old Testament of the Bible.

PENIS. Penis is a Latin word for tail. The name is also derived from pendere, meaning to hang down. The Romans had a great many terms for the male organ—e.g., cauda (tail), clava (club), gladius (sword), radix (root), ramus (branch), and vomer (plough). Penis was adopted as the anatomical term, and it has been used in English since the 17th century.

Anatomical Terms

Term	Meaning
scrotum skrō′tŭm	a bag; skin-covered pouch in the groin that is divided into two sacs, each containing a testis and an epididymis
testis (testicle) tes′tis	one of the two male reproductive glands, located in the scrotum, that produces sperm and the male hormone testosterone
sperm **spermatozoon** sper′mă-tō-zō′on	male gamete or sex cell produced in the testes that unites with the ovum in the female to produce offspring
epididymis ep-i-did′i-mis	coiled duct on top and at the side of the testis that stores sperm before emission
penis pē′nis	erectile tissue covered with skin that contains the urethra for urination and ducts for the secretion of seminal fluid (semen)
glans penis glanz	bulging structure at the distal end of the penis (glans = acorn)
prepuce prē′pūs	foreskin; loose casing covering the glans penis—removed by circumcision
vas deferens vas def′er-ens	duct that carries sperm from the epididymis to the ejaculatory duct (vas = vessel; deferens = carrying away)
seminal vesicle sem′i-năl	one of two sac-like structures lying behind the bladder and connected to the vas deferens on each side—secretes an alkaline substance into the semen to enable the sperm to live longer

THE MALE REPRODUCTIVE SYSTEM

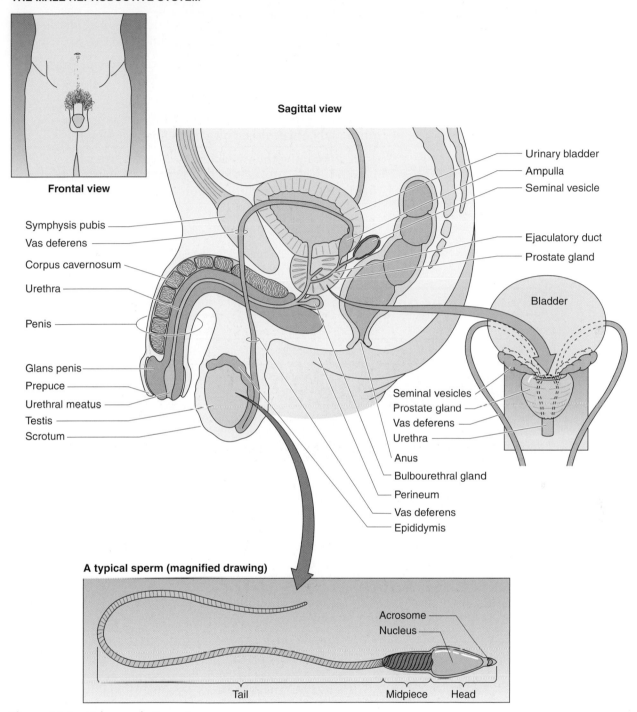

Figure 16.1   Male reproductive system.

Term	Meaning
semen sē′men	mixture of the secretions of the testes, seminal vesicles, prostate, and bulbourethral glands discharged from the male urethra during orgasm (semen = seed)
ejaculatory duct ē-jak′yū-lă-tōr-ē	duct formed by the union of the vas deferens with the duct of the seminal vesicle; its fluid is carried into the urethra

Term	Meaning
prostate gland pros′tāt	trilobular gland that encircles the urethra just below the bladder—secretes an alkaline fluid into the semen
bulbourethral glands (Cowper glands) bŭl′bō-yū-rē′thrăl	pair of glands below the prostate with ducts opening into the urethra—adds a viscid (sticky) fluid to the semen
perineum per′i-nē′ŭm	external region between the scrotum and anus in a male and between the vulva and anus in a female
spermatic cord sper-mat′ik kōrd	cord containing the vas deferens, arteries, veins, lymph vessels, and nerves that extends from the internal inguinal ring through the inguinal canal to each testicle

Symptomatic and Diagnostic Terms

Term	Meaning
SYMPTOMATIC	
aspermia ā-sper′mē-ă	inability to secrete or ejaculate sperm
azoospermia ā-zō-ō-sper′mē-ă	semen without living spermatozoa, a sign of infertility in the male (zoo = life)
oligospermia ol-i-gō-sper′mē-ă	scanty production and expulsion of sperm
mucopurulent discharge myū-kō-pū′rū-lent	drainage of mucus and pus
DIAGNOSTIC	
anorchism an-ōr′kizm	absence of one or both testes
balanitis bal-ă-nī′tis	inflammation of glans penis
cryptorchism krip-tōr′kizm	undescended testicle; failure of a testis to descend into the scrotal sac during fetal development; it most often remains lodged in the abdomen or inguinal canal, requiring surgical repair (crypt = to hide) (Fig. 16.2)
epididymitis ep-i-did-i-mī′tis	inflammation of the epididymis
hydrocele hī′drō-sēl	hernia of fluid in the testis or tubes leading from the testis (Fig. 16.3B)
hypospadias hī′pō-spā′dē-ăs	congenital opening of the male urethra on the undersurface of the penis (spadias = to draw away) (Fig. 16.4)

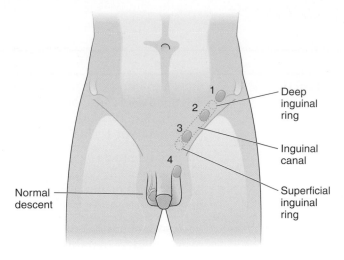

Figure 16.2 Cryptorchism. Four degrees of incomplete descent of the testis. 1. In the abdominal cavity close to the deep inguinal ring. 2. In the inguinal canal. 3. At the superficial inguinal ring. 4. In the upper part of the scrotum.

Deep inguinal ring

Inguinal canal

Superficial inguinal ring

Normal descent

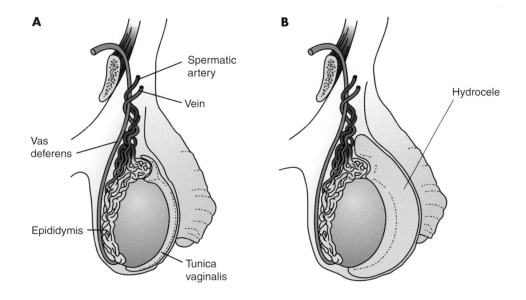

A

Spermatic artery

Vein

Vas deferens

Epididymis

Tunica vaginalis

B

Hydrocele

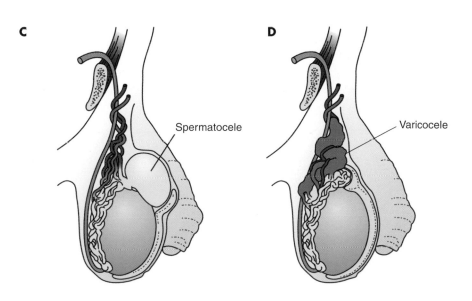

C

Spermatocele

D

Varicocele

Figure 16.3 A. Normal testes and appendages. **B.** Hydrocele. **C.** Spermatocele. **D.** Varicocele.

Term	Meaning
erectile dysfunction (ED)	failure to initiate or maintain an erection until ejaculation because of physical or psychological dysfunction; formerly termed impotence (im = not; potis = able)
Peyronie disease pā-rōn′ē	disorder characterized by a buildup of hardened fibrous tissue in the corpus cavernosum causing pain and a defective curvature of the penis, especially during erection (Fig. 16.5)
phimosis fī-mō′sis	narrowed condition of the prepuce (foreskin) resulting in its inability to be drawn over the glans penis, often leading to infection—commonly requires circumcision (phimo means muzzle) (Fig. 16.6)
benign prostatic hyperplasia/hypertrophy (BPH) bē-nīn′ pros-tat′ik hī-pĕr-plā′zē-ă/hī-per′trō-fē	enlargement of the prostate gland; frequently seen in older men, causing urinary obstruction (Fig. 16.7)
prostate cancer	malignancy of the prostate gland
prostatitis pros-tă-tī′tis	inflammation of the prostate
spermatocele sper′mă-tō-sēl	painless, benign cystic mass containing sperm lying above and posterior to the testicle, but separate from it (see Fig. 16.3C)

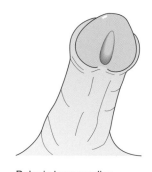

Balanic hypospadias

Figure 16.4 Hypospadias.

Penile hypospadias

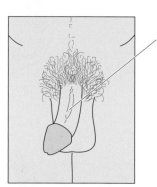

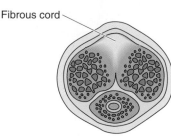

Fibrous cord

Transverse section

Figure 16.5 Peyronie disease.

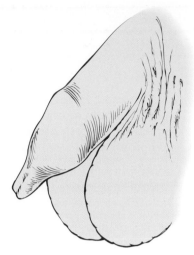

Figure 16.6 Phimosis.

Term	Meaning
testicular cancer tes-tik′yŭ-lăr	malignant tumor in one or both testicles commonly developing from the germ cells that produce sperm—classified in two groups according to growth potential
seminoma sem-i-nō′mă	most common type of testicular tumor, composed of immature germ cells—highly treatable with early detection
nonseminomas	testicular tumors arising from more mature germ cells that have a tendency to be more aggressive than seminomas; often develop earlier in life (includes choriocarcinoma, embryonal carcinoma, teratoma, and yolk sac tumors)
varicocele var′i-kō-sēl	enlarged, swollen, herniated veins near the testis (varico = twisted vein) (Fig. 16.3D)

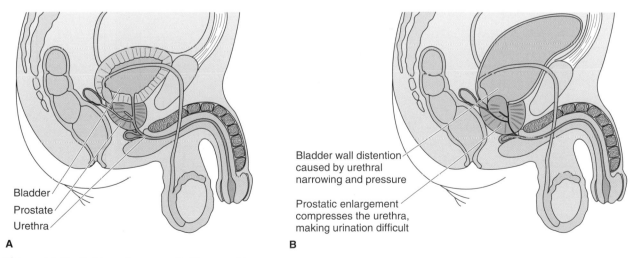

Bladder
Prostate
Urethra

Bladder wall distention caused by urethral narrowing and pressure

Prostatic enlargement compresses the urethra, making urination difficult

A

B

Figure 16.7 **A.** Normal prostate. **B.** Hypertrophic prostate.

Term	Meaning
SEXUALLY TRANSMITTED DISEASE (STD)	
Major Bacterial STDs bak-tēr′ē-ăl	
chlamydia kla-mid′ē-ă	most common sexually transmitted bacterial infection in North America; often occurs with no symptoms and is treated only after it has spread
gonorrhea gon-ō-rē′ă	contagious inflammation of the genital mucous membranes caused by invasion of the gonococcus, *Neisseria gonorrhoeae* (gono = seed; rrhea = discharge)
syphilis sif′i-lis	infectious disease caused by a spirochete transmitted by direct intimate contact that may involve any organ or tissue over time; usually manifested first on the skin with the appearance of small, painless red papules that erode and form bloodless ulcers called chancres (Fig. 16.8)
Major Viral STDs vī′răl	
hepatitis B virus (HBV) hep-ă-tī′tis	virus that causes inflammation of the liver as a result of transmission through any body fluid, including vaginal secretions, semen, and blood
herpes simplex virus type 2 (HSV-2) her′pēz	virus that causes ulcer-like lesions of the genital and anorectal skin and mucosa; after initial infection, the virus lies dormant in the nerve cell root and may recur at times of stress (see Fig. 17.9)

 GONORRHEA. Derived from the Greek root gono, meaning offspring or seed, and the suffix -rrhea, meaning flow or discharge, the word literally means flow of semen. It was once thought that the urethral discharge characteristic of the infection was a leakage of semen. Although the reasoning is wrong, attempts to change the term failed because its usage was too firmly established.

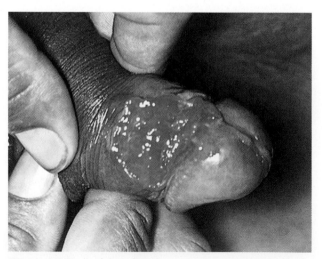

Figure 16.8 Syphilitic chancre.

Term	Meaning
human immunodeficiency virus (HIV) im′yū-nō-dē-fish′en-sē	virus that causes acquired immunodeficiency syndrome (AIDS), which permits various opportunistic infections, malignancies, and neurological diseases; contracted through exposure to contaminated blood or body fluid (e.g., semen, vaginal secretions)
human papilloma virus (HPV) pap-i-lō′mă **condyloma acuminatum** kon-di-lō′mah ă-kyū′mĭ-nāt′ŭm **pl. condylomata acuminata** kon-di-lō′mah′tă ă-kyū′mĭ-nah′tă	virus transmitted by direct sexual contact that causes an infection that can occur on the skin or mucous membranes of the genitals; on the skin, the lesions appear as cauliflower-like warts, and on the mucous membranes, they have a flat appearance (also known as venereal or genital warts) (see Fig. 17.10)

Diagnostic Tests and Procedures

Test or Procedure	Explanation
biopsy (Bx)	tissue sampling used to identify neoplasia
biopsy of the prostate	needle biopsy of the prostate often performed using ultrasound guidance (see Fig. 16.10)
testicular biopsy tes-tik′yū-lăr	biopsy of a testicle
digital rectal exam (DRE)	insertion of a finger into the male rectum to palpate the rectum and prostate (Fig. 16.9)

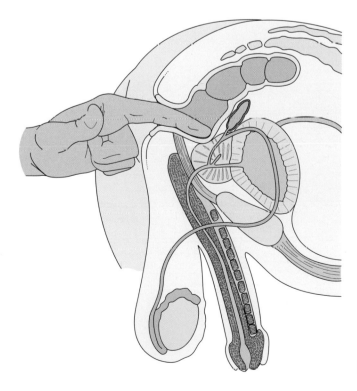

Figure 16.9 Digital rectal examination.

Test or Procedure	Explanation
prostate-specific antigen (PSA) test an'ti-jen	blood test used to screen for prostate cancer; an elevated level of the antigen indicates the possible presence of tumor
urethrogram yū-rē'thrō-gram	x-ray of the urethra and prostate
semen analysis sē'men	study of semen, including a sperm count, with observation of morphology (form) and motility; usually performed to rule out male infertility
endorectal (transrectal) sonogram of the prostate en'dō-rek'tăl trans-rek'tăl	scan of the prostate made after introducing an ultrasonic transducer into the rectum—also used to guide needle biopsy (Fig. 16.10)

Operative Terms

Term	Meaning
circumcision ser-kŭm-sizh'ŭn	removal of the foreskin (prepuce), exposing the glans penis
epididymectomy ep'i-did-i-mek'tō-mē	removal of an epididymis
orchiectomy ōr-kē-ek'tō-mē orchidectomy ōr-ki-dek'tō-mē	removal of a testicle

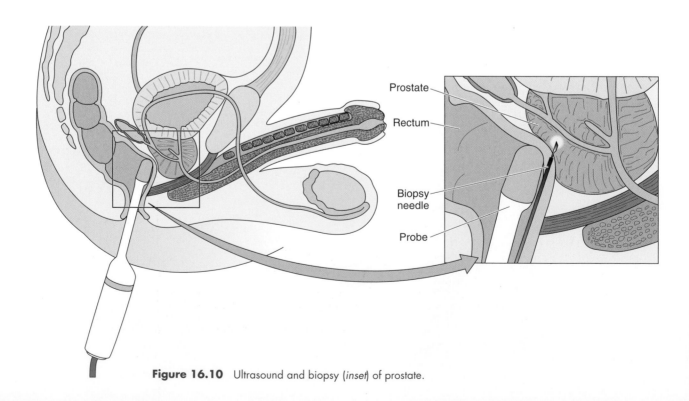

Figure 16.10   Ultrasound and biopsy (*inset*) of prostate.

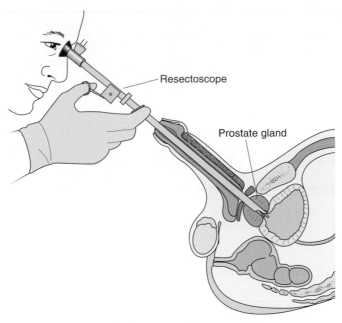

Figure 16.11 Transurethral resection of prostate (TURP).

Term	Meaning
orchioplasty ōr′kē-ō-plas-tē	repair of a testicle
orchiopexy ōr′kē-ō-pek′sē	fixation of an undescended testis in the scrotum
prostatectomy pros-tă-tek′tō-mē	excision of the prostate gland
transurethral resection of the prostate (TURP) trans-yū-rē′thrăl re-sek′shŭn	removal of prostatic gland tissue through the urethra using a resectoscope, a specialized urological endoscope—common treatment for benign prostatic hyperplasia/hypertrophy (BPH) (Fig. 16.11)

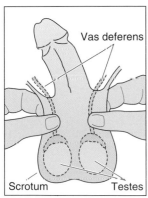
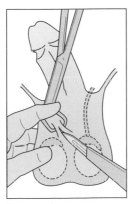
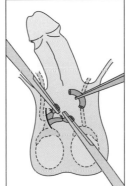
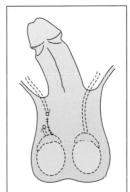

A
Locating the vas deferens

B
An incision is made over the vas deferens

C
The vas deferens is withdrawn through the incision, a section is removed, and the ends are tied.

D
The vas deferens is returned, and the scrotum incision is closed with sutures.

Figure 16.12 Vasectomy.

Term	Meaning
vasectomy va-sek′tō-mē	removal of a segment of the vas deferens to produce sterility in the male (Fig. 16.12)
vasovasostomy vā′sō-vă-sos′tō-mē	restoration of the function of the vas deferens to regain fertility after vasectomy

Therapeutic Terms

Term	Meaning
chemotherapy kem′ō-thār-ă-pē	treatment of malignancies, infections, and other diseases with chemical agents that destroy selected cells or impair their ability to reproduce
cancer immunotherapy im′ū-nō-thār-ă-pē	treatment of cancer by stimulating the patient's own immune response by transfer of immune components such as antibodies or T cells from an outside source to kill cancer cells
radiation therapy rā′dē-ā′shŭn	treatment of neoplastic disease by using radiation to deter the proliferation of malignant cells
brachytherapy	radiation technique involving internal implantation of radioactive isotopes, such as radioactive seeds to treat prostate cancer (brachy, meaning *short distance*, refers to localized application)
hormone replacement therapy (HRT)	use of a hormone to remedy a deficiency or regulate production (e.g., testosterone)
penile prosthesis pē′nīl pros′thē-sis	implantation of a device designed to provide an erection of the penis—used to treat physical impotence
penile self-injection	intracavernosal injection therapy causing an erection—used in treatment of erectile dysfunction

Summary of Chapter 16 Acronyms/Abbreviations

BPH	benign prostatic hyperplasia/hypertrophy	**HPV**	human papilloma virus
Bx	biopsy	**HRT**	hormone replacement therapy
DRE	digital rectal exam	**HSV-2**	herpes simplex virus type 2
ED	erectile dysfunction	**PSA**	prostate-specific antigen
HBV	hepatitis B virus	**STD**	sexually transmitted disease
HIV	human immunodeficiency virus	**TURP**	transurethral resection of the prostate

PRACTICE EXERCISES

For the following terms, on the lines below the term, write out the indicated word parts: prefixes (P), combining forms (CF), roots (R), and suffixes (S). Then define the word.

EXAMPLE

synorchism

_____ / _____ / _____
   P   R   S

syn/orch/ism
 P R S

DEFINITION: together/testis or testicle/condition of

1. oligospermia

_____ / _____ / _____
      P   R   S

DEFINITION: _____

2. perineoplasty

_____ / _____
     CF   S

DEFINITION: _____

3. testalgia

_____ / _____
     R   S

DEFINITION: _____

4. balanic

_____ / _____
     R   S

DEFINITION: _____

5. prostatomegaly

_____ / _____
     CF   S

DEFINITION: _____

6. orchidectomy

_____ / _____
     R   S

DEFINITION: _____

7. anorchism

_____ / _____ / _____
P   R   S

DEFINITION: _____

8. vasectomy

_____ / _____
R   S

DEFINITION: _____

9. aspermia

_____ / _____ / _____
P   R   S

DEFINITION: _____

10. cystoprostatectomy

_____ / _____ / _____
CF   R   S

DEFINITION: _____

11. balanitis

_____ / _____
R   S

DEFINITION: _____

12. orchioplasty

_____ / _____
CF   S

DEFINITION: _____

13. spermatocele

_____ / _____
CF   S

DEFINITION: _____

14. epididymotomy

_____ / _____
CF   S

DEFINITION: _____

15. vasovasostomy

_____ / _____ / _____
CF   CF   S

DEFINITION: _____

Identify the medical term for the following:

16. _____ absence of a testicle

17. _____ inflammation of the glans penis

18. _____ enlarged, herniated veins near the testicle

19. _____ specialized endoscope used to approach the
prostate when performing a **TURP**

20. _____ enlargement of the prostate

21. _____ removal of a portion of the vas deferens to produce male sterility

22. _____ disorder that causes a buildup of hardened fibrous
tissue in the corpus cavernosa in the penis

Match the following:

23. _____ fertility restoration   a. prostatectomy

24. _____ phimosis   b. seminoma

25. _____ BPH   c. STD

26. _____ cryptorchism   d. ED

27. _____ testicular cancer   e. orchiopexy

28. _____ penile self-injection   f. TURP

29. _____ prostate cancer   g. circumcision

30. _____ condyloma acuminata   h. vasovasostomy

Complete the following:

31. _____ orchism = undescended testicle

32. _____ sonogram of prostate = ultrasound scan of the prostate
made after introduction of a transducer into the rectum

33. _____ cele = fluid hernia in the testis

34. _____ spadias = condition of congenital opening of the male
urethra on the undersurface of the penis

35. _____ _____ exam = insertion of a finger
into the male rectum to palpate the rectum and prostate

36. _____ therapy = radiation technique involving implantation
of radioactive "seeds"

Match the following terms related to sperm:

37. _____ semen analysis   a. semen without living sperm

38. _____ oligospermia   b. inability to secrete sperm

39. _____ azoospermia   c. sperm morphology

40. _____ aspermia   d. scanty production of sperm

Write the term for the following abbreviations:

41. PSA _____

42. Bx_____

43. TURP_____

44. DRE_____

45. ED _____

For each of the following, circle the combining form that corresponds to the meaning given:

46. **testis**	prostat/o	epididym/o	orchi/o
47. **perineum**	peritone/o	perine/o	prostat/o
48. **sperm**	test/o	orchi/o	spermat/o
49. **vessel**	aden/o	angin/o	vas/o
50. **glans penis**	prostat/o	orchid/o	balan/o
51. **epididymis**	sperm/o	vas/o	epididym/o

Write in the missing words on the blank lines in the following illustration of the male anatomy.

52–59.

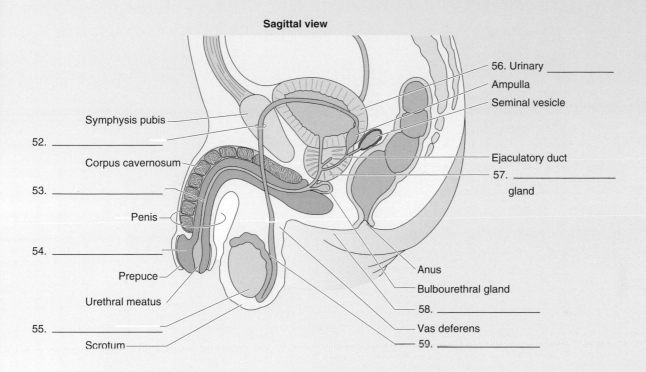

Sagittal view

56. Urinary _____
Ampulla
Seminal vesicle
Symphysis pubis
52. _____
Corpus cavernosum
Ejaculatory duct
57. _____
gland
53. _____
Penis
54. _____
Anus
Prepuce
Bulbourethral gland
Urethral meatus
58. _____
55. _____
Vas deferens
Scrotum
59. _____

For each of the following, circle the correct spelling of the term:

60. epididymis   epididymus   epedidimis

61. oligspermia   oligospermia   oligispermia

62. azospermia   asospermia   azoospermia

63. anorchesm   anorchism   anorschizm

64. balanitis   balanitus   balantis

65. creptorchism   criptorchism   cryptorchism

66. hypospadias   hypospadeas   hypespadias

67. clamidyia   chlamidya   chlamydia

68. syphilis   syphillis   syphyllis

69. fimosis   phimosis   phymosis

Give the noun that was used to form the following adjectives:

70. prostatic _____

71. epididymal _____

72. perineal _____

73. penile _____

74. gonorrheal _____

75. testicular _____

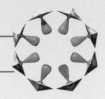

MEDICAL RECORD ANALYSES

MEDICAL RECORD 16.1

Chart Note

S: Twelve days ago this 34 y.o. male had a flu-like syndrome that lasted about 2–3 hours. For the past two days, he has felt lousy again and is experiencing left testicular pain and swelling s̄ avoiding Sx
Allergies: none
PH: negative
Habits: smoking—no
　　　　alcohol—occasional beer
ROS: otherwise negative

O: Slightly small testes bilaterally; tender Ⓛ epididymis; normal circumcised penis
UA: WNL

A: Ⓛ epididymitis

P: Rx: Maxaquin 400 mg #16
Sig: ii̅ STAT, then ī q.d. × 14 d; return in two weeks for follow-up

1. What was the patient's diagnosis?
   a. testicular pain and swelling
   b. inflammation of the testicle
   c. swollen veins near the testis
   d. inflammation of the coiled duct that stores sperm
   e. fluid hernia in a testicle

2. What was the condition of the patient's penis?
   a. small but normal
   b. prepuce had been excised
   c. inflamed
   d. swollen and tender
   e. not stated

3. What was the Sig: on the prescription?
   a. two every other day for fourteen days
   b. two immediately, then one a day for fourteen days
   c. one immediately, then one a day for fourteen days
   d. one as needed every day for fourteen days
   e. two a day for fourteen days

4. Did the patient have any trouble urinating?
   a. yes
   b. no

5. What was the condition of the right testicle?
   a. inflamed
   b. enlarged
   c. small
   d. normal
   e. had been excised

6. What was the result of the urinalysis?
   a. not stated
   b. normal
   c. not performed because the patient could not void
   d. hematuria
   e. glucosuria

MEDICAL RECORD 16.2

Larry Phelps, age 31, has been happily married to his wife Nancy for almost 5 years. They have two children. The second child caused some health problems for Nancy, and her obstetrician recommended that they have no more children because of the risk to her health. After trying different forms of birth control, Nancy and Larry decided that he would have a vasectomy. His doctor referred him to Dr. Jerard Derrick in the urology department at Central Medical Group.

Directions

Read Medical Record 16.2 for Larry Phelps (pages 530–531) and answer the following questions. This record is a series of three chart notes written by Dr. Derrick after first meeting with Mr. Phelps to schedule surgery, after the surgery and discharge, and after seeing Mr. Phelps in a follow-up 10 days later.

QUESTIONS ABOUT MEDICAL RECORD 16.2

Write your answers in the spaces provided.

1. Below are medical terms used in this record you have not yet encountered in this text. Underline each where it appears in the record and define below:

   sterility _____

   infiltrated _____

   resect _____

   ejaculation _____

   induration _____

2. The medical record suggests that Mr. Phelps signed which of these before surgery?
   a. last will and testament
   b. consent form
   c. application to sperm bank
   d. none of the above

3. In your own words, not using medical terminology, briefly summarize the procedure Dr. Derrick performed:

   _____

   _____

   _____

4. Complications of the surgery included the following:
   a. sterility
   b. fever
   c. nausea and vomiting
   d. bleeding
   e. all of the above
   f. none of the above

5. Translate the instruction for the immediate postoperative medication (how much, how often):

_____

_____

_____

6. Mark any of the following that were symptoms Mr. Phelps reported to Dr. Derrick on his follow-up visit 10 days after surgery:

a. fever

b. bleeding

c. pain in the scrotum

d. impotence

e. suture loosening

7. Dr. Derrick carefully examined Mr. Phelps in the follow-up visit and noted the following objective findings (mark all that are appropriate):

a. minor bruising in the scrotum

b. small area of hard tissue at left vasectomy site

c. bleeding at left vasectomy site

d. pain at left vasectomy site

e. very sore elevated mass at right vasectomy site

f. bleeding at right vasectomy site

g. pain at right vasectomy site

h. hard tissue areas along upper scrotum

i. black and blue penis

8. In your own words, define the diagnosis Dr. Derrick made in the follow-up visit:

_____

_____

_____

9. Translate Dr. Derrick's medication instructions after the follow-up visit:

Medication	*Amount*	*How Often*
_____	_____	_____
_____	_____	_____
_____	_____	_____
_____	_____	_____

CENTRAL MEDICAL GROUP, INC.
Department of Urology
201 Medical Center Drive • Central City, US 90000-1234

PROGRESS NOTES

PHELPS, LAWRENCE

June 4, 20xx

SUBJECTIVE: This 31-year-old male desires vasectomy for sterility. He and his wife have two children. He states that another pregnancy would put his wife at health risk.

OBJECTIVE: Normal genitalia with single vas bilaterally.

ASSESSMENT: The procedure, goals, and risks were thoroughly discussed with the aid of pictures. The vasectomy booklet and consent form were provided to the patient.

PLAN: Schedule bilateral vasectomy.

DL:ti   T:6/7/xx

J. Derrick, M.D.
J. Derrick, M.D.

June 10, 20xx

PROCEDURE: Bilateral vasectomy.

The patient was placed supine on the table; and the scrotum was shaved, prepped, and draped in the usual fashion. The right testicle was grasped, and the right vas was brought to the skin and was infiltrated with 1% Xylocaine. The vas was freed through a small incision. A segment was resected, and the ends were cauterized and tied with 3-0 silk suture. The skin was closed with 4-0 chromic suture. The same procedure was repeated on the left. There were no complications or bleeding.

PLAN: The patient is discharged to the care of his wife with an Rx for Darvocet-N, 100 mg, 1 q 4 h p.r.n. pain. He has been given a postvasectomy instruction sheet. He is asked to call if there are any problems. He was also instructed to submit a semen specimen for analysis after 15–20 ejaculations.

DL:ti   T:6/12/xx

J. Derrick, M.D.
J. Derrick, M.D.

Medical Record 16.2

CENTRAL MEDICAL GROUP, INC.

Department of Urology

201 Medical Center Drive • Central City, US 90000-1234

PROGRESS NOTES

PHELPS, LAWRENCE

June 20, 20xx

SUBJECTIVE: The patient has had pain in the right scrotum since surgery, which became worse yesterday with pain in his right back. He states he has had no fevers, nausea, or vomiting.

OBJECTIVE: 1) Mild scrotal ecchymoses inferiorly. Normal testes and epididymides.
2) Small induration at left vasectomy site without tenderness.
3) Exquisitely tender 1.5 cm nodule at right vasectomy site; no induration in upper scrotum or cord.

ASSESSMENT: Probable small hematoma at right vasectomy site.

PLAN: Rx: Cipro 500 mg b.i.d. x 5 d
Darvocet-N 100 mg q 4 h p.r.n. pain
ibuprofen p.r.n.

RTO in one week.

DL:ti   T:6/22/xx

J. Derrick, M.D.
J. Derrick, M.D.

Medical Record 16.2   *Continued*

MEDICAL RECORD 16.3

James Easley was having some difficulty urinating fully and was feeling gradually increasing pain in the perineal area. He went to see his personal physician, who after a digital rectal examination referred him to Dr. Lentz, a urologist at Central Medical Center.

Directions

Read Medical Record 16.3 for James Easley (page 534) and answer the following questions. This record is the ultrasound report dictated by Dr. Lentz after his session with Mr. Easley in the ultrasound suite at Central Medical Center.

QUESTIONS ABOUT MEDICAL RECORD 16.3

Write your answers in the spaces provided:

1. Below are medical terms used in this record you have not yet encountered in this text. Underline each where it appears in the record and define below:

   needle biopsy _____

   MHz _____

   bifocal _____

2. In your own words, not using medical terminology, briefly describe the ultrasound procedure Mr. Easley underwent:

   _____

   _____

   _____

3. In your own words, describe the position Mr. Easley was put in for the ultrasound:

   _____

   _____

   _____

4. Mark any of the following that are abnormal findings in Dr. Lentz's report:
   a. enlarged prostate gland
   b. hemorrhage
   c. hypoechoic lesion
   d. obstructed urethra
   e. prostatic calculi
   f. multiplanar rectum

5. Because of the results of the ultrasound, Dr. Lentz decided to perform an additional diagnostic procedure while Mr. Easley was in the ultrasound suite. In your own words, describe that procedure:

_____

_____

6. Explain why Dr. Lentz's report does not include a plan or recommendations for further actions:

_____

_____

_____

7. When and for how long should Mr. Easley take the Noroxin?

_____

_____

CENTRAL MEDICAL CENTER

21 Medical Center Drive   Central City, US 90000-1234

PROSTATIC ULTRASOUND

EXAMINATION: Transrectal ultrasound of the prostate gland with biopsy.

DIGITAL RECTAL EXAMINATION: Grade   enlarged prostate gland, benign-feeling.

PSA: 5.7 ng/ml

PROCEDURE: An ultrasound unit with a 7.5 MHz bifocal multiplanar rectal transducer was used to scan the prostate gland. The patient was placed in the left lateral decubitus position. The prostate and seminal vesicles were thoroughly scanned in the transverse and sagittal modes.

The abnormal findings included a hypoechoic lesion at the right base of the prostate gland in the central zone. There were numerous prostatic calculi. The prostatic volume was 22 cc, and the PSA density was 0.25 (calculation based on PSA value and size of prostate). A prostatic needle biopsy was performed because of the increased PSA density and the hypoechoic lesion. This was accomplished without incident.

The patient tolerated the procedure well and had minimal bleeding and discomfort. The patient left the ultrasound suite in satisfactory condition. The patient was placed on Noroxin 400 mg b.i.d. x 3 days.

Further recommendations will be made following the biopsy report.

R. Lentz, M.D.

RL:kj

D: 9/11/xx
T: 9/14/xx

PROSTATIC ULTRASOUND	PT NAME: EASLEY JAMES R.
	ID NO: SI-350013
	ATT PHYS: R. LENTZ, M.D.

Medical Record 16.3

Female Reproductive System

OBJECTIVES

After completion of this chapter you will be able to

- Define common term components used in relation to the female reproductive system
- Describe the basic functions of the female reproductive system
- Define the basic anatomical terms referring to the female reproductive system
- Define common gynecological symptomatic and diagnostic terms
- List the common gynecological diagnostic tests and procedures
- Define common gynecological operative and therapeutic terms
- Define common obstetrical symptomatic and diagnostic terms
- List the common obstetrical diagnostic tests and procedures
- Define common obstetrical operative and therapeutic terms
- Explain terms and abbreviations used in documenting medical records involving the female reproductive system

Combining Forms

Combining Form	Meaning	Example
cervic/o	neck or cervix	cervical ser'vĭ-kal
colp/o	vagina (sheath)	colposcope kol'pō-skōp
vagin/o		vaginal vaj'i-năl
episi/o	vulva (covering)	episiotomy e-piz-ē-ot'ō-mē
vulv/o		vulvar vŭl'văr
gynec/o	woman	gynecology gī-nĕ-kol'ō-jē
hyster/o	uterus	hysteroscopy his-ter-os'kŏ-pē
metr/o		metrorrhagia mē-trō-rā'jē-ă
uter/o	uterus	uterus ū'ter-ŭs

Combining Form	Meaning	Example
lact/o	milk	lactogenic lak-tō-jen′ik
mast/o	breast	mastodynia mas-tō-din′ē-ă
mamm/o		mammogram mam′ō-gram
men/o	menstruation	menopause men′ō-pawz
obstetr/o	midwife	obstetric ob-stet′rik
oophor/o	ovary	oophoritis ō-of-ōr-ī′tis
ovari/o		ovarian ō-var′ē-an
ov/i	egg	ovigenesis ō-vi-jen′ĕ-sis
ov/o		ovum ō′vŭm
pelv/i	pelvic cavity	pelvimetry pel-vim′ĕ-trē
salping/o	uterine (fallopian) tube	salpingitis sal-pin-jī′tis
toc/o	labor or birth	dystocia dis-tō′sē-ă
ADDITIONAL SUFFIX		
-arche	beginning	menarche me-nar′kē

Female Reproductive System Overview

The female reproductive system consists of the *uterus, ovaries, uterine (fallopian) tubes, vagina,* and *vulva* (Fig. 17.1). These structures are responsible for producing and maintaining female ova and providing a place for the implantation and nurturing of the fertilized ovum until birth. Treatment of the female reproductive system involves two medical specialties: *gynecology* and *obstetrics*.

Anatomical Terms

Term	Meaning
uterus ū′ter-ŭs	womb; pear-shaped organ in the pelvic cavity in which the embryo develops
fundus fŭn′dŭs	upper portion of the uterus above the entry to the uterine tubes

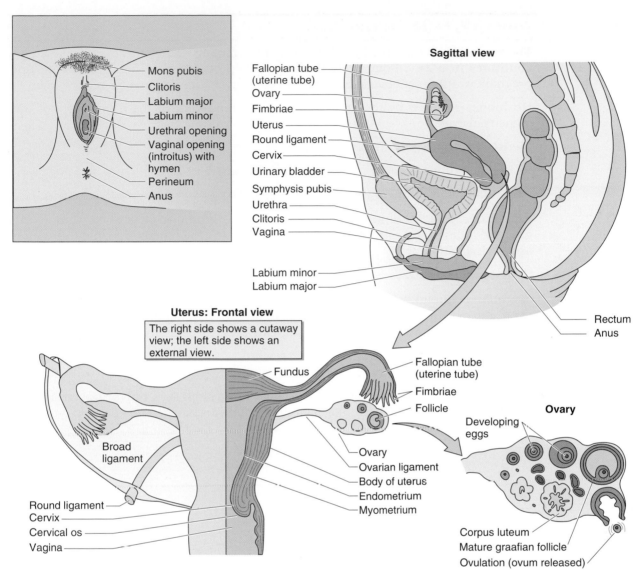

Figure 17.1 Female reproductive system.

Term	Meaning
endometrium en′dō-mē′trē-ŭm	lining of the uterus that is shed approximately every 28–30 days in the nonpregnant female during *menstruation* (see Table 17.1 on page 538)
myometrium mī′ō-mē′trē-ŭm	muscular wall of the uterus
uterine or fallopian tubes yū′ter-in fa-lō′pē-an	tubes extending from each side of the uterus toward the ovary that provide a passage for ova to the uterus
adnexa ad-nek′să	uterine tubes and ovaries (uterine appendages)
right uterine appendage **left uterine appendage**	right tube and ovary left tube and ovary
ovary ō′vă-rē	one of two glands located on each side of the pelvic cavity that produce ova and female sex hormones

FALLOPIUS. Gabriele Fallopius, a 16th-century Italian anatomist, made many important observations, especially concerning the female reproductive organs. His classical descriptions resulted in his name being associated with the uterine tubes. He compared the abdominal end of each tube to a trumpet.

Table 17.1   Menstrual Cycle

The menarche is the time in puberty when the female **menstrual cycle** begins and continues in a 28–30-day cycle throughout reproductive life, except at times of pregnancy, until menopause (generally occurring between 45 and 55 years of age).

Hormones secreted by the anterior pituitary gland control the four stages of the menstrual cycle:

Menstrual stage (period)   Days 1–5

Shedding of unused endometrial tissue in a bloody discharge

Follicular stage   Days 6–13

Secretion of follicle-stimulating hormone (FSH), initiating growth of an ovum in the graafian follicle, and release of estrogen by the maturing follicle, causing thickening and revitalization of the endometrial lining

Ovulatory stage   Days 14–16

Secretion of luteinizing hormone causes the follicle to rupture and release the mature ovum into the uterine tube; the ruptured follicle, remaining in the ovary, transforms into the corpus luteum, which then secretes progesterone and estrogen to further nourish the endometrium.

Premenstrual stage   Days 17–28

If conception does not take place, the corpus luteum stops secreting progesterone and estrogen, thinning of the endometrial lining occurs, and tissue breakdown culminates in menstruation.

Term	Meaning
cervix ser′viks	neck of the uterus
cervical os ser′vĭ-kăl os	opening of the cervix to the uterus
vagina vă-jī′nă	tubular passageway from the cervix to the outside of the body
vulva vŭl′vă	external genitalia of the female
labia lā′bē-ă	folds of tissue on either side of the vaginal opening known as the labia majora and labia minora
clitoris klit′ō-ris	female erectile tissue situated in the anterior portion of the vulva
hymen hī′men	fold of mucous membrane that encircles the entrance to the vagina
introitus in-trō′i-tŭs	entrance to the vagina
Bartholin glands	two glands located on either side of the vaginal opening that secrete a lubricant during intercourse
perineum per′i-nē′ŭm	region between the vulva and anus

Breast anatomy

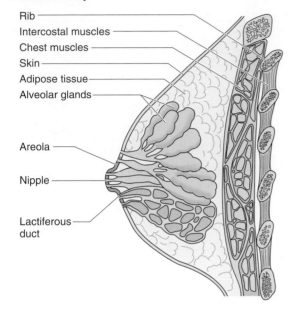

Rib
Intercostal muscles
Chest muscles
Skin
Adipose tissue
Alveolar glands
Areola
Nipple
Lactiferous duct

Figure 17.2 Breast.

Term	Meaning
mammary glands mam′ă-rē	two glands of the female breasts capable of producing milk (Fig. 17.2)
mammary papilla pă-pil′ă	nipple
areola ă-rē′ō-lă	dark pigmented area around the nipple
embryo em′brē-ō	developing organism from fertilization to the end of the eighth week (Fig. 17.3)
fetus fē′tŭs	developing organism from the ninth week to birth (Fig. 17.4)
placenta plă-sen′tă	vascular organ that develops in the uterine wall during pregnancy that provides nourishment for the fetus (placenta = cake)

MAMMA. Mamma is Latin for breast; the word is said to come from the cry of the infant for "mama," which is a sound common to most languages and is the root for mother in many. The word "breast" is derived from the German word for "bursting forth" or "budding."

Sperm and ovum

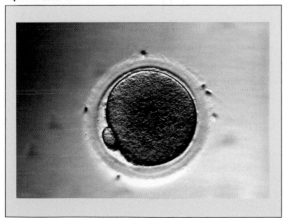

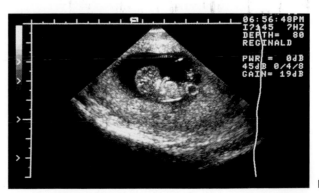

A   **B**

Figure 17.3 **A.** Sperm and ovum. **B.** Two-dimensional sonogram of 8-week embryo.

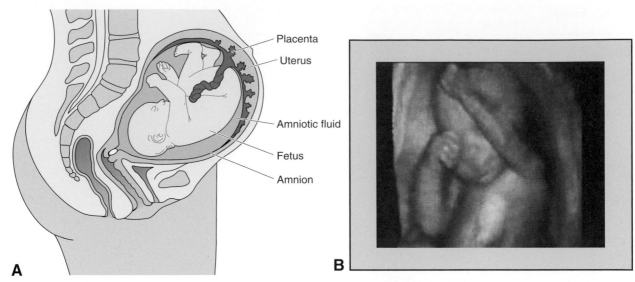

Figure 17.4 **A.** Fetus in utero. **B.** Three-dimensional sonogram of fetus "waking up."

Term	Meaning
amnion am'nē-on	innermost of the membranes surrounding the embryo in the uterus filled with amniotic fluid
amniotic fluid	fluid within the amnion that surrounds and protects the fetus
meconium mē-kō'nē-ŭm	intestinal discharges of the fetus that form the first stools in the newborn

Gynecological Symptomatic Terms
gī'nĕ-kō-loj'i-kăl

Term	Meaning
amenorrhea ă-men-ō-re'ă	absence of menstruation
anovulation an-ov-yū-lā'shŭn	absence of ovulation
dysmenorrhea dis-men-ōr-ē'ă	painful menstruation
dyspareunia dis-pa-rū'nē-ă	painful intercourse (coitus) (dys = painful; para = alongside of; eunia = a lying)
leukorrhea lū-kō-rē'ă	abnormal white or yellow vaginal discharge
menorrhagia men-ō-rā'jē-ă	excessive bleeding at the time of menstruation (menses)
metrorrhagia mē-trō-rā'jē-ă	bleeding from the uterus at any time other than normal menstruation
oligomenorrhea ol'i-gō-men-ō-rē'ă	scanty menstrual period
oligo-ovulation ol'i-gō-ov'yū-lā'shŭn	irregular ovulation

Gynecological Diagnostic Terms

Term	Meaning
cervicitis ser-vi-sī′tis	inflammation of the cervix
congenital anomalies (irregularities) kon-jen′i-tăl ă-nom′ă-lēz	birth defects causing the abnormal development of a female organ or structure (e.g., double uterus, absent vagina)
dermoid cyst der′moyd sist	congenital tumor composed of displaced embryonic tissue (teeth, bone, cartilage, and hair) more commonly found in an ovary; it is usually benign
displacement of uterus	displacement of the uterus from its normal position (Fig. 17.5)
anteflexion an-tē-flek′shŭn	abnormal forward bending of the uterus (ante = before; flexus = bend)
retroflexion re-trō-flek′shŭn	abnormal backward bending of the uterus
retroversion re-trō-ver′zhŭn	backward turn of the whole uterus—also called tipped uterus

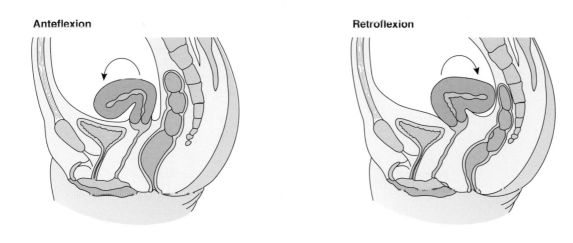

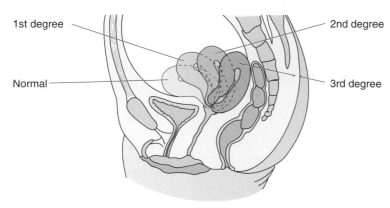

Figure 17.5 Displacements of the uterus.

Term	Meaning
endometriosis en'dō-mē-trē-ō'sis	condition characterized by migration of portions of endometrial tissue outside the uterine cavity
endometritis en'dō-mē-trī'tis	inflammation of the endometrium
fibroid fī'broyd **fibromyoma** fī'brō-mī-ō'mă **leiomyoma** lī'ō-mī-ō'mă	benign tumor in the uterus composed of smooth muscle and fibrous connective tissue (Fig. 17.6)
fistula fis'tyū-lă	abnormal passage such as from one hollow organ to another (fistula = pipe) (Fig. 17.7)
rectovaginal fistula rek-tō-vaj'i-năl	abnormal opening between the vagina and rectum
vesicovaginal fistula ves-i-kō-vaj'i-năl	abnormal opening between the bladder and vagina
cervical neoplasia	abnormal development of cervical tissue cells
cervical intraepithelial neoplasia (CIN) in'tră-ep-i-thē'lē-ăl nē-ō-plā'zē-ă **cervical dysplasia** dis-plā'zē-ă	potentially cancerous abnormality of epithelial tissue of the cervix, graded according to the extent of abnormal cell formation: CIN 1 mild dysplasia CIN 2 moderate dysplasia CIN 3 severe dysplasia (see Fig. 17.13B)

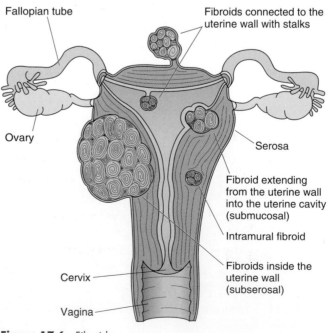

Figure 17.6 Fibroids.

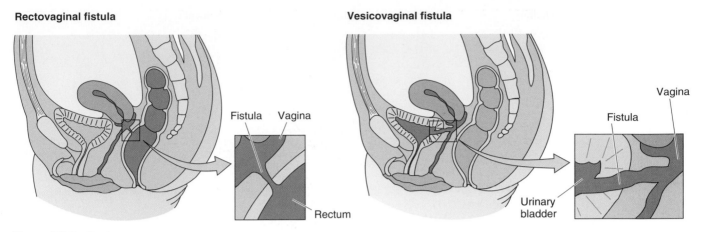

Figure 17.7 Fistulas.

Term	Meaning
carcinoma in situ (CIS) of the cervix kar-si-nō′mă in sī′tū	malignant cell changes of the cervix that are localized without any spread to adjacent structures
menopause men′ō-pawz	cessation of menstrual periods owing to a lack of ovarian hormones
oophoritis ō-of-ōr-ī′tis	inflammation of one or both ovaries
parovarian cyst par-ō-var′ē-an	cyst of the fallopian tube
pelvic adhesions pel′vik ad-hē′zhŭnz	scarring of tissue within the pelvic cavity as a result of endometriosis, infection, or injury
pelvic inflammatory disease (PID)	inflammation of organs in the pelvic cavity usually including the fallopian tubes, ovaries, and endometrium—most often caused by bacteria
pelvic floor relaxation	relaxation of supportive ligaments of the pelvic organs (Fig. 17.8)
cystocele sis′tō-sēl	pouching of the bladder into the vagina
rectocele rek′tō-sēl	pouching of the rectum into the vagina
enterocele en′ter-ō-sēl	pouching sac of peritoneum between the vagina and rectum
urethrocele yū-rē′thrō-sēl	pouching of the urethra into the vagina
prolapse prō-laps′	descent of the uterus down the vaginal canal
salpingitis sal-pin-jī′tis	inflammation of a fallopian tube

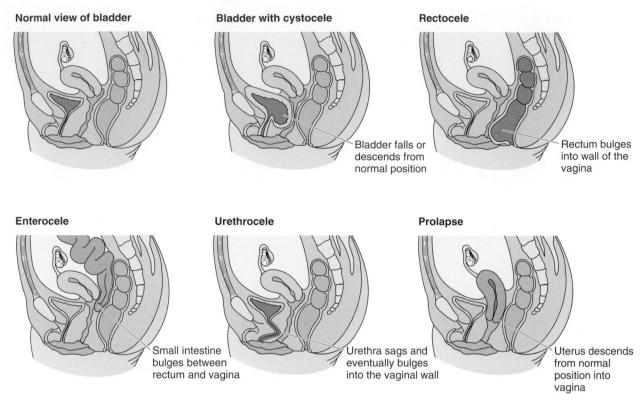

Figure 17.8 Pelvic floor relaxation.

SEXUALLY TRANSMITTED DISEASES (STDs)	
Term	**Meaning**
Major Bacterial STDs	
chlamydia kla-mid′ē-ă	most common sexually transmitted bacterial infection in North America; often occurs with no symptoms and is treated only after it has spread, such as to cause pelvic inflammatory disease
gonorrhea gon-ō-rē′ă	contagious inflammation of the genital mucous membranes caused by invasion of the gonococcus, *Neisseria gonorrhoeae* (gono = seed; rrhea = discharge)
syphilis sif′i-lis	infectious disease caused by a spirochete transmitted by direct intimate contact that may involve any organ or tissue over time; usually manifested first on the skin with the appearance of small, painless red papules that erode and form bloodless ulcers called *chancres*
Major Viral STDs	
hepatitis B virus (HBV) hep-ă-tī′tis	virus that causes an inflammation of the liver as a result of transmission through any body fluid, including vaginal secretions, semen, and blood
herpes simplex virus type 2 (HSV-2) her′pēz	virus that causes ulcer-like lesions of the genital and anorectal skin and mucosa; after initial infection, the virus lies dormant in the nerve cell root and may recur at times of stress (Fig. 17.9)

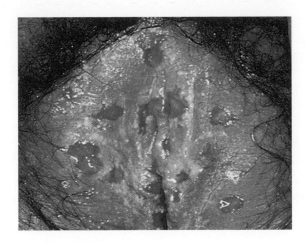

Figure 17.9   Herpes simplex virus type 2.

Term	Meaning
human immunodeficiency virus (HIV) im′yū-nō-dē-fish′en-sē	virus that causes acquired immunodeficiency syndrome (AIDS), permitting various opportunistic infections, malignancies, and neurological diseases—contracted through exposure to contaminated blood or body fluid (e.g., semen, vaginal secretions)
human papilloma virus (HPV) pap-i-lō′mă **condyloma acuminatum** kon-di-lō′mah ă-kyū′mĭ-nāt′ŭm **pl. condylomata acuminata** kon-di-lō′mah′tă ă-kyū′mĭ-nah′tă	virus transmitted by direct sexual contact that causes an infection that can occur on the skin or mucous membranes of the genitals; on the skin, the lesions appear as cauliflower-like warts, and on the mucous membranes, they have a flat appearance (also known as venereal or genital warts) (Fig. 17.10)

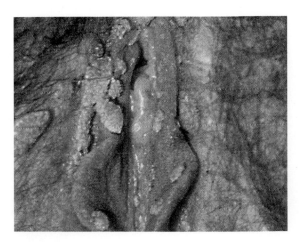

Figure 17.10   Condylomata acuminata (genital warts) caused by HPV.

Term	Meaning
vaginitis vaj-i-nī′tis	inflammation of the vagina with redness, swelling, and irritation—often caused by a specific organism, such as *Candida* (yeast) or *Trichomonas* (sexually transmitted parasite)
atrophic vaginitis ă-trof′ik	thinning of the vagina and loss of moisture owing to depletion of estrogen, which causes inflammation of tissue
vaginosis vaj′i-nō-sis	infection of the vagina with little or no inflammation characterized by a milk-like discharge and an unpleasant odor—also known as nonspecific vaginitis
BREASTS	
adenocarcinoma of the breast ad′ě-nō-kar-si-nō′mă	malignant tumor of glandular breast tissue
amastia ă-mas′tē-ă	absence of a breast
fibrocystic breasts fĭ-brō-sis′tik	benign condition of the breasts consisting of fibrous and cystic changes that render the tissue more dense—patient feels painful lumps that fluctuate in size during the menstrual cycle
gynecomastia gī′ně-kō-mas′tē-ă	development of mammary glands in the male, caused by altered hormone levels (Fig. 17.11)

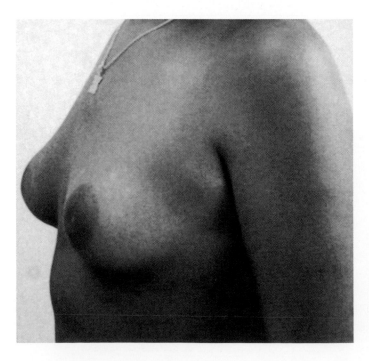

Figure 17.11 This 15-year-old boy presented with a 3-year history of gradual, bilateral breast enlargement known as *gynecomastia*. He was otherwise healthy and showed normal pubertal development. The cause in his case was idiopathic, but most are related to hormone imbalance as seen in tumors of the pituitary or adrenal glands. For cosmetic reasons and because of functional impairment (breast pain with running), he underwent breast reduction mammoplasty.

Term	Meaning
hypermastia hī-per-mas′tē-ă **macromastia** mak-rō-mas′tē-ă	abnormally large breasts
hypomastia hī′po-mas′tē-ă **micromastia** mī′kro-mas′tē-ă	unusually small breasts
mastitis mas-tī′tis	inflammation of the breast—most common in women when breast-feeding
polymastia pol-ē-mas′tē-ă	presence of more than two breasts
polythelia pol-ē-thē′lē-ă	presence of more than one nipple on a breast
supernumerary nipples sū-per-nū′mer-ār-ē	

Gynecological Diagnostic Tests and Procedures

Test or Procedure	Explanation
biopsy (Bx) bī′op-sē	removal of tissue for microscopic pathological examination (Fig. 17.12)
aspiration Bx as-pi-rā′shŭn	needle draw of tissue or fluid from a cavity for cytological examination—also called needle biopsy
endoscopic Bx en′dō-skōp′ik	removal of a specimen for biopsy during an endoscopic procedure (e.g., colposcopy)
excisional Bx ek-sizh′ŭn-ăl	removal of an entire lesion for microscopic examination
incisional Bx in-sizh′ŭn-ăl	removal of a piece of suspicious tissue for microscopic examination (e.g., cervical or endometrial biopsy)
needle Bx	removal of a core specimen of tissue using a special hollow needle
stereotactic breast Bx ster′ē-ō-tak′tik	use of x-ray or ultrasound imaging, a specialized stereotactic frame, and a computer to calculate, precisely locate, and direct a needle into a breast lesion for the removal of a core specimen for biopsy
sentinel node breast Bx sen′tin′l nōd	biopsy of the sentinel node (the first lymph node to receive lymphatic drainage from a tumor) in a breast with early cancer to determine metastases and, if no malignancy is found, avoid the extensive removal of axillary nodes that causes lymphedema (swelling under the arms); includes radionuclide imaging to locate the sentinel node (sentinel refers to *guarding* a point of entry)

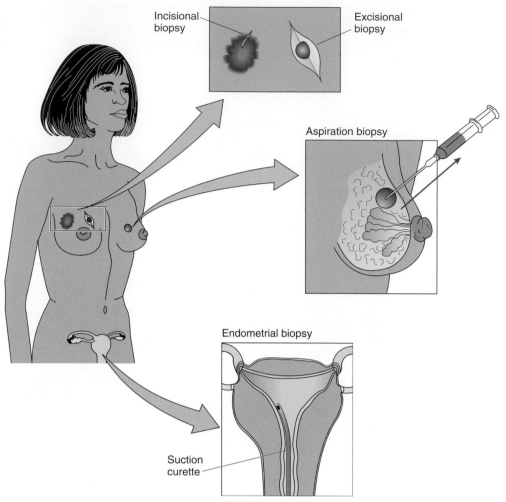

Figure 17.12 Biopsy.

Test or Procedure	Explanation
colposcopy kol-pos′kŏ-pē	examination of the vagina and cervix using a colposcope, a specialized microscope used to examine the vagina and cervix, often with a camera attachment for photographs—used to document findings and follow-up treatments (Fig. 17.13)
hysteroscopy his-ter-os′kŏ-pē	use of a hysteroscope to examine the intrauterine cavity for the assessment of abnormalities (e.g., polyps, fibroids, anomalies) (Fig. 17.14)
magnetic resonance imaging (MRI) rez′ō-nans	use of nonionizing images to detect gynecological conditions (e.g., anomalies of the pelvis or soft tissues of the breast) or stage tumors arising from the endometrium or cervix
Papanicolaou smear (Pap) pa-pĕ-nē′kĕ-low	study of cells collected from the cervix to screen for cancer and other abnormalities

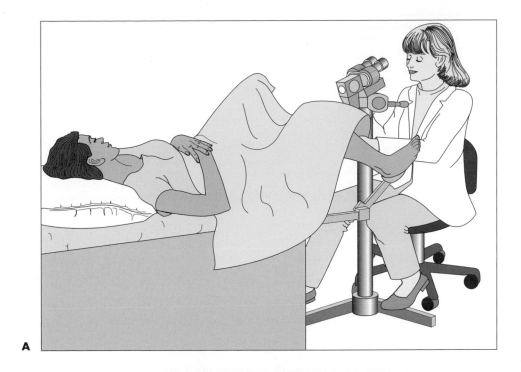

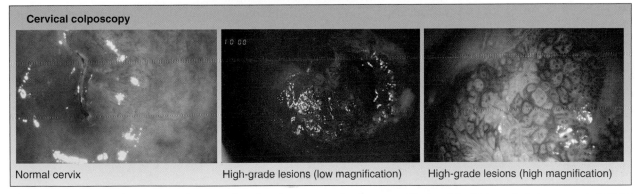

Cervical colposcopy

Normal cervix

High-grade lesions (low magnification)

High-grade lesions (high magnification)

Figure 17.13 **A.** Colposcopy. **B.** Photographs taken during cervical colposcopy. Biopsy of the high-grade lesions revealed CIN 3 (severe dysplasia).

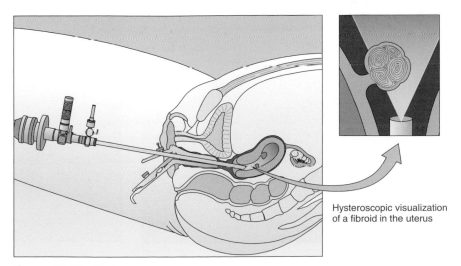

Hysteroscopic visualization of a fibroid in the uterus

Figure 17.14 Hysteroscopy.

Test or Procedure	Explanation
radiography rā′dē-og′ră-fē	x-ray imaging
hysterosalpingogram his′ter-ō-sal-ping-ō-gram	x-ray of the fallopian tubes after injection of a contrast medium through the cervix—used to determine tubal patency
mammogram mam′ō-gram	low-dose x-ray of breast tissue done to detect neoplasms (Fig. 17.15)
pelvic sonography sŏ-nog′ră-fē	ultrasound imaging of the female pelvis (Fig. 17.16)

endovaginal sonogram
    en′dō-vaj′i-năl
    transvaginal sonogram
    trans-vaj′i-năl son′ō-gram
	ultrasound image of the uterus, tubes, and ovaries made after introduction of an ultrasonic transducer within the vagina to detect conditions such as ectopic pregnancy or missed abortion

hysterosonogram (saline infusion sonogram)	transvaginal sonographic image made as sterile saline is injected into the uterus; used to assess uterine pathology or determine tubal patency; also known as sonohysterogram
transabdominal sonogram trans-ab-dom′i-năl	ultrasound image of the lower abdomen including the bladder, uterus, tubes, and ovaries to detect conditions such as cysts and tumors

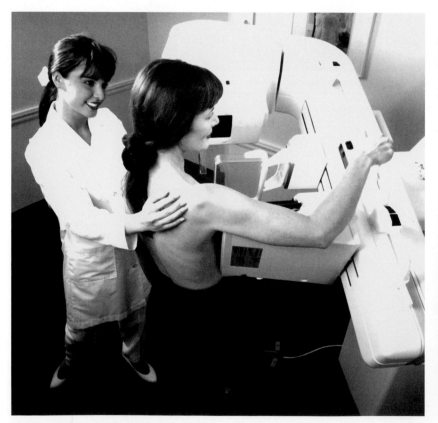
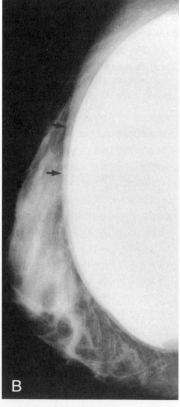

Figure 17.15 **A.** Mammography procedure. **B.** Mammogram of a patient with an implant. *Arrows,* pectoralis muscle anterior to the implant.

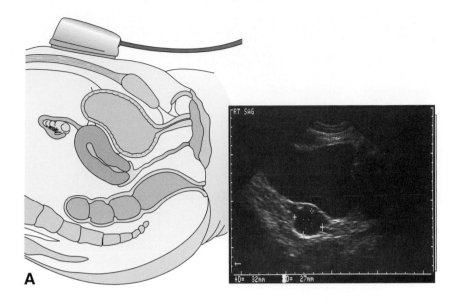

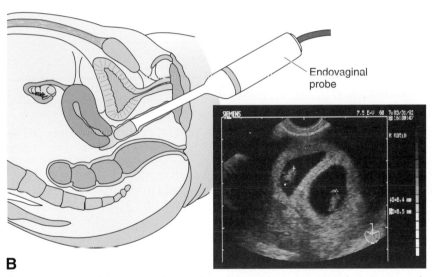

Figure 17.16   Pelvic sonography. **A.** Transabdominal imaging procedure. *Inset,* simple ovarian cyst. **B.** Transvaginal imaging procedure. *Inset,* twin pregnancies.

Gynecological Operative Terms

Term	Meaning
adhesiolysis ad-hē′zē-ōl′i-sis **adhesiotomy** ad-hē-sē-ot′-ōmē	breaking down or severing of pelvic adhesions
cervical conization ser′vĭ-kal kō-nī-zā′shŭn	removal of a cone-shaped portion of the cervix

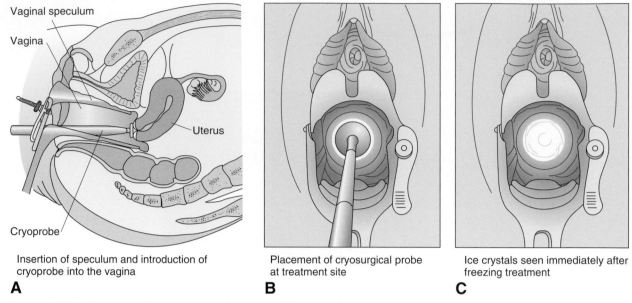

Vaginal speculum

Vagina

Cryoprobe

Uterus

Insertion of speculum and introduction of cryoprobe into the vagina

A

Placement of cryosurgical probe at treatment site

B

Ice crystals seen immediately after freezing treatment

C

Figure 17.17   Cryosurgical procedure: cryoconization of the cervix.

Term	Meaning
colporrhaphy kol-pōr′ă-fē	suture to repair the vagina
anterior repair	repair of a cystocele
posterior repair	repair of a rectocele
A&P repair	anterior and posterior repair of a cystocele and rectocele
cryosurgery krī-ō-ser′jer-ē	method of destroying tissue by freezing—used for treating dysplasia and early cancers (Fig. 17.17)

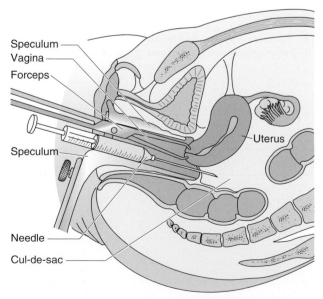

Speculum

Vagina

Forceps

Uterus

Speculum

Needle

Cul-de-sac

Figure 17.18   Culdocentesis.

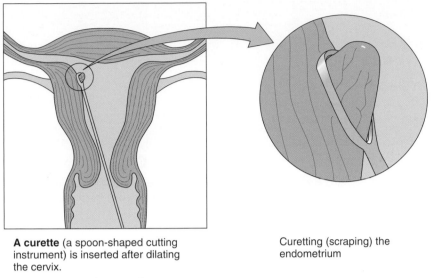

A **curette** (a spoon-shaped cutting instrument) is inserted after dilating the cervix.

Curetting (scraping) the endometrium

Figure 17.19 Dilation and curettage.

Term	Meaning
culdocentesis kŭl-dō-sen-tē′sis	aspiration of fluid from the cul-de-sac (cavity that lies between the rectum and posterior wall of the uterus)—used for diagnosing ectopic pregnancy and pelvic inflammatory disease (Fig. 17.18)
dilation and curettage (D&C) dī-lā′shŭn kyū-rĕ-tahzh′	dilation of the cervix and scraping of the endometrium to control bleeding, obtain tissue for biopsy, or remove polyps or products of conception (Fig. 17.19)
hysterectomy his-ter-ek′tō-mē	removal of the uterus
abdominal hysterectomy	removal of the uterus through an incision in the abdomen
vaginal hysterectomy	removal of the uterus through the vagina
total hysterectomy	removal of the uterus and cervix
laparoscopy lap-ă-ros′kŏ-pē	inspection of the abdominal or pelvic cavity with a laparoscope, an endoscope used to examine the abdominal and pelvic regions
laparoscopic surgery	surgical procedures within the abdominal or pelvic region using a laparoscope
laser surgery lā′zer	use of a laser to destroy lesions or dissect or cut tissue—used frequently in gynecology
loop electrosurgical excision procedure (LEEP) **large loop excision of the transformation zone (LLETZ)**	use of electrosurgical or radio waves transformed through a loop-configured electrosurgical device to treat precancerous lesions by simultaneous excisional biopsy and treatment of affected tissue (e.g., cervical dysplasia, human papilloma virus lesions); note that the transformation zone is the area of the cervix where neoplasia (abnormal cell formation) is most likely to arise (Fig. 17.20)

HYSTERIA. Hysteria is a Greek word meaning a uterine condition. Ancient Greeks believed that nervous symptoms were due to the uterus and therefore were experienced only by women. Plato described the uterus as an animal endowed with spontaneous sensation and emotion that was lodged in a woman, ardently desiring to produce children. If the uterus remained sterile long after puberty, it became ill-tempered and caused a general disturbance in the body until it became pregnant. The common prescription for the hysterical female in those days was marriage and childbirth!

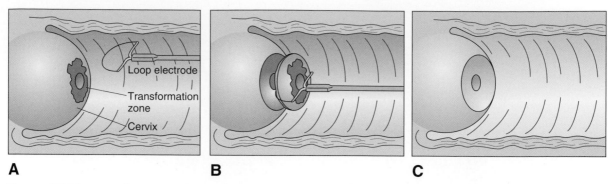

Figure 17.20 Loop electrosurgical excision procedure (LEEP) or large loop excision of the transformation zone (LLETZ). **A.** Electrode approach. **B.** Removal of the transformation zone. **C.** Excision site (region between the endocervix and ectocervix).

Term	Meaning
myomectomy mī-ō-mek′tō-mē	excision of fibroid tumors
oophorectomy ō-of-ōr-ek′tō-mē	excision of an ovary
ovarian cystectomy ō-var′ē-an sis-tek′tō-mē	excision of an ovarian cyst
salpingectomy sal-pin-jek′tō-mē	excision of a uterine tube
bilateral salpingo-oophorectomy bī-lat′er-ăl sal-ping′gō-ō-of-ō-rek′tō-mē	excision of both uterine tubes and ovaries
salpingotomy sal-pin-got′tō-mē	incision into a fallopian tube—often performed to remove an ectopic pregnancy (Fig. 17.21)
salpingostomy sal-ping-gos′tō-mē	creation of an opening in the fallopian tube to open a blockage
tubal ligation lī-gā′shŭn	sterilization of a woman by cutting and tying (ligating) the uterine tubes

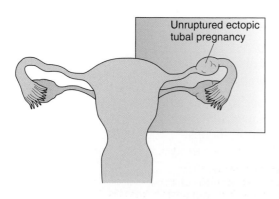

Unruptured ectopic tubal pregnancy

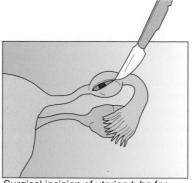

Surgical incision of uterine tube for removal of products of conception

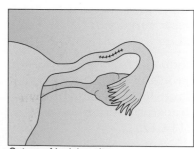

Suture of incision site

Figure 17.21 Salpingotomy.

Term	Meaning
BREASTS	
lumpectomy lŭm-pek′tō-mē	excision of a breast tumor without removing any other tissue or lymph nodes; most often followed by radiation and/or chemotherapy if cancerous
mastectomy mas-tek′tō-mē	removal of a breast (Fig. 17.22)
simple mastectomy	removal of an entire breast with underlying muscle and axillary lymph nodes left intact
radical mastectomy	removal of an entire breast, underlying chest muscles, and axillary lymph nodes
modified radical mastectomy	removal of an entire breast and axillary lymph nodes (Fig. 17.23A)

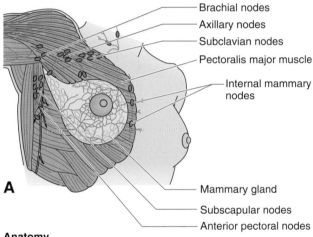

A

Anatomy
The breast, the underlying muscles, and the lymph nodes are the structures involved in breast cancer surgery. The lymph nodes, which act as barriers against bacteria or tumor cells, are useful in staging breast cancer.

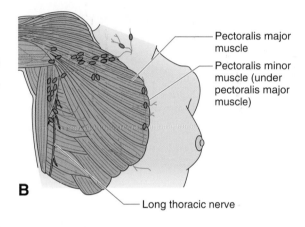

B

Simple Mastectomy
Only the breast is removed. The underlying muscle and associated lymph nodes are not removed.

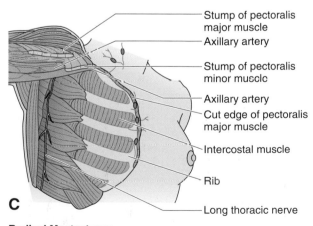

C

Radical Mastectomy
The breast, pectoralis muscles, and contents of the axilla (including lymph nodes and adipose tissue) are removed.

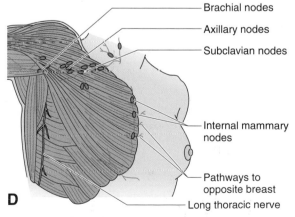

D

Modified Radical Mastectomy
The breast and lymph nodes of the axilla are removed. Occasionally, the pectoralis minor muscle is transected or removed to approach the lymph nodes.

Figure 17.22   A. Anatomy of the breast. **B–D.** Mastectomy alternatives.

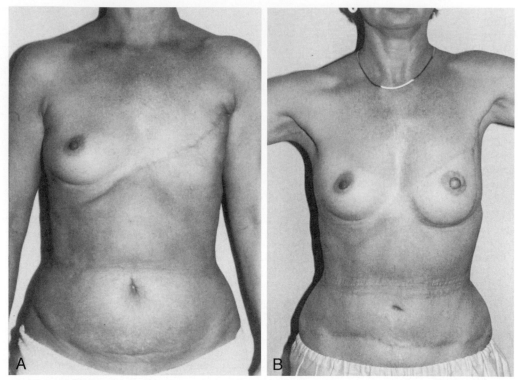

Figure 17.23 Augmentation mammoplasty. **A.** Left modified radical mastectomy in a 53-year-old woman (3 months postoperation). **B.** Same patient 10 months after augmentation mammoplasty.

Term	Meaning
mammoplasty mam′ō-plas-tē	surgical reconstruction of a breast
augmentation mammoplasty	reconstruction to enlarge the breast, often by insertion of an implant (see Fig. 17.23A and B)
reduction mammoplasty	reconstruction to remove excessive breast tissue (Fig. 17.24)
mastopexy mas′tō-pek-sē	elevation of pendulous breast tissue (see Fig. 17.24B)

Therapeutic Terms

Term	Meaning
chemotherapy kem′ō-thār-ă-pē	treatment of malignancies, infections, and other diseases with chemical agents that destroy selected cells or impair their ability to reproduce
radiation therapy	treatment of neoplastic disease by using radiation, usually from a cobalt source, to deter the proliferation of malignant cells
hormone replacement therapy (HRT)	use of a hormone (e.g., estrogen, progesterone) to replace a deficiency or regulate production

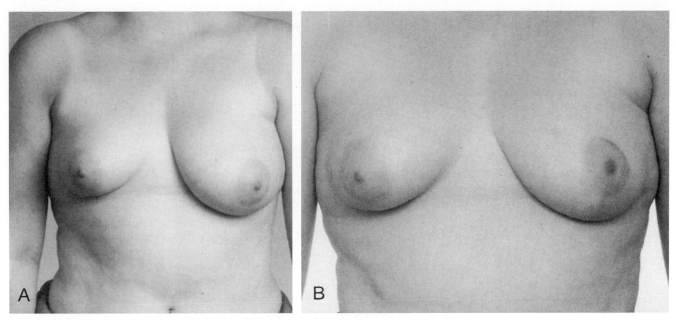

Figure 17.24 Mammoplasty and mastopexy. **A.** Micromastia of one breast and macromastia of the opposite breast in a 22-year-old patient. **B.** Same patient 15 months postreduction mammoplasty and mastopexy.

Term	Meaning
hormonal contraceptives	hormones used to prevent conception by suppressing ovulation
oral contraceptive pill (OCP)	birth control pill
contraceptive injection	injection of a hormone such as Depo-Provera into the body
contraceptive implant	insertion of a contraceptive capsule under the skin that provides a continual infusion over an extended time
barrier contraceptives	products that provide a physical barrier that prevents conception (e.g., condoms, diaphragms)
intrauterine device (IUD) in'tră-yū'ter-in	contraceptive device inserted into the uterus that prevents implantation of the fertilized egg
spermicidals sper-mi-sī'dălz	creams, jellies, lotions, or foams containing agents that kill sperm (cido = to kill)
uterine fibroid embolization (UFE)	catheter-guided injection of embolic agents into the arteries supplying blood to fibroid tumors, blocking circulation and causing shrinkage; minimally invasive procedure performed by a vascular and interventional radiologist in a angiographic laboratory

Obstetrical (OB) Symptomatic and Diagnostic Terms
ob-stet'ri-kal

Term	Meaning
SYMPTOMATIC	
gravida grav'i-dă	pregnant woman [Note: In an obstetrical history, gravida, or G, followed by a numeral indicates the number of pregnancies (Fig. 17.25).]
nulligravida nŭl-i-grav'i-dă	having never been pregnant
primigravida prī-mi-grav'i-dă	first pregnancy
para par'ă	to bear; a woman who has produced one or more viable (live outside the uterus) offspring [Note: In an obstetrical history, para, or P, followed by a numeral indicates the number of times a pregnancy has resulted in a single or multiple birth (see Fig. 17.25).]
nullipara nŭl-i-par'ă	woman who has not borne a child (nulli = none; para = to bear)
primipara pri-mip'ă-ră	first delivery (primi = first; para = to bear)
multipara mŭl-tip'ă-ră	woman who has given birth to two or more children (multi = many; para = to bear)
cervical effacement ĕ-fās'ment	progressive obliteration of the endocervical canal during delivery
estimated date of confinement (EDC) kon-fīn'ment	expected date for delivery of the baby—normally 280 days or 40 weeks from conception
estimated date of delivery (EDD)	
meconium staining mē-kō'nē-ŭm	presence of meconium in amniotic fluid
ruptured membranes rŭp'chūrd	rupture of the amniotic sac, usually at the onset of labor
macrosomia mak-rō-sō'mē-ă	large-bodied baby commonly seen in diabetic pregnancies (macro = large; soma = body)
polyhydramnios pol'ē-hī-dram'nē-os	excessive amniotic fluid
DIAGNOSTIC	
abortion (AB) ă-bōr'shŭn	expulsion of the product of conception before the fetus can be viable (live outside the uterus)
spontaneous abortion (SAB) spon-tā'nē-ŭs	miscarriage; expulsion of products of conception occurring naturally

The following abbreviations are used in recording an obstetrical history.

GPA terms:
G   gravida   number of pregnancies
P   para   number of viable birth experiences (may include multiple births)
AB abortus   abortions
     SAB   spontaneous abortion
     TAB   therapeutic abortion

Arabic numerals are placed after each abbreviation to indicate the number of pregnancies, viable births, or abortions.

Example:

Obstetric history: G2, P1, AB1 or gravida 2, para 1, abortus 1.
[The patient has been pregnant twice, had one birth experience that resulted in the delivery of at least one viable offspring, and had one abortion.]

TPAL terms:
T   term infants
P   premature infants
A   abortions
L   living children

Example:

Obstetric history: 5 term infants, 0 premature infants, 0 abortions, 5 living children or Obstetric history: 5-0-0-5.
[The patient has delivered five term infants, no premature infants, no abortions and has five living children.]

Occasionally, combined GPA and TPAL abbreviations are used. For example:

Obstetrical history: gravida 3, 4-0-0-4
[The patient has been pregnant three times, had four term infants, no premature infants, no abortions, and has 4 living children. (Numbers indicate one twin birth.)]

Figure 17.25   Obstetrical history abbreviations.

Term	Meaning
habitual abortion	spontaneous abortion occurring in three or more consecutive pregnancies
incomplete abortion	incomplete expulsion of products of conception
missed abortion	death of a fetus or embryo within the uterus that is not naturally expelled after death
threatened abortion	bleeding with threat of miscarriage

ECLAMPSIA.
Eclampsia is a
Greek word
meaning to flash out or
shine forth suddenly, first
used in the 18th century for
any sudden convulsion.
Today, it particularly refers
to toxemia of pregnancy.

Term	Meaning
cephalopelvic disproportion (CPD) sef′ă-lō-pel′vik	conditions preventing normal delivery through the birth canal—either the baby's head is too large or the birth canal is too small
eclampsia ek-lamp′sē-ă	true toxemia of pregnancy characterized by high blood pressure, albuminuria, edema of the legs and feet, severe headaches, dizziness, convulsions, and coma
preeclampsia prē-ē-klamp′sē-ă **pregnancy-induced hypertension (PIH)**	toxemia of pregnancy characterized by high blood pressure, albuminuria, edema of the legs and feet, and puffiness of the face, without convulsion or coma
ectopic pregnancy ek-top′ik	implantation of the fertilized egg outside the uterine cavity, often in the tube, ovary, or (rarely) the abdominal cavity (Fig. 17.26)
erythroblastosis fetalis ě-rith′rō-blas-tō′sis fē′tā′lis	disorder that results from the incompatibility of a fetus with an Rh-positive blood factor and a mother who is Rh negative, causing red blood cell destruction in the fetus—necessitates a blood transfusion to save the fetus
Rh factor	presence, or lack, of antigens on the surface of red blood cells that may cause a reaction between the blood of the mother and fetus, resulting in fetal anemia (which causes erythroblastosis fetalis)
Rh positive	presence of antigens
Rh negative	absence of antigens

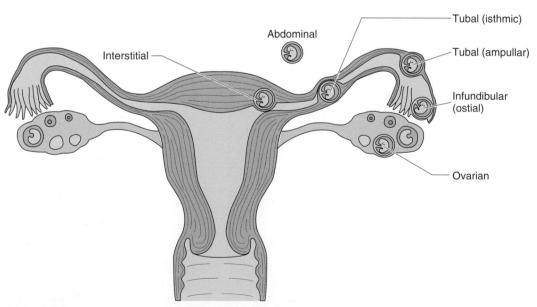

Figure 17.26 Ectopic pregnancy: sites of extrauterine implantation.

Term	Meaning
hyperemesis gravidarum hī-per-em′ĕ-sis grav-i-dā′rŭm	severe nausea and vomiting in pregnancy that can cause severe dehydration in the mother and fetus (emesis = vomit)
meconium aspiration mē-kō′nē-ŭm as-pi-rā′shŭn	fetal aspiration of amniotic fluid containing meconium
placenta previa plă-sen′tă prē′vē-ă	displaced attachment of the placenta in the lower region of the uterine cavity (Fig. 17.27)
abruptio placentae ab-rŭp′shē-ō pla-sen′tē	premature detachment of a normally situated placenta

Obstetrical Diagnostic Tests and Procedures

Test or Procedure	Explanation
chorionic villus sampling (CVS) kō-rē-on′ik vil′us	sampling of placental tissue for microscopic and chemical examination to detect fetal abnormalities (Fig. 17.28A)
amniocentesis am′nē-ō-sen-tē′sis	aspiration of a small amount of amniotic fluid for analysis of possible fetal abnormalities (Fig. 17.28B)
fetal monitoring	use of an electronic device for simultaneous recording of fetal heart rate and uterine contractions
pelvimetry pel-vim′ĕ-trē	obstetrical measurement of the pelvis to evaluate proper conditions for vaginal delivery
pregnancy test	test performed on urine or blood to detect the presence of human chorionic gonadotropin hormone (secreted by the placenta) that indicates pregnancy

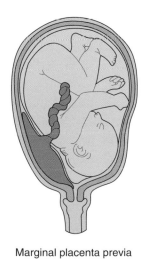 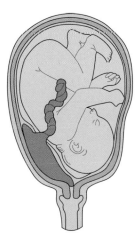 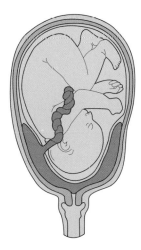

Marginal placenta previa   Partial placenta previa   Total placenta previa

Figure 17.27 Placenta previa.

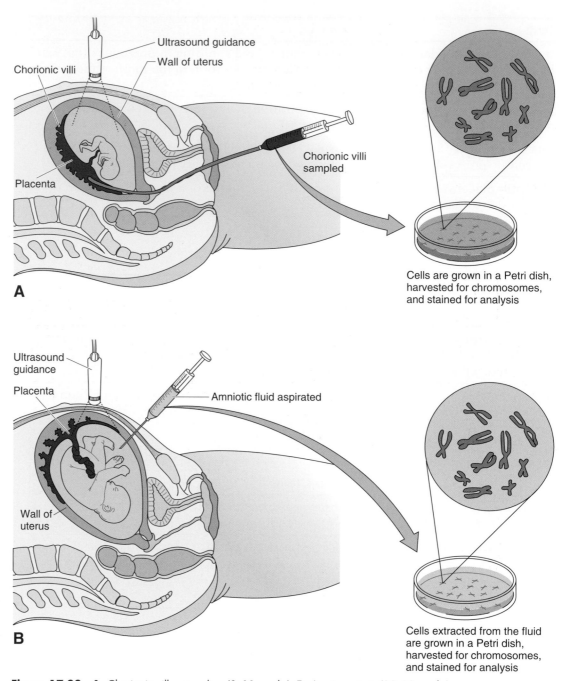

Figure 17.28 **A.** Chorionic villus sampling (9–11 weeks). **B.** Amniocentesis (15–18 weeks).

Term	Meaning
endovaginal sonogram **transvaginal sonogram**	ultrasound image of the uterus, tubes, and ovaries made after introduction of an ultrasonic transducer within the vagina—useful in detecting pathology (e.g., ectopic pregnancy, missed abortion) (see Fig. 17.16)
obstetrical sonogram	ultrasound image of the pregnant uterus to determine fetal development (see Figs. 17.3B, 17.4B, and 17.16B)

Obstetrical Operative and Therapeutic Terms

Term	Meaning
OPERATIVE	
cesarean section (C-section) se-zā′rē-ăn	surgical delivery of a baby by making an incision through the abdomen and into the uterus
episiotomy e-piz-ē-ot′ō-mē	incision of the perineum to facilitate delivery
THERAPEUTIC	
amnioinfusion am′nē-ō-in-fyū′zhŭn	introduction of a solution into the amniotic sac—most commonly an isotonic solution used to relieve fetal distress
therapeutic abortion (TAB)	abortion induced by mechanical means or by drugs for medical consideration
version	manual method reversing the position of the fetus, usually done to facilitate delivery
external version	abdominal manipulation
internal version	intravaginal manipulation
COMMON THERAPEUTIC DRUG CLASSIFICATIONS	
abortifacient ă-bōr ti fā′shent	drug that causes abortion (e.g., RU-486)
oxytocin ok-sē-tō′sin	hormone secreted by the pituitary gland that causes myometrial contraction—used for induction of labor
Rh immune globulin glob′yū-lin	immunizing agent given to an Rh-negative mother within 72 hours after delivering an Rh-positive baby to suppress the Rh immune response
tocolytic agent tō-kō-lit′ik	drug used to stop labor contractions

CESAREAN SECTION. The fetus is removed from the uterus through an incision in the abdomen. The procedure was first used to save the baby when the mother had died. Julius Caesar is said to have been born in this manner.

Summary of Chapter 17 Acronyms/Abbreviations

AB	abortion	IUD	intrauterine device
Bx	biopsy	LEEP	loop electrosurgical excision procedure
CIS	carcinoma in situ		
CIN	cervical intraepithelial neoplasia	LLETZ	large loop excision of the transformation zone
CPD	cephalopelvic disproportion		
C-section	cesarean section	MRI	magnetic resonance imaging
CVS	chorionic villus sampling	OB	obstetrics
D&C	dilation and curettage	OCP	oral contraceptive pill
EDC	estimated date of confinement	Pap	Papanicolaou smear
EDD	estimated date of delivery	PID	pelvic inflammatory disease
GYN	gynecology	PIH	pregnancy-induced hypertension
HIV	human immunodeficiency virus	SAB	spontaneous abortion
HPV	human papilloma virus	STD	sexually transmitted disease
HRT	hormone replacement therapy	TAB	therapeutic abortion
HSV-2	herpes simplex virus type 2	UFE	uterine fibroid embolization

PRACTICE EXERCISES

For the following terms, on the lines below the term, write out the indicated word parts: prefixes (P), combining forms (CF), roots (R), and suffixes (S). Then define the word.

EXAMPLE

ectocervical

_____ / _____ / _____
    P   R   S

<u>ecto/cervic/al</u>
  P   R   S

DEFINITION: outside/cervix or neck/pertaining to

1. vulvitis

_____ / _____
       R   S

DEFINITION: _____

2. polymastia

_____ / _____ / _____
      P   R   S

DEFINITION: _____

3. ovoid

_____ / _____
       R   S

DEFINITION: _____

4. tocolysis

_____ / _____
      CF   S

DEFINITION: _____

5. salpingotomy

_____ / _____
      CF   S

DEFINITION: _____

6. mammoplasty

_____ / _____
      CF   S

DEFINITION: _____

7. transvaginal

_____ / _____ / _____
        P   R   S

DEFINITION: _____

8. hysterorrhexis

_____ / _____
        CF   S

DEFINITION: _____

9. colposcopy

_____ / _____
        CF   S

DEFINITION: _____

10. mammography

_____ / _____
        CF   S

DEFINITION: _____

11. metrorrhagia

_____ / _____
        CF   S

DEFINITION: _____

12. ovariocentesis

_____ / _____
        CF   S

DEFINITION: _____

13. menarche

_____ / _____
        R   S

DEFINITION: _____

14. oophorectomy

_____ / _____
        R   S

DEFINITION: _____

15. oligomenorrhea

_____ / _____ / _____
        P   CF   S

DEFINITION: _____

16. dystocia

_____ / _____ / _____
        P   R   S

DEFINITION: _____

17. gynecologist

_____ / _____
CF   S

DEFINITION: _____

18. pelvimeter

_____ / _____
CF   S

DEFINITION: _____

19. episiotomy

_____ / _____
CF   S

DEFINITION: _____

20. colporrhaphy

_____ / _____
CF   S

DEFINITION: _____

21. hysterospasm

_____ / _____
CF   S

DEFINITION: _____

22. lactorrhea

_____ / _____
CF   S

DEFINITION: _____

23. ovigenesis

_____ / _____
CF   S

DEFINITION: _____

24. endocervical

_____ / _____ / _____
P   R   S

DEFINITION: _____

25. uterotomy

_____ / _____
CF   S

DEFINITION: _____

Complete the following:

26. _____ pause = cessation of menstruation

27. _____ menorrhea = painful menstruation

28. _____ menorrhea = absence of menstruation

29. _____ menorrhea = scanty menstruation

30. _____ rrhagia = excessive bleeding at time of menstruation

31. _____ rrhagia = bleeding from the uterus at any time other than the normal period

32. _____ mastia = development of mammary glands in male

33. _____ mastia = absence of a breast

34. _____ mastia = unusually small breasts—a common surgical remedy is _____ mammoplasty

35. _____ mastia = unusually large breasts—a common surgical remedy is _____ mammoplasty

36. masto_____ = surgical fixation of a pendulous breast

37. _____ ectomy = removal of a breast

38. _____ ectomy = removal of a breast lump

For each of the following, circle the combining form that corresponds to the meaning given:

39. **birth or labor**	tox/o	toc/o	troph/o
40. **vagina**	uter/o	metr/o	colp/o
41. **uterine tube**	vagin/o	oophor/o	salping/o
42. **menstruation**	men/o	mamm/o	mast/o
43. **cervix**	colp/o	cervic/o	salping/o
44. **egg**	oophor/o	ov/i	ovari/o
45. **vulva**	episi/o	vagin/o	metr/o
46. **uterus**	vagin/o	metr/o	oophor/o
47. **milk**	lact/o	leuk/o	lip/o
48. **ovary**	ov/o	oophor/o	salping/o
49. **breast**	men/o	metr/o	mast/o
50. **woman**	gen/o	gynec/o	hyster/o

Match the following:

51. _____ removal of a uterine tube   a. PID
     and an ovary

52. _____ white vaginal discharge   b. chlamydia

53. _____ condition when the baby's head   c. colporrhaphy
     is too big for the birth canal

54. _____ presence of more than   d. LEEP
     one nipple on a breast

55. _____ implantation of a fertilized   e. CPD
     egg outside the uterus

56. _____ most common bacterial   f. leukorrhea
     STD in North America

57. _____ excisional biopsy   g. polythelia

58. _____ painful intercourse   h. ectopic pregnancy

59. _____ surgical repair of a cystocele   i. salpingo-oophorectomy

60. _____ inflammation of entire   j. dyspareunia
     female pelvic cavity

Give the medical term for the following:

61. condition of benign lumps in the breast that fluctuate in size during the
    menstrual cycle _____

62. abnormal opening between the bladder and vagina _____

63. cutting and tying the uterine tubes _____

64. having more than two breasts _____

65. bacterial STD caused by a spirochete _____

66. study of cervical cells to screen for cancer _____

67. condition of migration of endometrial tissue _____

68. abnormal opening between the rectum and vagina _____

69. surgical remedy for a rectocele _____

Define the following abbreviations:

70. IUD _____

71. HPV _____

72. CVS _____

73. D&C _____

74. HBV _____

75. EDC _____

76. HSV _____

77. STD _____

78. TAB _____

79. HRT _____

Identify terms related to abortion:

80. _____ a naturally occurring miscarriage

81. _____ a miscarriage occurring in three or more consecutive pregnancies

82. _____ fetal expulsion with parts of the placenta remaining with bleeding

83. _____ fetal death within the uterus

84. _____ abortion induced by mechanical means or by drugs

85. _____ bleeding with the threat of miscarriage

Match the following:

86. _____ retroflexion   a. forward bend of uterus

87. _____ condylomata   b. toxemia of pregnancy

88. _____ para 2   c. backward bend of uterus

89. _____ prolapse   d. a pregnant woman

90. _____ cystocele   e. cancer

91. _____ gravida   f. genital warts

92. _____ rectocele   g. woman who has given birth twice

93. _____ eclampsia   h. first delivery

94. _____ CIN 2   i. protrusion of the rectum into the vagina

95. _____ primipara   j. descent of the uterus from its normal position

96. _____ anteflexion   k. cervical dysplasia

97. _____ CIS   l. pouching of the bladder into the vagina

Write in the missing words on the blank lines in the following illustration of the female reproductive anatomy.

98–105.

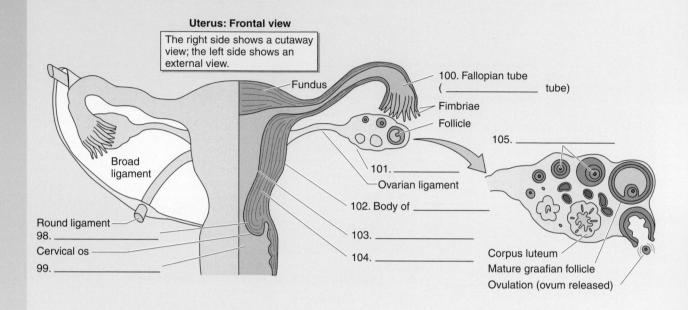

Uterus: Frontal view

The right side shows a cutaway view; the left side shows an external view.

Fundus

100. Fallopian tube (_____ tube)

Fimbriae

Follicle

Broad ligament

105. _____

Round ligament

98. _____

Cervical os

99. _____

101. _____

Ovarian ligament

102. Body of _____

103. _____

104. _____

Corpus luteum

Mature graafian follicle

Ovulation (ovum released)

For each of the following, circle the correct spelling of the term:

106.	gonoorhea	gonorrhea	ghonarhea
107.	dyspareunia	dyspariunia	dysparunia
108.	tokolytic	toecolytic	tocolytic
109.	polithelia	polythelia	polytelia
110.	meterorrhagia	metrorrhagia	metrorhagia
111.	dialation	dyelayshun	dilation
112.	salpingottomy	salpingotomy	salpigotomy
113.	nulligravida	nuligravida	nulligraveda
114.	meconeium	meconium	meconeum
115.	macrosomia	macrosomnia	macrasomia
116.	cureitage	curettage	curetage
117.	eclampshea	eklampsia	eclampsia
118.	amenorrhea	amennorhea	amenorhea
119.	abortifacient	abortafacient	abortofacent

Give the noun that was used to form the following adjectives:

120. chlamydial _____

121. areolar _____

122. syphilitic _____

123. cervical _____

124. dysplastic _____

125. endometrial _____

MEDICAL RECORD ANALYSES

MEDICAL RECORD 17.1

GYN Chart Note

S: This 44 y.o. female, gravida 2, para 2, c/o extremely heavy periods for the past several years that have been getting worse for the past 2 months and have been accompanied by moderately severe cramps. Pap smears have been normal. She has no bladder or bowel complaints.

O: On pelvic exam, the uterus is found to be retroverted and irregularly enlarged with several large fibroids palpable. There are no adnexal masses.

A: Leiomyomata uteri with secondary menorrhagia

P: Schedule vaginal hysterectomy; donate 1 pint of blood for autologous transfusion, if necessary

1. What is the patient's OB history?
   a. never been pregnant
   b. been pregnant only once
   c. had two miscarriages
   d. has been pregnant four times
   e. has had two live births

2. Identify the patient's most significant symptom:
   a. amenorrhea
   b. dyspareunia
   c. leukorrhea
   d. menorrhagia
   e. metrorrhagia

3. Which of the following was one of the objective findings?
   a. tipped uterus
   b. forward-bending uterus
   c. backward-bending uterus
   d. presence of several ovarian tumors
   e. migration of portions of endometrial tissue

4. What was the condition of the patient's uterine tubes?
   a. not stated
   b. normal
   c. inflamed
   d. enlarged
   e. had been previously removed

5. What was the Dx?
   a. congenital tumor composed of displaced embryonic tissue
   b. cyst of the uterine tube
   c. inflammation of the organs of the pelvic cavity
   d. smooth muscle tumors in the uterus
   e. ovarian tumors

6. What surgical procedure is planned?
   a. incision into uterine tube to remove the cyst
   b. excision of uterus
   c. excision of ovaries
   d. dilation of cervix and scraping of endometrium
   e. excision of tubes and ovaries

MEDICAL RECORD 17.2

Jane Foley has seen her gynecologist, Dr. Phyllis Widetick, yearly for a routine examination and Pap smear. Every year, the results have been normal. Jane is generally a healthy, active woman. This year, however, Dr. Widetick's examination and Pap smear found a problem. When the test results were in, Jane returned for additional testing.

Directions

Read Medical Record 17.2 for Ms. Foley (pages 575–576) and answer the following questions. This record is the history and physical report dictated by Dr. Widetick after her examination.

QUESTIONS ABOUT MEDICAL RECORD 17.2

Write your answers in the spaces provided.

1. In your own words, not using medical terminology, briefly describe the patient's chief complaint:

_____

_____

_____

2. In your own words, not using medical terminology, briefly describe what a Pap smear is:

_____

_____

_____

3. Explain the result of Ms. Foley's Pap smear:

_____

_____

_____

4. Because of this result, Dr. Widetick used colposcopy for further testing. Translate into nonmedical language what she discovered with this diagnostic procedure:

_____

_____

_____

5. What was the positive finding from the biopsy? Define this in your own words:

_____

_____

_____

6. Ms. Foley underwent all the following procedures. Put these in correct sequence by numbering them 1 to 6 in the order they were performed:

_____ follow-up examination

_____ visualization with colposcope

_____ ultrasound

_____ Pap smear

_____ routine physical examination

_____ Bx

7. The sonogram *definitely* showed what finding?

_____

What were the *possible* findings?

_____

_____

8. In nonmedical language, define the two previous surgeries Ms. Foley has had:

_____

_____

_____

9. How many children has Ms. Foley had?

_____

10. Mark any of the following abnormal findings from the present physical examination:
    a. enlarged uterus
    b. gross reflexes
    c. eroded cervix
    d. hypertension
    e. enlarged thyroid
    f. mobile right ovarian cyst

11. Define Dr. Widetick's final diagnosis, and explain what she will do next to treat Ms. Foley:

_____

_____

_____

CENTRAL MEDICAL CENTER

211 Medical Center Drive • Central City, US 90000-1234

TO BE ADMITTED: 9/3/20xx

HISTORY

CHIEF COMPLAINT:
Right ovarian cyst.

HISTORY OF PRESENT ILLNESS:
This is a 32-year-old Caucasian female who had a routine examination on June 21, 20xx, at which time the examination revealed the right ovary to be approximately two to three times normal size. Otherwise, all was normal. The Papanicolaou smear revealed atypical cells of undetermined significance. The patient returned for a colposcopy, and this revealed what appeared to be squamous epithelial lesions CIN 1–2. Biopsies were performed, which revealed chronic cervicitis and no evidence of CIN. The patient was placed on Lo-Ovral for two cycles and then was rechecked. The right ovary continued to enlarge and got to the point where it was approximately 4 x 5 cm, floating anteriorly in the pelvis, and was fairly firm to palpation. A pelvic sonogram corroborated the clinical findings in that superior to the right adnexa was a 4 x 5 cm mass, possibly with hemorrhage into either a paraovarian cyst or possibly a dermoid cyst. The patient is to be admitted now for an exploratory laparotomy.

PAST HISTORY:
There is no history of severe medical illnesses. The patient had the usual childhood diseases and has had good health as an adult.

PREVIOUS SURGERY: The patient had a hymenotomy and dilation and curettage in 20xx.

MENSTRUAL HISTORY: Menstrual cycle is 30 days, averaging a 4 – 7 day flow.

OBSTETRICAL HISTORY: The patient is a gravida 0.

FAMILY HISTORY:
Diabetes in the family. Mother and father are living and well.

REVIEW OF SYSTEMS:
Noncontributory.

(continued)

P. Widetick, M.D.
P. Widetick, M.D.

PW:bst
D: 9/1/20xx T: 9/2/20xx

HISTORY AND PHYSICAL Page 1	PT. NAME: FOLEY, JANE J. ID NO: IP-751014 ROOM NO: 331 ATT. PHYS: P. WIDETICK, M.D.

Medical Record 17.2

CENTRAL MEDICAL CENTER

211 Medical Center Drive • Central City, US 90000-1234

PHYSICAL EXAMINATION

GENERAL:
The patient is a well-developed, well-nourished Caucasian female who is anxious but in no acute distress.

VITAL SIGNS:
HEIGHT: 5 feet 5 inches. WEIGHT: 154 pounds. BLOOD PRESSURE: 110/82.

HEENT:
Normal.

NECK:
Supple; the trachea is in the midline. The thyroid is not enlarged.

CHEST:
LUNGS: Clear to percussion and auscultation. HEART: Regular sinus rhythm with no murmur. BREASTS: Normal to palpation.

ABDOMEN:
Soft and flat. No scars or masses.

PELVIC:
The outlet and vagina are normal. The cervix is moderately eroded. The uterus is normal size and anterior. The left adnexa is negative. The right adnexa has a firm, irregular cystic ovary that is anterior and approximately 5 x 5 cm. This is mobile and nontender.

EXTREMITIES:
Normal. Reflexes are grossly intact.

DIAGNOSIS:
Right ovarian cyst.

PLAN:
The patient is to be admitted for laparoscopy and probable ovarian cystectomy.

P. Widetick, M.D.
P. Widetick, M.D.

PW:bst
D: 9/1/20xx T: 9/2/20xx

HISTORY AND PHYSICAL PAGE 2	PT. NAME: FOLEY, JANE J. ID NO: IP-751014 ROOM NO: 331 ATT. PHYS: P. WIDETICK, M.D.

Medical Record 17.2 *Continued*

MEDICAL RECORD 17.3

Kathleen Montegrande is pregnant with her first child. She has regularly seen her obstetrician, Dr. Linda Fenton, throughout the pregnancy. The pregnancy has gone well so far, although the fetus is in a breech presentation. She has come for a routine obstetrical examination by Dr. Fenton, which confirms the breech presentation. She then reports to Central Medical Center when labor begins.

Directions

Read Medical Record 17.3 for Ms. Montegrande (pages 579–581) and answer the following questions. The first record is the history and physical examination report dictated by Dr. Fenton after Ms. Montegrande's last routine examination and before delivery. The second record is the discharge summary dictated from Central Medical Center by Dr. Fenton after Ms. Montegrande had her baby.

QUESTIONS ABOUT MEDICAL RECORD 17.3

Write your answers in the spaces provided:

1. Below are medical terms used in this record you have not yet encountered in this text. Underline each where it appears in the record and define below:

   Apgar score _____

   rubella vaccination _____

2. In your own words, not using medical terminology, briefly describe a breech presentation:

   _____

   _____

   _____

3. Which two tests that Dr. Fenton performed confirmed the breech presentation?
   a. sonography
   b. cesarean
   c. amniocentesis
   d. Bx
   e. pelvic examination
   f. colposcopy
   g. Pap smear

4. Mark any possible negative findings included in PMH:
   a. rheumatic fever
   b. closed cervix
   c. heart murmur
   d. mitral valve prolapse

5. Where did the autologous blood come from?

   _____

6. Explain what is important about the possibility of Ms. Montegrande's baby being Rh positive:

_____

_____

_____

7. In your own words, explain what "80% effaced" means:

_____

_____

_____

8. What is the main reason for Dr. Fenton's plan to perform a primary cesarean section?

_____

_____

_____

9. What two occurrences brought Ms. Montegrande to the Central Medical Center on March 6?

_____

_____

_____

10. In your own words, describe the surgery Ms. Montegrande underwent:

_____

_____

_____

11. What kind of suture did Dr. Fenton use to close the incision?

_____

12. Two other doctors were present in the surgical suite with Dr. Fenton:

Dr. Nelson was there to help care for (whom?) _____

Dr. O'Brien was there to help care for (whom?) _____

13. Mark any of the following surgical complications that occurred:
    a. uterine hemorrhage
    b. postop fever
    c. cervical erosion
    d. all of the above
    e. none of the above

CENTRAL MEDICAL CENTER

211 Medical Center Drive • Central City, US 90000-1234

HISTORY

HISTORY OF PRESENT ILLNESS:

The patient is a 31-year-old female, gravida 1 para 0, whose estimated date of confinement is March 8, 20xx. The patient has had a relatively normal pregnancy with normal blood pressures and approximately a 53-pound weight gain during her pregnancy. The infant has been noted to be in a breech position since mid-December 20xx and has remained in that position without any change. This position was confirmed by ultrasound and pelvic examination within the past few days. This patient is scheduled at this time to have a primary cesarean section because of the breech presentation. There is a small amount of amniotic fluid; and external version, I believe, would be injudicious at this time.

PAST MEDICAL HISTORY:

MEDICAL: Entirely negative except for possible mitral valve prolapse in this patient. She has never had any rheumatic fever and has had no other heart disease. She has had no high blood pressure, diabetes, thyroid trouble, varicose veins, or epilepsy. She has never had a blood transfusion. The patient specifically had requested to have one unit of autologous blood drawn earlier in her pregnancy, which is available. The patient is Rh negative, and she is not immune to rubella; therefore, she will need a RhoGAM shot if her baby is Rh positive and will need a rubella vaccination before leaving the hospital. The patient was given RhoGAM in our office on December 18, 20xx.

Her additional past medical history is noncontributory.

(continued)

L. Fenton, M.D.

L. Fenton, M.D.

LF:pn

D: 3/4/20xx
T: 3/5/20xx

HISTORY AND PHYSICAL Page 1	PT. NAME: MONTEGRANDE, KATHLEEN L. ID NO: IP-692580 ROOM NO: 377 ADM. DATE: March 8, 20xx ATT. PHYS: L. FENTON, M.D.

Medical Record 17.3

CENTRAL MEDICAL CENTER

211 Medical Center Drive • Central City, US 90000-1234

PHYSICAL EXAMINATION

HEENT:
Essentially normal.

NECK:
The thyroid is not enlarged. There is no lymphadenopathy in the neck or supraclavicular region.

CHEST:
Clear to percussion and auscultation.

CARDIAC: There are no murmurs or irregularities. There are no heaves, thrills, or thrusts.

BREASTS: Examination fails to reveal any masses.

ABDOMEN:
The uterus measures 42 cm by tape measurement. The infant is still in a breech position.

PELVIC:
The cervix is closed, approximately 80% effaced, and soft.

IMPRESSION:
TERM BREECH PREGNANCY IN PRIMIGRAVIDA FEMALE WHO IS RH NEGATIVE.

PLAN:
Primary cesarean section. I have explained the pros and cons of surgery and the possible alternatives. The patient and her husband do understand and have accepted the risks. The patient has one unit of autologous blood available, and she is in need of a rubella immunization prior to discharge from the hospital.

L. Fenton, M.D.

LF:pn

D: 3/4/20xx
T: 3/5/20xx

HISTORY AND PHYSICAL Page 2	PT. NAME: MONTEGRANDE, KATHLEEN L. ID NO: IP-692580 ROOM NO: 377 ADM. DATE: March 8, 20xx ATT. PHYS: L. FENTON, M.D.

Medical Record 17.3   *Continued*

CENTRAL MEDICAL CENTER

211 Medical Center Drive • Central City, US 90000-1234

DISCHARGE SUMMARY

DATE OF ADMISSION: March 6, 20xx   **DATE OF DISCHARGE:** March 9, 20xx

SUMMARY:
Mrs. Montegrande was scheduled to be admitted to this facility on March 8, 20xx, because of a primiparous breech presentation and came in on March 6, 20xx, at 0345 hours with a history of spontaneous rupture of the membranes and labor. She is a 31-year-old gravida 1 para 0 abortus 0 with an EDC of March 8, 20xx, and spontaneous ruptured membranes at approximately 0200 hours with onset of contractions probably before that, with a breech presentation confirmed on ultrasound. The cervix is posterior, 3 cm, and soft. There is some meconium staining. The patient was therefore set up for a primary cesarean section. The patient was taken to the operating room, where the primary cesarean section was accomplished; and she was delivered out of a frank breech presentation of a 7 lb 8 oz male infant, Apgars 9 and 9, with Dr. O'Brien, the pediatrician, in attendance. The assistant surgeon was Dr. Nelson.

The patient and infant are discharged on this date to home with full instructions; the patient will take Tylenol Double Strength for pain and will be seen in the office in two weeks for staple removal. She is to call if she has any problems with excessive bleeding or fever.

FINAL DIAGNOSIS:
PREGNANCY, UTERINE, DELIVERED.

COMPLICATIONS:
Primiparous breech.

TREATMENT RENDERED:
Low cesarean section.

L. Fenton, MD
L. Fenton, M.D.

LF:ti

D: 3/9/20xx
T: 3/10/20xx

DISCHARGE SUMMARY	PT. NAME:	MONTEGRANDE, KATHLEEN L.
	ID NO:	IP-692580
	ROOM NO:	377
	ATT. PHYS.	L. FENTON, M.D.

Medical Record 17.3 *Continued*

MEDICAL RECORD 17.4

Carla Woodward has been healthy all her life but is bothered by the unbalanced shape of her breasts. Finally, at age 23, she has chosen to see Dr. Karen McNeil, a plastic surgeon recommended by her personal physician.

Directions

Read Medical Record 17.4 for Ms. Woodward (page 584) and answer the following questions. This record is the consultation report dictated by Dr. McNeil after meeting with and examining Ms. Woodward.

QUESTIONS ABOUT MEDICAL RECORD 17.4

Write your answers in the spaces provided:

1. Below are medical terms used in this record you have not yet encountered in this text. Underline each where it appears in the record and define below:

   saline-filled _____

   silicone walled _____

2. In your own words, not using medical terminology, describe Ms. Woodward's chief complaint:

   _____

   _____

   _____

3. Summarize the two past surgeries Ms. Woodward has had. For each, identify the primary body system involved:

   _____

   _____

   _____

4. Ms. Woodward told Dr. McNeil that she has never had a mammogram, a diagnostic procedure used primarily for what purpose?

   _____

   _____

   _____

5. Dr. McNeil's physical examination focuses on Ms. Woodward's breasts. Describe the findings related to the breasts (first give the medical term for the finding, then define it):

	Medical Finding	*Definition*
Left breast	_____	_____
	_____	_____
Right breast	_____	_____
	_____	_____

6. In your own words, not using medical language, describe the surgery Dr. McNeil has proposed to Ms. Woodward:

_____

_____

_____

CENTRAL MEDICAL GROUP, INC.

Department of Plastic Surgery

201 Medical Center Drive • Central City, US 90000-1234

INITIAL CONSULTATION

PATIENT: WOODWARD, Carla S.

DATE: October 2, 20xx

HPI: This is a 23-year-old white female in general good health who has significant bilateral breast asymmetry with macromastia on the left breast and deformity and hypoplasia of the right breast. The patient denies having had any other problems except that her right thumb is shorter than her left thumb.

PMH: A left inguinal herniorrhaphy at age 15 and a laminectomy on March 1, 20xx, for treatment of a ruptured disk. The rest of her history is unremarkable.

MEDS: Vicodin 2-3 q d for the past 7 months secondary to her surgery.

ALLERGIES: None.

SH: The patient denies history of smoking or alcohol use and has never had a mammogram.

PE: The patient has a sternal nipple-notch distance of 27 cm on the left side and 22 cm on the right side. There are no breast masses or nipple discharge noted. The right breast is atrophic in the medial half of the breast, and the entire breast is hypoplastic. The left breast is large and ptotic. The patient reports being approximately an A-B cup on the right side and a C-D cup on the left side. She feels the right side is much too small and deformed, and the left side is too big.

PLAN: The patient would do well with a left breast reduction and a right breast augmentation/reconstruction of the deformity and atrophy. The risks and benefits of this surgery were discussed with the patient along with the risks and benefits of saline-filled, silicone-wall implants. The patient will think about our discussion today and contact me with a date.

K. McNeil, M
K. McNeil, M.D.

KM:mar

D: 10/2/20xx
T: 10/3/20xx

Medical Record 17.4

APPENDIX A

Glossary of Prefixes, Suffixes, and Combining Forms

Term Component to English

a- ....without
ab- ....away from
abdomin/o ....abdomen
-ac ....pertaining to
acous/o.................hearing
acr/o.....................extremity or
                        topmost
-acusis ....hearing condition
ad- ....to, toward, or near
aden/o ....gland
adip/o....................fat
adren/o..................adrenal gland
aer/o.....................air or gas
-al ....pertaining to
albumin/o ....protein
-algia ....pain
allo- ....other
alveol/o................alveolus (air sac)
ambi- ....both
an- ....without
ana- ....up, apart
an/o ....anus
andr/o ....male
angi/o...................vessel
ankyl/o ....crooked or stiff
ante-....................before
anti- ....against or opposed
                        to
aort/o ....aorta
appendic/o...........appendix
aque/o ....water
-ar.......................pertaining to
-arche ....beginning
arteri/o................artery
arthr/o ....joint, articulation
articul/o ....joint
-ary......................pertaining to
-ase......................enzyme
-asthenia ....weakness
ather/o ....fatty paste
-ation ....process
atri/o....................atrium
audi/o...................hearing
aur/i ....ear
auto-....................self
bacteri/o..............bacteria

balan/o ....glans penis
bi-.........................two or both
bil/i......................bile
-blast ....germ or bud
blast/o ....germ or bud
blephar/o ....eyelid
brachi/o ....arm
brady- ....slow
bronch/o ....bronchus (airway)
bronchi/o ....bronchus (airway)
bronchiol/o ....bronchiole (little
                        airway)
bucc/o ....cheek
capn/o ....carbon dioxide
carb/o..................carbon dioxide
carcin/o ....cancer
cardi/o..................heart
cata- ....down
-cele.....................pouching or hernia
celi/o ....abdomen
-centesis..............puncture for
                        aspiration
cephal/o ....head
cerebell/o ....cerebellum (little
                        brain)
cerebr/o ....cerebrum (largest
                        part of brain)
cerumin/o ....wax
cervic/o ....neck or cervix
cheil/o ....lip
chir/o ....hand
chol/e ....bile
chondr/o ....cartilage (gristle)
chrom/o ....color
chromat/o ....color
chyl/o ....juice
circum- ....around
cis/o.....................cut
col/o.....................colon
colon/o.................colon
colp/o...................vagina (sheath)
con- ....together or with
conjunctiv/o.........conjunctiva (to
                        join together)
contra- ....against or opposed
                        to
corne/o.................cornea

coron/o.................circle or crown
cost/o ....rib
crani/o ....skull
crin/o ....to secrete
cutane/o ....skin
cyan/o ....blue
cyst/o ....bladder or sac
cyt/o.....................cell
dacry/o.................tear
dactyl/o ....digit (finger or
                        toe)
de- ....from, down, or not
dent/i ....teeth
derm/o ....skin
dermat/o ....skin
-desis ....binding
dextr/o ....right, or on the
                        right side
dia-.......................across or through
diaphor/o ....profuse sweat
dips/o ....thirst
dis- ....separate from or
                        apart
doch/o ....duct
duoden/o ....duodenum
-dynia...................pain
dys- ....painful, difficult,
                        or faulty
-e ....noun marker
e- ....out or away
-eal ....pertaining to
ec- ....out or away
-ectasis ....expansion or
                        dilation
ecto- ....outside
-ectomy ....excision (removal)
-emesis.................vomiting
-emia ....blood condition
en- ....within
encephal/o ....entire brain
endo- ....within
enter/o ....small intestine
epi-.......................upon
epididym/o...........epididymis
episi/o ....vulva (covering)
erythr/o ....red
esophag/o.............esophagus

585

esthesi/o .... sensation
eu- .... good or normal
ex- .... out or away
exo- .... outside
extra- .... outside
fasci/o .... fascia (a band)
femor/o .... femur
fibr/o .... fiber
gangli/o .... ganglion (knot)
gastr/o .... stomach
-gen .... origin or
        production
-genesis .... origin or
        production
gen/o .... origin or
        production
ger/o .... old age
gingiv/o .... gums
gli/o .... glue
glomerul/o .... glomerulus (little
        ball)
gloss/o .... tongue
glott/o .... opening
gluc/o .... sugar
glyc/o .... sugar
glycos/o .... sugar
gnos/o .... knowing
-gram .... record
-graph .... instrument for
        recording
-graphy .... process of
        recording
gynec/o .... woman
hem/o .... blood
hemat/o .... blood
hemi- .... half
hepat/o .... liver
hepatic/o .... liver
herni/o .... hernia
hetero- .... different
hidr/o .... sweat
hist/o .... tissue
histi/o .... tissue
homo- .... same
hormon/o .... hormone (an
        urging on)
hydr/o .... water
hyper- .... above or excessive
hypn/o .... sleep
hypo- .... below or deficient
hyster/o .... uterus
-ia .... condition of
-iasis .... formation of or
        presence of
iatr/o .... treatment
-iatrics .... treatment
-iatry .... treatment
-ic .... pertaining to
-icle .... small
ile/o .... ileum
immun/o .... safe

infra- .... below or under
inguin/o .... groin
inter- .... between
intra- .... within
ir/o .... iris (colored
        circle)
irid/o .... iris (colored
        circle)
-ism .... condition of
iso- .... equal, like
-ist .... one who
        specializes in
-itis .... inflammation
-ium .... structure or tissue
jejun/o .... jejunum (empty)
kerat/o .... hard or cornea
ket/o .... ketone bodies
keton/o .... ketone bodies
kinesi/o .... movement
kyph/o .... humpback
lacrim/o .... tear
lact/o .... milk
lapar/o .... abdomen
laryng/o .... larynx (voice box)
lei/o .... smooth
-lepsy .... seizure
leuc/o .... white
leuk/o .... white
lex/o .... word or phrase
lingu/o .... tongue
lip/o .... fat
lith/o .... stone or calculus
lob/o .... lobe (a portion)
-logist .... one who
        specialized in
        the study or
        treatment of
-logy .... study of
lord/o .... bent
lumb/o .... loin (lower back)
lymph/o .... clear fluid
-lysis .... breaking down or
        dissolution
macro- .... large or long
-malacia .... softening
mamm/o .... breast
-mania .... abnormal impulse
        (attraction)
        toward
mast/o .... breast
meat/o .... opening
mega- .... large
megal/o .... large
-megaly .... enlargement
melan/o .... black
men/o .... menstruation
mening/o .... meninges
        (membrane)
meningi/o .... meninges
        (membrane)
meso- .... middle

meta- .... beyond, after, or
        change
-meter .... instrument for
        measuring
metr/o .... uterus
-metry .... process of
        measuring
micro- .... small
mono- .... one
morph/o .... form
multi- .... many
muscul/o .... muscle
my/o .... muscle
myc/o .... fungus
myel/o .... bone marrow or
        spinal cord
myos/o .... muscle
myring/o .... eardrum
narc/o .... stupor, sleep
nas/o .... nose
nat/i .... birth
necr/o .... death
neo- .... new
nephr/o .... kidney
neur/o .... nerve
obstetr/o .... midwife
ocul/o .... eye
-oid .... resembling
-ole .... small
olig/o .... few or deficient
-oma .... tumor
onych/o .... nail
oophor/o .... ovary
ophthalm/o .... eye
-opia .... condition of vision
opt/o .... eye
or/o .... mouth
orch/o .... testis (testicle)
orchi/o .... testis (testicle)
orchid/o .... testis (testicle)
orth/o .... straight, normal,
        or correct
-osis .... condition or
        increase
oste/o .... bone
ot/o .... ear
-ous .... pertaining to
ov/i .... egg
ov/o .... egg
ovari/o .... ovary
ox/o .... oxygen
pachy- .... thick
palat/o .... palate
pan- .... all
pancreat/o .... pancreas
para- .... alongside of or
        abnormal
-paresis .... slight paralysis
patell/o .... knee cap
path/o .... disease
pector/o .... chest

ped/o ....child or foot
pelv/i, pelv/o ....hip bone
-penia ....abnormal
                 reduction
per- ....through
peri- ....around
perine/o ....perineum
peritone/o ....peritoneum
-pexy ....suspension or
                 fixation
phac/o ....lens (lentil)
phag/o ....eat or swallow
phak/o ....lens (lentil)
pharyng/o ....pharynx (throat)
phas/o ....speech
-phil ....attraction for
-philia ....attraction for
phleb/o ....vein
phob/o ....exaggerated fear
                 or sensitivity
phon/o ....voice or sound
phor/o ....to carry or bear
phot/o..................light
phren/o ....diaphragm (also
                 mind)
physi/o ....physical, nature
plas/o ....formation
-plasia ....formation
-plasty ....surgical repair or
                 reconstruction
-plegia ....paralysis
pleur/o ....pleura
-pnea ....breathing
pneum/o ....air or lung
pneumon/o ....air or lung
pod/o ....foot
-poiesis................formation
poly- ....many
post- ....after or behind
pre- ....before
presby/o ....old age
pro- ....before
proct/o ....anus and rectum
prostat/o ....prostate
psych/o................mind
-ptosis ....falling or
                 downward
                 displacement
pulmon/o ....lung
purpur/o ....purple
py/o ....pus
pyel/o ....basin
pylor/o ....pylorus
                 (gatekeeper)
quadri- ....four
radi/o ....radius (a bone of
                 the forearm);
                 radiation (espe-
                 cially x-ray)
re-.........................again or back
rect/o ....rectum

ren/o....................kidney
reticul/o ....a net
retin/o ....retina
retro- ....backward or
                 behind
rhabd/o ....rod shaped or
                 striated
                 (skeletal)
rhin/o ....nose
-rrhage ....to burst forth
-rrhagia ....to burst forth
-rrhaphy...............suture
-rrhea ....discharge
-rrhexis ....rupture
salping/o ....uterine (fallopian)
                 tube; also
                 eustachian tube
sarc/o ....flesh
schiz/o ....split, division
scler/o ....hard or sclera
scoli/o..................twisted
-scope...................instrument for
                 examination
-scopy...................examination
seb/o....................sebum (oil)
semi- ....half
sial/o ....saliva
sigmoid/o............sigmoid colon
sinistr/o ....left, or on the left
                 side
sinus/o ....hollow (cavity)
somat/o ....body
somn/i ....sleep
somn/o ....sleep
son/o ....sound
-spasm ....involuntary
                 contraction
sperm/o ....sperm (seed)
spermat/o.............sperm (seed)
sphygm/o ....pulse
spin/o ....spine (thorn)
spir/o ....breathing
splen/o ....spleen
spondyl/o ....vertebra
squam/o ....scale
-stasis ....stop or stand
steat/o ....fat
sten/o ....narrow
stere/o ....three-dimensional
                 or solid
stern/o ....sternum
                 (breastbone)
steth/o ....chest
stomat/o...............mouth
-stomy ....creation of an
                 opening
sub- ....below or under
super-...................above or excessive
supra-...................above or excessive
sym- ....together or with
syn- ....together or with

tachy- ....fast
tax/o ....order or
                 coordination
ten/o ....tendon (to stretch)
tend/o...................tendon (to stretch)
tendin/o ....tendon (to stretch)
test/o ....testis (testicle)
thalam/o...............thalamus (a room)
therm/o ....heat
thorac/o ....chest
thromb/o ....clot
thym/o ....thymus gland
thyr/o, thyroid/o ..thyroid gland
                 (shield)
-tic ....pertaining to
toc/o ....labor or birth
tom/o ....to cut
-tomy ....incision
ton/o ....tone or tension
tonsill/o ....tonsil (almond)
top/o.....................place
tox/o ....poison
toxic/o ....poison
trache/o ....trachea
                 (windpipe)
trans- ....across or through
tri- ....three
trich/o ....hair
-tripsy...................crushing
troph/o.................nourishment or
                 development
tympan/o ....eardrum
-ula, -ule...............small
uln/o.....................ulna (a bone of the
                 forearm)
ultra- ....beyond or
                 excessive
uni-.......................one
ur/o ....urine
ureter/o ....ureter
urethr/o ....urethra
urin/o ....urine
uter/o ....uterus
vagin/o ....vagina (sheath)
varic/o ....swollen or twisted
                 vein
vas/o.....................vessel
vascul/o ....vessel
ven/o ....vein
ventricul/o ....ventricle (belly or
                 pouch)
vertebr/o ....vertebra
vesic/o ....bladder or sac
vesicul/o...............bladder or sac
vitre/o...................glassy
vulv/o ....vulva (covering)
xanth/o.................yellow
xeno- ....strange
xer/o ....dry
-y ....condition or
                 process of

English to Term Component

abdomen ....abdomin/o, celi/o, lapar/o
abnormal ....para-
abnormal impulse (attraction) toward ....-mania
abnormal reduction ....-penia
above ....hyper-, super-, supra-
across..................dia-, trans-
adrenal gland ......adren/o, adrenal/o
after ....meta-, post-
again ....re-
against ....anti-, contra-
air........................aer/o, pneum/o, pneumon/o
air sac ....alveol/o
airway ....bronch/o, bronchi/o
all ....pan-
alongside of ....para-
alveolus ....alveol/o
anus ....an/o
anus and rectum ..proct/o
aorta..................aort/o
apart ....ana-, dis-
appendix ....appendic/o
arm ....brachi/o
around ....circum-, peri-
artery ....arteri/o
articulation ....arthr/o
atrium ....atri/o
attraction for ....-phil, -philia
away..................e-, ec-, ex-
away from ....ab-
back ....re-
backward............retro-
bacteria ....bacteri/o
basin ....pyel/o
bear ....phor/o
before..................ante-, pre-, pro-
beginning............-arche
behind ....post-, retro-
below ....hypo-, infra-, sub-
bent ....lord/o
between ....inter-
beyond ....meta-, ultra-
bile ....bil/i, chol/e
bile duct..............choledoch/o
binding ....-desis
birth ....nat/i, toc/o
black ....melan/o
bladder................cyst/o, vesic/o, vesicul/o
blood ....hem/o, hemat/o
blood condition....-emia
blue ....cyan/o
body ....somat/o

bone ....oste/o
bone marrow........myel/o
both ....ambi-, bi-
brain ....cerebr/o (largest part), encephal/o (entire brain)
breaking down ....-lysis
breast ....mamm/o, mast/o
breathing ....-pnea, spir/o
bronchus ....bronch/o, bronchi/o
bud ....-blast, blast/o
burst forth ....-rrhage, -rrhagia
calculus ....lith/o
cancer ....carcin/o
carbon dioxide ....capn/o, carb/o
carry..................phor/o
cartilage..............chondr/o
cavity (sinus) ......atri/o, sin/o
cell ....cyt/o
cerebellum..........cerebell/o
cerebrum ....cerebr/o
cervix ....cervic/o
change ....meta-
cheek ....bucc/o
chest..................pectoro, steth/o, thorac/o
child ....ped/o
circle ....coron/o
clear fluid ....lymph/o
clot ....thromb/o
colon ....col/o, colon/o
colon, sigmoid......sigmoid/o
color..................chrom/o, chromat/o
colored circle........ir/o, irid/o
condition ....-osis
condition of..........-ia, -ism, ium, -y
contraction, involuntary ......-spasm
coordination ....tax/o
cornea ....corne/o, kerat/o
correct ....ortho-
creation of an opening ....-stomy
crooked ....ankyl/o
crown................coron/o
crushing..............-tripsy
cut ....cis/o, tom/o
death ....necr/o
deficient..............hypo-, olig/o
development ....troph/o
diaphragm ....phren/o
different..............hetero-
difficult ....dys-
digit (finger or toe)..............dactyl/o
dilation or expansion..........-ectasis
discharge ....-rrhea

disease ....path/o
dissolution............-lysis
division ....schiz/o
down ....cata-, de-
downward displacement ....-ptosis
dry ....xer/o
duct ....doch/o
duodenum ....duoden/o
ear ....aur/i, ot/o
eardrum..............myring/o, tympan/o
eat, swallow ....phag/o
egg ....ov/i, ov/o
enlargement ....-megaly
enzyme ....-ase
epididymis............epididym/o
equal ....iso-
esophagus ....esophag/o
eustachian tube....salping/o
examination ....-scopy
excessive ....hyper-, super-, supra-, ultra-
excision (removal) ....-ectomy
expansion or dilation.............-ectasis
extremity ....acr/o
eye ....ocul/o, ophthalm/o, opt/o
eyelid ....blephar/o
falling..................-ptosis
fallopian tube ......salping/o
fascia ....fasci/o
fast ....tachy-
fat........................adip/o, lip/o, steat/o
fatty paste ....ather/o,
faulty ....dys-
fear, exaggerated..phob/o
femur ....femor/o
few ....olig/o
fiber ....fibr/o
fixation ....-pexy
flesh ....sarc/o
foot ....ped/o, pod/o
form ....morph/o
formation............plas/o, -plasia, -poiesis
formation of ....-iasis
four ....quadri-
from ....de-
fungus ....myc/o
ganglion................gangli/o
gas ....aer/o
germ or bud..........-blast, blast/o
gland ....aden/o
glans penis..........balan/o
glassy ....vitre/o
glomerulus..........glomerul/o

glue ....gli/o
good ....eu-
groin ....inguin/o
gums ....gingiv/o
hair ....trich/o
half.....................hemi-, semi-
hand.....................chir/o
hard ....kerat/o, scler/o
head ....cephal/o
hearing.....................acous/o, audi/o
hearing
   condition ....-acusis
heart.....................cardio/o
heat ....therm/o
hernia ....-cele, herni/o
hip bone.....................pelv/i, pelv/o
hormone ....hormon/o
humpback ....kyph/o
ileum ....ile/o
incision ....-tomy
increase ....-osis
inflammation ......-itis
instrument for
   examination......-scope
instrument for
   measuring ....-meter
instrument for
   recording ....-graph
jejunum (empty) .jejun/o
joint ....arthr/o, articul/o
juice ....chyl/o
ketone bodies .....ket/o, keton/o
kidney ....nephr/o, ren/o
kneecap ....patell/o
knowing.....................gnos/o
labor.....................toc/o
large ....macro-, mega-,
              megal/o
larynx.....................laryng/o
left, or on the
   left side.............sinistr/o
lens.....................phac/o, phak/o
light ....phot/o
like ....iso-
lip.....................cheil/o
liver ....hepat/o, hepatic/o
lobe ....lob/o
loin (lower back) ..lumb/o
long ....macro-
lung ....pneum/o,
             pneumon/o,
             pulmon/o
male ....andr/o
many ....multi-, poly-
measuring,
   instrument for ..-meter
measuring,
   process of.........-metry
meninges ....mening/o,
             meningi/o
menstruation........men/o

milk ....lact/o
mind ....phren/o, psych/o,
             thym/o
mouth ....or/o, stomat/o
movement ....kinesi/o
muscle ....muscul/o, my/o,
             myos/o
nail ....onych/o
narrow ....sten/o
nature ....physi/o
near ....ad-
neck ....cervic/o
nerve ....neur/o
net ....reticul/o
new ....neo-
normal ....eu-, ortho-
nose ....nas/o, rhin/o
not ....de-
nourishment ....troph/o
oil ....seb/o
old age ....ger/o, geront/o,
             presby/o
one ....mono-, uni-
one who
   specializes in ....-ist
one who
   specializes in
   the study or
   treatment of......-logist
opening ....glott/o, meat/o
opening,
   creation of ....-stomy
opposed to ....anti-, contra-
order ....tax/o
origin ....-gen, -genesis,
             gen/o
other ....allo-
out ....e-, ec-, ex-
outside ....ecto-, exo-, extra-
ovary ....oophor/o, ovari/o
oxygen ....ox/o
pain ....-algia, -dynia
painful ....dys-
palate ....palat/o
pancreas ....pancreat/o
paralysis.............-plegia
paralysis, slight ....-paresis
perineum ....perine/o
peritoneum ....peritone/o
pertaining to ....-ac, -al, -ar, -ary,
             -eal, -ic, -ous,
             -tic
pharynx ....pharyng/o
phrase ....lex/o
physical ....physi/o
place.....................top/o
pleura.....................pleur/o
poison ....tox/o, toxic/o
portion.....................lob/o
pouching ....-cele
presence of ....-iasis

process.................-ation
process of ....-y
production............-gen, gen/o,
             -genesis
prostate ....prostat/o
protein ....albumin/o
pulse ....sphygm/o
puncture for
   aspiration..........-centesis
purple ....purpur/o
pus ....py/o
pylorus.............pylor/o
radius ....radi/o
record ....-gram
recording,
   process of.........-graphy
rectum ....rect/o
red ....erythr/o
resembling............-oid
reticulum ....reticul/o
retina ....retin/o
rib ....cost/o
right, or on the
   right side ....dextr/o
rod shaped............rhabd/o
rupture.................-rrhexis
sac ....cyst/o, vesic/o,
             vesicul/o
safe.....................immun/o
saliva ....sial/o
scale ....squam/o
sclera ....scler/o
sebum ....seb/o
secrete ....crin/o
seizure ....-lepsy
self ....auto-
sensation ....esthesi/o
sensitivity,
   exaggerated ......phob/o
separate from ......dis-
sheath ....vagin/o
sigmoid colon ......sigmoid/o
sinus.....................sinus/o
skeletal.................rhabd/o
skin ....cutane/o, derm/o,
             dermat/o
skull ....crani/o
sleep.....................hypn/o, narc/o,
             somn/i, somn/o
slow ....brady-
small ....-icle, micro-, -ole,
             -ula, -ule
small intestine......enter/o
smooth ....lei/o
softening ....-malacia
sound ....phon/o, son/o
specializes,
   one who ....-ist
speech ....phas/o
sperm.................sperm/o,
             spermat/o

spinal cord............myel/o
spine ....spin/o
spleen................splen/o
split ....schiz/o
sternum ....stern/o
stiff................ankyl/o
stomach ....gastr/o
stone ....lith/o
stop or stand ....-stasis
straight ....orth/o
strange ....xeno-
striated................rhabd/o
structure ....-ium
study of ....-logy
study of,
  one who
  specializes in ....-logist
stupor ....narc/o
sugar ....gluc/o, glyc/o,
                 glycos/o
surgical repair or
  reconstruction ..-plasty
suspension............-pexy
suture...................-rrhaphy
swallow ....phag/o
sweat ....hidr/o
sweat, profuse ......diaphor/o
tear......................dacry/o, lacrim/o
teeth....................dent/i
tendon ....ten/o, tend/o,
               tendin/o
tension.................ton/o
testis (testicle) ......orch/o, orchi/o,
              orchid/o, test/o

thalamus ....thalam/o
thick.....................pachy-
thirst ....dips/o
three.....................tri-
three-
  dimensional
  or solid ....stere/o
throat...................pharyng/o
through ....dia-, per-, trans-
thymus gland........thym/o
thyroid gland.........thyr/o, thyroid/o
tissue ....hist/o, -ium
to or toward..........ad-
together ....con-, sym-, syn-
tone ....ton/o
tongue ....gloss/o, lingu/o
tonsil ....tonsill/o
topmost ....acr/o
trachea.................trache/o
treatment.............iatr/o, -iatrics,
               -iatry
treatment,
  one who
  specializes in ....-logist
trop/o ....to turn
tumor...................-oma
turn ....trop/o
twisted ....scoli/o
two ....bi-
ulna ....uln/o
under ....infra-, sub-
up ....ana-
upon.....................epi-
ureter ....ureter/o

urethra.................urethr/o
urine ....ur/o, urin/o
uterine tube..........salping/o
uterus...................hyster/o, metr/o,
               uter/o
vagina ....colp/o, vagin/o
vein ....phleb/o, ven/o
vein, swollen or
  twisted ....varic/o
ventricle...............ventricul/o
vertebra ....vertebr/o,
               spondyl/o
vessel ....angi/o, vas/o,
               vascul/o
vision,
  condition of ......-opia
voice....................phon/o
voice box ....laryng/o
vomiting ....-emesis
vulva ....episi/o, vulv/o
water ....aque/o, hydr/o
wax.....................cerumin/o
weakness ....-asthenia
white ....leuc/o, leuk/o
windpipe ....trache/o
with ....con-, sym-, syn-
within ....en-, endo-, intra-
without ....a-, an-
woman.................gynec/o
word....................lex/o
yellow..................xanth/o

APPENDIX B

Abbreviations and Symbols

Abbreviations deemed error prone are printed in red.

ā	before
A	anterior; assessment
A&P	auscultation and percussion
A&W	alive and well
AB	abortion
ABG	arterial blood gas
a.c.	before meals
ACE	angiotensin-converting enzyme
ACP	American College of Physicians
ACS	American College of Surgeons
ACTH	adrenocorticotrophic hormone
AD	right ear
ADH	antidiuretic hormone
ADHD	attention-deficit/hyperactivity disorder
ad lib.	as desired
AIDS	acquired immuno-deficiency syndrome
AKA	above-knee amputation
alb	albumin
ALS	amyotrophic lateral sclerosis
ALT	alanine aminotrans-ferase (enzyme)
a.m.	morning
AMBS	American Board of Medical Specialties
amt	amount
ANS	autonomic nervous system
AOA	American Osteopathic Association
AP	anterior posterior
APKD	adult polycystic kidney disease
aq	water
AS	left ear
ASD	atrial septal defect
ASHD	arteriosclerotic heart disease

AST	aspartate aminotrans-ferase (enzyme)
AU	both ears
AV	atrioventricular
Ⓑ	bilateral
BAEP	brainstem auditory evoked potentials
BCC	basal cell carcinoma
BD	bipolar disorder
b.i.d.	twice a day
BKA	below-knee amputation
BM	black male; bowel movement
BP	blood pressure
BPH	benign prostatic hyperplasia/hypertrophy
BRP	bathroom privileges
BS	blood sugar
BUN	blood urea nitrogen
Bx	biopsy
c̄	with
C	Celsius; centigrade
C&S	culture and sensitivity
CABG	coronary artery bypass graft
CAD	coronary artery disease
cap	capsule
CAT	computed axial tomography
CBC	complete blood count
cc	cubic centimeter
CC	chief complaint; car-diac catheterization
CCU	coronary (cardiac) care unit; critical care unit
CHF	congestive heart failure
CIN	cervical intraepithelial neoplasia
CIS	carcinoma in situ
cm	centimeter
CNS	central nervous system
CO	cardiac output
CO_2	carbon dioxide

c/o	complains of
COPD	chronic obstructive pulmonary disease
CP	chest pain; cerebral palsy
CPAP	continuous positive airway pressure
CPD	cephalopelvic disproportion
CPR	cardiopulmonary resuscitation
CSF	cerebrospinal fluid
C-section	cesarean section
CSII	continuous subcutaneous insulin infusion
CT	computed tomography
cu mm	cubic millimeter
CVA	cerebrovascular accident
CVS	chorionic villus sampling
CXR	chest x-ray
d.	day
D&C	dilation and curettage
DC	Doctor of Chiropractic Medicine
DC, D/C	discharge; discontinue
DDS	Doctor of Dental Surgery
DEXA	dual-energy x-ray absorptiometry
DJD	degenerative joint disease
DKA	diabetic ketoacidosis
DM	diabetes mellitus
DO	Doctor of Osteopathic Medicine
DPM	Doctor of Podiatric Medicine
dr.	dram
DRE	digital rectal examination
DTR	deep tendon reflex
DVT	deep vein thrombosis
Dx	diagnosis
ECG	electrocardiogram

ECHO . . . . echocardiogram
ECT . . . . electroconvulsive
          therapy
ECU . . . . emergency care unit
ED . . . . erectile dysfunction
EDC . . . . estimated date of
          confinement
EDD . . . . estimated date of
          delivery
EEG . . . . electroencephalogram
EGD . . . . esophagogastro-
          duodenoscopy
EIA . . . . enzyme immunoassay
EKG . . . . electrocardiogram
EMG . . . . electromyogram
ENT . . . . ear, nose, throat
EPS . . . . electrophysiological
          study
ER . . . . emergency room
ERCP . . . . endoscopic retrograde
          cholangio-
          pancreatography
ESR . . . . erythrocyte
          sedimentation rate
ESWL . . . . extracorporeal shock
          wave lithotripsy
ETOH . . . . ethyl alcohol
F . . . . Fahrenheit
FACP . . . . Fellow of the
          American College of
          Physicians
FACS . . . . Fellow of the
          American College of
          Surgeons
FBS . . . . fasting blood sugar
Fe . . . . iron (ferrous)
FH . . . . family history
fl oz . . . . fluid ounce
FS . . . . frozen section
FSH . . . . follicle-stimulating
          hormone
Fx . . . . fracture
g . . . . gram
GAD . . . . generalized anxiety
          disorder
GERD . . . . gastroesophageal
          reflux disease
GH . . . . growth hormone
GI . . . . gastrointestinal
gm . . . . gram
gr . . . . grain
gt . . . . drop
gtt . . . . drops
GTT . . . . glucose tolerance test
GYN . . . . gynecology
h . . . . hour
H&H . . . . hemoglobin and
          hematocrit
H&P . . . . history and physical
HAV . . . . hepatitis A virus
HBV . . . . hepatitis B virus
HCT or Hct . . hematocrit

HCV . . . . hepatitis C virus
HD . . . . Huntington disease
HEENT . . . . . . head, eyes, ears, nose,
          throat
HGB or Hgb . hemoglobin
HIV . . . . human immuno-
          deficiency virus
HPI . . . . history of present
          illness
HPV . . . . human papilloma
          virus
HRT . . . . hormone replacement
          therapy
h.s. . . . . bedtime (hour of
          sleep); half strength
HSV-1 . . . . . . herpes simplex virus
          type 1
HSV-2 . . . . . . herpes simplex virus
          type 2
Ht . . . . height
HTN . . . . hypertension
Hx . . . . history
I&D . . . . incision and drainage
ICD . . . . implantable
          cardioverter
          defibrillator
ICU . . . . intensive care unit
ID . . . . intradermal
Ig . . . . immunoglobulins
IM . . . . intramuscular
IMP . . . . impression
IOL . . . . intraocular lens
          implant
IP . . . . inpatient
IUD . . . . intrauterine device
IV . . . . intravenous
IVP . . . . intravenous pyelogram
kg . . . . kilogram
KUB . . . . kidney, ureter, bladder
L . . . . left; liter
L&W . . . . living and well
LASIK . . . . . . laser-assisted in situ
          keratomileusis
lb . . . . pound
LEEP . . . . loop electrosurgical
          excision procedure
LH . . . . luteinizing hormone
LLETZ . . . . . . large loop excision of
          transformation zone
LLQ . . . . left lower quadrant
LP . . . . lumbar puncture
LTB . . . . laryngotracheo-
          bronchitis
LUQ . . . . left upper quadrant
m . . . . meter
ⓜ . . . . murmur
MCH . . . . mean corpuscular
          (cell) hemoglobin
MCHC . . . . . . mean corpuscular
          (cell) hemoglobin
          concentration
MCV . . . . mean corpuscular
          (cell) volume

MD . . . . muscular dystrophy;
          Medical Doctor
mg . . . . milligram
MI . . . . myocardial infarction
ml, mL . . . . . . milliliter
mm . . . . millimeter
MRA . . . . magnetic resonance
          angiography
MRI . . . . magnetic resonance
          imaging
MS . . . . multiple sclerosis;
          musculoskeletal
MSH . . . . melanocyte-
          stimulating
          hormone
MVP . . . . mitral valve prolapse
NCV . . . . nerve conduction
          velocity
NG . . . . nasogastric
NKA . . . . no known allergy
NKDA . . . . no known drug allergy
noc. . . . . night
NPO . . . . nothing by mouth
NSAID . . . . . . nonsteroidal anti-
          inflammatory drug
NSR . . . . normal sinus rhythm
O . . . . objective
O_2 . . . . oxygen
OA . . . . osteoarthritis
OB . . . . obstetrics
OB/GYN . . . . . obstetrics and
          gynecology
OCD . . . . obsessive-compulsive
          disorder
OCP . . . . oral contraceptive pill
OD . . . . right eye; Doctor of
          Optometry
OH . . . . occupational history
OP . . . . outpatient
OR . . . . operating room
ORIF . . . . open reduction,
          internal fixation
OS . . . . left eye
OU . . . . both eyes
oz . . . . ounce
p̄ . . . . after
P . . . . plan; posterior; pulse
PA . . . . posterior anterior
$PaCO_2$ . . . . . . arterial partial
          pressure of
          carbon dioxide
PACU . . . . postanesthetic care
          unit
PaO_2 . . . . arterial partial
          pressure of oxygen
PAP . . . . Papanicolaou test
          (smear)
PAR . . . . postanesthetic
          recovery
p.c. . . . . after meals
PD . . . . panic disorder
PDA . . . . patent ductus
          arteriosus

PE	physical examination; pulmonary embolism; polyethylene
PEFR	peak expiratory flow rate
per	by
PERRLA	pupils equal, round, and reactive to light and accommodation
PET	positron emission tomography
PF	peak flow
PFT	pulmonary function testing
pH	potential of hydrogen
PH	past history
Ph.D.	Doctor of Philosophy
PI	present illness
PID	pelvic inflammatory disease
PIH	pregnancy-induced hypertension
PLT	platelet (count)
p.m.	afternoon
PMH	past medical history
PMN	polymorphonuclear leukocyte
PNS	peripheral nervous system
p.o.	by mouth
post op	after operation
PPBS	postprandial blood sugar
PR	per rectum
pre-op, preop	before operation
p.r.n.	as needed
PSA	prostate-specific antigen
PSG	polysomnography
pt	patient
PT	physical therapy; prothrombin time
PTCA	percutaneous transluminal coronary angioplasty
PTH	parathyroid hormone
PTSD	posttraumatic stress disorder
PTT	partial thromboplastin time
PUD	peptic ulcer disease
PV	per vagina
PVC	premature ventricular contraction
Px	physical examination
q	every
q2h	every 2 hours
qd	every day
qh	every hour
q.i.d.	four times a day
q.n.s.	quantity not sufficient
q.o.d.	every other day

q.s.	quantity sufficient
qt	quart
R	right; respiration
RA	rheumatoid arthritis
RBC	red blood cell; red blood count
RIA	radioimmunoassay
RLQ	right lower quadrant
R/O	rule out
ROM	range of motion
ROS	review of symptoms
RP	retrograde pyelogram
RRR	regular rate and rhythm
RSD	reflex sympathetic dystrophy
RTC	return to clinic
RTO	return to office
RUQ	right upper quadrant
Rx	recipe; take thou
$\bar{s}$	without
S	subjective
SA	sinoatrial
SAB	spontaneous abortion
SAD	seasonal affective disorder
SC	subcutaneous
SCC	squamous cell carcinoma
SH	social history
Sig:	instruction to patient
SLE	systemic lupus erythematosus
SOB	shortness of breath
SPECT	single photon emission computed tomography
SpGr	specific gravity
SQ	subcutaneous
SR	systems review
$\overline{\overline{ss}}$	one-half
STAT	immediately
STD	sexually transmitted disease
Sub-Q	subcutaneous
SUI	stress urinary incontinence
suppos	suppository
SV	stroke volume
Sx	symptom
T	temperature
T_3	triiodothyronine
T_4	thyroxine
T&A	tonsillectomy and adenoidectomy
tab	tablet
TAB	therapeutic abortion
TB	tuberculosis
TEDS	thromboembolic disease stockings
TEE	transesophageal echocardiogram

TIA	transient ischemic attack
t.i.d.	three times a day
TM	tympanic membrane
TMR	transmyocardial revascularization
tPA, TPA	tissue plasminogen activator
TPR	temperature, pulse, respiration
Tr	treatment
TSH	thyroid-stimulating hormone
TURP	transurethral resection of the prostate
TV	tidal volume
Tx	treatment; traction
UA	urinalysis
UCHD	usual childhood diseases
UFE	uterine fibroid embolization
URI	upper respiratory infection
UTI	urinary tract infection
VC	vital capacity
VCU, VCUG	voiding cystourethrogram
VS	vital signs
VSD	ventricular septal defect
V_T	tidal volume
w.a.	while awake
WBC	white blood cell; white blood count
WDWN	well developed and well nourished
wk	week
WNL	within normal limits
Wt	weight
x-ray	radiography
y.o.	year old
yr	year
♀	female
♂	male
#	number or pound
°	degree or hour
↑	increased; above
↓	decreased; below
ө	none or negative
♀	standing
♀	sitting
O—	lying
×	times or for
>	greater than
<	less than
Ţ	one
ŤŤ	two
ŤŤŤ	three
ŤV	four

I, II, III, IV, V, VI, VII, VIII, IX, X
uppercase Roman numerals 1–10

Commonly Prescribed Drugs

The following alphabetical list of commonly prescribed drugs (trade and generic) is based on listings of prescriptions dispensed in the United States in 2003. The classification and major therapeutic uses for each are also provided. Trade name drugs begin with a capital letter; their generic names accompany them in parentheses. All generic names are set in lowercase.

Name	Classification	Major Therapeutic Uses
Accupril (quinapril hydrochloride)	angiotensin-converting enzyme (ACE) inhibitor	hypertension, congestive heart failure (CHF)
Accutane (isotretinoin)	retinoid	acne
acetaminophen and codeine	analgesic/antipyretic and opiate (narcotic) combination	moderate to severe pain, fever
Aciphex (rabeprazole)	proton pump inhibitor (PPI) (gastric acid secretion inhibitor)	peptic ulcer disease (PUD), gastroesophageal reflux disease (GERD)
Actonel (risedronate)	bisphosphonate (bone resorption inhibitor)	osteoporosis, Paget disease
Actos (pioglitazone)	oral antidiabetic	type 2 diabetes mellitus
Adderall XR (amphetamine mixed salts)	amphetamine	attention-deficit/ hyperactivity disorder (ADHD)
Advair Diskus (salmeterol/fluticasone)	adrenergic agonist (bronchodilator) and glucocorticoid (anti-inflammatory)	asthma
albuterol	adrenergic agonist (bronchodilator)	asthma, bronchitis
Allegra (fexofenadine)	antihistamine	allergy
Allegra D (fexofenadine/ pseudoephedrine)	antihistamine and decongestant combination	allergy with nasal congestion
allopurinol	xanthine oxidase inhibitor	gout
Alphagan P (brimonidine) ophthalmic solution	α_2-adrenergic agonist (antihypertensive)	glaucoma
alprazolam	benzodiazepine (anxiolytic, sedative, hypnotic)	anxiety

Name	Classification	Major Therapeutic Uses
Altace (ramipril)	angiotensin-converting enzyme (ACE) inhibitor	hypertension, congestive heart failure (CHF)
Amaryl (glimepiride)	oral antidiabetic	type 2 diabetes mellitus
Ambien (zolpidem)	hypnotic	insomnia
amitriptyline	antidepressant	depression
amoxicillin	penicillin (antibiotic)	bacterial infections
amoxicillin/clavulanate	penicillin (antibiotic) and β-lactamase inhibitor combination	bacterial infections
Apri (desogestrel/ ethinyl estradiol)	oral contraceptive	birth control
Aricept (donepezil)	acetylcholinesterase inhibitor	Alzheimer disease
Atacand (candesartan)	angiotensin receptor blocker (antihypertensive)	hypertension
atenolol	cardioselective β blocker/ β₁-adrenergic antagonist (antihypertensive, antiarrhythmic, antianginal)	hypertension, angina pectoris, cardiac arrhythmias
Atrovent (ipratropium)	anticholinergic (bronchodilator)	chronic obstructive pulmonary disease (COPD)
Augmentin (amoxicillin/ clavulanate)	penicillin (antibiotic) and β-lactamase inhibitor combination	bacterial infections
Avalide (irbesartan/ hydrochlorothiazide)	angiotensin receptor blocker (antihypertensive) and diuretic combination	hypertension
Avandia (rosiglitazone)	oral antidiabetic	type 2 diabetes mellitus
Avapro (irbesartan)	angiotensin receptor blocker (antihypertensive)	hypertension
Avelox (moxifloxacin)	fluoroquinolone (antibiotic)	bacterial infections
Aviane (levonorgestrel/ ethinyl estradiol)	oral contraceptive	birth control
Bactrim (trimethoprim/ sulfamethoxazole)	antibacterial and sulfonamide (antibiotic) combination	bacterial infections
Bactroban (mupirocin)	topical antibiotic	bacterial skin infections
Bextra (valdecoxib)	cox-2 inhibitor (nonsteroidal anti-inflammatory drug [NSAID])	pain, inflammation, fever, arthritis
Biaxin (clarithromycin)	macrolide (antibiotic)	bacterial infections
carisoprodol	skeletal muscle relaxant	skeletal muscle spasms and spasticity
Cartia XT (diltiazem)	calcium channel blocker	hypertension, angina pectoris, cardiac arrhythmias

Name	Classification	Major Therapeutic Uses
Cefzil (cefprozil)	cephalosporin (antibiotic)	bacterial infections
Celebrex (celecoxib)	cox-2 inhibitor (nonsteroidal anti-inflammatory drug [NSAID])	pain, inflammation, fever, arthritis
Celexa (citalopram)	selective serotonin reuptake inhibitor (SSRI) (antidepressant)	depression
cephalexin	cephalosporin (antibiotic)	bacterial infections
Cipro (ciprofloxacin)	fluoroquinolone (antibiotic)	bacterial infections
ciprofloxacin	fluoroquinolone (antibiotic)	bacterial infections
clonazepam	benzodiazepine (sedative/ hypnotic, anticonvulsant, anxiolytic)	epilepsy, seizures, anxiety (panic disorder)
clonidine	α_2-adrenergic agonist (antihypertensive)	hypertension
clotrimazole and betamethasone	topical antifungal and anti-inflammatory combination	fungal infections, some parasites
Combivent (ipratropium/ albuterol) inhalation aerosol	anticholinergic and adrenergic agonist combination (bronchodilators)	asthma, chronic bronchitis, emphysema
Concerta (methylphenidate) extended release	central nervous system stimulant	attention-deficit/ hyperactivity disorder (ADHD)
Coreg (carvedilol)	cardioselective β blocker/ β_1-adrenergic antagonist (antihypertensive, antiarrhythmic, antianginal)	hypertension, congestive heart failure (CHF)
Coumadin (warfarin sodium)	anticoagulant	thromboembolic disorders
Cozaar (losartan)	angiotensin receptor blocker (antihypertensive)	hypertension
cyclobenzaprine	skeletal muscle relaxant	skeletal muscle spasms and spasticity
Depakote (divalproex)	anticonvulsant	epilepsy, migraine prophylaxis, bipolar mania
Detrol LA (tolterodine)	anticholinergic	overactive bladder
diazepam	benzodiazepine (sedative/ hypnotic, anticonvulsant, anxiolytic)	anxiety, skeletal muscle spasm, epilepsy, seizures
Diflucan (fluconazole)	antifungal	fungal infections
Digitek (digoxin)	cardiac glycoside	congestive heart failure (CHF), cardiac tachyarrhythmias
Dilantin (phenytoin)	hydantoin (anticonvulsant)	epilepsy, seizures
diltiazem hydrochloride	calcium channel blocker	hypertension, angina pectoris, cardiac arrhythmias

Name	Classification	Major Therapeutic Uses
Diovan (valsartan)	angiotensin receptor blocker (antihypertensive)	hypertension
Diovan HCT (valsartan/ hydrochlorothiazide)	angiotensin receptor blocker and diuretic combination (antihypertensive)	hypertension
Ditropan XL (oxybutynin)	anticholinergic (urinary antispasmodic)	overactive bladder
doxycycline	tetracycline (antibiotic)	bacterial, rickettsial, and chlamydial infections
Duragesic (fentanyl)	analgesic, opiate (narcotic)	pain, sedation
Effexor XR (venlafaxine)	antidepressant	depression
Elidel (pimecrolimus) topical cream	immunosuppressant agent	atopic dermatitis
enalapril	angiotensin-converting enzyme (ACE) inhibitor	hypertension, congestive heart failure (CHF)
Endocet (oxycodone/ acetaminophen)	opiate (narcotic) and nonsteroidal anti-inflammatory (NSAID) (analgesic/antipyretic) combination	moderate to severe pain
Evista (raloxifene)	selective estrogen receptor modulator (SERM)	prevention and treatment of osteoporosis
Flomax (tamsulosin)	α_1-adrenergic antagonist (antihypertensive, vasodilator)	benign prostatic hypertrophy (BPH)
Flonase (fluticasone) nasal spray	glucocorticoid (anti-inflammatory, immunosuppressant)	allergic rhinitis
Flovent (fluticasone) oral inhalation	glucocorticoid (anti-inflammatory, immunosuppressant)	asthma control
fluoxetine	selective serotonin reuptake inhibitor (SSRI) (antidepressant)	depression
folic acid	vitamin	nutritional supplement
Fosamax (alendronate)	bisphosphonate (bone resorption inhibitor)	osteoporosis, Paget disease
furosemide	diuretic	hypertension, edema associated with congestive heart failure (CHF) or renal disease
gemfibrozil	antihyperlipidemic	hypertriglyceridemia, hyperlipidemia
Glucophage XR (metformin)	oral antidiabetic	type 2 diabetes mellitus
Glucotrol XL (glipizide)	oral antidiabetic	type 2 diabetes mellitus
Glucovance (glyburide/ metformin)	oral antidiabetic (combination product)	type 2 diabetes mellitus

Name	Classification	Major Therapeutic Uses
glyburide	oral antidiabetic	type 2 diabetes mellitus
Humalog (insulin lispro)	insulin; antidiabetic	type 1 and 2 diabetes mellitus
Humulin (insulin preparation)	insulin; antidiabetic	type 1 and 2 diabetes mellitus
hydrochlorothiazide	diuretic	hypertension, edema associated with congestive heart failure (CHF) or renal disease
hydrocodone and acetaminophen	opiate (narcotic) and nonsteroidal anti-inflammatory drug (NSAID) (analgesic/antipyretic) combination	moderate to severe pain
Hyzaar (losartan/hydrochlorothiazide)	angiotensin receptor blocker and diuretic combination (antihypertensive)	hypertension
ibuprofen	analgesic; nonsteroidal anti-inflammatory drug (NSAID)	pain, inflammation, fever
Imitrex (sumatriptan succinate)	triptan (antimigraine agent)	migraine headache
Inderal LA (propranolol)	β blocker (antihypertensive, antiarrhythmic, antianginal)	hypertension, angina pectoris, cardiac arrhythmias, migraine headache prophylaxis
isosorbide mononitrate	coronary vasodilator (antianginal)	angina pectoris
Kariva (desogestrel/ethinyl estradiol)	oral contraceptive	birth control
Klor-Con (potassium chloride)	potassium salt; electrolyte supplement	potassium deficiency
Lanoxin (digoxin)	cardiac glycoside	congestive heart failure (CHF), cardiac tachyarrhythmias
Lantus (insulin glargine)	insulin; antidiabetic	type 1 and 2 diabetes mellitus
Lescol XL (fluvastatin)	HMG-CoA reductase inhibitor (statin)	hyperlipidemia, hypercholesterolemia
Levaquin (levofloxacin)	fluoroquinolone (antibiotic)	bacterial infections
Levothroid (levothyroxine)	thyroid hormone	hypothyroidism
Levoxyl (levothyroxine sodium)	thyroid hormone	hypothyroidism
Lexapro (escitalopram)	selective serotonin reuptake inhibitor (SSRI) (antidepressant)	depression
Lipitor (atorvastatin)	HMG-CoA reductase inhibitor (statin)	hyperlipidemia, hypercholesterolemia

Name	Classification	Major Therapeutic Uses
lisinopril	angiotensin-converting enzyme (ACE) inhibitor	hypertension
lorazepam	benzodiazepine (sedative/ hypnotic, anticonvulsant, anxiolytic)	anxiety, preop sedation, epilepsy, seizures
Lotensin (benazepril)	angiotensin-converting enzyme (ACE) inhibitor	hypertension
Lotrel (amlodipine/ benazepril)	calcium channel blocker and angiotensin-converting enzyme (ACE) inhibitor combination	hypertension
Low-Ogestrel (norgestrel/ ethinyl estradiol)	oral contraceptive	birth control
Macrobid (nitrofurantoin)	antibiotic	bacterial infections of urinary tract
meclizine	anticholinergic	motion sickness, vertigo
metformin	oral antidiabetic	type 2 diabetes mellitus
methylprednisolone	glucocorticoid (anti- inflammatory, immunosuppressant)	inflammation, immunological disorders, allergies
metoprolol	cardioselective β blocker (β_1-adrenergic antagonist)	hypertension, angina pectoris
Miacalcin (calcitonin)	hormone	osteoporosis, Paget disease
Microgestin Fe (norethindrone ethinyl estradiol)	oral contraceptive	birth control
MiraLax (polyethylene glycol)	laxative	constipation
Mobic (meloxicam)	nonsteroidal anti- inflammatory drug (NSAID)	osteoarthritis
Monopril (fosinopril)	angiotensin-converting enzyme (ACE) inhibitor	hypertension
naproxen	analgesic, nonsteroidal anti-inflammatory drug (NSAID)	pain, fever, arthritis
Nasacort (triamcinolone) AQ topical nasal spray	glucocorticoid (anti-inflammatory, immunosuppressant)	allergic rhinitis
Nasonex (mometasone) topical nasal spray	glucocorticoid (anti- inflammatory, immunosuppressant)	allergic rhinitis
Necon (ethinyl estradiol/ norethindrone)	oral contraceptive	birth control
Neurontin (gabapentin)	anticonvulsant	postherpetic neuralgia, epilepsy (partial seizures)
Nexium (esomeprazole)	proton pump inhibitor (PPI) (gastric acid secretion inhibitor)	peptic ulcer disease (PUD), gastroesophageal reflux disease (GERD)

Name	Classification	Major Therapeutic Uses
Niaspan (niacin)	vitamin	dyslipidemia
nifedipine	calcium channel blocker	hypertension, angina pectoris
NitroQuick (nitroglycerin)	antianginal	coronary vasodilator
Norvasc (amlodipine)	calcium channel blocker	hypertension, angina pectoris
omeprazole	proton pump inhibitor (PPI) (gastric acid secretion inhibitor)	peptic ulcer disease (PUD), gastroesophageal reflux disease (GERD)
Omnicef (cefdinir)	cephalosporin (antibiotic)	bacterial infections
Ortho Evra (norelgestromin/ ethinyl estradiol)	contraceptive patch	birth control
Ortho Novum (norethindrone/ ethyl estradiol)	oral contraceptive	birth control
Ortho Tri-Cyclen (norgestimate/ ethyl estradiol)	oral contraceptive	birth control
oxycodone and acetaminophen	opiate (narcotic) and nonsteroidal anti-inflammatory drug (NSAID) (analgesic/ antipyretic) combination	moderate to severe pain
OxyContin (oxycodone)	opiate (narcotic) analgesic	moderate to severe pain
Patanol (olopatadine)	ophthalmic antihistamine	allergic conjunctivitis
Paxil (paroxetine)	selective serotonin reuptake inhibitor (SSRI) (antidepressant)	depression
Penicillin VK (penicillin V potassium)	penicillin (antibiotic)	bacterial infections
Percocet (oxycodone and acetaminophen)	opiate (narcotic) and nonsteroidal anti-inflammatory drug (NSAID) (analgesic/ antipyretic) combination	moderate to severe pain
phenobarbital	barbiturate (sedative/ hypnotic, anticonvulsant, anxiolytic)	insomnia, epilepsy, seizures, anxiety
phenytoin	hydantoin (anticonvulsant)	epilepsy, seizures
Plavix (clopidogrel)	antiplatelet agent	reduction in stroke or myocardial infarction risk by excessive clot prevention
Plendil (felodipine)	calcium channel blocker	hypertension, angina pectoris
potassium chloride	potassium salt; electrolyte supplement	potassium deficiency
Pravachol (pravastatin)	HMG-CoA reductase inhibitor (statin)	hyperlipidemia, hypercholesterolemia

Name	Classification	Major Therapeutic Uses
prednisone	glucocorticoid (anti-inflammatory, immunosuppressant)	inflammation, immunological disorders, allergy
Premarin (conjugated estrogens)	estrogen derivative	hormone replacement
Prempro (estrogen/medroxyprogesterone)	estrogen/progestin	hormone replacement
Prevacid (lansoprazole)	proton pump inhibitor (PPI) (gastric acid secretion inhibitor)	peptic ulcer disease (PUD), gastroesophageal reflux disease (GERD)
Prilosec (omeprazole)	proton pump inhibitor (PPI) (gastric acid secretion inhibitor)	peptic ulcer disease (PUD), gastroesophageal reflux disease (GERD)
promethazine	antihistamine; sedative and antiemetic	allergy; motion sickness, nausea
promethazine and codeine	antihistamine and opiate (narcotic) antitussive combination	cold and cough
propoxyphene and acetaminophen	opiate (narcotic) analgesic and nonsteroidal anti-inflammatory drug (NSAID) (analgesic/antipyretic) combination	mild to moderate pain
propranolol	β blocker (antihypertensive, antiarrhythmic, antianginal)	hypertension, angina pectoris, cardiac arrhythmias, migraine headache prophylaxis
Proscar (finasteride)	5α-reductase inhibitor	benign prostatic hyperplasia (BPH)
Protonix (pantoprazole)	proton pump inhibitor (PPI) (gastric acid secretion inhibitor)	peptic ulcer disease (PUD), gastroesophageal reflux disease (GERD)
Pulmicort (budesonide) inhalant	glucocorticoid (anti-inflammatory, immunosuppressant)	asthma
ranitidine hydrochloride	H_2 receptor antagonist	peptic ulcer disease (PUD), gastroesophageal reflux disease (GERD)
Remeron (mirtazapine)	atypical antidepressant	depression
Rhinocort Aqua (budesonide) nasal spray	glucocorticoid (anti-inflammatory, immunosuppressant)	allergic rhinitis
Risperdal (risperidone)	atypical antipsychotic (neuroleptic)	psychoses (e.g., schizophrenia)
Roxicet (oxycodone and acetaminophen)	opiate (narcotic) and nonsteroidal anti-inflammatory drug (NSAID) (analgesic/antipyretic) combination	moderate to severe pain

Name	Classification	Major Therapeutic Uses
Seroquel (quetiapine)	atypical antipsychotic (neuroleptic)	psychoses (e.g. schizophrenia)
Singulair (montelukast)	leukotriene receptor antagonist	asthma
Skelaxin (metaxalone)	skeletal muscle relaxant	skeletal muscle spasms and spasticity
spironolactone	potassium sparing diuretic	hypertension, edema
Strattera (atomoxetine)	selective norepinephrine reuptake inhibitor (SNRI)	attention-deficit/hyperactivity disorder (ADHD)
Synthroid (levothyroxine)	thyroid product	hypothyroidism
temazepam	benzodiazepine (hypnotic)	insomnia
terazosin	α_1-adrenergic antagonist (antihypertensive, vasodilator)	hypertension, benign prostatic hypertrophy
timolol	β blocker (antihypertensive, antiarrhythmic, antianginal)	hypertension, angina pectoris, cardiac arrhythmias, glaucoma (ophthalmic solution)
TobraDex (tobramycin and dexamethasone) ophthalmic solution	antibiotic and corticosteroid combination	external ocular bacterial infections
Topamax (topiramate)	anticonvulsant	epilepsy (partial seizures)
Toprol-XL (metoprolol)	cardioselective β blocker (β_1-adrenergic antagonist)	hypertension, angina pectoris, congestive heart failure (CHF)
trazodone	atypical antidepressant	depression
triamcinolone	glucocorticoid (anti-inflammatory, immunosuppressant)	inflammation, immunological disorders, allergy
triamterene and hydrochlorothiazide (HCTZ)	diuretic combination	hypertension, edema in congestive heart failure (CHF)
Tricor (fenofibrate)	fibric acid derivative	hyperlipidemia, hypertriglyceridemia, hypercholesterolemia
trimethoprim/sulfamethoxazole (TMP-SMX or co-trimoxazole)	antibacterial and sulfonamide (antibiotic) combination	bacterial infections
Trimox (amoxicillin)	penicillin (antibiotic)	bacterial infections
Trivora-28 (levonorgestrel/ethinyl estradiol)	oral contraceptive	birth control
Tussionex (hydrocodone and chlorpheniramine)	narcotic antitussive and antihistamine combination	cough and cold

Name	Classification	Major Therapeutic Uses
Ultracet (tramadol/ acetaminophen)	opioid analgesic and nonsteroidal anti-inflammatory drug (NSAID) (analgesic/ antipyretic) combination	pain
Valtrex (valacyclovir)	antiviral	herpes viruses
verapamil	calcium channel blocker	hypertension, cardiac arrhythmias, angina pectoris
Viagra (sildenafil)	phosphodiesterase (type 5) enzyme inhibitor	erectile dysfunction (ED)
Vioxx (rofecoxib)	cox-2 inhibitor (nonsteroidal anti-inflammatory drug [NSAID])	pain, inflammation, fever, arthritis
warfarin	anticoagulant	thromboembolic disorders
Wellbutrin SR (bupropion)	atypical antidepressant	depression
Xalatan (latanoprost) ophthalmic solution	prostaglandin	glaucoma
Yasmin 28 (drospirenone/ ethinyl estradiol)	oral contraceptive	birth control
Zetia (ezetimibe)	cholesterol absorption inhibitor	hypercholesterolemia
Zithromax (azithromycin dihydrate)	macrolide (antibiotic)	bacterial infections
Zocor (simvastatin)	HMG-CoA reductase inhibitor (statin)	hyperlipidemia, hypercholesterolemia
Zoloft (sertraline)	selective serotonin reuptake inhibitor (SSRI) (antidepressant)	depression
Zyprexa (olanzapine)	atypical antipsychotic (neuroleptic)	psychoses (e.g., schizophrenia)
Zyrtec (cetirizine)	antihistamine	allergy

References

Quick Look Drug Book. Baltimore: Lippincott Williams & Wilkins, 2004. Copyright ©2004 by Lexi-Comp, Inc.

RxList Top 200 Drugs of 2003, www.rxlist.com/top200.htm.

Stedman's Medical Dictionary for the Health Professions and Nursing, 5th ed. Baltimore: Lippincott Williams & Wilkins, Appendix: Commonly Prescribed Drugs and Their Applications, 2005.

Answers to Practice Exercises

CHAPTER 1 (PP. 7–8)

1. personal commitment
2. Answers will vary.
3. a. Act immediately to focus on goals.
   b. Don't try to take on too much at once.
   c. Divide materials into smaller, more manageable portions.
   d. Celebrate progress along the way, and look forward to future benefits for learning (note: class discussion will bring out other good ideas).
4. It promotes positive thinking and self-confidence that lead to success.
5. Answers will vary.
6. a. Find a comfortable place to study, and organize your study area.
   b. Listen to enjoyable music while studying.
   c. Replace negative self-talk with "can do" affirmatives.
   d. Think positively, and visualize yourself as a successful learner.

7. stress reduction and mental stamina
8. see it, say it, write it.
9. Preparation and the use of flash cards provide visual, kinesthetic, and auditory reinforcement of the senses helpful in memorization. Flash cards are portable and can be carried at all times.
10. When you annotate text material, you make notes in the margin as you read. This includes drawing lines to separate component parts of key terms and writing out their meanings.
11. a. Draw pictures of word components.
    b. Listen to audiotapes/pronunciations on CD-ROM.
    c. Make up songs or rhymes.
    d. Find a person or group to study with.

CHAPTER 2 (PP. 30–37)

1. pan / cyto / penia
     P   CF   S
   DEFINITION: all / cell / abnormal reduction
2. leuk / emia
     R   S
   DEFINITION: white / blood condition
3. tox / oid
     R   S
   DEFINITION: poison / resembling
4. meso / morph / ic
      P   R   S
   DEFINITION: middle / form / pertaining to
5. acro / dynia
     CF   S
   DEFINITION: extremity / pain
6. meta / stasis
      P   S
   DEFINITION: beyond, after, or change / stop or stand
7. ultra / sono / graphy
      P   CF   S
   DEFINITION: beyond or excessive / sound / process of recording

8. tachy / card / ia
      P   R   S
   DEFINITION: fast / heart / condition of
9. pyo / poiesis
     CF   S
   DEFINITION: pus / formation
10. aden / itis
      R   S
    DEFINITION: gland / inflammation
11. macro / cephal / ous
        P   R   S
    DEFINITION: large or long / head / pertaining to
12. para / centesis
       P   S
    DEFINITION: alongside of / puncture for aspiration
13. micro / lith / iasis
        P   R   S
    DEFINITION: small / stone / formation or presence of
14. ortho /ped / ic
       CF   R   S
    DEFINITION: straight, normal, or correct / foot / pertaining to

15. angio / megaly
     CF   S
    DEFINITION: vessel / enlargement
16. psych / iatry
     R   S
    DEFINITION: mind / treatment
17. carcino /genesis
     CF   S
    DEFINITION: cancer / origin or production
18. nephro / logist
     CF   S
    DEFINITION: kidney / one who specializes in the study
       or treatment of
19. rhino / sten / osis
     CF   R   S
    DEFINITION: nose / narrow / condition or increase
20. hypo / hydr / ation
     P   R   S
    DEFINITION: below or deficient / water / process
21. aero / gastr / algia
     CF   R   S
    DEFINITION: air or gas / stomach / pain
22. fibr / oma
     R   S
    DEFINITION: fiber / tumor
23. necro / philia
     CF   S
    DEFINITION: death / attraction for
24. scler / osis
     R   S
    DEFINITION: hard / condition or increase
25. hemo / lysis
     CF   S
    DEFINITION: blood / breaking down or dissolution
26. acro / phob / ia
     CF   R   S
    DEFINITION: topmost (or extremity) / exaggerated
       fear or sensitivity / condition of
27. cyto / meter
     CF   S
    DEFINITION: cell / instrument for measuring
28. cyano / tic
     CF   S
    DEFINITION: blue / pertaining to
29. extra / vascul / ar
     P   R   S
    DEFINITION: outside / vessel / pertaining to
30. hyper / troph / y
     P   R   S
    DEFINITION: above or excessive / nourishment or
       development / condition or process of
31. c. supra
32. d. re
33. c. pre
34. b. de
35. e. trans
36. c. super
37. b. infra
38. a. exo
39. b. dys
40. b. ab

41. b. pro
42. d. circum
43. c. hemi
44. f. ab-
45. g. inter-
46. h. para-
47. b. peri-
48. a. retro-
49. j. intra-
50. c. anti-
51. i. an-
52. d. ecto-
53. e. dia-
54. many
55. below or deficient
56. few or deficient
57. one
58. all
59. beyond or excessive
60. two or both
61. four
62. half
63. below or under
64. above or excessive
65. c. ante-
66. d. post-
67. e. tachy-
68. a. brady-
69. b. re-
70. d. without
71. b. foot
72. d. mouth
73. d. new
74. a. surgical repair
75. e. process
76. c. crushing
77. c. expansion
78. c. right
79. f. melan/o
80. a. tri-
81. j. erythr/o
82. g. quadri-
83. b. leuk/o
84. e. uni-
85. c. cyan/o
86. k. bi-
87. i. oligo-
88. d. dextr/o
89. h. sinistr/o
90. c. -gram
91. c. -osis
92. c. -ectomy
93. b. -ar
94. d. -rrhexis
95. c. -ula
96. a. -ism
97. nephritis
98. nephrolysis
99. nephrotomy
100. nephrogenous
101. nephropexy

102. nephrostomy
103. nephrectomy
104. nephrolithiasis
105. nephroma
106. nephrocele
107. nephrorrhaphy
108. nephroptosis
109. d. colostomy
110. a. vasorrhaphy
111. c. abdominocentesis

112. ovaries, ova
113. metastases
114. verrucae
115. condyloma
116. index
117. thrombi
118. c. nephrorrhaphy
119. a. abdominoscopy
120. b. pericardium

CHAPTER 3 (PP. 50–53)

1. onco / logy
   CF   S
   DEFINITION: tumor / study of
2. immuno / logist
      CF   S
   DEFINITION: safe / one who specializes in the study or treatment of
3. oto / laryngo / logy
   CF   CF   S
   DEFINITION: ear / voice box / study of
4. opto / metry
     CF   S
   DEFINITION: eye / process of measuring
5. gyneco / logy
      CF   S
   DEFINITION: woman / study of
6. patho / logy
      CF   S
   DEFINITION: disease / study of
7. ortho / ped / ic
      CF   R   S
   DEFINITION: straight, normal, or correct / foot / pertaining to
8. uro / logist
      CF   S
   DEFINITION: urine / one who specializes in the study or treatment of
9. neuro / logy
      CF   S
   DEFINITION: nerve / study of
10. psycho / logist
       CF   S
    DEFINITION: mind / one who specializes in the study or treatment of
11. osteo / path / y
       CF   R   S
    DEFINITION: bone / disease / condition or process of
12. ophthalmo / logist
        CF   S
    DEFINITION: eye / one who specializes in the study or treatment of
13. obstetr / ic
       R   S
    DEFINITION: midwife / pertaining to
14. an / esthesio / logy
       P   CF   S
    DEFINITION: without / sensation / study of

15. cardio / logy
    CF   S
    DEFINITION: heart / study of
16. dermato / logy
       CF   S
    DEFINITION: skin / study of
17. ped / iatrics
      R   S
    DEFINITION: child / treatment
18. endo / crino / logist
      P   CF   S
    DEFINITION: within / to secrete / one who specializes in the study or treatment of
19. nephro / logist
       CF   S
    DEFINITION: kidney / one who specializes in the study or treatment of
20. gastro / entero / logy
       CF   CF   S
    DEFINITION: stomach / small intestine / study of
21. hemato / logist
       CF   S
    DEFINITION: blood / one who specializes in the study or treatment of
22. j
23. q
24. l
25. p
26. f
27. n
28. o
29. e
30. b
31. d
32. i
33. h
34. g
35. a
36. k
37. c
38. m
39. obstetrics and gynecology
40. Doctor of Dental Surgery
41. ears, nose, and throat
42. American Board of Medical Specialties
43. Doctor of Optometry
44. Fellow of the American College of Surgeons

45. American College of Physicians
46. Doctor of Chiropractic Medicine
47. Doctor of Podiatric Medicine
48. Doctor of Osteopathic Medicine
49–53.
  gynecologist
  ophthalmologist
  otolaryngologist
  orthopaedist
  urologist

54. c
55. a
56. e
57. g
58. f
59. b
60. d

CHAPTER 4 (PP. 97–101)

1. chief complaint
2. occupational history
3. per rectum
4. bathroom privileges
5. postanesthetic recovery unit
6. past history
7. *discontinue or discharge
8. instructions to patient
9. emergency room
10. intensive care unit
11. rule out
12. nothing by mouth
13. living and well
14. blood pressure
15. *both ears
16. symptom
17. vital signs
18. review of systems
19. patient
20. *right eye
21. subcutaneous
22. history and physical
23. treatment or traction
24. diagnosis
25. history of present illness
26. female
27. decreased
28. d
29. e
30. g
31. a
32. j
33. i
34. b
35. c
36. f
37. h
38. d
39. h
40. f
41. i
42. g
43. j
44. b
45. c
46. a
47. e
48. vital signs every hour for 4 hours, then every 2 hours
49. one by mouth, 4 times a day, after meals and at bedtime

50. two and one-half grains of aspirin
51. 650 milligrams by mouth every 4 hours as needed for temperature more than 101°
52. one suppository through the rectum every night as needed
53. one drop in both eyes 3 times a day for 7 days
54. two capsules immediately, then one every 6 hours
55. tab Ť po tid ×7 d or Ť tab po tid ×7 d
56. suppos Ť PV hs or Ť suppos PV hs
57. 5 mL po qid
58. Ť or ŤŤ po q 3–4 h prn
59. gtt ŤŤ AS q 3 h or ŤŤ gtt AS q 3 h
60. cap Ť po bid am and pm or Ť cap po bid am and pm
61. ŤŤ po STAT, then Ť q 6 h
62. 30 mg po hs prn
63. 0100 hours
64. 1430 hours
65. 2400 hours
66. 1300 hours
67. 1900 hours
68. 0450 hours
69. e
70. h
71. g
72. f
73. i
74. d
75. b
76. j
77. a
78. c
79. every day, daily
80. every other day, every other day
81. left eye, left eye
82. right ear, right ear
83. both ears, both ears
84. greater than, greater than
85. discharge or discontinue, discharge or discontinue
86. yes
87. no
88. yes
89. yes
90. no
91. e
92. d
93. a
94. b
95. c

CHAPTER 5 (PP. 125–133)

1. dermato / logist
   CF   S
   DEFINITION: skin / one who specializes in the study or treatment of

2. ichthy / oid
   R   S
   DEFINITION: fish / resembling

3. onycho / lysis
   CF   S
   DEFINITION: nail / breakdown or dissolution

4. histo / troph / ic
   CF   R   S
   DEFINITION: tissue / nourishment of development / pertaining to

5. dys / plas / ia
   P   R   S
   DEFINITION: painful, difficult, or faulty / formation / condition of

6. hyper / kerat / osis
   P   R   S
   DEFINITION: above or excessive / hard / condition or increase

7. leuko / trich / ia
   CF   R   S
   DEFINITION: white / hair / condition of

8. myco / logy
   CF   S
   DEFINITION: fungus / study of

9. epi / derm / al
   P   R   S
   DEFINITION: upon / skin / pertaining to

10. lip / oma
    R   S
    DEFINITION: fat / tumor

11. sub / cutane / ous
    P   R   S
    DEFINITION: below or under / skin / pertaining to

12. an / hidr / osis
    P   R   S
    DEFINITION: without / sweat / condition or increase

13. histo / patho / logy
    CF   CF   S
    DEFINITION: tissue / disease / study of

14. par / onych / ia
    P   R   S
    DEFINITION: alongside of / nail / condition of

15. adip / osis
    R   S
    DEFINITION: fat / condition or increase

16. squam / ous
    R   S
    DEFINITION: scale / pertaining to

17. erythro / dermat / itis
    CF   R   S
    DEFINITION: red / skin / inflammation

18. de / squam / ation
    P   R   S
    DEFINITION: from, down, or not / scale / process

19. histo / tox / ic
    CF   R   S
    DEFINITION: tissue / poison / pertaining to

20. melano / cyt / e
    CF   R   S
    DEFINITION: black / cell / noun marker

21. xer / osis
    R   S
    DEFINITION: dry / condition or increase

22. purpur / ic
    R   S
    DEFINITION: purple / pertaining to

23. sebo / rrhea
    CF   S
    DEFINITION: sebum (oil) / discharge

24. xanth / oma
    R   S
    DEFINITION: yellow / tumor

25. a / steat / osis
    P   R   S
    DEFINITION: without / fat / condition or increase

26. melanoma
27. hypodermic
28. cherry angioma
29. excoriation
30. frozen section
31. closed comedo
32. antipruritic
33. onychomycosis
34. excisional biopsy
35. autograft
36. sclerotherapy
37. hyperpigmentation
38. steat/o
39. melan/o
40. myc/o
41. onych/o
42. erythr/o
43. trich/o
44. xer/o
45. seb/o
46. gangrene
47. pruritus
48. carbuncle
49. alopecia
50. curettage
51. acne
52. psoriasis
53. cellulitis
54. f
55. i
56. h
57. g
58. j
59. c
60. a
61. d
62. b
63. e
64. leukoderma
65. xanthoderma
66. xeroderma
67. erythroderma
68. scleroderma

69. rubella
70. varicella
71. rubeola
72. f
73. i
74. c
75. h
76. d
77. g
78. a
79. j
80. b
81. e
82. Bx
83. I&D
84. BCC
85. HSV-1
86. C&S
87. SLE
88. m
89. k
90. g
91. l
92. d
93. h
94. j
95. b
96. i
97. e
98. a
99. f
100. c
101. keratoses
102. bullae
103. nevi
104. maculae
105. ecchymoses
106. **electrodesiccation**—use of short, high-frequency, electric currents to destroy tissue by drying; the active electrode makes direct contact with the skin lesion; **fulguration**—use of long, high-frequency, electric sparks to destroy tissue; the active electrode does *not* touch the skin
107. **actinic keratoses**—localized thickening of the skin caused by excessive exposure to sunlight; **seborrheic keratoses**—benign, wart-like lesions seen especially on elderly skin
108. **vitiligo**—condition caused by the destruction of melanin that results in the appearance of white patches on the skin; **albinism**—a hereditary condition characterized by a partial or total lack of melanin pigment
109. **cicatrix**—scar; mark left by the healing of a sore or wound showing the replacement of destroyed tissue by fibrous tissue; **keloid**—an abnormal overgrowth of scar tissue that is thick and irregular
110. **dermatosis**—any disorder of the skin; **dermatitis**—inflammation of the skin
111. **incisional biopsy**—removal of a selected portion of a lesion for microscopic pathological analysis; **excisional biopsy**—removal of an entire lesion for analysis
112. **heterograft**—graft transfer from one animal species to one of another species; **allograft**—donor transfer between individuals of the same species such as human to human
113. **closed comedo**—below the skin surface with a white center; **open comedo**—open to the skin surface with a black center caused by the presence of melanin exposed to air
114. **cutaneous lupus**—lupus limited to the skin; evidenced by a characteristic rash especially on the face, neck, and scalp; **systemic lupus erythematosus**—more severe form of lupus involving the skin, joints, and often vital organs
115. **dysplastic nevus**—mole with precancerous changes; **malignant melanoma**—cancerous tumor composed of melanocytes; most develop from a pigmented nevus over time
116. squamous layer (stratum corneum)
117. basal layer (stratum germinativum)
118. epidermis
119. dermis
120. subcutaneous tissue
121. cicatrix
122. pruritus
123. petechia
124. verruca
125. ecchymosis
126. excision
127. psoriasis
128. impetigo
129. eczema
130. debridement
131. keratosis
132. bulla
133. nodule
134. seborrhea
135. petechia
136. ecchymosis
137. urticaria
138. eczema
139. macula (macule)
140. suppuration

CHAPTER 6 (PP. 175–184)

1. thorac / ic
      R   S
   DEFINITION: chest / pertaining to
2. myo / fasci / al
      CF   R   S
   DEFINITION: muscle / fascia (a band) / pertaining to
3. arthro / path / y
      CF   R   S
   DEFINITION: joint / disease / condition or process of
4. spondylo / lysis
      CF   S
   DEFINITION: vertebra / breaking down or dissolution

5. osteo / penia
   CF   S
   DEFINITION: bone / abnormal reduction
6. a / chondro / plas / ia
   P   CF   R   S
   DEFINITION: without / cartilage / formation / condition of
7. oste / algia
   R   S
   DEFINITION: bone / pain
8. poly / myos / itis
   P   R   S
   DEFINITION: many / muscle / inflammation
9. leio / myo / sarc / oma
   CF   CF   R   S
   DEFINITION: smooth / muscle / flesh / tumor
10. myelo / cyt / e
    CF   R   S
    DEFINITION: bone marrow or spinal cord / cell / noun marker
11. costo / vertebr / al
    CF   R   S
    DEFINITION: rib / vertebra / pertaining to
12. musculo / tendin / ous
    CF   R   S
    DEFINITION: muscle / tendon / pertaining to
13. orth / osis
    R   S
    DEFINITION: straight, normal, or correct / condition or increase
14. kypho / plasty
    CF   S
    DEFINITION: humpback / surgical repair or reconstruction
15. crani / ectomy
    R   S
    DEFINITION: skull / excision (removal)
16. arthr / desis
    CF   S
    DEFINITION: joint / binding
17. fibro / my / algia
    CF   R   S
    DEFINITION: fiber / muscle / pain
18. rhabdo / my / oma
    CF   R   S
    DEFINITION: rod-shaped or striated (skeletal) / muscle / tumor
19. sterno / cost / al
    CF   R   S
    DEFINITION: sternum (breastbone) / rib / pertaining to
20. intra / articul / ar
    P   R   S
    DEFINITION: within / joint / pertaining to
21. syn / dactyl / ism
    P   R   S
    DEFINITION: together or with / digit (finger or toe) / condition of
22. lumbo / dynia
    CF   S
    DEFINITION: loin (lower back) / pain
23. cervico / brachi / al
    CF   R   S
    DEFINITION: neck / arm / pertaining to

24. arthro / scopy
    CF   S
    DEFINITION: joint / process of examination
25. lord / osis
    R   S
    DEFINITION: bent / condition or increase
26. inter<u>costal</u>
27. <u>arthr</u>algia
28. myo<u>tomy</u>
29. spondylosyn<u>desis</u>
30. <u>leio</u>myoma
31. osteo<u>malacia</u>
32. <u>spondylo</u>listhesis
33. arthro<u>gram</u> or arthro<u>graph</u>
34. <u>osteo</u>tomy
35. epiphys<u>itis</u>
36. <u>cervical</u>
37. bony <u>necrosis</u>
38. <u>chondroma</u>
39. arthro<u>centesis</u>
40. osteo<u>plasty</u>
41. chondr/o
42. spondyl/o
43. myel/o
44. cervic/o
45. arthr/o
46. thorac/o
47. my/o
48. cost/o
49. scoliosis
50. osteoma
51. crepitation or crepitus
52. sequestrum
53. sagittal
54. traction
55. gout or gouty arthritis
56. subluxation
57. proximal
58. rickets
59. radiologist
60. h
61. f
62. c
63. e
64. a
65. g
66. b
67. d
68. **arthrogram**—x-ray of a joint; **arthroscopy**—procedure using an arthroscope to examine, diagnose, and repair a joint from within
69. **rhabdomyoma**—skeletal (striated) muscle tumor; **rhabdomyosarcoma**—malignant skeletal muscle tumor
70. **osteoarthritis**—most common form of arthritis that especially affects weight-bearing joints characterized by the erosion of articular cartilage; **rheumatoid arthritis**—most crippling form of arthritis characterized by a chronic, systemic inflammation affecting joints and synovial membranes causing ankylosis and deformity

71. **osteomalacia**—disease marked by softening of the bone; **osteoporosis**—condition of decreased bone density and increased porosity
72. **orthosis**—use of an orthopedic appliance to maintain a bone's position or provide limb support; **prosthesis**—an artificial replacement for a diseased or missing body part such as a hip, joint, or limb
73. **closed reduction, external fixation of a Fx**—external manipulation of a fracture to regain alignment along with application of an external device to protect and hold the bone in place while healing; **open reduction internal fixation of a Fx**—internal surgical repair of a fracture by bringing bones back into alignment and fixing them into place, often utilizing plates, screws, and pins
74. **ankylosis**—stiff joint condition; **spondylosis**—stiff, immobile condition of vertebrae
75. **leiomyoma**—smooth muscle tumor; **leiomyosarcoma**—malignant smooth muscle tumor
76. **lordosis**—abnormal anterior curvature of the lumbar spine (sway-back condition); **kyphosis**—abnormal posterior curvature of the thoracic spine (humpback condition)
77. **spondylolisthesis**—diagnostic term describing a forward slipping of a lumbar vertebra; **spondylosyndesis**—operative (surgical) term for spinal fusion
78. b
79. d
80. a
81. c
82. computed tomography
83. physical therapy
84. traction
85. range of motion
86. fracture
87. electromyogram
88. spondylosis
89. scoliosis
90. arthrodynia
91. ostealgia
92. sagittal
93. flaccid
94. sequestrum
95. ankylosis
96. chondral
97. dorsiflexion
98. osteoporosis
99. rhabdomyoma
100. medial
101. sagittal
102. anterior
103. frontal
104. posterior
105. superior
106. inferior
107. transverse
108. flexion
109. extension
110. abduction
111. adduction
112. rotation
113. eversion
114. inversion
115. pronation
116. supination
117. dorsiflexion
118. plantar flexion
119. skull
120. cranium
121. phalanges
122. clavicle
123. scapula
124. sternum
125. xiphoid process
126. humerus
127. ilium
128. ischium
129. ulna
130. radius
131. carpals
132. metacarpals
133. trochanter
134. femur
135. patella
136. tibia
137. fibula
138. tarsals
139. metatarsals
140. phalanges
141. sacrum
142. coccyx
143. calcaneus
144. orthosis
145. hypertrophy
146. radius
147. kyphosis
148. bursa
149. dystrophy
150. necrosis
151. osteoporosis
152. lordosis
153. ulna
154. scoliosis
155. prosthesis

CHAPTER 7 (PP. 222–228)

1. angio / graphy
   CF   S
   DEFINITION: vessel / process of recording
2. varic / osis
   R   S
   DEFINITION: swollen, twisted vein / condition or increase
3. pector / al
   R   S
   DEFINITION: chest / pertaining to
4. vaso / spasm
   CF   S
   DEFINITION: vessel / involuntary contraction

5. ven / ous
    R   S
DEFINITION: vein / pertaining to

6. aorto / coron / ary
    CF   R   S
DEFINITION: aorta / circle or crown / pertaining to

7. thrombo / phleb / itis
     CF   R   S
DEFINITION: clot / vein / inflammation

8. peri / cardio / centesis
    P   CF   S
DEFINITION: around / heart / puncture for aspiration

9. vasculo / path / y
     CF   R   S
DEFINITION: vessel / disease / condition or process of

10. athero / genesis
      CF   S
DEFINITION: fatty (lipid) paste / origin or production

11. stetho / scope
      CF   S
DEFINITION: chest / instrument for examination

12. myo / card / ium
     CF   R   S
DEFINITION: muscle / heart / structure or tissue

13. aorto / plasty
      CF   S
DEFINITION: aorta / surgical repair or
    reconstruction

14. veno / stomy
      CF   S
DEFINITION: vein / creation of an opening

15. arterio / sten / osis
      CF   R   S
DEFINITION: artery / narrow / condition or increase

16. phlebo / tomy
      CF   S
DEFINITION: vein / incision

17. cardio / aort / ic
      CF   R   S
DEFINITION: heart / aorta / pertaining to

18. ventriculo / gram
        CF   S
DEFINITION: ventricle / record

19. phleb / itis
      R   S
DEFINITION: vein / inflammation

20. angio / plasty
      CF   S
DEFINITION: vessel / surgical repair or
    reconstruction

21. endo / vascul / ar
     P   R   S
DEFINITION: within / vessel / pertaining to

22. cardio / tox / ic
      CF   R   S
DEFINITION: heart / poison / pertaining to

23. arterio / gram
      CF   S
DEFINITION: artery / record

24. ather / ectomy
      R   S
DEFINITION: fatty (lipid) paste / excision removal

25. athero / thromb / osis
      CF   R   S
DEFINITION: fatty (lipid) paste / clot / condition or
    increase

26. congenital anomalies
27. arteriosclerosis
28. arrhythmia or dysrhythmia
29. cardiomyopathy
30. anastomosis
31. gallop
32. echocardiogram
33. cor pulmonale
34. coronary angiogram
35. stress ECG
36. intracardiac catheter ablation
37. pector/o
38. phleb/o
39. angi/o
40. cardi/o
41. ather/o
42. coron/o
43. sphygm/o
44. thromb/o
45. arteri/o
46. ventricul/o
47. h
48. o
49. n
50. i
51. g
52. j
53. a
54. c
55. l
56. e
57. m
58. d
59. k
60. f
61. b
62. premature ventricular contraction
63. patent ductus arteriosus
64. arteriosclerotic heart disease
65. implantable cardioverter-defibrillator
66. congestive heart failure
67. coronary artery disease
68. hypertension
69. mitral valve prolapse
70. magnetic resonance angiography
71. ventricular septal defect
72. atrial septum
73. right atrium
74. tricuspid valve
75. right ventricle
76. left atrium
77. aortic valve
78. pulmonary semilunar valve
79. left ventricle
80. ventricular septum
81. e
82. h
83. b

84. a
85. j
86. c
87. i
88. d
89. f
90. g
91. ventricle
92. aorta
93. thrombus
94. myocardial
95. hypotension
96. diastole
97. ischemia

98. occlusion
99. infarct
100. aneurysm
101. atherosclerotic
102. thrombophlebitis
103. angiogram
104. defibrillation
105. antiarrhythmic
106. vasodilation
107. anticoagulant
108. hypertension
109. tachycardia
110. systole

CHAPTER 8 (PP. 256–263)

1. erythro / blast / osis
      CF   R   S
   DEFINITION: red / germ or bud / condition or increase
2. myelo / dys / plas / ia
      CF   P   R   S
   DEFINITION: bone marrow / faulty (bad, difficult) / formation / condition of
3. hemo / cyto / meter
      CF   CF   S
   DEFINITION: blood / cell / instrument for measuring
4. spleno / rrhagia
      CF   S
   DEFINITION: spleen / to burst forth
5. lymph / aden / itis
      R   R   S
   DEFINITION: clear fluid / gland / inflammation
6. immuno / tox / ic
       CF   R   S
   DEFINITION: safe / poison / pertaining to
7. reticulo / cyt / osis
      CF   R   S
   DEFINITION: a net / cell / condition or increase
8. thymo / path / y
      CF   R   S
   DEFINITION: thymus gland / disease / condition or process of
9. leuko / cyt / ic
      CF   R   S
   DEFINITION: white / cell / pertaining to
10. lymph / angio / gram
       R   CF   S
    DEFINITION: clear fluid / vessel / record
11. spleno / megaly
       CF   S
    DEFINITION: spleen / enlargement
12. pro / myelo / cyt / e
       P   CF   R   S
    DEFINITION: before / bone marrow / cell / noun marker
13. leuko / cyto / penia
       CF   CF   S
    DEFINITION: white / cell / abnormal reduction

14. splen / ectomy
       R   S
    DEFINITION: spleen / excision (removal)
15. chylo / poiesis
       CF   S
    DEFINITION: juice / formation
16. lymph / oma
       R   S
    DEFINITION: clear fluid / tumor
17. cyto / morpho / logy
       CF   CF   S
    DEFINITION: cell / form / study of
18. hemo / lysis
       CF   S
    DEFINITION: blood / breaking down or dissolution
19. an / emia
       P   S
    DEFINITION: without / blood condition
20. meta / stasis
       P   S
    DEFINITION: beyond, after, or change / stop or stand
21. neutropenia
22. leukocyte
23. hematopoiesis
24. splenomegaly
25. erythropenia, erythrocytopenia
26. thymic
27. agranulocytes
28. eosinophil
29. erythrocyte
30. pancytopenia
31. phag/o
32. thromb/o
33. chyl/o
34. plas/o
35. chrom/o
36. hem/o
37. immun/o
38. blast/o
39. white blood count, WBC
40. hemoglobin, HGB or Hgb
41. hematocrit, HCT or Hct
42. differential count

43. mean corpuscular (cell) volume, mean corpuscular (cell) hemoglobin, mean corpuscular (cell) hemoglobin concentration, anemia
44. phlebotomy
45. lymphoma
46. prothrombin time
47. erythrocyte sedimentation rate
48. partial thromboplastin time
49. complete blood count
50. l
51. j
52. k
53. g
54. c
55. e
56. f
57. b
58. d
59. i
60. h
61. a
62. immunosuppression
63. cross matching
64. acquired immunodeficiency syndrome (AIDS)
65. mononucleosis
66. plasmapheresis
67. **plasma**—liquid portion of the blood and lymph containing water, proteins, salts, nutrients, hormones, vitamins, and cellular components; **serum**—liquid portion of the blood left after the clotting process
68. **anemia**—condition affecting red blood cells that results in their diminished ability to transport oxygen to the tissues; **leukemia**—cancer of the blood-forming organs marked by abnormal white blood cells in the blood and bone marrow
69. **autologous blood**—blood donated by a person and stored for his or her future use; **homologous blood**—blood voluntarily donated by any person for transfusion
70. **antibody**—substance produced by the body that destroys or inactivates an antigen that has entered the body; **antigen**—a substance that, when introduced into the body, causes the formation of antibodies against it

71. **vasoconstrictor**—drug that causes a narrowing of blood vessels, decreasing blood flow; **vasodilator**—drug that causes dilation of blood vessels, increasing blood flow
72. **anticoagulant**—drug that prevents clotting of the blood; **hemostatic**—drug that stops the flow of blood within the vessels
73. **polycythemia**—increase in the number of erythrocytes and hemoglobin in the blood; **hemochromatosis**—hereditary disorder that results in an excessive buildup of iron deposits in the body
74. plasma
75. leukocytes
76. erythrocytes
77. thrombocytes
78. serum
79. right lymphatic duct
80. thymus gland
81. thoracic duct
82. lymphatic vessels
83. cervical lymph nodes
84. spleen
85. hematopoiesis
86. platelets
87. anisocytosis
88. poikilocytosis
89. hemolysis
90. lymphadenopathy
91. myelodysplasia
92. thrombocytopenia
93. hematocrit
94. splenectomy
95. plasmapheresis
96. vasodilator
97. venipuncture
98. leukemia
99. immunosuppression
100. thymus
101. hematopoiesis
102. spleen
103. septicemia
104. hemophilia
105. myelodysplasia

CHAPTER 9 (PP. 289–296)

1. pulmono / logy
    CF   S
    DEFINITION: lung / study of
2. thoraco / centesis
    CF   S
    DEFINITION: chest / puncture for aspiration
3. naso / sinus / itis
    CF   R   S
    DEFINITION: nose / sinus / inflammation
4. hyp / ox / emia
    P   R   S
    DEFINITION: below or deficient / oxygen / blood condition

5. pleur / itis
    R   S
    DEFINITION: pleura / inflammation
6. hyper / carb / ia
    P   R   S
    DEFINITION: above or excessive / carbon dioxide / condition of
7. alveol / ar
    R   S
    DEFINITION: alveolus (air sac) / pertaining to
8. tracheo / tomy
    CF   S
    DEFINITION: trachea / incision

9. oro / nas / al
      CF   R   S
   DEFINITION: mouth / nose / pertaining to
10. rhino / rrhea
       CF   S
    DEFINITION: nose / discharge
11. thoraco / stomy
        CF   S
    DEFINITION: chest / creation of an opening
12. tonsill / ectomy
        R   S
    DEFINITION: tonsil / excision (removal)
13. tracheo / bronch / itis
        CF   R   S
    DEFINITION: trachea (windpipe) / bronchus
        (airway) / inflammation
14. broncho / spasm
        CF   S
    DEFINITION: bronchus (airway) / involuntary
        contraction
15. laryngo / sten / osis
        CF   R   S
    DEFINITION: larynx (voice box) / narrow / condition
        or increase
16. spiro / gram
        CF   S
    DEFINITION: breathing / record
17. lob / ectomy
        R   S
    DEFINITION: lobe (a portion) / excision (removal)
18. peri / pleur / al
        P   R   S
    DEFINITION: around / pleura / pertaining to
19. stetho / scope
        CF   S
    DEFINITION: chest / instrument for examination
20. pneumon / ic
        R   S
    DEFINITION: air or lung / pertaining to
21. naso / pharyngo / scopy
        CF   CF   S
    DEFINITION: nose / pharynx (throat) / process of
        examination
22. bronchiol / ectasis
        R   S
    DEFINITION: bronchiole (little airway) / expansion
        or dilation
23. phreno / ptosis
        CF   S
    DEFINITION: diaphragm / falling or downward
        displacement
24. pector / al
        R   S
    DEFINITION: chest / pertaining to
25. uvulo / palato / pharyngo / plasty
        CF   CF   CF   S
    DEFINITION: uvula (grape) / palate / throat / surgical
        repair or reconstruction
26. pneumoconiosis
27. bronchiectasis
28. thoracoplasty

29. pneumonitis
30. spirometry
31. hypoventilation
32. eupnea
33. bradypnea
34. dyspnea
35. orthopnea
36. apnea
37. tachypnea
38. rhin/o
39. pneum/o
40. pharyng/o
41. thorac/o
42. laryng/o
43. spir/o
44. phren/o
45. or/o
46. pneumothorax
47. empyema, pyothorax
48. hemothorax
49. auscultation
50. bronchoscope
51. expectoration
52. pleurisy, pleuritis
53. percussion
54. thoracentesis, thoracocentesis
55. dysphonia
56. laryngitis
57. hypoxia
58. emphysema
59. epistaxis
60. bronchogenic carcinoma
61. cystic fibrosis
62. atelectasis
63. sputum
64. stridor
65. pulmonary embolism
66. tracheostomy
67. asthma
68. hyperventilation
69. pneumocystis pneumonia
70. chronic obstructive pulmonary disease (COPD)
71. peak expiratory flow rate
72. vital capacity
73. tuberculosis
74. cardiopulmonary resuscitation
75. chronic obstructive pulmonary disease
76. partial pressure of carbon dioxide
77. upper respiratory infection
78. tidal volume
79. pulmonary function testing
80. polysomnography
81. continuous positive airway pressure
82. k
83. h
84. g
85. f
86. i
87. l
88. d
89. e

90. b
91. a
92. j
93. c
94. CXR
95. ABGs
96. T&A
97. naso<u>pharynx</u>
98. <u>trachea</u>
99. <u>pleura</u>
100. upper <u>lobe</u> of lung
101. <u>diaphragm</u>
102. frontal <u>sinus</u>
103. <u>larynx</u> with vocal cords
104. left main <u>bronchus</u>
105. auscultation
106. tachypnea
107. eupnea

108. pleurisy
109. hemothorax
110. stethoscope
111. epistaxis
112. rhonchi
113. hemoptysis
114. rhinorrhea
115. emphysema
116. atelectasis
117. bronchodilator
118. orthopnea
119. pleura
120. hypoxia
121. dyspnea
122. pharynx
123. apnea
124. trachea
125. asthma

CHAPTER 10 (PP. 338–346)

1. gangli / oma
      R   S
   DEFINITION: ganglion (knot) / tumor
2. a / topo / gnos / ia
    P CF   R   S
   DEFINITION: without / place / knowing / condition of
3. cata / ton / ic
      P   R   S
   DEFINITION: down / tone or tension / pertaining to
4. dys / tax / ia
     P   R   S
   DEFINITION: painful, difficult, or faulty / order or coordination / condition of
5. brady / kines / ia
      P   R   S
   DEFINITION: slow / movement / condition of
6. meningo / cele
       CF   S
   DEFINITION: meninges (membrane) / pouching or hernia
7. dys / thym / ia
     P   R   S
   DEFINITION: painful, difficult, or faulty / mind / condition of
8. poly / somno / gram
     P   CF   S
   DEFINITION: many / sleep / record
9. spondylo / syn / desis
      CF   P   S
   DEFINITION: vertebra / together or with / binding
10. hemi / plegia
       P   S
    DEFINITION: half / paralysis
11. cranio / tomy
       CF   S
    DEFINITION: skull / incision
12. thalam / ic
       R   S
    DEFINITION: thalamus (a room) / pertaining to

13. neuro / gli / al
      CF   R   S
    DEFINITION: nerve / glue / pertaining to
14. dys / lex / ia
      P   R   S
    DEFINITION: painful, difficult, or faulty / word or phrase / condition of
15. somni / path / y
       CF   R   S
    DEFINITION: sleep / disease / condition or process of
16. hydro / cephal / ic
       CF   R   S
    DEFINITION: water / head / pertaining to
17. dys / arthr / ia
      P   R   S
    DEFINITION: difficult, painful, or faulty / articulation / condition of
18. acro / phob / ia
       CF   R   S
    DEFINITION: topmost / exaggerated fear / condition of
19. hypno / tic
       CF   S
    DEFINITION: sleep / pertaining to
20. eu / phor / ia
      P   R   S
    DEFINITION: good or normal / carry or bear / condition of
21. para / somn / ia
       P   R   S
    DEFINITION: abnormal / sleep / condition of
22. narco / lepsy
       CF   S
    DEFINITION: stupor (sleep) / seizure
23. stereo / tax / y
       CF   R   S
    DEFINITION: three-dimensional or solid / order or coordination / condition or process of
24. hemi / paresis
       P   S
    DEFINITION: half / slight paralysis

25. neur / asthenia
    R   S
DEFINITION: nerve / weakness
26. myelo / path / y
    CF   R   S
DEFINITION: spinal cord / disease / condition or process of
27. intra / crani / al
    P   R   S
DEFINITION: within / skull / pertaining to
28. a / phas / ia
    P   R   S
DEFINITION: without / speech / condition of
29. schizo / phren / ia
    CF   R   S
DEFINITION: split / mind / condition of
30. cerebro / spin / al
    CF   R   S
DEFINITION: cerebrum / spine / pertaining to
31. electroencephalogram
32. spondylosyndesis
33. craniectomy
34. cerebral atherosclerosis
35. hyperesthesia
36. dysphasia
37. analgesia
38. astereognosis
39. encephal/o
40. kinesi/o
41. lex/o
42. somat/o
43. myel/o
44. thym/o
45. esthesi/o
46. top/o
47. hypn/o
48. gnos/o
49. meningitis
50. diskectomy (discectomy)
51. Parkinson disease
52. Babinski sign
53. paresthesia
54. coma
55. spina bifida
56. e
57. j
58. i
59. k
60. b
61. g
62. h
63. f
64. c
65. d
66. a
67. computed tomography
68. magnetic resonance image or imaging
69. positron emission tomography
70. multiple sclerosis
71. central nervous system
72. cerebral palsy
73. transient ischemic attack
74. electroencephalogram
75. deep tendon reflexes
76. cerebrospinal fluid
77. magnetic resonance angiography
78. cerebrovascular accident
79. pons
80. cerebellum
81. spinal
82. callosum
83. thalamus
84. cranium
85. meninges
86. cerebrum
87. j
88. d
89. h
90. f
91. a
92. e
93. b
94. i
95. g
96. c
97. generalized anxiety disorder
98. attention-deficit/hyperactivity disorder
99. obsessive-compulsive disorder
100. electroconvulsive therapy
101. panic disorder
102. bipolar disorder
103. posttraumatic stress disorder
104. c
105. a
106. f
107. e
108. g
109. b
110. d
111. c
112. e
113. b
114. d
115. a
116. Alzheimer
117. schizophrenia
118. polysomnography
119. paranoia
120. atopognosis
121. dementia
122. epilepsy
123. catatonia
124. delusion
125. hallucination
126. poliomyelitis
127. epilepsy
128. euphoria
129. delusion
130. syncope
131. autism
132. psychosis
133. cerebrum
134. dysphasia
135. paranoia

CHAPTER 11 (PP. 372–377)

1. aden / itis
   R S
   DEFINITION: gland / inflammation
2. eu / glyc / emia
   P R S
   DEFINITION: good or normal / sugar / blood condition
3. thyro / toxic / osis
   CF R S
   DEFINITION: thyroid gland (shield) / poison / condition or increase
4. poly / dips / ia
   P R S
   DEFINITION: many / thirst / condition of
5. hormon / al
   R S
   DEFINITION: hormone (an urging on) / pertaining to
6. ket / osis
   R S
   DEFINITION: ketone bodies / condition or increase
7. poly / ur / ia
   P R S
   DEFINITION: many / urine / condition of
8. endo / crin / e
   P R S
   DEFINITION: within / to secrete / noun marker
9. thyro / ptosis
   CF S
   DEFINITION: thyroid gland (shield) / falling or downward displacement
10. thym / oma
    R S
    DEFINITION: thymus gland / tumor
11. acro / megaly
    CF S
    DEFINITION: extremity / enlargement
12. andr / oid
    R S
    DEFINITION: male / resembling
13. adreno / troph / ic
    CF R S
    DEFINITION: adrenal gland / nourishment or development / pertaining to
14. pancreato / gen / ic
    CF R S
    DEFINITION: pancreas / origin or production / pertaining to
15. glycos / ur / ia
    R R S
    DEFINITION: sugar / urine / condition of
16. dipso / gen / ic
    CF R S
    DEFINITION: thirst / origin or production / pertaining to
17. hypersecretion
18. hypoglycemia
19. Cushing syndrome
20. hyposecretion
21. hyperglycemia
22. sonography or ultrasonography
23. adrenal gland
24. shield
25. secrete
26. sugar
27. thirst
28. thymus gland
29. urging on
30. gland
31. hyperthyroidism or thyrotoxicosis
32. exophthalmos or exophthalmus
33. acromegaly
34. goiter
35. pituitary dwarfism
36. thyroid uptake and image
37. e
38. h
39. l
40. f
41. i
42. k
43. j
44. g
45. a
46. m
47. c
48. d
49. b
50. blood sugar
51. hormone replacement therapy
52. fasting blood sugar
53. diabetes mellitus
54. postprandial blood sugar
55. glucose tolerance test
56. diabetic ketoacidosis
57. para
58. thymus
59. adrenal
60. pituitary
61. thyroid
62. pancreas
63. hirsutism
64. exophthalmos
65. myxedema
66. goiter
67. androgenous
68. virilism
69. epinephrine
70. hypoglycemic
71. acromegaly
72. exophthalmos
73. metabolism
74. diabetes
75. hypoglycemia

CHAPTER 12 (PP. 403–408)

1. blepharo / ptosis
    CF   S
    DEFINITION: eyelid / falling or downward displacement
2. irido / tomy
    CF   S
    DEFINITION: iris / incision
3. ophthalmo / logy
    CF   S
    DEFINITION: eye / study of
4. vitr / ectomy
    R   S
    DEFINITION: glassy / excision (removal)
5. dacryo / lith / iasis
    CF   R   S
    DEFINITION: tear / stone / formation or presence of
6. lacrim / al
    R   S
    DEFINITION: tear / pertaining to
7. photo / phob / ia
    CF   R   S
    DEFINITION: light / sensitivity / condition of
8. kerato / plasty
    CF   S
    DEFINITION: cornea / surgical repair or reconstruction
9. aque / ous
    R   S
    DEFINITION: water / pertaining to
10. ir / itis
    R   S
    DEFINITION: iris / inflammation
11. corne / al
    R   S
    DEFINITION: cornea / pertaining to
12. phaco / lysis
    CF   S
    DEFINITION: lens (lentil) / breaking down or dissolution
13. retino / path / y
    CF   R   S
    DEFINITION: retina / disease / condition or process of
14. ocul / ar
    R   S
    DEFINITION: eye / pertaining to
15. conjunctiv / itis
    R   S
    DEFINITION: conjunctiva (to join together) / inflammation
16. presby / opia
    R   S
    DEFINITION: old age / condition of vision
17. opto / metry
    CF   S
    DEFINITION: eye / process of measuring
18. a / phak / ia
    P   R   S
    DEFINITION: without / lens (lentil) / condition or process of
19. hyper / opia
    P   S
    DEFINITION: above or excessive / condition of vision

20. sclero / malacia
    CF   S
    DEFINITION: sclera / softening
21. aphakia
22. exophthalmos
23. blepharochalasis or dermatochalasis
24. scleral buckling
25. blepharospasm
26. opt/o
27. presby/o
28. vitre/o
29. phot/o
30. scler/o
31. phac/o
32. irid/o
33. dacry/o
34. blephar/o
35. aque/o
36. conjunctivitis
37. blepharitis
38. asthenopia
39. mydriatic
40. hordeolum
41. cataract
42. macular degeneration
43. e
44. c
45. a
46. f
47. d
48. b
49. inward turning of the rim of the eyelid
50. instrument to measure intraocular pressure
51. outward turning of the rim of the eyelid
52. involuntary, rapid oscillating movement of the eyeball
53. f
54. h
55. a
56. e
57. i
58. b
59. j
60. d
61. c
62. g
63. eyelid
64. cornea
65. lens
66. sclera
67. vitreous
68. ciliary
69. retina
70. optic
71. asthenopia
72. pterygium
73. hordeolum
74. nystagmus
75. chalazion
76. mydriatic
77. scotoma

78. epiphora
79. dacryocyst
80. ophthalmoscope
81. conjunctiva

82. myopia
83. sclera
84. macula
85. exophthalmos or exophthalmus

CHAPTER 13 (PP. 426–429)

1. acous / tic
   R   S
   DEFINITION: hearing / pertaining to
2. oto / rrhea
   CF   S
   DEFINITION: ear / discharge
3. myringo / plasty
   CF   S
   DEFINITION: eardrum / surgical repair or
   reconstruction
4. aer / ot / itis
   R   R   S
   DEFINITION: air or gas / ear/inflammation
5. oto / tox / ic
   CF   R   S
   DEFINITION: ear / poison / pertaining to
6. cerumino / lysis
   CF   S
   DEFINITION: wax / breaking down or dissolution
7. salpingo / scope
   CF   S
   DEFINITION: eustachian tube / instrument for
   examination
8. hyper / acusis
   P   S
   DEFINITION: above or excessive / hearing condition
9. audio / metry
   CF   S
   DEFINITION: hearing / process of measuring
10. tympano / centesis
    CF   S
    DEFINITION: eardrum / puncture for aspiration
11. oto / dynia
    CF   S
    DEFINITION: ear / pain
12. aur / icle
    R   S
    DEFINITION: ear / small
13. myringo / tomy
    CF   S
    DEFINITION: eardrum / incision
14. cerumin / osis
    R   S
    DEFINITION: wax / condition or increase
15. audio / logy
    CF   S
    DEFINITION: hearing / study of

16. otosclerosis
17. otoscope
18. Ménière disease
19. acoustic neuroma
20. myring/o
21. audi/o
22. cerumin/o
23. salping/o
24. ot/o
25. aer/o
26. j
27. i
28. g
29. h
30. f
31. a
32. e
33. d
34. c
35. b
36. labyrinthitis
37. vertigo
38. tinnitus
39. stapedectomy
40. cerumen impaction
41. audiology
42. lavage
43. auricle
44. eustachian
45. pharynx
46. malleus
47. incus
48. stapes
49. cochlea
50. tympanic
51. aerotitis
52. cerumen
53. myringotomy
54. presbyacusis
55. vertigo
56. antihistamine
57. tinnitus
58. stapedectomy
59. deafness
60. eustachian

CHAPTER 14 (PP. 462–470)

1. trans / abdomin / al
   P R S

   DEFINITION: across or through / abdomen / pertaining to

2. gastro / entero / stomy
   CF CF S

   DEFINITION: stomach / small intestine / creation of an opening

3. sialo / litho / tomy
   CF CF S

   DEFINITION: saliva / stone / incision

4. glosso / rrhaphy
   CF S

   DEFINITION: tongue / suture

5. hemat / emesis
   R S

   DEFINITION: blood / vomiting

6. cheilo / stomato / plasty
   CF CF S

   DEFINITION: lip / mouth / surgical repair or reconstruction

7. appendic / itis
   R S

   DEFINITION: appendix / inflammation

8. celio / tomy
   CF S

   DEFINITION: abdomen / incision

9. chol / angio / gram
   R CF S

   DEFINITION: bile / vessel / record

10. colono / scopy
    CF S

    DEFINITION: colon / process of examination

11. ano / rect / al
    CF R S

    DEFINITION: anus / rectum / pertaining to

12. entero / col / itis
    CF R S

    DEFINITION: small intestine / colon / inflammation

13. oro / lingu / al
    CF R S

    DEFINITION: mouth / tongue / pertaining to

14. procto / sigmoido / scopy
    CF CF S

    DEFINITION: anus and rectum / sigmoid colon / process of examination

15. laparo / scope
    CF S

    DEFINITION: abdomen / instrument for examination

16. dys / phag / ia
    P R S

    DEFINITION: painful, difficulty, or faulty / eat or swallow / condition of

17. pancreato / duodeno / stomy
    CF CF S

    DEFINITION: pancreas / duodenum / creation of an opening

18. hernio / plasty
    CF S

    DEFINITION: hernia / surgical repair or reconstruction

19. bili / ary
    R S

    DEFINITION: bile / pertaining to

20. gastro / esophag / eal
    CF R S

    DEFINITION: stomach / esophagus / pertaining to

21. chole / docho / tomy
    CF CF S

    DEFINITION: bile / duct / incision

22. steato / rrhea
    CF S

    DEFINITION: fat / discharge

23. dent / algia
    R S

    DEFINITION: teeth / pain

24. pyloro / spasm
    CF S

    DEFINITION: pylorus (gatekeeper) / involuntary contraction

25. hepato / tox / ic
    CF R S

    DEFINITION: liver / poison / pertaining to

26. ileo / jejun / itis
    CF R S

    DEFINITION: ileum / jejunum / inflammation

27. peritoneo / centesis
    CF S

    DEFINITION: peritoneum / puncture for aspiration

28. bucco / gingiv / al
    CF R S

    DEFINITION: cheek / gum / pertaining to

29. chole / cyst / ectomy
    CF R S

    DEFINITION: bile / bladder or sac / excision (removal)

30. peri / rect / al
    P R S

    DEFINITION: around / rectum / pertaining to

31. hemi<u>col</u>ectomy
32. appen<u>dic</u>itis
33. <u>cheilor</u>rhaphy
34. cholelitho<u>tomy</u>
35. <u>stomato</u>plasty
36. chol<u>angio</u>gram
37. hyperbilirubin<u>emia</u>
38. gastric <u>resection</u>
39. diverticul<u>osis</u>
40. lapar/o
41. gloss/o
42. enter/o
43. dent/i
44. gastr/o
45. bucc/o
46. chol/e
47. stomat/o
48. hepat/o
49. phag/o
50. lith/o
51. proct/o
52. gastritis
53. anorexia

54. aphagia
55. buccal
56. flatulence
57. hernia
58. melena
59. eructation
60. proctoscope or rectoscope
61. colitis
62. barium swallow
63. ascites
64. cholecystitis
65. steatorrhea
66. diverticulitis
67. gastric ulcer
68. hepatomegaly
69. ankyloglossia
70. inguinal regions
71. hypochondriac regions
72. epigastric region
73. hypogastric region
74. lumbar regions
75. umbilical region
76. right upper quadrant
77. right lower quadrant
78. left upper quadrant
79. left lower quadrant
80. m
81. f
82. d
83. h
84. k
85. g
86. j
87. i
88. l
89. b
90. e
91. a
92. c
93. laparoscope
94. anoscope or proctoscope

95. gastroscope
96. colonoscope
97. peritoneoscope
98. esophagoscope
99. incarcerated hernia
100. excisional biopsy
101. nasogastric tube
102. endoscopic retrograde cholangiopancreatography
103. gastroesophageal reflux disease
104. left upper quadrant
105. gastrointestinal
106. magnetic resonance imaging
107. esophagogastroduodenoscopy
108. hepat/o or hepatic/o
109. cholecyst
110. enter/o
111. col/o or colon/o
112. gloss/o or lingu/o
113. gastr/o
114. proct/o or rect/o
115. an/o
116. anorexia
117. ascites
118. hematochezia
119. icterus
120. ankyloglossia
121. volvulus
122. cirrhosis
123. glossectomy
124. herniorrhaphy
125. hemorrhoidectomy
126. antacid
127. antiemetic
128. cathartic
129. melena
130. feces
131. icterus
132. ileum
133. endoscopy, endoscope
134. hemorrhoid
135. pancreas

CHAPTER 15 (PP. 497–503)

1. vesico / ureter / ic
      CF   R   S
   DEFINITION: bladder / ureter / pertaining to
2. bacteri / osis
       R   S
   DEFINITION: bacteria / condition or increase
3. trans / urethr / al
      P   R   S
   DEFINITION: across or through / urethra / pertaining to
4. uro / gram
      CF   S
   DEFINITION: urine / record
5. urethro / cyst / itis
       CF   R   S
   DEFINITION: urethra / bladder / inflammation

6. nephro / ptosis
      CF   S
   DEFINITION: kidney / falling or downward displacement
7. poly / dips / ia
      P   R   S
   DEFINITION: many / thirst / condition of
8. glomerulo / scler / osis
       CF   R   S
   DEFINITION: glomerulus (little ball) / hard / condition or increase
9. pyo / nephr / itis
      CF   R   S
   DEFINITION: pus / kidney / inflammation

10. uro / logy
　　CF　　S
　　DEFINITION: urine / study of
11. uretero / vesico / stomy
　　　CF　　　CF　　　S
　　DEFINITION: ureter / bladder / creation of an opening
12. glyco / rrhea
　　　CF　　　S
　　DEFINITION: sugar / discharge
13. meato / tomy
　　　CF　　S
　　DEFINITION: meatus (opening) / incision
14. pyelo / nephr / osis
　　　CF　　R　　S
　　DEFINITION: renal pelvis (basin) / kidney / condition
　　or increase
15. cysto / scopy
　　　CF　　S
　　DEFINITION: bladder / process of examination
16. supra / ren / al
　　　P　　R　S
　　DEFINITION: above / kidney / pertaining to
17. nephro / lith / iasis
　　　CF　　R　　S
　　DEFINITION: kidney / stone / formation or presence of
18. uretero / cele
　　　CF　　S
　　DEFINITION: ureter / pouching or hernia
19. albumin / ous
　　　R　　S
　　DEFINITION: protein / pertaining to
20. pyelo / graphy
　　　CF　　S
　　DEFINITION: renal pelvis (basin) / process of recording
21. nephritis
22. nephrosis
23. nephrotomy
24. nephrorrhaphy
25. nephrectomy
26. nephrolithotomy
27. urethral stenosis
28. extracorporeal shock wave lithotripsy
29. suprapubic catheter
30. resectoscope
31. Kegel exercises
32. occult blood
33. cystometrogram
34. peritoneal dialysis
35. scout film
36. cystitis
37. incontinence
38. enuresis
39. nocturnal enuresis
40. hydronephrosis
41. adult polycystic kidney disease
42. nocturia
43. oliguria
44. dysuria
45. ketonuria
46. hematuria
47. pyuria
48. g
49. d
50. i
51. h
52. a
53. k
54. c
55. b
56. f
57. e
58. j
59. albumin
60. intravenous pyelogram
61. extracorporeal shock wave lithotripsy
62. urinary tract infection
63. stress urinary incontinence
64. blood urea nitrogen
65. ur/o
66. dips/o
67. py/o
68. vesic/o
69. albumin/o
70. nephr/o
71. meat/o
72. pyel/o
73. lith/o
74. right kidney
75. ureters
76. urinary bladder
77. urethra
78. left kidney
79. cystoscope
80. pyelogram
81. oliguria
82. hydronephrosis
83. azotemia
84. urinalysis
85. glomerular
86. nephrectomy
87. diuretic
88. hemodialysis
89. catheterization
90. urine
91. glomerulus
92. meatus
93. uremia
94. urethra
95. nephrosis
96. UA
97. C&S
98. RP
99. KUB
100. VCU or VCUG

CHAPTER 16 (PP. 521–526)

1. oligo / sperm / ia
   P   R   S
   DEFINITION: few or deficient / sperm / condition of
2. perineo / plasty
      CF   S
   DEFINITION: perineum / surgical repair or reconstruction
3. test / algia
    R   S
   DEFINITION: testis or testicle / pain
4. balan / ic
     R   S
   DEFINITION: glans penis / pertaining to
5. prostato / megaly
      CF   S
   DEFINITION: prostate / enlargement
6. orchid / ectomy
      R   S
   DEFINITION: testis or testicle / excision (removal)
7. an / orch / ism
   P   R   S
   DEFINITION: without / testis or testicle / condition of
8. vas / ectomy
    R   S
   DEFINITION: vessel / excision (removal)
9. a / sperm / ia
   P   R   S
   DEFINITION: without / sperm (seed) / condition of
10. cysto / prostat / ectomy
      CF   R   S
    DEFINITION: bladder / prostate / excision (removal)
11. balan / itis
      R   S
    DEFINITION: glans penis / inflammation
12. orchio / plasty
      CF   S
    DEFINITION: testis or testicle / surgical repair or reconstruction
13. spermato / cele
       CF   S
    DEFINITION: sperm (seed) / pouching or hernia
14. epididymo / tomy
       CF   S
    DEFINITION: epididymis / incision
15. vaso / vaso / stomy
      CF   CF   S
    DEFINITION: vessel / vessel / creation of an opening
16. anorchism
17. balanitis
18. varicocele
19. resectoscope
20. benign prostatic hyperplasia or hypertrophy
21. vasectomy
22. Peyronie disease
23. h
24. g
25. f
26. e
27. b
28. d
29. a
30. c
31. cryptorchism
32. endorectal or transrectal sonogram of prostate
33. hydrocele
34. hypospadias
35. digital rectal exam
36. brachytherapy
37. c
38. d
39. a
40. b
41. prostate-specific antigen
42. biopsy
43. transurethral resection of the prostate
44. digital rectal examination
45. erectile dysfunction
46. orchi/o
47. perine/o
48. spermat/o
49. vas/o
50. balan/o
51. epididym/o
52. vas deferens
53. urethra
54. glans penis
55. testis
56. urinary bladder
57. prostate gland
58. perineum
59. epididymis
60. epididymis
61. oligospermia
62. azoospermia
63. anorchism
64. balanitis
65. cryptorchism
66. hypospadias
67. chlamydia
68. syphilis
69. phimosis
70. prostate
71. epididymis
72. perineum
73. penis
74. gonorrhea
75. testicle or testis

CHAPTER 17 (PP. 564–571)

1. vulv / itis
   R   S
   DEFINITION: vulva (covering) / inflammation
2. poly / mast / ia
   P   R   S
   DEFINITION: many / breast / condition of
3. ov / oid
   R   S
   DEFINITION: egg / resembling
4. toco / lysis
   CF   S
   DEFINITION: birth or labor / breaking down or dissolution
5. salpingo / tomy
   CF   S
   DEFINITION: uterine (fallopian) tube / incision
6. mammo / plasty
   CF   S
   DEFINITION: breast / surgical repair or reconstruction
7. trans / vagin / al
   P   R   S
   DEFINITION: across or through / vagina (sheath) / pertaining to
8. hystero / rrhexis
   CF   S
   DEFINITION: uterus / rupture
9. colpo / scopy
   CF   S
   DEFINITION: vagina (sheath) / process of examination
10. mammo / graphy
    CF   S
    DEFINITION: breast / process of recording
11. metro / rrhagia
    CF   S
    DEFINITION: uterus / to burst forth
12. ovario / centesis
    CF   S
    DEFINITION: ovary / puncture for aspiration
13. men / arche
    R   S
    DEFINITION: menstruation / beginning
14. oophor / ectomy
    R   S
    DEFINITION: ovary / excision (removal)
15. oligo / meno / rrhea
    P   CF   S
    DEFINITION: few or deficient / menstruation / discharge
16. dys / toc / ia
    P   R   S
    DEFINITION: painful, difficult, or faulty / labor or birth / condition of
17. gyneco / logist
    CF   S
    DEFINITION: woman / one who specializes in the study or treatment of
18. pelvi / meter
    CF   S
    DEFINITION: pelvic cavity / instrument to measure
19. episio / tomy
    CF   S
    DEFINITION: vulva (covering) / incision

20. colpo / rrhaphy
    CF   S
    DEFINITION: vagina (sheath) / suture
21. hystero / spasm
    CF   S
    DEFINITION: uterus / involuntary contraction
22. lacto / rrhea
    CF   S
    DEFINITION: milk / discharge
23. ovi / genesis
    CF   S
    DEFINITION: egg / origin or production
24. endo / cervic / al
    P   R   S
    DEFINITION: within / cervix / pertaining to
25. utero / tomy
    CF   S
    DEFINITION: uterus / incision
26. menopause
27. dysmenorrhea
28. amenorrhea
29. oligomenorrhea
30. menorrhagia
31. metrorrhagia
32. gynecomastia
33. amastia
34. hypomastia or micromastia; augmentation mammoplasty
35. hypermastia or macromastia; reduction mammoplasty
36. mastopexy
37. mastectomy
38. lumpectomy
39. toc/o
40. colp/o
41. salping/o
42. men/o
43. cervic/o
44. ov/i
45. episi/o
46. metr/o
47. lact/o
48. oophor/o
49. mast/o
50. gynec/o
51. i
52. f
53. e
54. g
55. h
56. b
57. d
58. j
59. c
60. a
61. fibrocystic breasts
62. vesicovaginal fistula
63. tubal ligation
64. polymastia
65. syphilis
66. Papanicolaou (Pap) smear

67. endometriosis
68. rectovaginal fistula
69. colporrhaphy—posterior repair
70. intrauterine device
71. human papilloma virus
72. chorionic villus sampling
73. dilation and curettage
74. hepatitis B virus
75. estimated date of confinement
76. herpes simplex virus
77. sexually transmitted disease
78. therapeutic abortion
79. hormone replacement therapy
80. spontaneous abortion
81. habitual abortion
82. incomplete abortion
83. missed abortion
84. therapeutic abortion
85. threatened abortion
86. c
87. f
88. g
89. j
90. l
91. d
92. i
93. b
94. k
95. h
96. a

97. e
98. cervix
99. vagina
100. uterine
101. ovary
102. uterus
103. endometrium
104. myometrium
105. developing eggs (ova)
106. gonorrhea
107. dyspareunia
108. tocolytic
109. polythelia
110. metrorrhagia
111. dilation
112. salpingotomy
113. nulligravida
114. meconium
115. macrosomia
116. curettage
117. eclampsia
118. amenorrhea
119. abortifacient
120. chlamydia
121. areola
122. syphilis
123. cervix
124. dysplasia
125. endometrium

Figure Credits

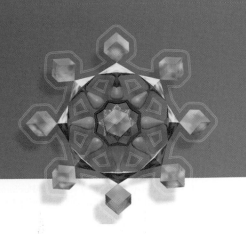

Figure 1.1   Redrawn from Bliss EC. Getting Things Done. New York: Bantam, 1976:67.

Figure 3.1   From Sheldon H. Boyd's Introduction to the Study of Disease, 11th ed. Philadelphia: Lea & Febiger, 1992:35.

Figure 3.2   From Hotel Dieu Museum, Beaune, France.

Figure 3.3   From Tate Gallery, London, United Kingdom/Art Resource, NY.

Figure 3.4   Thomas Eakins' *The Agnew Clinic*. From University of Pennsylvania School of Medicine, Philadelphia, PA.

Unnumbered Figure in Chapter 4.   Courtesy of Welch Allyn, Inc., Skaneateles Falls, NY.

Figure 4.14   Courtesy of Deutsches Roentgen-Museum, Remscheid-Lennep, Germany.

Figure 4.15   B. Courtesy of Toshiba Medical Systems.

Figure 4.16   Courtesy of ADAC Laboratories, a Philips Medical Systems Company, Bothell, WA.

Figure 4.17   B. Courtesy of Philips Medical Systems, Bothell, WA. ***Inset.*** Courtesy of Mission Regional Imaging, Mission Viejo, CA.

Figure 4.18   B. Courtesy of Acuson Corporation, a Siemens Company.

Figure 5.1   Squamous cell carcinomas and basal cell carcinomas. Reprinted with permission of Skin Cancer Foundation, New York, NY. Signs of melanoma (Figures 1–4). Courtesy of American Cancer Society, Atlanta, GA.

Figure 5.3   A–L and **N–Q.** Petechia. Courtesy of American Academy of Dermatology, Schaumburg, IL.

Figure 5.3   M. From Goodheart HP. Goodheart's Photoguide of Common Skin Disorders, 2nd ed. Philadelphia: Lippincott Williams & Wilkins, 2003.

Figure 5.4   From Dr. Barankin Dermatology Collection, Stedman's Medical Dictionary, 27th ed. Baltimore: Lippincott Williams & Wilkins, 2000.

Figure 5.5   From Goodheart HP. Goodheart's Photoguide of Common Skin Disorders, 2nd ed. Philadelphia: Lippincott Williams & Wilkins, 2003.

Figure 5.6   From Goodheart HP. Goodheart's Photoguide of Common Skin Disorders, 2nd ed. Philadelphia: Lippincott Williams & Wilkins, 2003.

Figure 5.7   From Goodheart HP. Goodheart's Photoguide of Common Skin Disorders, 2nd ed. Philadelphia: Lippincott Williams & Wilkins, 2003.

Figure 5.8   Sauer GC: Manual of Skin Diseases, 5th ed. Philadelphia: JB Lippincott, 1985.

Figure 5.9   From Goodheart HP. A Photoguide of Common Skin Disorders: Diagnosis and Management (0.683.30357.4). Philadelphia: Williams & Wilkins, 1999:268 (Figure 21-17).

Figure 5.10   From Roche Lexikon Medizin, 3rd ed. Munich, Germany: Urban & Schwarzenburg, 1993:877.

Figure 5.11   Courtesy of L. J. Underwood and R. D. Underwood, Mission Viejo, CA.

Figure 5.13   From Goodheart HP. Goodheart's Photoguide of Common Skin Disorders, 2nd ed. Philadelphia: Lippincott Williams & Wilkins, 2003.

Figure 5.14   Courtesy of Ellman International, Hewlett, NY. Randolph Waldman, MD, photographer.

Figure 5.16   From Goodheart HP. Goodheart's Photoguide of Common Skin Disorders, 2nd ed. Philadelphia: Lippincott Williams & Wilkins, 2003.

Figure 6.3   CT of skull. Courtesy of West Coast Radiology Center, Santa Ana, CA.

Figure 6.4   From Haines DE. Neuroanatomy: An Atlas of Structures, Sections, and Systems, 6th ed. Baltimore: Lippincott Williams & Wilkins, 2004.

Figure 6.8   From Cipriano J. Photographic Manual of Regional Orthopaedic and Neurological Tests, 2nd ed. Baltimore: Lippincott Williams & Wilkins, 1991.

Figure 6.10   LifeART image copyright ©2005. Lippincott Williams & Wilkins. All rights reserved.

Figure 6.12   From Malone TR (Ed). Hand and Wrist Injuries and Treatment. Baltimore: Williams & Wilkins, 1989:5.

Figure 6.14   X-rays. From Harris JH Jr, Harris WH, Novelline RA. The Radiology of Emergency Medicine, 3rd ed. Baltimore: Williams & Wilkins, 1993:440, 467.

Figure 6.15   Courtesy of Neil O. Hardy, Westpoint, CT.

Figure 6.16   B and **C.** Courtesy of Orange Coast College Radiologic Technology Program.

Figure 6.17   A and **B.** Courtesy of Neil O. Hardy, Westpoint, CT.

Figure 6.19   Courtesy of Orange Coast College Radiologic Technology Program.

Figure 6.20   From Moore KL, Dalley AF II. Clinical Oriented Anatomy, 4th ed. Baltimore: Lippincott Williams & Wilkins, 1999.

Figure 6.22   Photo courtesy of Lumenis.

Figure 6.24   Photo courtesy of 3M Health Care.

Figure 6.25   From Bucholz RW, Heckman JD. Rockwood & Green's Fractures in Adults, 5th ed. Lippincott Williams & Wilkins, 2001.

Figure 6.26   Photo courtesy of Camp Healthcare.

Figure 6.27   Courtesy of Smith & Nephew Systems, Inc., Memphis, TN.

Figure 6.28   Photo courtesy of Camp Healthcare.

Figure 6.29   Courtesy of RGP Prosthetic Research Center, San Diego, CA.

Figure 7.6   Courtesy of Welch Allen, Skaneateles Falls, NY.

Figure 7.10   From Rubin E, Farber JL. Pathology, 3rd ed. Philadelphia: Lippincott Williams & Wilkins, 1999.

Figure 7.16 Photo from Sheldon H. Boyd's Introduction to the Study of Disease, 11th ed. Philadelphia: Lea & Febiger, 1992:90.

Figure 7.17 From Pillitteri A. Maternal and Child Nursing, 4th ed. Philadelphia: Lippincott Williams & Wilkins, 2003.

Figure 7.18 **B.** Photo courtesy of Quinton Cardiology, Inc.

Figure 7.19 Photo courtesy of Quinton Cardiology, Inc.

Figure 7.20 **B.** Courtesy of Mallinckrodt Medical, St. Louis, MO. **C.** Courtesy of GE Healthcare.

Figure 7.21 Courtesy of Acuson Corporation, Mt. View, CA.

Figure 7.23 **A.** From Sheldon H. Boyd's Introduction to the Study of Disease, 11th ed. Philadelphia: Lea & Febiger, 1992. **B.** Courtesy of Edwards Lifesciences.

Figure 7.25 Courtesy of Hewlett-Packard, McMinnville, OR.

Figure 7.26 **A.** Redrawn from About Your Pacemaker. Sylmar, CA: Siemens Pacesetter, p. 18. **B.** Courtesy of Philips Medical Systems, Shelton, CT.

Figure 8.1 Components of the Blood. White blood cells and red blood cells. From Lee GR, et al. Wintrobe's Clinical Hematology, 9th ed. Philadelphia: Lea & Febiger, 1993. Platelets. Courtesy of Mosby's Medical Nursing and Allied Health Dictionary, 4th ed. St. Louis: Mosby-Year Book, 1994:1230.

Figure 8.3 From Lee GR, et al. Wintrobe's Clinical Hematology, 10th ed. Philadelphia: Lippincott Williams & Wilkins, 1999:910, 911 (Fig 30.4A).

Figure 8.4 From Lee GR, et al. Wintrobe's Clinical Hematology, 9th ed. Philadelphia: Lea & Febiger, 1993;1:758.

Figure 8.7 LifeART image copyright ©2005. Lippincott Williams & Wilkins. All rights reserved.

Figure 9.7 Sheldon H. Boyd's Introduction to the Study of Disease, 11th ed. Philadelphia: Lea & Febiger, 1992:340.

Figure 9.9 Sheldon H. Boyd's Introduction to the Study of Disease, 11th ed. Philadelphia: Lea & Febiger, 1992:344.

Figure 9.10 Photo courtesy of Temple University Health Sciences Center, Philadelphia, PA.

Figure 9.11 Courtesy of Felix Wang, MD, University of California Irvine.

Figure 9.12 **B.** Courtesy of SensorMedics, Yorba Linda, CA.

Figure 9.13 Courtesy of Respironics, Inc., Murrysville, PA.

Figure 9.14 Courtesy of Nellcor Incorporated, Pleasanton, CA.

Figure 9.15 Courtesy of Felix Wang, MD, University of California Irvine.

Figure 9.18 Courtesy of Respironics, Inc., Murrysville, PA.

Figure 9.19 Photo courtesy of DHD HEALTHCARE.

Figure 9.20 Courtesy of Siemens Medical Systems, Inc., Danvers, MA.

Figure 10.3 MRI. From Haines DL. Neuroanatomy: An Atlas of Structures, Sections, and Systems, 4th ed. Baltimore: Williams & Wilkins, 1995:29.

Figure 10.4 MRIs from Haines DL. Neuroanatomy: An Atlas of Structures, Sections, and Systems, 4th ed. Baltimore: Williams & Wilkins, 1995:131, 237.

Figure 10.6 From Pillitteri A. Maternal and Child Nursing, 4th ed. Philadelphia: Lippincott Williams & Wilkins, 2003.

Figure 10.11 From Cyber 3D Ultrasound Society, and GE Medical Systems, author Dr. Saied Tohamy, Egypt.

Figure 10.12 Courtesy of Mission Regional Imaging, Mission Viejo, CA.

Figure 10.13 From Pillitteri A. Child Health Nursing: Care of the Child and Family. Philadelphia: Lippincott Williams and Wilkins, 1999:532 (Figure 18-13).

Figure 10.15 Photo courtesy of Cadwell Laboratories, Inc.

Figure 10.16 Courtesy of SensorMedics.

Figure 10.17 Courtesy of General Electric Medical Systems, Milwaukee, WI.

Figure 10.18 Images courtesy of Philips Medical Systems.

Figure 10.19 PET scans courtesy of Newport Diagnostic Center, Newport Beach, CA.

Figure 10.21 Photo courtesy of Nicolet Vascular, Inc.

Figure 10.23 Courtesy of Carl Zeiss, Inc.

Figure 10.25 Courtesy of Varian Medical Systems, Palo Alto, CA.

Figure 10.26 Courtesy of Radionics, Burlington, MA.

Figure 11.3 From Weber J, Kelly J. Lippincott's Learning System: Health Assessment in Nursing. Philadelphia: Lippincott Williams & Wilkins, 1997:188.

Figure 11.4 From Weber J, Kelly J. Lippincott's Learning System: Health Assessment in Nursing. Philadelphia: Lippincott Williams & Wilkins, 1997:188.

Figure 11.5 From Sheldon H. Boyd's Introduction to the Study of Disease, 11th ed. Philadelphia: Lea & Febiger, 1992:640.

Figure 11.6 From Weber J, Kelly J. Lippincott's Learning System: Health Assessment in Nursing. Philadelphia: Lippincott Williams & Wilkins, 1997:188.

Figure 11.8 Courtesy of Felix Wang, MD, University of California Irvine.

Figure 11.9 Photo courtesy of Medtronic MiniMed.

Figure 12.4 From Tasman W, Jaeger E. The Wills Eye Hospital Atlas of Clinical Ophthalmology, 2nd ed. Philadelphia: Lippincott Williams & Wilkins, 2001.

Figure 12.7 From Tasman W, Jaeger E. The Wills Eye Hospital Atlas of Clinical Ophthalmology, 2nd ed. Philadelphia: Lippincott Williams & Wilkins, 2001.

Figure 12.8 Courtesy of Ellman International, Hewlett, NY. Robert Baran, MD, photographer.

Figure 12.9 From Roche Lexikon Medizin, 3rd ed. Munich, Germany: Urban & Schwarzenburg, 1993.

Figure 12.11 From Stedman's Medical Dictionary, 25th ed. Baltimore: Williams & Wilkins, 1990:1578.

Figure 12.13 **B–D.** Courtesy of Welch Allen, Skaneateles Falls, NY.

Figure 12.14 Courtesy of Nikon, Inc., Melville, NY.

Figure 12.15 Courtesy of Keeler Instruments, Inc., Broomall, PA.

Figure 12.16 Courtesy of Lumenis.

Figure 12.17 Courtesy of Jackie Moody, Irvine, CA.

Figure 13.2 Courtesy of Welch Allyn, Inc., Skaneateles Falls, NY.

Figure 13.3 Courtesy of Welch Allyn, Inc., Skaneateles Falls, NY.

Figure 13.4 Courtesy of Welch Allyn, Inc., Skaneateles Falls, NY.

Figure 13.6 Courtesy of BioLogic Systems Corporation.

Figure 13.7 Courtesy of Welch Allyn, Inc., Skaneateles Falls, NY.

Figure 13.8 Courtesy of Welch Allyn, Inc., Skaneateles Falls, NY.

Figure 13.9 Photograph provided by Cochlear Corporation, Englewood, CO.

Figure 14.2 From Anatomical Chart Company.

Figure 14.6 From Lindsay KL, Reynolds TB, Hoefs JC, Sanmarco ME. Ascites. West J Med 1981;134:415.

Figure 14.7 From Bickley LS, Szilagyi P. Bates' Guide to Physical Examination and History Taking, 8th ed. Philadelphia: Lippincott Williams & Wilkins, 2003.

Figure 14.15 Redrawn from poster created by Reed & Carnrick, Kenilworth, NJ. Endoscope and fiberoptics. Courtesy of Olympus America, Inc., Lake Success, NY. Photographs. Courtesy of Mission Hospital Regional Medical Center, Mission Viejo, CA.

Figure 14.17 From Ratcliff KM. Esophageal foreign bodies. Am Fam Physician 1991;44:827.

Figure 14.20 **A.** From Brant WE, Helms CA. Fundamentals of Diagnostic Radiology. Baltimore: Williams & Wilkins, 1994. **B.** Courtesy of Philips Medical Systems, Shelton, CT.

Figure 14.21 **A.** Courtesy of Acuson Corporation, a Siemens Company. **B.** Courtesy of Mission Regional Imaging, Mission Viejo, CA.

Figure 14.22 From Smeltzer SC, Bare BG. Textbook of Medical-Surgical Nursing, 9th ed. Philadelphia: Lippincott Williams & Wilkins, 2000.

Figure 15.3 From McClatchey KD, et al. Clinical Laboratory Medicine, 2nd ed. Baltimore: Lippincott Williams & Wilkins, 2001:538 (Figure 28.20).

Figure 15.4 From McClatchey KD, et al. Clinical Laboratory Medicine, 2nd ed. Baltimore: Lippincott Williams & Wilkins, 2001:539 (Figure 28.23).

Figure 15.5 From Sheldon H. Boyd's Introduction to the Study of Disease, 11th ed. Philadelphia: Lea & Febiger, 1992:436.

Figure 15.8 Courtesy of Mission Regional Imaging, Mission Viejo, CA.

Figure 15.10 Courtesy of Circon Corporation, Santa Barbara, CA.

Figure 15.11 Courtesy of Circon Corporation, Santa Barbara, CA.

Figure 16.3 From Rubin E, Farber JL. Pathology, 3rd ed. Philadelphia: Lippincott Williams & Wilkins, 1999.

Figure 16.6 From Weber J, Kelley J. Health Assessment in Nursing, 2nd ed. Philadelphia: Lippincott Williams & Wilkins, 2003.

Figure 16.8 Courtesy of L. J. Underwood and R. D. Underwood, Mission Viejo, CA.

Figure 17.3 **A.** Courtesy of Lucinda Veeck, New York, NY. **B.** Courtesy of Acuson Corporation, a Siemens Company.

Figure 17.4 From Cyber 3D Ultrasound Society, and GE Medical Systems, author Dr. Saied Tohamy, Egypt.

Figure 17.9 Mjolsness D. Gynecologic diagnosis: Primary herpes lesions. Patient Care 1990;Apr 30:85 (Figure 6).

Figure 17.10 From Micha JP. Genital warts: Treatable warning of cancer. Female Patient 1984; 9:31; Belle Mead, NJ: Excerpta Medica.

Figure 17.11 Courtesy of William B. Wadlington, MD, Nashville, TN.

Figure 17.13 **B.** Photographs courtesy of Cabbott Medical/Cryomedics, Langhorne, PA.

Figure 17.15 **A.** Courtesy of General Electric Medical Systems, Milwaukee, WI. **B.** From Brant WE, Helms CA. Fundamentals of Diagnostic Radiology. Baltimore: Williams & Wilkins, 1994:548.

Figure 17.16 *Insets.* Courtesy of Siemens Medical Systems, Inc., Danvers, MA.

Figure 17.23 Georgiade GS, et al. Textbook of Plastic, Maxillofacial and Reconstructive Surgery, 2nd ed. Baltimore: Williams & Wilkins, 1992:853, 863.

Figure 17.24 Georgiade GS, et al. Textbook of Plastic, Maxillofacial and Reconstructive Surgery, 2nd ed. Baltimore: Williams & Wilkins, 1992:795.

Index

Numbers in *italics* denote figures.

A

Abbreviations/acronyms, 592–593
  blood and lymph system, 255
  cardiovascular system, 221
  ear, 425
  endocrine system, 371
  error-prone, 79–80, *92*
  eye, 402
  female reproductive system, 563
  for history and physical, 55–57
  hospital, 79–80
  integumentary system, 124
  male reproductive system, 520
  medical record, 79–80
  medical specialties, 49
  musculoskeletal system, 174
  nervous system, 337
  pharmaceutical, 88–90
  prescription
    common, 91, *91*, 93–94
    error-prone, *92*, 93–94
  respiratory system, 288
  urinary system, 496
Abdomen
  anatomical divisions, 443–444
  clinical divisions, 444–445
Abdominal hysterectomy, 553
Abdominal sonography, 456, 458
Abdominocentesis, 459
Abduction, 148, 157
ABGs (arterial blood gases), 280
Ablation, intracardiac catheter, 212
ABMS (American Board of Medical
    Specialties), 42–43
Abortifacient, 563
Abortion, 558–559
  habitual, 559
Abruptio placentae, 561
Abscess, skin, 117
Absence seizures, 322
Absorption, 439
Abstract, discharge (*see* Discharge
    summaries)
Accent, primary, 18
Accommodation, visual, 391
Accupril, 594

Accutane, 594
ACE (angiotensin-converting enzyme)
    inhibitors, 219
Acetaminophen/codeine, 594
Aciphex, 594
Acne, 115, *116*
Acoustic neuroma, 419
Acquired immunodeficiency syndrome
    (AIDS), 248, 545
Acromegaly, 366
Acronyms/abbreviations (*see*
    Abbreviations/acronyms)
ACTH (adrenocorticotropic hormone),
    361, 362
Actinic keratoses, 118, *118*
Actonel, 594
Actos, 594
Acuity
  auditory, 421, 422
  visual, 396
Adderall XR, 594
Adduction, 148, 157
Adenocarcinoma, of breast, 546
Adenohypophysis (anterior pituitary
    gland), *360*, 361, 362
Adenoidectomy, 285
Adenoids, 272
ADH (antidiuretic hormone, vasopressin),
    361, 363
ADHD (attention deficit/hyperactivity
    disorder), 335
Adhesiolysis, 551
Adhesions, pelvic, 543
Adhesiotomy, 551
Adjective endings, 28
Adnexa, uterine, 537
Adrenalectomy, 370
Adrenal (suprarenal) glands, 359, *360*,
    361, 365
Adrenocorticotropic hormone (ACTH),
    361, 362
Adult polycystic kidney disease
    (APKD), 487
Advair Diskus, 594
Affect, 333
  flat, 333

Agnosia, 320
AIDS (acquired immunodeficiency
    syndrome), 248, 545
Albinism, 115
Albuminuria, 486, 490
Albuterol, 594
Alcoholic cardiomyopathy, 207
Alimentary canal, 439, 440
Allegra, 594
Allegra D, 594
Allergy and immunology, 44
Allografts, 123
Allopurinol, 594
Alopecia (baldness), 114
Alphagan P, 594
Alprazolam, 594
ALS (amyotrophic lateral sclerosis, Lou
    Gehrig disease), 320, 328
Altace, 595
Alveoli, *271*, 273
  normal vs. obstructed, *275*
Alzheimer disease, 320, *328*
Amaryl, 595
Amastia, 546
Ambien, 595
Amblyopia, 391
Amenorrhea, 540
American College of Physicians (ACP),
    42–43
American College of Surgeons (ACS),
    42–43
American Osteopathic Association
    (AOA), 43
Amitriptyline, 595
Amniocentesis, 561, *562*
Amnion, 540
Amniotic fluid, 540
Amoxicillin, 595
Amoxicillin/clavulanate, 595
Ampulla, rectal, 440, 442
Amputation, 169
Amyotrophic lateral sclerosis (ALS, Lou
    Gehrig disease), 320, 328
Anal fistula, 449, *451*
Anal fistulectomy, 460
Analgesics, 174, 333, 496